Prisons and their Moral

CLARENDON STUDIES IN CRIMINOLOGY

Published under the auspices of the Institute of Criminology,
University of Cambridge, the Mannheim Centre, London School of
Economics, and the Centre for Criminological Research, University of Oxford.

GENERAL EDITOR: PER-OLOF WIKSTRÖM (*University of Cambridge*)

EDITORS: ALISON LIEBLING AND MANUEL EISNER
(*University of Cambridge*)

DAVID DOWNES, PAUL ROCK, and JILL PEAY
(*London School of Economics*)

ROGER HOOD, LUCIA ZEDNER, and RICHARD YOUNG
(*University of Oxford*)

Recent titles in this series:

Accountability in Restorative Justice
Roche

Bouncers: Violence and Governance in the Night-time Economy
Hobbs, Hadfield, Lister, and Winlow

**The Criminological Foundations of Penal Policy: Essays in Honour of
Roger Hood**
Zedner and Ashworth (eds.)

**Policing and the Condition of England: Memory, Politics,
and Culture**
Loader and Mulcahy

**CCTV and Policing: Public Area Surveillance and Police
Practices in Britain**
Goold

Prisons and their Moral Performance

A Study of Values, Quality, and Prison Life

Alison Liebling
assisted by
Helen Arnold

OXFORD
UNIVERSITY PRESS

*This book has been printed digitally and produced in a standard specification
in order to ensure its continuing availability*

OXFORD
UNIVERSITY PRESS

Great Clarendon Street, Oxford OX2 6DP

Oxford University Press is a department of the University of Oxford.
It furthers the University's objective of excellence in research, scholarship,
and education by publishing worldwide in

Oxford New York

Auckland Cape Town Dar es Salaam Hong Kong Karachi
Kuala Lumpur Madrid Melbourne Mexico City Nairobi
New Delhi Shanghai Taipei Toronto
With offices in
Argentina Austria Brazil Chile Czech Republic France Greece
Guatemala Hungary Italy Japan South Korea Poland Portugal
Singapore Switzerland Thailand Turkey Ukraine Vietnam

Oxford is a registered trade mark of Oxford University Press
in the UK and in certain other countries

Published in the United States
by Oxford University Press Inc., New York

ISBN 978-0-19-929148-9

General Editor's Introduction

The *Clarendon Studies in Criminology* were inaugurated in 1994 under the auspices of the centres of criminology at the Universities of Cambridge and Oxford and the London School of Economics. The series was the successor to *Cambridge Studies in Criminology*, founded by Sir Leon Radzinowicz and J.W.C. Turner almost sixty years ago.

Criminology is a field of study that covers everything from research into the causes of crime to the politics of the operations of the criminal justice system. Researchers in different social and behavioural sciences, criminal justice and law all make important contributions to our understanding of the phenomena of crime. The *Clarendon Studies in Criminology* aim at reflecting this diversity by publishing high-quality theory and research monographs by established scholars as well as by young scholars of great promise from all different kinds of academic backgrounds.

Professor Sir Anthony Bottoms has claimed that, "if they are true to their calling all criminologists have to be interested in morality" (Bottoms 2002: 24). In *Prisons and their Moral Performance* Dr Alison Liebling, Director of the Prison Research Centre, Institute of Criminology, University of Cambridge, presents a fascinating theoretical account and empirical study of prisons and moral practices. Essentially it is a book about the dimensions of staff and prisoner moral and emotional relationships and their great importance for the nature and quality of life in and the management of prisons.

This is a very timely book, and one that is likely to have a major impact on how academics, policy makers, and practitioners think about prisons and their management. I suspect that this book will firmly establish Dr Liebling as the leading penal scholar in the UK.

Per-Olof H. Wikström,
University of Cambridge
March 2004

For Roger

Morality is a matter of face-to-face personal relations.

(Emmett 1966, p. ix)

I am not prepared to continue to apologise for failing prison after failing prison. I have had enough of trying to explain the very immorality of our treatment of some prisoners and the degradation of some establishments.

(Martin Narey, Speech to Prison Service Conference 2001)

It's getting rather deep, this!

(Prison Officer)

Contents

List of Figures

List of Tables

List of Abbreviations

ACAS	Advisory, Conciliation, and Arbitration Service
AI	Appreciative Inquiry
APS	Accelerated Promotion Scheme
BoV	Board of Visitors
CARATS	Counselling, Assessment, Referral, Advice, and Throughcare Service
CCG	Contracts and Competitions Group
CCTV	Closed Circuit Television
CIES	Correctional Institutions Environment Scale
CNA	Certified Normal Accommodation
COPES	Community-Oriented Programmes Environment Scale
CPT	Committee for the Prevention of Torture
CSC	Close Supervision Centres
DDG	Deputy Director General
DG	Director General
ETS	Enhanced Thinking Skills
HAC	Home Affairs Committee
HMCIC	Her Majesty's Chief Inspector of Constabulary
HMCIP	Her Majesty's Chief Inspector of Prisons
IEP	Incentives and Earned Privileges
IMB	Independent Monitoring Board
ITT	Invitation to Tender
KPI	Key Performance Indicator
KPT	Key Performance Target
LIDS	Local Inmate Database System
MDT	Mandatory Drug Testing
NAO	National Audit Office
OBP	Offending Behaviour Programme
OICS	Office of the Inspector of Custodial Services
ONS	Office of National Statistics
OPCS	Office of Population Censuses and Surveys
PASC	Public Administration Select Committee
PCO	Prison Custody Officer

PFI	Private Finance Initiative
PGA	Prison Governors' Association
POA	Prison Officers' Association
PPI	Prison Preference Inventory
PPRI	Prison Privatization Report International
PSCS	Prison Social Climate Survey
PSMB	Prison Service Management Board
PUMIS	Prisons Unified Management Information System
QoL	Quality of Life
RAPt	Rehabilitation of Addicted Prisoners Trust
SDA	Service Delivery Agreement
SLA	Service Level Agreement
SPSS	Statistical Package for Social Sciences
SSU	Special Security Unit
UKDS	United Kingdom Detention Services
VO	Visiting Order
VP	Vulnerable Prisoner
VPU	Vulnerable Prisoner Unit
WAS	Ward Atmosphere Scale
YOI	Young Offender Institution

Preface

At [another prison] they treat you with respect—as a human; like someone who has made a mistake.

(Prisoner, Risley)

This book attempts to solve some contemporary analytical and moral puzzles relating to the late modern prison. It has two main agendas. First, it constructs an analysis of recent prison history that shows how the role of values has changed considerably, both externally and internally, during a period of rapid modernization. Secondly, it recounts a related empirical study of the moral performance of five comparable prisons—a term arising out of extensive deliberation with staff and prisoners about what matters in prison. Together, these accounts are used to form an argument for the instatement of an explicitly moral agenda, and for continuous learning about the role of values, in penal practice, policy-making, and evaluation. The book has a further longitudinal aspiration, and we are hopeful that it might provide a basis for further comparative work on this subject in the future.

The study is, in one sense, the product of many earlier research endeavours. There have been some 'golden threads' in our research lives, which have persisted despite radical changes to prison life and some very different research topics, which finally receive some attention here. They are to do with the nature of the prison experience, and its relationship with who we are as human beings. We hope that the theoretical approach we have developed has a general application beyond the prison. Our study is about what it is to be affirmed in our humanness and what violates it. The book explores the existence of values, the use of power, the experience of justice and injustice, the role of trust, and, through these notions, the complexity of the prison world: the world of prisoners, staff, and managers, as they find it, and as we discovered and attempt to describe it, in five establishments. One of the arguments—a hypothesis—is that the apparent failure of the liberal penal project (associated most recently in England and Wales with the Woolf

Report)[1] is related to our lack of clarity about values. They fail to work because we are naïve and unclear about their meaning. The second hypothesis is that values matter—that as 'vulnerable human beings', we need to be in environments that acknowledge our dignity and permit our development.

We attempt to conceptualize and evaluate prisons, using a framework that develops throughout the book, which we call 'moral performance'. This term requires explanation. We are using it to denote several things. First, that prisons are, as others have argued, special moral places (Goffman 1987: 80; Sparks *et al.* 1996: 29). That is, that they are places where relationships, and the treatment of one party by another, really matter. They raise questions of fairness, order, and authority (others might say, legitimacy), but also some other questions about trust, respect, and well-being, in an exceptionally palpable way. Secondly, we show that difficult-to-measure moral aspects of prison life, or the practice of values in prison, *can* be measured and that this approach provides a more meaningful understanding of prison life and quality than standard or official approaches to performance measurement. Thirdly, we argue that certain prisons differ significantly in these moral practices; that is, in their treatment of prisoners. They differ broadly over time, and at any point in history they may differ significantly from one another. Fourthly, we support the argument that the managerially driven performance culture has been rightly criticized for focusing on what can be measured rather than on what matters. This does not mean that all attempts to gain management control or measure 'processes' and 'outcomes' are flawed, as we shall show.

Our study coincides with two major reform agendas which have precipitated considerable critical commentary: (i) the managerialist/post-managerialist reinvention of government and the public sector; and (ii) the Prison Service's own 'decency' agenda.[2] We reflect in detail on these related agendas, using our explorations as a descriptive case study of the modern search for public sector reform. The modernizing project—a systematic attempt to overcome the deficiencies of (old-style) bureaucracy—is often criticized for its neglect of values and its tendencies towards instrumentalism.

---

[1] See Home Office (1991*a*) and Chapter 1.

[2] We use the term Prison Service to refer to the Prison Service of England and Wales.

Some commentators, on the other hand, describe an apparent concern within a modernizing government and within some public (and private) sector organizations with values such as justice and respect; and with culture (Faulkner 2001). We argue that there is a complex paradox of this nature at play in penal life. There are clear signs of attentiveness to values at senior and policy levels within the Prison Service. But these signs, ideas, and practices have to be set against a constraining set of negative values. There is a lack of public and political sympathy for either the offender or for the Prison Service as an organization, and there are some impatient demands for modernization (from government and especially the Treasury) that can only be met by coercive means. Some important moderate ideas about the treatment of prisoners are making a significant impact on the daily texture of prison life, as ideas do. But control-oriented, anti-social, over-regulating ideas of hyper-efficiency and risk aversion are playing a part too in late modern penal life.

In the light of an unprecedented rise in the size of the prison population, and the above developments, a much-needed re-evaluation of the role of the prison is required. We hope the work we report here may form part of this re-evaluation. We propose that the questions of *exterior* legitimacy posed by Sparks (Sparks 1994), which relate to the prison's structural, political, and social properties, can only be satisfactorily addressed if we develop a fuller understanding of the *interior* quality of the prison, and the way these interact. Questions about how much imprisonment, of what kind, for what purpose and to what effect, should be answered whilst taking account of the analysis of prison life that follows. We argue that prisons (and other organizations) can be evaluated in ways that are meaningful, and that bring values to centre stage. We show that there *are* some major conceptual gaps in standard managerialist measurement approaches and procedures, which tend to concentrate on processes arguably unrelated to, for example, the staff–prisoner interface. This book places the staff–prisoner interface centre stage, not least because staff and prisoners agree that this aspect of prison life is 'what matters'. The question of how staff treat prisoners is, in the end, shaped by the messages they receive from those around them (governors, senior management, ministers, Home Secretaries, the media and their 'lay' friends and families) about what kinds of prisons are desirable, and achievable. Civic values are, paradoxically, deeply relevant to the prison condition.

They are least realizable when over-use, political use, or cynical use is made of the prison. This book represents a detailed attempt to make this case.

Part I, 'Penal Values and Prison Evaluation' considers the relevance of values to prison life, in practice and in research, and official evaluations of the prison. We begin, in Chapter 1, by developing a penological account of the period 1990–2003, a time of transition, and an important context for the remaining chapters. This introductory chapter describes the changing penal landscape during this period and shows how the role of values in penal life changed dramatically during the 1990s. It draws selectively on several research projects carried out throughout the period to illustrate the relationship between broad penal sensibilities 'out there' and the inner life of prisons. The chapter draws on a number of interviews conducted for the purposes of this account[3] and on broader criminological accounts of the decade. The chapter ends by describing the unprecedented increase in prison population size during the early years of the new century. A number of disturbances (including one each in two of the prisons in our study), and an alarming rise in suicides, indicate that despite some significant improvements detectable during the years 1999–2001, the penal system of 2002–3 was hovering on the brink of another major 'crisis of legitimacy'. This time, the crisis was precipitated largely by external pressures.

Chapter 2 reviews previous and current official attempts to evaluate prison quality. There has been a 'quality revolution', but this revolution has brought with it some untested assumptions about the *concept* of quality. Staff working in prisons express discomfort about the impoverished version of prison performance imposed by modern managerialist techniques. At the same time, they acknowledge that some aspects of the managerial revolution are necessary and long overdue. We suggest that a more satisfactory theoretical and conceptual approach to the prison and to the question of prison quality, without the inevitable distortions of managerialism, is both possible and necessary. We consider the early attempts by Moos and others to assess prison regimes in the quest for 'therapeutic effectiveness' and the move over time to more managerialist approaches

---

[3] Some of the interview excerpts have been left unattributed, in order to retain anonymity. Where this is impossible or confusing, excerpts have been attributed and drafts have been shown to the individuals concerned for approval.

to prison quality, including the contemporary proliferation of private–public sector comparisons. We revisit the public–private sector debate in the light of some of these comparisons, suggesting that there is considerable uncertainty about what just institutions might be, as well as uncertainty about what mechanisms might secure the elusive 'just prison'. There are major difficulties in both public and private sector approaches to prisons, but each sector also has some distinct advantages over the other. We question the extent to which notions of public *service* address or resolve the moral problems of contemporary imprisonment.

The research project drawn upon most directly throughout the remainder of the book began in the summer of 2000. This was one of a small number of the newly established Home Office Research Development and Statistics Directorate *Innovative Research Challenge Fund* projects. The research, 'Measuring the Quality of Prison Life', aimed, *inter alia*, to develop quantitative measures of qualitative dimensions of prison life which are widely referred to, but poorly understood. These dimensions were largely *values*. Chapter 3 describes how these value dimensions were selected. We worked closely with staff and prisoners in the identification of the 'key dimensions of prison life', and then engaged in exercises aimed at operationalizing these terms for evaluation. We devised a survey questionnaire based around these moral or value dimensions, and a set of 'appreciative protocols', which we used to generate considerable quantitative and qualitative data about the moral quality of life in five prisons. The next four chapters of the book describe this work, explore its findings and develop a new conceptual understanding of the quality of prison life.

Chapter 4 introduces the five prisons in the main part of our study. We consider some of the difficulties in making comparisons between prisons, and then briefly describe the characteristics, qualities, and *value cultures* of the five prisons selected for inclusion in our research.

Part II, 'The Meaning and Measurement of Key Dimensions of Prison Life' takes us further into the inner world of the five prisons, where we introduce each dimension, explore its meaning and application in the penal context, and then present a scale or set of items which reflect this meaning. We outline and explore the results, making comparisons between the prisons and reflecting on what these results tell us about prison life. Chapter 5 outlines the 'relationships' dimensions (respect, humanity, trust, staff–prisoner relationships, and support). Chapter 6 considers 'regime' dimensions (fairness, order, safety, well-being, personal development, family contact, and decency). Chapter 7 introduces two 'social structure' dimensions: power and prisoner social life, and two remaining individual items: meaning and overall quality of life. We show that, in general, there are higher levels of perceived safety and order in the prison than there are levels of fairness or respect, or especially, trust or personal development (i.e. constructive and meaningful occupation). But interesting and significant differences between prisons can be found. Material conditions are better than relational conditions in the late modern prison.

Part III, 'Penal Values and Prison Management' explores the modern managerialist framework in which prisons operate. In Chapter 8, we explore how life above prisoners shapes the prison experience. We consider relationships among prison staff, between staff and senior managers, and between governors and senior management of the Prison Service, showing how prisons are generally low trust organizations. At the end of this chapter we consider how prisons have *emotional* as well as *moral* climates, and we suggest that governors find themselves navigating, as well as shaping, these climates.

Chapter 9 reflects on some events to have taken place since we completed our research, and on their implications for our moral performance framework. We have drawn upon Braithwaite's work on political values (especially the concept of *value balance*) to make sense of the differences between the prisons in our study, and the role of values in prison quality more generally. An appreciation of the dual role of security and harmony values in political, civic, and penal life takes us beyond the typical contests and oscillations between the two that we began with in Chapter 1.

In Chapter 10, we review our findings, return to the key questions posed in the introduction and to the theoretical and criminological literature, in order to reflect on the implications of our work. We describe some 'essential features of the prison', and then consider the differences we found and their implications for the future study of prisons and their place in the criminological project.

Our 'Measuring the Quality of Prison Life' research was extended in September 2001, with Prison Service funding, in order to build on the findings and methodology, and to explore the possible links between Standards Audit measures of compliance with *process* (see Chapter 2) and prisoner satisfaction with delivery, or quasi-outcome measures (such as levels of fairness, respect, and safety). This work was completed in the autumn of 2002 and the findings will be published separately. A more sustained and longitudinal development of the work is currently in progress in a project intended to explore systematically the links between prison quality, or moral performance as we have developed the concept here, and levels of psychological distress experienced by prisoners. The work involves investigating in detail the links between prisoners' perceptions of their treatment, and suicide and distress rates in twelve prisons (see Liebling 2002; and Liebling *et al.* forthcoming). We hope that this book will serve as the reference point for that ongoing work, as well as constituting a reflective study of the prison in its own right. This book provides a distillation of much previous research already undertaken (for example, Liebling 1992; Bottomley *et al.* 1994; Liebling *et al.* 1997; Bottomley *et al.* 1997; Liebling and Price 1999; Liebling *et al.* 1999*a*; Liebling 2002), but is also intended to represent the methodological, empirical, and conceptual groundwork for work that is continuing.

The issues we explore in the chapters that follow raise many complex questions. We are aware that we have really only begun rather than finished a programme of research and reflection. At the very least we are endeavouring, in this book, to develop a clear argument using our empirical findings to date, and the related work of others. We are reinserting the language of justice or morality into the apparently instrumental, actuarial model of prison life we, and others (for example, Home Office 1991*b*; Sparks *et al.* 1996; Bottoms 2002), find lacking. This is something the prison staff and prisoners in our study strongly support.

Acknowledgements

My debts to others are considerable. Many individuals and organizations have made this book possible. The empirical study emerges most directly out of a Home Office Innovative Research Challenge project: Measuring the Quality of Prison Life, carried out between May 2000 and August 2001 and conducted with Helen Arnold. I am grateful to our sponsors for this funding and, in particular, for the freedom to conduct research without a policy steer.

The book was written by Alison Liebling but her friend, and colleague, Helen Arnold was a constant source of hard work and companionship. She conducted the largest share of the fieldwork for the main study. She worked with diligence and enthusiasm on the data entry and analysis, on the preparation of figures, quotations, and searches of the literature. She participated in discussions about the five prisons as well as the ideas in this book and she commented helpfully on early drafts of chapters. She has played a significant practical and conceptual role in this work. I am deeply grateful to her for all she has contributed.

Charles Elliott brought to the team his gifts in Appreciative Inquiry (AI). He has a capacity to express the value of others which brings people (and, sometimes, organizations) to life. We watched him achieve this, and tried to help, with admiration and affection. We have tried to learn his techniques from him, and to remain true to his best hopes for the method. He shaped the project's early stages in important ways.

Helen Griffiths painstakingly prepared tables and figures, checked references, proofread the manuscript, made corrections, and kept me laughing. I am indebted to her for her efficiency, her artistic and technical skills, and her exceptionally good humour. Others in the Prisons Research Centre—Ben Crewe, Linda Durie, Joel Harvey, Annick van den Beukel, and Shadd Maruna—have made this project a particularly companionable and exciting one. Sarah Tait joined us in 2002, and generously offered to proofread the evolving manuscript for errors as part of her introduction. Linda, Joel, and Annick have continued to develop the 'prison quality' measures with me, in subsequent work. I could not ask for a better team.

Keith Bottomley read and commented helpfully on the first draft of this manuscript before I dared show it to anyone else. His constant friendship and support, and his own personal and professional values, have influenced my development greatly. This time, I thank him for everything.

I am deeply grateful to Tony Bottoms, for long-standing intellectual guidance and friendship and, in particular, for commenting in considerable detail on drafts of every chapter. His suggestions for improvements were, as always, wise and demanding. Several other criminologists know the meaning of the verb, 'to Tonify'. He has been steadfast in his encouragement and support.

Hans Toch read and commented shrewdly and speedily on the draft of the whole manuscript, at my request. He alerted me to some of the connections between our work and the work of Herzberg and Lewin. His considerable knowledge, his adherence to humanism, his generosity, and his love of good wine have made him a new friend for life.

Peter Quinn proofread the whole manuscript, with an eagle eye. He returned it within a month, red-penned, and covered in amusing anecdotes as well as references to articles and books I probably should have read. It was a blessing to be kept so amused at the last lap, and I am grateful for his attention to detail.

Individual chapters (often more than one) were read and helpfully commented on at various stages by Stephen Rimmer, William Saylor, Mark Simpson, Phil Wheatley, Shadd Maruna, and Nigel Hancock.

I must thank the three anonymous assessors to whom Oxford University Press sent the original manuscript for review. All three provided detailed and constructive comments. Their identities were gradually rumbled. Kieran McEvoy provided encouraging and valuable comments, and prompted me in particular (but not enough, I am sure) to reflect on the role of human rights discourses in our moral performance framework. Roy King provided an encouraging and constructively critical account of our attempt to measure the prison's moral universe and a characteristically generous analysis of what he calls 'third generation' prisons research. I thank David Downes for his thoroughness, his most helpful comments and suggestions, for his encouraging words, and for spotting those weaknesses that I was most concerned about, while still strongly supporting the book's publication. I have attempted to take as many of these suggestions into account as I could in this final version.

Jan Schramm and Martin Narey kindly read the final manuscript. They both responded warmly and generously to it. I was more than ready to hear the words, 'don't change a thing' from Jan, and I remain grateful for the corrections to facts and other helpful comments from Martin.

The data for this project were collected with the collaboration and assistance of numerous individuals in establishments. We owe a great deal to the governors, staff, and prisoners at these five establishments, and to our workgroups in particular. We have been given a great deal of support and trust throughout this project, and could not have hoped for better co-operation. We would like to thank all those involved for letting us into, and for helping us to understand, their world. All five governors involved in the main research project were invited to read and comment on drafts of the chapters that concerned them most. They responded with warmth and openness to the account we had developed, and to our critical remarks. We are most grateful for their tolerance and willingness to subject their working lives to such scrutiny.

Jonathan Steinberg supported my excitement about this project from the outset. He knew that the book was about values before I did. He has provided understanding, inspiration, and calm reflection throughout. I owe him a very special debt.

There are many others who have assisted with this book in important ways, too numerous to mention. They are: Peter Atherton, Colin Austin, Ralf Bas, David Butterworth, Brodie Clark, Maureen Colledge, Peter Dawson, John Dring, Steve Gillespie, Martin Gunning, Kelly Hannah-Moffatt, Nathan Harris, Andrew von Hirsch, Graham Howes, Darrick Jolliffe, Marion Kant, Roxanne Lieb, Stephen Nathan, John Rynne, Andrew Sinclair, Michael Tonry, Malcolm Peacock, Ingrid Posen, John Pratt, David Roddan, William Saylor, Richard Sparks, Janos Suto, Robert Vahey, and Richard Wilson. The staff at the Radzinowicz Library, Institute of Criminology, Helen Krarup, Mary Gower, and Stuart Feathers, were most helpful as well as patient with this demanding but appreciative customer, as well as with others who chased books and articles on her behalf. John Louth, Gwen Booth, and Amanda Greenley at Oxford University Press have been kind and efficient editors. I am grateful to Willan Publishing for kind permission to reproduce Table 3 in Liebling 2002 as Table 1.3 here.

Finally, I owe much to Roger Haley, without whose love and support this book would probably not have been written. I thank the rest of my family too, for love and the best kind of friendship.

The book's weaknesses are, of course, all my own.

Alison Liebling
Cambridge, 2003

PART I

Penal Values and Prison Evaluation

1

The Late Modern Prison and the Question of Values

> The present state of our prisons, blighted by age, severe over-crowding, insanitary conditions and painfully slow progress in modernisation makes it necessary to consider urgent new ways of dealing with these problems which at present seem almost insoluble.
>
> (Home Affairs Committee 1987: 1)

In this chapter, we provide an account of some of the transformations to have taken place in penal practices, values, and sensibilities between 1990 and 2003. Our argument is that the failure of the liberal penal project, a project that looked so promising early on in the last decade, came about partly because of a failure to understand the meaning of the term 'liberal' in the penal context. We shall illustrate the turbulent nature of this period and its relation to the prison empirically. The history of this period led us to a more general preoccupation with the meaning and application of key terms, particularly those terms embracing the language of values in prison. The remainder of the book will address these broader, related themes.

Why have we adopted this term, the 'late modern' prison and what does it signify? We have chosen the term because it highlights the rapidly changing social context in which the prison currently exists—a context which shapes the prison but in which certain important features persist. The prison as a primary form of punishment was born in modernity,[1] an 'ambiguous legacy' of the

---

[1] To be distinguished from the *pre-modern* period, although the prison arguably retains even some pre-modern characteristics, such as its place-based nature and the role of tradition in its daily practices (see Giddens 1990; Sparks *et al.* 1996). *Modernity* refers to a phase in social development dating from the Enlightenment of seventeenth- and eighteenth-century Europe, also associated with the development

Industrial Revolution (Ignatieff 1978, p. xii) and many of the physical, architectural, symbolic, and material characteristics of the prison dating back to the late eighteenth century remain barely changed. This tension, between the forces of late modernity 'out there' and the micro processes of the prison, where staff and prisoners continue to exchange pleasantries, insults, disclosures, and deals, is precisely 'where the action is' (Goffman 1967: 194–214) in prison. In most prisons still, the landing is the same landing; time and place matter; and the essential prison experience remains fully recognizable by those who have always been there. Meanwhile, the world around the prison landing has been transformed. Since 1960, the new insecurity of employment; the use of information technology; the generalization of expectations and fears brought about by mass media; the 'desubordination' of lower socio-economic and minority groups; the questioning of authority and traditional values; the erosion of 'localized trust' (see Giddens 1990); and the rise of managerialism, have altered the frameworks in which penal practices are conducted.[2] It is necessary to tease out these tensions to depict the prison as it is today.

of industrial society in the nineteenth century. It is characterized as emphasizing bureaucracy, rationality, and science, and a notion of superiority, or social progress, via planned intervention (Berger *et al.* 1977: 13). Order, clarity, and economic growth are three of its key values. Bureaucracy and technology serve as important 'carriers' of modernization (ibid. 16). Despite the apparently civilizing aspirations of modernization, it brings risks of depersonalization and indifference to human suffering, or the 'effective administration of cruelties' (see Bauman 1989: 9; Berger *et al.* 1977). It can be alienating, mechanical, 'disenchanting' and individualistic (Kumar 1981). See, for example, Berger *et al.* on the decline of 'meaning and stability' (Berger *et al.* 1977: 85; also Bauman 1989; and Kumar 1981: 104–6).

[2] *Late modernity* is described as an extension and increasingly rapid development of many of the characteristics of modernity. Bottoms and Wiles argue that six important features of recent social change characteristic of late modernity are: economic changes; tendencies towards globalization and localization; technology and its consequences; changes in the sources of trust (from local and kinship relationships to less stable social relations and 'disembedded abstract systems'); changing forms of social differentiation; and managerialism (Bottoms and Wiles 1996: 10–31; also Bottoms 1995; Garland and Sparks 2000). In relation to the prison, Pratt describes a mixture of the apparently civilizing, traditional formal bureaucratic rationalism associated with modernity, alongside the return of certain, arguably pre-modern punishment practices 'designed to allow for emotional release' (Pratt 2000: 417–18; and 2002).

One of the important questions raised in this book is how far specific values traditionally associated with prison, albeit falteringly, exist or matter in this late modern context. How far do changing principles or ideas about the prison influence practice? Do prisons differ in the extent to which they take on, are shaped by, or resist 'macro ideologies'—and if they differ in their ethos, what accounts for these differences? We hope that we shall have provided at least partial answers to many of these questions by the end.

The Changing Penal Landscape, 1990–2003

[M]ost social phenomena and processes are most open to scrutiny in conditions of deep and rapid social change . . . the causal mechanisms of social life are more salient, the variables take more extreme forms, the dynamics are easier to grasp.

(Sztompka 1999: 151)

Most commentators are agreed that, over the course of the last decade or so, modern penality has undergone rapid and significant change (see O'Malley 1999; Pratt 2000, 2002; Garland 2001a; Feeley and Simon 1992). These changes are interlaced with continuities and resurgences: a complex web of penal trajectories can be identified, unevenly representing new tactics of punishment, alongside old preoccupations with emotion (Pratt 2000) and value (Bottoms 1995).[3]

In the account to follow, we set out the context for the study we have conducted and the argument we develop. We look at the changing penal context, at the changing role of values in penal life, and at what others have to say about the prison over this period. Our history is descriptive, in the sense that some very important

---

[3] Historians of the prison may be alarmed by the argument, in this introductory chapter, that a 'decade or so' can be divided into distinctive periods. Of course, they have a point. But it is interesting to note, in retrospect, the special nature of the period 1990–2 and its resonances with especially humanitarian, if not rehabilitative, sentiments that Garland and others would associate with an earlier period. Personally, we find the possibility that this period was an unusual interruption in a more enduring punitive historical turn unsatisfactory, analytically and otherwise. Zedner argues persuasively that normative and 'welfare-correctionalist' theorizing, policy-making, and practices have continued and that enduring traditions of welfare liberalism can be seen in Britain and other European countries (Zedner 2002).

events occurred, but it is also a history of ideas. There is a complex and important relationship between the two.

Other explorations of values in prison have, of course, been conducted. There are numerous examples of working parties, informal gatherings, and high-level attempts to explore the meaning of terms like 'justice' in the penal context during the 1980s and early 1990s (see e.g. Rutherford 1996: 87; Faulkner 2001; Windlesham 1993; and King and McDermott 1995: 3–4). Relevant empirical studies exploring values include an investigation of 'fairness' in prison (Ahmad 1996); a detailed study of legitimacy and order in prison (Sparks *et al.* 1996); studies carried out by the author and colleagues on staff–prisoner relationships (Liebling and Price 2001); an evaluation of incentives and earned privileges (Liebling *et al.* 1997; Bottoms 2003*b*); and McEvoy's study of paramilitary imprisonment in Northern Ireland (McEvoy 2001). We shall draw on these studies later. Garland's work on penal sensibilities is by far the most theoretically sophisticated analysis of values and their embodiment in penal processes and we shall draw on his work throughout (especially Garland 1990 and 2001*a*). The main point being made in this chapter is that official, public, and policy-related explorations of notions of justice more or less ceased between 1993 and at least 1999, at which point a new internal discourse (the 'decency' agenda) emerged, to which we shall come. These changing ideas shaped, and continue to shape, life in prison in important ways.

Perhaps one useful framework or point of departure is Rutherford's *Criminal Justice and the Pursuit of Decency*. Rutherford identifies three working credos: the punishment credo—which privileges the punitive degradation of offenders; the efficiency credo—which emphasizes issues of management, pragmatism, efficiency, and expedience; and the caring or 'humanity' credo—which he describes as an attitude towards suspects and prisoners based on 'liberal and humanitarian values' (Rutherford 1993). Arguably, Rutherford has conflated censure with official vindictiveness in his 'punishment' credo (see von Hirsch 1993; Barbalet 1998); and 'care' with 'justice' in his 'care' credo: important points to which we shall return.[4] It is important to note that his book was completed in 1992. In the decade to follow, the pursuit of these particular credos has altered, their substance may have developed in new

---

[4] We are indebted to Tony Bottoms for this observation.

directions, and other credos have emerged, including what we have called the 'effectiveness' credo (see below).

TABLE 1.1. Rutherford's three working credos

Credo One: Punishment	Credo Two: Efficiency	Credo Three: Care

Moral condemnation
Dislike of offenders
Degradation
Unfettered discipline
Expressive function
  of sanctions
	Pragmatism
	Management, system-based
	Smooth administration
	Process oriented
	Lack of correctional
	  ideology
	Separation of action from
	  beliefs or sentiments
		Liberal, humanitarian
		Empathy with offenders
		Optimistic, inclusive
		Belief in constructive work
		Open and accountable
		  procedures
		Links with social policy

Rutherford was concerned with senior practitioners (prison governors, senior probation officers, and so on) and their ideologies ('beliefs and sentiments'; Rutherford 1993, preface). Later, we explore penal values as they are understood and practised mainly by prisoners and prison staff respectively, but in the context of the changing shape of broader management and public-political ideologies. Rutherford's framework is a helpful place to begin. Table 1.1 draws on his account to show the key features of each working credo (for a full account of Rutherford's credos and an alternative reworking of them, see Rutherford 1993; and Cavadino et al. 1999).

Several commentators have pointed out that Credo Two (otherwise referred to as managerialism) can be combined with Credo One or Credo Three (see e.g. Lacey 1994; Cavadino et al. 1999).

How might Rutherford's credos apply in the Prison Service today? It is interesting to observe that the punishment credo has reappeared in terms of the contribution it makes to policy and rhetoric and that feelings of resentment or degradation form an important part of it (see e.g. Pratt 2000, 2002). The 'efficiency' credo would now probably incorporate some of the 'due process' elements placed by Rutherford in his 'care' credo. The 'care' credo would not include the word 'liberal'. Liberal values have been discredited and all but abandoned in criminal justice practice. This is so in prisons in particular, in the wake of a series of escapes from high security prisons in the mid-1990s, and public outcry at serious offences committed by prisoners on home leave and early release schemes throughout the 1990s (see further below). Some important changes to the penal landscape have taken place which shape and constrain the values expressed, practised, and yearned for, and we shall outline them here. Between 1990 and 2003 the Prison Service has had five Director Generals: Chris Train (1982–91); Joe Pilling (1992–3); Derek Lewis (1993–5); Richard Tilt (1995–9); and Martin Narey (1999–2003), with a sixth taking up post on promotion from Deputy Director General just as the book was being completed.[5] The penal values represented during each Director General's reign arguably represent distinguishable phases in what has been a complex and troubled period. As this near parting with liberalism is a central part of the context in which we have carried out our research, and a key theoretical stage in our analysis, we shall try to tell this story below.

Prisons, Regimes, and the 'King and McDermott Exposé'[6]

In a much-cited article published in the *British Journal of Criminology* in 1989, King and McDermott suggested that the apparent crisis in British prisons was a crisis of management (of staff) rather than a crisis of overcrowding, sanitation, and resources (King and McDermott 1989). Regimes (including time spent out of cells, time spent in and numbers of prisoners attending, especially work, but also education, training, and association) were consistently worse in 1985–7 than they had been in 1970–2. This was despite widely declared constructive aspirations and a determined effort emerging at the time to introduce the values of economy, efficiency, and effectiveness, and management accountability, into Prison Department activities (King and McDermott 1989: 109; Train 1985). It was also despite pre-'Fresh Start' increases in staffing levels,[7] and improvements to staff–prisoner ratios (King and McDermott 1989: 123). This was without account being taken of 'huge increments' in the amount of overtime worked (King and McDermott 1989: 124;

[5] Martin Narey, one of the main protagonists of this chapter, was promoted from Director General of the Prison Service, to the first post of Commissioner of Correctional Services, in March 2003. See later.

[6] This part of our account was informed by discussions with Tony Bottoms (2003, pers. comm.).

[7] Fresh Start was introduced by Director General, Chris Train. It introduced fixed working hours (ending overtime) and the unification of uniformed and non-uniformed grades, clearer line management, and enhanced pay, thus leading to the abolition of the role of chief officer. See Liebling and Price (2001); and King and McDermott (1995: 10 and 29–36).

also Home Office 1979). The article's findings and implications were discussed at length at several seminars and high-profile meetings. Some of the deterioration in regimes was a result of troubles in the dispersal estate and an increasing emphasis on security and control (King 1994a). Other explanations included the increasing intransigence of the Prison Officers' Association, and the powerful grip of the POA over what happened in prisons.[8]

It was this kind of failure to deliver acceptable standards of daily provision in most prisons that led King and Morgan to favour the potentially achievable 'humane containment' goal for the Prison Service over the hopelessly unrealistic, aspirational, 'good and useful life' statutory formulation of the Prison Service's aims (King and Morgan 1980; Bottoms 1990; King and McDermott 1995, chapter 1; Stern 1993, chapter 4).[9] Human warehouses would surely be preferable to *inhuman* warehouses (King and McDermott 1995: 9)? What use were 'good intentions', if they were 'devoid of real meaning' and not aimed at 'specifying achievable objectives' (King and McDermott 1995: 9)? Industrial relations disputes, poor systems of managerial control, an increasing prison population and deteriorating prison conditions made for impoverished regimes and a lack of justice.

New working arrangements for prison officers, a determined flirtation with new management systems (including the new practice of regime monitoring), and a long-standing (but unsuccessful) debate about the possibility of introducing minimum standards led to increasing concern with questions of aims, achievements, and 'performance' (King and McDermott 1995; Train 1985; Dunbar 1985). Modest improvements were accomplished. But they were not sufficient, or sufficiently deeply embedded in the cultures of otherwise materially improving establishments. Collective protests, and other troubles, were increasing and spreading from the maximum security estate to lower security category C prisons and local prisons (Home Office 1977, 1982, 1987, 1991a, 1994). Problems of penal order were beginning to dominate debates about the modern prison (Sparks *et al.* 1996, chapter 1; Fitzgerald and Sim 1979; Thomas and Pooley 1980; Home Office 1984; Ditchfield 1990).

---

[8] See Stern (1993, e.g. at 59–60 and 75–7).
[9] Rule 1 of the 1964 Prison Rules, as amended, now preserved at rule 3 of the 1999 Prison Rules as amended. See n. 10.

The Liberal Penal Project: Woolf, Justice, and a New Penal Agenda

> Were these proposals to be followed, then we believe that they would substantially influence the way prisoners come to view the prison system. While not preventing all disruptions, they could marginalise those who claim they must resort to deeply damaging and costly disturbances on the grounds that there is no other way to have their voices heard.
>
> (Home Office 1991*a*, para. 14.438)

The Woolf Report was based on an independent public inquiry into a major series of disturbances at Manchester Prison (Strangeways) and other prisons during April 1990. It set out, in its 600 pages, a promising liberal penal project, which surprised and delighted commentators, practitioners, and policy-makers alike. Its methods had been open, its framework wide-ranging, and its account of the problems leading to the disturbances fair. The Woolf Report was hailed as the most impressive analysis of the English penal system since the Gladstone Report of 1895—'a landmark' (Player and Jenkins 1994: 1). Its diagnosis of the main problems of the Prison Service were: instability arising from overcrowding; poor conditions and regimes; staff shortages and inadequate staff training; and poor staff attitudes towards prisoners. The Report also suggested, as many others had before, that there was a moral crisis in the penal system, or lack of clarity about purpose, which also contributed to the disturbances (Home Office 1991*a*: 239; Home Office 1979; Bottoms 1990; Garland 2001*a*). Its recommendations were widely welcomed, and they resulted in several major practical developments: the appointment of a Prisons Ombudsman, revised grievance procedures, the creation of a Criminal Justice Consultative Committee and 24 area committees, better contact with families, and improved sanitation facilities. Some of the broader recommendations of the Report (for example, closer co-operation between different parts of the criminal justice system; better overall standards of justice; a separate statement of purpose and improved conditions for remand prisoners; and a system of accredited standards) were seen as providing a reform agenda which might last 25 years.

Woolf's major argument was that the balance between security, control, and justice should always be carefully maintained, and that prisoners should be treated with humanity and fairness. Justice, for Woolf, meant due process, fairness, and standards of care consistent with the letter and spirit of Prison Rules 1 and 2 (Morgan 1992).[10] This balance would ensure that fewer prisoners felt aggrieved enough to take collective action against their ill-treatment, as they had at the time of the Strangeways and other disturbances. Relationships with staff, a greater degree of responsibility for prisoners, and a minimum basic threshold of quality of life (a legitimate expectation) would constitute important components of this balancing act. It was significant that Woolf's analysis was very much in line with the broader 'well-formulated' and largely liberal penal and criminal justice climate of the time (Downes and Morgan 2002; see also Cavadino *et al.* 1999). This policy climate supported decarceration (the Criminal Justice Act 1991 attempted to place limits on the use of imprisonment), an explicit recognition of the limited role of imprisonment, and a determination to offer more constructive disposals in the community (Cavadino and Dignan 1997; Rutherford 1996).[11] There were some important limitations to Woolf's analysis, few of which received attention at the time (see Ryan 1992; Sim 1994; Richardson 1993; Morgan 1997), but which also need setting out here. We turn first to what happened in practice.

A White Paper, *Custody, Care and Justice*, was published shortly after the publication of the Woolf Report, and was drafted by a 'Woolf implementation unit' within the Prison Service, led by the civil servant who had acted as secretary to the Woolf inquiry (Morgan 1992). The government announced its acceptance of the 'direction set' by Woolf's recommendations, and a period of major reform began.[12] The White Paper continued and developed some of

[10] Rule 1 (as it then was) provides that 'the purpose of the training and treatment of prisoners is to encourage and assist them to lead a good and useful life'; Rule 2(3) provides that 'at all times prisoners must be treated so as to maintain and enhance their self-respect and sense of personal responsibility'.

[11] The Criminal Justice Act 1991 was based on a 'just deserts' model of punishment consisting of due process, proportionate sentences, and use of custody limited to the most serious offences (Cavadino and Dignan 1997: 49–51; Home Office 1991*b*). In practice it was a hybrid Act, with (amongst other things) increased sentences for violent and sexual offenders.

[12] A senior commentator described this White Paper as a masterpiece of drafting: it committed the government and Prison Service to all of the principles, to the 'sort of service ministers wanted . . . without a single commitment in terms of the money to do that' (2002, pers. comm.).

the themes outlined in an earlier Green Paper (*Punishment, Custody and the Community*; Home Office 1988). The 1991 White Paper described imprisonment as 'an expensive way of making bad people worse' (Home Office 1991*b*, para. 2.7).

The story of the public and political backlash that followed (the 'law and order counter-reformation') is well-known (see e.g. Cavadino and Dignan 1997: 103–4; Cavadino *et al.* 1999: 20–2; and Garland 2001*a*).[13] As Garland suggests, changes in the emotional tone of crime policy, from 'humanity' to 'resentment', were characteristic of contemporary penality in the UK and the USA over this period (Garland 2001*a*). What we want to add to this rather familiar (at least, to criminologists) story is a much less familiar account of how these climate changes were reaching into life on prison landings. Prisons underwent a 'crisis of authority', but this was a crisis of a very different kind from that described by Fitgerald and Sim in the 1970s (Fitzgerald and Sim 1979; Cavadino and Dignan 1997: 133–4).

Immediately following the publication of the Woolf Report in 1991, Joe Pilling, the newly appointed Director General of the Prison Service, published an influential lecture, 'Back to Basics: Relationships in the Prison Service'. This lecture was circulated with a note from the then Director of Inmate Administration, Ian Dunbar, to all governors: 'We now see relationships, and even more fundamentally the values on which good relationships must be based, as central to our vision for the new Prison Service Agency to be launched next year' (Dunbar 1992: 1).

In this lecture, Pilling took up the 'fundamentally important' concepts of respect, fairness, individuality, care, and openness, arguing, like Woolf, that the Prison Service needed to re-legitimize itself (Pilling 1992). Pilling argued that these five concepts constituted 'humanity' and would, if practised, deliver the promise of the Prison Service's Mission Statement, which states: 'Her Majesty's Prison Service serves the public by keeping in custody those committed by the courts. Our duty is to look after them with humanity and help them lead law-abiding and useful lives in custody and after release.' He also used the term 'trust'. His lecture was grounded

---

[13] Among the reasons given are poor public presentation of the Criminal Justice Act 1991, a severe economic recession, which made the 'middle classes' anxious, and rising fear of crime (see e.g. Cavadino *et al.* 1999: 26).

in the 'renewed optimism' around at this time—about the moral practice of imprisonment and its prospects for achieving change, through the encouragement of personal responsibility and by taking 'calculated risks' (Pilling 1992: 9). He did distinguish between the obligation to nurture 'a sense of hope' and any return to the idea that 'imprisonment in itself is a good thing' (Pilling 1992: 11). One of the many interesting observations in his paper was that these values should be adopted at all levels of the Service. We shall return to Pilling's influential paper later, in Chapter 5.

Several practical changes arising from Woolf have been, and continue to be, implemented although others have not. In addition to the changes outlined already, prisons were generally designed and built with slightly smaller wings, divided into spurs since the early 1990s (for example, Doncaster and Woodhill were 'new generation designs', and other prisons such as Whitemoor were built with small spurs).[14] Telephones were introduced, and prisoners were allowed better and more generous visits and home leave facilities. In this sense, the Woolf project has continued to reach into prison life at the level of policy and practice, and there has been no overriding 'abandonment' of the Woolf agenda, as some critics have argued.[15] There have been some important departures, however, and we shall consider these below.

At the level of ideology or sensibilities, Woolf's message had a much more troubled passage. What the Woolf agenda did to the *inner life* of prisons, almost from the moment of publication, was to send a clear signal that staff should treat prisoners civilly, and that order in prison was dependent to a large degree on justice, and

---

[14] Later in the decade, many existing prisons were asked to take on additional accommodation, which consisted of houseblocks with galleried wings of 120, gated in the middle. These larger wings were considerably cheaper to build and were easier to supervise, requiring fewer staff (see Fairweather and McConville 2000). Despite lower staffing levels, they are regarded by many prisoners as safer than previous designs.

[15] More recently (2002–3), televisions in cells have been introduced for all prisoners except those on basic regimes. Release on temporary licence has been 'eased', Home Detention Curfew has been introduced for prisoners coming towards the end of relatively short sentences, and prisoners are becoming involved in reparation and restorative justice practices. These are all liberal initiatives, albeit with varied and complex causes. Under the decency framework, laxity is forbidden but some might argue that, internally at least, Woolf's meaning of the term 'justice' has returned to favour. See further below.

on the meeting of legitimate expectations. Newly opening prisons, most of them local prisons and many of them privately managed, took the Woolf Report as a blueprint, and sought to deliver, in the new managerialist language appearing at that time, model regimes based on activity, justice, and security, as Woolf had recommended (see e.g. James *et al.* 1997; and Chapter 2). Order, it was promised, would follow. There were good theoretical reasons for this. Reasonable and legitimate treatment encouraged compliance, defused tensions, and fostered good relationships between staff and prisoners, which had long been known to be crucial to stability in prison (along with other situational measures; see Sparks *et al.* 1996; Home Office 1984).

Prisons and the Problems of Security, Order, and Justice

In practice, several unexpected problems arose. The first was the problem of order. Despite impressive new regimes, levels of violence and drug-taking soared, particularly in these new 'Woolf-like' prisons (Prison Service 1994*a*). Prisoners did not willingly take up the (albeit limited) constructive activities on offer, but chose to stay in bed and mix on their barely supervised wings, where private sector competition had removed all but the essential staff. In some establishments at least, 'justice' became 'laxity', because staff understood the change of focus to mean the avoidance of conflict, and the cultivation of tolerant relationships with prisoners.[16] On their own new performance measures, prisons were looking decidedly troubled (see Table 1.2).[17] It was significant, as we shall argue

[16] Jacobs's account of the emergence of a liberal administration at Stateville during the 1970s illustrates similar confusion between 'rehabilitation' and laxity or disorganization (Jacobs 1977: 73–93).

[17] It is difficult to gather *evidence*, beyond escape figures (which are stark), for the existence of laxity in prison regimes during 1992–4. This is partly because '[senior management] were, officially, trying not to notice'. Bodies like the Inspectorate 'would have observed good relationships, and been satisfied with that' (2003, pers. comm.). Escapes and assaults peaked during 1991–4 (see Table 1.2). There is evidence of high levels of drug use, and high adjudications during 1993–4 in particular, but arguably a relatively low level of formal 'policing' was part of the climate, especially, but not exclusively, in the maximum security estate (Liebling 2002). The earliest audits found that many prisons were barely compliant with policy instructions, and thus the poor early results constitute evidence that prisons were 'doing things in a different way' (2003, pers. comm.). Escape figures are a convincing illustration of procedural laxity, as most of the investment in security, post-Learmont, was in the maximum security estate, and yet most of the improvement in escape rate

below, that the Home Office changed Woolf's carefully chosen language of 'security, order and justice' to 'Custody, *Care* and Justice' in the 1991 White Paper.[18] This choice of language was in line with other related thinking about prison matters at the time,[19] although the White Paper gave equal weight to matters of security, management, programmes, and standards.

This confounding of the terms 'justice' and 'care' and confusion over the word 'liberal' requires special consideration. It is part of our argument in this book that one of the explanations for a move away from liberal working credos is a lack of clarity about what the terms 'liberal' and 'justice' mean. The term 'liberal' has been associated in popular and public debates, and as we argue throughout, in some practices, with laxity, indulgence of the offender, a failure to demand responsibility for action, and poor outcomes in terms of public safety. This usage must be clearly distinguished

has occurred in the medium security estate. 'The level of investment did not change, but behaviour did' (ibid.). The change was from a climate in which managers and prison staff were 'relaxed about everything' (and where therefore levels of informal discretion were high) to one where 'procedures matter' (see Bottoms 2003b). Not *all* prisons have entered this 'new world', and not *all* prison regimes were 'lax' in the sense meant here, during this period. There is, however, a detectable overall trend.

[18] The word 'care' causes considerable controversy in prisons, with some staff finding it unutterable, and many studies of the prison officer claiming that the key conflict they face is the tension between custody and care. Staff who take on specialist welfare roles are known, somewhat sceptically, as 'care bears' by other staff (see Liebling and Price 2001). It is interesting that the Scottish Prison Service have a 'Director of Rehabilitation and Care' and some prisons in England and Wales have had a 'Head of Care'. The term 'care' has an unclear meaning and can lead to infringements of (for example) principles of respect, or 'benevolent tyranny' (Bottoms and Stelman 1988: 41). This is not to say that care for persons is not important: 'a social work practice which makes a point of respecting persons and their choices, but which does not offer care, is ultimately only an abstraction devoid of human commitment and compassion' (ibid.). The point is that the word can be rather slippery.

[19] It is significant that the two reports on which the White Paper drew were the Woolf Report (co-authored by the then Chief Inspector of Prisons, Judge Stephen Tumim), and The HMCIP Review of Suicide Prevention Procedures. The latter report, amongst others, led to a new strategy for suicide prevention launched in 1994, called 'Caring for the Suicidal' (see HMCIP 1990a; Prison Service 1994b). The White Paper elaborated on the term 'care' as follows: 'staff have a responsibility not only for the custody but also for the care of prisoners. This must be reflected in staff training [and] must be demonstrated through providing programmes and conditions for prisoners which treat them with humanity, dignity and respect' (Home Office 1991b: 4).

TABLE 1.2. Escapes, assaults, and drug use, 1989–2003

Indicator	1989	1990	1991	1992–3	1993–4	1994–5	1995–6	1996–7	1997–8	1998–9	1999–2000	2000–1	2001–2	2002–3
Escapes from prisons	116	201	315	269	171	151	52	33	23	28	30	11	15	5
Escapes from prison escorts	163	113	132	131	102	51	36	20	10	7	8	8	11	12
Escapes from escort contractors	—	—	—	—	23	15	34	78	72	55	59	58	40	33
Escape rate (%)	0.54	0.76	1.03	0.79	0.60	0.41	0.24	0.23	0.17	0.14	0.06	0.03	0.04	0.02
Assault rate (%)	7.7	8.6	9.4	10.2	12.3	11.6	10.6	9.3	9.4	9.4	10.0	9.9	9.9	9.1
Rate of positive tests for drug use (%)	—	—	—	—	—	—	—	24.4	20.8	18.3	14.2	12.4	11.6	11.7
Average population	48,500	44,523	44,754	44,628	45,819	49,314	51,614	56,671	62,584	65,228	64,816	64,576	67,474	71,498

Sources: Prison Service (1994a) and Prison Service Headquarters. Note that escapes and assaults peak during the period 1991–4.

from 'liberalism' as a central idea in academic discourse (Neal 1997).[20] Woolf's *intention* may have been to communicate a version of liberalism meaning 'favourable to or respectful of individual rights and freedoms' (*New Shorter Oxford English Dictionary* 1993), based on the democratic and 'contractual' ideal. This central idea (as with many important ideas) was actually quite difficult to translate into practice. As Ryan observed: 'No number of formal rules will secure justice unless the prison officers deliver it in their daily rounds, in their intimate relationships with those over whom they exercise great and sometimes regrettably, unyielding power. About how to persuade officers to deliver justice in this sense, the Report has very little to offer' (Ryan 1992: 10–11).

This confusion over how to deliver justice in practice was confounded by the association of the word 'justice' with 'care', in the White Paper and elsewhere. The White Paper itself was full of the attention to balance initiated by Woolf. It even said, explicitly, that 'constructive relationships must not engender laxity' (Home Office 1991*b*: 3). But White Papers, like policy instructions, are rarely read by practitioners (Liebling 2000, 2002).[21] The term 'justice' was intended to communicate the inviolability of individual rights (consistent with use made of the term by political and other theorists of justice) and the relevance of individual redress of legitimate expectations (Home Office 1991*a*; Sandel 1982). The term 'justice' takes on a less precise meaning in practice when it is linked to the trickier concept of care. We shall return to this point towards the end of the chapter, and in our explorations of the terms 'respect' and 'fairness' later in the book.

Joe Pilling did not survive the transition to Agency status,[22] but was replaced by the first Chief Executive of the Prison Service, Derek Lewis, recruited from the private sector. Lewis launched a new *Framework Document* (Prison Service 1993), and introduced eight key performance indicators, and six goals, against which the success (or performance) of the Service was to be evaluated.

---

[20] See also e.g. Abbey on Taylor's 'complex liberalism' (Abbey 2000: 111–27); and later.

[21] If prison staff had (had time to) read the White Paper in full, its (and Woolf's) carefully balanced messages might have survived better translation into practice.

[22] It was said anecdotally that Joe Pilling had alienated Kenneth Clarke, because Pilling had said that he was fundamentally committed to a public service (pers. comm.).

He made the following promise:

The move to Agency status signalled the beginning of fundamental management changes designed to make the Prison Service a more effective, better performing organisation. 1993–4 saw the assignment of greater responsibility and accountability to governors, the introduction of targets for establishments, rigorous measurement of performance, the publication of a new code of operating standards and the added stimulus of competition from the private sector ... (Prison Service 1994a: 2)

The two newly opening privately managed prisons (Wolds and Blakenhurst) both experienced major threats to order. They achieved unprecedented hours out of cells, but drug-taking was high, staff felt uncomfortably unsafe, and, in these prisons and elsewhere, levels of assaults on staff and prisoners were increasing (see James *et al.* 1997; Prison Service 1994a). There was considerable opposition to the contracting out of the management of prisons from campaigning organizations, the public sector and its unions, and from many academic critics, on moral grounds (Ryan and Ward 1989; Christie 1993).[23] Its introduction was defended by the government and by Prison Service senior managers on the grounds that competition would lead to improvement overall, particularly in the treatment of prisoners. The public sector was, after all, in need of modernization.

When Michael Howard took over from Kenneth Clarke as Home Secretary in 1993, there was a distinct change in tone, in relation to both the use of custody and the nature of prison regimes. Howard consolidated and enhanced the corrective backlash to the Criminal Justice Act 1991, 'switching the emphasis, rhetorically and substantively wherever possible, from "just deserts" sentencing to incapacitation and general deterrence' (Nellis 2001: 29). In addition, according to a leaked memorandum, the new Home Secretary wanted to take a 'radical look at the nature of the prison experience'. Prison regimes were 'lax' and Howard thought that prisoners should 'spend less time in leisure activities and more time working' (King and McDermott 1995: 53).

---

[23] And from the Labour Party in opposition: 'It is not appropriate for people to profit out of incarceration—this is surely one area where a free market certainly does not exist' (Shadow Home Secretary, Jack Straw, Mar. 1995, in Mathiasen 2001).

Prisoners (and, in some cases, prison governors) were in need of firmer discipline.

The second unexpected problem to arise in prison life was exposed by a series of escapes from maximum security prisons. The first involved six high-security prisoners, five of whom had been convicted of terrorist offences. They managed to escape from Whitemoor Prison's Special Security Unit (SSU). The second involved three maximum-security prisoners from a second maximum security establishment, Parkhurst (Liebling 2002: 111–19). In both cases, prisoners had managed to accumulate and test equipment, apparently unobserved. The escapes were linked, in the scathing Woodcock and Learmont Reports that followed, to a serious breakdown in the balance of power in long-term prisons, and to staff under-enforcement of the rules, in the interests of good relationships and a quieter life (Home Office 1994, 1995). In the potentially highly charged, newly technological environment of Whitemoor's SSU, staff believed their special high security unit within a maximum security prison was escape-proof. The fear of disorder was considerably higher than the fear of escape. Line management responsibility was unclear, practices were rarely audited, and governors visited the Unit infrequently. No one in line management above the governor 'had worked in a prison in any capacity' (Home Office 1994: 74). The Prison Service was publicly humiliated, to the shame and rage of a radical Conservative government which had, by this stage, entered their 'punitive turn' (Sparks 1996: 76),[24] when an inquiry found that prison officers were shopping for category A prisoners and allowing personal possessions to reach unacceptable levels. There were, of course, complex sociological and historical reasons for this liberal style of long-term imprisonment (see Liebling 2000, 2002; Advisory Council on the Penal System 1968; McEvoy 2001). But if this was liberalism, its time had come:

The Service fell into trying to deliver the philosophy behind Woolf if not the reality—there were real issues of expenditure, but it was a big turning

---

[24] This reconfiguring of punishment resulted in a deeper and heavier version of imprisonment for a far higher number of prisoners. The prison population rose at an unprecedented rate from 1993 onwards, from a low of 40,722 in the December following the publication of the Woolf Report (King and McDermott 1995) to 73,911 at the time of writing (Home Office 2004; Prison Service 2003). See Fig. 1.1.

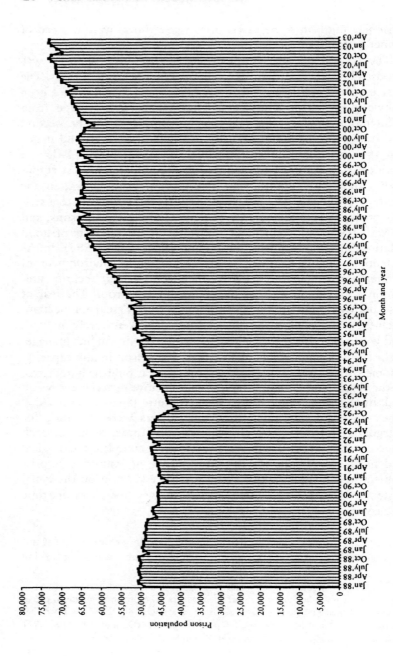

FIGURE 1.1.   Prison population, England and Wales, 1988–2003

point about the sort of Prison Service we were going to have. The Prison Service saw Woolf, saw the White Paper, were intoxicated by it, and it was just simply the fact the security didn't matter. There was a time during that period when nobody could have said how many people we had unlawfully at large. (Narey 2002)

Woolf, of course, had never said that security did not matter. Nor had he recommended a non-technical version of liberalism. But it was too late. The escapes gave the radical Conservative Howard all he needed to berate the Prison Service for its indulgent, inappropriate, badly managed and poorly monitored regimes. Howard famously insisted that prison regimes should be 'decent but austere', where 'decent' meant a basic but not indulgent minimum standard of privileges and conditions. Everything above the basic minimum 'should be earned by good behaviour and hard work' (Prison Service 1995; see also O'Grady 2002; and Farrington et al. 2002 on the new 'high intensity' regimes for young offenders). Howard also coined the slogan, 'Prison Works', by which he meant that longer sentences and higher prison populations were acceptable and were to be encouraged, if necessary, in the modern war on crime; he 'did not flinch' from measures which would increase the prison population (Cavadino and Dignan 1997: 12). Other cataclysmic demonstrations of the apparent dangers of liberalism during the 1990s (for example, the Bulger murder, a murder by a prisoner on home leave, an alleged corruption scandal in the country's best-known resettlement prison[25]), and the changing course of 'law and order' politics, altered the language and practice of penology in England dramatically (see Downes and Morgan 2002). This was despite—or partly as a result of—the English penal system's most determined flirtation with liberal justice principles only two years earlier.

Derek Lewis was removed from his post following the second major set of escapes from a maximum security prison in 1995. His leadership lasted until his dramatic major clash with Michael Howard over who had responsibility for the escapes.[26] Lewis's 'hoped-for independence' was never real. His period in office was

---

[25] But see Home Affairs Select Committee (2001).

[26] Anne Widdecombe, then Howard's Junior Minister for Prisons, famously said, after the row that culminated in Howard's decision to sack Derek Lewis, that Howard had 'something of the night' about him (see O'Grady 2002; Lewis 1997).

turbulent and was made more so by an ambitious and right-wing Home Secretary who was exposed to several humiliating crises. In 1995: 'Mr Howard simply handed him a revolver and said he wanted him dead by five o'clock. Mr Lewis refused. Okay, said Mr Howard, by dawn. Mr Lewis still refused. In that case, said Mr Howard, with "great sadness", you hang. On went the noose, whoosh went the trap, snap went Mr Lewis' neck' (Jenkins 1995; Lewis 1997, ch. 13).

The Service was devastated. Lewis had not been well liked by operational people more used to their own kind, but he was all they had:

The Service at the time of Derek Lewis' departure felt terribly beleaguered. It was very badly damaged. It was performing extremely badly. We can't expect the sort of investment I want to see if we don't keep security as the bedrock, and that had been abandoned. Everybody knows that there were three category A escapes from Whitemoor and two from Parkhurst, but people forget that in the first five years of the 1990s there were nineteen category A escapes. In 1993, in total—these are not escapes from escorts or hospitals and courts—there were more than 300 escapes from prison, compared to fourteen last year with a much bigger population . . . So I think the Service had lost its way very badly indeed. (Narey 2002)

Cavadino *et al.* suggest that one reading of these events might be that a 'Strategy A' (punitive) Home Secretary exercised 'such personal hands-on influence' that what had been a 'Strategy B' (managerialist) strategy came under 'intolerable strain' (Cavadino *et al.* 1999: 132).[27] Woolf had been attempting to employ Strategy B techniques in pursuit of an ultimately Strategy C goal (justice for inmates) (Cavadino *et al.* 1999: 135).[28]

We shall see below that, in a reactive turnaround, 'Strategy A' began to dominate, politically and in the courts at least, from this point on (see also Cavadino *et al.* 1999: 138–41). The 'rediscovery of the criminal' that characterized New Labour's term in office was accompanied by a determined 'rediscovery of the prisoner' by those working in and managing prisons (see Downes and Morgan 2002: 297; Bottoms 2003*b*; and Wiener 1994).

---

[27] These Strategies relate to Rutherford's Credos One, Two, and Three, outlined earlier.

[28] Although as we have argued, Strategy C, as Rutherford describes it, is 'care' rather than 'justice'.

Managerialism, Privatization, and the Delivery of Penal Values

Underpinning many of the above developments, particularly the attempt to improve and modernize the management of prisons, has been the onset of managerialism. This has been variously characterized as the search for more efficient, effective output-oriented techniques for organizing and improving public services, and as an 'ideology of total, finely calibrated control' (Nellis 2001: 33). The term is used to describe a process of public sector transformation started under the Conservative government, from the early 1980s, but very much continued under New Labour. This transformation involved the 'remaking of the British state—its institutions and practices as well as its culture and ideology' (Clark and Newman 1997, p. ix; see also Pollitt 1995; McEvoy 2001: 254–8). Its aim was to overcome the deficiencies of the bureaucratic ways of the machinery of government (Clarke and Newman 1997: 20) by introducing private sector practices and mechanisms into well-meaning but inefficient organizations. Managerialism brought with it close attention to budgets, target-setting, strategic plans, competition, best practice, performance measurement, and the concept of 'value for money', and, many have argued persuasively, a move away from any discussion of purpose and ethics (Nellis 2001).

Critics argued throughout the 1990s that managerialism was displacing older normative concerns and ideals in criminal justice and in prisons in particular (see Feeley and Simon 1992; Bottoms 1995).[29] It represented a departure from an 'old way of life': the welfare state 'compromise between capitalism (the free market) and socialism (public provision through the state)', the ameliorative aspirations of many public institutions, including the prison, and an ethos of 'public service' (Clark and Newman 1997: 1 and *passim.*). A clear value base had been embedded in notions of citizenship, bureaucracy, and professionalism. This framework was destabilized during the 1980s in the face of 'complex pressures of public spending restraint', shifting (New Right) ideologies, and the

---

[29] Van Swaaningen, amongst others, suggests that managerialism and *moralism* or *moralizing* do 'need each other badly', for example, in the identification and control of dangerousness and risk (van Swaaningen 1997: 183). This relationship is to be distinguished from the use of managerialist strategies to pursue values such as justice.

exposure of bureaucratic inefficiencies in the public sector (Clarke and Newman 1997: 13). The state was seen as acting as an inhibitor of innovation and efficiency—whereas the market would increase and enhance consumer choice. Bureaucrats were the enemy of the people: 'Hiding behind the impersonality of regulations and "red tape" to deny choice, building bureaucratic empires at the expense of providing service, and insulated from the "real world" pressures of competition by their monopolistic position' (Clark and Newman 1997: 15).

Professionals were self-interested and had become too powerful. 'Worse still', argued Clarke and Newman:

Welfare professionals were often the product of 1960s and 1970s 'liberalism' which was viewed as undermining personal responsibility and family authority and as prone to trendy excesses such as egalitarianism, anti-discrimination policies, moral relativism or child-centredness. Such attacks undercut the implicit claim of the 1945 organisational settlement that the professional bureaucracies of the welfare state could be trusted to represent the 'public interest'. (Clarke and Newman 1997: 15)[30]

This critique of bureaucracy and (the less overt critique) of professionalism was applied wholesale to prisons. They were poorly managed, increasingly expensive, wasteful, bureaucratic, and shamefully out of date (Home Office 1979; Home Affairs Committee 1987; King and McDermott 1989; Lygo 1991). There were truths in the claims described by Clark and Newman, then. Regimes were impoverished (King and McDermott 1989), although (importantly) nobody knew this with any accuracy until King and McDermott published their 1989 article.[31] There were major concerns about ineffectiveness, lack of accountability, and extravagance (replicated in much of the public sector during the 1980s). New public management developed into the reinvention and modernization of public sector organizations in the interests of

---

[30] Hennessy describes, in his account of the early reforms of Whitehall and the Thatcherite anti-Civil Service bias underpinning the intensity of this period, that 'the theory of the welfare state . . . has not actually until recently included any emphasis at all on efficiency, effectiveness or value for money'. The protagonists of the 'failed Keynesian-Beveridgite consensus' were the new demons and a crusade against waste and inefficiency began (Priestley, in Hennessy 2001: 590 and *passim*).

[31] Bottoms, pers. comm.

'value for money' and improved overall performance (Raine and Willson 1997). Those driving this agenda saw it as the only effective way to achieve 'quality' by accelerating the momentum of reform. Public sector managers should, after all, know what resources they were managing and to what effect. Scrutiny, of an unprecedented kind, was born (see Hennessy 2001, ch. 14). The movement saw a decline in the influence of professionals in the management of their organizations, and some tensions between the values of non-managerialist 'expert professionals' and the need for greater 'public accountability' (Power 2001: 45). The main cultural shift was 'from an administrative to a managerial culture' (Wilson and Doig 1996: 53). This meant an increase in management control over organizations via a combination of shorter management chains, devolution of some functions (like budgets), tighter accountability, and an insistence on continuing improvement, as measured by newly proliferating performance indicators. The time was right for a mixed economy (King and McDermott 1995: 48)—the 'new solution' to the prisons crisis and an 'additional resource' for government (Home Affairs Committee 1987, para. 4). The Derek Lewis era of privatization and performance represented the Prison Service's first serious attempt to adopt modern managerialist techniques in practice,[32] and this development has of course continued.

The use of private companies to build, manage, and eventually finance prisons was conceived as 'an experiment' (Home Affairs Committee 1987, paras. 10 and 15) and was to be restricted, in the first instance, to facilities for prisoners on remand (Windlesham 1993). Politically and ideologically, the choice between privatization (which would bring growth, innovation, competition, cost savings, and improvements in standards) and decarceration (which would entail risk, continuing uncontrolled costs, and continuing union resistance to change), particularly in the face of active lobbying by interested companies, was clear. Monopoly had led to complacency and 'a failure to innovate' (Young 1987: 4). A competitive bid was held for the management of Wolds Remand Centre, and shortly afterwards for several additional prisons holding both

---

[32] The early precursors can be seen on paper, in (for example) Train 1985; and Dunbar 1985, whose term 'dynamic security' is still one of the best expressions of the delicate balancing act in which prison staff engage. These early efforts in strategic management accountability were less revolutionary because there were no satisfactory mechanisms for ensuring that such 'on paper' expressions infiltrated practice.

sentenced and remand prisoners (Windlesham 1993; James *et al.* 1997). These newly built, modern prisons would offer 'value for money' and 'humane, challenging and purposeful' regimes (Windlesham 1993: 300). This move would pave the way for a broader programme of institutional and penal reform.

Critics argued throughout that this internal penal reform agenda largely managed to avoid questions of value, failing to resolve the 'moral crisis' of the late 1980s, and proceeding with an impoverished concept of service delivery characteristic of the 'new penology' (Feeley and Simon 1992). The language and practice of 'systemic efficiency' usurped the language of morality (Feeley and Simon 1992: 452). The Conservative government introduced privatization not because of any 'penological principle' but because of their 'conviction of the need for radical reform outside the prevailing consensus' (Windlesham 1993: 421–2). Sparks suggested that privatization—the logic of managerialism taken to its natural conclusion in criminal justice—was offered as a weak solution to the legitimation problems of the modern penal system (Sparks 1994). Privatization, and experiments with market testing, formed part of a pragmatic, 'control model' approach to the delivery of penal services. 'The delivery of penal services' was an instrumental notion with little relevance to the ethics of imprisonment. The type of quantification (performance measurement) and the regime aspirations arising out of these developments, argued Feeley, Simon, and others, left crucial questions of moral responsibility and individual transformation untouched.

Harding, and others in favour of private sector competition, have claimed, on the other hand, that the debate about the morality or otherwise of the privatization of prisons can only be resolved using empirical data. They suggest that opponents of privatization have to be careful not to be defenders of public squalor (Harding 1997). If recidivism rates were lower, prisoner health were better, the experience of imprisonment were less painful, or a more legitimate distribution of power and authority in daily prison life were found in some private sector establishments, would these facts not constitute part of a moral argument? We think Harding may be wrong about the moral relevance of these facts, but not for the reasons so far offered by Sparks (1994; see Chapter 2).

The modernizing of prisons, a process in which privatization played a significant but certainly not exclusive role, was part of a much larger reform movement, regarded by many as part of the creation of a new state (Clarke and Newman 1997). More and better management would lead to better and more efficient public services (Wilson and Doig 1996) and 'delivery' for 'the customer' or citizen, as the new Citizen's Charter promised (Hennessy 2001). This drive for greater efficiency and effectiveness included new, mechanical, and hierarchical processes of monitoring and measurement, or new forms of control (Pollitt *et al.* 2002), about which we shall have much more to say in the next chapter. Identifying and devising measurable processes and, where possible, outputs became part of the new reform ethic. This was particularly the case in the UK (Pollitt *et al.* 2002). This 'new craft' of performance audit and monitoring brought with it tensions between the need for technical sophistication, speed, and simplicity, and sensitivity to the cultures of institutions that had 'taken-for-granted' ways of doing complex things (Pollitt *et al.* 2002: 201–3). There was considerable 'pain and agony' over this management transformation (Priestley, cited in Hennessy 2001: 589).

Prisons were among the later organizations to become transformed into quasi-autonomous agencies during the late 1980s and early 1990s. Their invention was the contested climax of the 'Conservative reforms of the state' (Richards and Smith 2002: 104; Hennessy 2001: 618–27). A White Paper issued in 1982 (Cmd. 8616) required 31 government departments to critically review their operating procedures and their systems of financial management under the Financial Management Initiative.[33] The intention of agencies was to improve and modernize the management and performance of large public organizations by introducing market mechanisms and habits and by allowing greater managerial, financial, and personnel autonomy. Agencies would concentrate on implementation of policy. They would each have an accountable chief executive, who would be responsible for providing a service. Strategic policy-making would remain in the hands of a smaller Whitehall elite. There was considerable opposition to this move (e.g. from the Treasury), so that 'by the time of Thatcher's resignation in

---

[33] Several nationalized utilities were privatized during the late 1980s, and just before the introduction of agency status, legislation was passed that enabled the market to be brought to prisons, in 1992. Mrs Thatcher was no longer Prime Minister, but her great 'coup' was to pave the way for privatization within the Prison Service (see James *et al.* 1997: 56–7).

November 1990, only 34 agencies had been established' (Richards and Smith 2002: 109). This activity intensified during the Major government so that by 1997, '138 agencies had been established which accounted for 66 percent of the Civil Service' (Richards and Smith 2002: 110). This development brought an infusion of people from the private sector into the executive agencies, including the appointment of Derek Lewis as the first Chief Executive of the Prison Service (Lewis 1997: 4–11). Lewis reflected that the Director General of the Service 'should be given the freedom to manage day-to-day operations without ministerial involvement; and the appointment of the new head should be determined by open competition, with candidates from the Civil Service being considered alongside candidates from the private sector—still a relatively new and controversial approach' (Lewis 1997: 5).

Lewis is credited with bringing strategic direction and leadership, a performance framework, and a culture of financial accountability into the Prison Service during his reign ('1,104 days', Lewis 1997). This is despite considerable unease in the early stages (a 'lack of enthusiasm' about this 'brash intruder', Lewis 1997: 17). He describes the Home Office as having a 'stifling, woolly culture', as attracting people who shared its 'liberal and humanitarian ethos', and he was curious about the apparent development of 'a distinct Home Office policy on law and order, largely independent of the government of the day. It was felt that such weighty matters were too important to be left to transitory ministers, who needed to be guided and restrained by their senior civil servants, rather like delinquent schoolboys' (Lewis 1997: 25).

This is a gross simplification but his reaction to what he found during his short tenure, and to the types of people he first met, indicates the intended cultural and managerial revolution brought about by the influx of private sector and related managerialist thinking into prison life and management since the early 1990s.

The privatization of prisons, from 1992 onwards, took place within this context of impatience with the slow pace of public sector reform, continuing resistance by powerful unions (particularly the Prison Officers' Association, despite Fresh Start), and a need to overcome the problems of legitimacy identified by Woolf in his 1990 Report. The turn away from a private sector Chief Executive in 1995 by no means represented a move away from the new managerialist practices of competition and privatization. But this return to the

Service for leadership did signal some recognition that a public sector Director General might heal a deeply wounded organization.

Recovery and Safety, 1995–1999

Lewis was replaced in 1995 by the well-liked, public sector, Richard Tilt, in what was regarded as an unprecedented security, performance, and audit era. Some hoped that Tilt's appointment would signal a first small step back in the direction of public sector values. These hopes were linked to his public sector role but they were also related to his personal and professional qualities. He was the first Director General to have governed a prison; and, for this reason, he inspired loyalty. Tilt accepted the post as a temporary measure but was persuaded to stay for a further two years. From the outset, Richard Tilt was being described as the man who would bring some stability back to the Prison Service. He was 'a safe pair of hands':

It was incredibly important to the Prison Service that that happened . . . the emotions were all perfect. The Service got someone with huge credibility, he had governed Gartree, he had led on industrial relations, and more to the point he had also been over to the Home Office and managed one of the police divisions for a couple of years. (Narey 2002)

What Narey means here is that Richard Tilt (amongst some others) represented 'the human face' of the Prison Service. His continuing role signalled the possibility of continuity with older and more traditional values, but in a new, modern, framework. Tilt appointed a staff officer to sort out how business was to be conducted. He also appointed Phil Wheatley as Director of the high security estate. This was a further significant appointment and represented a change of tone at senior levels (Liebling 2002). The performance agenda started by Lewis, but somewhat resisted by the field, was finally made real.

What followed, from 1995 onwards, was a series of reshapings of parts of the high security estate and senior management in the Prison Service, together with a set of general policies aimed at controlling the behaviour of prisoners but also the behaviour of prison staff. Perhaps more importantly, and radically, the behaviour of governors trusted with shaping these policies in their own prisons was also brought under stringent control (Liebling *et al.* 1997;

Liebling 2000). These policies included Mandatory Drug Testing (MDT); the ending of the handing in of property by visitors; the move away from telephone cards to a 'Personal Identification Number system' of approved telephone numbers; a policy of incentives and earned privileges (IEP); the reduction of home leave and temporary release; and massively increased internal and perimeter security, including the use of closed circuit television (CCTV). This new security and control agenda constituted a departure from the spirit of (and, in some cases, specific proposals accepted from) the Woolf Report and wiped any scent of 'liberalism' away from prison life.[34] This represented an agenda which was clearly echoed outside prisons, in the Probation Service (for example, in the emphasis on enforcement and 'more demanding' forms of punishment in the community; see Nellis 2001: 28; also Nellis 1999, 2000), in 'zero tolerance' policing, and in neo-liberal and neo-conservative political strategies on crime and its control (see Simon 2000; O'Malley 1999). Entitlements were once again 'privileges', to be earned. The message now communicated to those working in prisons was, 'staff must regain control'; and 'the sentence must be effectively delivered'. The term 'justice'—at least in relation to the prison—became something of an embarrassment.[35] Prisoners were firmly reminded of their lack of entitlement to all but the minimum level of privileges, unless they were prepared to earn 'enhanced' levels through good behaviour. What started as a Woolf-like concern to secure 'willing compliance' via high basic threshold standards in prison, with additional incentives on top (Home Office 1991a: 374–8), was translated at the drafting stage into a more punitive and restricted system of 'sticks and carrots', with considerable losses for most prisoners in their levels of privileges (Liebling et al. 1997; Bottoms 2003b). Thus a two-handed strategy of 'compacts' intended to provide 'legitimate expectations' became instead a more one-handed example of the New Right move to make prisoners self-governing, enterprising, accountable agents of their own incarceration (Garland 1996; O'Malley 1999). Prison officers became more powerful, and more able to distribute differential standards of living for

[34] But not *necessarily* justice. In some cases, these changes reduced perceptions of legitimacy, but in other cases, they increased it. See later, and Liebling (2002).

[35] A research proposal submitted by a colleague from another university on justice in prisons was turned down on the grounds that the topic was 'not a current priority'.

prisoners (Liebling 2000). A national evaluation of this change in policy and climate in prisons during 1995–6 showed changes in prisoner perceptions of some key dimensions of life in prison, as recorded in Table 1.3.

TABLE 1.3.   Overview of outcome effects of policy changes in five prisons, 1995–6

	Local	Training	Dispersal	Young offender	Women's open	All cases
Behaviour	↓	↑				
Order		↑↑	↑			
Relations with staff	(↓)			↓	↓↓	↓
Staff fairness	↓	↓	↓	↓	↓	↓
Regime fairness¹	↓	(↓)	↓	↓	↓	↓
Woolf dimension²	↓	(—)	↓	↓	↓	↓
Making progress	↓	↓	(↓)	↓ (↓)	↓	↓
Participation	↓	↓		↓		↓

Notes:

[1] This dimension (five items) included a question on whether prisoners felt they were being 'looked after with humanity'. About half of those interviewed thought they were 'a little'. See Liebling *et al.* (1997).

[2] The 'Woolf dimension' consisted of a series of questions relating to consistency and clarity of treatment including, 'how clear are staff in telling you the rules?'; 'how consistently do staff interpret the rules?'; 'are you given reasons for decisions?'; and 'how good is the speed of response to requests and applications?'.

Source: Liebling 2002: 127.

These overall results mask some complex and important *within prison* differences, which are discussed elsewhere (Liebling *et al.* 1997; Bottoms 2003*b*).[36] We can see from the direction of the arrows a clear drop in perceptions of fairness and justice (or legitimacy) which is theoretically consistent with the pursuit of Strategy A type policies from 1995–7. As Cavadino *et al.* 1999 suggest:

Strategy A is likely to incur a serious and unavoidable 'legitimacy deficit' by virtue of its reliance on coercive measures that deny prisoners both the respect to which their humanity entitles them and also their residual civil

[36] For example, at the training prison, there were no losses on fairness and relationships in one half of the establishment, because of significant improvements made to levels of safety over this period in that part of the establishment. Prisoners were prepared to 'trade' a greater level of restriction for significant gains on safety. See further, Bottoms (2003*b*).

status as members of the moral community of citizens. To the extent that Strategy B is used in pursuit of the coercive ends identified by Strategy A (what we have called 'punitive managerialism'), it is likely to incur a similar legitimacy deficit. (Cavadino *et al.* 1999: 141–2)[37]

This project (carried out between 1995 and 1996, during this period of dramatic policy change) formed the origin of our emerging interest in measuring the prison (Liebling *et al.* 1997) and in the relationship of ideas and penal values to prison regimes.

Richard Tilt was regarded as a 'fine man', who in many ways embodied humanitarian values, and yet he presided over what many saw as a 'dehumanizing moment' in Prison Service history (Liebling 1999; Sparks 1997). This period reached its nadir when a pregnant woman prisoner gave birth in an outside hospital, shackled to an officer. A few months later, a man died of cancer, handcuffed to his bed (see Coyle 2003). These incidents were not perceived as legitimate by the external public.[38] Tilt and others said the security agenda had gone too far. Tony Pearson said in a powerful and honest condemnation on a radio broadcast that he felt 'deeply ashamed to be in the Prison Service' (Narey 2002). The corporate conscience had been stirred.

The New Penal Agenda

> Our new society will have the same values as ever. It should be a compassionate society, but it is compassion with a hard edge.
>
> (Tony Blair, speech to Labour Party Conference,
> 30 Sept. 1997; in Cavadino *et al.* 1999: 53)

Martin Narey returned to the Prison Service from the Home Office in 1997 as head of security policy, just as New Labour took up office. The post of Director of Regimes was created in December 1997 in order to 'push' on making regimes constructive. This was being done on the back of a one-line statement in the Labour Party manifesto, which said that they would provide this. Narey was

---

[37] As Bottoms suggests, there are two aspects of legitimacy here: the *internal* legitimacy of policies such as IEP, and the '*external* legitimacy of penal policies vis-à-vis the wider audience of citizens at large' (Bottoms 2003b: 81). Both kinds of legitimacy are at issue throughout this chapter.

[38] Suggesting that, in the eyes of wider society, the pendulum can swing too far.

invited to apply for the post. This was the beginning of an upturn in optimism as, along with the manifesto commitment, came 'the promise of some money' for regimes (Narey 2002). He held this post for only a year. Richard Tilt announced that he would not be returning to office for a further term, despite a clear offer. When Tilt announced his early retirement after three years in post, there was an (unsuccessful) search within the senior civil service for 'someone who would pull the Prison Service back into the Whitehall family' (pers. comm.) without trusting the Service 'to an insider'. That is, there was a move away from the 'chief executive' role, and a recognition that (for example) parliamentary questions should be fielded by the Home Secretary. The Prison Service has not looked for a private sector Director General since.

But this was by no means the end of managerialism, nor was it the end of private sector competition to achieve reform. When Narey became the Director General in 1999, with Phil Wheatley as his Deputy, a new 'robust' approach to failing prisons, and performance in general, was taken.[39] Before long, and despite an early perception that 'the liberals had gone' and the new younger, performance-minded generation had taken over, a new apparently moral framework was developed: the 'decency' agenda. There was some evidence that the 'return to power' for prison officers (Liebling 2000), and the dramatic internal move away from declarations about justice, provided a climate in which staff violence against prisoners—a characteristic of a much earlier period—was able to reappear (HMCIP 1999d, 2001; Hansard 1999). It is interesting to note that in Narey's first speech to the Prison Service Conference, the language of morality was used instead of the language of performance. The decency framework attempted to strike a balance between the need for political acceptability, the need for improved performance, an end to violence by staff, and yet a robust and challenging but humane approach to offenders. This agenda was characterized by many as 'very New Labour' (pers. comm.).

---

[39] What constitutes a failing prison has changed slightly over time. A 'failing' prison is generally one which fails to meet its key performance indicators (KPIs), and which achieves poor compliance ratings on Standards Audits (see Ch. 2). They may also, but not necessarily, have confusion of function or purpose, poor industrial relations, decrepit buildings, weak or frequently changing management, little provision of activity for prisoners, high sickness absences, and, occasionally, allegations of brutality by staff.

This meant that the new senior management of the Prison Service represented modernization, acceptance of 'the market' (i.e. private sector competition), progress, effectiveness, personal responsibility, and 'tough' justice: a centre right, neo-liberal position (Downes and Morgan 2002; Dunbar and Langdon 1998).[40] There was, from 1999 onwards, a clear recognition within government and in the Prison Service that some set of principles and values (a 'third way') was required in order to provide coherence and credibility to the modernizing project (Faulkner 2001). Notions of citizenship, decency and respect offered the early beginnings of these lines of thought (Faulkner 2001; Giddens 2001). We shall return in more detail to the Prison Service's adoption of this agenda, its significance, and its prospects, in the concluding chapter. When Narey was promoted to Commissioner of Correctional Services in 2003, and his Deputy, Wheatley, took over as Director General, this was a sign that the robust performance management approach taken by both in an unparalleled partnership throughout the period 1999–2003 had been regarded by ministers as a resounding success. The Prison Service was held up as a shining example of successful public sector reform (Falconer 2003).

The Effectiveness Credo

Prisoners' legitimate expectations had risen dramatically in the light of the post-Woolf era, and politically, as well as in practice, the pendulum had swung too far. Their legitimate expectations were revised downwards under the new illiberal framework described above. This framework required prisoners to 'engage fully in the process of their own incarceration': attending offending behaviour courses, complying with the requirements of their sentence plan, and voluntarily avoiding the use of drugs became part of the 'new legitimacy'. Effective prisons were capable of following their own rules, delivering reasonable (but not excessive) standards,

---

[40] Narey is described in a *New Statesman* article as 'an odd mixture: part Whitehall issue, part reformist with an almost Wildean concern for souls in pain. He has proved excellent (thus far) on prison escapes and good on drugs. On education and offending behaviour programmes, he claims heartening results. Others—citing unambitious and missed performance indicators—are less impressed' (*New Statesman* 2002b: 30–1). Another *New Statesman* article questioned the extent to which New Labour had a 'moral or intellectual base' (*New Statesman* 2001: 12).

securing compliance by a mixture of control, incentives, disincent-
ives, and legitimate (but not indulgent) treatment, and offering a
menu of accredited offending behaviour programmes increasingly
tailored to particular populations and criminogenic needs, and
designed to challenge thinking and behaviour (rather than 'understand' it; see Hannah-Moffatt 2004).[41] There were new attempts to
replace recreational education with evidence-based basic skills
courses (against some significant opposition). This mixture of better standards, adherence to process, control over 'privilege-drift',
intervention in criminal attitudes and lifestyles, and a more robust
approach to performance on public safety issues (i.e. more emphasis
on outcomes) became the dominant working credo of the late
1990s and early twenty-first century.

TABLE 1.4.   A new working credo

New Credo: Effectiveness
Standards for all aspects of work Protection of public a key ideology Regimes and programmes subject to accreditation Reducing reoffending as key outcome Best value from resources Links with other agencies to maximize effectiveness

Table 1.4 sets out this new credo, 'effectiveness'. The new credo
superseded (and drew on, to different degrees) the three credos
identified by Rutherford. Making the sentence—and therefore the
punishment—effective was one of its main tenets. There were some
pressures which kept the expression of more 'liberal-humanitarian'
values on the agenda and fairly deeply embedded in Prison Service
statements of their business, but, we argue, at least at first, largely
for the wrong (i.e. instrumental) reasons. These included the
Human Rights Act 1998, existing legislation and mechanisms of
external review, some surviving working ideologies, and concern
about rising suicide rates and race relations issues. Those who
speculated at this stage (1999–2001) as to how far humanitarian
values were contained in or had been abandoned by this new
apparently dominant working credo were deeply pessimistic. We
shall address these issues in later chapters. What is clear is that the

---

[41] As Bottoms observed, this agenda is very 'correctionalist' (Bottoms 2002).

'liberal humanitarianism' espoused during the early life of the Woolf Report had been largely jettisoned by 1999,[42] and if there was a new humanitarianism emerging in 2001–3, it was not of a liberal variety (but see below). That is not to say that humanitarian values disappeared but they were (as they had previously been understood) clearly in conflict with other urgent agendas. We shall explore this argument, and some of the possible explanations for the case we make, below.

Humanitarian Values and Unintended Outcomes

There are two major and related difficulties implicit in the account so far. The first is confusion over the concept of liberal justice. The second is the apparently instrumental or consequentialist vision of justice and legitimacy implicit in the Woolf Report and explicit in responses to and characterizations of it. This led to the subsequent consequentialist, outcomes-driven adoption of what are deontological (self-evident) normative values by the Prison Service. We shall look at these issues in turn. Any commitment to a set of principles should be inextricably linked to a set of beliefs about what sort of society we want. In practice, they seem to have become linked to a set of beliefs about 'what works'. This leaves them in a strangely vulnerable position when they do not 'work'.

First is the concept of liberal justice. We have already suggested that one explanation for a move away from liberal working credos is a lack of clarity about what the term 'liberal' means. Despite its clear association in law and academic discourse with rights and freedoms, it became 'laxity', in some prisons, in part because of its confusion with 'care', and, in turn, with a lack of clarity about what the term 'care' might mean, and what might deliver it, in a prison. The problem of justice in the maximum security estate during the period 1990–5 (and earlier; see Liebling 2002) was, paradoxically,

---

[42] Loss of faith in 'liberal humanitarianism' can be linked to the rise in crime; declining security; the involvement of individual 'carers' in abuse cases, and so on. Faulkner argues that the 1950s and 1960s (often associated with the liberal era) was no golden age, with complacency and elitism often accompanying apparent optimism and confidence (Faulkner 2001: 108). Stenson describes how the term 'liberal' has come to hold new meanings in contemporary language, and has been used as a term of abuse, especially in criminal justice (Stenson 2001: 17; Faulkner 2001: 44 and 102–4). Cavadino and colleagues describe penal policy during the first decades following the Second World War as 'laissez-faire' (Cavadino et al. 1999: 129). This label applies to some aspects of penal practice.

not how to prevent officers from over-using their power (although this remained an important problem both in selected areas within maximum security establishments, for example in segregation units, and elsewhere). The less analytically obvious difficulties arose in the opposite direction. It was not over-use, but *under-use* of power that posed a problem. In practice, at least in some key establishments, the liberal agenda followed post-Woolf (in addition to the already inherent 'defects of total power'; see Sykes 1958) led to staff relinquishing 'the rules' in order to be flexible and to achieve order (see Liebling 2000; also Home Office 1994, 1995). This was despite considerable emphasis placed by Woolf on situational measures, on incentives, and on security. Woolf's model of prisoner compliance was a 'mixed economy' model (Bottoms 2002). Prison officers, and arguably some senior managers, were trying to be 'fair' to prisoners, but with a limited (and, in fact, distorted) notion of justice or fairness in mind. The aspiration of value balance (see Chapter 9), so important in this complex world, and certainly recognized by Woolf, was never accomplished. The daily practices of prison officers (and their senior managers) in some prisons matched the popular interpretation of the term liberal as 'open, tolerant, generous treatment' and as 'freedom from restraint'. The consequences for the Service were dire.

The second issue is the instrumental or consequentialist vision of justice and legitimacy implicit in the Woolf Report and explicit in responses to and characterizations of it. Humanity and justice on the one hand, and security and control on the other, were important because they would solve the crisis the Prison Service faced and lead to improved order in prison:

My belief is that many, perhaps most, prisoners will respond positively if shown respect and a degree of trust by staff . . . Good relationships can be preserved in spite of the inevitable frictions of prison life. Indeed they help to ensure that tensions do not boil over, and therefore they positively assist our goal of maintaining good order. (Pilling 1992: 10)[43]

Good relationships may increase the chances of compliance with penal regimes, but they cannot guarantee it. As Tiles argues, the sources of validity of value systems must be that they are 'good'

---

[43] And later, 'staff will not deliver unless they feel valued' (p. 11).

and 'right' according to general conceptions of 'what humans should try to achieve or preserve in their lives as a whole' (Tiles 2000, p. xi). Values and general principles need something other than instrumental justification or sources of authority (Tiles 2000; Seligman 1997). Consequentialism is not enough.

The subsequent outcomes-driven adoption of what (we have argued above) are deontological normative values by the Prison Service during the early 1990s was seriously flawed. The Woolf agenda was adopted because here was a blueprint for the 'model prison'. Senior practitioners used it as a guide to action (see James *et al.* 1997); and prison officers understood that the key message of the Woolf Report was the call for improved day-to-day treatment of prisoners. In the complex history of staff–prisoner relationships in the Prison Service, relationships with prisoners were to be an 'instrument of justice' (see Liebling and Price 1999).[44] The expectation of those who adopted the Woolf thesis was that legitimate treatment by 'the system' and by prison officers who embodied that system would generate willing compliance among prisoners. When this expectation was not fulfilled, Woolf's liberal notion of the responsible individual prisoner with legitimate expectations was quickly abandoned. It was substituted by (or incorporated into) a new and powerful form of penal control with the 'contract'—or compact—forming part of the prisoner's domination instead of his or her liberation (as predicted in Sim's critical analysis of Woolf's framework; see Sim 1994: 40).

One of the transformations in the penal sphere over the last half of the decade, then, was an increased concern with security, and a move away from self-consciously 'liberal' or open regimes in the face of growing disorder and violence in prisons during the early 1990s (see Liebling 2002; Home Office 1995). Garland's account of the culture of control—a move from penal welfare to risk management, a need for public and political credibility, the systematic addressing of a perceived control deficit—has direct application to the inner life of prisons over this period (Garland 2001*a*). The justice agenda was privileged briefly between 1990 and 1992, albeit without any clear thinking at an operational level about what that

---

[44] Relationships between staff and prisoners had been, as we have argued elsewhere, instruments of order, and became instruments of security, via 'intelligence' in the post-1994 era (Liebling 2000).

agenda meant. In a swift reactive turnabout, a security and control agenda was pursued single-mindedly, from about 1994. This had repercussions of its own. Around 1999, attempts at a more balanced approach to prison life began to emerge, at least from within the Prison Service, if not from those determined to use the prison increasingly, to achieve multiple social, political, and populist ends. At the Prison Service Conference 2001, Narey declared:

I am not prepared to continue to apologise for failing prison after failing prison. I've had enough of trying to explain the very immorality of our treatment of some prisoners . . . We have to decide, as a Service, whether this litany of failure and moral neglect continues indefinitely . . . It's a matter of caring, a matter of determination, and, I accept, not a little courage in taking on a culture in all too many places which we have allowed to decay . . . The prize is . . . a Prison Service of which we need no longer be ashamed. (Narey 2001: 3)

This time, the term 'care' is being used in relation to performance. Prisons had to improve. In 2000, Lord Laming was invited to lead a working group on 'targeted performance improvement' to 'assist the Prison Service in its commitment to tackle underperforming prisons' (Home Office 2000: 1; and see n. 39).[45] All the prisons identified as 'failing' were within the public sector and most were local prisons, which reflected a general neglect of the (pre-trial and court servicing) local end of the prison system over many decades (King and Morgan 1980). Poor performance was regarded in this analysis as a 'failure of management' and it was often linked with the long-term development of dysfunctional staff cultures. Such establishments, once identified, would be 'rigorously line managed'. Those staff and managers who were 'clearly either unable to cope with the demands of the job, or openly disregard the requirements of their job description' should have a period of support and training followed by 'further action' (Home Office 2000: 13).

Achieving a renewed balance between competing values—security, fairness, safety, order, and decency—involved a new recognition that regulation of the prison environment (i.e. the regulation of

---

[45] The report was criticized for its lack of analysis of the causes of failure, and its failure to draw on empirical evidence. The Deputy Director General (DDG) and one of the non-executive directors were part of the committee. Lord Laming subsequently joined the Prisons Board. We shall look more closely at the impact of this exposure of failing prisons and attempts to improve them in Chapter 8.

prisoner and staff behaviour) could *contribute* to as well as pose a challenge to legitimacy. Managers needed to be clear about what staff were doing. Hand-wringing, or declaring humanitarian values without management systems to back them up, was futile. Managing prisons was challenging and complex, and was made all the more difficult by increasing population throughput (Home Office 2000: 2). Laming argued that evaluations of performance, including a comparative review of the performance of new private prisons, should be routinely conducted.

By 2002–3, just as the official policy language of the prison's interior life achieved something of a new balance, the exterior penal policy framework looked likely to make most of the Prison Service's internal and newly moral aspirations unachievable. The penological inconsistency of modern criminal justice, with its volatile and contradictory policies and practices, make the provision of a theoretically satisfactory account of penal change all the more difficult (Zedner 2002; O'Malley 1999) and yet all the more important.[46]

We have shown that, over the course of just over a decade, the inner life of prisons has been shaped first in one direction and then another, following a series of near catastrophic events. The reinvention of the prison (Garland 2001*a*) has an internal as well as an external dynamic. In a familiar 'dialectic between freedom and control' (Garland 2001*a*: 198), the years 1990–2003 have seen a shift from the post-Strangeways and other disturbances, and the Woolf Report drive for justice and humanity (*relegitimation*), to the 1993 calls for austerity and the post-escapes *redisciplining* of the prison and the prison experience, to what seems to be the current '*new effectiveness-plus*' agenda. The *new effectiveness-plus* agenda consists of standards for all aspects of work; impatience with 'failing prisons'; protection of the public as a key ideology; regimes and programmes which are subject to accreditation; reducing reoffending as a key outcome (by certain restricted and 'approved' methods); best value from resources; risk aversion; and stronger links with other

---

[46] O'Malley suggests that contemporary penality pursues 'nostalgic' (neo-conservative) and 'innovative' (neo-liberal) policies simultaneously, resulting in considerable incoherence (O'Malley 1999: 175). Two competing trends of thought—one with a social authoritarian strand and one with a free-market strand—form this complex and contradictory political rationality, to create a 'neo-liberal/New Labour amalgam' (O'Malley 1999: 185). See also Rose (1996) on the meaning of neo-liberalism (a free market, combined with 'firm government-at-a-distance').

agencies. There are deontological strands to this agenda as terms like 'decency' become incorporated into the Prison Service's own sense of what constitutes 'performance'. On the one hand, the bid to identify and challenge failing prisons involves relegitimating establishments where racism, brutality, and poor performance have been found, but this relegitimation project is being pursued under a new effectiveness framework, where 'performance' seems to be imperfectly linked to moral values, such as justice and fairness. Managerialism has appeared as a common thread underpinning and facilitating change, but lacking a clear or inherent value base of its own. It has been variously deployed as an end in itself (Feeley and Simon 1992), (briefly) as a tool for securing justice, and as a tool for securing institutional control. There are mixed views about the extent to which the focus of current performance measures and the decency agenda are compatible (see later chapters). The modernizing penal project is clearly under way, but with an unclear sense of direction.

Some critics have argued that the introduction of Next Steps Agencies and associated reforms have 'altered the balance of power between ministers and civil servants' (Richards and Smith 2002: 111), reducing the influence of Whitehall and giving greater 'steering power' to ministers. There is no doubt that a programme of reform, continued under New Labour, which intends to change the culture of the civil service and its public sector organizations from 'snag-hunting' to a 'managerially-oriented can do' culture, has been under way with even more energy since New Labour's second term (Richards and Smith 2002). There is far greater emphasis on 'delivering what ministers want' (ibid. 112), that is, on operational effectiveness. Civil servants no longer have the monopoly on policy advice, but a growing number of special advisers have a 'disproportionate amount of power', according to critics. Policy-making is more politicized (e.g. Sixsmith 2002). There are numerous special advisory units (such as the Prime Minister's Delivery Unit, and the Office of Public Services Reform), whose operations are not transparent and whose advice sometimes conflicts with that of traditional civil servants. The traditional civil service values of integrity, neutrality, 'speaking truth under power' (and elitism) are under threat (Richards and Smith 2002: 104).[47] Some have argued that

---

[47] But see their reassertion in 'The Civil Service Code' on http://www.cabinet-office.gov.uk.

levels of trust between ministers and civil servants have declined, and that this modernization programme has weakened democratic checks on government.

This context is important as it explains an almost frenetic concentration on 'delivery' at senior levels in the Prison Service and the background conditions under which the Prison Service is being modernized (some suggest, more successfully than other organizations). Ministerial interference in policy ('interest') has been high, to the extent that many would argue that the Prison Service no longer operates as an agency in practice.[48] The question we want to address in this book is what all this activity has achieved in terms of prison quality or the prison experience, and what can be said empirically, as well as conceptually, about the role of values in the management and organization of daily prison life. Some notion of liberal values has to be fundamental to any modern society which makes claims to democracy, fairness, decency, and legitimacy, even when (or perhaps especially when) thinking about the prison. The alternative (coercion and illegitimacy) is simply not sustainable, and requires unthinkable degrees of force. When social policies conflict with liberal democratic ideals and values, these conflicts must surely be resolved in favour of those ideals. As King argues, these conflicts 'should warn us that liberal democracy is a dynamic not a static set of institutions and values, the content of which should never be assumed but instead periodically scrutinised' (King 1999: 308).

Penal Values and Penal Sensibilities

> Where the liberating dynamic of late modernity emphasised freedom, openness, mobility, and tolerance, the reactionary culture of the end of the century stresses control, closure, confinement, and condemnation.
>
> (Garland 2001a: 198)

Garland has argued that the forms, functions, and significance of punishment in modern society reach well beyond instrumental or technical aspirations of crime control. Systems of punishment have

---

[48] As this book was going to press, Agency Status was formally brought to an end, and the Prison Service was brought firmly back into the Home Office under the new National Offender Management System (see Home Office 2004, and Chapter 8).

social meanings and expressive functions, which may account for the persistence of the prison despite evidence of failure and uncertainties of purpose. There are tensions, internal conflicts, and ambiguities in the penal process, which are related, Garland argues, to its other social functions. The prison interacts with (shapes and is shaped by) cultural and historical features of the social world. He proposes, then, that penality is a deeply social issue, not a technical task (Garland 1990; see also Pratt 2002). Prisons have a far more complex social significance which is not reducible to a single meaning or purpose. Confined to its 'instrumental crime-control pretensions', punishment is not comprehensible, not least because, considered within these limited technical horizons, it does not work (Morgan 1991: 431).

One of the officially expressed aims of HM Prison Service is: 'Effective execution of the sentences of the courts so as to reduce reoffending and protect the public' (Prison Service 2001: 9). Various statements of purpose and principle go on to state that this will be achieved 'with humanity', 'decency', and 'respect' (Prison Service 2001). Garland's account suggests that the prison does much more than 'protect the public' and 'reduce reoffending'. In some ways, these are its most difficult and contested tasks and there are arguably 'more reliable social mechanisms' that are better placed for achieving these aims (Garland 1990: 289). Prisons communicate meaning not just about crime and punishment but also about power, authority, legitimacy, normalcy, morality, personhood, and social relations (Garland 1990: 252; Ignatieff 1978). It follows from this account of penality—or systems of punishment more broadly—that prisons need to be understood as serving many functions, some of which are more obvious than others. We need to describe the reality of the prison against the backcloth of contemporary sensibility. But these ideas about punishment and its purpose, and penal values, influence practice and constitute penal sensibility, as we have begun to show in this chapter. The prison is a social institution, which embodies and expresses public sentiment, serves to 'enforce the law, regulate populations, realise political authority . . . enhance solidarities, emphasise divisions and convey cultural meanings' (Garland 1990: 284). Garland argues that part of the function of the prison is 'the pursuit of values such as justice, tolerance, decency, humanity and civility' and that these things should be 'intrinsic and constitutive aspects of its role' rather than a diversion from its 'real' goals or an inhibition on its capacity to be 'effective' (Garland 1990: 292). In other words, the role of the prison is a moral and symbolic one.

In the light of Garland's analysis, can we describe what has happened to the late modern prison over the last 13 years? How do prisoners describe their treatment now? What relationship is there between contemporary discourse about values and the daily practices of the prison? Is it possible to describe and evaluate penal values in ways that prove analytically useful?

We have suggested above that the events described earlier in this chapter took place within a broader context of penal and political sensibilities, which influenced their meaning, and public, political, and policy reactions to them. Outside the prison, but shaping policy formation and its translation into daily life, there exists a more general set of feelings about crime, punishment, and penal policy (Garland 1990, 2001a). These broad 'penal sensibilities' shape prison life internally: at the level of policy formulation but also at the level of daily practice and sentiment. Garland suggests that: 'The social and economic determinants of "the outside world" certainly affect the conduct of penal agents (police officers, judges, prison officials, etc.) but they do so indirectly, through the gradual reshaping of the rules of thought and action within a field that has what sociologists call a "relative autonomy"' (Garland 2001a: 24).

Our analysis suggests that this relationship can be closer and more direct than Garland and others suggest—via policy, but also via sensibilities and visions held by prison officials of the offender and of the purposes of punishment. It is significant that prison officers, senior managers, and prisoners are members of the public too. Sparks et al. suggest that prisons are 'vulnerable to historical and political change' (Sparks et al. 1996: 55; see also Jacobs 1977). As Sparks and colleagues argue: 'Both the high politics of penal policy and the informal practices of the custodians significantly affect the experience of imprisonment for inmates ... There is very little work in prison sociology that treats these questions at all seriously' (Sparks et al. 1996: 59).

We suggest that this vulnerability may be, perhaps increasingly, direct.[49] Our question here is whether there is a relationship

[49] One of the achievements of managerialism has been to make the influence of political will in prison life possible.

between shifting penal sensibilities as described in Garland's texts, and the changing 'high politics' and policy climate, and penal values as delivered over time in the daily round of prison life. In what way is the 'carceral texture of society' (Christie 1993) related to the daily texture of the prison?

Penal Policy and Prisoner Evaluations, 1992–2003

The final part of our argument in this introductory chapter is the most speculative, and draws on a cumulative series of research projects to develop between them a longitudinal account of aspects of the quality of prison life in England throughout most of the period 1990–2003.[50] As we have argued above, this has been a significant and rapidly changing period in terms of penal policy and, in Garland's language, 'penal sensibilities'. If we return to 1995 and the introduction of IEP (see Table 1.3 above), and using data from other research projects, what we see is a widespread shift in the depth and weight of imprisonment between 1995 and 1996.[51] There is some evidence that this sudden downward shift in internal legitimacy *continued*, and then has been forced upwards again since about 1999, under the 'failing prisons' and 'decency' agendas. In other words, we have between 1990 and 1999 something of a match between decreasing and then increasingly punitive penal sensibilities at a social and criminal justice level (reflected in Figure 1.1, showing prison population changes), and the inner life of prisons (Figures 1.2 and 1.3, showing prisoner perceptions of their treatment over time).[52] Staff became, over this period, first more preoccupied

[50] Throughout this period, three questions have been asked, albeit in slightly different ways and for different purposes, allowing for some comparisons to be made over time. These questions are, 'How would you describe relationships between staff and prisoners?', 'Are you being treated with respect?', and 'Are you being looked after with humanity?'

[51] See Downes (1988); and King and McDermott (1995). The term 'depth' refers to security procedures, and the term 'weight' refers to the psychological burden of imprisonment: relations with others, access to redress, and so on.

[52] Figure 1.2 is based on data from several research projects conducted by the author. It includes 100 randomly selected prisoners at each point, in two comparable local prisons (1995 and 1996 data are from Wormwood Scrubs and 1999, 2001, and 2002 data are from Wandsworth). Figure 1.3 is based on data from 39 prisoners in Woodhill, and 43 prisoners from Wolds, in 1992–3; 100 prisoners each in three adult male prisons in 1995 and 1996; and 100 prisoners each in ten prisons in 2001 and 2002. It is likely that Wolds and Woodhill were better than average local prisons. Data from the 1991 National Prisoner Survey show that 41% of prisoners

with justice (or leniency), but then, following the escapes from Whitemoor and Parkhurst, more powerful, and arguably they adopted the changing view of the offender identified by many: from socially deprived citizen to undeserving and culpable stranger (Garland 2001*a*). What we see in these exploratory figures is a close match between increasing use of imprisonment and increasing social rejection and 'zero tolerance' *within* the prison. It was arguably intended between 1995 and 1998 that the prisoner should experience imprisonment as more painful. The prison was deliberately dehumanized and made more punishing. A return of visible staff violence in some establishments (e.g. Wormwood Scrubs, Portland, and Dartmoor) could be linked to the messages staff were receiving about who prisoners were.

What we see more recently is something of a departure between these two trajectories from 1999. The prison population continues to rise, but the new language of 'tackling failing prisons' arises alongside a drop in annual suicide rates in 2000–1 (Fig. 1.2). This period is characterized internally by the challenging of staff violence towards prisoners, and a new 'decency' agenda which seeks to relegitimize the prison and untangle the obsession with increasing depth and weight that characterized the late 1990s. Garland's account of the 'Culture of Control' explains the years 1995–8 better than it does the years 1999–2001.[53] During the latter period, the Prison Service began to pursue an explicitly moral agenda, but on its own, and quite effectively at the level of discourse, if not always in practice. By 2002–3 the rise in the size of the prison population was, arguably, reversing these humanizing moves and we see drops in prisoner perceptions of their treatment once again (as well as increases in suicide rates).

Where does this take us? Two major issues arise from this account. The first relates to the methodological and conceptual problem of whether it is possible accurately to operationalize (and

---

felt they were treated well 'by officers in this prison' (there was no question on relationships *per se* in that survey). This figure was lower amongst remand prisoners (30%). Seventy-one per cent said most prison officers treated them fairly (White *et al.* 1991; OPCS 1992). There are large differences *between* local prisons, and therefore no group of (especially local) prisons can be said to be representative. These figures are suggestive only.

[53] See the interesting critique of Garland's pessimistic analysis in his 2001 study by Zedner (2002).

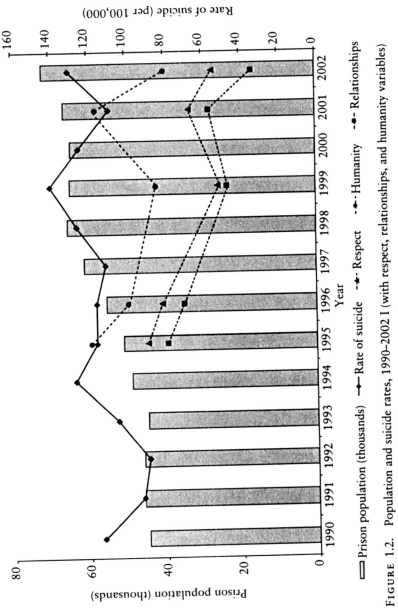

FIGURE 1.2.   Population and suicide rates, 1990–2002 I (with respect, relationships, and humanity variables)

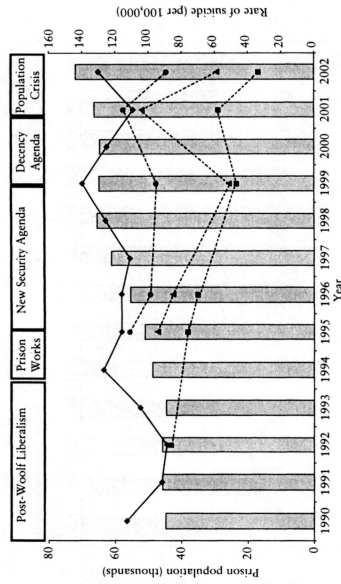

FIGURE 1.3.   Population and suicide rates, 1990–2002 II (with respect, relationships, and humanity variables)

then account for) prisoners' perceptions of their treatment in prison. The second constitutes a broader explanatory task: using this methodology, and the empirical and theoretical literature at our disposal, is it possible to develop an informative, critical understanding of the late modern prison? As Carlen argues, the prison's continuing need for legitimacy may explain the current concern with decency, where decency means reasonable relational as well as material treatment (Carlen 2002a). Garland put the case in relation to the use of imprisonment generally, as follows: 'Imprisonment has emerged in its revived, reinvented form because it is able to secure a newly necessary function in the workings of late modern, neo-liberal societies: the need for a "civilised" and "constitutional" means of segregating the problem populations created by today's economic and social arrangements' (Garland 2001a: 199).

We propose that his argument extends to the prison's inner life. Reform in many ways strengthens the capacity of the prison to punish and in that sense, careful theorization of what is going on and what such reforms mean is required. Carlen suggests that the emerging languages of auditable performance and decency during the 1990s exist to paper over the cracks in the legitimacy of imprisonment (Carlen 2002b; see also Mathiesen 1974).[54] Critics of the prison may be disarmed by the evidence that prisons are striving to become decent places. Can prisons ever be anything other than places of punishment? Prisons are being 'made to work', via accredited programmes, and a rigorous insistence on improving performance, against a rising tide of punitive sentiment. We agree with many of Carlen's concerns, including those about performance and its measurement. But we also believe there is value in measurement, provided that what we measure helps us to reflect critically and theoretically on the nature of imprisonment. Garland suggests that we have, as a nation, become newly trusting of penal authority, as it serves a new social and cultural purpose (Garland 2001a). This is a matter of external legitimacy. We need to look separately at the questions of quantity and quality or legitimacy inside the prison before evaluating how and why these matters interact. As prisoners were saying to us in 2001–3, the major 'legitimacy

---

[54] Mathiesen argues that the new prison, when it is established, is fundamentally 'like the old prison' and that a true alternative must constitute a contradiction to the existing order. This is the difference between 'reform' and 'revolution' (Mathiesen 1974).

deficit' (Sparks 1994) in contemporary penal life is its *quantity*. It is possible that the facts of quantity have rendered ineffective many of the 'relegitimation' strategies being pursued internally between 1999 and 2001. Developments in 2003–4 are looking less than optimistic (and see e.g. Haney 1997 on the USA).

Justice, Quality, and Moral Performance

This book is centrally concerned with ideas and practices of values and their relation to the concept of prison quality. Woolf referred to a basic threshold quality of life in prison. Others have argued that 'standards' of prison life are set by physical living conditions and mainly material goods—access to showers and telephones, hours spent out of cells, and the state of sanitation. We are not taking issue with the importance of these basic living conditions to prisoners, and we have included in our research some (albeit limited) information on these material items. However, our concern is with less easily quantifiable features of the prison experience, and in particular, with perceptions of justice, fairness, safety, order, humanity, trust, and opportunities for personal development. We have called these dimensions, when considered together, the 'moral performance' of the prison, and we shall have much more to say about this choice of terminology in later chapters. We embarked on our work with the taken for granted assumption (based on substantial evidence: see Bottoms and Rose 1998; Sparks *et al.* 1996; Liebling and Price 1999) that how material goods are *delivered*, how staff *approach* prisoners, how managers treat *staff*, and how life is *lived*, through talk, encounter, or transaction, constitute (above a minimum threshold) key dimensions of prison life. This is what staff and prisoners said to us in the deliberative exercises we describe in Chapter 3. They had in fact been saying so for many years. It is in these areas of prison life that we find significant variation over time, but also between prisons. These are the things that 'matter'. Taking Garland's analysis, in addition to the conversations we shall describe, they matter at several different levels. Careful consideration of their meaning and measurement will help us to describe and reflect on what is going on in late modern prison life.

This book is essentially about penal values and penal practices, how they differ and change, and how they might be understood and evaluated. We suggest that prison quality can be conceptualized and prisons evaluated using a moral framework. This chapter has set the scene, arguing that values and sensibilities shape and are central to prison life, but pointing out that practitioners, critics of the prison, and senior managers and advisers are often vague and uncertain as to the meaning of key terms. We move, in Chapter 2, to previous attempts to evaluate prison life and quality. We make the case that whilst these preoccupations with measurement have been helpful, the concepts of quality and performance have been narrowly conceived.

2

The Measurement and Evaluation of Prison Regimes

> The concept of prison performance is complex and multi-dimensional. No single indicator, nor even any small number of indicators, should be taken too seriously by itself. Multiple indicators are required to capture the many tradeoffs that must be made between the various and sometimes conflicting criteria of quality in the operation of a prison. Since no organisation can maximise all values at once, the more criteria and indicators we use, the more accurately we can reflect the total pattern of an institution's strengths and weaknesses.
>
> (Logan 1993: 39)

> Human environments have significant impacts on human functioning.
>
> (Moos 1975: 3)

Introduction

Accounts of 'what goes wrong' in prisons make abundant references to 'tension', 'low morale', prisoner 'fragmentation', staff 'capriciousness', or intimidating cultures (e.g. Dinitz 1981; Home Office 1991a; HMCIP 2000c). We read of 'fear, hate, anger, rage, frustration and paranoia' (Dinitz 1981: 5), of power and its resistance and also, sometimes, of affection and loyalty. Successive reports of the Chief Inspector, and specific inquiries into disturbances, deaths, and suicides, speak of 'cultures of brutality', 'intimidation', and 'prisons in the dark ages' (HMCIP 1998, 1999d, 2001a). The now scant critical penological literature likewise describes anger, anguish, and 'festering sores' in violent institutions (Scraton et al. 1991: 17; van Swaaningen 1997; Sim 1994; and Hillyard et al. 2004). Compared to these emotive and general descriptions, official measures of narrowly conceived performance indicators (such as hours out of cell) or contemporary research evaluations which focus on specific policy effects, or at best, policy implementation, seem barely relevant. Why is this so?

Our primary task in this chapter is conceptual as well as descriptive. How is the quality of a prison or of prison life assessed? How does the literature help us? In 1992, Logan argued that 'there is no established methodology for measuring or comparing prison quality' (Logan 1992: 528). What are appropriate techniques for conceptualizing the quality of a prison? Do modern performance leagues make sense? To what extent do staff and prisoners recognize the picture of their prison world painted by audit teams, inspectorates, or management information systems—developments described collectively as part of a 'quality revolution' in the life of modern organizations? Are there meaningful ways in which to reflect, accurately, what matters in prison?

Theories about the nature of prisons have been concerned with their essential similarities (Clemmer 1940; Sykes 1958; Goffman 1962; Polsky 1962). This is despite a rich and varied literature on their differences (e.g. Street *et al.* 1966; Giallombardo 1966; Heffernan 1972; Heal *et al.* 1973; Sparks *et al.* 1996; Kruttschnitt *et al.* 2000). This book is concerned with both of these key questions. Are there 'essential features' of the prison experience on the one hand (as Goffman's 'total institution' thesis suggests),[1] which may help us to conceptualize 'quality', and to what extent do these features differ between prisons, on the other?

The early interest of social science in the prison was primarily in relation to its *social organization* (e.g. Clemmer 1940). That is, the prison consisted of a number of interacting human groups who 'exercise power over one another, communicate, and at times are in conflict, but in general form a unit that operates as a going concern' (Grosser 1960: 1). Most early sociological studies of the prison therefore tended to focus on a single establishment (e.g. Clemmer 1940; Sykes 1958; Mathiesen 1965; Jacobs 1977 in the USA; and Sparks 1971; Emery 1970; Morris and Morris 1963; Cohen and

---

[1] Goffman suggested that 'what is distinctive about total institutions is that each exhibits to an intense degree' attributes such as a breakdown in the barriers ordinarily separating work and play, surveillance, a 'basic split' between inmates and supervisory staff, with 'narrow hostile stereotypes' held of each other, and all needs organized by the institution (Goffman 1961: 15–22).

Taylor 1972; King and Elliott 1977; and Carlen 1983 in the UK). The aim of these studies is to describe 'the prison' and its effects; especially, how prisoners organize themselves, to survive psychologically or to offset the pains and deprivations of imprisonment. The primary focus of interest is power, discipline, and control; and the roles adopted or collective stance taken towards the institution.[2] Many of these studies consider values, for example, the 'strikingly pervasive value system' arising amongst prisoners (Sykes and Messinger 1960: 185). This value system is 'publicly professed' and is, according to many sociologists of the prison, normally oppositional (Sykes and Messinger 1960: 186). Mathiesen, on the other hand, suggested that a certain amount of 'consensus between ruler and ruled regarding basic norms and values' existed (Mathiesen 1965: 47), although he also proposed that this consensus was somewhat 'superficial' and strategic. We shall return to these issues later, in Chapter 3. Early studies were not concerned with administrative causes of variations in these value systems (Cressey 1958) until a little later (e.g. McCleery 1961; Street et al. 1966). It is probably fair to say that sociological interest in prison management goals and styles and their effects has remained rather limited (see, however, Jacobs 1977; Barak-Glantz 1981; DiIulio 1987; Adler and Longhurst 1994; Kruttschnitt et al. 2000; and Chapter 8).

Early sociological studies of prison life, then, questioned whether there existed enduring and universal properties or features of the prison's inner life (Sykes and Messinger 1960; Goffman 1961). The 'universal' assumptions (e.g. of Sykes and Goffman) were challenged (by Grusky 1959; Berk 1966; and Street et al. 1966), when they found differences in inmate culture and attitudes, and the nature of staff–prisoner relationships, according to various organizational goals and formal structures.[3] The apparently enduring features included inmate grouping, leadership, solidarity (and sometimes,

---

[2] The sociological study of the prison was at its strongest during the 1940s to the 1970s in the USA, during a time of major change (particularly liberalization) and prison population transformation, towards a younger, and more ethnically varied population (Simon 2000). Exemplary reviews of the sociological prisons literature can be found in Sparks et al. (1996, ch. 2); McEvoy (2001, ch. 2); and Zamble and Porporino (1988).

[3] The early sociological studies were primarily observational, whereas the 'testing' period of the 1960s and 1970s involved more extensive use of questionnaires, with little emphasis on observation.

friendship), hierarchy, status, and modes of adaptation (such as co-operation, withdrawal, rebellion, and resistance; see Clemmer 1940; Sykes 1958; Cressey 1961). Studies described, sometimes painstakingly, these 'argot roles' and the subcultures that arose from these adaptations. Attention was paid to the functioning of the prison economy and the effects of prisonization (i.e. shifting the values, beliefs, wishes, drives, ambitions, and habits of prisoners as they became accustomed to the prison). There was considerable concern with processes of alienation, institutionalization, and mortification, during which prisoners' self-respect and dignity were stripped away, only to be replaced by new values and defences (Clemmer 1940; McCorkle and Korn 1954; Goffman 1961; Morris and Morris 1963). There was considerable critical interest in the coercive power of prison officers and its effects (e.g. Thomas and Petersen 1977; Thomas and Pooley 1980). In relation to staff–prisoner interactions, studies focused on notions of opposition, proximity, and familiarity between staff and prisoners, censoriousness,[4] and collusion (see Chapter 7). We might say that these early studies were intended to *describe* and *explain* (to analyse) rather than to *evaluate*. What mattered in prison research tended to be the sociological concepts of interest to sociologists. Subsequent empirical analyses have often found the key concepts of interest (such as 'prisonization' and the 'effects of imprisonment') to be too crude or broadly conceived to yield useful results (Zamble and Porporino 1988: 9; Liebling 1999).

More formal evaluation came later and was primarily linked to the concept of treatment. These studies focused more optimistically on training and the success or otherwise of different regimes (e.g. Moos 1975; Bottoms and McClintock 1973; Genders and Player 1995; and the studies reviewed below), or more pessimistically on the mortifying effects of institutionalization (Cohen and Taylor 1972). In the latter types of studies, comparisons were usually drawn with different establishments or regimes thought to be related to distinct (treatment-related) outcomes. Evaluation methods were conceptually linked to treatment, so studies focused on those aspects of prison life thought to be related to this outcome. More recent

---

[4] The critique by individual prisoners that staff are not following the rules and that closer adherence to them would be less depriving: a 'weak' form of resistance identified by Mathiesen in his Norwegian study (Mathiesen 1965).

and proliferating post-prison reconviction studies (for example, meta-analyses) have lamented the lack of either descriptive or quantitative data from the relevant prisons with which more sense might be made of very varied results (Solicitor General Canada 1999). Measurement of prison regimes in most contemporary studies, where it exists at all, tends to be linked to standards or accreditation processes, and driven by a confinement or 'service delivery' model of the prison. We shall consider some of these studies below.

This chapter selectively reviews the available research and attempts to clarify some of the conceptual difficulties posed by the questions of performance and quality. The term quality can mean 'standard', 'basic character', 'property', 'special feature', 'the relative excellence of a thing', 'condition', 'tone', or 'rating at a certain value' (*New Shorter Oxford Dictionary* 1993). These overlapping definitions are important since few attempts to measure quality venture beyond a narrowly conceived concept of 'standards'. There are few attempts to integrate individual indicators (e.g. the number of assaults, or compliance with a single policy instruction) around broad themes or dimensions although, as we shall see, a number of studies have attempted to move in this direction.

Key Performance Indicators, Auditing, and Inspections

> If management reform really does produce cheaper, more efficient government, with higher-quality services and more effective programmes, and if it will simultaneously enhance political control, free managers to manage, make governments more transparent and boost the images of those ministers and mandarins most involved, then it is little wonder that it has been widely trumpeted. Unfortunately however, matters are not so simple.
>
> (Pollitt and Bouckaert 2000: 6)

As part of the increasing concern with management and accountability described in Chapter 1, and encouraged by the new possibilities offered by information technology, and the future-oriented leanings of late modernity, various forms of operational data are collected and disseminated in and about many organizations. This information revolution has inevitably occurred within the Prison

Service, as it has in public services more generally. Services are assessed against a framework of targets or standards set by the body carrying out the evaluation.[5]

The two most significant types of data available in relation to the prison are Key Performance Indicators and Targets (KPIs and KPTs), and Standards Audit ratings of compliance with specified policy processes. There is a third, more independent evaluative body, the Prisons Inspectorate, which has a distinct and arguably more 'moral' role. The fourth source of data about prison quality, boards of visitors, have recently been relaunched as 'Independent Monitoring Boards', so we shall also look briefly at their role. How far do these sources fulfil their tasks? Can we judge the quality of a prison from the data generated precisely for this purpose (and if not, why not)?

Key Performance Indicators and Key Performance Targets

> Performance information shows how well an organisation is performing against its stated objectives. Knowing how well the organisation is currently doing is essential in developing strategy and policies to meet the organisation's aims.
>
> (HM Treasury 2001: 6)

The introduction of KPIs in UK prisons in 1992 was part of a general shift towards a greater emphasis on the development and maintenance of long-term penal strategies, expressed and measured in relation to specific goals. They illustrate, as well as symbolize, the changing nature of modern institutions, from largely static, tradition- and past-oriented social organizations to dynamic, self-reinventing, reflexive (self-inquiring), future-oriented, global social organizations, managed by expert abstract 'strategic' systems (Giddens 1990, 1991; Bottoms 1995) and long-term planning.

---

[5] A Public Administration Select Committee (PASC) Inquiry on 'public service targets and associated matters' is under way, concerned by messages from professionals and others that 'target regimes being set from the centre' are 'oppressive and demoralising', that they 'distort priorities' and that 'people feel bullied'. Employees in the NHS, in Education, and in the Prison Service are afraid to challenge such targets, and yet many feel they are like 'the emperor's new clothes' (www.publication.parliament.uk/pa/cm200203). On the other hand, public services have been for decades 'in denial' about failing institutions, and managers at a loss as to how to improve them.

TABLE 2.1.   Prison Service key performance indicators, 1994–2003

1994–5 (8)	1995–6 (9)	1996–7 (9)	1997–8 (9)	1998–9 (6)
• To ensure that the number of escapes from prison establishments and from escorts is fewer than in 1993–4. • To reverse, over the period 1993–6, the rising trend of assaults on staff, prisoners, and others. • To ensure that in 1994–5 the average number of prisoners held three to a cell in accommodation which is intended for one prisoner is fewer than in 1993–4, subject to ensuring that no prisoners are held in police cells unless this is absolutely unavoidable. • To provide 24-hour access to sanitation in at least 3,500 more cells, including new and renovated accommodation, thus ensuring that at least 95% of prisoners have access to sanitation at all times.	• To ensure no category A prisoners escape. • To ensure that the total number of escapes from prison establishments and from escorts, expressed as a percentage of the average prison population, is at least 25% lower than in 1994–5. • To ensure that the rate of assaults on staff, prisoners, and others, expressed as a percentage of the average prison population, is lower than in 1994–5. • To ensure that no prisoners are held three to a cell in accommodation which is intended for one prisoner, subject to ensuring that no prisoners are held in police cells unless this is absolutely unavoidable. • To ensure that all prisoners have access to sanitation	• To ensure no category A prisoners escape and to ensure that the number of escapes from prisons and from escorts is at least 10% lower than in 1995–6. • To ensure that the number of assaults on staff, prisoners, and others is lower than in 1995–6. • To ensure that the rate of positive testing for drugs is lower in the fourth quarter of 1996–7 than in the first quarter of that year. • To ensure that no prisoners are held three to a cell designed for one. • To ensure that prisoners spend, on average, at least 26.5 hours per week in purposeful activity. • To ensure that by 31 March 1997 at least 60% of prisoners are held in establishments which unlock all prisoners on the standard or enhanced regime for at least 10 hours per weekday.	• To ensure no category A prisoners escape and to ensure that the number of escapes from prison and from escorts, expressed as a proportion of the prison population, is lower than in 1996–7. • To ensure that the number of assaults on staff, prisoners, and others, expressed as a proportion of the average population, is lower than 9%. • To ensure that the rate of positive testing for drugs (the number of random drug tests that prove positive expressed as a percentage of the total number of random tests carried out) is lower in 1997–8 than in 1996–7. • To ensure that the percentage of the prison population above the uncrowded capacity of the estate is no more than 13%	• To ensure no category A prisoners escape. • To ensure that the number of escapes from prison and prison escorts is lower than in 1997–8. • To ensure that there are at least 3,000 completions by prisoners of programmes accredited as being effective in reducing reoffending, of which 680 should be completions of the sex offender treatment programmes. • To ensure that the number of assaults on staff, prisoners, and others is lower than 9%. • To ensure that by 31 March 1999 at least 60% of prisoners are held in establishments which unlock all prisoners on the standard or enhanced regime for at least 10 hours per weekday. • To ensure that prisoners spend, on average, at least 24 hours per week in purposeful activity.

1999–2000 (13)	2000–1 (18)	2001–2 (13)	2002–3 (16)
• To ensure no category A escapes.	• To ensure no category A escapes.	• To ensure no category A escapes.	• To ensure no category A escapes.
• To ensure that the number of escapes from prisons and escorts is lower than 0.05%.	• To ensure that the number of escapes from prisons and escorts is lower than 0.05%.	• To ensure that the number of escapes from prisons and escorts is lower than 0.05%.	• To ensure that the numbers of escapes from prisons and escorts is lower than 0.05%.
• To ensure that the number of escapes from contracted out escorts is no more than 1 per 20,000 prisoners handled.	• To ensure that the number of escapes from contracted out escorts is no more than 1 per 20,000 prisoners handled.	• To ensure that the number of escapes from contracted out escorts is no more than 1 per 20,000 prisoners handled.	• To ensure that the number of escapes from contracted out escorts is no more than 1 per 20,000 prisoners handled.
• To ensure that the number of positive adjudications of assault on prisoners, staff, and others is lower than 9%.	• To ensure that the number of positive adjudications of assault on prisoners, staff, and others is lower than 9%.	• To ensure that the number of positive adjudications of assault on prisoners, staff, and others is lower than 9%.	• To ensure that the number of positive adjudications of assault on prisoners, staff, and others is lower than 9%.
• To ensure that the rate of positive results from random drug tests is lower than 18.5%.	• To ensure that the number of prisoners held two to a cell designed for one does not exceed 18%.	• To ensure that the number of prisoners held two to a cell designed for one does not exceed 18%.	• To ensure that the number of prisoners held two to a cell designed for one does not exceed 18%.
• To ensure that the number of prisoners held two to a cell designed for one does not exceed 18%.	• To ensure that the rate of positive results from random drug tests is lower than 16%.	• To ensure that the number of ethnic minority staff in the Prison Service is at least 4.1% by April 2002.	• To ensure that the number of ethnic minority staff in the Prison Service is at least 4.5% by April 2003.
• To ensure that prisoners spend on average at least 24 hours per week in purposeful activity.	• To deliver 28,000 prisoners to a voluntary drug testing compact by April 2001.	• To ensure that the average staff sickness does not exceed 10 working days per person by April 2002.	• To ensure that the average staff sickness does not exceed 9 working days per person by April 2002.
• To ensure that there are at least 3,600 completions by prisoners of offending behaviour programmes	• To ensure that there are at least 5,000 completions by prisoners of offending behaviour programmes accredited as being effective in	• To ensure that the average cost per uncrowded prisoner place does not exceed £35,910.	• To achieve the target for the average cost per uncrowded prisoner place.
		• To ensure that the average cost per prisoner does not exceed £37,418.	• To achieve the target for the average cost per prisoner.
			• To deliver 7,100 accredited offending behaviour programme completions in 2002–3, including 950 sex offender treatment programmes.

TABLE 2.1.   (*Continued*)

1994–5 (8)	1995–6 (9)	1996–7 (9)	1997–8 (9)	1998–9 (6)
• To ensure that prisoners spend, on average, at least 25.5 hours per week in purposeful activity. • To ensure that by March 1995 at least 36% of prisoners are held in establishments where prisoners are unlocked on weekdays for at least 12 hours. • To ensure that all prisoners have the opportunity to exceed the minimum visiting entitlement throughout 1994–5. • To ensure that the average prisoner place does not exceed £24,500.	at all times by the end of February 1996, provided that the prison population does not increase significantly above current projections and there is no major unplanned loss of accommodation. • To ensure that prisoners spend, on average, at least 25.5 hours per week in purposeful activity. • To ensure that by 31 March 1996 at least 38% of prisoners are held in establishments where prisoners are unlocked on weekdays for at least 12 hours, provided this can be supported by an active and constructive regime. • To ensure that all prisoners have the opportunity to exceed minimum visiting entitlements, subject to qualifying under earned incentive schemes.	• To ensure that at least 1,300 prisoners complete programmes accredited as being effective in reducing reoffending, of whom 650 should complete the sex offender treatment programme. • To ensure that the average prisoner place does not exceed £24,388. • To ensure that, on average, staff spend at least six days in training.	(population surplus to planning in-use as a percentage of the CNA population (calculated on annual averages)). • To ensure that prisoners spend on average at least 22.5 hours per week engaged in purposeful activity. • To ensure that, by 31 March 1998, at least 60% of prisoners are held in establishments which normally unlock all prisoners on the standard or enhanced regime for at least 10 hours per weekday. • To ensure that there are at least 2,200 completions by prisoners of programmes accredited as being effective in reducing reoffending, of which 670 should be completions of the sex offender treatment programmes. (Accredited courses: during 1997–8 there will be four such courses. These

1999–2000 (13)	2000–1 (18)	2001–2 (13)	2002–3 (16)
accredited as being effective in reducing reoffending, of which 700 should be sex offender treatment programmes. • To ensure that the average cost per uncrowded prison place does not exceed £26,208. • To ensure that the average cost per prisoner does not exceed £27,392. • To ensure that the average staff sickness does not exceed 12.5 working days per person. • To ensure that 95% of correspondence receives a reply within 20 days by October 1999.	reducing reoffending, of which 1,020 should be completers of sex offender treatment programmes. • To reduce the proportion of prisoners discharged from their sentence who are at least at level 1 or below for basic skills in literacy by 10% by April 2001. • To reduce the proportion of prisoners discharged from their sentence who are at least at level 1 or below for basic skills in numeracy by 10% by April 2001. • To ensure that prisoners spend on average at least 24 hours per week in purposeful activity. • To ensure that the average cost per uncrowded prison place does not exceed £27,031. • To ensure that the average cost per prisoner does not exceed £26,118. • To ensure that the average staff sickness does not exceed	• To deliver 23,400 accredited educational or vocational qualifications in 2001–2, including 18,000 level 2 basic skills awards. • To ensure that prisoners spend on average at least 24 hours per week in purposeful activity. • To deliver 6,100 accredited offending behaviour programme completions in 2001–2, including 1,160 sex offender treatment programmes. • To ensure that the rate of positive results from random mandatory drug tests is lower than 12% by April 2002.	• To ensure prisoners spend on average at least 24 hours per week in purposeful activity. • To ensure that the rate of positive results from random mandatory drug tests is lower than 10% by April 2003. • To achieve at least a 20% reduction in the rate of self-inflicted deaths per 100,000 of the prison population compared with 1999–2000. • To deliver the targets for accredited educational or vocational qualifications, including basic skills awards. • To deliver the target for numbers of prisoners getting jobs or training places after release. • To achieve the new target on health care for 2002–3.

TABLE 2.1.   (*Continued*)

1994–5 (8)	1995–6 (9)	1996–7 (9)	1997–8 (9)	1998–9 (6)
	• To ensure that the average cost per prisoner place does not exceed £24,600.		are the Sex Offender Treatment Programme, the Sex Offender Booster Programme, the Reasoning and Rehabilitation Course, and the Enhanced Thinking Skills Course.) • To achieve at least a 1.3% reduction in real terms compared to 1996–7 and ensure that the average cost of a prison place does not exceed £24,610. • To ensure that, on average, staff spend at least six days in training.	

Notes: Number of KPIs in parentheses.

In this constantly changing yet risk-averse late modern world, the 'future is continually drawn into the present' by means of 'the reflexive organisation of knowledge environments' (Giddens 1991: 3). Organizations must continually measure, reinvent, and improve themselves. The pace of social, and therefore organizational change is extraordinary, and its scope profound (Giddens 1991: 16). The effects of this reorganization of time and space are 'existentially troubling' for the individual (Giddens 1991: 21). In this untrusting, disembedded new world, more and more of the activities of organizations are susceptible to monitoring and 'chronic revision' (Giddens 1991: 20). Managerially, this development is useful, as it permits unprecedented levels of information and control. In the interests of improvement, a will to precision, effectiveness, and regulation (an attempt to 'colonise the future', Giddens 1991: 111) permeates late modern organizational life.

1999–2000 (13)	2000–1 (18)	2001–2 (13)	2002–3 (16)
	11.25 working days per person.		
	• To ensure that 95% of correspondence receives a reply within 20 days.		
	• To respond to calls to the HQ switchboard in an average of 12 seconds and to have no more than 5% abandoned calls as a proportion of attempted calls.		

KPIs were introduced in most organizations in this modernizing context. They started in the Prison Service as organizational-level targets, with individual establishments coming under significant pressure from area managers to contribute as effectively as possible to the national target. Each Prison Service goal (as expressed in the Corporate Plan) has one or more KPI intended to reflect its achievement (Lygo 1991; King and McDermott 1995). So, for example, the goal of 'keeping prisoners in custody' is measured by the number of escapes; 'maintaining order' is measured by the number of assaults, and so on. KPIs are negotiated annually with ministers, which means the Prison Service cannot freely choose its own or the most appropriate targets. They have changed considerably over time, reflecting shifting priorities and improvements in thinking about the limitations of measures selected (see Table 2.1). Table 2.1 shows that the target numbers of hours unlocked and in purposeful activity, for example, increased between 1994–5 and 1997–8 and then decreased slightly. Target costs per place decreased between 1994–5 and 1996–7, then seemed to increase dramatically as headquarters' costs began to be taken into account. The period 1998–2003 has seen a significant move away from 'inputs' (such as number of days in training) towards 'outcomes' (such as reducing deaths, completing drug treatment, and getting jobs). Increasing emphasis is placed on staff-related and headquarters' targets, such as reduced staff sickness and recruitment of ethnic minority staff. Numbers of indicators decreased, and then increased again as 2003 saw new measures on 'health care'[6] and reducing suicides. It is noticeable that the key Prison Service aim of 'reducing reoffending' (Prison Service 2002b) is not measured by an outcome (reconviction rates) but by an input (completion of accredited and basic skills courses), although there is a Home Office Public Service Agreement which includes 'reducing the rate of reconvictions of all offenders punished by imprisonment or by community supervision by 5% by 2004 compared to the predicted rate'; and 'reducing the rate of repeat offending amongst problem drug-misusing offenders by 25% by 2005 (and by 50% by 2008)' (Prison Service 2002b: 24).

KPIs have become part of the culture of new public management aimed at improving the provision of public sector services described in Chapter 1. This 'new governance' technique is so called because it is government driven, and attempts to discipline managers into controlling and motivating the workforce to maximize an organization's value and effectiveness (Power 2001: 41).[7] KPIs are change agents, intended to bring about 'organisational introspection', modernization, and improvement (Power 2001: 54). They are intended to be a tool for strategic management. They

[6] This includes moving closer to NHS standards and 'modernising a significant part of the prison health estate' (Prison Service 2002b: 14).

[7] Pollitt and Bouckaert point out that 'the powerful have been better able to postpone or deflect the tide of measurement than other groups. Thus, within health services, the activities of nurses and receptionists have been measured far more intensively than clinical decision-making by doctors. In the NPM [New Public Management] countries, at least, the public can read plenty of reports containing measures of the performance of teachers, police, social workers, social security clerks and specialist agencies, but few, if any, measuring the performance of MPs or ministers' (Pollitt and Bouckaert 2000: 88).

are used to analyse and monitor performance within organizations, and to indicate where attention and resources need to
be directed. In this sense they can be used to exert senior management control from a distance ('management by target', senior
manager, in Sinclair 2002: 27). They also form a method of doing
business with the Treasury, as requests for additional funding by
the Prison Service are increasingly tied to performance on specified
targets.

A recent study of the role of KPIs in the management of prisons
and their performance concluded that what they bring to prison
management (and therefore quality) is clarity or direction (Sinclair
2002). Of the KPI targets set each year, an average of 63 per cent
have been met since their introduction in 1993 and improvements
can be seen in 80 per cent of cases (Sinclair 2002: 29–30). Some
indicators are deliberately 'target-stretching', and others are low-
ered when they prove impossible to meet. As Sinclair argued, the
Prison Service does not have control over its environment (for
example, population size, which impacts on regime delivery); and
KPIs do not take into account different populations and their
propensity to assault, for example. There are significant omissions,
so that, for example, health care, personnel matters, and prisoner
evaluations are not included in these measures (but see later).
Senior managers are aware that 'we still measure what we do,
rather than what we *should* be doing' (pers. comm.).

Some governors have commented that the introduction of KPIs
constituted the single most important transformation in the role of
governor and in the way the Service is managed (see Chapter 8).
They clarify objectives and can be used to demonstrate to staff
where the strengths and weaknesses are in their own organization
(as well as how they are 'performing' in relation to like establishments). Because they are quantitative, and providing that individual governors believe in them, the introduction of KPIs 'for the first
time gave staff confidence that they knew what they were being
asked to deliver' (Sinclair 2002: 4). Whilst they constitute an imperfect measure of 'what is going on', they do focus attention on
performance generally. Governors are well aware that their competence is judged by whether or not they succeed in meeting KPI
(and now their more numerous KPT) targets. They have reduced
idiosyncracy, but also, arguably, innovation; and they arise from a
mechanistic image of organizations (G. Morgan 1997). There is

considerable debate about whether KPIs constitute distracting outputs rather than outcomes:

When managers are enjoined to concentrate on concrete outputs (training courses completed) they tend to lose sight of outcomes and, therefore, to stress efficiency rather than effectiveness . . . when, alternatively, managers are asked to concentrate on outcomes and effectiveness, it is hard to hold them responsible and accountable, for several reasons. This is because the attribution of outcomes to the actions of individual units or organizations is frequently obscure or doubtful, and also because, for many public programmes, measurable outcomes manifest themselves over such extended time periods that they cannot provide a sensible basis for annual accountability exercises anyway. (Pollitt and Bouckaert 2000: 166–7)

Critics often point out that, whether in the Prison Service or in other organizations, they do not always reflect the declared strategic direction of the Service (e.g. they reflect security as a bottom-line goal but not 'humanity'; see Table 2.1). Those KPIs which do measure a relevant goal often measure only one aspect of it, and this they may do ineffectively, despite constant refinement. KPIs 1 to 3 (escapes) are the clearest and methodologically most robust indicators of a relevant goal (keeping prisoners in custody) but there are difficulties thereafter. The number of assaults is taken to be a proxy measure of 'safety' and 'order'. The figures used refer only to recorded findings of guilt at adjudication for assault and so fail to take account both of the separate charge of fighting and of assaults which staff ignore or fail to see. Other indications of safety which staff and prisoners may judge relevant but which are not reflected in performance measurement include levels of bullying, minor and major disorder, use of IEP, and so on. 'Percentage overcrowded' is not by itself an informative indicator of 'a decent environment'. Establishments inevitably massage their statistics in various ways, for example, showing videos in workshop areas which might otherwise be closed and claiming these hours as 'work'. KPIs are a limited way of measuring performance, although they can, to some extent, measure change over time. They can, however, have important distorting effects on organizations. The current Chief Inspector of Prisons has suggested that they create a 'virtual prison system' far removed from reality (*New Statesman* 2002*a*).

KPIs (and their shortcomings) have led to the proliferation of a larger number of input-based Key Performance Targets (there are 48), which are more detailed and are weighted according to agreed priorities for different types of establishment. These are, unlike KPIs, essentially local rather than national measures. If 'no escapes' is a performance indicator, then cell searches, staff training, estate maintenance, incident rehearsal, and security audit ratings (activities that support the achievement of security) form the related performance targets. In 2001, the Prison Service started using a 'weighted scorecard' method, which is a mathematical model using standardized scores for KPTs. A weighting is applied to reflect the importance placed on each KPT in each (type of) establishment. This model takes account of each establishment's function, and shows up specific areas of weakness (and strength). This provides a more sophisticated and detailed measurement of aspects of each prison's performance. Using these 'weighted scorecard' measures, establishments achieve a rating according to their performance against targets, their cost per place (compared to the average for that type of prison), and any progress made (Gillespie 2002; and see www.hmprisonservice.gov.uk). KPT and KPI scores are used to form dimensions, reflecting 'security', 'safety', 'decency and health', 'organizational effectiveness', and 'regimes'. Outlier overall poor performers receive additional pressure and attention (and sometimes, additional resources). Outlier high-cost establishments, even if they are high performers, are brought under pressure to reduce costs.[8] There exists, then, an empirically based performance-cost scale, along which establishments are distributed. This scale is supplemented by 'star ratings' (which draw on other sources of information about each establishment). On the basis of this kind of information, establishments with negative assigned reputations can be deemed to have changed, others can be deemed to have declined. The lowest performers (at least two per year) are 'market tested' or

---

[8] This more sophisticated model gets round the problem characteristic of much public sector reform that all units are forced to make equal savings, regardless of quantities of 'fat' or the scale of inefficiencies. It is one of many paradoxes of public sector reform that those organizations or units which are most efficient and effective in service delivery to start with often find themselves able to make the most radical reform (see Pollitt and Bouckaert 2000: 160). Such unforeseen consequences for better performing units lead to losses in legitimacy. See further below, and Chapter 8.

required to follow a 'performance improvement plan' (see below). If senior managers (including area managers) are doing their jobs properly, there should be 'no surprises' in these figures. That there are some surprises (e.g. when the Inspectorate visit) suggests that they are far from perfect.

The critique of KPIs, and the performance culture, suggests that they constitute 'window dressing'; they undermine leadership; they are subject to manipulation; and they only measure what is measurable (see e.g. King and McDermott 1995; Feeley and Simon 1992; Power 2001; O'Neill 2002). Few of the KPIs currently in use relate directly to the Prison Service's stated objectives. Targets tend to be set in areas that are amenable to measurement, rather than in areas that 'matter'.[9] As one commentator put it, they measure 'progress through the jungle', but they do not necessarily indicate whether this is 'taking them further into or out of the jungle' (Sinclair 2002: 11). Wormwood Scrubs has been used as an example of a prison that was 'failing' and yet apparently effective according to its KPI performance (see HMCIP 2000c, 2002a). These shortcomings are contrary to the declared spirit of the managerialist ethos, whereby greater control over important organizational goals is being sought.

Whilst these criticisms undoubtedly have significance, it has not been established that KPIs are wholly irrelevant to performance or prison quality. Then Director General Martin Narey said, in his speech to the Prison Service Conference in 2001: 'I acknowledge that KPIs may not provide the full picture, but . . . show me a prison achieving all its KPIs and I will show you a prison which is also treating prisoners with dignity' (Narey 2001: 5).

There may be an association between performance on targets and 'moral performance' (prisons that do things well do most things well), but the association is not necessarily causal. Sinclair (2002) found that the existence of KPIs by itself does not drive performance in any simple manner. The KPI on escapes existed before the escapes from Whitemoor and Parkhurst (see Chapter 1). It was after these escapes, and a public expression of increased emphasis on 'security,

---

[9] In the examination of witnesses for the PASC inquiry into public service targets, the spokesman for education said: 'In many cases we measure what is easily measured rather than what is important . . . we need to develop a broader basket in primary and secondary education for things that matter as children grow up and get into adult life . . . We over concentrate on measurable things.' (Examination of witnesses; (www.publication.parliament.uk/pa/cm200203) Tues. 10 Dec. 2002).

security, security', that the number of escapes dramatically declined. Likewise, the reduction of prison suicides during 2001/2 occurred before a performance indicator was introduced and could be linked to personal statements of commitment made by the Director General. Sanctions exist for underperforming prisons, including performance testing (e.g. Reading and Leicester)[10] and the threat of market testing or privatization (e.g. Brixton; see later). The development of performance measurement and testing has resulted in a change in the distribution of skills required amongst senior management teams in charge of establishments: auditors, accountants, and good presentation skills are increasingly significant. As others have noted, there has been less focus in research or in the literature on what organizations *do with*, or how they *respond to*, the increasing quantities of performance data available to them (see Smith and Goddard 2002).[11] Performance *measurement* has been privileged over performance *management* (ibid.; and see Chapter 8). The story of Wandsworth prison, which we tell in the next chapter and which shaped our own study, illustrates this.[12] One of the characteristics of British public services, according to the PASC inquiry, is a tendency to deny failure, or fail to address the relevant problems, until a precipitating event makes this impossible. Diagnosing problems and addressing them have been given less emphasis under modernization than creating targets which are of limited quality, too numerous, and too centrally driven.

What matters is whether performance data measure or reflect a prison's performance accurately. KPIs and KPTs certainly provide an increasing amount of information to the Service and to ministers, and an increased feeling of accountability. Most prisons are now working towards Service Delivery Agreements (SDAs) which

---

[10] Performance testing is a mechanism for improving the quality and decreasing the cost of low performing establishments in a performance league by setting demanding targets to be achieved within a deadline. Often this comes with additional resources or other forms of 'special management attention'. Successful bids outlining how improvements will be achieved result in the award of a contractual Service Level Agreement, for a period of five years. The SLAs are independently monitored.

[11] 'There may be a role for some generic social research to establish more effective links between the production of evidence and its influence on organisational policy and practice' (see Smith and Goddard 2002: 254; also Davies *et al.* 2000).

[12] More questions need asking about *why* organizations are, or become, poor performing (www.publication.parliament.uk/pa/cm200203).

resemble private prison contracts and which are based, like those contracts, on this kind of target-setting. The terms are agreed between the Home Secretary and the Chancellor of the Exchequer, and then between the area managers and their governors. These agreements often bring additional resources, but they are tied to the delivery of tightly specified outputs, such as an increased level of completed accredited offending behaviour programmes. This development is regarded as a new and powerful form of high-level strategic control and a new and effective mode of accountability for public spending.

KPIs have precipitated a cultural change within the Service, from an input (staff-led) organization of the kind described by King and McDermott in the previous chapter, to an outputs-focused Service, with some apparent improvements in regime delivery. Governors and staff 'care about how my prison is doing on those charts' (governor, in Sinclair 2002: 57) almost regardless of whether or not the charts are measuring the right thing.[13] On the other hand, there is a considerable critique of target-setting and its effects in general (e.g. on morale and on activity), especially in hierarchical organizations, on the extent to which they measure 'quality', and more specifically, of the choice and number of targets used. We shall return to this critique below.

Standards Audit

> SENIOR OFFICER: 'Have we got any ticks in any of the boxes yet?'
> AUDITOR: 'Only little ones.'
>
> (Fieldwork notes)[14]

Audit has become a benchmark for securing the legitimacy of organisational action in which auditable standards of performance have been created not merely to provide for substantial internal improvements to the quality of service but to make these improvements externally verifiable via acts of certification.

> (Power 2001: 10–11)

---

[13] In a discussion with prison staff about 'what gave them most satisfaction', staff said that achieving a 'good audit' rating was a great boost. When asked if they felt a good audit score reflected good practice (in this example, in suicide prevention policy), they said 'largely, no' and yet maintained that the result, by itself, was satisfying.

[14] The quote is taken from a fieldwork observation of an audit; see further Liebling and Durie (in progress).

The second 'performance measurement' mechanism is the use of process auditing. This practice arose for very similar reasons to those described above, but it has a distinct emphasis on daily practices and procedures. It had a special relevance in the prisons context, given the inattention to process and procedure found in Whitemoor's SSU, described in Chapter 1.

The 'audit explosion' is related to a distinct 'phase in the development of advanced economic systems' (Power 2001: 14), and is consistent with the move towards targets outlined above. A practice originating in the world of finance, the process of auditing is now applied to non-financial practices and systems and is used to scrutinize them closely. Auditing, like performance measurement, represents a 'new rationality of governance', whereby central control reaches deeply into organizations, bringing with it expectations of self-control, individual accountability, and unprecedented levels of knowledge about internal organizational arrangements (Power 2001).

Considerable discussion about standards in prison took place during the 1980s as concern about unacceptable conditions in (mainly local) prisons proliferated (see Vagg 1994). An attempt to introduce a code of minimum standards in prisons in England and Wales following the Woolf Report faltered in the 1990s (Home Office 1991a; Vagg 1994), but paved the way for a comprehensive set of operational standards which have a different focus. Minimum standards would specify 'an agreed means of determining whether or not prison conditions were adequate' (Vagg 1994: 205). Operational standards specify *processes*, or the minimum establishments should be 'doing' in relation to specified policy areas. They are intended to provide a benchmark, help set targets, and provide a means for the assessment, monitoring, and improvement of performance. They constitute a proxy measure of prison quality or performance. They actually assess compliance with procedures or local operational policy (performance against baselines).

The Prison Service Standards Audit Unit was established in 1994 to audit operating standards and the policies and strategic priorities to which they relate. The first audits were related exclusively to security procedures and were introduced in 1995 as a direct result of the finding, after the high profile 1990s escapes, that prison staff were not following basic security procedures (Home Office 1994, 1995). Operational standards audits began soon after, in 1996, and were revised and renamed performance standards in 1999. The purpose of standards is: 'To ensure all staff apply agreed policies and procedures in a consistent way and achieve consistently high levels of performance' (Prison Service 2002d: introduction).

Establishments are audited every two years. There are currently 61 standards, and revisions are introduced in regular reviews conducted by Standards Audit Unit. The standards include security, regime features such as provision of work, education, offending behaviour programmes, sentence planning, and health care, as well as general issues of treatment such as race relations, suicide, and self-harm prevention, and the use of force (Prison Service 2002d). They also include a module on 'KPI and KPT Data Quality', which is aimed at ensuring that these data are accurate and reliable. For this module there are 18 key audit baselines, for example: 'A member of the senior management team signs and returns the monthly validation sheet having taken the action required . . . to investigate and correct discrepancies' (Prison Service 2002d: standard 29).

Standards form the basis for assessment of the key work (or 'performance') of individual officers (in principle) so that a system of 'staff performance and development' is linked to contributions made to certain audit baselines. Establishments take the audit process (a visit by the audit team) very seriously.[15] Audits have the same kind of impact on an establishment as a full inspection. Considerable preparation is involved and establishments see their impending audit (announced several months in advance) as a key date by which any planned or required improvements to procedure should be in place. Unlike an inspection (see below), the standards audit process rarely involves contact with prisoners. This process is about what staff do and whether they are doing it 'properly'.[16]

Establishments attract a 'score' on individual modules, and a 'rating' overall (such as 'good', 'acceptable', or 'deficient'), according to levels of compliance with specified processes. Some standards are weighted, so that they carry a disproportionate impact on the overall score. The auditing process depends to a large extent on accurate recording of practices, and there is increasing emphasis on self-auditing, so that establishments should, over time, be 'doing

---

[15] Standards Audit Unit consists of an in-house department staffed by ex-governors, psychologists, and other civil service grades.

[16] Although see references to the adoption of our survey in Chapter 3.

this to themselves' (as Power describes). The audit process does not assess the suitability of policy or the achievement of relevant outcomes. Achieving a 'good' on, for example, sentence management, suicide prevention, or incentives and earned privileges, does not necessarily mean that the prisoner's sentence is being carefully planned, his or her needs are being met, or that incentive levels are appropriately linked to behaviour (see Liebling and Durie in progress).[17] Considerable effort is expended within establishments to achieve good ratings. Considerable scepticism is expressed about the value and meaning of the process, as well as the relative ease with which establishments can achieve an 'acceptable' or 'good' score.[18]

Standard-setting and scoring arises as part of a process of questioning (and controlling and modernizing) what organizations are doing, and whether they are doing these things in an acceptable way (Scrivens 1994: 87; Pollitt *et al.* 2002; Clarke and Newman 1997). A report on the use of standards in health care carried out by the World Health Organization highlighted three different questions that can be asked:

1. At what level are they set? Is their agenda *regulation* (i.e. setting minimum standards) or *accreditation* (a more aspirational agenda)?
2. What type are they? (Do they measure structure, process or outcomes?); and
3. What scaling or scoring system is set?

We might add a fourth question:

4. What are they measuring? Is it what is easily quantifiable rather than 'what matters'?

The Prison Service has adopted a regulation approach and a process emphasis. The level at which they are set is, arguably, relatively low

---

[17] For example, we found that producing good sentence plans (an input) attracted good scores in the sentence management audit module, but prisoners still rated the management of their sentence or time in prison quite negatively in prisons with good sentence plans. Good practice ceased at the point where the evaluation questions ended, with the production of an acceptable sentence plan.

[18] Power suggests that scoring levels are set relatively low, and that this is consistent with the purpose of standards auditing which is to reassure and legitimate (Power 2001). Carlen argues similarly that such processes look like critique but actually stifle it (Carlen 2002*b*).

with most prisons achieving acceptable ratings most of the time (see Rex *et al.* 2003).[19] Some argue that the audit process serves as a 'stimulus to professional strivings to improve practice' and make relevant changes (see Scrivens 1994: 95). Others are more cynical, believing that the performance and audit figures are irrelevant, meaningless, and systematically fabricated.[20] Power has suggested that the excessive checking involved in 'the audit society' is pathological. He describes auditing as a 'ritual of verification' which is rarely based on a solid understanding of what practices matter. It is related to a deeper set of issues about 'the organisation of trust in developed societies' (Power 2001, p. xvi). The need to check suggests doubt, mistrust, risk, and danger (ibid. 1; also Giddens 1990). The alternative to checking is *trust*. Power suggests that auditing systems are primarily about 'reaffirming order' (rather than constituting a true system of accountability) and that: 'Institutionalised pressures exist for audit and inspection systems to provide comfort and reassurance, rather than critique' (Power 2001, p. xvii).

This yearning for order via control, without trust, may, as we might anticipate, have unintended consequences. As O'Neill argues: 'Perhaps the culture of accountability that we are relentlessly building for ourselves actually damages trust rather than supporting it' (O'Neill 2002: 19). Inappropriately precise and rigid measurement systems used in complex organizations can lead employees to 'conclude that they are not valued or understood as professionals' (Sitkin and Stickel 1996: 210) and can lead to a reaction of distrust (see also Giddens 1990, 1991) and non-compliance (Braithwaite 2002). If broader objectives are used rather than precise measures: 'It may be more feasible for individual members of the organisation to conform to both the spirit and the letter of the rule while adapting that rule to the requirements of their particular task' (Sitkin and Stickel 1996: 210).

This, the above authors suggest, leads us to the literature on perceived justice, which shows that the manner of an individual's treatment (in addition to outcomes) is highly significant in judgements about the fairness of an authority. Fair measurement systems (which

---

[19] Rex and colleagues found, in a study of the accreditation process for offending behaviour programmes, that the Prison Service gained accredited status with apparent 'ease' compared to the Probation Service. There may, of course, be several reasons for this (including longer experience). See Rex *et al.* 2003.

[20] See www.lean-service.com.

are perceived as fair and appropriate by employees) matter in organizational life. Co-operation and fairness are linked amongst employees as well as among prisoners and citizens more generally (see Bottoms 1999, 2002; Tyler 1990; Paternoster *et al.* 1997; and later chapters). It is this tension between 'rigid measurement' and perceptions of fairness (e.g. being treated as moral agents rather than as aggregates, and recognition of the complexity of one's work) that underlies resistance to, and reservations about, their proliferation. Employees feel 'wrongly accused', for example, if they have been performing well in a poor performing organization (Sitkin and Stickel 1996: 212). This, amongst other things (such as the existential trouble described by Giddens), may account for their defensive rejection of such aggregate reviews.[21] To restore trust, O'Neill argues: 'We need not only trustworthy persons and institutions, but also assessable reasons for trusting and for mistrusting' (ibid. 98). The idea of a 'trustworthy institution' is an important one, with relevance to modernization and to the drawing in to public sector organizations of private sector practices (see further Kramer and Tyler 1996 and below).

Audit is, as Power argues, a 'sociologically significant activity', with, we argue, important and barely understood effects on prison life. It may bring with it evasions and fabrications; it is unclear how closely satisfying the requirements of audit brings about increases in the concept of 'quality'. Audit is seen by many practitioners as 'meaningless' compared to KPIs, which do set priorities.

Despite our own and others' mixed feelings about the process and its effects, we found that there *was* a relationship between establishments' scores on audit and scores on our measure of prison quality, although again this relationship may not be causal. Prisons that had good processes, as assessed by audit, tended on the whole to also treat prisoners better (Liebling and Arnold 2000). But the relationship was indirect. A gap existed between what a prison had to do to attract a good audit rating and whether or not the establishment was achieving the intended outcomes. Staff in establishments expressed some unease with this approach to scoring, and would have preferred the evaluations to have been more robust and meaningful, that is, more carefully linked to the 'work they were meant to be doing'.

---

[21] Staff at Wandsworth reacted in exactly this manner to a damning Inspectorate visit, as we shall explain below and further in Chapter 3.

The Prisons Inspectorate

> The Chief Inspector treads a delicate path. He is not constitu-
> tionally independent of the chain of responsibility for the Prison
> Service. But he can and does exercise independence of judgment.
>
> (Morgan 1985: 121)

The third official source of information about the quality of a prison
comes from Her Majesty's Inspectorate of Prisons. This body
arguably has a more explicit 'moral' and qualitative role than the
KPI, KPT, and standards auditing tasks outlined above. The post of
Her Majesty's Chief Inspector of Prisons was formally established in
1981 as a result of the deliberations of the May Committee (Home
Office 1979). It is an independent body, reporting to the Secretary
of State on the treatment of prisoners and the conditions of prisons
(section 5A Prison Act 1952, as amended by section 57 of the
Criminal Justice Act 1982). This charter included the requirement
that regular inspections should concentrate on: 'The morale of
staff and prisoners; the quality of the regime; the condition of the
buildings; questions of humanity and propriety; and the extent to
which the establishment is giving value for money' (para. 4; Morgan
1985: 110).

The stated aim for the creation of the Prisons Inspectorate was to
'open up the prisons to the public gaze' (Morgan 1985; Vagg 1994).
They carry out full inspections (about 20 per year) and about the
same number of short and follow-up inspections of individual establishments. They also carry out an increasing number of thematic
reviews on issues of special interest and concern (e.g. women,
unsentenced prisoners, resettlement, suicide, and life sentence prisoners). They occasionally investigate major incidents, as directed by
the Secretary of State (e.g. HMCIP 1987). They have recently been
invited to include Prison Service performance or service delivery
on race relations matters in their remit. This is the first indication
of any power the Prisons Inspectorate have to inspect the Service
rather than establishments.

Full inspections are normally announced in advance, whereas
short inspections are normally unannounced and may concentrate
on particular issues arising from previous inspections. Every prison
establishment should receive a full inspection at least every five
years. The strength and expertise of the Inspectorate team has
grown considerably since its inception. Thirty full-time staff are

employed by the Inspectorate, and specialists (e.g. in health, education, immigration, or drug treatment) are frequently invited to accompany teams on individual inspections. There are three inspection teams, a research and development section, and a secretariat. Each team has four core members, including a team leader, who is usually an ex-governor.

During a full inspection, the team investigates the way prisoners are treated; the quality of the regime (including opportunities for prisoners to work and receive education); and how the establishment prepares prisoners for release. They also investigate the quality of health care; how the establishment is managed; and the physical condition of the buildings. A full inspection lasts between five and ten working days, and involves between five and 20 individual inspectors. The Prisons Inspectorate, unusually, do not inspect in relation to the organization's published standards (a position they defend by reference to the original statute),[22] but concentrate on the quality of the regime and the treatment of prisoners.

Informal and open-ended (non-scoring) methods are used, although it has become increasingly common for inspections to include surveys of prisoners, and there is now a set of expectations, developed by the Inspectorate in 1999, which are outcome-based, and which inform visits (HMCIP 2001d: annexe 7). They constitute the 'criteria for assessing the treatment of and conditions for prisoners' and they are designed 'to assist [them] in making accurate and consistent judgements about what is happening to prisoners, and in making recommendations' (ibid. 1).[23] The expectations have, underlying them, a concept of the 'healthy prison' (HMCIP 1999a), which incorporates four main areas of concern: safety, respect, family contact, and purposeful activity (see Chapter 3). They are detailed

[22] Current Prison Inspectorate methods have evolved with a distinct purpose in mind, dating back to the disturbances of the 1970s. More recently established inspectorates tend to have more managerialist purposes and approaches (Lloyd 2002). The increasingly wide availability of management information within criminal justice agencies makes the Prison Inspectorate's 'quality' role (and observational methods) seem highly appropriate.

[23] 'Expectations take account of existing statutory United Kingdom Prison and Young Offender Institution Rules, European Prison Rules, Prison Service Standards, and United Nations and World Health Organisation statements that offer guidance, particularly in declaring principles about the way in which prisoners are to be treated. The majority of them are in harmony with existing Prison Service Standards' (HMCIP 2001d: 1).

(for example, there are 26 subject areas, with 48 expectations on 'reception and induction' alone, including an expectation that 'prisoners are allowed to make essential contacts with family and friends before being locked up for the first night'). There are 66 expectations on 'good order', and so on (HMCIP 2001*d*: 5–113). 'Expectations', which guide the inspection process, operate as checklists or 'aides-memoirs rather than formal guidelines' (Vagg 1994).

Governors often find inspection reports (and the inspection process, which includes verbal feedback on good practice and areas for improvement at the end of the visit) valuable. For those wishing to glean useful background information about a particular establishment, Inspectorate reports are informative. Some reports are highly critical and receive considerable publicity (e.g. HMCIP 1997*b*, 2001*c*), although others are surprisingly uncritical (Morgan 1985: 111–12; HMCIP 1999*b*). All inspection reports are published, normally within a few months of the visit (although there is often a negotiating process, and the timing of publication may be influenced by the Director General). Annual Reports and Thematic Inspection Reports are also published. The Inspectorate has no enforcement role. Its effectiveness depends to some extent on this 'shaming' function, and on succeeding in interesting the press. The publication process (and the time this takes) is therefore vitally important, and takes place in stages. The Service and the Home Secretary are normally given first sight of each report, and an opportunity to reply.

The relationship between the Inspectorate (particularly individual Chief Inspectors) and the Director General can be tense, but arguably this may be a measure of their effectiveness in exposing matters of concern. Different Chief Inspectors have had different styles and take a particular focus. There have been five post-holders: William Pearce (1981–2), Sir James Hennessy (1982–8), Judge Stephen Tumim (1989–95), Sir David Ramsbotham (1995–2001) and (currently) Anne Owers, CBE (2001–).

The inspection model is 'the best resourced and most professionalised' in Europe (and probably elsewhere; Vagg 1994). It is highly regarded abroad and has recently been adopted by the government of Western Australia (see OICS 2001).[24] As Morgan

---

[24] The Office of the Inspector of Custodial Services of Western Australia was established in June 2000. The first incumbent, Professor Richard Harding, has set a lively tone. Inspections are 'intended to scrutinise . . . standards and practices and

argues, the effectiveness of the inspecting role depends on achieving a balance between independence and experience ('insider intelligence'), on the availability of data, and on the methods used (Morgan 1985: 112). There have been tensions for ex-governors holding key positions in the Inspectorate seeking a return to the Service, although Morgan notes that the first and second Deputy Chief Inspectors both became Deputy Directors General of the Prison Service (Morgan 1985: 113). There have been recent moves to encourage younger governors to work as team leaders in the Inspectorate.

Inspectorate reports constitute a well-informed and detailed assessment of quality, but with few measures or easily calibrated criteria. This had led to controversy over particular inspection verdicts (such as the 'culture of brutality' identified at Wandsworth in 1999; see HMCIP 1999c; and Chapter 3). Certain critical Inspectorate reports have been robustly rebuffed by Director Generals, who have occasionally accused the Inspectorate of unclear and unreliable methods. Other critics have suggested they may occasionally 'pursue specific agendas' or 'decide in advance the flavour of their report' in specific cases (pers. comm.). On the other hand, extremely critical reports (such as the 2002 report on HMP Dartmoor's 'outdated culture of disrespect and over-control') have been welcomed as 'hard-hitting but perceptive' (HMI Press Service 2002: 1). Importantly, the purposes of inspection—to improve standards and curb abuses of power—are distinct from, but might increasingly draw upon, research. Their effectiveness should be evaluated in relation to these aims, and the extent to which they are regarded as independent, rather than the extent to which they accurately reflect a prison's quality. They contribute enormously to the information flow about prison life and standards, and their reports may lead to important policy changes (for example, the ending of 'slopping out', and reform of the troubled Close Supervision Centres; see HMCIP 1990b, 2000e).[25]

produce public information about corrections policies, systems and strategies' (OICS 2001). The framework adopted relates to the Ministry's theoretical approach to imprisonment: the Inspectorate's main themes are custody, care and well-being, rehabilitation and reparation.

[25] Although importantly, often they do not lead to change despite repeated and fiercely stated requests (see consecutive reports on Wormwood Scrubs 1997, 1999, 2000, and 2002).

Independent Monitoring Boards

> It is in monitoring the . . . well-being of prisoners that BoVs can provide a uniquely valuable service.
>
> (Home Office 2001a: 15)

Formerly known as boards of visitors (BoVs), independent monitoring boards consist of lay representatives who voluntarily take on responsibility for overseeing individual prisons and the treatment of prisoners in them (Vagg 1985, 1994). They visit all areas of establishments, hear prisoners' complaints, and until 2003, they authorized the segregation of prisoners. A quarter of a century ago, 'BoVs provided the only independent oversight of prisons in the United Kingdom' (Home Office 2001a: 12). Now, the Chief Inspector of Prisons, and the Prisons Ombudsman, have 'considerably more impact' (ibid.). BoVs used to conduct disciplinary hearings, where alleged offences were serious, or repeated, but this power was removed in 1992, in the interests of clarifying and enhancing their watchdog role (Home Office 1991a). Under section 6(3) of the Prison Act they 'report to the Secretary of State any matter which they consider it expedient to report'. Known informally as independent 'watchdogs' (the 'eyes and ears of the Home Secretary', Vagg 1994: 5), their role has been criticized on several grounds. Their profile too closely resembles that of justices of the peace (they were originally visiting magistrates); they lack independence (often seeing themselves as in 'partnership' with the governor); they rely on a continuing relationship with establishments; they cannot draw comparisons between prisons; and their reports are bland and ineffective (Vagg 1994: 36 and 142; Home Office 2001a). Individual boards operate at different levels of effectiveness. They sometimes play an important role in the investigation of and response to critical incidents.

Their re-launch in April 2003, under the new title, 'independent monitoring boards' (IMBs), coincides with a symbolic move to new accommodation, shared with the Prisons Ombudsman.[26] This

---

[26] The now well-established role of Prisons (and Probation) Ombudsman operates as an 'independent adjudicator' of prisoners' complaints. He publishes a detailed annual report. This role offers an important mechanism of accountability and legitimacy in the eyes of many prisoners, but for several reasons (including different propensities to complain among different populations and the possibility

decision followed a review of boards of visitors arising from the Laming Report on prison performance. The Laming Report expressed concern that issues identified by the boards often received an inadequate response. Their role was unclear, and their practices were out of step with the modern performance-driven Service. Monitoring and checking the quality of prison life was now a specialist activity requiring detailed understanding of targets and the process of target-setting (Home Office 2000a: 17). It was often unclear what constituted 'abuse', for example, yet boards had a responsibility under Prison Rule 77(4) to 'inform the Secretary of State of any abuse which comes to their knowledge' (Home Office 2000a: 15). There was an 'essential tension' between 'broad issues' (e.g. poor relationships between staff and prisoners) and 'specific issues' (the complaint of an individual prisoner) (Home Office 2000a: 18–19). The same degree of uncertainty arose over what constituted good practice.

The revisions to their role allow greater access to area managers, and a new Prison Rule places a 'duty on the area manager to look promptly into and make a formal decision on any matter concerning segregation raised by a board' (Home Office 2001a: 62). The role is lay 'quality assurance'; that is, they represent 'the standards of the community in the prison' (Home Office 2001a: 26). Guidance offered to IMB members suggest that they are: 'Primarily concerned with observing and reporting on the extent to which prisons are being administered in accordance with Prison Rules, with the Prison Service's own Statement of Purpose and with international standards of decency and humanity in the treatment of prisoners' (National Advisory Council 2003).

Their revised Statement of Purpose states that their role is: 'To safeguard the interests of prisoners by monitoring and reporting to Ministers and the community on the extent to which the Prison Service holds prisoners in a safe, decent and healthy environment and prepares them for release' (National Advisory Council 2003). The formal changes to their organization represent an attempt to strengthen both their monitoring powers and their credibility (Home Office 2001a).

---

that better prisons encourage, or, at least, do not inhibit complaints), complaints to the Prisons and Probation Ombudsman do not constitute a reliable indicator of prison quality.

We have reviewed the development and use of official performance measures mainly within the Prison Service, above. We move
below to other existing attempts to evaluate prison quality, from
a number of different perspectives.

The Evaluation Literature

In this section we (selectively) consider classic and recent social
scientific and more evaluative contemporary official approaches to
prison quality, identifying a number of important lessons as well as
a number of important limitations in current and previous work.
There have been many such studies, and we can divide them into
two broad categories. They are:

1. The academic prison evaluation literature. This includes
   treatment studies (e.g. the Moos *Correctional Institutions
   Environment Scale* (CIES) and the adjustment literature to
   emerge from these beginnings); and management studies (e.g. the
   Federal Bureau of Prisons' *Prison Social Climate Survey*).
2. Cost, performance, and other comparisons between public and
   private sector prisons (e.g. Logan's *Prison Quality Index* (1992);
   some case study evaluations; and some of the more analytic
   accounts).[27]

We shall show how questions of prison quality have changed in
nature as management needs and public–private sector competition
have come to dominate the research agenda.

The Academic Prison Evaluation Literature

(a) Treatment Studies

Most early attempts to assess prison quality were conducted in a
quest for 'therapeutic effectiveness'—what kinds of penal regimes
led to what outcomes on release? This work emerged out of a

---

[27] Much of the early privatization literature is historical and conceptual and
together constitutes a valuable overview of the arguments for and (more usually)
against privatization (see e.g. Ryan and Ward 1989; Lilly and Knepper 1993;
Christie 1993; Shichor 1999) but implicitly or explicitly rules out empirical investigation as irrelevant to the case being made. The empirical literature rarely engages
fully with these important critiques (see Liebling and Sparks 2002).

growing recognition that environments or settings, and in particular, how individuals and groups perceived these environments, influenced behaviour.[28] The framework within which such studies were conceived consisted of a set of beliefs about the 'people-changing' nature of institutions and their potentially rehabilitative effects (see e.g. Street *et al.* 1966),[29] in addition to a broad interest in the nature of individual and group adaptations to these environments. Moos, for example, applied the methods he had developed in his evaluations of treatment environments in psychiatric and community settings to correctional environments during the 1960s and 1970s.[30] His scale was originally developed to provide a measure of the 'social climate' of psychiatric wards (or schools, military bases, work milieus, and families) and was based on a number of items, which were used to form subscales. These subscales or dimensions were empirically derived from respondents in these environments and applied across a wide range of settings. They were felt to be 'useful in characterising the social and organisational climates of a variety of groups and institutions' (Moos 1975: 20).

Moos constructed a 90-item scale—the Correctional Institutions Environment Scale (CIES)—which assessed nine dimensions of the social climate of correctional programmes. It was adapted from the Ward Atmosphere Scale, used in hospitals. New items were devised, informed by the relevant literature, discussions with staff and residents on various correctional programmes, and certain

[28] The term 'press' was used to refer to the relationship between the phenomenological world of the individual and the environment. The word was used to indicate a significant external or environmental and directional determinant of behaviour. Individuals have needs (e.g. for achievement, affiliation, autonomy, and order) and environments satisfy or frustrate these needs to varying degrees (Moos 1975: 19). Murray argued that there is a point at which the world of the individual merges with that of others, 'that people tend to share common interpretations of the events in which they participate' (Jones and Cornes 1977: 91). This was 'beta press' (a more collective version of 'press'). Moos argued that group mean scores on the CIES subscales provided a measure of some of this 'beta press' (Murray 1938).

[29] This concern with change was underpinned by a 'rise in humanitarian values' and the professional/therapeutic optimism of the time (Street *et al.* 1966; see also Home Office 1959; Janowicz 1966, p. vi).

[30] Moos was not the first to describe and assess social climates in prisons (see Street *et al.* 1966), but his is the most detailed and influential attempt. The early versions of environment scales devised by Moos were the Social Climate Scale, the Ward Atmosphere Scale (WAS), and the Community-Oriented Programmes Environment Scale (COPES).

statistical criteria (for example, items should discriminate significantly among units; and each scale should have ten items each, half scored true and half scored false). Items with low item-to-subscale correlations were eliminated; other subscales were collapsed into one. The three broad categories of dimensions developed were clearly linked to therapeutic concepts so that, for example, relationship dimensions included involvement, support, and expressiveness; personal development included autonomy, practical orientation, and personal problem orientation and was a proxy for 'treatment'; system maintenance included order and organization, clarity, and officer control. Table 2.2 contains his CIES Scale and the subscale dimensions (Moos 1975: 41).

TABLE 2.2. Moos's correctional institutions environment scale (CIES) (subscale descriptions)

Relationships Variables
1. *Involvement*: measures how active and energetic residents are in the day-to-day functioning of the programme (i.e. interacting socially with other residents, doing things on their own initiative, and developing pride and group spirit in the programme).
2. *Support*: measures the extent to which residents are encouraged to be helpful and supportive towards other residents, and how supportive the staff is towards residents.
3. *Expressiveness*: measures the extent to which the programme encourages the open expression of feelings (including angry feelings) by residents and staff.

Treatment Programme Variables
4. *Autonomy*: assesses the extent to which residents are encouraged to take initiative in planning activities and take leadership in the unit.
5. *Practical orientation*: assesses the extent to which the resident's environment orients him (*sic*) towards preparing himself for release from the programme: training for new kinds of jobs, looking to the future, and setting and working toward goals are among the factors considered.
6. *Personal problem orientation*: measures the extent to which residents are encouraged to be concerned with their personal problems and feelings and seek to understand them.

System Maintenance Variables
7. *Order and organization*: measures how important order and organization are in the programme, in terms of residents (how they look?), staff (what they do to encourage order?), and the facility itself (how well is it kept?).
8. *Clarity*: measures the extent to which the resident knows what to expect in the day-to-day routine of his programme and how explicit the programme rules and procedures are.
9. *Staff control*: assesses the extent to which the staff use regulations to keep residents under necessary controls (e.g. in the formulation of rules, the scheduling of activities, and in the relationships between residents and staff).

TABLE 2.3.   Selected examples of subscale items

Involvement	The residents are proud of this unit.
	Discussions are pretty interesting on this unit.
Support	Staff are interested in following up residents once they leave.
	Staff go out of their way to help residents.
Expressiveness	Residents are encouraged to show their feelings.
	Staff and residents say how they feel about each other.
Autonomy	The staff act on residents' suggestions.
	The staff give residents very little responsibility.
Practical orientation	There is very little emphasis on making plans for getting out of here.
	Residents are encouraged to plan for the future.
Order and organization	The day-room is often messy.
	This is a very well-organized unit.
Clarity	If a resident's programme is changed, someone on the staff always tells him (*sic*) why.
	If a resident breaks a rule, he knows what will happen to him.
Staff control	Once a schedule is arranged for a resident, he must follow it.
	All decisions about the unit are made by the staff and not by the residents.

These subscales were not conceived as wholly independent from each other but as realistic, recognizable, and interrelated aspects of prison life. A moderate degree of subscale intercorrelation has been reported (Jones and Cornes 1977: 104). Selected examples of the items are included in Table 2.3. Items from each scale were interspersed randomly throughout the questionnaire.[31] The items were scored 'true' or 'false'.

Moos and his colleagues devised several (short and long) versions of this scale and, unlike our own work which we shall describe later, staff and prisoners were asked to answer exactly the same items. Moos conducted test-retest reliability checks and tests of stability of the scale, and found that 'the CIES profile is stable when the program is stable'; and that it was 'sensitive to program change when change occurs' (p. 45). The scale was consistent with findings on other perceived environment scales in that assessments were (perhaps surprisingly) relatively independent of background

---

[31] The items included in his 90-item questionnaire can be found in Moos (1975: appendix A).

variables such as age, sex, and length of stay (Moos 1975: 47).[32] The scale was administered to random samples of inmates using paper and pencil questionnaires, under conditions of anonymity. A version of the scale intended to determine 'ideal program' characteristics was also used in some of the studies conducted by Moos and his colleagues. Comparisons between real and ideal programmes indicated that substantially higher levels of involvement, support, autonomy, and clarity were desired by residents. Certain structural characteristics (e.g. size of programme, staff–resident ratio) were linked to evaluations, so that larger programmes with lower staff–resident ratios tended to result in lower ratings on certain relationships dimensions, such as support and expressiveness (see Moos 1975: 73–7).

Moos developed an empirical typology of correctional treatment programmes based on a cluster analysis of the subscale scores above. He classified programmes as therapeutic, relationship-oriented, action-oriented, insight-oriented, control-oriented, and disturbed behaviour programmes. Each type of programme emphasized different subscales so that, for example, the disturbed behaviour programmes were high on expressiveness and staff control. The usefulness of the typology was linked to developing typologies of offenders, who might be suited to different types of treatment interventions.

The CIES was developed in order to evaluate specific treatment programmes in the context of residents' evaluation of their social milieu. The scale could be used to test whether new treatment programmes generated or were consistent with the kind of climate intended. It could identify variations in apparently similar programmes, and it could be used to explore (and partly explain) differences in personality changes, across different institutions or units. The outcomes of interest were residents' morale and self-esteem, modes of adaptation and coping, behavioural rating, personality test changes, and success or failure on parole. Moos found, for example, that high scores on relationships subscales were linked to high perceptions of personal development, and that, conversely, high scores on staff control were negatively correlated with personal development and with relationships. High involvement was

---

[32] Others have found that 'troublesome' prisoners systematically rate their environment more negatively; see Wood *et al.* (1966); Liebling (2001).

linked to positive changes in self-appraised levels of independence and 'calmness' (Moos 1975: 166–7). Moos concluded that individuals on units with more 'positive social climates' showed more beneficial changes on a range of self-appraisal dimensions. Only slight differences were found between expected and actual parole survival (measured in months spent in the community) between the 'best' units and the 'worst'. Some items within the social climate scale were more closely correlated with 'community tenure' (post-release survival) than were others. Interestingly, Moos found that items related to quite high levels of staff control as well as items related to expressiveness, openness, and encouragement were associated with 'high tenure units' (Moos 1975: 168–72).[33] There are, of course, major difficulties with the idea that experience in one environment will affect behaviour in another (see Moos 1975: 177–8). Social milieu, once out of prison, is 'an important determinant of individual behaviour'. Put more strongly: 'Recidivism may not mean that institutional correctional programs have failed: it may reflect the failure of the relevant social environments in the community' (Moos 1975: 179). We can be more confident that the way an environment is perceived will affect current or institutional behaviour to an important degree (see, for example, Sparks et al. 1996).

Moos's work constitutes an important early attempt to conceptualize and measure social climate, in a reliable way.[34] The scale he devised can be used systematically to describe and compare institutional climates, longitudinally and cross-sectionally. It can be used in evaluations of the effects of training, new treatment programmes, or other interventions. Moos argues that 'a variety of

[33] One of the shortcomings of these early attempts to relate institutional climate to post-release survival is that institutions rather than individuals are compared. That is, the success rate of all inmates released from a particular unit are compared with all those released from another unit, rather than, for example, exploring the post-release survival rates of those individuals *within* a generally highly rated unit who rated the unit highly.

[34] Some of the methodological problems he encounters provide us with an interesting model with which to compare our own work: for example, what size samples are adequate? How is anonymity ensured? Can different populations be compared? Does length of time incarcerated affect evaluations? Do background variables affect evaluations? Are only those dimensions which discriminate significantly between institutions useful? Should 'normative samples' be used as a baseline for assessing quality, so that institutions are evaluated against the average? (Moos 1975: 39 and *passim*; and see later chapters).

methods are needed to assess correctional programs' (1975: 78), and he recognizes that this kind of research is developmental. His main concern was the relationship between attitudes and the 'more objective institutional outcome': success on parole (p. 154). We would argue (as others have: e.g. Saylor 1984) that the transition in use of the instrument from mainly psychiatric treatment settings to prison environments was never satisfactorily made. On the other hand, his work takes us back to some of the basic questions about the environments of institutions that seem to have been overlooked in official performance measures. Moos argued that environments have 'personalities': they may be more or less supportive or controlling, they have different goals and values. They may change, and they are shaped by their surrounding conditions (Moos 1975: 3–13). Using broad categories of dimensions 'provides us with a convenient framework' for making comparisons and reflecting on differences between environments (ibid. 25). Assessing social climates in institutions periodically may also be useful in *bringing about change*, by feeding back results to staff and residents and identifying strategies for addressing low scores according to their own goals and values, sometimes followed by further assessment (see Moos 1975: 91–105). It may also be useful in identifying institutional tensions.

Moos's model is limited because his measures are conceptually and ideologically linked to 'treatment' or behaviour modification, of a particular kind. His work is focused on responses to contrasting treatment programmes and on the prediction of individual prisoner behaviour. The interest in staff is limited to their perceptions of prisoner-oriented behaviours and attitudes, and staff perceptions of the 'treatment' climate are always found to be more positive than prisoners' perceptions. There is no separate attempt to evaluate how staff see their working climate as it is experienced by them (Saylor makes this point, arguing that this aspect of Moos's scale is contrived and inappropriate; Saylor 1984: 6). Replication studies provide mixed levels of support for the dimensional structure or the subscales as they were conceived by Moos (Duffee 1975; Wright 1979; Wright and Boudouris 1982; Saylor 1984). It was unclear how they had been selected, and what their theoretical and empirical properties were. Several critics questioned his use of the term 'climate', suggesting that it needed further theoretical as well as empirical elaboration (Wright and Boudouris 1982). However, the CIES was immensely influential and widely used, and its development and use represent significant conceptual and empirical beginnings.

In a UK application of this framework, Jones and Cornes conducted a detailed comparison of prisoner and staff assessments of three open and two closed prisons during the 1970s using versions B and C of the Moos CIES,[35] adapted for use in British prisons (Jones and Cornes 1977). Their study was supported by observational research. Jones and Cornes found interesting and unexpected differences between prisons, some of which were related to the length of sentence being served in each prison:

> . . . a greater degree of intelligibility and co-operativeness appears to enter into a regime, the longer the sentence which is being served. This is shown by progressively higher scores at a significant level for Involvement and Clarity, as one moves from short term to medium and long term. There is a similar rising gradient for Support, Expressiveness, Autonomy and Personal problem orientation, although the differences between short and medium term in these cases are not statistically significant. Equally meaningful is a parallel statistically significant decline with increase in length of sentence in the more discipline-oriented subscale of Staff control. (Jones and Cornes 1977: 116–17)

The closed prisons were more similar to each other than the open prisons (making them more essentially 'like a prison'). The open/ closed distinction was not the most important distinction. The authors suggested that longer-term institutions tended to develop 'more sympathetic regimes' (Jones and Cornes 1977: 117); that is, they were more treatment-oriented and less discipline-oriented. Clarity of objectives, the governor's conception of the type of regime he or she wished to create, and in this study, the capacity of the governor in the long-term open prison to select his own prisoner intake, contributed most to the organizational climate. A significant source of discrepancies in prisoners' perceptions of individual prisons was the variable 'staff control'. High levels of staff control were negatively perceived. Likewise the most significant source of variation among staff was perceived 'inmate autonomy'. High levels of

---

[35] The authors used the longer version B, but analysed version C, following extensive revisions to version B for application to a correctional environment by the original author (Jones and Cornes 1977: 92–3). The scales used were: involvement, support, expressiveness, autonomy, practical orientation, personal problem orientation, order and organization, clarity and staff control (Jones and Cornes 1977, appendix I: 241–3).

inmate autonomy were negatively perceived by staff. The authors argue that these variables are likely to be assessing similar aspects of each prison's regime. We might call this aspect of a prison's regime the distribution of power between staff and prisoners (see Chapter 7).

Whilst Jones and Cornes do provide mean scores for each subscale, for prisoners and for staff for each prison, there is little discussion of what the subscales mean, or interpretation of the scores achieved. There is no discussion of data from individual questions. Their study was conceived partly as a test of the CIES and its applicability to British prison regimes. They conclude that the scale was a useful aid in the assessment of prison regimes, but that it included many redundant items and it was capable of further refinement. They argued that a new tool should be assembled with more attention paid to the penological literature and the scale reconstructed 'from the ground up' (Jones and Cornes 1977: 93; and see below).

Others developed, from the work pioneered by Moos, interesting analyses of differences in, for example, probation hostels and attendance centres and linked these differences to differences in absconding rates (Heal et al. 1973; Clarke and Martin 1971; Sinclair 1971). Sinclair, and Heal et al. developed dimensions relating to 'strictness' (e.g. 'if a boy argues with staff he will get in trouble'); 'work' (e.g. 'it is easy to skive here when you should be working'); 'staff support' ('staff have very little time to encourage the boys'); 'satisfaction' ('this place is better than I expected'); and 'behaviour' ('there is a fight here almost every day'). Paternalistic regimes (strict discipline, with understanding and warmth) were associated with lower failure (absconding and reconviction) rates (Sinclair 1971: 94–113). However, failure rates for individual hostels could vary considerably over time. These institutional differences were, in turn, strongly related to warden changes (Sinclair 1971). Differences between hostels were more highly related to short-term (institutional) behaviour than to long-term success or failure although institutional failure rates did correlate with reconviction rates (Sinclair 1971: 77).

Gunn and colleagues used three scales (support, control, and clarity) from the CIES in their evaluation of the Grendon regime to show that the social climate of a treatment institution is relatively stable over time (Gunn et al. 1978: 93–8 and 291–6). They explored wing differences using these three scales, finding that wings varied on authoritarianism (control) and helpfulness (support) but not on clarity (Gunn *et al.* 1978: 95–8).

Saylor argues that the pervasiveness of the CIES in corrections research 'may be due to the paucity of any alternative climate instruments [rather] than to the appropriateness of the CIES' (Saylor 1984: 4). Later variations of the CIES (and other related attempts to measure prison quality) included the 'Custodial Adjustment Questionnaire' in the UK (Thornton 1987), Toch's 'Prison Preference Inventory' in the USA (which is designed to provide a measure of the individual's 'sentiments towards his environment'; see below); the Prison Environment Inventory (Wright 1985); and the Federal Bureau of Prisons' Social Climate Survey.

From Treatment to Adjustment: Hans Toch's 'Prison Preference Inventory'

Toch's work was developed more or less within the rehabilitative framework above. He talked of *adjustment*, or our 'capacity to adapt' (Toch 1992*a*: 5), a more moderate concept, but he was concerned about the dangers of a shift away from rehabilitative aspirations. Prisons could so easily become sterile human warehouses. They should be neither inhumane nor psychologically harmful (Toch 1992*a*: 7). They should be 'sane' places, where positive goals, such as self-betterment, are built-in features of the institution. The amelioration of damage and suffering required a certain *congruence* between the individual and his or her environment. This transaction between the environment and the individual, or the *appraisal* of the environment by the individual, is of critical importance in understanding the experience of imprisonment. Stress occurs when the environment taxes or exceeds the resources of an individual: 'Stress . . . shows us what happens when the environment challenges our capacity to adapt . . . it highlights ways in which we process information, assess it and react to it; it highlights the plasticity and vulnerability of human beings . . . Stress is the testing ground of mankind's frailty and resilience' (Toch 1992*a*: 5).

His main concern was to identify which features of the environment are either stressful or ameliorative. He developed seven characteristics of the prison environment from the preferences and aversions expressed by the 700 prisoners interviewed in his original study: privacy, safety, structure, support, emotional feedback, activity, and freedom. Individuals had different psychological concerns, aversions, or priorities (Toch 1992a: 165–6) and some of these were linked to personal characteristics (e.g. younger prisoners had less concern with structure; married prisoners, and those with drug problems, had a greater concern for emotional feedback). Other differences were related to criminal justice variables (such as experienced versus inexperienced prisoners) or contextual matters, such as the type of prison. Freedom typically emerged as the primary concern for all prisoners, although safety was also a primary concern for vulnerable or victimized prisoners. The concept of freedom, for example, included many issues relating to dependence and autonomy: styles and degrees of rule enforcement, the need for respect, feelings of being infantilized, and the urge to rebel. Privacy included a concern for anonymity, the avoidance of external stimuli, and the avoidance of encroachment by others. There were trade-offs between different characteristics. Those in prison for the first time had less concern with privacy, for example, in the interests of gleaning information about how to do their time. Toch describes how 'niches' with different characteristics may be created or sought, which enhance environmental congruence, in which individuals can cope best, or even thrive. A structured instrument was devised based on these dimensions—the Prison Preference Inventory (PPI)—using 56 forced paired comparisons: ('I would prefer ... knowing my people still love me ... or ... A guard who overlooks infractions'; and 'I'd be more bothered by ... being used ... or ... being told what to do'). After several revisions, the internal reliability or consistency of each dimension increased to between 0.42 for activity and 0.70 for privacy.[36] The instrument was tested on 1,604 New York prisoners, and other scales were introduced (such as a self-confidence measure) in later studies (Toch 1992a: 332–4). Several of the dimensions were found to be inversely related to each other (e.g. freedom was negatively associated with safety; and activity was inversely related to emotional feedback).

Toch's scheme provides us with detailed understanding of the salient characteristics of prison environments, and of some of

---

[36] The full version of the Prison Preference Questionnaire can be found in Toch (1992a, appendix A). For a detailed review of this and other 'adaptation' measures, see Adams (1992).

the important differences between individuals and groups in *responses* to these environments. His main concern was in understanding and, if necessary, classifying prisoners for survival. This transactional (and potentially shifting) 'measure' should be distinguished, at least in part, from the task described so far, of seeking to evaluate social climates or prison environments *per se*. Toch's analysis alerts us to these important questions of individual differences in perceptions of the environment, and we shall return to this point later.

(b)   Management Studies

Once the 'naïvely optimistic' treatment ideology had truly waned (Dinitz 1981: 16; Home Office 1979), a shift of emphasis from 'correctional' to 'custodial' goals can be identified in evaluation attempts (see King and Morgan 1980; Dinitz 1981; Home Office 1985; Logan 1992; US Department of Justice 1993). Major disturbances in US prisons and elsewhere (Fogel 1975; Irwin 1980; Colvin 1982; Useem and Kimball 1989; Home Office 1984; Ditchfield 1990), and related practical problems of industrial action, growing security concerns, and population growth (Home Office 1966; King and Morgan 1980; Home Office 1985), were linked to increasing prisoner dissatisfaction with the conditions of their confinement. There were obvious gaps between prison systems' aspirations to rehabilitation and the reality of impoverished but expensive regimes (Caird 1974; King and McDermott 1995). Dinitz ends his account of the New Mexico riot with a suggestion that prisons should aspire to be lawful, safe, industrious, and hopeful (Dinitz 1981: 11–16). If they could not treat, then they should house the offender humanely. Terms like 'dignity' and 'justice' began to appear in the literature, and became the basis for powerful claims for reasonable rather than ineffective and authoritarian 'medical' treatment (von Hirsch 1976; Sim 1990). The objectives of penal systems became less aspirational, but the efforts made to deliver and monitor these apparently more achievable objectives increased (Dunbar 1985; King and McDermott 1995; US Department of Justice 1993). The delivery of 'humane containment' (King and Morgan 1980), or humane containment plus various additional 'good things' such as opportunities for self-improvement (Home Office 1979; Bottoms 1990), was linked to the achievement of order and the requirements of formally burgeoning standards of justice (Zeeman *et al.* 1977; DiIulio 1987).[37] The 'confinement model' brought with it a move away from social and individual change, and a focus instead on 'relatively precise concepts' that were 'susceptible to operationalisation and empirical measurement' (Logan 1992; see further below). A new evaluation era was born.

The Federal Bureau of Prisons' 'Prison Social Climate' Survey

Perhaps the most comprehensive and methodologically promising work in this tradition has been carried out by Saylor and colleagues at the Federal Bureau of Prisons (Camp *et al.* 2002; Camp 1999; Saylor 1984). The work is empirically impressive, and the authors have conducted several reviews of the work carried out by Moos and others (see Saylor 1984).[38] The Prison Social Climate Survey was specifically developed by the Federal Bureau of Prisons to replace the CIES, which had been in use in those US prison facilities that requested it since the early 1970s. Despite its widespread use, the CIES instrument was found to lack validity once rigorously tested. This was partly because of a lack of evidence to support the model in the analysis of data, partly because it had been generated with mainly juvenile populations, and partly because of its origins in the treatment/medical model of corrections (Saylor 2002). It was also unsatisfactory that staff and prisoners answered the same questions, as different issues were relevant to each group. At the very least, the instrument was dated. Administrators seemed more interested in the response rate (which represented their 'sense of

---

[37] DiIulio's study looked at indicators of 'order, amenity and service' using institutional data from three contrasting penal systems in the USA (Texas, Michigan, and California). He suggested that differences in system-wide levels of prison quality were related to differences in prison management or 'keeper' philosophies (a control model, a responsibility model, and a consensus model, respectively; DiIulio 1987). See Simon for an interesting critique of DiIulio's rather broad approach and methodology (Simon 2000).

[38] Although their approach is, as the authors themselves argue, pragmatic; that is, primarily unsociological. There are prison surveys carried out in England (on prisoners, see White *et al.* 1991; on staff, see Woodman and Dale 2002) and more frequently and comprehensively, on staff and prisoners in Scotland (Wozniac and McAllister 1992; Wozniac *et al.* 1994; and Wozniac *et al.* 1998). These studies are used 'as a mechanism to inform and support the process of strategic planning' (Wozniac *et al.* 1998: 7), but in the case of the Scottish survey in particular are very informative.

command') rather than in the substantive results, which they found either 'useless or incomprehensible' (Saylor 2002). The Prison Social Climate Survey was conceived to replace it (Saylor 1984). As its instigator, Saylor recalled: 'I wanted to take a very different perspective from the one Moos had taken. I wanted to create measures that would stand on their own, that is, not require comparison to some normed population' (Saylor 2002).

Saylor and his colleagues developed a 'pragmatic climate instrument . . . that would address a broad range of issues of concern to prison management' (Saylor 1984: 6). This included a 'reservoir of items', with no prior attempt to generate dimensions. The items are loosely grouped into sections, but the authors are keen to allow administrators to analyse results in whatever way they see fit. The surveys used for staff and prisoners are separate. Each begins with a socio-demographic section, and has four other substantive sections seeking opinions about aspects of prison regimes, such as quality of services and programmes; personal safety and security; quality of life (which incorporates crowding, accidents, noise, dirt, visits, food, and grievances); personal well-being (which includes questions on physical and emotional health); and job assignments (Federal Bureau of Prisons 1990).

The questionnaires were designed in such a way as to allow for the completion of only some of the sections of the questionnaire by individual respondents (they might be asked to complete one or more of the four subsets and the demographic section, for example). The survey has been used more widely with staff samples (the staff version has been administered annually since 1988) than with prisoner samples (the prisoner version has been used on a more ad hoc or as needs basis). Most of the published work arising from these surveys has been concerned with analysis of the staff data (Wright and Saylor 1991; Saylor and Wright 1992; Camp 1994; Camp et al. 1997, 2002). Inmate surveys have been increasingly employed in evaluations of privatization, however (see Camp et al. 2003 and later). Their measures provide comparative data (departures from the mid-point) rather than numeric indicators of performance.

Saylor, Camp, and colleagues raise important methodological and conceptual problems (e.g. should prisons be evaluated against norms, or against some benchmark or external standard?). They argue that most attempts to measure organizational climate use either an aggregate subjective (i.e. psychological or experiential) approach, or an objective approach (i.e. they use institutional-level indices such as assault rates). Few studies attempt both (but see Jones and Cornes 1977, above; and Poole and Regoli 1980). The questionnaire items constructed by Saylor *et al.* are intended to reflect both individual and collective levels of perception, and their analytic work has demonstrated strong links between organization-level data and individual-level data.

As Camp argues, staff and prisoners normally do not have detailed knowledge of important aspects of prison operations, such as the budget, technical details relating to the physical plant, personnel data, security, and so on (Camp 1999) which, arguably, constitute important contextual information. There have also been doubts raised as to the trustworthiness of staff and (especially) inmate evaluations of a prison. The effects of union leaders, malcontents, and inevitably disaffected prisoners have been assumed to skew survey results in a negative direction.[39] However, average survey responses do differ, and these differences can be shown to be independent of the individual or demographic characteristics of the staff and prisoners providing the data (Camp 1999; Camp *et al.* 1997, 1999). They have found that safety and security are particularly difficult concepts to operate (especially for staff) in ways that produce high reliability scores (Camp *et al.* 2003). They find that staff and prisoners tend to evaluate prison conditions in highly congruent ways.

Camp *et al.* have made considerable attempts to control for known differences between individual staff and prisoners in the way they evaluate their prison environment, and for certain institutional characteristics. In the case of prisoners, the socio-demographic characteristics of age, race, marital status, citizenship, education level, offence, time served, drug use, and security level have been controlled for. Camp *et al.* have found that their measures derived from inmate data tend to be more reliable than their measures derived from staff data (Camp *et al.* 2003). They conclude that research should continue 'to identify the most appropriate survey questions that yield desirable information about differences between prisons' (Camp 1999: 266).

---

[39] Saylor has argued that, in the prison context, staff doing a job well could necessarily lead to negative evaluations by some prisoners on some measures; managers may have the same fears about their subordinates. It may be important to select dimensions (such as safety) where good performance by staff leads to positive evaluations by prisoners, and so on (see Camp 1999).

So, the search for a valid evaluation approach continues. Since the PSCS (Prison Social Climate Survey) has been used most widely in recent evaluations of privatization, we shall turn now to that rapidly developing literature, and to some of the other evaluation attempts that have arisen as a result of the prison privatization initiative.

Cost, Performance, and Other Comparisons between Public and Private Sector Prisons

> Quality . . . is the most important aspect of the whole privatization debate.
>
> (Harding 2001: 285)

Many practitioners and critics of public institutions argue passionately that measurement has become 'a fetish' with the general onset of new managerialism; that is, the setting of clear objectives for organizations about the services they intend to deliver, the measurement of their achievements in relation to these objectives, and a commitment to raising 'performance', as we suggested in the first part of this chapter. A major conceptual gap exists in these measurement attempts, some of which we have outlined already. The advent of privatization, and a related proliferation of comparative studies of prison cost and quality, have increased interest in the business of measuring the quality of prison life well beyond the official interests outlined earlier. The re-emergence of privatization during the 1980s and 1990s in an increasing number of jurisdictions brought with it an intense (and vested) concern with the measurement of prison quality and cost (or 'value for money').

The reasons for the (re)introduction of privatization vary slightly between countries but they include: escalating prison costs; escalating prison populations (alongside a political unwillingness to decarcerate); deteriorating regime conditions; growing impatience with powerful unions; some aspiration to improve the quality of prison regimes; and, in the USA, lawsuits. These factors coincided with a neo-liberal loss of faith in the public sector to do anything efficiently or well (James *et al.* 1997; Jones and Newburn forthcoming).

The justification for private sector involvement in the UK was that public sector efforts (including apparently good intentions and high ideals) were, in practice, useless if not underpinned by administratively efficient and accountable systems (James *et al.* 1997).

Privatization was thought to bring with it cost reductions, managerial innovation, capital investment, and an increased focus on outputs (Ryan and Ward 1989; Lomas 2001). The state remained the regulator and 'purchaser' of services (see Harding 1997), but competitive bidder companies (in the UK: Group 4, Premier Prisons, Securicor, and UKDS) were invited to demonstrate that they could outperform the public sector, at a lower cost, in the design and delivery of regimes and buildings. The private sector was effectively invited to provide more 'humane' and reasonable treatment than the public sector had been achieving throughout the 1980s and early 1990s. Despite the clarity of this challenge, there have been few carefully designed comparisons of public and private sector prisons. Many of the proponents of privatization have in any case argued that the main 'test' of the success or otherwise of privatization was whether improvements in value for money were seen in the *public* sector. This is the 'cross-fertilization' case (Harding 2001). Commentators disagree about whether the apparent improvements witnessed in the public sector are real (or result from strategic management of figures) and whether, if so, they can be wholly attributed to private sector competition. Other explanations for apparent improvements to performance include the introduction of more effective tools for performance management, a clarification of priorities, increased funding in key areas, major security improvement programmes, and stronger leadership (Lomas 2001). Governors often claim that private sector competition has helped them enormously in the management and control of their own staff, and frequently admit to using the threat of privatization as a key bargaining tool in securing agreements to cost-reduction strategies and efforts to improve their establishments' performance.

The public–private sector debate is full of vested (commercial and ideological) interests which make systematic analysis difficult, but all the more important. The question of what *constitutes* prison quality can be helpfully explored by looking at this literature in particular. There are two main sources of evaluation literature in this field: (i) published official comparisons, which tend to rely on secondary and official performance measures, and (ii) the unpublished results of competitions held, which tend also to rely on formal performance data and the content of individual bids.

(i)   Published Official Comparisons

A study carried out by the Home Affairs Committee (HAC) compared the performance of the first three privately managed prisons in the UK with three comparator public sector prisons, selected on grounds of similarity of size and function (Home Affairs Committee 1997). The difficulties of any such comparison between prisons were acknowledged (e.g. due to the different age and design of the buildings; the different mix of prisoners—i.e. different security categories, the proportion of prisoners on remand or convicted, the levels of overcrowding, and so on). There were three main criteria of 'performance': (i) financial savings; (ii) improved quality; (iii) evidence of a positive influence on the public sector.

On cost, the private sector was found to be 9 to 15 per cent cheaper than the public sector, but the differential was already coming down by 1997 at about 2.5 per cent each year.[40] In five years, the public sector had closed the gap by 8 per cent. These efficiency gains were clearly spurred by competition from the private sector, which was able to reduce costs through lower staffing levels, lower rates of pay, longer working hours, less annual leave, and lower pensions. Indicators of quality included the number of assaults, escapes, hours unlocked, and the views of the controllers,[41] boards of visitors, and the Chief Inspector of Prisons. The rate of assaults was significantly higher in all of the private prisons than in newly opened public sector prisons. Wolds had a rate of 27.3 per 100 prisoners per year (the average for the comparator prisons was 10.8); Blakenhurst had a rate of 33.7 (the average for its comparators was 12.5); Doncaster had a rate of 33.7 (the average for its comparators was 12.3). All assault rates fell in the second year of operation (although levels were still high). HAC noted a consensus that all privately managed prisons suffered from 'teething troubles' (especially in the area of control and

[40] Some critics have suggested that private companies engage in loss-leading or low-balling (bidding at unrealistically tight levels) in the early stages in order to establish a foothold in the market. See Harding (2001).

[41] Controllers or contract monitors are public sector governor grades who work in private prisons as 'overseers' of the contract. They also conduct disciplinary adjudications in the UK, thus (some argue) keeping the 'allocation' of punishment in the hands of the state (see Logan 1990; Harding 1997, 2001; but also Sparks 1994 and Moyle 2001). See Harding (1997) on the notion of 'capture'.

discipline) due to the (deliberate) inexperience of staff.[42] The rate of escapes was similar, and the levels of activity were higher in the private prisons. The hours unlocked were greater; and levels of purposeful activity per week were generally higher: Wolds 29 hours (average 24); Blakenhurst 25 hours (average 19); Doncaster 24 hours (average 18).

The Home Affairs Committee argued that their evidence supported the view that private sector competition had encouraged innovation in regimes, management, design, and the use of technology. It had speeded up change in the public sector. Most of the examples of best practice arose disproportionately from the private sector and, unsurprisingly, their own evaluations were positive. Group 4 argued that they provided better conditions for remand prisoners than had previously existed; UKDS referred to improved processes for visits, and their strict internal auditing; Premier Prisons advocated their new systems for involvement of the community and prisoners' families, and the cleanliness of the prison. There was some praise from HMCIP Reports and from the Association of Chief Probation Officers (Home Affairs Committee 1997). A positive emphasis was placed in the private sector prisons on quality, custody, and staff–prisoner relationships.

The HAC verdict was, despite early troubles, a vote of confidence for private prisons: 'We consider that, after some early teething troubles, privately managed prisons are now operating well in terms of the quality and performance and the regimes they run; and that their performance overall has been at least as good as that of publicly run prisons and in some areas better' (Home Affairs Committee 1997, pp. xiv, l).

---

[42] Private companies have generally deliberately avoided employing custody officers with Prison Service experience, in order to avoid the existing POA culture. Some of the results were also explained by other factors: Premier Prisons argued that their high rate of assaults was due to the high proportion of young offenders held, and that the behaviour of these prisoners was better than at previous establishments. UKDS/Blakenhurst argued that their assault rates were high because of long hours of unlock. However, HAC generally accepted the evidence that all three private prisons suffered difficulties of control and a steep learning curve during the first 18 months of each prison's life, as prisoners tested out staff and management. In each case, start-up rates were pushed too fast, as the prison population increased and spaces were urgently needed. All improved levels of control subsequently (some would argue at the cost of staff attitudes).

The Home Office published a 'review of the comparative costs and performance of privately and publicly operated prisons' in 1999 (Woodbridge 1999). This showed that cost differences between the private and public sector were lower than typically assumed once 'in-use places' were compared.[43] In addition, these differences were reducing (from 13–22 per cent in 1994–5 to 11–17 per cent in 1995–6; to 8–15 per cent in 1996–7; to 2–11 per cent in 1997–8, depending on the cost measure used; Woodbridge 1999: 36). Four private prisons were included in the study, and each was, inevitably, imperfectly matched with two or three comparator prisons. There were differences between the private prisons, so that some generated much larger cost savings than others. Performance was measured using officially recorded KPIs, that is: number of escapes and absconds, assaults as a percentage of the population, hours of purposeful activity, number of accredited courses delivered, percentage of population tested for drugs, and number of hours unlocked on weekdays (Woodbridge 1999). The performance of each sector was similar, although 'privately operated facilities tended to provide more purposeful activity and out of cell hours than comparators, and more flexible visiting hours' (Woodbridge 1999). The level of assaults was relatively high at two of the private prisons, although much of this difference was accounted for by the presence in these establishments of high numbers of prisoners under 21 years of age.

A second review was published in 2000 (Park 2000), which showed that no further cost savings had been made. Some improvements were made in the selection of comparators. The results can be summarized briefly as in Table 2.4. This table shows whether each of the private prisons was better, worse, or no different from its comparators (with the actual figures in brackets). It should be noted that assaults at Doncaster were high as a result of its young offenders, as suggested above (the figure for adults only was 6.7 per cent). 'Mixed' means that the private prison performed better than one or two of its comparators, but also worse than one or two of its comparators.

---

[43] Two measures of prison cost are given in KPI figures: cost per place (based on certified normal accommodation, or the number of prisoners officially allowed) and cost per prisoner (based on the number of prisoners actually held, which is often higher in the public sector).

TABLE 2.4.   Selective performance of private prisons compared to comparators[1]

Performance indicator	Blakenhurst	Buckley Hall	Doncaster	Wolds
Assaults	Worse (18.8)	No diff. (2.9)	Worse (19.7)	Mixed (11.0)
Purposeful activity	Better (21.8)	Better (26.8)	Mixed (17.0)	Better (29.1)
Accredited courses	Worse (20.0)	No diff. (0.0)	Worse (0.0)	Mixed (26.1)
Positive drug tests	Worse (38.6)	Worse (37.6)	Better (12.6)	Worse (17.8)
Hours unlocked	Better (10.8)	Better (13.5)	No diff. (10.3)	Better (11.7)

Notes:
[1] Assaults are expressed as a percentage of the population; purposeful activity is 'hours per week'; accredited courses is the number of courses completed; drug tests are the percentage of the population testing positive; and number of hours unlocked relates to weekdays.

The study concluded that little or no cost savings were made once in-use places were used, and that 'privately operated prisons tended to provide more purposeful activity and more flexible visiting hours' (Park 2000: 26).

These types of comparisons are helpful, but technical and somewhat superficial. The reports produced and their results are not peer reviewed, and thus serve managerial purposes more clearly than they serve the need to develop understanding. It is interesting to note that Buckley Hall and Blakenhurst have both returned to the public sector in the latest round of competitive tendering.

A more detailed attempt to make reliable comparisons in England and Wales has recently been made by the National Audit Office (NAO 2003). In this study, comparisons were made between seven PFI prisons (designed, constructed, managed, and financed by the private sector), two privately managed-only prisons, and twelve public sector prisons (including one operating with a service level agreement).[44] The comparisons drew on a combination of survey data from staff and prisoners, selected KPI data, standards audit ratings, and inspectorate reports. The study also explored the

[44] This means, in this case, that the prison is managed by the public sector as a result of a successful in-house bid against the private sector.

performance of seven PFI prisons against the requirements of their contracts.[45] All but one of the PFI prisons had suffered financial deductions for poor performance (for example, for disturbances, key compromises, assaults, escapes, positive drug tests, self-harm, low activity, and programme hours). These tended to be highest in the first year of operation, and then to reduce, except in one case where financial penalties had increased over time. The study found that there was considerable variation within both sectors. The best PFI prisons were outperforming most of the public sector prisons included in the study, but the worst private prison was considerably worse than most of the poor performing public sector prisons in the study (NAO 2003). The private sector 'had the edge' on activities, relationships, and treatment of prisoners, but they performed less well on security and safety. They had relatively high levels of assaults. Private prisons produced more reliable data, due to the requirements of the contract (and a culture of recording activities fully).

The major difference between the public and private sector was in the attitude of staff towards prisoners. This was due to inexperience, low levels of unionization, and a commitment by many private prison directors to 'good relationships'. PFI prisons employed a higher proportion of female staff (34 per cent compared to 21 per cent in the public sector). Apart from this distinction, surprisingly little innovation had taken place in PFI prisons. There were problems of high staff turnover, particularly in some establishments. A case study of the worst performing PFI prison (Ashfield) suggests that the problems arising included: difficulties with staff recruitment and retention; unsafe staffing levels; poor contract monitoring (as well as inconsistencies between different contractual arrangements); insufficient training; frequent changes of management; a lack of 'policies and procedures'; and lack of experience and staff knowledge of policies and procedures (NAO 2003). The staffing difficulties were related to relatively poor terms and conditions (particularly in a high

---

[45] As the authors point out, performance against contract is an imperfect measure of quality. Contracts cannot reflect the full complexity of what is required, and they do not reflect changing Prison Service requirements (e.g. a shift in emphasis towards the provision of basic skills education). Likewise, there are problems with the use of penalties as a measure of relative performance, including different scales for different contracts, different thresholds, and diverse responses by controllers to underperformance (see NAO 2003; also Harding 1997).

employment part of the country).[46] There were changes in the population after contract signature (to include juveniles) and once the establishment opened (to include sentenced young offenders).

Most of these difficulties are described in the NAO Report as difficulties in *regulation*. The study concludes that measuring performance is a highly complex business. Increasing the number of quantitative measures did not improve the ability to make significant distinctions between prisons. Using a subgroup of the available performance measures differentiated between prisons as well as when all available indicators were used. Again, this study suggested that more thought should be given to the analysis of performance (NAO 2003: 26–7).

An alternative, but less readily available source of information are the documents prepared for bids in competitions.

(ii) The Unpublished Results of Competitions[47]

In England and Wales, competitions between private sector companies bidding for new ('greenfield') sites and between the public and private sector for existing sites are managed by the Prison Service's Contracts and Competitions Group (CCG). They issue the Invitation to Tender (ITT), assess the bids, make recommendations to the Prison Service Management Board[48] and agree the contracts with the preferred bidders (Lomas 2001). The ITT specifies what service is required, and this specification should reflect the Prison Service's published objectives. The Blakenhurst ITT, for example, specified that bids should be devised around the following objectives:

1. To protect the public by holding in custody those committed by the courts in a safe, decent, and healthy environment.
2. To reduce crime by providing constructive regimes which address offending behaviour (Lomas 2001: 52).

Tender documents for other prisons have required highly specific innovations, such as the creation of a 'high dependency unit' for

---

[46] Newly appointed prisoner custody officers at Ashfield were paid £15,250 per year. Newly appointed prison officers in the public sector were paid £17,000 per year (NAO 2003: 40). Private sector staff also had less generous pensions.

[47] We are grateful in the section below to Martin Lomas, whose M.St. thesis at the University of Cambridge explored the process of market testing in detail.

[48] From 2003–4, the Correctional Services Management Board; see Chapter 8.

women prisoners at Ashford, or a new therapeutic community at Dovegate (Genders 2002). The specifications are highly detailed and they are closely linked to performance indicators and other desired outputs. The competitive process generally results in high-quality ambitious bids which are, in practice, challenging to deliver—despite the fact that as in many types of contracts (including research contracts) 'deliverability' is a key criterion in any assessment of the bid's quality. There is a 'quality collar' which indicates that the lowest bidder does not have to be the most successful. Any extra expense has to be justified in terms of higher quality. Strict confidentiality between bidders can mean that successful teams can 'win by too much'. Cost-cutting and aspirations to 'perform' can go too far in this climate, resulting in an overstretched workforce and high risks to the establishment's functioning.[49] The evaluation is conducted strictly and according to specified criteria and an agreed marking scheme (an assessment 'strait-jacket') which means in practice that the outcome of competitions should be as exacting and fair as possible (Lomas 2001) and may be politically unwelcome. The evaluation process is open to public scrutiny, and appeals can be formally investigated. Despite these process safeguards, considerable scepticism regarding outcomes is often expressed by those involved (and by informed observers).

This process inevitably leads to the accumulation of experience and skills in the 'performance' area, in managers and staff learning to think in terms of delivery and performance, and in a culture of constant striving towards innovation and improvement.[50] The bidding and evaluation process is costly and time-consuming, but it does have a creative impact, as bidding teams reflect intensively on what a 'winning bid' might look like (and therefore on what sort of prison they would ideally manage). We shall reflect on some of the dangers of this climate in Chapter 8. Few of these documents reach the public domain, and in many cases even contracts are unavailable for public (or academic) scrutiny, for commercial reasons. The bid document forms the basis of a contract or service delivery

---

[49] There seemed to be some recognition by the Labour government and Prison Service senior management during 2003, at least in principle, that there were *limits* to competition, and to cost-cutting, and that these limits had almost been reached. However, see Home Office 2004.

[50] Governors who have returned to the public sector after a spell in the private sector report bringing back with them 'a much clearer focus on performance and delivery' (pers. comm.).

agreement that specifies precisely what 'outputs' establishments are expected to achieve. Fines are levied where failures occur (see Genders 2002; NAO 2003).[51] They constitute a potentially inform-ative source of data about what penal aims are being pursued and about how different companies (and sectors) set about trying to achieve these aims.

(iii)   Academic Research Evaluations

There are several published studies from the USA, Australia, and the UK reporting on findings from evaluations of private sector prisons, often by comparison with selected public sector prisons.[52] The most helpful are the study by Logan (1992), a handful of qualitative case study comparisons, and some more recent mainly quantitative studies. Despite the introduction of private sector competition being regarded by many as the 'penal experiment of the century', research access has been restricted and the publication of results from research has been carefully controlled.

In the USA, Logan's (1992) work offers a refined development of the confinement or 'doing justice' model of imprisonment. His con-ceptual scheme was 'inspired in major part by analyzing the man-agement concerns of the Bureau of Prisons as revealed in its Prison Social Climate Survey', reviewed above (Logan 1993: 37). Under this model, the mission of a prison is to 'keep them in, keep them safe, keep them in line, keep them healthy, and keep them busy— and to do it with fairness, without undue suffering, and as effi-ciently as possible' (ibid. 25). The relevant criteria for assessing performance which flowed from this model were, according to Logan, divisible into eight distinct dimensions. He then developed a set of empirical indicators that could be used as performance measures for prisons and that concentrate on the 'competent, fair

---

[51] Private prisons have incurred fines for contract breaches relating to (for example) incidents of self-harm, concerted indiscipline, assaults, failures to complete manda-tory drugs tests, failure to see a medical officer on reception into custody, failures to provide a sentence plan, and failures to provide prisoners with a discharge report (Genders 2002: 294).

[52] For the purposes of this section of the chapter, we have omitted articles which focus exclusively on arguments for and against privatization, or on theoretical/ ideological issues. Such studies contribute significantly to knowledge in this field but they do not address the empirical question of central concern in this section. We shall return to the broader issues of moral evaluation later.

and efficient administration of confinement as a form of deserved punishment' (Logan 1992: 579).[53] The dimensions were:[54]

(1) *security*: security procedures, drug use, significant incidents, community exposure, freedom of movement, and staffing adequacy;
(2) *safety*: safety of staff, safety of inmates, dangerousness of inmates, safety of environment, and staffing adequacy;
(3) *order*: inmate misconduct, staff use of force, perceived control, and strictness of enforcement;
(4) *care*: stress and illness, health care delivered, dental care, counselling, and staffing for programmes and services;
(5) *activity*: involvement and evaluation of: work and industry, education and training, recreation, and religious services;
(6) *justice*: staff fairness, limited use of force, number and type of grievances, the grievance process, the discipline process, legal resources and access, and justice delays;
(7) *conditions*: space in living areas, social density and privacy, internal freedom of movement, facilities and maintenance, sanitation, noise and food, commissary and visitation, and community access;
(8) *management*: job satisfaction, stress and burn-out, staff turnover, staff and management relations, staff experience, education and training, salary and overtime, and staffing efficiency.

Logan compared the quality of confinement in three women's prisons, one each of different management types: federal, state, and private. Quality of confinement was defined along the eight dimensions above and was measured using 333 indicators derived from staff and prisoner surveys, field observations, and institutional records (Logan 1992; Logan 1993: 42–57). A 'Prison Quality Index' (ranging from 0 to 1) was calculated for each item for each prison

---

[53] Some of his data are drawn from interviews, some from self-completion methods (which had low return rates). Logan argues that the dimensions are 'relatively concrete concepts'. His measures are comparative only (i.e. he reports which prisons are 'better' or 'worse' than others, but no assessment of the overall standard or quality of service). He compounds data from staff, prisoners, and the institution to form a net effect. The survey includes several unreliable indicators, such as an 'estimated rate of being assaulted', the 'perceived frequency of accidents occurring', and the 'perceived frequency that staff have used force against inmates'.

[54] Broad categories of empirical indicators are included.

to enable comparison of any two prisons across an unequal number of measures and the ranking of each establishment relative to all the others. Logan found that the private prison outperformed the state and federal prisons across all dimensions, with the exception of care (where the state prison outscored the private prison 'by a modest amount') and justice (where the federal and private prisons achieved equal scores, both slightly higher than the state prison). The private prison outscored the state prison by quite a wide margin on security, management, order, and safety.

The state prison outscored the private prison on 'care'. Logan suggests that this is one aspect of a theoretically coherent cluster of dimensions (designated a 'welfare model': activity, conditions, and care), where the state prison also outscored the federal prison. On a second cluster ('governance model') which included justice, order, security, safety, and management, the private prison and the federal prison outscored the state. These results were obtained by including all the sources for each of the indicators together. On the results of inmate surveys only, the state prison outscored the private prison on all dimensions except activity (no prisoners were surveyed at the federal prison). On staff surveys only, the private prison outscored the state prison on all dimensions. Despite the complexity of the above results, Logan concluded that the private prison performed relatively better, and proposed that the reasons were: greater operational and administrative flexibility, higher morale, enthusiasm and a sense of ownership amongst line staff, and stricter 'governance' of inmates.

There are some important limitations to Logan's methodology. He only uses one prison of each type, so that a single prison has to stand for the whole sector, despite known variations in each sector's performance. None of his dimensions have been tested for validity, reliability, discrimination, or other statistical properties (Logan 1993: 38 n). He uses some indicators in more than one dimension. There is no empirical or theoretical rationale for the definitions used for each dimension, or case made for the eight dimensions which apparently 'flow' from the confinement model he articulates. So for example, under Logan's confinement model, the dimension 'activity' does not have to include programmes or activities that lead to the 'betterment' of prisoners, as long as they are consistent with 'the orderly, safe, secure, and humane operation of a prison' (Logan 1993: 28–9; see also Camp *et al.* 2002 for a critique of Logan's 'safety' and 'management' dimensions). As we argue throughout, the question of *what these words mean in practice* has never been satisfactorily addressed. The term 'without undue suffering' (p. 31) is assumed to have a mainly material significance. Measurement, in other words, comes before meaning. Logan argues, however, that the key purpose of this evaluation exercise is to choose the criteria (i.e. *do the thinking*) rather than settle the question of what standards of measurement should be used.

Three mainly qualitative case studies have looked in more detail at social practices and relationships in more or less matched public and private sector prisons in the UK and in Australia, where greater emphasis has been placed than in the USA on using private sector competition to bring about cultural and attitudinal change (see Bottomley *et al.* 1997; Moyle 1995; Rynne 2004).

The first was a study by Bottomley *et al.* (1997) of the first UK private sector prison (Wolds, opened in 1992). The formal aims of this research were 'to consider what lessons may be learned which could be applied to publicly operated prisons, and how far these lessons might shape future penal policy. To assess the quality of management, regime delivery, and staffing and to explore the roles of staff and management' (Bottomley *et al.* 1997; James *et al.* 1997). The research had been initiated by the research team, following an earlier approach to members of the team from one of the unsuccessful bidders at the tendering stage to become involved in an evaluation of some kind. In the event, the Home Office was persuaded *ex post facto* to introduce and fund a formal evaluation only once the successful company had been identified and the prison opened (see James *et al.* 1997: 56–8; and Windlesham 1993: 266–307 and 419–27). The evaluation thus began quite late in this so-called experimental prison's life. The second private prison (Blakenhurst) opened immediately after the research team had settled in to Wolds, and the third (Doncaster) followed swiftly after that.

However, some interesting lessons were learned. The methods used consisted mainly of observation of life in the prison and selected participation (e.g. in meetings, and on association); structured and semi-structured interviews with prisoners (new receptions and others), staff (prisoner custody officers, unit supervisors, and senior managers) and specialists; and analysis of documents. Owing to the continuing political sensitivity of the research (there were vested interests and strong feelings of both support and opposition), several changes were introduced to the research project as the early findings emerged. The cost-effectiveness component in the original proposal was dropped as other studies were commissioned to assess the financial implications of contracting out (James *et al.* 1997: 65); and a comparative dimension was introduced, extending the research into a new public sector prison, in order to explore whether the problem of 'teething troubles' was a characteristic of private prisons or new prisons *per se*. There were some other limitations to the research, as 'commercial-in-confidence' considerations meant that the team could not have access to the contract. The board of visitors declared that in order to maintain their independence, they wished not to become involved.

Prisoners viewed the regime at Wolds largely favourably (with the important exception of the vulnerable and unprotected 'few'; see also Sparks *et al.* 1996). Nearly 80 per cent of the prisoners interviewed regarded it as a better prison than others they had been to (Bottomley *et al.* 1997). This was for three main reasons: the physical and material conditions; the openness of the regime; and the attitudes of staff (Bottomley *et al.* 1997). Staff–prisoner relationships were exceptionally good, where 'good' means staff were benign and unobtrusive (see later). Their relative inexperience, lack of unionization, and distinct backgrounds (they lived locally and often applied for the job as a result of an advert in the local paper) contributed to a distinct ethos, seen in other privately managed prisons in the UK (and in Australia), whereby prisoners were treated with unusual levels of fairness and respect.[55] The hours unlocked were unusually long (12 to 14 hours per day), a feature of many newly opening prisons in a post-Woolf era. Staff were less favourable, and felt rather isolated, unsafe, and unsupported. They expressed concerns about low promotion prospects, in the leaner staffing structure offered by the private sector. Senior and (especially) middle management were generally poorly regarded; staff morale was low; and there were serious staff shortages.

There were several problems with the regime at Wolds: the high level of drugs used; the high levels of medication offered by non-Prison Service health-care providers; the relatively high levels of

[55] For example, 84% of prisoners interviewed felt that officers treated them fairly at Wolds, compared to 41% at the highly regarded, newly opened public sector Woodhill prison (Bottomley *et al.* 1997). Seventy per cent of prisoners at Wolds found the officers helpful, compared to 41% at Woodhill, and so on.

violence between prisoners; high levels of boredom; a much lower than expected take-up of activities; the unanticipated length of stay of prisoners (which added to perceptions of boredom); unexpected costs; the level of isolation of the establishment from others; unprecedented media attention; and the more typical problems of opening a new prison (i.e. establishing routines and an 'ethos', training staff, negotiations over boundaries with prisoners, and so on). This pattern, of positive prisoner and negative staff evaluations, matched some informal reports of other private prisons.

Four key elements were seen as central to the achievement of a relatively well-regarded regime at Wolds: the contract between the Home Office and Group 4; the employment of staff with no prior experience of prison work; the existence of a flatter management structure which enhanced communication, minimized lines of accountability, and encouraged a more responsive management style; and the use of compacts, setting out what was expected of prisoners (Bottomley *et al.* 1997; Home Office 1991*a*). This early evaluation was exploratory, and has not been repeated in any of the other private prisons opened in the UK to date.

A second in-depth study was carried out over a similar period at Borallon Correctional Centre, in Queensland, Australia (Moyle 1995, 2000). Borallon was the first privately managed correctional centre to open in Australia, in 1990. One of the main aims of privatization in Australia was to 'bring about cultural and attitudinal change' in the management and delivery of correctional regimes (Moyle 1995: 51). Some prison staff in Queensland had been openly critical of and resistant to the 'humanizing' policies being introduced by the Queensland Corrective Services Commission (Moyle 1995: 51). At an institutional level, this cultural change was largely achieved. Similar findings were reported to those above, with staff–prisoner relations regarded positively, but with staff feeling in a relatively weak position and believing staffing levels to be too low. Prisoners were self-consciously empowered, which meant that they felt relatively well treated and that they could contribute to the shaping of the regime, for example, suggesting the use of vending machines and a children's sand pit during visits, giving adults more time together during visits (Moyle 1995: 53). The establishment's staff had 'progressive attitudes', and officers described themselves as 'less security conscious' and more 'conciliatory' (p. 52). Staff attitudes towards punishments were very

clear: 'taking them away from their families and taking their freedom is their punishment. There is no need to treat them badly
once they are in here' (in Moyle 1995: 53; see also Bowery 1999 on
Junee Correctional Centre in New South Wales).[56] This is strikingly
similar to the attitudes found at Doncaster (see later chapters).
The work provided for prisoners was not meaningful and was
dependent on external contracts but prisoners responded positively
to the attitudes of staff.

Moyle is more sceptical of the use of private sector competition
to achieve reform than these findings might suggest. He argues that
the profit motive conflicts with the need to provide constructive
work; that staffing levels are often dangerously low; and that given
the right management lead, public sector correctional officers can
deliver modern (e.g. 'case management') regimes. He also argues
that accountability is reduced, due to commercial interests and an
unwillingness to share successful ideas and practices (Moyle 2000).

The third comparative study (still in progress) is also being carried out in Australia. It is likely to report similar cultural improvements in the private sector, with prisoners generally preferring staff
attitudes in private prisons, compared to comparator prisons. Private
sector approaches are clearly being used in several Australian states
to 'force out' undesirable cultural (attitudinal) characteristics of staff
working in public sector prisons. There are, however, significant
differences between companies in both culture and performance
(Rynne 2004).

There seems to be evidence from these Australian and UK studies
that some private sector prisons differ substantially (often positively)
in their organizational cultures, and therefore in their treatment
of prisoners, whatever the *exterior* legitimacy of their operations.
Many studies find evidence of 'progressive trends', including a
more humane and less custodial approach by staff towards prisoners, in the private prisons studied. Evaluations find a high concentration of public sector correctional experience at a senior level;
little experience at middle/lower levels; and a high concentration of
public sector correctional experience at prisoner level. They find
low staff–prisoner ratios (sometimes leaving staff and prisoners

[56] This four-year comparative longitudinal study is based on operational data
only. The author found considerable variation as well as some improvements over
time (Bowery 1999; also 1994, 1996, 1997).

feeling vulnerable); and they find some savings, in most cases, without losing quality, as it is measured by official performance figures. However, all three studies have also suffered from restrictions on access to key documentation, and a certain amount of reluctance to co-operate with the research. Several private prisons experiencing major difficulties (and where staff have been found to be over-using their power) have not been formally evaluated at all (see HMCIP 2003). The ideal of 'scrupulous examination' (Chan 1992: 244) has not been met.

Returning to the more common quantitative approaches to public–private sector comparisons, one of the most detailed studies was carried out by Charles Thomas in Florida in 1997. Thomas used contract renewals, prisoner litigation, and accreditation and audit results to compare public and private sector facilities in the USA. A contract may be renewed only if the contractor is providing at least the same quality of service as the state at a lower cost or if the contractor is providing services superior in quality to those provided by the state at essentially the same cost. In other words, legislation required private sector establishments to be superior on cost, equivalent on quality; or vice versa. Thomas used several broad thematic categories in his assessment of 'quality': 'public safety' (where the indicators are disturbances, escapes, and injuries to visitors); 'protecting the state and prisoners' (where the indicators are number of homicides, assaults, arson, and inciting a riot); 'programmes' (where the indicators are work, education, and substance abuse); and 'maintaining professional standards' (where the indicators are audits, litigation, grievances, disciplinary data, and employee training). He found that the private sector was achieving cost savings of 13.8 per cent, when compared with all equivalent prisons, and that the quality of performance was generally superior to the state-operated facilities, although one or two state prisons had performance records equal or superior to the private sector (Thomas 1997). His measures (e.g. prisoner litigation, or audit results) are quite crude, and could be measuring other things (e.g. compliance with process, in the case of audit) rather than 'performance' or 'quality'.

Contrary to much of the critical commentary on privatization, which suggests that it is inextricably linked to incapacitation ideologies of imprisonment, its resurgence has coincided with an apparent return to rehabilitative aspirations, albeit in a new and somewhat contentious guise (see Hannah-Moffatt 2001; and Genders 2002). A study by Lanza-Kaduce and colleagues used reconviction rates as a 'proxy' indicator of prison quality (Lanza-Kaduce et al. 1999). One hundred and ninety-eight releasees from two private facilities in Florida were 'precision matched' with 198 releasees from public prisons (on offence, race, number of prior incarcerations, and age). The authors used five different indicators of recidivism (arrest, conviction, sentence, sentence of imprisonment, and technical violations). They also categorized the new offences by seriousness, on a scale of one to five. They found statistically significantly lower rates of recidivism among releasees from the two private sector prisons (17 per cent compared to 24 per cent for the public sector releasees), and that the private sector releasees were convicted of less serious offences, after a 12-month period. The 'time to failure' was similar (107 days compared to 115 days for the public sector releasees). All the prisoners in the study were medium/minimum custody (some prisoners had moved between the public and the private sector, but the authors omit to consider this as a weakness in design). The authors concluded that: 'Only one conclusion can be drawn from the results: Private prison releasees were more successful than were their public prison matches' (Lanza-Kaduce et al. 1999: 42).

The study was severely criticized on methodological grounds: the study period was too short, the unmatched cases had more similar rearrest rates,[57] and because of a conflict of interest—the authors had a financial interest in the performance of the private sector establishments (see Geis et al. 1999). Of interest here are the three possible explanations the authors put forward for their results: the methodological limitations of their study; the effects of programmes; or what they call 'contextual effects', which relate to the organizational culture of an establishment, and whether this culture supports treatment over custody. The importance of this cultural dimension has been demonstrated before, as the authors point out (see Street et al. 1966). The authors argue that the statutory and contractual

---

[57] One-third of the private prison releasees (93 cases) could not be matched. This higher rearrest rate suggested that the non-matched releasees from the private prisons differed from the matched releasees. The authors point out that the severity of these reconvictions was still lower than for the public sector releasees. Comparing all samples together, the rearrest rate for the public releasees was 19%, and for the private releasees was 14% (see Lanza-Kaduce et al. 1999: 41).

obligations, under which the private sector operates in the USA, support and reinforce a treatment priority. This is further supported by the efforts of contract managers, whose task it is to secure compliance with these obligations. Whatever the validity of their results, their argument about the importance of the culture of a prison is a significant one. Their claim that their results reflect substantive differences in operations needs investigating further.

The case for a rigorous investigation of prison quality receives further endorsement by Pratt and Maahs (1999), who conducted a meta-analysis of 33 evaluation research studies (based on adult male facilities only). They concluded that private prisons are no more cost-effective than public sector prisons (see also Camp *et al.* 2003) and that the size (economy of scale) of an establishment, its age, and security level are the key predictors of cost. Consistent with the above, the authors note that their evaluation would have been more rigorous and informative if they had been able to include 'quality' as part of their assessment. As Feeley argues, assessments to date are 'tentative' (Feeley 2002: 397).

Camp *et al.* have used survey data from their Prison Social Climate Survey to explore public–private sector comparisons (see Camp *et al.* 2002, 2003). In particular, they have found in a demonstration project comparing a single private prison with three comparator prisons in California that prisoners rated the three public prisons as less safe and as having less sufficient staff available to protect prisoners, than the (more costly) private prison. The private prison was quieter (e.g. in the evening and at night), and had less gang-related activity, but scored less well on sanitation and food (Camp *et al.* 2003). This work is ongoing, and published work has so far focused on results from the more frequently administered staff surveys and on methodological issues than on results from the less frequently administered prisoner surveys. Using a small number of measures that survived rigorous exploration, the authors found that after controlling for institutional and demographic differences, staff working at public prisons rated higher than expected on organizational commitment (i.e. commitment to the Federal Bureau of Prisons) whilst those at the private prison rated higher than expected on institutional commitment (i.e. commitment to their own establishment; Camp *et al.* 2002). The authors argue that theoretical explanations for differences in performance should be developed. They suggest that such explanations are likely to include differentials in the power balance among competing interest groups, such as unions, managers, and staff (Camp and Gaes 2001).

In a broader but less detailed national survey of local, state, and federal jurisdictions housing adult offenders in public and private facilities, the authors found that lower labour costs in private sector prisons were associated with higher rates of escapes and poor basic security practices. These were linked to lower staffing levels, lack of experience, insufficient training, and high staff turnover. They describe the use of private sector practices as 'an experiment in the organisation of work in prisons', suggesting that more research is needed on the effects of lower labour costs on the 'quality of the correctional product' (Camp and Gaes 2002). It may also be important to distinguish between private prison companies in such research.

Public versus Private Sector Values: Posing a Question

Harding argues that private prisons have become integral to penal administration and that critics who pursue fundamental moral objections are naïvely blind to more tangible matters such as regime quality, value for money, public accountability, and the efficacy of regulatory procedures. He suggests that, increasingly, the matter of whether the impact of the private sector has improved standards and outcomes in the prison business as a whole settles these questions. Harding states that there is clear evidence of system-wide improvement. Hennessy's thorough examination of this period shows that the Conservative government of the 1980s intended to 'hang on to' public sector 'ownership', 'rules', and 'ethics' in its search for improved managerial control (Hennessy 2001: 624). The type and level of accountability built into the first private prison in the UK was careful and unusually tight (Harding 1997). Yet there is also emerging evidence that the private sector can succumb to the same failures as the public sector or worse (see e.g. accounts of Blakenhurst and Ashfield Prisons in *Prison Privatisation Report International* 2002, Nos. 53, 50, 49, and 47; HMCIP 2002b;[58] of Victoria (Kirby 2000) and several establishments in the USA

[58] In October 2002, the first privately managed penal institution for juveniles and young offenders, Ashfield, was described as 'a threat to the safety of prisoners and staff'. A critical report accused the operator of 'putting profit before the welfare

(PPRI 2002, Nos. 46, 49, 50; Mobley and Geis 2001; Shichor and Sechrest 2002; Camp and Gaes 2001). There have been considerable problems, in several privately managed establishments, of high staffing turnover, lack of experience, and complaints from staff about safety and employment conditions (see e.g. PPRI 49 and 53; Bottomley *et al.* 1997; Camp and Gaes 2001, 2002, and above).[59] When the worst things have happened, Harding argues that it is usually found that the regulatory system has been inadequate (which suggests that the public authorities have therefore been complicit in the failure; Harding 1997, 2001). We want to take the debate in a slightly different direction.

It looks from the evidence reviewed above as if some private sector staff, at least in the UK and in Australia (where regulation is relatively tight), treat prisoners better than some public sector staff treat prisoners, where 'better' means more respectfully. This is partly because they are more powerless (see Chapter 8), and partly because they are carefully socialized. The better treatment of prisoners by some, but not all, private sector staff in these two jurisdictions is worthy of note. There are some risks, of collusion and weaker security practices, as indicated above, which we shall come to later. Let us remain, for the moment, with this finding relating to respect. Our own observations, *at this level of daily practices*, have persuaded us that the public–private sector debate is far from straightforward. However, beyond staff, there may be some less visible instrumental practices (such as making a decision to increase profits, investing in security companies engaged in military activities, or lobbying for prison and other correctional expansion) which raise serious doubts about the possibility in practice of keeping

and safety of young people' (PPRI 49: 6). Its director was removed and a public sector prison governor was brought in (PPRI 50 and 53). The two sectors worked together for five months to produce a 'comprehensive plan for improvement'. Staff recruitment, retention, experience and training, a precisely worded (and therefore limiting) contract, and a weak and inexperienced senior management team were the main problems (HMCIP 2003; and PPRI 53).

[59] Camp and Gaes found that 'privately operated prisons have problems in maintaining basic security procedures' and that these problems are linked to high turnover and lack of experience of front-line staff and middle managers, which is in turn linked to lower levels of pay (Camp and Gaes 2002: 16 and *passim*). They conclude: 'The data presented here indicate that less costly workers in private prisons have not produced an acceptable level of public safety or inmate care to date' (Camp and Gaes 2002: 18).

a public service ethos centre stage, via the contract. As Taylor said in a discussion of the future of the centre-left in Britain, 'capitalism is amoral . . . it will go wherever profit is to be made' (Taylor 2001: 220). These financially driven but less visible activities raise crucial questions about the morality of private sector involvement in prisons and may lead us to settle questions in a different way (see e.g. PPRI 51: 3). Again, we doubt whether immoral practices are only true of private companies (recall the shackled prisoners, and examples of staff brutality against prisoners), but we can at least state the problem or consider the privatization question in a new way.

The moral problem is twofold. First, we are unclear about what just institutions are. We are even less clear about how to measure them. This chapter has reviewed numerous studies, and several official measures of 'performance'. There are clearly difficulties in establishing a clear and meaningful consensus on this basic issue. *Is* the question of prison quality, when properly posed, a question about just—legitimate—institutions? We think it cannot be otherwise. Rawls suggests, in his *Theory of Justice*, that justice would be chosen as a 'first principle' by reasonable people in a situation that is fair. This fits with our 'ordinary considered judgment' (Rawls 1980; Daniels 1975; and see further, Chapter 6) and determines how our basic social institutions should be designed. Justice is the 'most fundamental virtue' (Raphael 2001), a basic ideal and 'the most "political" or institutional of the virtues' (Ryan 2001: 1). Ryan likewise argues that the 'legitimacy of a state rests upon its claim to do justice' (Ryan 2001: 1). The principles of justice are, according to Rawls and others, those which free and rational persons would agree should govern their forms of social life and their major institutions: 'Justice is the virtue that holds society together and allows us to pursue the common good for whose sake society exists' (Ryan 2001: 9).

A social institution is just only when every person whose conduct falls under the rules has good reason to act in accordance with the rules (Rawls 1980; Ryan 2001). This (Kantian) conception of the just institution rests on an assumption of the *moral equality* of persons (i.e. that people are equally deserving of concern and respect) rather than on any utilitarian notion of people as *aggregates*: 'Each person possesses an inviolability founded on justice that even the welfare of society as a whole cannot override' (Rawls 1980: 3).

When individuals lose their freedom, the sacrifice of this good can only be justified in the name of a just, civil society (a social contract theory). Rawls proposes that justice has a moral priority over other 'goods' (such as utility and efficiency) and thus it places limits on the pursuit of other ends. This is not to say that other ends are not important, simply that they are *limited* by considerations of justice. Justice is often consistent with utility, but cannot be substituted by it (Ryan 2001: 5).

Rawls was concerned with major social institutions such as the political constitution, the organization of the economy, and political rights. Modern social institutions would be unlikely to satisfy his criteria (and many criminologists would hold inequality responsible for considerable quantities of crime in the first place). Several aspects of Rawls's theory have been disputed by moral and political theorists (see e.g. collections by Daniels 1975; and Ryan 2001). Prisons have several additional inherent deficits which limit the applicability of Rawls's theory of justice, such as the in-built loss of liberty and an extreme imbalance of power. But Rawls's 'ideal theory' of the primacy of justice (Daniels 1975, p. xv) does provide a useful framework for a new and challenging evaluation of late modern institutions (even if we have not yet established its meaning in the penal context; see Chapter 6). His analysis also provides considerable clarification of some of the expressed dissatisfaction with the excesses of managerialism. If persons should not be treated as aggregates (as they sometimes feel they are treated under managerialism), and justice is the first virtue of institutions (and yet remains unmeasured), then we have theoretically solid grounding for the explorations that follow.

Rawls suggests that just institutions nurture a sense of justice. Others have argued persuasively that there is a 'lack of connection between principles of justice and their actualisation in particular institutions, policies and acts' (O'Neill 2000: 5). It seems that there are several good reasons for using principles of justice for evaluating the nature and quality of prisons as social institutions. The concept of justice should then be properly conceived. We shall pursue these themes throughout the account that follows.

Here we come to our second moral problem. There also seems to be considerable uncertainty about what kinds of *mechanisms* might secure just institutions. There have been major failings in both public and private sector approaches to prisons (some critics would argue that these failings are inherent in the nature of prisons). The assumption that there is a 'public service ethos' in the public sector that underpins decent, honest, and accountable behaviour, whether in prisons or anywhere else, may be over-simplistic (see Pollitt and Bouckaert 2000). It is possible that public sector values 'such as democracy, accountability, equity and probity' (ibid. 2000: 9) are common and self-conscious at higher levels in the civil service, but that weak management and complex bureaucracies mean these ideals are infrequently instilled effectively 'at the coal face'.[60] Values of individual accountability and of representing the organizational ethos seem to be common in the private sector at ground level (at least in some of the private sector prisons we have studied), but inevitably the occupational ethos of for-profit companies is rather more mixed.[61] Private sector management techniques are more effective in controlling the workforce, in particular, in ending the employment of individuals who misbehave.[62] On the other hand, the new privatized economy keeps conscientious workers on tenterhooks for less palatable commercial reasons too. There are major difficulties and tensions inherent in the use of private sector companies in traditionally public sector spheres, and in the whole-sale adoption of private sector management approaches in public service tasks (see e.g. Pollitt and Bouckaert 2000; also House of Commons 2002). Public servants are perceived as inherently 'more trustworthy than business people', for example (Pollitt and Bouckaert 2000: 158). Pollitt and Bouckaert argue that the public sector is 'distinctive' and 'collective'. What do they mean? The House of Commons Public Administration Select Committee refer to the traditional public service values of impartiality, account-ability, trust, equity, probity, and service. They suggest that a distinction should be drawn between the notions of the public *sector* and public *service*, and that 'it might in principle be pos-sible to retain a public service ethos even where services are

[60] It is interesting to note increasing emphasis on 'ethics in the workplace' in the corrections literature (see e.g. Stohr *et al.* 2000; Pollock 1998 in the USA) and in prac-tice (see the new Prison Service Professional Standards Unit, in England and Wales).

[61] We have witnessed directors of privately managed prisons reluctantly follow-ing the instructions of their company directors to reduce staffing levels, and make additional savings. We are also witnessing this tension in several public sector pris-ons, however. The moral conflict may be related to the threshold above which profit, or efficiency savings, are pursued.

[62] As one governor said, 'the single power that I lack which would improve the quality of life for my prisoners is the power to sack poorly performing staff'. This is arguably changing, albeit slowly, in the public sector.

delivered by private sector providers' (House of Commons 2002: 11). They warn against any assumption that 'the public sector is the unique repository of the virtues of selflessness, service and caring' (ibid. 12). Monopolies as well as considerations of profit 'can hamper good service'. They do acknowledge, however, that the public service ethos 'may be put under strain by the profit motive. The ethos needs protecting and, where necessary, reinforcing in these circumstances. The private sector can be a useful servant for public services, if properly supervised; what it can never be is their master' (House of Commons 2002: 13).

It may be highly significant that just as we outlined in Chapter 1, when the Prison Service adopted what are essentially deontological values for instrumental reasons (justice for order), these values were all too quickly abandoned under critique (or in crisis). The fundamental problem with private sector management of prisons may be that private sector managers are inherently preoccupied with this basic instrumental (commercial) form of reasoning in a sphere of activity where this instrumental approach is particularly morally dangerous.[63] This is precisely the problem the Select Committee's Report has set out to address. We have set out how the public and private sectors differ in a tentative and schematic way at Figure 2.1.

The purpose of this figure is to describe and consider an apparent paradox. Each sector has a distinct advantage over the other: the public sector arguably operates within an established value base. The state is owner and a public sector ethos emphasizing integrity and transparency underpins all high-level operations. This provides a normative framework under which day-to-day services are organized and provided. The goals of a public sector penal system are, arguably, public reassurance, quality, and social justice.

Two difficulties arise, from this point on. The first is that there are many obstacles which prevent these high ideals from routinely

[63] The Public Administration Select Committee of the House of Commons has set out a new Public Service Code to 'bolster the public service ethos' and make adherence to this code binding for all those who deliver public services, including the private sector. It states that all service providers should 'put the public interest first', and they also state that it is a 'myth' that 'only public sector workers and organisations can uphold the ethos of public service' (www.parliament.uk/commons/selcom/pubpnt31.htm). See also House of Commons (2002). That such a call has been made provides support for the relevance of the scheme outlined in Fig. 2.1.

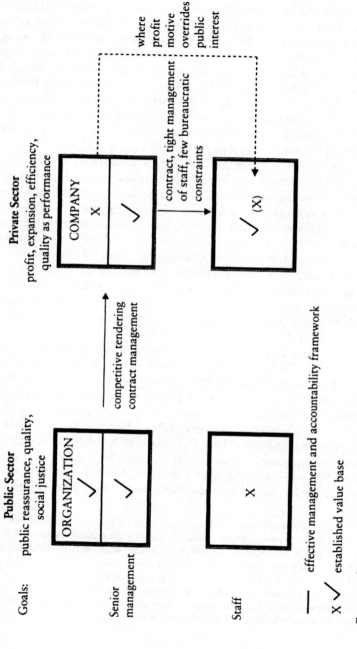

FIGURE 2.1. A schematic sketch of structures and mechanisms of value bases in two sectors

reaching into life on prison landings. These include, for example, protracted union activity, inadequate quality control, slippage of standards, bureaucratic inertia, fragmentation among headquarters' groups and between headquarters and the field, inadequate buildings, lack of management expertise, and uncertainty of purpose. With some important exceptions, attitudes, conduct, and 'performance' are patchy and fall far short of this ideal. Remedies for such ills may be more easily achievable at an institutional level in the public sector than in the private sector, however (e.g. whereas the contract inhibits management takeovers in the private sector, these are possible in the public sector). As the House of Commons review of the 'Public Service Ethos' argued: 'A public service ethos is only as good as the service it delivers. It is not enough to celebrate it in the abstract; it has to be given concrete expression in the way public services work for the citizens who use them and depend on them' (House of Commons 2002: 25).

The second difficulty is that the lofty goals referred to above are limited by cost-cutting and increasing concern with efficiency. The public sector is being made to operate in competition with the private sector, on cost as well as on 'quality'. So we have a public sector with sound declared values unable to produce a well-established value base among its staff (taken as a whole). Certain matters of exterior legitimacy are reasonably satisfactorily addressed[64] but matters of interior legitimacy (the treatment of prisoners by staff) often fall short of best practice.

On the right-hand side of Figure 2.1 we have the private sector. Here the state is purchaser. The goals pursued by private companies are profit and expansion, efficiency, and quality (as measured by 'performance').[65] These goals are theoretically compatible with

[64] Others, such as over-use of the prison, are clearly not.

[65] It is fair to say that the primary goal of for-profit organizations is profit and expansion. Group 4/Falck's corporate vision, for example, includes becoming a 'leading global provider of security and security related services' (where 'the term "leading" should be seen as a combination of being among the very largest in the global market, and the leading provider in terms of quality'; see www.group4falck.com; the 'corporate vision and strategy' page). The company advertises a target annual growth rate of 8–9.5% and promises its shareholders that it will take a 'proactive role in acquisitions'. Premier Prison Services Ltd. advertise their company's mission as emphasizing 'not only the security of the operation but also the care of the prisoners in our charge'. It is interesting to note that sections on 'ethics' and 'social responsibility' can be found on Group 4's website, stating, for example, that

increased efficiency and quality overall, via competition, innovation, careful oversight (Harding 2001) and each company's financial stake in its own reputation (Moyle 2000: 74). The House of
Commons has suggested that the quality of management is 'decisive'
in ensuring that a public service ethos is shielded from the profit
motive. It is difficult to argue, despite some concessions to 'ethics'
and 'social responsibility', that for-profit companies operate with an
established value base. This is not to suggest that individuals working for private prison companies do not take their public sector values with them when they take up career offers in the private sector.
Many individual governors leave the public sector frustrated in their
attempts to run a decent prison by the kinds of bureaucratic inertias
already referred to.[66]

The use of a competitive tendering process, and the existence of
a detailed contract, carefully scrutinized by the awarding body,
ensures that what is delivered is what is desired: reasonable treatment of prisoners by carefully controlled staff. The 'contingent
workforce' (Moyle 2000) is more closely managed by a flatter
structure, fewer protections, and clearer goals. In some countries,
formal systems of 'public standard' accreditation, linked to contract renewal, encourage more frequent attainment of minimum
standards in private sector prisons (Thomas 1997; Moyle 2000:
324). Matters of interior legitimacy are, broadly speaking, better
addressed, at least in many of those prisons that have been subject
to evaluation.[67] This apparently superior interior legitimacy is
achieved, where it occurs, via an economic, rational choice, or

'Group 4 Falck works both nationally and internationally on the basis of principles
regarding such issues as human rights, racism and child labour'. A code of conduct
exists for employees, which they all sign. The company's statement under 'social
responsibility' focuses on establishing the company on 'a sound financial footing'
and 'creating jobs'. Despite these sections (a development presumably encouraged by
ethical consumer movements), it is fairly uncontroversial to suggest that a private
company's main commitment is to its investors (see www.ethicalconsumer.org).

[66] No attempt has been made in this study to formally explore the values and
aspirations of any individuals working in private sector companies managing prisons, beyond this corporate level exploration of the secondary literature and available
websites. This, and other senior management level comparisons between the sectors,
would be an interesting but complex line of research to pursue.

[67] Moyle warns of a 'halo effect' whereby the first few contractors will perform
well under close scrutiny in order to secure larger and longer-term contracts (Moyle
2000: 61).

instrumental model of institutional behaviour. A new cultural ethos is achieved, via instrumental means.

There are problems: lack of transparency, the presence of an overriding commercial interest, excessive delegation of power, and the potential for abuse when systems of regulation fail. There are few effective remedies at the institutional level when things do go wrong (it may be easier to dismiss individual staff members in the private sector but it is difficult for the public sector to take back a struggling institution under the terms of tightly drawn up contracts). When the profit motive overrides the public interest, the performance of staff deteriorates. The sources of 'legitimacy deficit' seem to be located at different levels in the two sectors. They lie in lack of management oversight, capability, or power in the public sector (i.e. at relatively low levels in the organization). There are substantial institutional barriers that make management particularly difficult in the public sector (such as high levels of bureaucracy and resistance by the Prison Officers' Association), despite, at the highest level, a famously robust approach to performance management. It seems to be at establishment level (at some establishments in particular) that most difficulties appear. The sources of legitimacy deficit lie, on the other hand, in unfettered financial interest or incentive in the private sector (i.e. at the highest levels of the organization).[68] Responsibility for such unfettered financial interests is arguably shared with the purchaser. We have suggested already that the public sector shares some of this morally dangerous ground with the private sector when it reaches a certain 'efficiency' threshold in the resourcing of individual prisons.

Good 'moral performance' in the private sector is secured (where it occurs) by a combination of efficient private sector management techniques, and a clear public sector steer on what the required values should be, via the contract. Without these public sector restraints (and values), there would be no limits on what could be done, for profit. This is not to suggest that those individuals who

---

[68] Moyle gives examples of decisions (e.g. the transfer out of a private sector prison in Australia of difficult prisoners) taken by managers influenced by commercial considerations (such as 'protecting the company's business name'); Moyle (2001: 90–2). See also Mobley and Geis (2001: 211); Shichor and Sechrest (2002); and Camp and Gaes, who distinguish between the primary goals of owners/shareholders and those of managers and workers, who may have a broader range of interests (Camp and Gaes 2001: 289).

leave the public sector in the hope that they might be able to manage better prisons in a private sector framework do not take their ameliorative and individual moral values with them. But once there, they are required to put profit and competition first. The question is perhaps whether, and up to precisely what point, efficiency and ethicality (or social justice, to put it another way) are compatible. In support of some of the radical management reforms outlined in the previous chapter, what use are public sector values without their effective translation into practice? Can the state machine, without competition, put 'flesh on the bones' of its own social democratic claims (Hennessy 2001: 728)? Hennessy notes: 'One of the remarkable differences between the public and the private sector is that the former can take very clever people and put them in an environment where it is impossible to achieve anything, and the latter can take rather dull people, point them at the rabbit and have them achieve marvels' (Stephen Taylor 1987, in Hennessy 2001: 730).

The public sector had much to learn from the private sector about techniques, about leadership, change, and competition. The difficulty has been the adoption of these new managerialist techniques, and the invitation extended to powerful corporate interests to make them happen, without incurring the abandonment of the traditional or core values of trustworthiness, integrity, and 'public service' around which the Civil Service was originally established. These are the values for which it has long been admired by many other jurisdictions (Hennessy 2001, chapter 1): 'The concept of public service is fundamentally about integrity, doing what is right . . . none of this is incompatible with modernisation. The things that matter in public service are not changing. A Civil Service that didn't change would invite wholesale winding up' (Wilson 2002, pers. comm.).

But there are limits to centrally driven managerialism if moral legitimacy is to be retained (or rebuilt) in a 'progressive century' (Lawson and Sherlock 2001). Hennessy suggests that the latest versions of 'a search for efficiency-with-economy in the public services as outlined in Sir Richard Wilson's annual report to the Prime Minister in December 2000' would have met with the approval of 'Mr Gladstone himself' (Hennessy 2001: 743). Others remain deeply critical about the scope, style, and speed of the current modernizing project, its politicized nature, and the direction in which it takes us. These matters extend far beyond the scope of one book, and well beyond the expertise of its author. It is important to have looked, however briefly, at the social and political context in which the late modern prison is being shaped, as a 'special case' among many public sector services currently under transformation. It is in this rapidly transforming world that penal values and issues of prison quality have arisen, as political and commercial as well as empirical and theoretical questions.

The issues raised above—apparently superior performance in places, a lack of rigorous evaluation, the absence of an established or enduring moral framework at senior management levels in the private sector—make more complex the already problematic ethical debate about public versus private sector management and ownership of prisons. Add to this, concern about an apparently failing public sector and its struggle to reform (as outlined in Chapter 1). The values we want to discuss as our argument develops may not be *inherently* (or any longer, exclusively) public sector values, but this may be partly as a result of the effects of private sector competition and culture on the workings of the public sector.

Martin Narey's speech to the Prison Service Conference in 2001 included a rallying tone of support to the public sector, in the light of two successful bids against the private sector by the public sector: 'Who could possibly have imagined such astonishing achievements two years ago? Who could have expected a Director General to say, as I say now, that the private sector need to improve their act if they are to regain their competitive edge?' (Narey 2001: 6).

We have reviewed many attempts to conceptualize and measure prison quality, and our account has taken us into complex and contested territory. We suggest that in this area of organizational life, there must be satisfactory ways of thinking about the concept of quality. There needs to be a 'vested interest in the truth' (Hennessy 2001: 740).

So What is 'Quality'?

There has been a 'quality revolution' in public services generally (Power 2001: 59), but this revolution has brought with it some untested assumptions about the concept of quality and, arguably, some undesirable effects on the institutions subjected to new modes of evaluation. Quality has been linked, imperfectly, to the concepts of performance and effectiveness as outlined above. Staff and others express regular discomfort about this impoverished version of 'quality', whilst acknowledging that some aspects of the managerial revolution are necessary and long overdue. We suggest that there is a conceptual problem at the heart of these evaluation efforts. There are major gaps in the conceptual framework around which managerialist but also scholarly measurement techniques have been developed to date (and this is unlikely to be true only of the prison). The 'performance agenda' has been rightly criticized for being narrowly conceived, with key performance measurements arising because they constitute 'things that can be measured' rather than because they reflect accurately the concept at issue or the most important aspects of prison life. Neither the processes nor the outcomes address what really matters in institutions.

In contemporary comparative prison studies, far greater methodological sophistication has been achieved in relation to studies of comparative costs (Woodbridge 1999) than in relation to the quality of regimes or performance overall. There are some important exceptions, and these studies have been discussed in some detail. The recent meta-analysis of cost-effectiveness research studies carried out by Pratt and Maahs (1999) concluded that issues of quality remained an empirical uncertainty, and that their own study was limited by this failure to include measures of quality (Pratt and Maahs 1999: 367). There is no accepted consensus in the literature (or in practice) of what is meant by quality or how it should be measured. Part of the difficulty is a preference or need for quantifiable measures of what are basically qualitative dimensions of prison life. These 'measurables' are invariably a poor translation of whatever qualitative concept is being sought. Often, the measures used are selected because they exist: that is, the measurement of prison life has been driven by the nature of the information collected rather than by any satisfactory framework for thinking about what is important. Current dissatisfaction with available measures and their failure to identify, for example, 'failing prisons' reflects the inadequacy of this easily quantifiable material (Home Office 2000).

We have noted some imaginative scholarly attempts to identify and operationalize the concept of 'prison quality'. But there are, despite significant strides, nine main limitations to past and current measurement or evaluation techniques, which each attempt may share to a greater or lesser degree. Taken together, they reflect an underlying major theoretical gap in approaches to this task. They are:

(i) failure to address key dimensions in statements of aims (such as 'humanity');

(ii) lack of clarity about the meaning of key terms (such as 'respect' and 'justice');

(iii) a managerialist concern with performance-as-service-delivery, and poor operationalization of this narrowly conceived agenda;

(iv) limitations in the use of specific measures: such as recorded assaults as a measure of 'safety';

(v) a 'process compliance' and 'componential' framework for standards, where one practice is apparently unrelated to another;[69]

(vi) insufficient information from prisoners and staff about a sufficiently broad and relevant range of areas of prison life;

(vii) failure to compare information from diverse sources (e.g. standard audits and performance data);

(viii) failure to analyse or interpret data in detail; and

(ix) low 'face validity'; that is, the rejection by staff (and prisoners) of the accuracy of the world painted by these methods.

Despite a rich 'prison measurement' literature, there are few theoretical approaches to the prison that fully conceptualize and justify the use of a broad range of environmental dimensions and assess them empirically or systematically. We are less concerned with the public–private sector competition, or with a managerialist performance-driven agenda, than with the more fundamental question of how to evaluate the quality of a prison. We are especially concerned with what we have come to call the prison's moral climate, or in the light of the above account, its moral performance. Our conclusions may have implications for the former two projects, but we wish to consider the question of prison life without the inhibitions and inevitable distortions of the managerialist or 'service-laced' agenda. This enterprise involves some clearer thinking,

[69] See Berger *et al.* (1977), and Bottoms (1995) on the use of this term. An example is the policy on IEP, whereby establishments can achieve a good audit on IEP despite achieving poor audit ratings on sentence planning and personal officer schemes, on which IEP is supposed to depend. See Liebling *et al.* (1997); Bottoms (2003*b*).

first about *what matters* (to whom and why). Only then can we set about operationalizing these key dimensions of prison life, once they have been identified. Clearly, methods for assessing the quality of a prison environment are needed, whether to fulfil the needs of the new 'decency agenda', for other instrumental reasons relating to recidivism research, or because, as Toch (1992*a*), and Zamble and Porporino (1988) have argued before, we have a moral duty to understand prison environments and their psychological effects. It is to this principal question—of what matters—that we turn in the next chapter.

3
Identifying What Matters in Prison

Gym and education—the regime—are no substitute for individuality and psychological peace. The fact that material provisions are the very things they go for is a symbol of prisoners' scorn for these things. They just want to be treated decently.

(Medical officer, HMP Bristol, after the 1990 riot; fieldwork notes)[1]

Interviewed an officer due to be transferred before the summer—outside in the sun. Took over an hour. Then I found [small unit prisoner] painting gnomes. He wanted to talk about a research project he had to do for his psychology degree. We talked about possibilities. For some reason, anger came up . . . and how it is managed very formally in this setting. He wanted to study it. That precipitated an hour-long outburst. I no longer had to ask questions. It was an assault by staff—five years earlier—his legs, the front of his shins, he was hit with a baton, kicked and bruised. He was unable to walk for 6 days. It left him feeling very confused (at one stage, suicidal). He spoke so fast. This had never been dealt with. It changed his personality. He went from extrovert to introvert. He stays on the edge, never joins in the community. He couldn't make sense of the brutality he'd suffered. Neither could I.

(Fieldwork notes, 1992)

We have argued so far that there are conceptual and methodological limitations to current prison evaluation techniques, particularly in relation to the measurement of prison quality. This is true of official performance measures of the prison and of research

---

[1] Prisoners had destroyed the gym and the education department. See Home Office (1991a).

attempts to evaluate prison quality to date. The search for 'what matters' in prison has been overshadowed by a narrow focus on what can easily be measured.

Approaches to the prisons research craft vary from the exploratory and quasi-anthropological (e.g. Clemmer 1940; Sykes 1958; Morris and Morris 1963; Cohen and Taylor 1972; Sparks *et al.* 1996) to the 'head-counting', psychological testing methodology often favoured by official sponsors (e.g. Banister *et al.* 1973; Bolton *et al.* 1976). Most studies veer towards one or other of these extremes. All social research raises 'fundamental problems of ethics and responsibility' (King and Elliott 1977: 33).[2] We have obligations to our research participants, our sponsors (where relevant), our scholarly communities, and also to the standing and role of social science. The best research, on the whole, manages to draw together the 'sociologically imaginative' (Sparks *et al.* 1996: 341) with the empirically precise. This is our aspiration in the study we shall now describe. In this chapter, we outline how we conducted the research on which much of the remainder of the book is based. We begin with a brief summary, before embarking on a more detailed account of the evolution of our approach and the methodology employed.

Our Approach

The main research project we shall draw upon was carried out under the Home Office's Innovative Research Grant scheme, under the title, 'Measuring the Quality of Prison Life and Locating the Energy for Change'. It was thus intended to be open and innovative. The invitation to tender was received at a time when we had a pressing methodological agenda to pursue.

We used two main approaches. The first was appreciative inquiry (AI) (a focus on best experiences), which we deployed in three distinct ways: in the identification of 'what matters'; in the interviews conducted throughout the survey exercises in each prison; and in an exploratory process of change at HMP Wandsworth. AI is a way

---

[2] Useful accounts of doing prisons research can be found in Clemmer (1940, appendix A (in 1958 edn.)); Sykes (1958); Mathiesen (1965); Cohen and Taylor (1972); Genders and Player (1995, ch. 2); Sparks *et al.* (1996, appendix A); Liebling (1992, ch. 4; and 1999); King (1999); and King and Elliott (1977, ch. 2).

of looking at an organization, which concentrates on strengths, accomplishments, best practices, and peak moments. It is an approach to organizations (and individuals) based on the articulation of a vision of what is 'best' rather than an analysis of what is not.

AI begins with exercises aimed at imaginative conversation and continues into loosely structured interviews (Liebling *et al.* 1999*a*). The method is informed by, and has certain similarities with, symbolic interactionism and grounded theory. It is creative and mainly qualitative; it is concerned with theory generation and with the development of sensitizing concepts; and it is concerned with 'lived experience', narrative, and meaning (see Glaser and Strauss 1967; Rock 1979; Matza 1969). It is also distinct from them in important ways. It is less concerned with the predictive validity of theories generated from the data; it is more concerned with individual and organizational transformation; and it includes an explicit use of *generative questions*. These questions are few in number, they generate emotion as well as experience, they are based exclusively on narrative, and they are based on real memories of specific experiences (Elliott 1999: 214; Ludema *et al.* 2001). They also involve a deliberate focus on emotion and peak experiences (see Elliott 1999; also Barbalet 1998 and Stocker 1996 on the compatibility of emotion with reason). We shall describe these stages of the research more fully later in this chapter. This part of our research was largely *inductive*.

Our second main approach (a more *deductive* component) was the development and administration of a detailed quality of life survey, which was informed and supplemented by the method of AI. We worked closely with groups of staff and prisoners in the identification of themes for the survey, trying to 'imagine' each prison at its best, drawing on experiences of 'appropriate treatment' and agreeing a set of dimensions each group would wish to see reflected in any attempt to measure it. The themes to emerge included things like, 'a more productive sentence', 'personal growth', 'a view of the future', 'a change of emphasis', 'more support', 'acknowledgement that you are a human being', 'empathy with your situation', and 'being treated like an individual'. A series of appreciative interviews were conducted based loosely around these early themes, and the results were discussed in workgroups aimed at reaching a consensus about the areas in need of further exploration. Inevitably, illustrations arose of both positive and negative experiences:

I don't think the staff understand that we're only remand prisoners. They should be more careful what they say and with their attitude. Say, when someone gets a 20-year sentence. Years ago, you didn't get sentences like that. When I got a 14-year sentence, it took me two years to come to terms with it. It would have caused murders, their attitude, in my day. A lot of them take the piss. (Prisoner, Wandsworth)

We used reframing exercises (Elliott 1999; and see below) to identify the positive value being expressed, or yearned for:

INTERVIEWER: So what I hear you saying is that sensitivity to your situation in here is very important?
PRISONER: Yes. Absolutely.

This search for what is life-giving out of what is experienced as painful was made in order to move beyond or unseat 'existing reified patterns of discourse' (Ludema *et al.* 2001: 189) and to create space for the deeper and less circumscribed expression of individual experience. Instead of containing conversation at the level of the problem, we attempted to move beyond the problem, but in an affirmative and exploratory way. This was consistent with the overall approach to social research taken by AI: 'The questions we ask are fateful. They set the stage for what we later "discover" . . . The concept of the unconditional positive question assumes that whatever . . . topic we want to study, we can study it unconditionally and, in so doing, significantly influence the destiny of our organizations and our social theory' (Ludema *et al.* 2001: 189).

There was, despite the exploratory nature of this approach, considerable consensus during these exercises about what mattered. This was surprising, and allowed for much more detailed comparisons to be made between prisons than we had originally expected. After considerable discussion and deliberation, the key dimensions identified were: respect; humanity; staff–prisoner relationships; support; trust; fairness; order; safety; well-being; personal development; family contact; power; meaning; and decency. 'Respect' and 'humanity' almost always emerged first and were given the strongest emphasis. We shall describe this process in more detail later. These dimensions are empirical and theoretical constructs, in the sense that we devised each via conversation; these conversations were inevitably informed by the literature, and we revised them according to the analysis. They seemed to us, and in consultation with our colleagues, to resemble the values of almost any civil society.

Staff and prisoners then helped us to devise questions that reflected each dimension under investigation. Once the design of the survey was complete, questionnaires were administered in five comparable prisons. We continued to use appreciative questions in interviews, before or after administering the more structured questionnaire, in order to allow for continual clarification of meaning.

Prisoners felt most strongly about being locked up for long periods of time; staff having so much power over them; and staff attitudes (see Chapter 9). Many prisoners experienced imprisonment as deeply punishing: 'My feeling is that it's punishment. It seems as if everything is to make you suffer. Everything is done as punishment. It's mental torture. I *feel* it as a punishment, even though I'm on remand. They drain people, make it feel bad . . . They shouldn't be so heavy handed—they do it with an attitude' (prisoner, Belmarsh).

We carried out the surveys in a year-long exercise including interviews with a total of 512 prisoners and 121 staff. We interviewed approximately 100 randomly selected prisoners in each of five prisons. Our interviews with staff were less systematic and participants were not randomly selected. For this reason, this book is primarily concerned with the theoretical issues arising from the survey we devised for use with prisoners and the results from these. We shall draw on the work we carried out in the staff survey in Chapter 8 in particular, as we found that what staff had to say was increasingly important in understanding the developing 'moral performance' theme. We shall report in detail on the use of prison staff workgroups in this chapter, as staff contributed significantly to the development of the prisoner survey questionnaire, as well as to the development of their own.

The research approach was twofold. Everything we did had strong qualitative roots, as well as a quantitative goal. Our ideas arose from the data (as in grounded theory) but have inevitably been shaped by prior theory (as in Layder's (1998) adaptive theory). We have attempted to use some innovative methods designed to do justice to the complexity of prison experience, whilst also striving for meaningful quantification. The research was exploratory, and in that sense, we have learned a great deal about different research styles and tools, and if it were possible to begin again, we might have carried out some aspects of the research differently.[3] In the remainder of this chapter we shall outline briefly how and why we came to alight on the method of AI, how we used it, and how we designed and conducted the interview-based survey. We outline some of the research questions and puzzles that led us to this project in the first place.

Background and Context to the Current Study

The research has its origins in several previous studies, relevant aspects of which we shall mention briefly below. It arose as the culmination of countless interviews, conversations, and regular returns to some fundamental questions. In this sense, it is about what matters to us as well as what matters to prisoners and staff. We shall say more about the 'Whitemoor study', as this was where we first used AI. The formal research proposal was precipitated by a specific event. So we also need to recount our first encounter with Wandsworth.

In a two-year evaluation of the early operation of the first privately managed prison in the UK, we found that newly recruited non-unionized and non-experienced private sector custody officers treated prisoners with very high levels of courtesy and respect, but the private sector prison was relatively under-policed, suffered from high assault rates, and lacked safety (see Chapter 2). Drugs and alcohol were more widely available than in a comparator publicly managed prison. Staff reported high levels of dissatisfaction with staffing levels, management, communication, and job satisfaction, and high levels of anxiety and stress and a lack of discipline and control in the establishment (James *et al.* 1997). These findings

---

[3] The most difficult question was whether or not to tape-record our interviews. We recorded few of the prisoner interviews, but relied instead on detailed note-taking, where notes were written up soon afterwards. This had the major advantage of economy of time, and the instant identification of salient issues, but had the major disadvantage of losing some of the 'rawness' of others' accounts. This book constitutes an experiment in (generally) leaving the tape recorder behind. We still have mixed feelings. Perhaps the most exciting new technique we adopted was the use of workgroups, for which we thank Charles Elliott. We shall describe these, and the exercises involved, fully below.

were consistent with other evaluations and with Inspectorate and other reports on many other subsequently opened privately managed prisons, as we suggested in Chapter 2. Prisoners have asked the directors of at least two privately managed prisons to *reduce* the number of hours out of cells. This research experience, and our efforts to teach students about the complexity and significance of public–private sector comparisons, marked the beginning of a developing interest in comparing prisons, and in the vexed questions of relative legitimacy (Sparks 1994).

Shortly after this project was completed, several members of the Cambridge University Institute of Criminology became involved in an evaluation of the national policy of Incentives and Earned Privileges (IEP). This involved a before and after study of the impact of this and other newly introduced policies on all aspects of prison life (Liebling *et al.* 1997; Bottoms 2003*b*). In particular, we were interested in the impact of the policy on prisoner behaviour and levels of order in each of five establishments. We were also, largely as the result of relevant work by Sparks *et al.* on legitimacy and 'the problem of order', interested in perceptions of justice and fairness. We knew that a different form of 'policing' would have very different consequences in many areas of prison life (Liebling 2000). We found, using composite measures based on highly structured before and after interviews with over 1,000 prisoners, that prisoner behaviour and levels of order did not improve overall, but measures of staff–prisoner relationships, staff and regime fairness, some Woolf-like measures of clarity and consistency of treatment, making progress in prison, and participation in regime activities, all declined (Chapter 1, Table 1.3). These measures of fairness were all, in their turn, linked to prisoner behaviour and levels of order, which IEP sought to improve (Liebling *et al.* 1997; Bottoms 2003*b*).

The key learning points for us were that major shifts in prison life could be measured, and that policies could have unintended effects, many of which were linked to the context in which they were introduced. Because several other newly restrictive policies were introduced at the same time, we inadvertently captured one of the most significant periods of changing penal practice and sensibilities in recent history (see Liebling 2002; Bottoms 2003*b*; and Chapter 1). We also found, in confirmation of the Sparks *et al.* work, that *values* as well as *interests* influenced behaviour in prison.

We moved on to a study intended to explore an interesting finding that emerged from the IEP study. We had found a strong link between officers' use of IEP and their relationships with prisoners, particularly in one of our establishments: a long-term maximum security prison. Where staff–prisoner relationships were distant and uncomfortable (as they were on one wing in particular), increased use was made of the formal sanction newly available for staff of a 'basic' regime, that is, the reduction of prisoners' privileges (see Liebling 2002). Staff resorted to *formal* powers when their *informal* powers were under-utilized (Liebling 2000; see also Muir 1977; Banton 1964; and Reiner 1997 on policing). This wing went on to have a major disturbance, and we had sufficient data to demonstrate that there was an empirical relationship between a breakdown of order and the use by staff of too much power of the wrong sort (Liebling 2000). On other wings, and in other establishments, staff had managed to introduce a package of very restrictive policies, whilst apparently retaining a certain amount of legitimacy in the eyes of prisoners (although this did decline in most places). As a result of this turn of events, we were invited to carry out an exploratory observational study of staff–prisoner relationships and the work of prison officers more generally in a maximum security prison, to look more carefully at staff–prisoner relationships and the use of formal and informal power.

This project clearly required an unusual level of trust to be established between ourselves and prison officers (Liebling and Price 1999). We had absorbed the message from the recipients of the IEP research that, in the research process, we tend to uncover problems and shortcomings in practice—that research is, by its nature, 'problem-oriented'. Prison staff, in particular, are highly sensitive to the damage that research(ers) can do to them, and has done to them in the past. One only has to read the descriptions of prison staff by, for example, Cohen and Taylor (1972), or Morris and Morris (1963), to see that staff are superficially and stereotypically regarded by many prison researchers (see King and Elliott 1977: 36–51; for an alternative approach, see Liebling and Price 2001; Crawley 2001).

At about the time we were beginning to think about how to set about this research, Charles Elliott, an economist and a consultant in organizational change, introduced us to the method of AI. It occurred to us that this might be an effective way to approach prison officers.

Appreciative Inquiry and an Exploration of Staff–Prisoner Relationships at HMP Whitemoor

The essential purpose of AI is organizational *change*. We used it in a very limited and exploratory way in Whitemoor, simply to ask an unusual set of questions. Instead of 'how do you get on with management here?', or 'have you got the resources you need to do your job?', we asked, 'when do you perform at your best, as a prison officer?', 'tell me about your best moment in the job', 'what was going on at the time, to make this day so special?' and so on (see Liebling and Price 2001). We found, through this method, that we could dig deeper into a prison, if we were sensitive to people's achievements as well as to their problems and difficulties (Liebling et al. 1999a).

We also adapted the kinds of questions we asked of prisoners, so that we were inviting them to tell us about when life 'worked best' in this prison, or 'if you had one wish for staff–prisoner relationships here, what would it be?' These questions, despite the constraints of prison, solicited creative and energetic answers.

The method of AI generated enthusiasm. We used it in Whitemoor Prison simply as a mode of inquiry. It is intended to be used in organizations as a mode of transformation. Its theoretical claim is that inquiring about best experiences and accomplishments generates energy in the direction of best practice, which can then be used to move the organization in that direction. We certainly detected that kind of energy amongst prison staff in our Whitemoor study, but we had not set out to test that part of the process. This caused us some soul-searching, as we had effectively stimulated the staff in this direction, and they expressed a powerful need to be carried forward in some process of change. We thought we had found a new way of finding 'the truth about a prison', and we uncovered some previously neglected dimensions in the work of prison officers (Liebling and Price 2001) and in the experiences of prisoners. Perhaps most important, the participants in the research process found it rewarding, and (unlike some research) emotionally 'safe', and the results relevant and worthy of discussion.

We decided to use AI as a key approach in the quality of prison life study we are about to describe. There were two main reasons for this. The first was that previous efforts to evaluate the prison had been narrowly quantitative and largely unimaginative (as we argued in Chapter 2). The results of such evaluations could be shallow, inaccurate, and misleading. The second reason was that evaluations tended to be problem or 'deficit' oriented. In previous research (for example, Liebling 1992; Liebling and Krarup 1993), the author and colleagues had relied upon a kind of 'testimony' approach to the research encounter. This deficit orientation constituted what we believed to be a 'humanistic', empathetic valuing of the person. Listening, with a few structured questions to start the conversation off, achieved a good research outcome and constituted a defensible ethical position. Or did it? We had witnessed this approach having potentially damaging effects on staff and prisoners and their subsequent behaviour. The 'problem-oriented interview' was capturing only part of the story and leaving interviewees feeling cathartically relieved, but with a largely negative narrative delivered, and with (we imagined) some negative emotions to carry out of the interview with them, despite efforts to counteract or avoid this. The 'humanistic' or testimony method of depth interviewing, based on the establishment of rapport, had the unfortunate limitation that it generated largely problem-oriented data, or a very selective account of 'the truth' (Liebling *et al.* 1999a; Alasuutari 1995: 53). The 'honest, confidential, heart-pouring talk' favoured by many qualitative researchers, and certainly until this point by the author, might in fact miss the point (Alasuutari 1995: 53).

We were looking for a way of capturing 'the essence' of a prison (or of an individual's experience of that prison), without making either of these mistakes. As Wright Mills argued, one useful way of thinking about themes is to consider their antitheses: 'If you think about despair, then also think about elation; if you study the miser, then also the spendthrift' (1970: 235).

This refocusing on (for example) elation paradoxically allows a deep conversation about (for example) despair to go on, but gently, and within the context of other emotions. There was a way, it seemed, of capturing a wider range of experience.

We have drawn on AI in our overall approach to each establishment, and each individual, in our design of the research instruments, in the focus of our questions, and in the way the research was launched and generally conducted. We used AI workshops, which we shall describe below, to identify the 'things that matter' when thinking about the evaluation of prison life. We have departed from AI to the extent that we were seeking to work towards measurement and quantification. The verb '*to appreciate*' can mean 'to estimate the value of', or 'to recognise as valuable' (Bagnall 2000). It can also mean 'to estimate *rightly*', 'understand', 'be sensitive to', 'esteem adequately', or 'form an estimate of worth or quality' (*New Shorter Oxford English Dictionary* 1993). These definitions capture the spirit and intention of AI as we have used it here. In using it as our principal tool, at least in the first instance, we might be corrupting its integrity. We reject this claim and hope, conversely, that we have contributed to its validation and utility *mainly* (in our case) as a guide to evaluation *but also* (as we describe elsewhere: see Liebling *et al.* 2001) as one possible tool for organizational transformation. As a research method, it is participatory, respectful, and empowering, and it takes us closer to the 'truth about an organization' than we have been before. It has a special relevance to the measurement and cultivation of *values*.

A Brief Survey of HMP Wandsworth, 1999

After what we experienced as an unconstrained and creative research process in Whitemoor, we received a daunting request. In 1999, we were invited to carry out a brief survey of the quality of life at Wandsworth, following a contested and damning Chief Inspector's Report.[4] The Report described a powerful culture of brutality, dominated by the POA (HMCIP 1999c: 3–8). Similar cultures had been described at Feltham and Wormwood Scrubs (HMCIP 1998, 1999d), but 'in no prison that I have inspected, has the "culture" that we found caused me greater concern than in HMP Wandsworth' (HMCIP 1999c: 6). The Inspection had been incomplete, and one senior member had suggested in private that the Report might be exaggerated. The Report contained an extended critique of performance measurement:

I find myself asking how Prison Service line management, with its Visions, Statements of Purpose, Prison Rules, Operating Standards and so on, quite apart from all it publicises about its aims and performance—all of which profess exactly the opposite of what we have found—can have allowed such treatment and conditions to exist. (HMCIP 1999c: 3)

---

[4] A question arises here about how these invitations arise and how (or whether) threats to independence are identified and resisted. We shall consider these issues towards the end of this chapter.

The Chief Inspector expressed irritation that, when critical reports were written, 'the Director General expresses surprise' (HMCIP 1999c: 4). This was:

> not because he does not know what he wants prisons to deliver, but because the information he is given about them is not about the quality of outcomes for prisoners but about budgets, Key Performance Indicators and measurements of the quantity of laid down processes. In other words I fear that the agenda on which I [am] required to report to Ministers, based as it is on an Act of Parliament, and the Prison Service's own Statement of Purpose . . . is far removed from one governed by budgets and Key Performance Indicators . . . which concentrate on completely different outcomes . . . Therefore it is not surprising that we report on things which line management do not appear to notice because they are not looking for them. If senior line management does not concentrate on the correct treatment and conditions of prisoners, it is hardly surprising that line management in prisons take their cue from them, and devote their attention to those aspects upon which their superiors require them to concentrate. (HMCIP 1999c: 4)

The then Director General of the Prison Service challenged the Report, suggested that the methods were 'suspect', and requested (via an area manager then working in the London South Area) a methodologically trustworthy survey, which could be conducted swiftly and with a minimum of 100 prisoners. We had many reservations about this request (see Liebling 2001). It was a potentially sensitive exercise; the very request seemed a bit 'cloak-and-dagger' and we were given almost no time to prepare or conduct the survey. We were also intrigued, however, by the measurement question, and the role of different (i.e. supportive versus 'condemning') approaches to institutional change (see Braithwaite 2002; and later). In the end, for better or for worse, we requested some assistance (in the shape of a governor then under training), and hastily assembled a team of willing research assistants. We wanted to see if this kind of work could be quickly but robustly achieved. We adapted a previous questionnaire (used in the evaluation of IEP described above), including only those questionnaire items which had formed the composite variables in the original study (reducing the questionnaire from 30 pages to six). We also included a more open 'appreciative' set of questions, following our experience at Whitemoor. This was intended to deepen our understanding of life at the prison, and to allow variation and elaboration to emerge. If prisoners could identify an encounter they regarded as respectful, we wanted them to describe it, so that when we wrote our report, staff and others would recognize the (real) presences as well as the (real) absences of respectful treatment.

We completed the interviews, with a random sample of 100 prisoners, in one week. We were able to produce reliable measures of the Chief Inspector's 'healthy prison' indicators: whether prisoners felt safe, whether they felt treated with respect, whether they were assisted in maintaining meaningful contact with their families, and whether they participated in activities. We were also able to give examples of where and when prisoners did feel treated well. Prisoners felt safe from threats and bullying by other prisoners; they did not generally feel respected by staff; they took part in a limited number and range of activities for a limited part of the day; and they were assisted to a minimal degree to maintain contact with their families (Liebling *et al.* 1999*b*). There were, however, times and places where respectful treatment occurred. We also conducted (against the wishes of our research sponsors) about 20 informal interviews with prison staff. We were able slightly to modify the Chief Inspector's claim that there existed a 'culture of brutality' at Wandsworth and, through these supplementary informal interviews with staff, to explain some of the cultural features of the establishment: for example, a high commitment to discipline and regulation, and a general, but not universal, lack of respect for prisoners. Prisoners said, 'it's OK here if you don't ask for things'. They also said,

There was one compassionate prison officer. He cared. He helped me with my sentence plan, made me feel better, completely different. (Prisoner)

When an officer decides you can have a phone call, after you've been banged up for 48 hours; when they explain why you're banged up, and say, 'we feel sorry for you lot'. Most of them say that. (Prisoner)

I was shaving my head with a couple of razors, but they weren't sharp enough and I left all these bits. I caught a lady officer and she came back with a razor, very rapid, like; she saved me from embarrassment. She understood what it would have been like in front of these looking an idiot. (Prisoner)

Limited as these examples are, they form part of the story about Wandsworth. Prisons operate with different *degrees* of respect and disrespect, different degrees of legitimacy and illegitimacy (Sparks 1994). These differences, and the reasons for them, needed to be understood.

Staff at Wandsworth had all their pride invested in security and discipline and very little in activities or relationships. They felt invisible, powerless, and almost dehumanized by an unpredictable and struggling shift system. Several of the staff were unhappy with the behaviour of their colleagues but needed comradeship in the face of few alternatives. They were an 'insecure community', angry about being left 'without a governor' for a long period. They expressed a mixture of shame and defensiveness about how 'out of control' they had become. Staff were very sensitive about reviews which failed to reflect their few specific achievements 'against the odds' (see the remark in Chapter 2 about good staff in poor organizations). They were engaged in the 'pursuit of security', in Zedner's language, as a goal and as an activity, where the focus had shifted from actual dangerousness to perceived potential risk (Zedner 2000, 2003). We shall return to Wandsworth later, as, stimulated by this early but very brief survey experience, we included it in the current study.

This strengthened our interest in the question of how to evaluate a prison: what is it important to measure? How do we get under its skin? How do we capture, empirically, distinctions between prisons, which can be good or bad in so many different ways? Professionals and scholars were agreed that existing performance indicators were flawed. Performance data were routinely collected at Wandsworth (as well as other prisons later found to be 'scandalous'; see HMCIP 2001c, 2002d). Why did these data not alert the Service to these hazards of quality? It seemed possible for a prison to practise violence and abuse of prisoners, and yet be meeting its performance targets.[5] At just this point in our thinking, the invitation to tender for methodologically innovative research projects arrived.

---

[5] Selected performance data for Wandsworth are included in Chapter 4. The data show nothing untoward. Wandsworth did achieve two 'deficients' in its Standards Audits in 1998 and 2000. These findings did not lead to action or major concern, suggesting that Pollitt's point (made in the previous chapter) that performance data tend to be more concerned with measurement than management might be right.

Measuring the Quality of Prison Life

Our intention, when applying for the grant, was to develop the work we had started, trying to combine an 'appreciative' approach with a more quantitative outcome. We had identified a knowledge gap and we were dissatisfied with previous and official method-ologies. We had become persuaded that the *relational* aspects of a prison's life, and its linked *ethos* or culture, were crucial to the prison experience, and yet were not adequately captured by official data collection methods. As one of the prisoners we interviewed put it:

> When I first came in, I had no pillow. I approached two officers—they were chatting, so I waited. Eventually, one of them asked me what I wanted. He said, 'You're not entitled to a pillow' and carried on chatting. They were not concerned about me. That seems minor, but it's crucial. It can turn you into a different person. (Prisoner, Belmarsh)

We were informed, but not constrained, by the empirical and the-oretical literature. Our primary interest was in capturing accu-rately, using imaginative methods where we could, how the prison experience is *lived* and what *shapes* it. The formal aims of our research were:

- to employ the method of AI in the development of a detailed survey of the quality of prison life in five carefully selected pris-ons with different levels of performance, and some important controls;
- to develop quantitative measures of qualitative dimensions which are widely used but poorly understood;
- to explore whether this approach delivers a supplementary source of operationally useful information to other available performance data;
- to evaluate the impact of a full AI in one 'prison with difficul-ties', using a before and after design;[6] and
- to pursue a cumulative interest in evaluating prison quality, and in exploring changes over time; to develop a rounded sociolog-ical understanding of prison life.

---

[6] We have reported on this part of our study elsewhere (Liebling *et al.* 2001; Liebling and Arnold 2002).

So we had multiple objectives: exploration of the AI method; the identification of 'what matters' in prison life; clarification of the meaning of certain key ideas; and the generation of a new evaluation tool, which would generate knowledge about areas of prison life that matter, but which tend not to be measured.

Measuring What Matters in Prison

The task we set ourselves was to find a reliable way of forming a quantitative assessment of the nature and quality of a prison, without losing too much of the closeness generated by qualitative methods. We wanted to do so with values at the forefront of our minds. The Prison Service makes claims about 'humanity' and 'justice', but how far do these ideals translate into daily practices in particular establishments? Our study was informed by a strong tradition of the measurement of prison quality in the USA (as reviewed in Chapter 2). However, the purpose of retaining the AI dimension was to generate continuing discussion, to discover what staff and prisoners thought 'mattered most', and to seek examples of when prisoners felt treated with respect, or fairness, and so on, in order to gain a closer understanding of these concepts. We were determined to keep the interview open, sensitive, and balanced. We were more interested in the psychological experience of imprisonment than in material circumstances.[7] We were seeking a high degree of precision, particularly because these things may differ in subtle and complex ways. We needed data that were amenable to quantification. But we also wanted to retain meaning, depth, and individual contact.

The Research Setting

Most of the research we shall describe was carried out in five establishments (see Chapter 4). We wanted some similarities (e.g. function) but some expected differences in performance, in order to test our survey 'measure'.

---

[7] We know from other studies that staff attitudes towards prisoners, and their relationships with them, may be more important than material features of the regime in overall evaluations, above a certain threshold (see Ch. 5). This may differ in certain international contexts, particularly where material conditions are extremely poor (see e.g. King 1994b).

Local prisons were mainly chosen for this study for several reasons. A local prison serves the courts, tends to house unsentenced and mainly short sentence prisoners, and claims, as its name suggests, a degree of 'locality' to the communities its prisoners come from, although this is not always the case.[8] Local prisons are still the most numerous, and almost all prisoners pass through them. More recently, there has arguably developed a 'two tier' system of local prisons—those newly built establishments now often owned and managed by the private sector and their newly built public sector competitors; and the traditional, often architecturally decrepit establishments that were built between 1800 and 1900, many of which struggle to perform a modern penal role in buildings that were designed with other more limited penal purposes in mind. The two-tier system is not exclusively divided according to age and architecture, however—some ancient establishments have managed to exorcise the ghosts of Du Cane and his followers, but others have not. There is probably a greater range of quality and 'performance' among local prisons than among prisons of any other category. Most of the worst 'performance' staff cultures and attitudes are concentrated in local prisons, but some of the best practice can also be found in locals.[9] Here we had an interesting problem to consider, and a diversity of environments. We selected one category C prison to provide some degree of comparison with the four local prisons.

Access was negotiated locally, but the selection of establishments was informed by discussions with area managers and the then Deputy Director General. The first private prison selected suggested

---

[8] Historically, the English local prison has represented 'the English prison' because they date back to a period when penal policy was a matter for local ratepayers and magistrates. As Sparks argued, 'for many prisoners the general local prison *is* the English Prison system. Comparatively few have ever been in an open prison or a closed training or central prison; a large fraction have accumulated all, or most, of their prison experience in the "local nick", which serves their home neighbourhoods' (Sparks 1971: 90). This influenced the extent of public interest in them and the efforts made to recoup costs by the use of productive labour (see McConville 1998). Their local nature also ensured that there was a lack of uniformity in the regimes they offered. This was addressed by nationalization in 1877.

[9] Many of the failing prisons identified post-Laming were local prisons. Strategic decisions taken in the 1950s resulted in a concentration of attention on the training estate. King and Morgan argue that this unwitting neglect of a key part of the prisons estate has contributed to its long-term failure (King and Morgan 1980).

an alternative establishment in its place as the original establishment was undergoing a market-test. Once the five prisons were agreed, we had no difficulties in securing formal or informal access, and their full participation in the study. The fieldwork took place between August 2000 and August 2001.

In effect, the five establishments constituted a 'construction sample' (see Heal *et al.* 1973); that is, we developed and tested our survey tool in detail in this study. We subsequently applied and validated the revised scale in a further 14 establishments, using a less time-consuming methodology, in two further studies. The more labour-intensive approach reported in this book was necessary to achieve our aims: clear conceptual as well as empirical understanding.

The research team spent five weeks in each establishment. During the early stages of our research in each prison, we held several workgroups with staff (and, where we could, with prisoners), devising a set of 'things that matter' in prison. It was interesting that staff and prisoners produced the same set of dimensions, suggesting a moral consensus or shared vision of social order and how it might be achieved.[10] We outline this process below.

The Role of the Workgroups

In each prison, we spent the first four days of the main fieldwork period with a workgroup of staff. This had to be arranged in advance, which meant that those who volunteered (or were selected) had a reasonable idea about what we were trying to do. We specified the ideal number and composition in advance: ten to twelve people, varied membership, but with several uniformed officers of different grades and representatives from specialist grades. Notices were sent out to staff and, in most cases, volunteers were sought (sometimes individuals were invited, for example, from the Prison Officers' Association). We asked if we could have the participants from 10 a.m. to 4 p.m., uninterrupted, for three consecutive days. This was a lot to ask of busy local or training prisons. During the

---

[10] If this kind of value consensus is possible among apparently opposing groups in prison, this suggests they are of an enduring and universal quality. Mathiesen assumed 'a certain amount of consensus . . . between ruler and ruled regarding basic norms and values' in prison (Mathiesen 1965: 13). He also suggested, tentatively, that this consensus might be superficial and strategic (but he was referring to already established rules).

time they spent with us, the staff were completely free of other commitments.

In each prison, we were based in an office, and we were given keys, passes, and a liaison officer. We normally met with the governor (and often with other members of the senior management team) and had introductory discussions. We asked for a brief tour of each establishment during the first morning, and an informal meeting with the workgroups during the afternoon.

Staff annotated our first walk around the prison, with an account of how things were:

There is more focus now here on our *duty of care*. Things have improved here—it is much calmer. They want their showers, food, visits, etc. If they don't get these basic things, their entitlements—to exercise, mail etc., that's when they get grumpy. It has a lot to do with staff attitudes. What you want are staff who will *deliver the regime*. They look at who's on today and they know what they're going to get. (Senior officer, Belmarsh)

Our workgroups (variously) consisted of officers, senior and principal officers, administrative grades, education officers, chaplains, and physical education instructors. We facilitated warm-up exercises,[11] then divided the workgroups into small teams and asked the teams to draw a 'history wall' of each prison, highlighting highs and lows and marking important events and transitions. This generated intense concentration, and considerable discussion. The exercise helped us to ground ourselves a little in the mood, history, and 'collective' memory of each establishment, and to identify some of its sensitivities. We learned about achievements and disappointments, the industrial relations climate, the comings and goings of different governors, awards won (and wings lost), about deaths in custody—and, in one case, an officer suicide. Establishments changed their function (e.g. from female to male, or remand to training), opened new wings, offered new courses, and achieved an 'acceptable' rating on an audit. We learned, from the feedback exercises, what these events meant to the staff concerned, and how

[11] For example, using a marble game. We asked small teams to invent a new game of marbles, then send an ambassador to another group to communicate the results without speech. This worked—everyone engaged in it, all the individuals began to develop their role, and there was a great deal of laughter. The exercise bonded the workgroup, broke down barriers, and linked enjoyment and creativity to work.

they were related to the tone or ethos of the prison. There were slumps, good Inspectorate visits (and bad ones), and popular and less popular governors. There were disciplinary inquiries, budget cuts, changes to shifts, and closures of staff social clubs. These exercises opened everyone up. Our workgroup members were the knowledgeable ones, and we were there to learn.

We then asked the teams to identify what we called 'headwinds' and 'tailwinds'. This was another energetic exercise, with the teams often identifying similar themes, but discussing (not just for our benefit, but because they became engaged) the subtleties of each 'headwind', and its impact on their establishment. They raised issues of management style, the threat of privatization, POA activity, the need for a clear identity for their establishment, uncertainty about the future, the reputation of their establishment, and structural or building changes. Staff in two prisons felt their senior managers were 'too confrontational'. Staff in most of the prisons felt 'they expect too much'. Tailwinds included, for example, staff commitment, strong leadership, teamwork, good humour, appreciation, innovative work with prisoners, and relationships or 'rapport' with prisoners.[12]

The next task was to consider what values might emerge for the prison from a strengthening of the tailwinds and if the headwinds were removed? This was the first exercise in imagination. The workgroups were to put the headwinds to one side. What would happen? Where would the prison move to? The sorts of themes identified by the teams were:

- better working conditions;
- a more productive sentence;
- reducing reoffending;
- moving together in the same (clear) direction;
- community;
- personal growth for staff and prisoners;
- more support—for example, counselling and rehabilitation;
- balance, a shift of emphasis (from security alone);

---

[12] The use of 'headwinds' and 'tailwinds' resonates somewhat with Lewin's 'force field analysis', particularly his concepts of 'driving' and 'resisting' forces (see Lewin 1997: 351–77). Conflict situations arose, according to Lewin, when the forces acting (in this case, on the person) are opposite in direction and about equal in strength (ibid. 352).

- openness and trust between departments;
- a long-term future (no threat of market testing/privatization); and
- professionalism.

Throughout this process, we departed with all our notes and flip charts in the evenings, then returned each morning with a slightly digested account of the previous day's work. We tried to move from the kinds of issues raised above, to an identification of the values underlying them. What did these lists on flip charts say about 'what mattered'? This process took considerable time, and there was much animated discussion, and sometimes disagreement—particularly about the detail.

Eventually, we collectively refined our list of 'things that matter'. The most important things, the groups said, were relationships between staff and management; and between staff and prisoners. What should be measured, staff and prisoners said, were things like:

- the general atmosphere ('we can all sense unrest among staff and prisoners');
- staff relationships (teamwork; or friction amongst staff);
- staff relationships with prisoners;
- prisoner–prisoner relationships ('one group should not have too much power over others');
- relationships between uniformed staff and governor grades ('how open their door is');
- staff feeling valued by management (not 'them and us'); and by the wider public ('are inmates more important?');
- prisoners and staff feeling treated fairly, listened to, treated and communicated with as individuals;
- appreciation;
- respect;
- job satisfaction/the opportunity for development, for staff and prisoners;
- making positive contributions to the community;
- consultation and participation;
- support from line managers ('not just on KPIs, budgets, and plans');
- awareness of each other's roles;
- the ability to work across disciplines; communication.

Staff identified an 'element of *care*' in 'delivery': 'It is doing your job—but properly' (officer).

While these discussions were going on, we devised some questions from what staff and prisoners were saying to us. We did this 'from scratch' in the first prison, then added questions or revised them slightly in the following establishments.

We pulled together all we had heard and tried to identify headings or themes around which our questions would be devised. We discussed a provisional list with the staff workgroups. Words could be 'torpedoed', substituted, or reframed. We ended up with a list of concepts:

- respect;
- support;
- fairness;
- humanity;
- safety;
- order (including security and control);
- development;
- power/authority;
- trust;
- validation/appreciation;
- communication;
- relationships;
- tension (or well-being);
- alienation (or belonging);
- staff only: job satisfaction; and
- loyalty.

Achieving the same level of discussion with prisoners as we had achieved with staff was inevitably more difficult. When we did work with prisoners, it was in shorter bursts, although we did manage to hold a workgroup in four of the five prisons. These workgroups generated a similar list of dimensions in each prison, almost duplicating the themes raised by staff. Methodologically, this was crucial. It allowed us to move from the inductive to the deductive rapidly and with increasing confidence. It allowed us to make far more systematic comparisons between prisons than we had hoped for originally. Considerable consensus about what mattered emerged despite 'the conditions of late modernity' (Taylor 1999). It is often argued that we inhabit a post-traditional world, where moral questions have been repressed and there can be no common interest or perspective (Giddens 1991). Yet in each prison, via very different types of conversations, we were led towards the same set of concepts. We made very few changes to the original interview schedule as a result (although we did make some). To incarcerated prisoners and to staff, it seemed very clear that certain values mattered. This powerful re-experiencing of the same 'end-point' alerted us to the fact that, in contemporary late modern societies, prisons are highly unusual places. They could be said to constitute place-based, or neighbourhood-based communities, in which people can 'know each other' (see Bottoms 2000; Taylor 1999). Unlike old-style villages, of course, there are stark power relations and a fractured but significant 'caste-like' division between staff and prisoners. This makes it less surprising that issues of power, respect, and governance arise in such a powerful way. We return to these themes in later chapters.

We asked prisoners what they would want measured, and what sorts of questions might be appropriate; and we invited small groups to complete our draft questionnaire and discuss it with us. Feedback from all of these exercises was incorporated into the final version. Several questions were dropped, invented, or reworded as a result of these discussions.[13]

We used the list of dimensions, and the notes taken from the discussions, to devise our four main research instruments (see below). Staff and prisoners offered questions, or revised wording of questions, as we sought to develop the specific items or questions which would reflect each of the concepts. We deliberately sought variation and elaboration, but ended up with very few changes to the list of concepts and only minor changes to the questionnaire.

Our workgroups hardly constituted 'the original position' (see Rawls 1980; and Chapter 6), nor were our participants behind a 'veil of ignorance' about who they were and what their future roles

---

[13] Changes were made to the wording of some questions rather than to the conceptual scheme, which remained remarkably intact. For example, statement 87 ('This prison is poor at maintaining good order and discipline') was revised to omit the term 'discipline' after the first prison. Additional items were added to the two development dimensions and to the decency dimension following further elaboration, and so on. Two 'population characteristics' questions were also added after the first prison ('Is this your first time in prison?' and 'Have you ever been in this prison before?'). These were matters of detail and refinement, rather than changes to the substance of the questionnaire.

might be, but they were, for the period of these exercises, free from special interests and other confounding influences (Pettit 1993). As a method of discovery about 'what matters', our workgroups were lively and effective. Staff told us constantly that this exercise was engaging, and that they had enjoyed themselves. Prisoners wanted to become involved, but were harder to 'keep', as their time was more restricted. But we did manage continually to check the emerging themes, and the specific questions, with individuals. A number of prisoners conducted appreciative interviews with each other, and wrote up notes to give us.

Staff and prisoners found the process of interviewing each other formally (and of being interviewed in this 'appreciative way') illuminating. 'This is very in-depth, isn't it? The questions and answers are not as simple as you might expect. It is not light-hearted, you need to concentrate. This talks about every corner of the prison— it's a small number of questions, yet . . . If it gets listened to, it'll be great' (officer).

Staff called the final version of our survey a 'tick-box questionnaire'. They liked the questions (and both staff and prisoners expressed surprise when they completed it, at its relevance to their condition). Our volunteer interviewers were surprised at what they found: 'When we were talking about trust, this officer put governors in the same category as the inmates—"not at all". That shocked him— how little trust he had for senior management. It was seeing it in black and white' (officer).

We discussed what emerged substantively from the interviews, but also the questions—were they the right questions, could we express them more easily? The officers talked amongst themselves, in our presence, about their prison and 'how it was'. The process made them helpfully reflective.

So we identified 16 concepts, from which we developed 14 dimensions. These dimensions can be conceptually separated into relationship dimensions, regime dimensions, social structure dimensions, and two individual items.

A. Relationship Dimensions

Respect
Humanity
Relationships
Trust
Support

B. Regime Dimensions

Fairness
Order
Safety
Well-being
Personal Development
Family Contact
Decency

C. Social Structure Dimensions

Power
Social Life

D. Individual Items

Meaning
Quality of Life

These dimensions then reflect, albeit quite subtly, some serious normative thinking about the sort of institution a prison ought to be, as well as identifying areas on which establishments are known to vary. Our method of discovery was organized conversation, with the aim of establishing general principles of universal applicability in the prison setting. The two main groups of dimensions—relationships and regime—arguably reflected the values of most civic communities. We had not intended to 'do political philosophy', but we were struck by the relevance of the values identified to broader social and political thinking.

Using the above dimensions as a conceptual framework, and following further discussions, we developed a series of questions that addressed the dimension of interest. In the light of the research objective, to generate a measurement tool, we converted each question into statements. The final questionnaire consisted of 102 items, expressed in the form of statements about prisoners' treatment in, and experience of, their current prison. Prisoners responded to each statement on a five-point Likert Scale, from 'strongly agree' to 'strongly disagree'. Scoring varied so that some of the items were worded positively and some were worded negatively.[14] We allocated

---

[14] Sixty-five of the 102 questions in the structured questionnaire for prisoners were worded 'positively' (where agreement with the statement constituted a positive response about the prison) and 37 were worded 'negatively' (where agreement with the statement indicated a negative perception of prison life). This was to minimize acquiescence bias.

each item to a provisional scale, which represented a specific dimension. The items were randomly distributed throughout the questionnaire. We adjusted the placement of items (and eliminated some) based on a detailed statistical analysis of the results, and on the basis of further discussions. The items included and internal reliability scores will be illustrated in our discussion of the results and the analysis in Chapters 5 to 7. The questionnaire was therefore clearly formatted and standardized. The neutral score or 'pass mark' was designated as three, and anything above that was a positive score. Between three and 22 question items were devised for each dimension and the overall dimension score was the composite mean score for all the items, ranging, again, from one to five. Table 3.1 shows the individual items used to measure some of these dimensions.

We devised a structured questionnaire for prisoners; a (less) structured questionnaire for staff; an unstructured 'appreciative protocol' for prisoners; and an unstructured 'appreciative protocol' for staff.

TABLE 3.1.   Statement items for humanity, relationships, and well-being

Humanity	Staff–prisoner relationships	Well-being
I am being looked after with humanity here.	Relationships between staff and prisoners in this prison are good.	The atmosphere in this prison is relaxed and friendly.
I am treated as a person of value in this prison.	Personally, I get on well with the officers on my wing.	My experience of imprisonment in this particular prison has been stressful.
Some of the treatment I receive in this prison is degrading.	Staff are confrontational towards prisoners in this prison.	I can be myself in this prison.
Staff here treat me with kindness.	There is a strong sense, or culture, of 'them and us' in this prison.	I feel tense in this prison.
I am not being treated as a human being in here.	The level of staff interaction with prisoners is low.	My experience in this prison is painful.
		Morale amongst prisoners here is high.
		Generally I fear for my psychological safety.

Our AI interviews continued throughout the survey process, and sought continual clarification of meaning: what does it mean to be treated with respect? Can you give me an example of a time when you have felt fairly treated here? What does it mean to feel safe in a prison? As the literature suggests, concepts like justice and respect are asymmetric, that is, we are clearer about what injustice and disrespect are than we are about what justice and respect *might be* in practice (Lucas 1980; Bottoms 1998). We have good reason to believe (as outlined in Chapter 1) that staff cannot easily 'deliver' things like fairness, respect, decency, without some clear thinking about the precise meaning of the terms. It is clear from events of the early to mid-1990s described in Chapter 1, for example, that staff had widely different visions of what was meant in practice by Woolf's term 'justice'.

All of the research instruments were devised with a considerable contribution from staff and prisoners, and with a much clearer conceptual framework about 'what matters' than in previous studies. Both questionnaires were used in most of the interviews, so that prisoners were interviewed quite openly, and then they were asked to complete our 102-item questionnaire. In each prison, the AI interview schedule was tailored to the establishment and to specific aspects of our discussion, so a different one was used in each prison. The structured questionnaire only changed in minor ways, where questions 'did not work' or better suggestions were made. Examples of the AI protocols for staff and prisoners are as follows:

Appreciative Protocol—HMP Risley: Prisoners

1. Can you tell me about an occasion when you feel you have been treated with fairness and/or respect here?
2. Some days are better than others. Can you tell me what it is like when life is at its best here?
3. Can you describe for me, in as much detail as you like, an occasion when you have been assisted in maintaining contact with your family?
4. What does being treated with humanity in prison mean to you? Can you illustrate that?
5. When are relationships with staff at their best? If you had one wish for staff/inmate relationships here, what would it be?

6. What changes should take place if this were to be the best prison in the country?
7. The Director General has said that he wants prisons to be decent places. What do you think he means? Can you give me an example?
8. Can you tell me about a time when you have received help or support from a member of staff or another prisoner in this prison?
9. Which is the most constructive activity you do/have done in here that will be helpful to you on release? What gives you the most sense of purpose or achievement?
10. What makes you feel safe here? Can you tell me a story about that?

Appreciative Protocol—HMP Risley: Staff[15]

1. Of the many changes that have taken place at Risley over the last twelve months, which has had the most positive effect on the way Risley works? (Probe: Many of these changes have been difficult, but given this . . .)
2. What do you think is the best piece of work you have done this year? Can you think of an occasion when you or a colleague

---

[15] Herzberg used workers' accounts of real events that made them feel good or bad about the job in his studies of worker motivation developed during the 1950s (Herzberg *et al.* 2002). This approach was based on the 'Critical Incident' method developed by Flanagan for the selection of pilots during the Second World War (Flanagan 1954). The authors carried out a content analysis of specific stories of sequences of 'either high or low morale' (Herzberg *et al.* 2002, p. xix). The stories were usually vivid and full of deep emotion (ibid. 20). They found that factors leading to high morale tended to be intrinsic to the work (achievement and feelings of self-actualization) whereas factors leading to low morale tended to be related to external or contextual factors (relations with supervisors, company policy, and administration). This genre of research was motivated mainly by the search to improve worker productivity. Appreciative Inquiry shares some aspects of its methodology (e.g. the use of real examples to illustrate answers) with this approach. It generates vivid stories and deep emotion. Its distinct emphasis on 'the best' experiences is one of AI's more contentious (and important) characteristics. This emphasis is, like the studies that preceded it, linked to its ambition to envision and move towards an improved state of affairs (what gives the organization 'life and energy'; see Liebling *et al.* 1999a).

received proper recognition for good work? How did that make you/him/her feel?

3. Tell me about an occasion where staff were really motivated to make something happen.

4. How do you feel that staff–management relations could be improved? (Probe: Can you give an example of a good experience of staff–management relations to illustrate?)

5. Give me an example of a time when you were asked to contribute your ideas to develop or improve something at Risley. In what way did you feel you benefited through your involvement? How did you feel?

6. Can you think of an occasion where good communications (horizontally and vertically) have assisted you with your work at Risley?

7. Can you think of an example where you worked with people from another department and achieved a better outcome as a result? What could be done to improve the interdisciplinary approach?

8. When have you felt most clear about your role in the prison? Through what experiences has your understanding of your role been best developed? Do you feel this prison has a sense of direction? When have you felt that it has?

9. Can you describe an occasion where your relationship with prisoners has had a positive effect? How did this leave you feeling personally and professionally?

10. If we (the research team) were to come back to Risley in six months' time, what would you hope we might see?

In each prison a random sample of 100 prisoners was interviewed, using the 'appreciative protocol' and the highly structured questionnaire (see Table 3.2 for demographic characteristics).[16] The prisoner samples were systematically randomly selected using the Local Inmate Database System (LIDS) as the sampling frame in each prison (a complete listing of all prisoners in the population by wing/cell location). We 'over-sampled' to allow for voluntary participation and the possibility that some prisoners would be transferred

---

[16] The response rate was high: Belmarsh 93.3%; Holme House 97.9%; Risley 96.2%; Doncaster 98.3%; Wandsworth 96.0%. In total 531 prisoners were approached. Nineteen declined the interview, yielding an overall response rate of 96%.

TABLE 3.2. Prisoner sample demographics

	Belmarsh	Holme House	Risley	Doncaster	Wandsworth
Sample population	83	94	101	114	60 (120)[b]
Ethnic origin[a]					
White British	62.7	97.9	83.2	88.5	60.0
White other	8.4	—	1	1.8	11.7
Black African	4.8	—	—	1.8	5.0
Black Caribbean	8.4	—	2	—	6.7
Black British	6.0	—	8.9	1.8	11.7
Black other	1.2	—	—	0.9	—
Asian Pakistani	1.2	1.1	—	0.9	1.7
Asian Indian	1.2	—	1.0	0.9	—
Asian Bangladeshi	—	—	—	0.9	—
Asian other	—	—	—	0.9	—
Chinese	—	—	1.0	—	—
Other	6.0	1.1	3.0	1.8	3.3
Location					
Ordinary	86.7	86.2	98.0	87.7	66.7
Segregation	1.2	3.2	2.0	2.6	1.7
VPU[c]	8.4	5.3	—	7.9	30
HCC[d]	2.4	2.1	—	1.8	1.7
Other	1.2	3.2	—	—	—
Status					
Remand	35.4	6.4	—	23.7	13.3
Convicted/ unsentenced	17.1	6.4	—	6.1	10.0
Sentenced	47.6	87.2	100.0	70.2	76.7
Regime level					
Basic	3.7	3.2	—	5.3	1.7
Standard	78.0	61.7	37.6	48.7	70.0
Enhanced	18.3	35.1	62.4	46.0	28.3
Average time in the prison	6 months	9 months	11 months	4.3 months	8.5 months
Previous prison experience					
First time in prison	—	11.7	40.6	20.2	30.0
Served time previously in the prison	—	67.0	23.8	63.2	40.0

Notes:
[a] All figures are in percentages. All prisoner populations were adult males, with the exception of Doncaster where 34.2% of those sampled were young offenders (under 21).
[b] 120 prisoners were included at Wandsworth, but half the sample completed a previous version of the questionnaire, for comparative purposes.
[c] VPU: Vulnerable Prisoner Unit.
[d] HCC: Health Care Centre.

or released. In each prison, the 'target' sample comprised approximately 15 per cent of the total prisoner population. Staff selection was less formal and more opportunistic. Between 20 and 49 staff were interviewed in each prison. In both cases, participation was voluntary and this was stressed at the outset. Participants were assured that they were free to decline to answer any individual question or withdraw from the interview at any time. Confidentiality and anonymity were assured in each case. Interviews were, generally, not tape-recorded but detailed notes were taken throughout the interviews, as well as during or after more informal discussions with staff and prisoners. Participants were assured that excerpts from interviews might be used in the final report, but under no circumstances would their names or identifying characteristics be included in any report or publication. The results have been presented without reference to individuals.

We are reasonably confident that prisoners answered our questions as honestly and accurately as they could. The inclusion of the questionnaire as part of a much more discursive interview meant that they had an opportunity to illustrate their views, elaborate on certain questions, or clarify the meaning of any item. They were seen individually and without any staff present. The consistency within establishments and the nature of the differences between them suggest that we were finding 'real' differences in how each establishment was perceived. There was considerable agreement between prisoners' perceptions of the environment and other official and informal views of each establishment. The results suggest that there are important variations between establishments in these key areas of prison life.[17]

We also had access to management information about each establishment. Performance and audit data were collected, and observations aimed at understanding each establishment as 'deeply' as possible were carried out. We spoke regularly but informally to senior managers in each establishment.

Data Analysis

The structured questionnaire data were entered and analysed using SPSS.[18] Each response to the prisoner structured questionnaire was

---

[17] Even where two prisons had the same 'score' on a single dimension, the *composition* of the score (i.e. the contribution made by different items) could be significantly different (see e.g. the differences in the *form of safety* described at Wandsworth and Doncaster, in Ch. 6).   [18] Statistical Package for Social Sciences.

coded on a 1 (strongly disagree) to 5 (strongly agree) scale (this coding was reversed for negatively worded items). This provided a consistent way of reading the results. The higher the value, the stronger the agreement, and the 'better' the quality of life. Any missing answers (of which there were few) were coded as the neutral value of 3.[19] Scores on each dimension for each prisoner were represented as the mean (calculated by dividing the sum of responses to each of the items making up each dimension by the number of items). The overall dimension score for each prison was then calculated as the mean of these values. The data from each of the prisons, then, were subject to a number of descriptive analyses (frequencies, means, standard deviations) and to tests of reliability and item-to-dimension and item-to-item correlations. Logistical regression was used to explore the power of a dimension to discriminate between the establishments.

The questionnaire survey served three possible functions:

(1)   to provide a detailed assessment of life in an individual prison;
(2)   to identify and measure differences between prisons; and
(3)   to measure differences longitudinally (over time) in particular establishments.

If we take Holme House as an example (see Chapter 4) the results closely reflected but also helped clarify the 'feeling' those who knew the prison had about it. It was a generally very good, well-performing

[19] Too high a proportion responding in this category poses a difficulty for interpretation. If most prisoners score '3', this can look more positive than intended. High numbers choosing the 'neutral score' suggests that the question is not meaningful enough to prisoners as a whole (e.g. if they were not engaged in activities we asked about); that it is a difficult question to answer; or that prisoners had mixed feelings (as they often did in relation to staff, taken as a whole). The proportion of prisoners responding in this way was smaller than we initially expected, but varied according to each statement. Among the lowest proportions were the statements, 'The rules and regulations in this prison are made clear to me' (average 8%; and 3.2% at Holme House, for example), and 'I am given adequate opportunities to keep myself clean and decent' (average 4%; and no one at Holme House: all but one chose 'agree' or 'strongly agree'). The highest proportions were for the statements, 'Staff in this prison show concern and understanding towards me' (average 39%), 'Staff in this prison often display honesty and integrity' (average 40%) and 'I don't trust the other prisoners in here' (average 35%). The average proportion of prisoners choosing this category throughout the study was 24.7%. We decided, for the above reasons, to treat the 'neither agree nor disagree' category as data (see Ditton *et al.* 1999: 98 n).

public sector establishment, with high levels of order and safety, good family contact, but lower levels of respect and trust. Staff had a firm 'upper hand' and despite a generally good level of regime delivery, they could be careless with prisoners. Prisoners said, 'I'd say I'm treated fairly, but it's not respect'. This prison was well organized and safe, but staff operated with a 'control model' of penal order with which they felt comfortable but about which prisoners had mixed feelings. It was described as a 'screw's nick' (see Chapter 7).

The survey's second purpose was to identify and measure (sometimes subtle) differences between prisons. We found that prisons differed—that the quality of the prison experience, or the extent of punishment and painfulness, varied significantly, as we shall show in Chapters 4 to 6.

The third purpose of our quality of prison life survey was longitudinal: to measure differences over time in particular establishments. This might be to assess specific interventions or to monitor change over time. We have reported on the findings from this part of our study elsewhere (Liebling and Arnold 2002).

Finally, before we present the substantive findings from the research, we offer some reflections on some of the methodological and 'political' issues arising from how this research came about. We also consider where it may take us in the future. We do this partly so that those who are interested in our results can assess the extent to which we may have influenced the findings. We also attempt this because we want to place on record our aspirations for, and feelings about, the research instrument we have developed. We consider some of the limitations of the methods we have used in Chapter 10.

Reflections on the Research Process: Trust, Influence, and 'Losing Control of the Data'

> [T]o speak a true word is *potentially* to transform the world.
>
> (Bottoms 2000: 33, citing Friere 1972)

Any research in prison is fraught with difficulties of a practical, methodological, moral, and political nature (Bottoms 2000; King 2000; Liebling 2001; McEvoy 2001).[20] We have conducted this

---

[20] There are also difficulties of an emotional nature; see Liebling (1999); Smith and Wincup (2000); Genders and Player (1995); and in other areas of criminological research, Maher (1996, appendix); and Ferrell and Hamm (1998).

work within the formal infrastructure of criminological research (Morgan 2000), which requires that it is relevant, potentially useful, policy-friendly, but also (we assert) high quality. We are 'outside outsiders' (see Reiner 2000: 222) but with unusually enduring inside links and relationships and holding a quasi-official status which is formally supported by the Prison Service.[21] We operate with an implicit understanding that we approach our research tasks honestly, carefully, sometimes diplomatically, and with a studious independence of mind. We are trusted to do the job (a genuine privilege) and therefore encounter fewer constraints than many less experienced (or privileged) researchers. This has its dangers.[22] We had fundamental and scholarly questions in mind at the outset (how *should* we think about the inner life of a prison?), but our work is likely to have influence in the short term, and not always in ways that are to our liking. We built on relationships of trust, established over time, to persuade staff (and prisoners) to open up to us, and to participate in our research. That the research was originally conceived and initiated by us renders it slightly less constrained than might otherwise have been the case (Morgan 2000). We have experienced no constraints on the publication and dissemination of our results. But there is a slightly uneasy and unintended 'fit' between the orientation of our work and the need of senior managers for additional, new, and better performance tools (see Chapters 2 and 8 in particular).[23]

Our intention, as set out earlier in this chapter, was to identify what matters, and then to capture the presence as well as the absence of (for example) respect, so that a prison like Wandsworth could be understood in all its complexity, with its very real (almost unique) combination of poor and reasonable treatment of prisoners. This seemed a more worthwhile exercise than simply branding the prison 'brutal' or 'failing', on the basis of less reliable information. This is not to deny, but to gain greater purchase on, the nature and extent (and meaning) of brutality at Wandsworth. For those staff who were exasperated by the behaviour of their colleagues, and trying to do well in a failing institution, it mattered very much that we were attempting to paint a true and balanced picture.

[21] The Prisons Research Centre was formally established in May 2000 for a period of five years, with Prison Service funding of £18,200 per year.
[22] Constraints *can* be informative and well-intentioned.
[23] The research was funded into a second phase by the Prison Service Standards Audit Unit. See Liebling and Durie in progress.

We believe our work constitutes a strong case for the comparative empirical study of the 'moral performance' of prisons, as we suggest in the concluding chapter. These aspects of prison life do matter, and they can be measured (we elaborate in Chapters 5 to 7). In this sense we are pleased, but nervous, that the Prison Service had, at the time of writing, adopted a slightly shorter, revised version of our survey instrument, and established a new unit that will (with our oversight) continue to carry out these surveys. Some will accuse us of acting in support of the re-legitimization of the prison, which they see as a strategy intended to justify its increasing use (Carlen 2002a; and see Mathiesen 1974 on the distinction between positive and negative reforms). Our agenda, as we see it, is rather different.[24] We argue that our research illuminates and supports the argument that prisons are special moral places (Sparks *et al.* 1996). We can derive from the dimensions of prison life that matter most a conceptual scheme that re-establishes links between the prisoner-as-person/citizen and the state. That how one is treated and regarded matters so much, especially in the prison, forces us to consider the prison not simplistically as an instrument for social exclusion, but as a state-run institution[25] where symbolic and significant constructions of the state's relationship with the individual continue to be forged. Our most direct theoretical contribution lies, we hope, in the attempt we are making to contribute to a reappraisal of 'the essence of imprisonment' (Carlen 2002a). We wish to clarify what it is that makes the prison experience painful, and in some identifiable circumstances, immoral, and the practice of imprisonment always morally dangerous.

The substantive results from the research reported here (and subsequent studies) tell us that prisons differ in their moral performance and that, at best, apparently 'high performing' establishments only deliver 'fairness', 'respect', 'humanity', and 'safety' to a limited extent. The more troubled prisons score very poorly on these value dimensions. There are serious implications of a 'differential delivery of punishment' and a 'differential delivery of pain', with some prisons being experienced by prisoners as much more distressing than others. The implications of our work are that we should seriously reconsider current uses of the prison (see Chapter 10).

---

[24] See further Wiener, who argues, like Garland and others, that not everything is about social control (Wiener 1994: 1–9).   [25] See Chapter 2.

Having made this clear, we are nervous, primarily as scholars in pursuit of cumulative understanding, about elevating social problem-solving to the status of a *primary* goal. As Hecht says: 'If one's goal is to legislate the eradication of a problem, one tends to lose the ability to consider what the individuals who constitute that "problem" are doing and saying and how they see their place in the world' (Hecht 1998: 24).

What we see in our work, now that it is done, is an empirical reminder that human beings yearn to be in social environments which contain certain *virtues* (like fairness and respect; see Duguid 2000; MacIntyre 1999) and that the experience of being in punitive and disrespectful environments is traumatic and damaging. It may be theoretically relevant that certain values emerged (such as the concepts of respect and dignity) whereas others did not (e.g. the concept of honour, an unfashionable, less individualized concept; see Rock 1979: 95; and Berger *et al.* 1977).[26] Our study suggests that we should drastically reduce our reliance on the prison, and that we should reconsider the 'what works' literature against what we know about the relevance of prison environments. There are risks that major distortions are beginning to appear in the way prisons are developing (and expanding), and that the public are being misled into believing that programmes are a 'holy grail', without regard to the *context* in which they are delivered. An anger management programme is surely less useful in a prison environment where prisoners are continually frustrated or intimidated. Without respect, dignity, or fairness, how is 'personal development' possible? In any case, we would argue, as would most of our research participants, these dimensions matter because they matter, and not (just) because they might 'work'. They take us away from resources and politics towards a fundamental set of values: it reminds us that even in a prison, the dignity of the individual remains a right with few limitations (Van Zyl Smit 2002).

---

[26] Berger *et al.* suggest that the hierarchical concept of honour has been replaced by the individual and egalitarian and rights-based notions of dignity and humanity, by modernity, which they suggest includes the declining hold of institutions over the individual (Berger *et al.* 1977: 78–89; also Seligman 1997: 153, who talks of the 'triumph of the private'). 'The concept of honour implies that identity is essentially . . . linked to institutional roles. The modern concept of dignity, by contrast, implies that identity is essentially independent of institutional roles' (Berger *et al.* 1977: 84).

The following chapters seek to construct a framework for things that matter in prison. We take a theoretical and empirical journey with the key values or dimensions of prison life identified in this chapter, drawing on selected literature and on our discussions with staff, prisoners, and others. The language used to name each dimension reflected staff and prisoner views about these concepts. For example, 'personal development' was a much broader concept than 'resettlement', which applied only to prisoners about to leave; 'family contact' could be meaningless if it did not allow for sustained communication of a kind that permitted the relationship 'to develop'; and so on.[27] Each dimension was revised slightly as the analysis of the data proceeded and we reflected on what staff and prisoners were saying in the open interviews about each concept. These adjustments were made mainly in the first establishment selected, but other slight amendments were introduced as we improved our understanding of each concept with every prison studied. Where we have amended dimensions, we have continued to compare 'the old' dimension alongside 'the new', for consistency.

Chapter 4 introduces the five prisons in the main part of our study in more detail.

---

[27] In this case, we have retained the label 'family contact', but the point made about its nature is an important one.

4

Particular Prisons and their Qualities

In the last chapter we described how we set about identifying 'what matters' in prison. There was a surprising but marked consensus between establishments, and between staff and prisoners, about the importance of certain values in prison life. We turn in this chapter to the vexed methodological question of selecting prisons. Is it possible to take five particular prisons, in any research, in order to understand 'the prison'? Always problematic in any prisons research is the question of the representativeness or otherwise of the prisons selected (Liebling 1999). We introduce the five prisons in our study more fully, describing their characteristics, outlining their 'qualities', and drawing on our own data briefly to describe the distinct value cultures in each.

Prisons and their Differences

There are 138 prisons in England and Wales, which range in size from 94 to 1,510 prisoners (East Sutton Park, for women; and Liverpool local prison, respectively). They carry out distinct functions, so there are local prisons (which serve the courts, but also have a resettlement function), training prisons (open and closed; for longer-term prisoners), high security prisons, women's prisons, prisons for young offenders, and prisons for juveniles. Many prisons are multifunctional. There do seem to be some 'essential similarities' between prisons (even across continents), and we shall say more about these 'essential features of the prison' below and in later chapters. Prison staff (and particularly governors) are expected to move between prisons, often on promotion. This means that prisons change (the question of how *much* they change is a key issue) as prisoners, staff, and senior managers come and go. The differences between prisons can be overt and physical (age and architecture are two important variations), organizational (they have different functions and accommodate different populations), and cultural (see Kruttschnitt *et al.* 2000).

There are clear physical demarcations between prisons built during different historical periods, with perhaps the starkest contrast found between prisons built in the Gothic, Victorian style (such as Wandsworth and the original Holloway) during an era of formidable state power and 'social engineering' (Rock 1996: 19); and prisons built since the late 1980s (such as Belmarsh, Holme House, and Doncaster) during a less visible, less certain, and more 'civilized' era (Pratt 2002). Old prisons (which include about half of the existing local prisons) have memories (and passing ideologies) almost seeping from their walls (Rock 1996; Fairweather and McConville 2000). They are deliberately 'extravagant, ornate, imposing, [and] melodramatic' (Rock 1996: 17). The very buildings embody organization and control. Most older prisons have plaques displayed prominently in creaking corridors, on which the names of previous governors (and, sometimes, chief officers) are proudly inscribed. Newer prisons are disguised, unobtrusive, hidden from public view, the architecture, conditions, and language somewhat sanitized (Pratt 2002). Their names no longer locate them (children in local schools sometimes enter competitions to name them imaginatively). New prisons have less emphatic boundaries, and far less dramatic gateways, suggesting a move away from the symbolic trappings of the 'total institution'. Yet they are built further from cities, so may be located in remote and inaccessible places, and their very invisibility constitutes an important exclusionary function (Pratt 2002: 52–9). The power that flows within them seems less visible or overt. But even newer prisons quickly accumulate 'biographies' of their own (Liebling and Price 2001). They are by no means immune to disturbances, interpersonal conflicts, nor to any of the other routine dramas and tragedies of prison life. They, too, are profoundly shaped by dramatic experiences: such as an escape, a suicide, the death of an officer, or a sudden change of role. New prisons are significantly influenced by their geographical location, as a high proportion of the workforce will be locally recruited. The selection of a site on which to build a prison may be for economic reasons, rather than to meet the constantly shifting geographical needs of the prison population. Doncaster and Holme House, for example, were built in areas where unemployment rates were high and land was relatively cheap. The labour force is characteristic of other workforces in those areas. This is particularly so of Doncaster, where staff joined the company by applying for jobs advertised in the local press. It is significant that a prison is disproportionately staffed by ex-miners, redundant middle-managers, or 'ordinary working folk'.

So prisons differ, in significant and numerous ways. On the one hand, we are making a case for the comparative empirical study of the prison. On the other, we are cautioning the reader that, contrary to the typical 'performance league' approach, such comparisons are fraught with difficulties.

We suggested, in Chapter 2, that the *institution* rarely receives as much attention as the prisoners in prison research. What mattered was the prison's *effects on the prisoner*, during and after custody. There are some exceptions, particularly where the focus of the research is on change over time (Bottoms and McClintock 1973; Jacobs 1977; King and Elliott 1977; Rock 1996). Rock's meticulously detailed 'reconstruction' study of Holloway, for example, sketches different evolving narratives about this well-known institution, which has symbolically represented approaches to, expectations of, and hopes for women in prison over most of a century (Rock 1996). Alongside his telling of the policy tale (and the changing criminology of women, to which his account of the institution is intimately connected), he reconstructs the social life of the establishment—the relationships between staff and prisoners, among prisoners, and the 'role releases' practised by both, in formal and informal ways. His account takes place against the changing landscape of the 'mutant' prison—a hybrid between therapeutic treatment and secure containment—over a period when women (and women prisoners) were changing sociologically and ideas about their treatment were confused (Rock 1996: 264). He shows how the design and operation of the prison seemed (albeit unevenly) linked to these changing perceptions of the female offender, from the 'sad' but not dangerous creature of the early twentieth century, to the mad woman of the 1970s to late 1980s, to the 'bad' but reasoning woman of the late twentieth century. Each conception (in practice, not mutually exclusive) shapes the prison, its social life, and its mode of control. This is a model of 'single site' prison sociology—except that, as his account is a historical study, the author wasn't 'there'. Still, he achieves the commendable aim of establishing the prison as an institution composed of multiple layers and shaped by shifting ideologies.

Studies that attempt to compare prisons tend to make their comparisons cautiously (apart from those that are specifically concerned with the evaluation of prison quality, reviewed in Chapter 2). They focus on the research question of central interest: levels of violence (Edgar *et al.* 2002; Sparks *et al.* 1996; Mandaraka-Sheppherd 1986), other threats to order (Sparks *et al.* 1996), fairness (Ahmad 1996), race relations (Genders and Player 1989), regimes (King 1991; King and McDermott 1989, 1995; Hannah-Moffatt 2001), health and health care (Smith 1996), or management style (DiIulio 1987; Kruttschnitt *et al.* 2000). Often the selection of establishments is not made for comparative purposes at all, but is intended to allow the research to cover a wider range of types of establishment, in order to make generalizations (e.g. Genders and Player 1989; although see pp. 99–108). The focus is firmly on policy, or a particular issue, rather than on the exploration of similarities and differences between establishments.

Many studies, then, do not make the prisons visible enough to relate qualities of the institutions to the individual-level variables of interest. Comparisons between prisons are rarely systematic or unconstrained by a narrow field of interest. To develop a rounded sociological understanding of prison life and quality, we need both a deep sociological 'appreciation' of individual establishments *and* a way of making tangible comparisons between prisons in areas of prison life that matter. We have sought, within the constraints of a funded research contract, to delve a little into each prison and to emerge understanding what we could about its mood, ethos, and direction. This was partly achieved by the intensive workgroup exercises described in the previous chapter. We also collected institutional data, made other observations, took copious notes, and talked amongst ourselves and to others about each establishment as the research progressed.

Five Prisons and their Qualities

In the remainder of this chapter, we look a little more closely at the prisons in our study. We want to give something of the feeling of life inside them, as we found it, and as staff and prisoners described it, in order to place the reader in a position to reflect clearly on the results that follow. We shall include a brief account of the overall prisoner evaluations, and staff perceptions, in order to set the scene.

Selection

We selected the five establishments in consultation with the Prison Service. We included four local prisons, one of which is privately managed (and in its second term). The establishments were chosen mainly on the grounds that they had a diverse range of perform-ance, geographical location, and age. The function was similar in four cases, which provided a way of exploring variation between prisons with population type (mainly adult men) controlled for. We wished to focus on local prisons mainly because locals seem to have the widest spread of performance (see Chapter 3). We included one category C training prison, which was 'relevant but different', and introduced a small test of generalizability to other populations. We did not include a women's prison in our sample, as other studies suggested that women might evaluate prisons in a significantly different way (Toch 1992a; Liebling *et al.* 1997). Doncaster held 30 per cent young offenders, which introduced one further test of our survey's relevance to a different population, within the male estate. Table 4.1 shows the function of each prison, their ages, geographical area, average population, and cost per place. It also includes how each establishment's performance, quality, or reputa-tion was described to us by those we asked. Belmarsh and Doncaster were 'core locals', which meant they could accommodate category A prisoners. This accounts for their higher cost per place, as more staff are needed to carry out the more demanding security tasks.

TABLE 4.1.   Selection of establishments: descriptive data

Prison	Belmarsh	Holme House	Risley	Doncaster	Wandsworth
Function	Core local	Local	Category C	Core local	Local
Opened	1991	1992	1964	1994	1851
Area	SE London	N East	N West	S Yorkshire	SW London
Average population	766	943	773	1,072	1,302
Sector	Public	Public	Public	Private	Public
Apparent performance	Mixed	Good+	Poor	Good+	Poor−
Cost per place	£32,309	£15,744	£18,207	£27,658	£19,636

Belmarsh was seen as a mid-performing establishment, with some clear strengths and a marked 'high security' status. It had been built to replace the other, much older, and notoriously traditional London locals. It was built on the same site as a new Crown Court, with an underground connection between them, to enable exceptional risk category A prisoners housed in its large Special Security Unit to appear in court without the drama and expense of police escort vans.[1] Holme House was also new, and was regarded as a 'beacon' public sector prison, with some qualifications. We were told that there was something 'not quite right' about its staff–prisoner relationships, which observers often noted, but on which no one could put their finger. As it was achieving its performance targets, this would be an important test of our research. Risley was regarded as rather troubled and at risk of market-testing. It had been the subject of damning media and Inspectorate attention during the late 1980s in the light of several rooftop disturbances and suicides (it was popularly known at the time as 'Grisly Risley'). Despite some improvements, and several changes of function, it was finding it difficult to shake off this image. Doncaster was regarded as something of a 'star' prison (following turbulent beginnings; see Home Affairs Committee 1997; HMCIP 1996). It was managed by the private sector, under a contract with Premier Prisons. At the time of selection, we were not aware that it would outperform our other prisons on most of our dimensions of interest. But that is to anticipate a complex story. Wandsworth had been singled out for condemnation by the Chief Inspector of Prisons 18 months before our work on this project began, as we described in the previous chapter. However, it was going through a concerted change process.

Performance Data

We requested performance data for each of the establishments from Prison Service Headquarters (see Table 4.2). Key performance target data were also made available to us for the financial year 2001–2 (see Table 4.3). These figures do not allow accurate comparisons to be made, as most data would need to be transformed into rates per 100 prisoners (as shown for the assault rate). However, this would also be an unreliable exercise, as the prisoner population in each

---

[1] Category A prisoners are prisoners who must not escape as they pose a high risk to the community. Exceptional risk category A prisoners have usually been convicted of terrorist offences. See Price (1999).

TABLE 4.2.   Selected performance data for the five research establishments, 1999–2000

Indicator	Belmarsh	Holme House	Risley	Doncaster	Wandsworth
Complaints to Ombudsman	47	7	12	12	21
Assault rate (%)	16.7	3.2	3.0	19.5	5.2
Assaults on prisoners	34	6	13	142	16
Assaults on staff	94	24	10	67	50
Self-inflicted deaths	0	1 (2)	1	1 (2)	3
Rate of positive drug tests (%)	10.5	10.3	15.4	10.2	6.1
Escapes[1]	0	0	1	0	0
Temporary release failures	0	0	0	0	0
Time out of cell	8.8	5.0 (9.5)	9.8	10.3	8.0
Average purposeful activity	12.8	16.6	22.3	18.3	18.4
Association time	21.6	15.1 (15.6)	33.8	37.2	16.8
Offending behaviour programmes	46	63	27	0	72
Sick absence	17.6 (15.8)	14.6 (12.7)	22.8	N/a	17.8
Average hours owed	6.1	6.7	9.6	N/a	5.1
Training days per staff	6.1	4.6 (4.4)	3.5	N/a	7.0

Notes: Figures in parentheses supplied by Headquarters. Figures not in parentheses supplied by establishments or by the Prison Ombudsman.
[1] A KPI escape is counted when the prisoner is not recaptured within 15 minutes, or if the prisoner commits an offence even if recaptured within 15 minutes.

establishment can fluctuate. There are also differences in the populations that could account for some of the differences, so that, for example, Doncaster would be expected to have a higher assault rate, largely due to its younger population. There may be some additional problems with the reliability of the data (such as variation in recording practices).[2] None the less, we can see that Belmarsh and Wandsworth generated significantly more complaints than the other prisons. Belmarsh and Doncaster had significantly higher assault rates (and numbers), although Wandsworth recorded a high number

---

[2] Contract prisons often face larger penalties for not recording (and being found out) than for the reported incident (pers. comm. 2003).

TABLE 4.3.   Key performance target data, 2001

Prison	Belmarsh	Holme House	Risley	Doncaster	Wandsworth
Prison Service Area	High security	North east	Mersey and Cheshire	Yorkshire and Humberside	London
Escapes	0	0	0	2	0
Assaults %	13.7	3.3	2.4	10.2	6.2
Accidents (injuries) %	0.1	0.5	0.3	N/a	0.1
Accidents (all) %	30.9	15.6	11.6	N/a	9.2
Doubling %	0	9.4	3.3	58.7	37.2
Overturned adjudications %	0.3	0.3	0.2	N/a	0.9
Requests and complaints %	59.3	82.4	91.1	N/a	37.9
Self-audit rating in self-harm procedures (1 to 5)	4	4	2	N/a	4
Cost per uncrowded place £	37,588.7	18,554.8	19,739.3	28,124.8	21,516.9
Operational capacity %	91.5	96.5	97.7	97.1	98.5
Staff training[a] (days per year)	4.5	6.4	9.5	N/a	3.3
Staff sickness[a]	20.4	10.4	15.4	N/a	17.1
Mandatory drug testing %	12.7	11.8	23.9	10.5	8.7
Purposeful activity (hours per week)	11.0	15.5	25.2	20.1	17.1
OBP completions[b]	7	84	77	N/a	126
Time unlocked[c] (hours per weekday)	5.8	5.7	11	11.4	7.2
Basic skills in literacy[c]	49	95	90	67	88
Basic skills in numeracy[c]	39	83	103	46	84
CARATs[c]	457	484	180	384	611
Drug treatment[c]	0	128	0	N/a	96
Detoxification[c]	849	948	0	2,143	1,199
Key work skills[c]	139	3,016	1,132	209	116

Notes:
[a] Not available for privately managed prisons.
[b] Not available for some privately managed prisons.
[c] Not available for two of seven privately managed prisons.

of assaults on staff. Risley had the highest rate of positive drug tests and Doncaster had the longest amount of time out of cell for prisoners during the day. Wandsworth and Holme House delivered the largest number of accredited offending behaviour programmes.

The last three figures in Table 4.2 relate to staff, and show that Risley had the highest staff sickness rate (although Belmarsh and Wandsworth were higher than the national average). Staff at Risley were also 'owed the most hours', which means many staff were being asked to work additional hours, to cover for absences. Wandsworth achieved the highest number of training days for staff. Some of this information relating to staff is not available from private prisons, for reasons of 'commercial confidentiality'. These figures relate to the period closest to our fieldwork.

Below, we paint a more detailed pen picture of each prison, in the order that we researched them. Our accounts represent the prisons as they were at the time of our research (2000–1). Like all prisons, they will each look different today. Many of the characteristics we describe below we have seen before (in other research projects) and continue to see again elsewhere (in ongoing work). Our characterizations are intended to provide a way of making sense of the data to follow, in the interests of developing a greater understanding of the nature of prisons in general, and their differences.

HM Prison Belmarsh

Belmarsh is a modern local on the outskirts of south-east London (at Woolwich). It opened in 1991, and was built to a modern galleried design. When it first opened, it gained a reputation for high levels of assaults and a degree of disorder. It housed category A prisoners, which gave it a distinct status and function. This meant that all staff and prisoners were subject to a very rigorous set of security procedures. Its governor was (unusually for a prison of this size, security status, and location) female.

Belmarsh was included in our study because it was regarded as quite a good, modern London local. It had failed its security audit 'during the Whitemoor era', which had dramatically influenced its subsequent direction. It had an average population of 766 prisoners at the time of our research, accommodated in four houseblocks, each of which was divided into three spurs. The houseblocks each had three landings. During an Inspectorate visit in 1998, HMCIP reported: 'The atmosphere on houseblocks was calm. The relationships between staff and prisoners were excellent. Staff were in control but not overbearingly so and took time both to listen to prisoners' worries and queries, and to enjoy a joke' (HMCIP 1998: 1.05).

About a third of prisoners remained locked up for most of the core day. If prisoners had a job, this significantly improved their quality of life: 'The quality of my life is good because of my job; I am out of my cell a lot. Belmarsh is a good remand prison because you get more time out of cell compared to other London locals where there is 23-hour bang up' (prisoner). Most prisoners mentioned the long hours locked up, the rush to achieve what they needed to do when on the wing, and the lack of constructive activities as significant limitations at Belmarsh. Prisoners rated the prison badly on relational items (see Fig. 4.1). Staff attitudes towards prisoners varied from concerned to dismissive:

They treat you like nothing, not like human beings. Even on remand you are treated as if you are guilty, until proven innocent. (Prisoner)

The system is designed to crush your spirit, to stop you 'fighting' . . . Most prisoners just accept the ill-treatments . . . You try and harvest some dignity by beating the system to get something as trivial as an extra towel. (Prisoner)

Prisoners described a 'them and us' culture, and said that staff were generally confrontational, and often shouted, 'but if you give it back, that's the end of your time here'. They could often identify one or two particular officers who behaved differently, and who had helped them: 'Senior officer——is brilliant. He's interested in you and asks every day how you are, if you have any problems come and see me, if you want to make a phone call. He genuinely cares, not just about your offence' (prisoner).

Prisoners on remand, or in prison for the first time, felt in particular that this dismissive attitude was both surprising and unfair (although a handful of convicted prisoners said they did not feel they deserved to be treated with respect or fairness, or to have luxuries in prison). Prisoners said that officers 'look forward to banging you up', and many described their periods of unlock as 'all rush, rush, rush to get things done'. On some items, like feeling safe and being encouraged to maintain contact with their families, prisoners rated the prison favourably. Staff responded promptly to alarm bells, which prisoners found reassuring. Prisoners also told us about incidents whereby staff had intervened effectively in personal crises or serious violence between prisoners on the exercise yard:

They treat me as an individual. I am a cleaner so I have got to know them better. I had a knife pulled on me in the exercise yard. About ten black guys. I robbed them outside but they were in here and I was surrounded. Five staff got me off the yard—I told them the trouble and they brought me up here, moved me to another houseblock, and in with a new cell mate. They went out of their way to help me, and to make sure I was safe and moved. (Prisoner)

Belmarsh was (like many prisons) in flux, with major strengths in security, order, and control, but with a related cynicism in staff attitudes towards prisoners. Prisoners felt they were regarded 'as a nuisance'. Staff reported considerable confidence in the degree of control they held, and some pride in (for example) the prison's induction procedures and its therapeutic community. Belmarsh was struggling to incorporate other, more relational dimensions into its regime, according to its (relatively new) governor. The prison was clearly 'over-achieving' on security ('Belmarsh does security with knobs on . . . we are better than the security manual', senior manager), with disproportionate pride and staff time invested in its security function. It was very difficult to 'persuade a prison' (i.e. its staff) to do less of something prestigious and significant, like security. It was especially difficult for this to become the central message from a new senior management team to an experienced group of staff. The staff were proud of their security record, and knew that Belmarsh had a high status within the Service (and in the local area) mainly because of its security function.

At the time of our research, senior managers were perceived rather negatively by staff. They described the senior management group as split, with something of an ideological rift between two interpretations of the role of the staff (e.g. as 'carers' or 'disciplinarians'). There seemed to be little trust for the senior management group, although this feeling was expressed together with a genuine wish for more contact and communication (suggesting higher levels of trust than staff were willing to admit). Staff complained that the governor was not visible enough.[3]

---

[3] Both of these issues may have been exacerbated by some complex feelings (some expressed, others implicit) in a nearly all male environment about the governor being a woman (particularly in this case as the 'ethic of care' is widely regarded as essentially *feminine* and the 'ethic of security and discipline' is regarded as highly *masculine*). These 'resistances to female authority' were complex, but have been documented elsewhere (see Cawley 2000).

Staff were energetic and passionate about the prison and its future. They talked a lot about their work with prisoners, and about extending trust and respect to them. They gave us examples of help they had offered, and of suicide attempts averted, tensions reduced, conversations held, and efforts made to sort out problems. They were keen to develop more 'throughcare' and 'resettlement' work. There was some evidence that the prison had improved recently and that 'there's less growling; attitudes are better' (prisoner). Staff welcomed being *asked to do things*. Despite complaints from prisoners about staff attitudes, staff were much closer to prisoners than to their senior managers (inevitably given the nature of their work, but more so than at other prisons). Mixing with prisoners was 'the bread and butter of their work': 'With inmates, they have to trust us and we have to trust them. It does exist between us. For example, it might be a cleaner who rings the alarm bell when a member of staff is threatened' (officer).

Staff described occasions when they had been thanked by prisoners—often in front of other officers—for work they had done. But overall, officers were far closer to each other than they were to prisoners. Officers were deeply loyal to each other. We were told continually that teamwork, backing, and practical means of support were important qualities staff looked for in each other. There were relatively high sick levels, a lack of expressed loyalty to senior management, and a relatively weak regime. Life at Belmarsh was energetic but divided: prisoners, staff, and senior managers all saw their environment through 'them and us' lenses—with staff in the unfavourable position as 'the other' from above and below. Some staff attitudes reflected a resentment of this position and a seeking of refuge in security and 'maintaining the upper hand'. Some prisoners said their one wish for the prison was that the Prison Service would 'privatize it'.[4]

HM Prison Holme House

Holme House had been purpose-built on Teesside (in Stockton-on-Tees), 'one of the most economically and socially deprived areas in the country' (HMCIP 2002c: 1). The prison opened in 1992, and

---

[4] A market test of Brixton was under way at the time of our research, which in the event did not attract any private sector interest. Prisoners saw the onset of competition as a challenge to the worst aspects of staff attitudes in many London local prisons.

had an average population of 943 at the time of our research. It was the largest prison in the north-east. It was not a typical local prison. There were relatively few prisoners on remand; the length of stay was longer than usual, and there were significant numbers of category C prisoners who were nearly all allocated work. It was a more 'active' and training-oriented establishment than our category C prison (see below). It was modern and clean. This contributed to an overall positive evaluation by prisoners.

The prison operated at about 100 prisoners below its certified normal accommodation (CNA),[5] which encouraged the Prison Service to send regular overcrowding drafts from the 'wrong parts of the country', and it provided a few places 'on loan' for the Immigration and Nationality Department (HMCIP 2002c). The residential units were known as 'Bullingdon model' design, although there was an additional houseblock ('Bedford Unit') which operated as the category C unit, and a sixth houseblock which included a small therapeutic community for substance abusers. There was a separate health-care centre and segregation unit. Most of the prisoners were unemployed on arrival, and many were heavy drug users.

Holme House was well ordered and organized (in terms of consistency of regime delivery) and safe. Staff felt very much in control. The staff were described in the most recent Inspectorate Report as 'professional but formal' (HMCIP 2002c: 12). The prison had a 'control' model of operation, and prisoners expressed some reservations about this basic orientation. Staff were very prisoner-focused and often mentioned their desire to be involved in 'rehabilitative' work. Overall, staff seemed pleased to be working at Holme House, and they talked in very positive terms about their managers.

Prisoners felt they were generally treated fairly at Holme House. There were complaints of discrimination or unfairness in the distribution of privileges (especially televisions). Some prisoners felt there was an element of favouritism and differences in treatment depending on offence (those convicted of drug offences felt particularly disadvantaged, as well as those on the vulnerable prisoner unit). There was little complaint by prisoners about the restrictions

---

[5] This had considerable benefits for prisoners who had, as a result, more access to activities. This situation changed with the rise in the prison population in 2002 (see Ch. 9).

security levels imposed on their quality of life, although several category C prisoners mentioned the compromise between being located nearer home and being transferred to a category C prison with its increased freedom, work, and opportunities for release on temporary licence.

Despite its role as a local prison there were considerable opportunities to participate in activities, including gym (which offered several courses and qualifications), an offending behaviour course (problem-solving training), education, and work. However, the majority of available work was domestic (cleaning on wings) and, as a result, prisoners were critical of the lack of opportunities to gain what they considered to be relevant work experience for their release.

Relationships between prisoners at Holme House were good. A high proportion were from the local area and therefore knew each other. Many had been in Holme House in the past (some had not been in any other prison) and several mentioned that they knew some of the staff from outside. Relationships between staff and prisoners were more complex. They seemed better when there had been an opportunity to build up over time, either as a result of prisoners staying for a lengthy period (many served their whole sentence at Holme House after a period on remand), or because individual prisoners had been in and out of the prison over the years since it had opened. Some prisoners complained about staff attitudes and the language used by some officers. There was some discrepancy between staff and prisoner perceptions: staff considered relationships between staff and prisoners to be good but prisoners had mixed feelings. Staff thought relationships were 'right' as a result of the control they had. Prisoners thought there was a lack of respect and help in some areas. Some prisoners chose not to interact with staff, or ask for help from anyone other than prisoners. There was a consensus that staff had considerable power and that the level of control they exerted was significant in the prevention of bullying.

One of the major issues at Holme House was the availability of drugs, which had a negative influence on prisoner relationships and the atmosphere in the prison. A large number of prisoners were described as 'smack heads'. Drug use brought about problems of withdrawing on arrival, and of getting into debt and bullying. Doing time at Holme House was 'easy', although there was a prevailing view that it was 'a screws' jail'.

Staff were friendly, helpful, and displayed an assured confidence in their work. 'This place is so well organized and staff have so much control. There are no confrontations like we used to have. I've only had one lock-on in nine and a half years and to be honest that's down to management' (officer).[6]

Many commented on the success of Holme House. One of their main 'wishes for the prison' was that this good work would continue.

Holme House is actively anti-drugs, actively pursuing more time out of cell for prisoners . . . and has good staff–prisoner relationships . . . Staff here want the best for Holme House, for prisoners, and for staff. (Senior officer)

If I have to work, there is nowhere else I would rather come to work than here. It is a good prison. It's as good as you're ever going to get. (Officer)

HM Prison Risley

Risley was located in the north-west between Warrington and Manchester. It opened as a remand centre for men and women in 1964. In 1990, it ceased to function as a remand centre and converted to an all-male category C training prison. The women were transferred to nearby Styal prison in 1999. It held 773 prisoners at the time of our research. Risley occupied a rather decrepit site, despite the addition of new buildings. It had some new 'living blocks' (LB1–LB3), constructed in the early 1990s, and some additional 'quick build' accommodation (A Wing), built in 1995, which had allowed the prison to expand and also to begin to establish a 'new culture'. The prison operated an 'integrated regime', that is, the vulnerable prisoners were mixed with other prisoners, throughout the prison. This was with mixed success. About 130 of the prisoners located in Risley were sex offenders.

The most recent Inspectorate Report described Risley as 'anti-governor, anti-change, and anti-work' (HMCIP 2001*b*, preface) and said it had a 'very heavy Prison Officers' Association background'. The newly arrived governor was engaged in a 'battle for the hearts and minds' of staff. The prison was simply not focused on 'the treatment of or conditions for prisoners' (ibid.). According to the Inspectorate:

It was clear that the Governor enjoyed the full support of his Area manager, and that, in addition to the vast majority of his management team, he

---

[6] A lock-on is where an officer uses 'Control and Restraint' and puts on a wrist lock.

already had a number of staff behind him, notably those who realised that the old reputation was unsavoury, and that the old practices and attitudes have no place in today's Prison Service. (HMCIP 2001b: 2)

The prison had a 'lax attitude to security' (HMCIP 2001b: 3), to the extent that the new governor had requested a security audit on his arrival, only to find that the report was 'one of the worst that had ever been written on a prison' (ibid.). This had shaken staff: 'who were made to realise that, in addition to not doing nearly enough to look after their prisoners with the humanity mentioned in the Prison Service's Statement of Purpose, they were failing in their first duty which was to keep them in custody securely' (HMCIP 2001b: 4).

Risley was an interesting establishment because of its reputation, the higher than expected prisoner ratings found in our survey, and because of the strength of staff feeling about their condition. The prison had been threatened with market-testing, and a new 'high flying' governor had been 'brought in to sort it all out'. Staff were finding the change process, particularly the fact that there were major threats underlying it, difficult. Severe cuts were being made to staffing numbers, and expectations about what staff might do during a typical shift were increasing. Prisoners did not rate the prison badly, and many spoke sympathetically about the position of the staff. They appreciated the relatively generous time out of cell, but there was little constructive activity available, leading to boredom on the wings. There were high levels of association and prisoners appreciated the availability of televisions.

Some of the prisoners' dissatisfaction with Risley was related to the change process it was going through—which staff and prisoners both 'blamed on the new governor'. The prison had recently introduced new procedures for movement around the prison, for example, and this, and the new emphasis on security generally, was 'stirring everyone up'. The highly prized levels of freedom and trust were under threat ('This place is like Ibiza in the summer—lots of sunbathing outside the governor's office. That's all got to stop'; governor). Many changes had been introduced in quick succession, which left the prison feeling organizationally chaotic. Prisoners and staff complained of not knowing where they stood. Prisoners complained of inconsistency and unfairness. Despite these changes, a significant number of prisoners said that the level of 'freedom' they had at Risley was one of the best things about the prison.

Relationships between staff and prisoners were comfortable but 'remote'. Staff had a *laissez-faire* approach to prisoners, which resulted in good but undirected interactions. Officers expressed confusion about whether they were 'jailers' or 'social workers', and there were divisions on this matter. Staff did not use their authority effectively. Prisoners described a lack of positive interaction, and a lack of staff presence (this was sometimes put in the positive sense that 'staff leave you alone and don't hassle prisoners'). There were, however, plenty of examples of constructive interventions, particularly by personal officers. Generally, relationships could not be described as wholly positive nor negative, nor as particularly helpful or supportive, yet they were far from obstructive and intimidating. At their worst, relationships between staff and prisoners were characterized by mutual indifference, or comfortable animosity ('you're here, we're here, and none of us are happy'), yet neither saw the other as their main source of dissatisfaction. Many prisoners identified a member of staff who was helpful and who 'did their best' under the current circumstances. Staff were regarded by prisoners as the 'unwilling victims' of a new mode of working, who were themselves unsure of the rules.

Staff had very good relationships with each other, and with their line managers. They held the governor (a young, bright, ambitious man with a reputation for toughness) accountable for most of their anxieties about the prison and its future. Risley had been threatened with a market test, which meant that the future depended on how well, or whether, the governor could lead the prison out of a long period of 'underperforming'. There were major concerns about the transition period but an underlying willingness to take the prison forward in a new direction, and high levels of loyalty to the establishment. There was also a certain amount of fear, and a lack of trust of the senior management team. Jobs were threatened. There was more POA activity and influence than we had witnessed in other establishments, which made for difficult relationships between staff and management. Many of the staff were eager to point out to us that their own views and wishes were not necessarily represented by the POA. But staff had grievances about reductions in staffing levels, which negatively affected their perceptions of safety. They complained of a lack of information and consultation, despite some best efforts made by the governor. Many of the staff felt that the changes being made were necessary. Others welcomed them, but they were less comfortable about the style in which changes were taking place. There was a lot of talk of 'too many people in ivory towers'. Some staff were reluctant to see 'home-grown' programmes and activities with no accreditation status discontinued with the promise of more formal programmes to be conducted in the future. There was some 'in-fighting' at middle management level and an 'alliance to maintain the status quo' ('Even the senior management team are "locked in" to how Risley is'). There seemed to be a lack of 'ownership' amongst staff of the establishment's quality or direction.

Risley had not made the transition from its role as a mixed local to its role as a category C training or resettlement prison. There was a lack of any sense of identity or cohesion in the prison, and a lack of focus on work, training, or preparing prisoners for release. Uncertainty about the future had unsettled staff.

HM Prison and YOI Doncaster

> HMP and YOI Doncaster remains a good prison, affording good value for the public money ... and from which many examples of good practice have been, and could be, transported into the Prison Service. All concerned can ... take pride in their achievements.
>
> (HMCIP 1999e: 8)

Doncaster is a modern 'new generation design' prison located in the centre of Doncaster, in South Yorkshire. It opened in 1994, and was built to accommodate 771 sentenced and remand prisoners but often held more (at the time of our research it held 1,072 prisoners). Thirty per cent of its population were young prisoners, including juveniles. It held a small number of category A prisoners, which made it a 'core local' (like Belmarsh) with higher security ratings than other locals (which were normally designated category B). The establishment was operated by Premier Prisons, and was in its second term at the time of our research. Unusually, it had only had one director since it opened. The inspection report cited above included some comments from prisoners that 'staff were OK but were easy to manipulate' (HMCIP 1999e: 2.1).

Prisoners were keen to communicate to us how strongly they felt about the regime at Doncaster. Their views were unusually positive.

There were three aspects of prison life at Doncaster that made it 'stand out' for prisoners: the nature of the regime, that is, the amount of time spent out of cell (prisoners said they 'did not feel caged'); the quality of the physical environment; and being treated with respect by the staff on their wing. It was noticeable that prisoners expressed their approval of the regime using terms like 'civility', 'respect', 'trust', and 'care'. The whole prison was, according to prisoners, 'underpinned by trust, respect, responsibility, self-worth, dignity, participation . . . and access to senior management'. Doncaster's regime was outstanding in this respect, and the attitude of staff to prisoners was markedly different from anything we had seen so far in the public sector.

> This is the best prison I've ever been in . . . you notice the difference straight away . . . they don't use C and R (control and restraint) techniques, they walk you to the seg . . . they go out of their way to help you . . . there's no atmosphere when you stand next to an officer . . . there are no barriers, they are willing to listen . . . you can be an individual . . . this works . . . even the way they word your sentence plan . . . you get your dignity, the way they speak . . . there's nothing to resist, rebel against . . . it changes you, trust builds up . . . we get more help, with less staff, reports are done on time . . . it changes the way you think. They let you develop. This is a good place to leave from . . . I never give them any grief . . . you flourish . . . they try to make you feel human. (Prisoners, group discussion)

There are three important caveats to this picture. First, the lower internal reliability scores for our dimensions at Doncaster suggests that some contradictions may have appeared in the interviews (see Chapters 5 to 7). Secondly, although the dimension scores were significantly higher at Doncaster when compared with those at the other prisons we studied, they still had an upper limit, and these scores did include some negative evaluations. Thirdly, staff expressed some fears, and prisoners some concerns, about staffing levels, occasional neglect of searching procedures, and a feeling that staff were not being sufficiently financially rewarded despite an exceptionally committed approach to their work. The prison was undergoing a renegotiation of the terms of its contract at the time of our research, and the director was under pressure to make savings. Staff reacted to this prospect with indignation and fear ('So this is our reward!'). From turbulent beginnings ('when staff were green'), the prison had stabilized over a number of years, until a recent expansion of the regime and some reductions in staffing had 'stretched staff' again:

In 1994 it was terrible. I used to cry when I put my uniform on. We were receiving 30 prisoners per day over two or three weeks. You didn't know when you'd go home. After the seven weeks' training swarms were leaving. We had no back up or support from the public sector. But then it all came together from 1995. Management started to appear, we got our regimes in order, staffing started to level out, there were some promotions and we started to get support from those who had been in our shoes 18 months earlier. We had some intensive control and restraint level three training. We knew what we were doing. By 1997, prisoners started to appreciate Doncaster and so did other HMP prisons. They could see we were doing a good job with half the staff. The hostility we had been getting in reception from other staff started to improve. (Prison custody officer)

There were some implications for Doncaster of a newly opening prison elsewhere in the country. Some transfers of the more experienced staff to this prison (not all of whom went willingly) left Doncaster depleted, and many of the remaining staff demoralized. Despite these feelings, levels of staff pride in their work, and their treatment of prisoners, were exceptional. Relationships between departments were very co-operative.

Relationships among prisoners, and between staff and prisoners, were very good (although they were not necessarily 'right'; see later). Staff were seen as generally down-to-earth, helpful, and friendly. Prisoners described a high level of interaction with staff, which was most notable during association times, when both groups participated in wing recreational activities. The atmosphere was relaxed and a good-natured humour was present much of the time. This level of interaction seemed to rule out a 'them and us' culture. Prisoners said that staff were 'the same as us': they were from the local area, were 'normal' people with problems just like them, and they were 'just doing their job'. Prisoners could see 'beyond the uniform' and felt that staff could talk to them as people. Staff, generally, did not shout or swear at prisoners or talk down to them. They addressed them by their first names or a nickname. Prisoners were eager to give us examples of being listened to, being treated with respect, being given responsibility, and of the constructive feel to the prison. They said there was no 'hostility' in staff and no 'falseness'. Some prisoners were dissatisfied with staff attitudes, complaining that staff were not always helpful. Others said that being in prison was still difficult and painful, despite the efforts of the staff to be 'easygoing'. One member of staff commented that, 'We were giving in to them a bit. One prisoner told us we had to "say no" more!'.

The 'basics' (visits, activities, and association) were delivered to a high standard at Doncaster. This meant that prisoners experienced few problems in maintaining contact with family and friends. Because they spent a large proportion of time out of their cells, in association on the wings, prisoners had ample opportunity to use the telephones. The opportunities for visits were generally praised (although there was still agreement that the amount of time for visits was not long enough) and prisoners felt they could buy an adequate number of telephone cards. In addition, prisoners were provided with two second-class letters per week. The prison was modern and clean and had good facilities. Prisoners considered the regime to be generally fair, with some exceptions: the process of being 'written up' (put on report) by staff was unfair; the prison was slow in responding to applications; and there were some petty rules that were inconsistently applied.

Prisoners at Doncaster described a relaxed environment, although they also described incidents of assault on the wings. Others mentioned the low number of fights that had occurred in the preceding months and the 'chilled out' atmosphere. Bullying appeared to be dealt with—if not by removal of the perpetrator onto a separate unit by staff, then it was 'sorted out' amongst the prisoners themselves. A high level of drug use was reported on some wings, and we sometimes wondered whether prisoners had taken drugs before some of the interviews. The availability of drugs led to an increase in tension and prisoners feeling less safe (they were more likely to become involved in trouble as a result of debts and fights over supplies).

One of the most frequently heard criticisms of the regime at Doncaster was boredom; much of the time out of cell consisted of periods spent on the wings and there were limited opportunities for constructive employment. Although many prisoners had a job in the prison, these jobs normally consisted of wing-based domestic work that was spread thinly to 'occupy' a larger group than necessary. The work was therefore completed in a short period of time and prisoners returned to the general 'hanging out' they felt characterized the prison. Education and a daily opportunity to attend the gym were appreciated.

There were a few observations by staff and prisoners about the extent of leniency in the regime and whether discretion was kept within appropriate boundaries. Staff–prisoner relationships were unusually close—there may have been some manipulation of staff by prisoners. There was insufficient supervision by staff (and, arguably, of staff), which led to a chaotic feel to wing life. At times, the prison had a 'traditional dispersal' feel to it—a liberal regime within a secure perimeter—with the attendant risks of potential appeasement or conditioning. Prisoner demands were almost always met, and as a result, their expectations were very high. It was an 'easy jail' for prisoners, with little direct challenging of their behaviour. However, as prisoners said, this 'worked', and sometimes did bring about what seemed to be a genuine transformation in prisoner attitudes and behaviour. Staff sometimes expressed a wish for a more structured approach to earned privileges. In general, they commented that 'structures and systems' were not their forte.

Staff had been successfully persuaded by a dedicated Director (who had opened the prison and still worked there after nearly ten years) that respect gets returned ('prisoners respect the prison, and they respect staff'). Staff were good-humoured, enthusiastic, and proud of their work, and of the way prisoners related to them.[7] They seemed clear about their objectives, and delivered an impressive regime in a non-authoritarian style. They were clear that 'the Director's main commitment is fairness and decency'. Many staff also observed that 'he's passionate about the place . . . goes out of his way to help you'. However, they felt undervalued ('the culture here is all about prisoners, not staff') and thought there was some tension in the prison. They regarded themselves as doing 'a good job', but several were contemplating leaving, for better paid work elsewhere.[8] A relatively high turnover meant that experienced staff were often moving on. Staff discussed with us a deliberate attempt

---

[7] One of the striking differences in our workgroups at Doncaster was that several of the staff who participated took notes throughout our exercises and discussions. This did not happen in any of the other prisons, and presumably reflects a cultural difference between public and private sector officers.

[8] Some staff expressed a desire for the prison to be 'taken over by the public sector', as their pay and conditions of service would improve.

not to take their feelings of being 'hard done by' on to the wings ('we'd be back to fighting them every day').

There was some similarity between Doncaster and Risley in that there was a risk that staff–prisoner relationships were becoming more mutually supportive than staff–management relationships, as a new phase in Doncaster's life (a renewed bid) required 'even more, for less'. Staff said 'we get all our praise and recognition from prisoners'. There were several comments (also heard in other prisons) made about 'not wanting to give the Director bad news', in the 'new performance culture'. On the other hand, we were told that 'senior management really care about the prison', and 'they are very close to the ground'; 'it's all first names here, all the way up to the Director'.

The 'Doncaster spirit' involved little emphasis on paperwork or formality. There were high numbers of female staff, with male and female roles easily accepted, and not a hint of 'macho posturing', by staff or prisoners. The whole prison saw itself as 'like a family'. There were areas where questions of balance, or 'professionalism', required further thought. For example, prisoners knew that cell searches were carried out relatively infrequently, but commented enthusiastically and in contrast to their previous experiences, that, 'when I had my cell searched, they left it cleaner than I left it! I shall look forward to my next search in two weeks!' We were surprised by Doncaster, and intrigued to understand more.

HM Prison Wandsworth

Wandsworth was described by the Chief Inspector of Prisons in 1999 as a 'thoroughly unhealthy prison'. It opened in 1851 in south-west London (as Surrey County Prison). The prison is built in the tradition of a large, radial design characteristic of the Victorian era, with six wings (A to F) and a 'centre', and an additional three wings (G to K) and a centre, in a second, smaller radial block. Each wing had four landings, so each was known as the 'ones', the 'twos', and so on. The wings were large, with a few small pool tables and the occasional table-tennis table strewn along the centre corridor of each. The prison had an average population of 1,302 at the time of our research. A substantial refurbishment programme had begun, but was incomplete, so that some of the wings were in a much better state of repair than others. The prison had an imposing gateway entrance, and the buildings had a typical sombre and intimidating feel, with pigeons everywhere, barbed wire above the walls, and tiny, barred windows out of which prisoners shouted to visitors and to each other. It suffered from many of the problems associated with older, large London locals: a culture of 'resistance' to change and strict discipline. The staff were described in a follow-up inspection as 'dominating and intimidating' (HMCIP 2000*b*, preface). The Prison Officers' Association had a high profile at the prison (with posters and leaflets prominently displayed), and the industrial relations climate was turbulent. The segregation unit was described as 'filthy' and 'reprehensible' (ibid.).

We had conducted a brief survey at Wandsworth shortly after this Inspectorate visit (as described in Chapter 2), so our survey exercise in 2001 was a 'return visit' and we had some prior knowledge of what the prison had been like before. Following the Inspectorate Report, an impressive new governor had been 'drafted in', additional resources had been found, and an 'action planning' exercise (including a full AI) had been carried out. There seemed to be a general consensus that the atmosphere was more relaxed than it had been when we first visited.[9]

Prisoners complained about the lack of time out of cell and activities; the limited opportunities to use the telephone, have a shower, clean their cell, change their clothes, or attend education, the gym, work, and courses, and the lack of association and exercise (which was often cancelled). The amount of time prisoners spent locked up ('bang-up') was described as inhumane and 'against human rights'. The lack of staff meant that regime delivery was inconsistent. Prisoners disliked this inconsistency and complained of 'not knowing where they stood'. The reverse was the case in relation to the rules relating to expected behaviour, which were made very clear.

One of the basic complaints at Wandsworth was the distribution of privileges (e.g. the provision of portable televisions on some wings and pocket-sized hand-held televisions which required batteries on others). The IEP scheme was inconsistent; prisoners did not know what they had to do to get the enhanced regime. They felt there was an element of favouritism in moving up a level; it was easy to get a 'negative slip under your door', but to get a positive

---

[9] There were areas of good practice: for example, the 'Care and Separation Unit' (the segregation unit), the PE Department, the RAPt Course, the VPU, and visits. However, prisons with only 'areas of good practice' may be neglecting important basic regime provisions.

report was unrealistic (you had to stop a fight, save someone from suicide, or help staff in some way). Everything was done 'by application' and replies were slow, especially in response to requests for work and education. The restricted and unpredictable regime increased prisoners' perceptions of the likelihood of favouritism. Getting anything was left open to the discretion of officers.

The emphasis in the establishment was on order and control, particularly during prisoner movements. There was evidence of two types of relationships: some were supportive, helpful, and friendly. These relationships were reported by prisoners who were trusted and liked, and who worked on the wings. Others were 'unresponsive', and were characterized by indifference, a lack of sympathy and concern, and a general disregard (or neglect), which were experienced by prisoners who had minimal contact with staff: 'I don't keep relationships with staff, you don't have a relationship with them unless you are working as a cleaner, then they talk to you in a friendly manner, laugh and chat, so then you form a relationship. Otherwise you're just a name and number' (prisoner).

Cell bells were only supposed to be used in emergencies but were often used as the only means of communicating with staff (to ask to be let out; or to signal some distress). This contributed to a cycle of staff neglecting to answer cell bells, and prisoners resorting to their use even more.

Prisoners felt safe as a consequence of the strict regime and the limited opportunities to interact with each other, especially on the wings. However, some prisoners said their sense of safety depended on who their cell mate was. There were suggestions that some prisoners did not feel safe with staff:

I feel safe from prisoners . . . from staff, no comment. I don't feel very safe . . . it's not so much the inmates you have to worry about, it's the staff, and it's not a small minority . . . a few staff here are over-the-top in handling inmates . . . Like sometimes, if you say something to them I'll think 'I bet they come in and do something later', you know, start getting heavy . . . Bullying, there is hardly any from prisoners but quite a lot from staff . . . some staff overstep the mark. (Prisoners, group discussion)

These feelings seemed to be founded partly on the reputation of Wandsworth. Few of our interviewees reported either witnessing or personally experiencing any violence. However, one prisoner reported, in interview, that he had been beaten by an officer several weeks beforehand.

Prisoners reported a fairly relaxed atmosphere in the prison despite their limited opportunities to use their time in a constructive way. This was due to the changing attitudes of staff towards them, which were improving. Staff were more respectful and prisoners expressed a view that staff were trying to do their best.

The biggest grievance for staff at Wandsworth was staffing shortages: lack of staff resulted in restricted regime delivery. Staff felt bitter, weary, and undervalued, and therefore unsupported and unappreciated in their work by management. Staff expressed a sense of frustration in that not even prisoners' basic entitlements were being provided and that other operational, security, and administrative tasks, such as searches and sentence planning, were either being neglected or were not being achieved to a satisfactory standard. This led to a feeling among staff that they were being prevented from 'doing their job'. Relationships with prisoners suffered as a result: tensions arose from prisoners' sense of injustice at the nature of the regime.

Staff felt that management did not understand the reality of the job. They did not feel they were listened to or consulted. They wanted (even) stronger leadership, more consultation, open and honest communication, and 'stability, commitment and visibility' from the senior management team.

Despite these frustrations, there was some strength in the camaraderie, trust, and loyalty amongst officers. Satisfaction was derived from the relationships between staff, from teamwork, commitment, and pulling together to achieve in the face of adversity, from 'getting through against almost impossible odds'. A recent trend of high numbers of staff leaving ('in droves') in the face of local recruitment campaigns within policing and the railways was undermining this sense of 'team spirit': 'I joined because I like dealing with people. The skills in this job are interpersonal—it attracts people who like dealing with people. So if you leave to be a train driver, you'd miss that' (officer).

Staff satisfaction came from achieving specific things for, and communicating with, prisoners ('I've achieved association today and we've not achieved that for three weeks; today we had the staff to do it'), although opportunities for effective prisoner contact were limited. When staff described their vision of how they would like to see the prison develop, there was a heartfelt consensus:

> The governor would be able to do all the things he wants to do; the regime for prisoners, they would get more. Staff morale would go up. There shouldn't be three or four hundred prisoners on the yard—more than once in the last two years we have retreated to a place of safety. More staff would mean a wider regime and not the tension we see when they are banged up 23 hours a day, so you won't have the arguments and frustration building up. (Officer)

Staff wanted to deliver 'the proper regime'—searching and sentence planning, the personal officer system, and a speedier response to applications. They talked of delivering a 'richer regime', with more contact with prisoners, and more constructive programmes. There was a strong feeling that the establishment was on the 'up':

> The atmosphere is now much more relaxed; there is less tension between staff and inmates. Control and discipline are good and there is the right balance between discipline and friendly relationships with the prisoners much happier as a result. That is progress . . . and would be even more marked if staff shortages could be solved. At the moment sentence plans and parole reports are done on the hoof—which is unfair to prisoners. (Senior officer)

> There have been positive changes—sanitation and health and safety, and we've certainly got more help-groups for prisoners, we recognize the drugs problem. Four wings have been revamped and that makes a big difference, the living conditions. (Officer)

Prison Staff Perceptions of the Distribution of Power

Staff at Holme House reported a generally better 'quality of life' than their peers at Doncaster. Staff at Belmarsh and Holme House reported high levels of order, and staff at Holme House reported high levels of safety and well-being. Staff at Doncaster reported lower levels of fairness and loyalty, perceptions that were arguably related to their private sector status (see Table 4.4, and Chapter 8).

The way staff talked about who had how much power in the establishment arose often in conversation, and it had arisen in our search for 'things that matter', so we included several questions on power and authority in the staff questionnaire. Only the staff at Holme House reported that officers had the right amount of power and responsibility. Half the staff at Belmarsh, Doncaster and more than half at Wandsworth thought they had 'not quite enough' or

TABLE 4.4.   A comparison of staff views on the quality of prison life in five prisons: 'dimension' scores

Dimension	Belmarsh n=19	Holme House n=24	Risley n=49	Doncaster n=33	Wandsworth n=17
Respect	2.98[b]	3.26	3.33	3.64[a]	3.50
Humanity	3.39	3.79[a]	3.27[b]	3.46	3.50
Support	3.66	4.05[a]	3.26[b]	3.58	3.41
Relationships	3.34[b]	3.94[a]	3.51	3.71	3.76
Trust	2.90[b]	3.11[a]	3.01	3.03	3.08
Fairness	3.62	3.91[a]	3.62	3.47[b]	3.54
Order	4.38[a]	4.38	3.36[b]	3.80	3.46
Safety	4.56	4.67[a]	4.37	4.12	3.53[b]
Tension/well-being	3.03[b]	4.32[a]	3.21	3.15	3.38
Development	3.13	3.42[a]	2.30	2.97	2.87[b]
Job satisfaction	2.90[b]	3.47	3.18	3.59[a]	3.21
Appreciation	3.59[a]	3.39	3.09[b]	3.30	3.42
Power	—	—	3.65[a]	3.55	3.24[b]
Communication	3.16	3.36[a]	2.30[b]	3.27	3.06
Loyalty	4.05	4.30	4.40[a]	3.98[b]	4.08
Belonging	3.37	3.76[a]	3.27	3.57	3.26[b]
Quality of life (Scores from 5)	2.92[b]	3.76[a]	3.04	3.25	3.00

Notes: Scores out of 5. Scores accompanied by the letter 'a' indicate the most positive score. Scores accompanied by the letter 'b' indicate the most negative. All figures in this table are indicative only, given the small sample sizes. Responses in relation to treatment by line and senior managers only (not peers) are included in the mean scores. The dimensions are provisional, and we made no attempt to explore reliability. See Chapter 8 for a fuller and more qualitative account of staff perceptions.

TABLE 4.5.   Staff perceptions of the distribution of power, in descending order

Belmarsh	Holme House	Risley	Doncaster	Wandsworth
Governor grades	Governor grades	Governor grades	Senior managers	Governor grades
Principal officers	Principal officers	Principal officers	Operational managers	Prisoners
Prisoners	Senior officers	Prisoners	Prisoners	Principal officers
Senior officers	Officers	Officers	Unit managers	Senior officers
Officers	Prisoners	Senior officers	Prisoner custody officers	Officers

'not enough'. When we ranked the answers staff gave for different groups in the prison, staff at four out of the five establishments placed 'prison officers' lowest in the hierarchy. Staff at Wandsworth thought prisoners 'had more power' than principal officers (see Table 4.5). These responses do not reflect empirical realities at all precisely, but they do match qualitative differences in levels of supervision and control of prisoners, and they tell us a great deal about how officers *feel*. Staff said things like:

There's no clear management structure, especially on the living blocks. We are not sure who's got the power or authority to make decisions. It's a very unclear structure. (Officer, Risley)

The staff are completely pissed off—they are fed up with the way they are treated, the amount of work they have to do, not being listened to. Between these walls you're like a separate community—a forgotten community. We are not allowed to speak out. People listen to the inmates—and we are just bypassed. To be honest with you, I am looking for another job. If they gave us support, the staff, we'd be fine—but . . . we can't deliver what we're being asked to deliver. We just want some *acknowledgement* of what it is like. I can't say anything very positive at all. We tell the inmates not to bother with us—go straight to the governors and area managers— they get listened to more than we do. We feel a bit invisible. (Officer, Wandsworth)

It seems that governors put the feelings of the inmates before those of staff and this imbalance causes resentment. Any authority we have is eroded. As front-line troops we should have our decisions, made by knowledge of the inmates and circumstances, backed up by managers. (Officer, Wandsworth)

Even senior managers recognized this level of uncertainty: 'No one is sure where the power lies. They are all used to hidden agendas. There is a lot of organizational anxiety' (senior manager, Belmarsh).
    By contrast, at Holme House and Doncaster:

I have to use my discretion on a daily basis, especially when mixing with prisoners on association; you let your guard down a bit because they're your trustees and you have to build relationships, not only for security reasons. I use my judgement all the time; whether to let them out, or stay in the shower an extra five minutes. It is quite strict here, they are closely super- vised; one prisoner wanted to go and get some water, and I thought, well, he hasn't got a kettle in there, he's banged up all the time so I let him out and told him to be quick. But you don't want to be labelled a soft touch. You have to get kudos first. It's a very macho world; you have to walk the walk and talk the talk. (Officer, Holme House)

We carry a phone card and we can use it at our discretion, we never have to consult any manager. (PCO, Doncaster)

How staff felt was related to their relationships with senior managers; and these relationships were linked (possibly causally) to their relationships with prisoners. Staff attitudes, in other words, were empirically linked to organizational and managerial features of each establishment.

Prisons and their Value Cultures

So what do we learn from this brief account of each prison? Figure 4.1 shows the results for each dimension, with 'three' as the neutral score, and the basic differences between establishments. We shall provide a more detailed account in subsequent chapters. Anything above or below the line indicates a mean positive or mean negative score, respectively. There were important differences between prisons on most of the dimensions (although there were also some important similarities; see later chapters). There were also differences in the *range* of scores, with some dimensions (e.g. safety and order) tending to attract higher mean ratings than others (e.g. power, trust, and personal development). It is true, then, that (these) prisons are high regulation, low trust environments, with deep power differentials. But it is instructive and important to note that prisons differ, even on dimensions where, overall, scores are relatively high or relatively low. It is too simplistic to claim that 'the prison is a low trust environment', given these differences.

We were informed in our analysis of the results by Karstedt's analysis of cross-cultural value patterns in 39 countries (Karstedt 2001). Karstedt categorized countries according to their position above or below the median on a scale of several value dimensions, yielding dominant cultural patterns in each country. In this part of our analysis, we followed this technique, although we preferred to identify those values above the neutral score (rather than above the mean), as some values are clearly more in evidence than others. If we remove the dimension 'family contact' (as all prisons attracted an average rating over '3' on this dimension), but consider the remaining dimensions rated as '3 or above' in each establishment, some interesting 'cultural differences' emerge (see Fig. 4.2).

These differences made sense to us in the light of other information we had gleaned about each prison. Risley, struggling and slightly aged, with no clear identity, had a somewhat impoverished, but not hostile regime. Staff–prisoner relationships were easygoing,

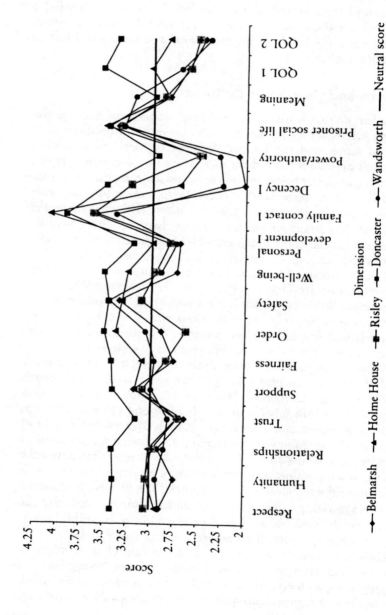

FIGURE 4.1.   A comparison of prisoner views on the quality of life in five prisons: dimension scores

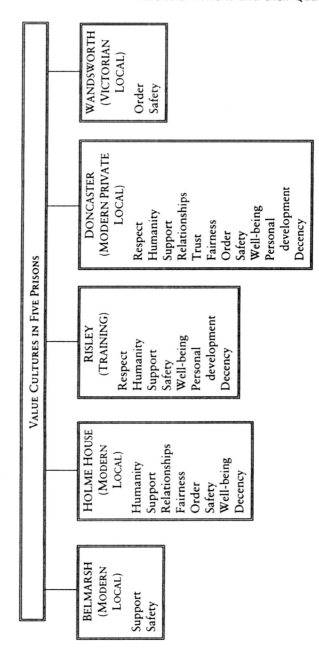

VALUE CULTURES IN FIVE PRISONS

BELMARSH (MODERN LOCAL)	HOLME HOUSE (MODERN LOCAL)	RISLEY (TRAINING)	DONCASTER (MODERN PRIVATE LOCAL)	WANDSWORTH (VICTORIAN LOCAL)
Support	Humanity	Respect	Respect	Order
Safety	Support	Humanity	Humanity	Safety
	Relationships	Support	Support	
	Fairness	Safety	Relationships	
	Order	Well-being	Trust	
	Safety	Personal development	Fairness	
	Well-being	Decency	Order	
	Decency		Safety	
			Well-being	
			Personal development	
			Decency	

FIGURE 4.2.   Value cultures in five prisons: values attracting a mean score of '3 or above'

but there was little order to the prison. Belmarsh and Wandsworth were poorly related on most dimensions, and each had a recognizable but distinguishable negative culture. Wandsworth was over-concerned with discipline, whereas Belmarsh was over-concerned with security. Holme House and Doncaster, on the other hand, were modern, active prisons, striving to provide a constructive regime. Doncaster had a more explicitly 'respectful' culture, but staff seemed not fully in charge. In Holme House, where staff were very much more in control, prisoners felt treated fairly, 'but it's not respect'.

It is interesting to note that each establishment had quite different expressed organizational goals (Belmarsh: security; Holme House: re-education; Risley: survival; Doncaster: 'prison *as*, not for, punishment'; and Wandsworth: discipline).[10] The two prisons with limited success at value dimensions and with more traditional custodial goals (Belmarsh and Wandsworth) had the least trusting staff–management relations (see Chapter 8). Staff were far more trusting of and open to us at Risley, Holme House, and (especially) Doncaster, although at all five prisons we quickly established a close and trusting relationship with our staff workgroups.

We began this chapter with a question about whether there are indeed 'essential features' of the prison which should be answered alongside our pursuit of the question of differences. There were certainly some common features of prison life identified among prison staff. They reported higher than expected levels of job satisfaction, and high levels of order, safety, and loyalty to their establishments. They saw their world at wing, or at most, at establishment level, and they did not share (or understand) the 'strategic visions' of their senior managers. Staff felt that management did not understand the reality of the job they did. They did not feel they were listened to or consulted, and they were highly conscious of the stringent financial climate, staffing shortages, and of the potentially damaging consequences of their already low staffing levels. They wanted strong leadership, more consultation, open and honest communication, and 'stability, commitment, and visibility' from their senior management teams. There were some links between staff and prisoner evaluations of prison quality, so that on the

[10] See Street *et al.* (1966) for an early account of the significance of organizational goals in institutional life.

whole higher staff evaluations seemed to correspond with higher prisoner evaluations. Similar to previous studies (James *et al.* 1997), staff in a generally well-regarded public sector prison reported slightly higher levels of 'satisfaction', or quality of life scores, than staff in a well-regarded private sector prison. Public sector staff reported higher levels of public valuation of their task. There is considerable evidence in the literature that employee perceptions of their working environment affect levels of satisfaction and performance or effectiveness (Fisher *et al.* 1995). Negative perceptions of the working environment can affect levels of stress, motivation, and absenteeism and can therefore result in reduced productivity. Arguably, in any comprehensive and explanatory evaluation of prison quality, staff perceptions should form an important part of what is being assessed.[11] We have only made a start on this process.

We shall return to the question of the 'essential features of the prison' in our concluding chapter.

---

[11] We have developed a detailed staff questionnaire in ongoing work on the relationship between prison quality and prison suicide. We shall report on this work in future publications.

PART II

Key Dimensions of Prison Life

5

Relationships Dimensions

Introduction

> The reader will often find philosophical ideas applied to or tested
> by the concrete experience of individuals. For this I make no
> apology; an idea has to bear the weight of concrete experience or
> else it becomes a mere abstraction.
>
> (Sennett 1998: 11)

> We owe it to our staff to be clear about what we ask of them.
>
> (Pilling 1992: 5)

The aims of the chapters that follow are threefold: the clarification
of meaning; an exploratory account of the role and significance
of each of 14 dimensions to prison life; and an account of our
measurement technique. We draw on the 'concrete experience' of
individuals, relating these experiences to significant theoretical
themes in the literature. The Prison Service has not been theoretically sophisticated when such well-worn terms as 'respect' and
'humanity' have been used, as we suggested in Chapter 1. A higher
level of sophistication and clarity is needed, whilst recognizing that
we can only progress so far in one account. The empirical scales and
their content therefore remain provisional, and subject to further
elaboration and review. We hope we shall say enough to develop
a convincing expository scheme.

We seek to discuss these concepts positively, where possible. As
Lucas argued in relation to justice, many of these concepts are
'asymmetric' (Lucas 1980). That is, it is easier to be clear about and
recognize 'injustice' than it is to express what justice is. The same
is true for respect, humanity, order, and so on. A treatise with the
title, 'Humanity', has, in the end, far more to say about 'inhumanity' (Glover 1999). However difficult and open-ended our task, it
is important to consider these values for what they are, in addition

to what they are not. Prisons are not all about conflict and they differ, along important moral dimensions. By exploring these differences, we can construct a tentative but morally relevant empirical account: how much trust, fairness, and co-operation is there in the prison? To what is this related? This exercise has taken us in the direction of normative and political theory, via more grounded methods than other scholars of prison quality have tended to use.

The values identified are not, in themselves, virtues. They are corruptible and subject to distortion.[1] We are not arguing that human (or penal) values are fixed or that we have discovered ultimate truths. On the contrary, we approach our task tentatively, but with a serious commitment to further dialogue. Our work reformulates the problems of the prison in a moral language (Misztal 1996: 8), a transformation that staff and prisoners welcome, and which is in tune with their sense of what makes prison life what it is. In this sense we hope, with their assistance, to 'illuminate things formerly obscure' (see e.g. Becker 1970).

Respect

Joe Pilling said in his well-received lecture (1992), 'Back to Basics: Relationships in the Prison Service', that the terms, 'respect', 'fairness', 'individuality', 'care', and 'openness' required particular emphasis in the complex and sensitive environment of the prison. His justificatory exposition (Sparks 1994: 21) coincided with the publication of the Woolf Report and other significant moves to relegitimize the prison. But what did this vocabulary mean? We argued in Chapter 1 that the ill-fated term 'justice' was imprecise and impossible to implement in a prison, without some clarity about its meaning. Is it possible to achieve greater clarity about this important collection of words so that we can consider to what extent they can be practised in the prison?

'Respect' is a term often appearing in official vision statements, training documents, and self-defining commentary (e.g. Prison Service 2002a), but less often reflected upon, theoretically or empirically, inside or outside the prison. We shall see later that the concept of respect for others may provide the basis of a newly

---

[1] The history of the Prison Service between 1990 and 1995 illustrates how 'justice' can become 'laxity', as suggested in Chapter 1.

emerging normative structure (Boutellier 2000: 156–7; Bottoms 2002) and in this sense it provides a focus or central point, to which we shall return later. Pilling spoke about respect as 'basic human dignity and worth . . . Respecting prisoners means addressing them courteously, by the name they prefer; asking not ordering; listening to what they are saying; being sensitive to their feelings about being locked up . . . It is the key to healthy relationships. It is the key to good control' (Pilling 1992: 6).

Kant argued that respect for others—treating them as ends not means—was a universal guide to moral conduct. The principles of moral equality and individual autonomy formed the basis of co-operative life. There is a link between this notion of respect and human freedom. Respect acknowledges the autonomy of the other and places limits on what others might do 'in their interests'. It places limits on care (Dworkin 1977) and on compassion and pity which can 'wound' (Sennett 2003: 127–50). In this sense, the dignity of the person requires an element of freedom to be 'left intact' (O'Neill 2000: 178). But this freedom requires respect for others— a limited or specific version of autonomy with obligations attached. Respect also incorporates a level of accountability and responsibility for action, so that to respect a person requires us to see them as moral agents—fully responsible beings—a 'proper object of praise and blame' (Quinton 1991: 40). To be respected as a person is to be recognized as a fellow being to be reasoned with and not to be subject to manipulation or force (Quinton 1991: 42). Loss of this autonomy (as in slavery, for example) is dehumanizing. Respect incorporates an acceptance of difference. Awareness of, or respect for, the other as a person requires the avoidance of stereotypes, fears, suspicions, and discrimination (Zehr 1991a). It is to behave without condescension (Gaita 1998: 2). Sennett argues that: '[B]ehaviour which expresses respect is often scant and unequally distributed in society . . . what respect means is both socially and psychologically complex' (Sennett 2003: 59).

Respect is a form of positive consideration or 'recognition' (Sennett 2003: 54). It does not occur 'simply by commanding that it should happen', but involves a complex series of negotiations. It may require a form of autonomy that means 'accepting in others what one doesn't understand about them' (Sennett 2003: 262). Gaita (1998) argues that respect for others is first constituted and subsequently made possible through *attachments*. Self-respect and respect for others are linked, as they both require an identity that does not require taking power over others (see Zehr 1991*b*: 5; also de Zulueta 1993; and Boutellier 2000: 144).

What limits are set by respect? Quinton argues that:

... there is no incompatibility between treating someone with respect and, in the first place, disapproving of things he does or the aspects of his character which are responsible for them and, secondly, of bringing pressure to bear on him with a view to preventing the acts or improving the character they manifest ... To say to someone, who is acting, as one believes, wrongly, that one does think so and why and then, when that has no effect, to say 'well, if you think that is all right you had better go ahead and do it' and to abstain from all further pressure on him is a failure of duty ... (Quinton 1991: 43)

So the concept of respect might include challenging specific aspects of a person's behaviour, in the sense suggested by Quinton, above.[2] A sanction (like a sentence of imprisonment) is not in principle or *in itself* a denial of respect—but in its application it can turn into being such. Von Hirsch has argued that the application of a sanction may *constitute* respect, as it treats the individual as blameworthy, responsible, and autonomous (von Hirsch 1976 and 1993).

The notion of respect places positive obligations on others to explain their actions: our ontological security or sense of safety, order, and meaning requires this kind of accounting for one's actions. The 'three pillars of wholeness'—autonomy, order, and relatedness— are embedded in the concept of respect (Zehr 1991*b*: 2–3). Respect and 'the experience of justice' are very closely linked, as we shall show later. Some have argued that 'violence only abates with respect' (Pepinski and Quinney 1991).

Respect was a key value in prison, and was always one of the first to emerge in our discussion about 'what mattered'. The Prison Service has committed itself, at the level of official discourse at least, to 'treating prisoners with decency and with respect' (Prison Service 2000*b*: 25). There is a Prison Service Principle which encourages prisoners 'to address their offending behaviour and respect others' (ibid. 9).

The term 'respect' could have many meanings, including fear and wariness (see Liebling and Price 2001: 101; Bourgois 1995): 'I have a large, well-known family so other prisoners treat me with respect. The officers? A few know my family so I get treated with less

---

[2] This should be distinguished from bullying, which implies a lack of respect and more than a little pressure.

respect!' (prisoner, Holme House). We are not using it in that way here. It was most commonly used in the sense that:

They talk to me like a human being, not 'do this! Do that!'. They have a chat; it is nice just to talk. It's nice when they tell you things . . . you like to hear about what is going on outside. (Prisoner, Wandsworth)

The gym screws, they treat lads with a lot of respect. They give you a lot of confidence; they show you what to do, not tell you. They're like one of the lads. (Prisoner, Holme House)

When I arrived at reception I was treated like anybody else and that was fair. I was treated like the next man, with respect and dignity. (Prisoner, Wandsworth)

Some staff show respect, respect for you as an individual, then it is natural to show it back. One officer says 'hello' or 'good morning', asks if you are OK and never just walks past you; it's the way he asks, you know he means it and he's interested. (Prisoner, Belmarsh)

The Governor on this wing has treated me with respect . . . although the answer was not what I wanted, I did speak to her and she showed me respect. She spoke to me as a normal person, not a thug. She listened and considered what I had to say and went out of her way to explain everything so I understood. (Prisoner, Risley)

Sometimes respect was contingent on location or IEP level,[3] or staff member:

I got nicked, just when I was up for enhancement. I was told by one officer I would have to wait for three months before I could get it. Another one told me six months and another six weeks. One officer came up to me and told me I should have had it ages ago. He got me the form, filled it out with me and I got it the same day; that was cool. When you get enhanced you get respect back. (Prisoner, Holme House)

Since I've been on this wing I've been treated with respect; it's like a different jail, you're given more time on the landing and more respect; I'd say 99 per cent treat you with respect. They let you have showers before a visit; they'll open up 15 minutes before to give you time to get ready; they sit and talk to you, they mix with you on association and watch the football. On here, it's the best you're gonna get in prison; it's relaxed and sociable. (Prisoner, Holme House)

---

[3] Incentives levels (basic, standard, and enhanced) are related to prisoner behaviour and reflect differential entitlements to privileges, such as extended visits and additional spending power. See, briefly, Chapter 1; also Bottoms (2003b).

Gym staff . . . work with you, make suggestions and constructive criticism, and don't question your motives as landing staff do. (Prisoner, Doncaster)

Prisoners drew fine distinctions between fairness and respect: 'I am usually treated with fairness, but not respect' (prisoner, Holme House). Prisoners commented that respect was 'more than civility': 'Civil is how you treat everyone. Respect is more than that. This prison is good at being civil to prisoners, but not so far as treating them with respect' (prisoner, Holme House).

Respect was distinguishable from 'being nice' or 'kind regard'. Both respect and fairness were sometimes unreliable: 'Fair, respectful treatment is hugely dependent on staff members' mood at the time' (prisoner, Doncaster).

Respect was, then, related to individuality ('if they don't just treat you like a number'; 'some call you by your first name and you're not all tarred by the same brush'). Prisoners sometimes linked the notion of individuality to the feeling of 'being known': 'Once when I was pulled for having a go at a nurse and they threatened to put me on basic, but the senior officer didn't think that was right as he knew me, and I didn't get put on basic. In fact the officer wanted to recommend me for enhanced!' (prisoner, Belmarsh).[4]

Respect was a precise concept and prisoners had no difficulty giving specific examples of what it was and what it was not, when asked to 'tell me about a time when you have felt treated with respect, in here':

The best thing that had ever happened was when a friend of his left to go to another prison. He asked an officer if he could pass on a note to him saying goodbye, instead the officer let him out of his cell to go and say goodbye in person. They had about a minute. He said 'I nearly fell over; I would have understood if he couldn't have passed the message on'. My interviewee became more cynical later though, thinking the officer only allowed this because he didn't want any trouble from him; there was an underlying reason for the niceness, which did not mean respect. (Fieldnotes, Belmarsh)

[4] If the link to 'being known' was essential, this would suggest that respect cannot be shown in a context where people meet for the first time (such as in a court). This is not the case, but the example illustrates an empirical link in the prison between established relationships and the granting of respect, in a context where individuality is difficult to sustain. Many prison sociologists make the latter point.

This remark provides support for our earlier argument that concepts like respect, and other related values, such as fairness, are deontological rather than instrumental. Respect shown *in order to* achieve compliance is not respect.

The role of *apology* in respect became apparent to us during previous research on the nature of staff–prisoner relationships, and some discussions arising out of that research with our colleagues.[5] To apologize *is* to fully recognize the other as an autonomous person with their own worth, to acknowledge that an injustice has been done to them, and to seek to restore what has been lost by the unjust act (Tavuchis 1991): 'One officer was rude to me and I told him there was no need to be like that and later on he apologized. I was getting a Rizla from someone's door, but he got me out later and said sorry, it was because he was so busy, he snapped. That was alright. Cool' (prisoner, Wandsworth).

Staff agreed: 'He has made mistakes. Then he should apologise, as an adult to an adult. That is respect' (senior officer).

Apology was not common (it was regarded as 'dangerous ground' or a loss of authority by many staff). As Lucas argued in relation to justice, it was easier to identify lack of respect:[6]

The majority of staff show no respect to prisoners, they see themselves as enforcers of punishment that has been ordained by the courts. (Prisoner, Wandsworth)

The principal officer on houseblock *x* didn't believe me; that's where there is a lack of respect. You are automatically assumed to be a liar. Prisoners cannot be thought to tell the truth and that hurts; I pleaded guilty to murder; why should I lie about other things? (Prisoner, Belmarsh)

When they call, you answer straight away and don't talk back; the officers can scream and shout at you. (Prisoner, Belmarsh)

Being called by your second name is horrible, the way you're addressed is not nice. I hate them shouting [second name!]. Even if they called you 'mate' or 'pal' that would be better. (Prisoner, Holme House)

Prisoners associated respect with 'being treated as an individual', with staff 'getting to know you as a person, so they would have the

---

[5] We are especially grateful to Tony Bottoms for this insight and for alerting us to the work of Tavuchis (1991). See also Bottoms (2003*a*: 94–9).

[6] We have given examples of being treated with positive respect in this account but we had to develop a very specific methodology in order to achieve this.

ability to say this person is not likely to lie'. 'Proper respect' was 'when one officer made the time to sit down with me and didn't judge me for my offence, but took the time to explore with me why I became involved in drugs and committed my offence' (prisoner, Belmarsh). Respect for the other as a person required the avoidance of suspicions and discrimination, which was difficult in the environment of the prison (rather as apology was difficult and contentious). These values conflict with other (overriding) values, such as security and power. Respect was a form of positive consideration, or further, it was recognition of the inherent dignity and worth of the person, and of differences between individuals.

Definition of respect An attitude of consideration; to pay proper attention to and not violate. Regard for the inherent dignity and value of the human person.

We developed three statements to form the dimension 'respect':[7]

Statement 65   I feel that I am treated with respect by staff in this prison (0.878)

Statement 26   Staff address and talk to me in a respectful manner (0.841)

Statement 95   This prison is poor at treating prisoners with respect (0.822)

Table 5.1 shows the statements as they were worded (i.e. without any re-coding in a positive direction for statements worded negatively) and the responses. Throughout the account to follow, highest and lowest scores are shown using *a* (highest) and *b* (lowest).

About half of the prisoners at Belmarsh, Holme House, Risley, and Wandsworth felt that staff addressed them in a respectful manner, compared to a significantly higher 72 per cent at Doncaster (Table 5.1*a*). About a third of prisoners in all of the prisons (more

---

[7] The mean from all prisoners in the sample was calculated and this constituted the dimension score. Initial analyses resulted in some revisions to the dimensions in the light of reliability scores (see Table 5.3), and the item-to-item and item-to-dimension correlations. Correlation explores the strength and direction of relationships between two variables and is expressed as a correlation coefficient, which ranges from minus 1 to 1. The closer to 1 (or minus 1) the coefficient, the stronger the relationship (either positive or negative). The item correlations with the dimension are shown in descending order of strength, in parentheses.

at Doncaster) felt they were treated with respect by staff. It is significant that even in a relatively 'low respect prison', 31 per cent of prisoners at Belmarsh agreed or strongly agreed that they were 'treated with respect by staff in this prison'.

TABLE 5.1.   Percentage of prisoners who agree/strongly agree with statements about respect and humanity

	Belmarsh	Holme House	Risley	Doncaster	Wandsworth
(a) Respect—Statements					
1. Staff address and talk to me in a respectful manner.	48.2	47.9[b]	53.4	72.0[a]	48.4
2. I feel that I am treated with respect in this prison.	31.3[b]	34.1	38.7	43.0[a]	33.3
3. This prison is poor at treating prisoners with respect.	54.2[b]	47.9	36.6	23.7[a]	50.0
(b) Humanity—Statements					
1. I am being looked after with humanity here.	38.5[b]	62.7	60.4	73.7[a]	51.7
2. I am treated as a person of value in this prison.	14.4[b]	26.6	23.8	38.6[a]	35.0
3. Some of the treatment I receive in this prison is degrading.	61.5[b]	42.5	37.6	24.5[a]	43.3
4. Staff here treat me with kindness.	30.1	28.8	27.8[b]	36.9[a]	30.0
5. I am not being treated as a human being in here.	38.6[b]	22.3	20.8	8.8[a]	28.3

Note: Throughout this account, scores accompanied by the letter 'a' indicate the most positive score. Scores accompanied by the letter 'b' indicate the most negative.

Two of the comments prisoners made about Doncaster were that staff 'used nicer nicknames' and officers did not 'bark their names'.
To test for significant differences between the prisons, we used mean scores on individual items. The results are shown below. All of the significant differences were between Doncaster and the other

TABLE 5.2. Prisoner views on respect and humanity: individual item mean scores

Item/statement	Item scores (1–5)					ANOVA (Mean difference)									
	B	HH	R	D	W	B&HH	B&R	B&D	B&W	HH&R	HH&D	HH&W	R&D	R&W	D&W
(a) Respect															
Staff address and talk to me in a respectful manner.	3.19	3.19	3.33	3.66[a]	3.15[b]	N/s	N/s	0.47*	N/s	N/s	0.47*	N/s	N/s	N/s	0.51*
I feel that I am treated with respect by staff in this prison.	2.98[b]	2.99	3.08	3.31[a]	2.98[b]	N/s	N/s	N/s	N/s	N/s	N/s	N/s	N/s	N/s	N/s
This prison is [good] at treating prisoners with respect.	2.52[b]	2.64	2.77	3.26[a]	2.57	N/s	N/s	0.75**	N/s	N/s	0.62*	N/s	0.49*	N/s	0.70*
(b) Humanity															
I am being looked after with humanity here.	(5) 2.95[b]	(2) 3.43	(3) 3.39	(1) 3.70[a]	(4) 3.15	0.47	0.43	0.75**	N/s	N/s	N/s	N/s	N/s	N/s	0.55*

I am treated as a person of value in this prison.	(5) 2.46[b]	(3) 2.79	(4) 2.66	(1) 3.04[a]	(2) 2.80	N/s	N/s	0.59*	N/s	N/s	N/s	N/s	N/s	N/s
The treatment I receive in this prison is [not] degrading.	(5) 2.48[b]	(2) 2.91	(3) 2.90	(1) 3.32[a]	(4) 2.72	N/s	N/s	0.84**	N/s	N/s	N/s	N/s	N/s	0.61*
Staff here treat me with kindness.	(2) 2.96	(5) 2.84[b]	(4) 2.93	(1) 3.19[a]	(3) 2.95	N/s	N/s	N/s	N/s	N/s	N/s	N/s	N/s	N/s
I am [not] being treated as a human being in here.	(5) 2.84[b]	(3) 3.22	(2) 3.32	(1) 3.66[a]	(4) 3.05	N/s	0.47*	0.81**	N/s	0.43	N/s	N/s	N/s	0.61*

Notes: B = Belmarsh (n = 83); R = Risley (n = 101); HH = Holme House (n = 94); D = HMP & YOI Doncaster (n = 114); W = HMP Wandsworth (n = 60). Item scores in bold indicate those that achieved the 'passmark' score of 3. * The mean difference is significant at the p < 0.05 level. ** The mean difference is significant at the 0.001 level. Comparison figures without asterisks indicate the mean difference at the p < 0.1 level (not enough to achieve difference is significant at the 0.001 level). Comparison figures without asterisks indicate the mean difference at the p < 0.1 level (not enough to achieve significance). N/s—not significant. (Ranking in parentheses.)

prisons, and were found in statements 1 and 3 (see Table 5.2*a*). The non-significant differences are still informative, as they indicate whether mean scores are above or below 3 on each item, and they show variations in a consistent direction between prisons.

We have outlined how the dimension scores were calculated in Chapter 3. A score above 3 represents a positive average view on the questions in that dimension taken as a whole. Two of the establishments had a score of 3 or above for respect (Table 5.3).

TABLE 5.3.   Scores on dimension one: respect

Prison	Reliability	Mean score
Doncaster	0.7181	3.4094
Risley	0.8668	3.0594
Holme House	0.8262	2.9397
Wandsworth	0.7863	2.9000
Belmarsh	0.7307	2.8956

The overall internal reliability of this dimension across all prisons was high, at 0.80.[8] There were significant differences between Doncaster and the other establishments (the difference between Doncaster and Risley did not quite reach a 0.05 level of statistical significance).[9] The detailed results from significance tests on all dimensions, for all prisons, are included in the Appendix.

Dimension Correlations[10]

Respect was significantly positively correlated with all other dimensions. It was most highly correlated with (in descending order): humanity (0.822); relationships (0.755); trust (0.746); fairness (0.730); and support (0.725). We shall consider the significance of these relationships, and explore them in more detail, later.

[8] We use Cronbach's alpha for all the reliability scores to follow. Cronbach's alpha is expressed as a correlation coefficient. The nearer this is to 1, the more internally reliable or consistent is the scale. Cohen and Holliday (1982) suggest the following 'rule of thumb' when interpreting any correlation coefficient: 0.19 and below = very low; 0.20 to 0.39 = low; 0.40 to 0.69 = acceptable; 0.70 to 0.89 = high; and 0.90 to 1 = very high.

[9] We have provided the significance level only for results which fall at or below the 0.05 level (95% confidence interval).

[10] This analysis was conducted using Pearson's r (Product Moment correlation coefficient), a two-tailed test.

Humanity

> ...while we live, while we are among human beings, let us cultivate our humanity.
>
> (Seneca, *On Anger*)

> The traditional appeal of modern penal reformers has been to emphasise the humanity of offenders and the cruelty of current penal practices. The new penology not only has trouble recognising the cultural investment in the figure of the criminal, it has trouble with the concept of humanity.
>
> (Simon and Feeley 1995: 173)

As shown in Chapter 1, the Prison Service's Statement of Purpose identifies 'humanity' as a central duty informing the way in which prisoners must be treated. Humanity is, in this sense, the most important and prominent principle in the Prison Service vocabulary. It is surprising, therefore, that there is little discussion in official literature of what this term means (however, see Coyle 2003). It has, like the word 'morality' and most other associated terms, an 'open texture' (Hart 1963: 164). All systems of ethics make some reference to terms like 'humanism' or 'humanity' (the Chinese term is *ren*; Hansen 2000). The exposure of 'crimes against humanity' at the end of the Second World War caused a dramatic shift in public thinking about the importance of human rights, and the limits of what could be done to another human being, although there is substantial evidence of both atrocities and public outrage before then (Neier 1998). The term 'humanity' (except when used to mean 'people' in general) is other-regarding, and indicates how we should treat a 'neighbour', or our fellow human beings. To do right is to recognize and treat others as fully human. The term is linked, then, to notions of citizenship (Nussbaum 1997) and concern for others. We are incomplete creatures, who are vulnerable on our own (Nussbaum 1997: 91; MacIntyre 1999). The human animal (like other animals) has 'social traits like parental care, cooperative foraging and reciprocal kindness... which... show plainly that such creatures are not in fact crude, exclusive egoists, but beings who have evolved the strong and special motivations needed to form and maintain a simple society' (Midgley 2000: 7–8).

Our humanity might be said to be what we normally recognize in each other (however, see n. 12 below). It constitutes the origin of morality, and is based on fellow feeling and a need for social organization and community living. It arises from and signifies our sociability or, at least, our humanity makes our sociability possible. Our sociability can be partial and narrow (normally starting with the family), or it can be broader. Humanity is, according to Steinberg, what encouraged the Italians to protect the Jews (Steinberg 1991).[11] It is linked to respect—for the dignity of others (see above) but it includes sympathy or kind regard for their condition. It acts as a constraint against cruelty and as the root of compassionate action. Recognizing the humanness of the other prevents us from inflicting suffering on them. Indignation about crime is (often) tempered by consideration of humanity and the 'desire to heal' (Allard 1991: 15–16). To 'treat with humanity', then, means to treat someone as an individual and as a person. Proximity nourishes humanity (except under certain conditions; see Chapter 7). Distance makes it easier to forget.[12]

The term *inhumanity* tends to be used in a restricted and technical way by the courts to indicate 'environmental ill-treatment'. Evans and Morgan argue, for example, that a 'high threshold has been set' in their study of the practices and deliberations of the European Committee for the Prevention of Torture and Inhuman and Degrading Treatment or Punishment (Evans and Morgan 1998: 253–4). There are few positive statements of what the term 'humanity' means in this international context (for a recent attempt, see Coyle 2003).[13]

Glover has argued that to treat someone with humanity means treating them with kindness, civility, and mercy (see also *Collins Dictionary of the English Language* 1986). Do these terms help us

---

[11] Steinberg argues, in his account of early twentieth-century Italian culture, that the primary virtue of humanity was often surrounded by secondary vices: unpunctuality, bureaucratic inefficiency, evasiveness, and corruption. These vices may be in service to the primary virtue, humanity. In Germany, by contrast, the secondary virtues of efficiency and incorruptibility were harnessed to inhumanity (Steinberg 1991: 170; also Glover 1999: 390).

[12] As Glover argues, technology and distance combine to make inhumanity uniquely possible. Bauman, and others, have made the same point (Bauman 1989).

[13] There are many examples of what 'inhumanity' might mean, including rulings of unsatisfactory conditions in CPT reports of their UK visits to Brixton, Leeds and Wandsworth in 1990, for example. In these cases the cumulative effect of overcrowding, lack of integral sanitation and inadequate regime activities amounted to 'inhuman and degrading treatment' (Evans and Morgan 1998: 243–4).

to clarify what humanity *is*? *Kindness* is shown by consideration, generosity, or support. It involves an emotional response, and is often triggered by visible reminders of another's humanness: photographs of the family; letters from a significant other; or, in an example used by Glover, 'seeing the fascist soldier holding up his trousers as he runs' (Glover 1999). Kindness, like other virtues, may need to be cultivated, as we are 'divided against ourselves' and may not find human kindness easy (see Aristotle 1976). Some times and environments may be more conducive to kindness than others. Cruelty is the opposite of kindness and is just as amenable to cultivation. *Civility* is of interest to historians of the prison and criminal justice because of its fluctuating significance in public life (Pratt 1998; see also Gatrell 1994). It can variously mean decency, consideration, and polite, orderly, good, or moral behaviour. The *civilian* or public servant should be decent, honest, and polite. We believe that our modern public institutions should be civil: that is, that they should avoid debasement or humiliation of individuals. Pratt argues that the civilizing of modern Western societies has been an uneven and in many ways unnatural process, with a greater emphasis on foresight and self-restraint than we can live up to, even with stringent external controls (Pratt 2000, 2002). The 'armour of civilised conduct crumbles very rapidly' and decivilizing influences reappear (as arguably they have since 1995, Pratt's main point). His case is that:

The greater the tendency towards state monopoly of the power to punish, the stronger the sense of mutual identification, and the higher the threshold of sensitivity and embarrassment, the more this lends itself to a penality encased in bureaucratic rationalism. By corollary, the more emphasis we find on emotive and ostentatious punishment, the more we are likely to see, by reference to trends in the opposite direction of these features, either a slower adaptation to the civilizing process, or a decivilizing interruption to it. (Pratt 2000: 422)

In the modern prison, considerable effort is expended in trying to expel 'distasteful' and violent punishment—or the unacceptable face of punishment. Civility is part of humanity to the extent that it recognizes and is sensitive to the unintended suffering of the individual person. It departs from humanity when it becomes wedded to bureaucratic, non-emotive, rational, and anonymous systems (see

Pratt 2000: 16; also Bauman 1989; Elias 1996) and, in particular, when those systems lose their ameliorative ethos.

And what about *mercy*? In our account (and in the definition we have settled on) we agree that *mercy* or compassion is embedded within the concept of humanity. Mercy places limits on the use of power, and is intended to demonstrate recognition of and sympathy for the condition of the individual. Some have argued that mercy can also constitute or belong to justice (see later below).[14] Mercy tempers judgement because it is attentive to the human qualities of the individual. We can already see, then, that there are potential conflicts between official aspirations to treat prisoners with respect and humanity, and some structural features of the prison (the need to deal with prisoners en masse).

In prisons, the term 'humanity' plays a prominent role in penological thinking, but we find very few attempts to explore the meaning of the term 'humanity' or to articulate what it might require in practice.[15] This is despite its appearance in 1988 in a new Prison Service Statement of Purpose, which has remained ever since the official statement of the aims of the Service (see Chapter 1, p. 12). It has proved difficult to reconstruct precisely how the word 'humanity' made it into this Statement of Purpose, beyond establishing that the terms 'humane' and 'humanity' were 'on many people's lips at the time' (see King and McDermott 1995: 11–15; Dunbar 2002). The Statement of Purpose was itself the culmination of a series of discussions between the then Director General (Chris Train) and the Chief Inspector of Prisons (James Hennessy). These discussions were taking place in the light of the demise of the treatment and training ideal and the resulting lack of 'moral purpose' or 'sense of direction' that remained (Dunbar 1985; see also Home Office 1979; King and Morgan 1980; Stern 1993; Bottoms 1990). The Statement arose as part of an attempt to set clear principles and standards for the treatment of prisoners, which could be linked to tangible aspects of practice, and to find ways of measuring and monitoring regime delivery (Train 1985). It was intended to be a 'moral statement' and a general framework within which individual establishments could operate (Dunbar 1985: 82) and which could

---

[14] Bottoms, for example, argues that mercy, or compassion, can be rationally exercised in the interests of justice (Bottoms 1998: 67–8; Harrison 1992).

[15] Coyle's recent (2003) publication represents such an attempt.

be linked to 'attainable objectives'. But the Statement had to go further than its recent predecessor: a Statement of Tasks of the Prison Service, which had received much criticism for its bland operational tone and its uninspiring emphasis on the efficient use of resources (Train 1985; Bottoms 1990; King and McDermott 1995). An additional factor in the search for moral language was the actual treatment of some prisoners (e.g. hunger strikers) by some staff in individual prisons (particularly London locals) during the 1980s. A way of 'setting limits' for the staff, and reminding them of their 'duty of care . . . when they were left on their own', was needed (Dunbar 2002). As Sparks has noted, the time has come for scholars of the English penal system to inquire 'what work this word is doing there' (pers. comm., and forthcoming). The Statement has become popular with prison staff, but it has not satisfied its critics (Bottoms 1990; Home Office 1991a; Home Office 1995).[16]

John Howard was impressed by the 'humanity' of the Dutch in his 1777 study of 'The State of Prisons in England and Wales' and elsewhere (Howard 1929: 61). By this, he meant the cleanliness, industriousness, and attentiveness to religious and moral instruction he observed, and the practice of early release and the avoidance of life sentences 'to prevent despair' (Howard 1929: 46–8). We find many references to the need for 'humanitarian reform' elsewhere (e.g. Cross 1971), and much debate about what constitutes 'inhumane' and 'humane' treatment (Home Office 1979; King and Morgan 1980; Mott 1985). The law has a rather restricted interpretation of the term 'inhuman and degrading treatment' (see Evans and Morgan 1998; and Chapter 10). We have tried to allow for a less negative, legalistic definition, based on what prisoners said. The term 'humanity' refers, we think, to something more than prisoners' living conditions.

An influential, but brief attempt to consider the meaning of the term 'humanity' in the penal context was published by Pilling, the incoming Director General of the Prison Service, in 1992 (see Chapter 1, and above). Pilling claimed that the term consisted of the five fundamentally important concepts outlined above (p. 206),

[16] Or a female senior manager whom I overheard saying angrily, in the foyer of Cleland House (Prison Service Headquarters) in 1992, 'If anyone else uses the word "humanity" today, I'll drive a stake through their heart!'

which he brought together under the theme of relationships (Pilling 1992). At about the same time, Woolf suggested that several things flowed from the term 'humanity', including an 'obligation of the Prison Service to use no more security than is necessary to look after those in its custody' (Home Office 1991*a*, para. 10.11). He proposed that the Statement of Purpose was flawed, or insufficient, because the term 'humanity' did not necessarily include justice (paras. 10.19–10.20). His own concept of justice did include humanity, which, in its turn, implied that prisoners had a 'legitimate expectation' of facilities and opportunities to address their offending behaviour (see G. Morgan 1997: 1150–1; Home Office 1991*a*, paras. 10.24–10.34). Sparks and Bottoms argued that this requires 'the recognition of prisoners in terms of both their citizenship and their ordinary humanity' (Sparks and Bottoms 1995). They suggest that the term 'humanity' emphasized respect for prisoners (including recognition of their intrinsic worth as persons), care (including the provision of humane conditions and a commitment to minimize the harmful effects of removal from normal life), and hope for the future (including opportunities for betterment; Sparks and Bottoms 1995). In our interviews, prisoners often linked the term 'humanity' to opportunities for development (see also Johnson 1996).

Logan argued that:

Humans are not meant to be idle.[17] That simple fact, rather than any hypothesized link to rehabilitation, is what justifies programs inside prisons. Such programs may also help authorities to maintain order, but that, too, is a secondary benefit. The primary justification for work, recreation, education and other programs is that they are essential to the human condition . . . their total absence would be inhumane and thus not an ordinarily intended aspect of punishment. Thus, meaningful activity is a component of prison quality that is essential to prisoner welfare. (Logan 1992)

Thus he linked humanity to activity. Humanity was also linked, via the concept of activities, to meaning (see Chapter 7). It was very closely linked to 'respect and dignity'. Prisoners argued that being treated with humanity was something broader than

---

[17] We agree with Logan. We also agree with a comment on a draft of this chapter by Tony Bottoms, however, that they also need 'time out' and that without this they can become 'dehumanized'.

'humane' treatment:

> Being treated with humanity means you're not just a name and a number and you've got your self-respect. (Prisoner, Risley)

> Being treated with humanity is being treated like a person. (Prisoner, Holme House)

> To me, being treated with humanity means being provided with adequate, reasonably comfortable and clean accommodation and being acknowledged as a person with individual needs, desires, concerns, strengths, and weaknesses. (Prisoner, Doncaster)

Prisoners thought humanity was about being treated as a person rather than as a 'prisoner' or a 'criminal': 'At Altcourse they treat you with respect—as a human; like someone who has made a mistake' (prisoner, Risley).

The term 'humanity' also had a material dimension, and a 'responsive' nature suggested by the term *concern*, earlier:

> They treat you with humanity and dignity here—it's the way they speak, how they come over, no aggression, they ask. They make you react differently. It's a good layout, we are out a lot, the food's great, you have loads of access to the phone. There is nothing to rebel against here. There is less stress. We have two lifer days a year, where you can spend a whole day with your family. It's worth its weight in gold . . . In my previous prison, staff . . . said I only speak to staff when I want something, all these clichés and stereotypes. Here they just ask if you want a game of pool—they treat you like normal people, they relate to you like normal people. At first it's frightening—the big layout, and this lack of intimidation . . . When you come here, it reminds you of how civil people can be. It changes you. Trust builds up. (Prisoners, group discussion, Doncaster)

> They asked if I wanted to be padded-up with a smoker or a non-smoker; they ask you what you want for dinner . . . They don't need to because you're a prisoner, but they do. (Prisoner, Doncaster)

> They have always behaved professionally towards me; one example was during my trial and my glasses frame broke. An officer noticed a bit had fallen off and he said 'Give it to me, I'll see if I can do something'. He returned five minutes later and fixed it temporarily. I thought he had forgotten but three weeks later he checked and brought in the proper bit and fixed it. That was nice because he didn't have to do it. He treated me as a human being as opposed to a prisoner. (Prisoner, Belmarsh)

Prisoners' answers to our open questions about humanity often involved many references to other related dimensions: for example, support, respect, trust, and relationships:

I received a lot of support from one particular officer who has always shown fairness and equality; he always acted almost as a friend, which is very rare . . . You can talk to staff if you have a problem and if you're upset, they understand. I have talked to staff about family problems. I got upset and they've calmed me down. Sometimes just talking on the same level, not seeing the uniform, or us as prisoners, just being people, that helps. (Prisoner, Doncaster)

Here they have a laugh with you, play pool, have a little bet, and they pay up! We bet for chocolate bars. They give you straight answers and help you as much as they can and don't swear unless they're messing about. They see that being in prison is not to punish you more than having your liberty taken away. (Prisoner, Doncaster)

Humanity is about being treated fairly, leaving you alone on association and putting trust in you. (Prisoner, Risley)

I had to go to outside hospital and they took the mechanical cuffs off me. The Officers took their epaulets off and their Prison Service coats off; that showed respect. I was choked up to be given that amount of trust, no one had done that in 11 years. I felt free for once; they showed a lot of faith in me and no one in the hospital could know I was a prisoner. I felt a normal person again and a human being for once. (Prisoner, Belmarsh)

The term went further than respect, indicating kindness or care:

Life is at its best when I have access to my family, either by phone or a visit, but it's hard to get on the phone; prisoners are anxiously waiting to speak and they don't understand. Once, the day I was sentenced, I was late back and banged up; I asked to talk to my wife and they let me use the phone. I think that was humane. (Prisoner, Belmarsh)

The officers' attitudes are so important. There are the ones who get on with their job who are not cruel, you can have a laugh with them. They are just being like that to get through the day but it has a snowballing effect. It allows you to act like a human being. Others don't let you act like a human, they push you so far down, that's one in every twenty I'd say. (Prisoner, Wandsworth)

There are little pleasantries which makes you keep feeling human. (Prisoner, Wandsworth)

In our quantitative analysis (see below), humanity was strongly correlated with respect, fairness, trust, relationships, and support. What seems distinct about the accounts of the term 'humanity' above is the emphasis on *personhood*. In their answers, prisoners linked humanity most closely to respect—which was often interpreted as 'being treated as a human being', where staff 'don't talk down to you'; they 'treat you as a person of value'. We considered combining the dimensions 'respect and humanity' but felt that they had slightly different meanings: respect meaning *recognition of the individual, their worth, and autonomy*, and humanity meaning (at least) reasonable material conditions and (at its strongest) *kind regard for the person*. We found that scores were (just) distinct enough to continue to distinguish between them (however, see later).

Not being treated with humanity was to be 'nothing', to have no value (see Chapter 4, p. 177). Prisoners at establishments with lower levels of humanity wished 'staff would be more polite and genuine' (prisoner, Belmarsh). Not being allowed to think or feel was inhumane:

The way I look at it, we have no control over our lives. They do our thinking for us, so in that way we have none [humanity]. We're not allowed to think for ourselves in jail; they tell us when to eat, when to go to work, when we can do things. (Prisoner, Holme House)

Humanity is the way you're treated, not like animals and having bare cells. It's hard to explain, but when you come to prison you're stripped of your liberty, you can't have feelings, you have to bottle them up, you have to shut down and block things out. (Prisoner, Holme House)

Humanity was a combination of material and interpersonal conditions. Decency, safety, dignity, fairness, and equality were mentioned often:

What would make this prison a decent place? Make it more hospitable, I wouldn't say easy but more humane. It can be degrading and I see people slash themselves up; some people when they come in are weak and scared. It should be a safe place; I think this is safer than some because you can see the officers about—in some prisons you never see them on the wing. You should be let out your pad more and there should be exercise every day no matter what. (Prisoner, Holme House)

[INTERVIEWER: 'What does being treated with humanity in prison mean to you?'] Fairness . . . just in a human way; we are expected to live here but they can't just push things onto us all the time. You don't have much dignity in prison, that's the only thing. There should be equality no matter what colour, race, or creed, or if you're a sex offender. (Prisoner, Doncaster)

There is nowt humane about being in prison, you have to share everything with people you don't know; mattresses, cutlery . . . there are no toilet seats and we've had cold showers . . . It's all about cleanliness and hygiene. Like in the laundry, they had no washing powder so they used shampoo instead! You have to share spoons between two because there's not enough and there is no time to sterilize them. It's hygiene—we used to have our own—and they're all dirty, there is HIV and hepatitis in prison and we're sharing cutlery—we could buy them from canteen. (Prisoner, Doncaster)

Definition of humanity   An environment characterized by kind regard for the person, mercy, and civility, which inflicts as little degradation as possible.

In our survey, the dimension 'humanity' consisted of five statements:

Statement 94   I am not being treated as a human being in here (0.789)
Statement 10   I am being looked after with humanity in here (0.767)
Statement 21   I am treated as a person of value in this prison (0.761)
Statement 29   Some of the treatment I receive in this prison is degrading (0.758)
Statement 47   Staff here treat me with kindness (0.754)

Table 5.1b shows the proportion of prisoners who agreed or strongly agreed with each statement. A total of 57.4 per cent of all the prisoners in the study agreed or strongly agreed that they were being 'looked after with humanity'. However, lower scores were found for 'being treated as a person of value', and 'being treated with kindness'. Even at Doncaster, where prisoners reported high scores on being 'looked after with humanity', only 39 per cent and 37 per cent felt they were being 'treated as a person of value' and 'with kindness' respectively. This discrepancy accounts for the slightly lower reliability score at Doncaster (see Table 5.4), and suggests that even in a 'high humanity' prison, levels of kindness and value may have upper limits in the penal context. Some prisoners gave examples of being 'treated as a person of value'. But it is noticeable that the percentages of prisoners agreeing with questions 2 and 4 in this dimension reduce, compared to the relatively high numbers agreeing with the statement that 'I am being looked after with humanity'. It is possible that questions 2 and 4 constitute a more substantive form of assent to the dimension of humanity, particularly as prisoners will recognize statement 1 due to its close links with the Statement of Purpose. Prisoners do distinguish here, and in 'respect', between 'formal civility' and a form of treatment which suggests more human depth or a fuller meaning to the term 'humanity' not captured by question 1 alone.[18]

Table 5.2b shows single item means, with all the scores and any significant differences between the prisons expressed positively. It shows that the *ranking* of prisons for items 1, 3, and 5 are almost identical, whereas this is not the case with the two other items. There might be a case for distinguishing in future studies between the 'mainly material' and 'mainly relational' aspects of this dimension, or for creating a new dimension out of statement 2, from 'respect' ('I am treated with respect by staff') and 2 and 4, from 'humanity' ('I am treated as a person of value' and 'staff here treat me with kindness').

Prisoners linked humanity with respect and trust.[19] At Doncaster, their sense of humanity was linked to the amount of time out of cell; the quality of the physical environment (both related to conditions); and being treated well by the staff on their wing (a more interpersonal matter). No significant differences between the prisons were found in question 4, 'staff here treat me with kindness'. Doncaster scored above 3, whereas the other four prisons scored just below 3 on that item. For the other questions, the significant differences tended to be between Doncaster, and Wandsworth and Belmarsh, although there was also a significant difference between Risley and Belmarsh on the item, 'I [am not] treated as a human being in here'.

The overall internal reliability of the dimension 'humanity' across all prisons was high, at 0.82. Three out of five prisons scored '3 or above'. Wandsworth scored just below 3, and Belmarsh scored lower. Doncaster was significantly higher on humanity than all four

---

[18] We are grateful to Tony Bottoms for this important insight.
[19] There were very high correlations between the items 'I feel that I am treated with respect by staff', 'I trust the officers in this prison' (0.601) and 'Staff in this prison often display honesty and integrity' (0.588).

public sector prisons. There were some important differences between the establishments on specific items (and we would argue that the difference between Risley/Holme House and Belmarsh is, on the face of it, substantial), but no statistically significant differences between the four public sector prisons on this dimension overall. We shall return to this 'surprising similarity' later.

TABLE 5.4.   Scores on dimension two: humanity

Prison	Reliability	Mean score
Doncaster	0.6714	3.3842
Risley	0.8914	3.0386
Holme House	0.8161	3.0383
Wandsworth	0.7945	2.9333
Belmarsh	0.8190	2.7398

Humanity was most strongly positively correlated with: respect (0.822); fairness (0.774); trust (0.759); relationships (0.749); and support (0.741).

Staff–Prisoner Relationships

What makes a good officer? . . . I don't know. It must be a pretty hard balance because I mean you've got to try and develop your interpersonal relationships with others so that you can control an environment without resorting to violence every minute of the day . . . there's a line drawn and although you can have a crack with them, everybody's aware there's a line that cannot be crossed . . . I don't think it's just a matter of being able to turn up here . . . I think there's a lot more to it.

(Prisoner; in Liebling *et al*. 1997: 90)

The best thing about this prison, for me, has been the relationships I have built up with people in here, you really get to know a person . . . It is the way you are treated and the facilities are good. Prison has taught me confidence in approaching staff, and talking to people in authority.

(Prisoner, Doncaster)

Staff–prisoner relationships are, as many have argued, central to prison life (Home Office 1984; Sparks *et al*. 1996; Liebling and

Price 2001). Scholars of the prison have argued that the attitudes and activities of prison officers are a major determinant of the prison experience (Glaser 1964; Hawkins 1976: 88): 'A hostile, superior, contemptuous, or dismissive attitude on the part of a staff member constitutes an attack on the prisoner's self-esteem and inspires resentment both against the staff member and against the values and standards which he symbolises' (Hawkins 1976: 92).[20]

Arguably, all of the dimensions in this chapter are about staff–prisoner relationships or the interpersonal conditions of imprisonment.[21] It is a well-established maxim in UK prisons that staff–prisoner relationships matter. As the Control Review Committee said in their review of a number of disturbances in maximum security prisons:

At the end of the day, nothing else that we can say will be as important as the general proposition that relations between staff and prisoners are at the heart of the whole prison system and that control and security flow from getting that relationship right. Prisons cannot be run by coercion: they depend on staff having a firm, confident and humane approach that enables them to maintain close contact with prisoners without abrasive confrontation. (Home Office 1984, para. 16)

The dimensions generated from our research demonstrate the extent to which this is the case, as at least five of them concern relational matters. It is commonly said that in 'good' prisons, relationships between staff and prisoners provide the glue which holds establishments together (see above; also Sparks *et al.* 1996; Liebling and Price 2001). The reverse is sometimes starkly illustrated, as recent prosecutions of prison officers at Wormwood Scrubs and exposure of brutality at other prisons show (see HMCIP 1999*d*, 2000*c*; Home Office 1991*a*). As Pilling said: 'Let us not kid ourselves that any of this is straight-forward. I wonder if there is any job in which the day-to-day relationships which have

---

[20] The question of what contribution prison staff make to the prison experience is an empirical one (*how much*, and in *what way?*), deserving of further exploration (see Liebling 1992: 148–9; Johnson and Price 1981; and Bondeson 1989). Biggam and Power (2002) argue that relationships between prisoners and families may contribute more to the prison experience. Prisoners may seek support from staff more often in practice than they are generally willing to admit in interviews (see later).

[21] We deal with prisoner–prisoner relationships in Chapter 7.

to be nurtured are so complex and delicate, or which requires such a range of personal qualities and skills?' (Pilling 1992: 5).

A key difference between prisons (and one which may in certain circumstances be more important to prisoners' evaluation of regimes than material differences) lies in the nature and quality of staff–prisoner relationships (see Sparks *et al.* 1996: 171–5). There is, as yet, little empirical research on the nature of these relationships, on differences between prisons, or on the characteristics of prison officers that are associated with positive relationships. There are, of course, formal and informal boundaries to relationships between staff and prisoners, and some reservations expressed by both groups about the use of the term (see Liebling and Price 2001). There is evidence that staff and prisoners may hold different preferences about relationships, with prisoners preferring clear boundaries and staff sometimes preferring quite high levels of involvement (e.g. Ben-David and Silfen 1994; also Dobash *et al.* 1986: 188–92; Cohen and Taylor 1972).

Many sociological studies of prison life begin by showing that the relationship between staff and prisoners tends to be characterized by mistrust and hostility, or a 'basic split' (Clemmer 1940; Cressey 1961; Sykes 1958; Morris and Morris 1963; Goffman 1961), but some argue that considerable variations occur, according to establishment type (e.g. whether the prison is treatment or custody oriented) and over time. Far from the oppositional relations described in the earliest sociological studies, however, other studies have shown that staff–prisoner relations can be accommodating and apparently collusive, in complex ways that involve a relationship with administration and which may leave the staff holding two positions at once (i.e. a stance towards prisoners, and a conflicting stance towards administration; see Shapira and Navon 1994). Sykes described this 'cracked monolith' (the false notion that staff have all the power) in his classic US study (Sykes 1958; see also Ohlin 1956; Glaser 1964, chapter 6;[22] and McCleery 1960). Shapira and Navon found a mutual dependence, and a blurred boundary between staff and prisoners in their Israeli study:

The feeling of 'no other choice' accompanying the use of force by the staff, added to the restricted means of punishment and the tendency to 'buy

[22] Glaser's chapter on inmate–staff relationships has the subtitle, *The Traditional Gap and its Many Crossings* (Glaser 1964: 119).

peace for concessions' which is widespread in Israeli prisons, present to our mind a relationship between inmates and staff totally different from that depicted by Goffman (1961). Instead of a staff that 'tends to feel superior and righteous' we have here a staff that is in a dilemma and often compromises and makes concessions. Instead of inmates feeling 'inferior, weak, blameworthy and guilty', we have inmates capable of manoeuvering, of applying pressure, of threatening and in the end—getting what they want. Instead of a great social distance between inmates and staff, we find co-operation between the two social categories, which goes as far as developing a relationship of mutual dependence. Instead of a clearly defined boundary between the two social strata, we find bounds between guards and inmates blurred to a large extent, intimate relations between prisoners and social workers and the adoption of a policy of 'concessions in exchange for peace' even on the part of the highest ranking officials. (Shapira and Navon 1985: 139)

Likewise, prisoners in our study said: 'Relationships work better when you have common ground, when something happens which affects staff and prisoners, like some policies, if both groups are upset about it there is a commonality which improves things a bit . . .' (prisoner, Belmarsh).

This kind of mutual identification could sometimes become collusive (see Home Office 1995; Sparks *et al.* 1996: 193). Or it could simply lead to a sympathetic view by prisoners of the prison staff condition:

No one has ever approached me about anything; I don't blame the officers, I'm surprised at how reasonable and polite 60–70 per cent of the officers are. They are . . . unmotivated and frustrated. A lack of proper control by the governors is where it begins. A less restrictive regime would improve relationships, but most prisoners see that staff are under pressure. (Prisoner, Belmarsh)

A study by Ben-David and Silfen identified five staff–prisoner relationship 'prototypes', ranging from punitive to integrative. Their study was carried out in a psychiatric ward rather than a prison, although the authors argue that there are sufficient similarities for the study to be relevant to the prison setting. The five prototypes were:

- the *punitive type*—who abstains as much as possible from communication with inmates, maintains an authoritative status

by ordering and demanding submission and obedience, and
stereotypes all inmates as 'bad' or 'mean';
- the *custodial type*—who relates to inmates as 'kept' people and
views guards' tasks as one of keeping the ward [wing] and the
inmates clean. Inmates are expected to obey orders, and communication is limited to role requirements;
- the *patronage type*—who is protective, generally an authoritative figure who grants assistance, protection, and guidance to
inmates perceived as weak and who answers inmates' instrumental needs and requests. Inmates are expected to co-operate
with guidance efforts but not to 'obey' or 'submit';
- the *therapist type*—who views inmates as patients—as suffering
from illness—and views his or her role as one of advising or
guiding willingly co-operative patients. Interaction is limited to
professional, therapeutic interactions, and relationships are
controlled by ethical and professional considerations; and
- the *integrative or personal type*—who has an egalitarian orientation and is flexible, adaptable, and readily available for interaction. Inmates are perceived as people with status almost equal
to that of the staff. Their mode of interaction varies with need
and circumstance and may be punitive, therapeutic, or custodial
(Ben-David and Silfen 1994: 132; see also Ben-David 1992).

Ben-David and colleagues argue that the greater the anxiety and
insecurity experienced by staff (personal, professional, and job-
related), the more likely it is that staff will be punitively oriented.
According to the authors, 'few occupations entail daily contact with
such a variety of sources of anxiety, fear and insecurity'
(Ben-David *et al.* 1996: 95). Apart from the threat of physical
danger, staff feel their power has been eroded due to 'an ongoing
series of prison reforms', the introduction of specialists, the threat of
legal action, and lack of support by management (Ben David *et al.*
1996: 95–6; also Jacobs 1977; Thomas 1972). Fear can lead to
flight or fight, causing staff either to 'retreat towards ritualism and
keeping a low profile' or a 'punitive and tough attitude towards
inmates and penal policy' (Ben-David *et al.* 1996: 96). Other studies
have characterized prison staff orientations towards prisoners in
typological ways, distinguishing between 'enforcer types', 'reciproc-
ators', 'avoiders', and the 'professional' (Gilbert 1997; and Muir
1977 for the origin of this typology, which applied to policing styles).

Interestingly, it is not the 'lax' or accommodating officer who is liked by prisoners (there are dangers for prisoners in 'avoidance' of rule breaking by other prisoners; see Liebling and Price 2001: 46–9), but the 'professional', who is prepared to use authority when this is required, but who does not over-use it (Liebling 2000). Glaser comments that officers credited as having been a rehabilitative influence on prisoners 'gave them self-respect': 'This did not mean that the officers were unusually lenient, lax, or permissive; it meant only that they treated the men with a personal interest and without pretension or condescension' (Glaser 1964: 144).

There is no question that relationships exist in prison between staff and prisoners, despite a certain amount of discomfort with the term. Prison officers apply the rules *through* relationships; that is, through typifications and assumptions (as well as real knowledges) of the person and the situation (see Liebling and Price 2001). There is some evidence that the nature and quality of staff–prisoner relationships changed in England and Wales after the publication of the Woolf Report in 1991, and the subsequent White Paper *Custody, Care and Justice* (Home Office 1991*b*), in favour of more liberal, closer relationships with higher regard for prisoners' rights and legitimate expectations (see Chapter 1). This arguably more liberal period ended with the escapes from Whitemoor and Parkhurst prisons in 1994/5, when it was shown that staff were not following procedures tightly enough. Accusations of 'appeasement' by staff and 'conditioning' by prisoners led to a renewed concern for 'boundaries', 'relationships within role', and closer attention to procedure or rule enforcement. As we shall argue, these oscillations and tensions constitute a key dynamic in prison life.

Staff attitudes towards prisoners may be affected by the policy and political climate (see Chapter 1), the *establishment*'s climate or culture (see Chapter 8), and their own character.

Prisoners raised questions of respect and trust as soon as we asked about staff–prisoner relationships:

When are relationships at their best? When screws get to see what lads are really like, when they get a chance to see them out of their pads. My wish would be that they treat you with more respect and don't categorize you but deal with you, recognize you, as individuals. They think we are all the same, staff get twisted . . . some staff talk to you as if they want you to retaliate . . . . (Prisoner, Holme House)

They're prepared to give anyone a chance to prove themselves, that is the best thing about the relationships. (Prisoner, Wandsworth)

There was a difference between what officers would do in front of each other, and what they might do on their own:

I get on with the officers. They talk normally to you when they are on their own with you, talk to you like a human being. They talk differently when another officer is there. When they are on their own they don't need to put an act on of 'being in control'. When other officers are there it's the 'them' and 'us' thing. Ninety-nine per cent of the officers are good though. (Prisoner, Wandsworth)

Staff on certain wings could differ in their overall approach to prisoners: 'It's like a different jail, this wing, compared to the rest. The screws are more laid back and don't rush you behind your door. If you ask them to do something they do it, or they let you know if they can't' (prisoner, Holme House).[23]

Prisoners drew distinctions between what officers were like in general, and what the best officers were prepared to do:

The majority of screws just haven't got time for you. A few will do anything for you and do sort stuff out for me, they'll come straight back to you, not fobbing you off and will tell you if they haven't managed to sort it out. I get on OK with my personal officer; I had a couple of problems at home and he let me have a phone call and he was the one who referred me to CARATS. (Prisoner, Risley)[24]

They often commented that the uniform seemed to make a difference: 'The civilian staff don't judge you, whoever you are they sort of get on with you, whereas [uniformed or discipline] staff talk down to you' (prisoner, Risley).

Good relationships were characterized by the feeling of getting 'behind the uniform', to the person: 'If you are wrong they come down on you but if you play by the rules, which are not strict anyway, they are easy going. At the end of the day, if you look through the uniforms they are human beings' (prisoner, Risley).

[23] We prepared individual reports to each of the establishments participating in this study, which included an analysis of wing differences.

[24] Counselling, assessment, referral, advice, and throughcare service (for assistance with drug use).

We have distinguished in earlier work between 'good' (i.e. close) relationships and 'right' (i.e. balanced) relationships (Liebling and Price 2001: 76 and 104–6). Close relationships had the disadvantage that staff used more discretion and life could become less predictable for prisoners: 'I would wish for them to be more consistent. At the end of the day they are humans and everyone is different but some use and make up their own rules and some turn a blind eye to things, but you need to know where you stand; its consistency basically' (prisoner, Risley).

But as the key to a good relationship was individuality, there was some tension between the need for consistency and the 'judicious use of exceptions' (Bottoms 1998):

Relationships between staff and inmates come in many forms. Some inmates stand out to staff as trouble causers; others stand out as sensible. This plays a lot on the inmate–staff relationship. If I had a wish for staff–inmate relationships, I'd wish that when one inmate causes a member of staff problems, being abusive and unco-operative, that the member or members of staff involved don't take it out on other inmates to relieve the stress. (Prisoner, Doncaster)

The experience of imprisonment was qualitatively different when relationships in general—or individual interactions—were distant or poor:

If you are taken to the block they are not the staff you get on with and have friendships with. That's where it breaks down for me—their job will come first and it destroys relationships. (Prisoner, Belmarsh)

Some staff go out of their way to provoke and rile you and see if you react and then nick you. It's not unheard of for them to come in your pad and push you around a bit so they can cart you off to the seg. (Prisoner, Holme House)

The worst thing about this prison is the way staff treat you, most are OK but some call you a wanker, or a piece of shit; they talk down to you. The best thing is when they say thanks to you when you have done a good job, something you didn't have to do. (Prisoner, Holme House)

Prisoners wanted staff to understand them and to treat them carefully: 'My one wish for staff–inmate relationships would be for more staff training, on a psychological level, in terms of how to deal with people at all levels and from different cultures. I wish staff would be more polite and genuine' (prisoner, Belmarsh).

We saw examples of this, for instance, individual officers reacting patiently when confronted by an angry prisoner: 'If you can hold back and just say, "Now why did you say that, what's the problem? Come on then, have your say". Sometimes it all ends in tears and they just needed you to listen' (officer, Risley).

Many prisoners thought the level of interaction with staff was low. Some felt that staff were confrontational towards prisoners and about half thought there was a 'strong them and us' culture in the prison (see Table 5.5):

I get more support from the prisoners than from the staff. Lads are helping lads and club together rather than going to the staff because that wouldn't make it work. You forge friendships with the prisoners in here and not the staff because it is them versus us. I wouldn't want to have them call me by my first name—I feel threatened by them and want to keep my distance. (Prisoner, Risley)

Definition of relationships   The manner in, and extent to which, staff and prisoners interact during rule-enforcing and non-rule-enforcing transactions.

In our survey, the dimension 'relationships' consisted of five statements:

Statement 5	Relationships between staff and prisoners in this prison are good (0.754)
Statement 63	There is a strong sense, or culture, of 'them and us' in this prison (0.733)
Statement 76	The level of staff interaction with prisoners in here is low (0.652)
Statement 18	Personally, I get on well with the officers on my wing (0.647)
Statement 37	Staff are confrontational towards prisoners in this prison (0.628)

Table 5.5 shows the proportion of prisoners who agreed or strongly agreed with each statement. There are some interesting variations here, with Belmarsh and Wandsworth having low overall dimension scores, but for slightly different reasons.

Sixty-four per cent of prisoners at Doncaster, but only 42 per cent of prisoners at Belmarsh, Holme House, and Risley, and a lower 33 per cent of prisoners at Wandsworth felt that relationships between staff and prisoners were good (Table 5.5). Some prisoners, at all establishments, strongly disagreed with this statement. Almost three-quarters of prisoners at all establishments felt they got on very well with the officers on their wing (this was lowest at Wandsworth, but relatively high at Belmarsh). More than half of prisoners agreed that staff are confrontational towards prisoners at Belmarsh, which is difficult to reconcile with the response above (unless there is a stark difference at Belmarsh between officers who know prisoners individually, and 'officers in general' or officers when they are together). There were some comments about staff 'barking' orders, or intimidating (particularly new) prisoners, for example at Risley. Sixty-four per cent of prisoners at Belmarsh (26 per cent at Doncaster) thought there was a strong 'them and us' culture in the prison. A striking difference can be seen between Doncaster and the other establishments in the response to question 5: only 20 per cent of prisoners at Doncaster agreed that 'the level of interaction with staff is quite low'; about half agreed with this statement at the four other establishments. This is despite (or because of) relatively low staffing levels at Doncaster. This has the intended effect of making

TABLE 5.5. Percentage of prisoners who agree/strongly agree with statements about relationships

Statement (relationships)	Belmarsh	Holme House	Risley	Doncaster	Wandsworth
1. Relationships between staff and prisoners in this prison are good.	42.1	41.5	41.6	64.0[a]	33.4[b]
2. Personally, I get on well with the officers on my wing.	78.4	71.2	67.4	80.7[a]	63.4[b]
3. Staff are confrontational towards prisoners in this prison.	51.8[b]	46.8	35.7	26.4[a]	43.3
4. There is a strong sense of 'them and us' in this prison.	63.9[b]	55.3	48.5	26.3[a]	55.0
5. The level of staff interaction with prisoners here is low.	50.6	41.5	42.6	20.1[a]	58.3[b]

TABLE 5.6. Prisoners' views on relationships: individual item mean scores

Item/statement	Item scores (1–5)					ANOVA (Mean difference)									
	B	HH	R	D	W	B&HH	B&R	B&D	B&W	HH&R	HH&D	HH&W	R&D	R&W	D&W
Relationships between staff and prisoners in this prison are good.	3.20	3.09	3.06	3.63ª	3.02ᵇ	N/s	N/s	0.43	N/s	N/s	0.55*	N/s	0.57*	N/s	0.61*
Personally, I get on well with the officers on my wing.	3.87	3.79	3.69	3.94ª	3.65ᵇ	N/s	N/s	N/s	N/s	N/s	N/s	N/s	N/s	N/s	N/s
Staff are [not] confrontational towards prisoners in this prison.	2.58ᵇ	2.77	2.85	3.09ª	2.68	N/s	N/s	0.51*	N/s	N/s	N/s	N/s	N/s	N/s	N/s
There is [not] a strong sense, or culture, of 'them and us' in this prison.	2.27ᵇ	2.55	2.51	3.06ª	2.43	N/s	N/s	0.80**	N/s	N/s	0.51*	N/s	0.55*	N/s	0.63*
The level of staff interaction with prisoners here is [high].	2.65	2.88	2.75	3.28ª	2.47ᵇ	N/s	N/s	0.63**	N/s	N/s	0.40	N/s	0.53*	N/s	0.81**

prisoners dependent on a small number of individual officers (and the officers more than usually dependent on goodwill; see James *et al.* 1997: 69–73).

Table 5.6 shows mean scores and significant differences. It is interesting to note that the significant differences between establishments are in statements 1, 3, 4, and 5, and not in statement 2 (how prisoners get on personally with the officers on their wing).

The overall internal reliability of the dimension 'relationships' across all prisons was high, at 0.71, but a bit variable (note the lower reliability for Doncaster and Wandsworth). Prisoners frequently commented during the interview that they wanted to distinguish between 'officers in general', which normally meant 'on my wing', and 'the few officers who stand out, who I try to approach most of the time'. They found it difficult to generalize on these questions. Prisoners tended to have quite strong negative feelings about those officers they felt were unsympathetic, but also quite strong positive feelings (which they wanted recorded or captured by the study) about those officers they did like, who they felt treated them fairly. We shall consider the role of relationships again in the dimension 'fairness', in Chapter 6.

Two of the five prisons scored 3 or above on relationships (Table 5.7). The only statistically significant differences were between Doncaster and the other four prisons, although Belmarsh and Wandsworth both attracted low scores (particularly on items relating to 'confrontation'). The dimension 'relationships' was significantly positively correlated with all other dimensions. It was most highly correlated with: respect (0.755), humanity (0.749), fairness (0.730), trust (0.704), and support (0.678).

TABLE 5.7.   Scores on dimension three: relationships

Prison	Reliability	Dimension score
Doncaster	0.5957	**3.4000**
Holme House	0.7014	3.0149
Risley	0.8071	2.9743
Belmarsh	0.6366	2.9133
Wandsworth	0.5723	2.8500

Trust

> . . . quality of life and subjective well-being are strongly correlated
> with the presence of generalised trust.
>
> (Sztompka 1999: 15)

> . . . to paralyze the trusting impulse it is enough to dehumanise . . .
> the target of trust, to purge it of its human traits: individuality,
> identity, dignity, autonomy.
>
> (Sztompka 1999: 65)

Without trust, it would be difficult to get up in the morning
(O'Neill 2002: 4). We need trust because humans have agency
(Seligman 1997), and 'all guarantees are incomplete' (O'Neill
2002: 6). Basic trust, Erikson argued, brings confidence. It eases
discomfort and encourages hope rather than despair.[25] We 'cannot
flourish without trust' (Hollis 1998: 4). Its absence in an individual
can be linked to psychosis, depressive illness, and problems of
identity (Erikson 1995). The 're-establishment of a state of trust
has been found to be a basic requirement of therapy' (Erikson
1995: 223). According to Sztompka, writing later and more sociologically, trust is a tool for navigating our way in conditions of
uncertainty, where others have freedom. It may be particularly
relevant in conditions where one party is relatively helpless, and
has little control over circumstances. It is intertwined with expectations, which may be cognitive, emotional, and moral. Trust is an
interactive notion (unlike hope and confidence, which are more
individual). It is 'a bet about the future contingent actions of others' (Sztompka 1999: 25) and it consists of two main components:
belief and commitment, of varying types and degrees. It is, like
many of our other dimensions, an *asymmetric* concept, in the sense
that trust may be built in one way, and slowly, yet destroyed in
another, and in an instant. Offering trust brings with it vulnerability, the extent of which may be dependent on the type of trust
offered and the amount of risk involved. The consequences of
misplaced trust may be adverse, in practical and psychological
respects (Sztompka 1999: 31). For example, we may lose faith in
our capacity to evaluate others. Erikson argued that respectful
treatment could lead to trust, and both were in turn related to

---

[25] This relationship is reciprocal: 'trust reflects an optimistic view of the world
and the belief that you can control your own fate' (Uslaner 2002: 12).

dignity (Friedman 1999: 92).[26] As Sztompka argues (and see below), trust is linked to humanity.

The word 'trust' is loaded and constrained in the prison context. As in many circumstances, admitting that one trusts a prisoner as a member of staff is tantamount to jettisoning the basic wisdom of 'jail craft': 'never trust a con'. Beneath this façade, and contrary to much that is written about the prison, trust exists, unevenly.[27] Trust is won, lost, and redirected in subtle and instructive ways. There are 'trusted' positions—the orderlies, the listeners,[28] wing representatives—and there are labels of distrust—the obligatory yellow stripes worn by those considered to pose an escape risk. There are bonds, of durable and less durable varieties and there is, importantly, social co-operation more often than there is not. At least a minimum level of trust is essential to social co-operation even in the prison. Trust is, in the prison and elsewhere, a 'fragile commodity': 'if it erodes in any part of the mosaic it brings down an awful lot with it' (Dasgupta 1988).

Only in conditions of maximum physical coercion is there no room at all for trust. In a sense, acts of trust and distrust characterize the prison: 'You have to trust them and they trust me. You have to feel that if you don't know something you can ask and don't try to bluff your way through' (officer).

Prison officers extend reserved forms of trust to individual prisoners, and these acts may defy the rules (Liebling and Price 2001): 'I trust some prisoners and have a good relationship with most. If I was on my own and something happened, I believe they would look after me. Prisoners trust me to keep things confidential. In some cases, I trust prisoners enough to give them my keys (obviously I never would!)' (officer).

[26] 'When the adult was open, confident, genuinely respectful, and caring, the child would respond openly, respectfully and trustingly . . . this personal relationship of trust and self-revelation only occurred if the supervising adult treated the youngster's art-work, compositions, and other representations with the same dignity that the adult expected in response to his own work' (Friedman 1999: 92). Seligman suggests, likewise, that trust is related to civility (Seligman 1997: 66).

[27] Sykes and Messinger assert that prisoners have 'lost the privilege of being trusted' (Sykes and Messinger 1960: 14). Whilst this is the case in general, their statement is in need of qualification and elaboration. Seligman talks of trust in *roles* as well as trust in the 'open spaces' between roles (Seligman 1997: 18).

[28] Listeners are Samaritan-trained volunteer prisoner counsellors, who provide support to other prisoners.

Prison officers have a 'working personality' that demands of them that they generally distrust prisoners (like police officers with suspects; see Skolnick 1966). Paradoxically, in other asymmetric relationships (e.g. between professional and client), levels of trustworthiness in the more powerful partner is an imperative (Levi and Pithouse forthcoming).

Trust may operate in concentric circles—as a prisoner I trust this officer, so I trust the social role or position of the prison officer, so I trust the prison system, so I trust the social order (see Bottoms 2002). Trust and distrust are 'contagious' (Sztompka 1999: 50) and can spread upwards and downwards: 'When distrust appears it has a tendency to expand upwards, from more concrete toward more general levels' (Sztompka 1999: 50). So in a prison, who trusts, where do we find trust, and to what extent? Is it unevenly distributed, so that normal patterns of reciprocity cannot function? To what is it related? Do prisoners trust staff? Do they trust governors? Under what circumstances?

Sztompka argues that in the everyday functioning of public institutions: 'If citizens are treated with dignity, they are more apt to extend trust' (Sztompka 1999: 198 n.).

The principles of democratic accountability are all 'fundamentally important for producing trust' (Sztompka 1999: 188; see also Braithwaite and Levi 1998). They provide the structural and cultural preconditions for trust, helping to establish: 'normative certainty, transparency of social organisation, stability of the social order, accountability of power, enactment of rights and obligations, enforcement of duties and responsibilities, and the personal dignity, integrity, and autonomy of the people, as well as their feeling of empowerment' (Sztompka 1999: 143).

The number of protest events (and, in the community, electoral abstentions) may be an indicator of low levels of trust in a society. A 'trust culture' is predictable, stable, and open (and may be 'anchored in tradition'; Sztompka 1999: 122–3; see also Giddens 1991). Trust and co-operation are, then, linked. Trust 'underlies order in civil society' (Sztompka 1999: 102; Braithwaite and Levi 1998).[29]

Prisons, of course, are not democracies. In conflictual societies, where there are low levels of trust, those who extend it 'will be

---

[29] Others have argued, similarly, that fair procedures and a decent manner of treatment increase co-operation (Tyler and Blader 2000; see Ch. 6).

censured for stupidity, naivety, credulity, and simple-mindedness. Cynicism, cheating, egoism, evasion of laws, outwitting the system, turn into virtues' (Sztompka 1999: 179). Vigilance becomes a substitute for trust.

In a moral community, 'us' means those we trust, toward whom we are loyal—or whose trust we are careful not to breach (Sztompka 1999: 5). When prisoners and staff talk of 'us' and 'them', this is, in part, what they mean.[30] There are structural limits on the likelihood of trust being 'built into' prisoner and prison officer roles (Seligman 1997), but these limits are not unqualified. Trust is a 'quality of a relationship', but, in prison, this relationship is a guarded one.[31] It is acceptable, even prudent, to operate with high levels of distrust. The 'rules' allow a certain amount of mutual suspiciousness: 'It's a game of cat and mouse. We're trying to catch them out, they're trying to get one over on us' (officer, in Liebling and Price 1999).

But if distrust reaches upper limits, it can produce escalation of mutual suspicion (Sztompka 1999: 62) and hostility. Trust operates as a 'lubricant of co-operation' (ibid.), but is also necessary for individual mental health (Erikson 1995; Levi and Pithouse forthcoming). It grows with use and decays with disuse (ibid.).[32]

Where prisoners trust staff, what is it that they trust them to do? What is it reasonable to expect? Expectations vary according to role. Are there normative rules about the role of the prison officer which shape expectations and thereby determine the circumstances in which an officer can be trusted? Individuals can be expected to be competent, efficient, reliable, law-abiding, fair, predictable, honest, and helpful, for example (Sztompka 1999: 55–6). Research has shown that these kinds of expectations may vary according to

---

[30] It is important to point out that not all prisoners trust other prisoners, so there are some qualifications to this 'talk'.

[31] Uslaner distinguishes between trust of strangers (a moral value) and trust of those we already know (a more strategic form of trust; Uslaner 2002). Hollis, similarly, distinguishes between predictive and normative trust (Hollis 1998: 10–12). Prisons make these distinctions unworkable. Uslaner shows that generalized trust decreases with inequality (ibid.).

[32] In a culture of distrust: 'People start to dream about a father figure, a strong autocratic leader, a charismatic personality . . . who would purge with an iron hand all untrustworthy ("suspicious" or "alien") persons, organisations, and institutions, and who would restore, if necessary by force, the semblance of order, predictability, and continuity in social life' (Sztompka 1999: 118).

gender, occupational status, educational level, and other variables (Sztompka 1999: 58–60).[33] Is competence or efficiency important in prisoner evaluations of the officer? The criterion most often mentioned during interviews was honesty, or 'straight-talk'. Prisoners and staff are experts in the detection of inauthenticity (Goffman 1967; Liebling and Price 2001).

Sztompka argues that to expect or wish for efficiency and competence 'is a relatively strong bet of trust' (Sztompka 1999: 53). We witnessed a very low level of trust by staff in their senior managers in one of our prisons, and quite low levels in three of the others (in the fourth we found slightly higher levels; see Chapter 8; and Liebling *et al.* 2001). This is important in understanding prisons and their differences, but also in setting the context in which staff–prisoner relationships 'go on'. Compared with staff views of those above them, staff levels of trust of prisoners may be considerably higher than expected. In two of the prisons in our study, staff reported (to their own surprise) that they trusted prisoners slightly more than they trusted their senior managers. This has important sociological (and managerial) consequences.

The violation or abuse of trust ('the lie') has psychological and social consequences and constitutes 'an offence against mankind' (Levi and Pithouse forthcoming; O'Neill 2000: 78–9, 2002). Trust is selective: we choose to trust, and by doing so, we take a risk.[34] 'The question is how much trust there is (between whom, for which purposes) rather than whether "people" trust or distrust others' (Levi and Pithouse forthcoming). As Levi and Pithouse argue (forthcoming), trust is a linear rather than binary concept.[35] It

---

[33] 'There is a . . . certain personality syndrome correlated with trustfulness. It includes . . . activism rather than passivism, optimism rather than pessimism, future orientation rather than a present or traditionalist orientation, high aspirations rather than low aspirations, success orientation rather than adaptive orientation, innovative drive rather than conformity-proneness' (Sztompka 1999: 125). Rutter showed that those individuals most likely to trust were more likely to be trustworthy themselves and to enjoy better social and personal adjustment (Levi and Pithouse forthcoming; Rutter 1982).

[34] The extent to which, and the speed at which, staff and prisoners were prepared to trust us was humbling, and suggests that a defensive posture masks a yearning to place trust in others.

[35] Levi and Pithouse distinguish between 'contractual trust', 'competence trust', and 'goodwill trust' (Levi and Pithouse forthcoming). This is an important categorization, with relevance to some of Paternoster *et al.*'s criteria for procedural fairness

grows organically out of embedded social relationships (Gambetta 1988) and is in this sense dependent upon time: 'Trust is established through honesty . . . through people doing as they say they'll do' (officer).

Misztal argues, like others, that empirical differences in achieved levels of trust can explain levels of co-operation in social and political environments (Misztal 1996: 2; Hollis 1998). Prisoners linked trust to compliance: '[INTERVIEWER: 'Is there anything you have seen in other prisons which you would like to happen here?'] I'd say more freedom. They need to have more trust, to a degree. If they trusted us we could conform more when we come out of our cells' (prisoner, Wandsworth).

As the present study was intended to explore the meaning of and experience of trust (amongst other concepts), we asked open-ended questions before devising the questions intended to capture closely levels as well as types of trust. How did staff and prisoners think about and experience trust? We were interested in both levels of trust extended towards staff, and the experience of being trusted: the 'flow of trust'.

Trust by prisoners in staff meant having confidence that they would do what they said they would do: stop fights, keep confidences, complete paperwork, return with answers, and treat them as individuals. They tended to develop trust in particular officers, 'the ones that have a different outlook, where it's not all about ego' (prisoner). We asked prisoners to give us examples of occasions when they had placed their trust in staff:

I had hit another prisoner in the gym, but I hadn't been caught. I needed to get it off my chest, as I was really angry and wanted to bash him up. I confided in an officer, who just advised me to let it go. The officer knew I'd had trouble with this inmate before, but he pointed out that I'd lose time if I assaulted him (I am going out in seven weeks). The officer didn't report me or nick me, and told me he was glad I'd trusted him with the information. Then he told me something personal and trusted me back. (Prisoner, Holme House)

A question asking prisoners to 'Tell me about a time when you feel you have been treated with fairness or respect here' was answered

(Paternoster *et al.* 1997; see Ch. 6). We are primarily concerned with 'goodwill trust', although adherence to rules and legitimate expectations, and professional competence will inform prisoners' evaluations (see e.g. Liebling and Price 2001).

with a reference to trust placed in one individual by staff:

When I got here they called me in the office for sentence planning but one female officer could see I wasn't up to it and said, 'we'll do it later'. She said if I ever needed to talk I could come to her. I told her about my case and everything, explained it all and she told me to keep fighting. She thought I had been stitched up. She said it sounded like I was set up and that she was on my side. She believed me, she could tell what I said was true and said these things do happen. She shouldn't really help me but she gives me advice on my case and the appeal. (Prisoner, Holme House)

Prisoners were cautious about trusting staff and other prisoners, but found they could not function without some trust:

Not 100 per cent because you can't in here; you have to trust them to a certain extent. You can't do everything on your own, you have got to confide in someone sometimes but you have to be careful because some people take it as weakness. With prisoners, I confide in them, mostly people do, about your family. Like I don't see my kids and it's really hard and it's better to get it off your chest. (Prisoner, Holme House)

You can't let your emotions get to you. The only person I trust in here is myself . . . and my pad mate, because you have to. (Prisoner, Holme House)

As we have argued elsewhere, staff and prisoners trade in *gradations* of trust (Liebling and Price 2001). Lack of trust was sometimes accounted for by prisoners (often encouraged by staff—see Sparks *et al.* 1996, on Albany) by focusing on senior managers, rather than on officers: 'There should be more trust, of prisoners. No one gets home leave, because if one lad doesn't come back that's a black mark for the prison. They don't trust prisoners, when one doesn't come back they think we're all like that. It's not the officers, it's higher up than that' (prisoner, Holme House).

Prisons are normally seen as 'low trust' environments. We found that they are, but that the existence of some trust is analytically important. Prisons differ significantly in degrees of trust. Trust was mentioned often and was highly valued:

I trust the majority of staff. It used to be 'them versus us' but things have changed. I can be relaxed because I trust people so I'm not looking over my shoulder; there isn't a tense atmosphere here. (Prisoner, Belmarsh)

On my last sentence here I was on Houseblock six, where you start at the bottom and work your way up the ladder; I got to be the unit co-ordinator, at the top. I was in a trusted and responsible position. You are on first-name terms there and can build up a close relationship so I was treated with respect and trusted. (Prisoner, Holme House)

. . . one officer, the lads were being funny with me because I came in with them and I got offered the [trustee] job, given the privilege, and I got some threats from them. I had this trouble before in my last prison, so I went back to the officer and declined the job and he talked me round. [Staff] said there was no bullying and that they dealt with bullies; I trusted them and it has paid off. I trust them to deal with it properly . . . I have faith in what he said. (Prisoner, Risley)

I trust them all. Trust is being able to tell them something important and they'll keep it to themselves. I trust staff more than prisoners, because they are not in here, they just work here. (Prisoner, Doncaster)

Prisoners also talked about when trust had been placed in them:

Life is at its best here when I am doing my job; on the wing there is nothing to do all day . . . It's hard to get a job though . . . I got mine through a mate. It's a trustworthy job and I appreciate that my boss does trust me to an extent. (Prisoner, Risley)

The best thing about this prison is the aspect of trust. An incident happened and I told them it was nothing to do with me; they believed me and it paid off for both of us. (Prisoner, Doncaster)

They do put trust in some prisoners, if they get to know them. (Prisoner, Wandsworth)

Prisoners needed to be trusted to do things—keep medication in their cell, have an extra five minutes before lock-up, or make a phone call. In the constrained environment of a prison, trust was a basic requirement:

We have to trust in their word, that they are doing what they say they will do. (Prisoner)

You place your trust in prison officers every day. Every time you put your post in the bubble [staff office] you are trusting that they will post it. Every time you leave your pad unattended you are trusting them. Being able to trust them makes you feel more comfortable. (Prisoner, Holme House)

You have to trust the officers, there is no one else to trust. If there were more staff there would be a lot more trust placed in prisoners. (Prisoner, Wandsworth)[36]

> **Definition of trust**   Reliance on the honesty, reliability, and good sense of a person; the level of responsibility or confidence invested in and experienced by individuals.

Our definition (and our discussion) arguably deals mainly with individualized trust. We did not explore prisoner trust and distrust of 'the system' or any other 'collective' form of trust in our survey. We shall return to the question, first raised in Chapter 2, of trust in organizations in later chapters.

In our structured survey, the dimension 'trust' consisted of four statements:

Statement 58   I feel that I am trusted quite a lot in this prison (0.793)

Statement 15   I trust the officers in this prison (0.777)

Statement 45   This prison is good at placing trust in prisoners (0.773)

Statement 71   Staff in this prison often display honesty and integrity (0.753)

Table 5.8 shows the percentage of prisoners who agreed or strongly agreed with each statement. It is interesting to note that prisoners did not trust staff much at Risley, despite having reported relatively high levels of respect. Trust may be related to predictability, as well as 'friendliness', so that Risley is experienced as a prison in which little confidence about outcomes is possible. Belmarsh has the lowest scores on prisoners feeling trusted (which corresponds with its high security status and ethos). Prisoners likewise felt that staff were least trustworthy at Belmarsh (see question 4). Doncaster clearly had higher than average levels of trust, in both directions.

Three of the four statements discriminated between the prisons, with only the statement 'I feel that I am trusted quite a lot in this prison' not attracting significantly different answers (Table 5.9).

---

[36] It is interesting to note the contradiction between this faith expressed by the prisoner, and the evidence that increasing officer numbers, above a certain level, may encourage staff to talk to each other rather than to prisoners.

The overall internal reliability score of the dimension 'trust' across all prisons was high, at 0.78. Only one of the five prisons (Doncaster) scored 3 or above on trust and this prison was significantly higher on trust than Holme House, Risley, and Belmarsh (but not Wandsworth, interestingly; Table 5.10). Trust was significantly positively correlated with all other dimensions. It was most highly correlated with: humanity (0.759); respect (0.746); fairness (0.739); support (0.725); and relationships (0.704).

TABLE 5.8. Percentage of prisoners who agree/strongly agree with statements about trust and support

Statements	Belmarsh	Holme House	Risley	Doncaster	Wandsworth
(a) Trust					
1. I trust the officers in this prison.	31.3	28.7	21.8[b]	39.5[a]	25.0
2. This prison is good at placing trust in prisoners.	12.0[b]	22.4	23.8	37.7[a]	20.0
3. I feel that I am trusted quite a lot in this prison.	28.9[b]	35.1	30.7	36.8[a]	36.7
4. Staff in this prison display honesty and integrity.	22.9[b]	34.1	31.7	43.9[a]	31.7
(b) Support					
1. I receive support from staff in this prison when I need it.	43.3	54.2	44.5	65.8[a]	41.6[b]
2. I have been helped significantly by a member of staff in this prison with a particular problem.	60.3[a]	52.1	51.5	47.4	43.4[b]
3. Staff in this prison show concern and understanding towards me.	33.7	30.9	27.8	38.6[a]	21.7[b]
4. Staff in this prison are generally not available to talk to.	32.5	29.8	29.7	16.7[a]	46.6[b]

Table 5.9.   Prisoner views on trust and support: individual item mean scores

Item/Statement	Item scores (1–5)					ANOVA (Mean difference)									
	B	HH	R	D	W	B&HH	B&R	B&D	B&W	HH&R	HH&D	HH&W	R&D	R&W	D&W
(a) Trust															
I trust the officers in this prison.	2.69	2.56	2.51[b]	3.17[a]	2.75	N/s	N/s	0.48	N/s	N/s	0.60*	N/s	0.65*	N/s	N/s
This prison is good at placing trust in prisoners.	2.40[b]	2.49	2.59	3.04[a]	2.60	N/s	N/s	0.65*	N/s	N/s	0.55*	N/s	0.45*	N/s	N/s
I feel that I am trusted quite a lot in this prison.	2.66[b]	2.85	2.78	3.08[a]	2.88	N/s	N/s	N/s	N/s	N/s	N/s	N/s	N/s	N/s	N/s
Staff in this prison often display honesty and integrity.	2.81[b]	2.97	2.97	3.33[a]	3.02	N/s	N/s	0.53*	N/s	N/s	0.37	N/s	0.36	N/s	N/s
(b) Support															
I receive support from staff in this prison when I need it.	3.22	3.30	3.10[b]	3.66[a]	3.10[b]	N/s	N/s	0.44	N/s	N/s	N/s	N/s	0.56*	N/s	0.56*
I have been helped significantly by a member of staff in this prison with a particular problem.	3.53[a]	3.38	3.35	3.41	3.22[b]	N/s	N/s	N/s	N/s	N/s	N/s	N/s	N/s	N/s	N/s
Staff in this prison show concern and understanding towards me.	2.96	2.87	2.90	3.20[a]	2.80[b]	N/s	N/s	N/s	N/s	N/s	N/s	N/s	N/s	N/s	N/s
Staff in this prison [are generally] available to talk to.	3.01	3.12	3.01	3.32[a]	2.85[b]	N/s	N/s	N/s	N/s	N/s	N/s	N/s	N/s	N/s	0.47

TABLE 5.10. Scores on dimension
four: trust

Prison	Reliability	Mean score
Doncaster	0.7841	3.1557
Wandsworth	0.7255	2.8125
Holme House	0.7554	2.7181
Risley	0.8065	2.7153
Belmarsh	0.7246	2.6386

Support

[H]uman beings of all ages are happiest and able to deploy their
talents to best advantage when they are confident that, standing
behind them, there are one or more trusted persons who will
come to their aid should difficulties arise.

(Bowlby 1979: 103)

Finally, in this chapter, the dimension 'support'. This is closely related
to both the concept of trust and the concept of relationships, as
we shall show. Support means being able to rely on another, having someone to talk to, being important to another person, or
having a role model (Harvey 2002). Being supported involves the
feeling of being cared for and receiving information that one has
some value (ibid.). Social support has been shown to be positively
associated with health (Brown and Harris 1978; Argyle 1987;
Bowlby 1969, 1979). It plays a 'stress-buffering' role, 'protecting
individuals from the detrimental impact of stressful life events' and
acting as a 'coping assistant' (Harvey 2002; Biggam and Power
1997; Hobbs and Dear 2000). Albrecht and Adelman argue that
support consists of: 'Verbal and non-verbal communication
between recipients and providers that reduces uncertainty about the
situation, the self, the other, or the relationship, and functions to
enhance a perception of personal control in one's life experience'
(Albrecht and Adelman 1987: 19).

Relationships between staff and prisoners can hardly be expected
to be the companionable interactions described by Bowlby, Holmes,
and others (e.g. Holmes 1993). They are heavy with power imbal-
ances and high levels of dependency. Interactions with officers in
uniform have huge symbolic meaning. Prison officers may not
always see themselves as a source of social support to prisoners.
Supportive relationships are constituted *despite*, rather than

through, inherently low levels of trust. But it is clear from our account above that, despite these constraints, officers can play a crucial role in the support of prisoners, as they are key providers (or withholders) of practical and emotional support throughout a period of custody (Biggam and Power 1997). They have the power to distribute recognition, civility, and affirmation, as well as material privileges, as we shall see later (see Mathiesen 1965; also Liebling 2000). Biggam and Power found that anxious, depressed, and hopeless young prisoners wished for higher levels of practical and emotional support from officers they knew best on a wing and from their personal officers (Biggam and Power 1997). Prisoners may find support easier to solicit from prison staff than from fellow prisoners (Zamble and Porporino 1988; although see Hobbs and Dear 2000). Biggam and Power found that perceived deficits in support from officers were 'the major predictors of anxiety, depression and hopelessness' (Biggam and Power 1997: 226).

The provision of support is a specific aspect of prison staff practice and constitutes an important part of their role. Prisoners gave many examples of support they had received:

The first week here I was depressed and an officer came up to me and said 'Are you OK?', I said 'Not really', he said 'Do you want to talk?', I said 'Not really', but I was happy he came up to me and I feel like I could go back to him and talk if I needed to because he showed concern and interest. (Prisoner, Belmarsh)

Everyone's been OK to me, staff have helped out every time I've asked for things, my belongings or some advice, everyone has given me an honest answer and even spoken about my problems and the reasons why I'm in here. They are quite understanding. I trust the ones I spoke to. (Prisoner, Belmarsh)

They seem to know when you're on a downer. I've seen them approach prisoners to see if they are OK. Some don't have that line between inmate and officer, although some prisoners don't want that to happen. They can't be seen talking to staff because that makes them a grass. (Prisoner, Holme House)

I wouldn't tell the staff this but they are very good. Some are lazy but they're fine. I wouldn't take my problems to them, though, but I never speak about my problems. If you have a problem you can go to them and they listen to genuine grievances. It's gentler; that's the only way I can describe it; staff will meet you halfway. (Prisoner, Holme House)

When my partner died, staff gave me all the support they could and made all the enquiries possible. They made sure I was OK. Because there is a risk

of self-harm I have received lots of understanding from my personal officer and lots of concern. I was referred to Psychology, who were brilliant,
and it's an ongoing thing. It's one of the only things getting me through it.
(Prisoner, Risley)

If you're struggling with something they help you; if you go to them with
a problem they will help you as much as they can. I've been able to talk to
someone if I've needed to, they try and advise you about what is best to
do. They are helpful on here—as much as they can—I don't have a bad
word to say about any of the regulars on here. (Prisoner, Risley)

The provision of support was linked to prisoners' evaluations of
fairness: 'I've never been treated unfairly in here by them. I don't
think they [staff] could be better. If you need to talk and they are
busy they'll say "Can you come back in twenty minutes?" and
when you go back they'll be there for you; if you need to sit and
talk they will sit and talk to you' (prisoner, Risley).

Sometimes the specific provision of support came mainly from
non-uniformed staff: 'The CARAT workers have helped me;
they've done a lot for me. They've made things clear to me and I'm
going to be sorted out with outside placements. Health care have
been good, getting tests and that. I've had to sort myself out and
depend on the officers' (prisoner, Doncaster).

As Biggam and Power found, prisoners generally felt the need for
more support from prison officers:

I would wish that staff would listen to inmates much more and they tend
to taint people with the same brush, but there are genuine people with genuine problems in here and they shouldn't just fob you off. (Prisoner,
Wandsworth)

I think we need more support; asking us if we need to talk instead of us
having to ask. People don't help you enough, they just bang you up. They
need to reason with you, talk to you about your offence. I wouldn't ask for
help because then you don't know if they are really listening, or if it's just
because you've asked. (Prisoner, Doncaster)

There were clear distinctions between staff who were supportive
and those who were not: 'Four or five members of staff do help
prisoners. The rest, there is no relationship at all, they treat us
mostly like animals, preferring to bang the door rather than listen
and solve problems' (prisoner, Wandsworth).

The denial of support was linked to a lack of respect. Providing support demonstrated that the individual mattered:

I'd want to tell staff to treat prisoners with respect, and don't forget some are proper upset about being here. There is not enough help for those that can't handle it properly. The bell is for emergency only. I heard one officer say 'you'd better be swinging in there boy', which isn't funny really because he could be feeling like that, you don't know. They can see people who need help but my impression is that they seem to laugh it off. Some people are suffering and their mind is deteriorating; they only get help when they're smashing down their door. (Prisoner, Wandsworth)

Definition of support   To help, carry the weight of or bear the pressure; to give aid or courage; approval and strength. To ease the strain.

In our survey, the dimension 'support' consisted of four statements:

Statement 6   I receive support from staff in this prison when I need it (0.833)

Statement 49   Staff in this prison show concern and understanding towards me (0.796)

Statement 19   I have been helped significantly by a member of staff in this prison with a particular problem (0.757)

Statement 67   Staff in the prison are generally not available to talk to (0.677)

Table 5.8*b* shows the proportion of prisoners who agreed or strongly agreed with each statement. We find some of the 'special character' of Belmarsh in its unusually high levels of agreement with the statement, 'I have been significantly helped by a member of staff in this prison with a particular problem'. Many prisoners at Belmarsh spoke at length about the trauma experienced during their early days in custody and linked their examples of support to this period. This difference almost disappears, however, when means are used (see Table 5.9*b*), suggesting that other prisoners at Belmarsh strongly disagreed with this statement. We can see that, as with the dimension 'humanity', notions of 'concern and understanding' may be a stronger test of the notion of support than our other questions. Levels of availability clearly differ, in opposition to staff numbers on the wings.

Only statement 1 discriminated significantly between establishments, once mean scores were used. Doncaster was significantly higher than Risley and Wandsworth, on receiving 'support from staff when I need it'.

The overall internal reliability of the dimension 'support' across all prisons was high, at 0.77. Four prisons scored 3 or above on support. Higher levels of support than trust are reported. The only significant difference was between Doncaster and Wandsworth. The difference between Risley and Doncaster almost reached statistical significance.

Support was significantly positively correlated with all other dimensions. It was most highly correlated with: humanity (0.741), respect and trust (0.725), relationships (0.678), and fairness (0.652).

TABLE 5.11. Scores on dimension five: support

Prison	Reliability	Mean score
Doncaster	0.7441	3.3991
Belmarsh	0.6371	3.1807
Holme House	0.7700	3.1676
Risley	0.7918	3.0891
Wandsworth	0.8428	2.9917

We explored all the items belonging to dimensions discussed in this chapter together, using a factor analysis.[37] This was conducted in order to explore whether different (or additional) patterns could be found in the data, and whether alternative scales could be devised.

Two factors arose: a general factor containing twelve of the 'relationships' items, and a factor we called 'frustration' or 'alienation' including most of the negatively worded items (Table 5.12).

[37] 'A mathematically complex method of reducing a large set of variables to a smaller set of underlying variables' (de Vaus 1999: 257). The aim of a factor analysis is 'to examine whether, on the basis of people's answers to questions, a smaller number of more general factors that underlie answers to individual questions can be identified' . . . 'in other words [e.g. when asking questions about what people consider to be important] some variables tend to cluster together' (de Vaus 1999: 157). Factor analysis identifies items which belong together statistically and combines them into scales. De Vaus cautions us that one problem with factor analysis is that regardless of the variables used a set of 'underlying factors will be produced, whether they make sense or not' (p. 258). They may also cluster together because they are causally related. It is important therefore to be guided by our conceptual work in this process of analysis (de Vaus 1999: 158).

TABLE 5.12.   Two factors arising from the original 'relationships' dimensions

Factor 1: Relations with staff (12 items (0.93))	Factor 2: Frustration/alienation (four items (0.82))
Staff in this prison show concern and understanding towards me (0.818) (S)	This prison is poor at treating prisoners with respect (0.819) (R)
I feel that I am treated with respect by staff in this prison (0.809) (R)	I am not being treated as a human being in here (0.773) (H)
Staff here treat me with kindness (0.790) (H)	There is a strong sense, or culture, of 'them and us' in this prison (0.670) (Rel)
I receive support from staff in this prison when I need it (0.764) (S)	Some of the treatment I receive in this prison is degrading (0.657) (H)
I am treated as a person of value in this prison (0.743) (H)	
Relationships between staff and prisoners in this prison are good (0.741) (Rel)	
Staff address and talk to me in a respectful manner (0.733) (R)	
I trust the officers in this prison (0.720) (T)	
Personally, I get on well with the officers on my wing (0.707) (Rel)	
Staff in this prison often display honesty and integrity (0.685) (T)	
I feel that I am trusted quite a lot in this prison (0.647) (T)	
I am being looked after with humanity in here (0.605) (H)	

Notes: S: support; R: respect; H: humanity; Rel: relations; T: trust.

This factor may have arisen as a result of these items attracting a stronger response from prisoners than other items. Alternatively, it may be that prisons where staff have poor attitudes (and a 'them and us' culture) result in an overall poor treatment in many related areas of prison life.

Here, Belmarsh emerges as lowest on the general 'relationships' factor and also on 'frustration/alienation' (Table 5.13). Wandsworth is next lowest, but achieves slightly above 3 on relationships. There is a greater difference between Doncaster and the other prisons on the new 'frustration/alienation' factor. It may therefore be a useful additional factor to use in further analysis, as it is more discriminating than the general relationships factor. We prefer to retain the conceptual and empirical distinctions between the concepts of 'trust', 'respect', 'humanity', and 'relationships' because establishments attract different scores on these dimensions and they are meaningful to (and were selected by) prisoners. We might improve our measurement of each by devising new items in the light of further fieldwork and reflection. It might be productive to use the above general 'relationships' and 'frustration' factors in addition, or to explore additional combinations of items based on the correlation matrix.[38]

TABLE 5.13. Mean scores on the revised dimensions, 'relationships' and 'frustration'

Prison	Factor 1: Relationships	Factor 2: Frustration/alienation
Belmarsh	2.9960[b]	2.5271[b]
Holme House	3.0550	2.8324
Risley	3.0338	2.8762
Doncaster	3.4094[a]	3.3268[a]
Wandsworth	3.0208	2.6917

Notes: Significant differences: relationships—D and B (p < 0.05), HH (p < 0.05), R (p < 0.05), W (p < 0.05); Frustration/alienation—D and B (p < 0.001), HH (p < 0.005), R (p < 0.005), W (p = 0.001); the difference between Belmarsh and Risley is almost statistically significant, at p = 0.09. a indicates highest; b indicates lowest scores.

Conclusions

The main purpose of this chapter was to explore the meaning and measurement of key relational dimensions of prison life. We have shown how and why these dimensions matter, and how their presence or absence makes one prison experience better, or worse, than another. Prisoners reported higher levels of support than respect, humanity, and relationships in all five prisons in our study, and they reported significantly lower levels of trust. These distinctions were despite the fact that these dimensions—respect, humanity, relationships, trust, and support—were all highly correlated with

[38] Available from author.

each other. We can see from the accounts given by prisoners that they are closely linked, but they are also distinguishable, conceptually and empirically.[39] Relationships require certain degrees of support, and respect, and perhaps, finally, trust, in order to become established and to function. The prisons in our study differed significantly in their scores on each of the dimensions. Most of the differences in the 'relationships' category were between Doncaster and the other prisons, but there were also some differences on some items: between, for example, Belmarsh and Holme House on humanity (see p. 214). Prisons have different 'profiles' in the kinds of relationships that exist, so that Belmarsh has relatively high levels of support, despite rather low levels of respect, humanity, and trust.

It is important to note that trust can exist in the prison environment, and that relationships can function despite relatively low levels of trust. As Sparks *et al.* noted: '[Staff and prisoners] share the same physical and social space. They cannot sustain a state of submerged warfare all the time. They develop familiarities. They banter. There are acts of concern and kindness. It is a situation marked by contradictions' (Sparks *et al.* 1996: 196).

There are two contrasting truisms relating to prison life: first, that prison is full of tension and conflict; and secondly, that prison life is all about relationships. We have begun, in this chapter, to reconcile this apparent contradiction, and to construct ways of describing and evaluating different degrees and types of relationships which characterize different prisons. We have also tried to identify different aspects of relationships, and to show that prisons differ in these important areas of prison life. Our illustrations from the interviews show that individual prisoners may experience each prison in different ways, but the results suggest that there are significant mean differences that reflect, more accurately than other methods, each prison's character. If we summarize the findings so far using rank orderings (where 1 is highest and 5 is lowest), we begin to see some

[39] Of the five relationships dimensions, respect, humanity, relationships, and trust discriminated better between prisons. The only question in the dimension 'support' that discriminated clearly between prisons was item 1: 'I receive support from staff in this prison when I need it' (despite an acceptable reliability score for the dimension as it stands). It was clear from what prisoners said that support was the most difficult concept to distinguish from relationships. We therefore incorporated the apparently more discriminating item in the dimension 'support' in the dimension 'relationships' in the revised version of our Prison Quality Scale.

interesting features of each prison's quality of life, as evaluated by prisoners (Table 5.14). Doncaster comes first on everything (however, see the discussion in Chapter 9 on why all was not necessarily well at Doncaster). Belmarsh, somewhat surprisingly, comes second on 'support'. Holme House scores lower than Risley on 'frustration', 'respect', and 'humanity'. But Risley scores lower than three of the other prisons on 'trust' and 'support'. Wandsworth scores surprisingly high (relative to the other prisons) on 'trust'.

TABLE 5.14.   Five prisons ranked by dimensions

Prison	Respect	Humanity	Relationships	Trust	Support	Factor 1 (Rels.)	Factor 2 (Frust.)
Doncaster	1	1	1	1	1	1	1
Belmarsh	5	5	4	5	2	5	5
Holme House	3	3	2	3	3	2	3
Risley	2	2	3	4	4	3	2
Wandsworth	4	4	5	2	5	4	4

There were some surprising similarities between the four public sector prisons in this study on many of the relational dimensions, suggesting something of an overarching culture which is distinctive (and relatively low on respect and relationships), at least in the prisons included in this study. This apparent cultural finding (which resonates with our discussion in Chapter 2) reduces the statistical significance of some subtle differences in each prison's style. Some differences that approached significance were found, however, and the results reflected understandable variations in prisoners' perceptions of their treatment in specific areas of each prison's life.[40]

We move, in the next chapter, to another set of dimensions that matter and to areas of prison life where clearer differences emerged.

[40] We have found greater variation (and some outperforming of private sector prisons) in ongoing work (see Liebling submitted).

6

Regime Dimensions

Introduction

In this chapter we consider some dimensions about which others have had a great deal to say. 'Fairness' and 'order', for example, are conceptually two of the most important aspects of prison life (Bottoms 1999, 2003b). They are also, as others have noted, two of the central ideas in political theory. Prisons can be said to constitute a 'special case' of the problem of social co-operation (Sparks et al. 1996: 29). We shall develop this analysis, both to deepen our understanding of the prison and what goes on there, and to speculate on the significance of these dimensions, of fairness and unfairness, safety and danger, and so on, to the prison experience.

This group was called 'regime' dimensions because they are arguably centrally related to the more formal day-to-day delivery of many aspects of prison life. But we shall see later that there are also some important links between several of the dimensions in this conceptual category and the previous set. We shall explore them individually, before concluding this chapter with an exploratory analysis of the relationships between them. The dimensions in this conceptual group are fairness, order, safety, well-being, personal development, family contact, and decency.

Fairness

> [Fairness] does not mean that the answer will always be 'yes' and that is not what most prisoners expect. It does mean giving prisoners opportunity to get across their point of view and taking it seriously. It means applying rules with consistency, avoiding petty discrimination, and being proportionate in the use of sanctions for misconduct. Indeed it means ensuring equal treatment whatever a person's race, creed or ethnic group.
>
> (Pilling 1992: 6)

A society satisfying the principles of justice as fairness comes as close as a society can to being a voluntary scheme, for it meets the principles which free and equal persons would assent to under conditions that are fair.

(Rawls 1980: 13)

Rawls's theory of justice as fairness is derived from an imaginary 'original position',[1] in which rational actors are behind a 'veil of ignorance'.[2] In this state, they choose the principles of justice. The terms 'fairness' and 'justice' can be used interchangeably for our purposes (Lucas 1980; although see Raphael 2001). These principles are that basic rights and duties are assigned equally, and that inequalities of wealth and authority are just 'only if they result in compensating benefits for everyone, and in particular for the least advantaged members of society' (Rawls 1980: 14–15). According to Rawls, fairness should *generate trust* (Rawls 1980: 497–8). Others have argued that fairness 'involves an ability to consider consistently and without contradiction the interests and intentions of others' (Siegal 1982: 1). It requires impartiality (Barry 1989). On the other hand, it expresses the 'value of persons' (Raphael 2001: 248). Lucas describes justice as: 'a dynamic equilibrium under tension, wanting to treat the individual as tenderly as possible, yet being prepared, for sufficiently compelling reasons, to take a tough line' (Lucas 1980: 18).

Justice requires balance (or a 'mean between excess and defect', as Aristotle argued).[3] It is a basic or primary value, central to law, ethics, and politics (Raphael 2001).[4] Justice requires that 'our award should be just right', but the feeling of an infringement of

---

[1] The 'original position' is a hypothetical (some say too artificially contrived) situation in which free and rational actors find themselves in a situation of equality; it corresponds to the state of nature in traditional social contract theories (Rawls 1980: 11–12).

[2] That is, 'no-one knows his place in society, his class position or social status' or their 'fortune in the distribution of natural assets and abilities, intelligence, strength' and so on, when making their choices about the principles of justice. This ensures that no one is advantaged or disadvantaged 'by the outcome of natural chance or the contingency of social circumstances' (Rawls 1980: 12). This mechanism ensures that equal concern and respect is afforded to each person (Dworkin 1975: 50–1).

[3] See Raphael (2001: 43) and Aristotle's *Nicomachean Ethics* (1976).

[4] Satisfying legal justice may be different from satisfying the requirements of moral justice (Raphael 2001).

justice is, justifiably Lucas argues, 'greater if we err on the side of less than if we err on the side of more' (Lucas 1980: 18). Fairness (a form of particular justice to an individual) depends on *how* decisions are taken, the *frame of mind* in which they are taken, and the results (ibid. 4). In other words, fairness is intrinsically bound up with the *quality of the behaviour* of individuals, especially those in power (Tyler 1990). Judgements of fairness depend to a significant extent on the *manner* of one's treatment as well as (sometimes, more than) outcomes (Paternoster *et al.* 1997; Tyler and Blader 2000).[5] Fairness is related to, but is more than, equality. It often requires the resolution of competing claims and interests. Raphael argues that, whilst utility is not irrelevant to fairness, 'some of the most perplexing conflicts are conflicts between the principle of utility and an aspect of justice' (Raphael 2001: 201).[6]

So how, then, is fairness possible in a prison, where freedom has been lost and 'the proper distribution of the benefits and burdens of social cooperation' cannot be equal? Rawls was concerned, in these early statements of his work, with 'the special case of a well-ordered society' (Rawls 1980: 572), which makes his theory seem of little relevance to the prison at first sight.[7]

Rawls's framework is non-utilitarian; that is, he is conscious of the discrepancies between many of the implications of utilitarian thinking and 'our ordinary moral convictions' (Rawls 1996, p. xvii). Rawls argues that 'in justice as fairness the principles of justice are prior to considerations of efficiency' (Rawls 1996: 69). Prisons can only be more or less fair, and they may be less immune than other institutions from considerations of efficiency and utility. But we can judge the fairness of a prison by reference to certain principles or criteria derived from less inherently depriving situations: is there

---

[5] Judgements about fairness often involve perceptions of the treatment of others. In this sense it is not an exclusively self-regarding value. 'Young children are quick to complain that action which discriminates in favour of one child or one group is unfair, and they do not confine this complaint to thought of their own advantage but are ready to speak up for the claims of others' (Raphael 2001: 208).

[6] We sometimes distinguish between 'what is right in the circumstances' and 'what is just' (Raphael 2001: 212).

[7] In later revisions of his work (Rawls 1996), he argues that societies are no longer united in their moral beliefs but may still be united in their conception of justice. He thus draws a distinction between moral and political philosophy; that is, between moral and political visions of justice. In the prison, there are often shared beliefs about what is 'fair' (Sparks *et al.* 1996, and later).

discrimination? Are decisions made impartially? Are there formal avenues for complaint?

There has been considerable recent empirical and theoretical interest in fairness in prisons (Home Office 1991a; Ahmad 1996; Bottoms and Rose 1998; Sparks *et al.* 1996; Liebling and Price 2001; and Bottoms 2003b). This research has developed rapidly since the link was explicitly made between a major series of disorders in English prisons and the perceptions of prisoners that they were not being treated *fairly*.[8] Fairness, according to the Woolf Report, included due process or procedural justice (e.g. being informed about reasons for decisions made) but also decent facilities, programmes, means of redress, and the manner of prisoners' treatment by staff (Home Office 1991a).

An unpublished doctoral study, arising out of discussions held at the time of the Woolf Inquiry (see Sparks *et al.* 1996, appendix B), constitutes the most comprehensive empirical analysis of fairness in prison to date. Ahmad set out to explore 'the perceived fairness of day-to-day life in prison' (Ahmad 1996: 64) by conducting detailed structured interviews with 230 prisoners in three prisons of different types: a local prison, a category C prison, and a maximum security prison. He argued that fairness in prison had three main components: the fairness of staff; the fairness of the regime; and the fairness of procedures (for example, disciplinary and grievance procedures). Ahmad argued that there is 'a direct relationship between the nature of rule enforcement and the quality of life that inmates experience inside the prison' (Ahmad 1996: 26). He found that prisoners emphasized interpersonal aspects of fairness (which he suggests included being 'treated with respect and humanity'; Ahmad 1996: 84). Prisoners wanted 'understanding and concern', and 'equality' (ibid.).[9] Rules, procedures, and relationships together

---

[8] There was some important work on disciplinary and grievance procedures prior to this date, which led to significant improvements, in particular to the conduct of disciplinary hearings in prison, and to the kinds of punishments that could be given (e.g. Ditchfield and Duncan 1987; Quinn 1993; Loucks 1994, 1995; and Vagg 1994). We are looking more broadly at fairness overall rather than at adjudications or grievance procedures, although similar issues of principle arise. Adjudications are a good example of the 'them and us' structure that often arises in prison, but which is 'hidden from view' much of the time (Cunningham 1996: 39; see also Boyle 1985; McDermott and King 1988).

[9] These might be in tension, of course. We shall return to this point below.

provided fairness. If the staff were perceived as fair, then the regime was also likely to be perceived as fair (and vice versa). Relational aspects of staff behaviour, such as personal contact, helpfulness, and positive attitudes, were strongly related to judgements about staff fairness. Ahmad hypothesized that prisoners saw staff as having more control over these variables than over specific details of the regime, which they could blame on the governor (Ahmad 1996: 144). Features of a regime that contributed strongly to prisoners' judgements about fairness included the amount of time they spent locked up, the frequency and conduct of searches, and privacy (e.g. on the telephone; ibid. 188–90).

Secondary multivariate analysis of Ahmad's data, conducted by Bottoms and Rose, showed that: 'when prisoners assess overall staff-prisoner relationships in a prison, their perceptions of the fairness of the uniformed staff are of central importance to their judgment of the overall quality of staff-prisoner relationships' (Bottoms and Rose 1998: 223).

Perceived staff fairness was seen as the 'main determinant of perceived overall regime fairness' (ibid.; and see Fig. 6.1). Prisoners' perceptions of staff–prisoner relationships, and prisoners' perceptions of staff fairness, were very highly related. Perceptions of fairness in prison were 'substantially more dependent' on perceptions of staff fairness and staff–prisoner relationships than they were on 'the objective quality of various specific regime features' (i.e. material provision), or prisoners' evaluations of the fairness of these regime features: 'In a very real sense, therefore, it would seem that staff actually embody, in prisoners' eyes, the regime of a prison, and its fairness' (Bottoms and Rose 1998: 227).

This is a crucial insight, and it has significant implications for our understanding of prisons, the way in which they are evaluated by prisoners, and for our thinking about the work of prison officers. It is less surprising, following this analysis, that relationships are central to prison life.

Ahmad's research, and the secondary analysis above, provide empirical support for the relational vision of justice expressed by critics of the 'rules and rights' school of justice (see Gilligan 1982; Heidensohn 1986; Burnside and Baker 1994). In the prison, as elsewhere, both the 'Portia' and the 'Persephone' models of justice (rationality and proceduralism; and care and subjectivity, respectively) matter. These models, or aspects of justice, are sometimes

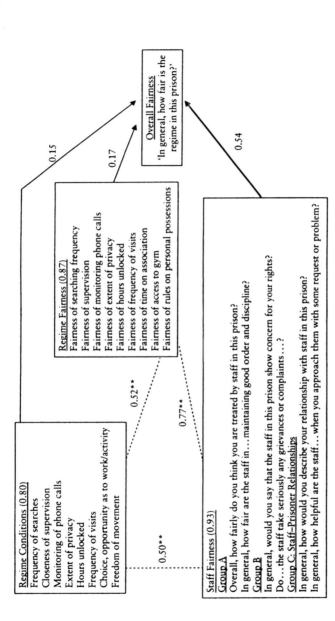

FIGURE 6.1. Fairness in prison: a multivariate analysis

Notes: Alpha values (reliability scores) are given in parantheses. Beta values (effect sizes) on the dependent variable 'overall fairness' are shown next to each arrow. All are statistically significant, but the value for 'staff fairness' is much higher than the values for 'regime conditions' and 'regime fairness'. Relationships between the three key independent variables are shown on dotted lines. ** indicates that they are all significant at the p < 0.01 level (see further Bottoms and Rose 1998).

Source: Adapted from Bottoms and Rose (1998), and further discussions with the authors.

regarded as 'essentially masculine' and 'essentially feminine' (Heidensohn 1986: 293). However, this assumption that the tension is essentially gendered does not hold in prison (or in other institutions where rules are numerous, and one party is especially powerless). Rules are 'open textured': that is, words are vague and ambiguous; no two situations are exactly alike; and rules may be used with very different purposes in mind (Twining and Miers 1982; Hart 1961). Discretion is inevitable where there are rules (and there are too many rules to follow in prison life to make it through the day). Rules and contexts have to be interpreted (Dixon 1997; Liebling 2000; Dworkin 1977).[10] Rules are a 'resource', rather as relationships can be, in prison.[11] To consider prison life and work as either simply a matter of rule-enforcement, or as unconstrained by rules, is a sociologically impoverished conception (Price and Liebling 1998). There is a tension between any detached application of the rules, and the resolution of real, complex moral and social problems. Perceptions of fairness depend on a 'more contextual mode of judgment' than rules and procedures allow (Heidensohn 1986: 296; O'Neill 2000: 53). Formal justice, which assumes equality, must be tempered by care, or mercy, and must be sensitive to differences between cases. As we have argued elsewhere, and as others insist, rules can never offer 'complete guidance' (Liebling 2000; O'Neill 2000: 54; Dixon 1997). What follows is that: 'If principles and rules cannot fully guide action, they must be complemented by judgment' (O'Neill 2000: 55). Flexibility on its own can soon degenerate into arbitrariness and anarchy. Some resolution between rules in the book and their application in action must therefore be found, via clear principles and sound judgement. But principles, to which we have multiple allegiances, often conflict. Kant described judgement as a 'peculiar talent' (O'Neill 2000: 62), albeit one that can be developed. O'Neill suggests that 'some account must be given' of when we fail to adhere to all the principles to which we express allegiance. A degree of moral failure is inevitable, but to strive for justice, we

---

[10] There is 'strong' discretion (with few constraints) and 'weak' discretion (constrained by specified criteria); it can also be provisional (subject to review). See Hawkins (1992).

[11] Dixon calls this account of rules the culturalist approach; it is to be contrasted with the legalistic-bureaucratic model, whereby rules determine action (see Dixon 1997).

should make our institutions as just as we can, and our reasoning clear (O'Neill 2000: 63–4). What is just is 'what can be approved of from an impartial standpoint' (Barry 1989: 362).

This analysis has considerable relevance to prison life, where prison officers engage, knowingly or otherwise, in refined exercises of judgement continually (Hay and Sparks 1991; Liebling and Price 2001; Stohr *et al.* 2000; Sparks *et al.* 1996).[12] We shall consider this point more fully in our account of the dimension 'order', below.

Fairness, according to prisoners, required a complex balance between consistency and flexibility in their day-to-day lives:

I like it in a jail where you know the rules and they don't keep changing all the time; here you know where you stand. (Prisoner, Belmarsh)

You get treated fairly mostly all the time. Last week the cleaning officer gave everyone a Mars Bar because we had all worked well. There are sixteen of us, cleaners and servery workers. I was shocked, something like that had never happened before, and he didn't have to do it but it was nice because it proves someone appreciates the work you do. (Prisoner, Holme House)

I think it is fair, there's no really big bad points about it. They tell you you get nothing and plenty of it when you come in but you can work your way up and get privileges and you know if you mess about they will take them off you so you know where you stand, and they warn you about things first. (Prisoner, Holme House)

An example of fairness is when there was a football match on and it went to extra time; it was time to bang us up but they let us stay out and watch it. (Prisoner, Doncaster)

Fairness is a hard line to go by because sometimes fairness from staff is not based on you as a person—if another inmate was to cause problems it can affect the attitude of that member of staff towards other inmates in general. So to be treated with fairness is not just based on prison rules or an inmate's rights, or from the behaviour of that inmate, it goes on the frame of mind the member of staff is in. (Prisoner, Doncaster)

Just as over-individualized decisions could lead to arbitrariness, consistency did not always lead to fairness (as prisoners are saying, above)—although *parity* (treating like cases alike) might. Harrison addresses the problem that there is an important distinction

---

[12] See Muir (1977, ch. 7) on the importance of this ability in policing.

between 'the mechanical operation of rules' and 'the question of justice' in a particular case.[13] This is often the case in prison. Harrison suggests that mercy, or compassion, can be rationally exercised (Bottoms 1998: 67–8; Barry 1989). In practice, Bottoms argues: 'Demands for mercy within a legal system especially arise when a given general rule seems likely to lead to an inappropriate (or unjust) result in a specific case; in other words, such demands "are really often arguments about the need for flexibility" in the application of rules' (Bottoms 1998: 68).

Rules are 'blunt instruments', which do not take into account the complexity or individuality of a particular case (Harrison 1992; Hawkins 1992; Padfield and Gelsthorpe 2003). Real differences between individuals and situations justify differential applications of a rule, provided that the application of the rule—its enforcement or suspension—would be similar in any similar case. How can this sort of flexibility avoid becoming arbitrary decision-making? How can we be certain of 'what counts as a relevant consideration'? Harrison argues as follows:

> What it requires is the trained application of the reasons of law to individual cases . . . If justice is to be done, the decision should be taken for reasons and be rationally defensible. Such a rational defence will include emphasising all the special features of the particular case . . . Judgment is needed, but the best judgment is informed by, and sensitive to, reason. The best judgment is not just about one case in isolation, but is sensitive to the possible implications of that judgment on other cases. (Harrison 1992: 122)

What this means is that discretion should be 'bound' by guidelines which are 'flexible enough to be adaptable to meet the special circumstances of particular cases' (Bottoms 1998: 69). Such guidelines 'draw upon and yet also develop the *deep structures* of' (in this case) penological practice and thinking (in Giddens's language, the 'practical consciousness' of prison officers).[14] As Bottoms argues:

> Bringing an occupation's 'practical consciousness' into the realm of formal discussion and deliberation may well be an appropriate way to begin to develop 'the trained application of the reasons of law to individual cases', as Harrison puts it, precisely because the collective 'practical consciousness'

---

[13] Gilligan and others have argued that 'justice', 'impartiality', and 'equality' may be abstract, cold virtues, and that human beings want their interests treated mercifully, not impartially (Gilligan 1982; Harrison 1992).   [14] See pp. 287–8.

often contains some extremely useful pointers to good practice. But equally, in this process of explicit articulation of previous practice, it will very likely become apparent that appropriate good practice guidelines will need to go beyond the insights of 'practical consciousness'—which insights may at crucial points be overly vague ... or even, on careful reflection, actually insupportable when critically considered. (Bottoms 1998: 70)

What this means is that open dialogue about detail—about boundaries, decision-making, and the use of power, drawing on daily practice—is crucial to the development of 'the right' *deep structures*, or practices. Right behaviour is 'conduct for which reasons could be given' (Harrison 1992: 115). Actions are not justified by their *source* (because one has the power to decide) but by their *content* (i.e. can the decision be justified?). Without this constraint, we have 'power without accountability'. Harrison argues: 'Every use of power, of the power of states against citizens, should be subject to review' (Harrison 1992: 118). Discretion should be conceived as not 'arbitrary judgment' but 'rather, the ability to discern correctly' (Harrison 1992: 119). The 'peculiar talent' of judgement is crucial in prison, where so much power to decide (on small but important detail) rests with prison staff. There is a need for flexibility, but also a demand for consistency that places a constraint on flexible decision-making. There should be some means for dealing with 'exceptions', without reaching 'outside it to arbitrary judgment' (ibid. 120). If there are *principles*, as well as rules, then judgement is guided, and flexibility is possible. Where disagreements arise, there is a need for dialogue and (Harrison says) reason: 'It's all to do with self-confidence, with seeing the bigger picture ... This is where management come in' (senior manager, in Liebling and Price 1999; and see Chapter 8).

What prisoners want is a version of Harrison's 'flexibility within clear boundaries'. There is much to be said about where the appropriate boundaries might lie (as suggested in Chapter 1; see also Liebling (2002), and Chapter 9): 'They interpret the rules fairly consistently, but they break the rules in our favour a lot of the time, like in using the phones' (prisoner, Wandsworth).

There was a great deal of support for the importance of 'process' over 'outcomes', as suggested by the procedural justice literature (Paternoster *et al.* 1997; Tyler and Blader 2000):

My visiting order got lost for my girlfriend to come and visit. They called to see if another one was sent out and explained the process to me. They were consistent with the rules so that was fair. I waited 28 days. I had been told the procedure and it actually happens. Although I don't agree with the procedure itself I think it is fair because they were consistent with whatever procedure was in place. (Prisoner, Wandsworth)

Fairness is getting off with quite a lot but not too much. An incident happened the other week when I talked back and was abusive to an officer on the wing. He banged me up and told me that I had to move wing. Later that day he got me on my own and explained why I needed to move wing. He explained that the new prisoners on the wing had to learn that you can't talk to an officer in that way. After the incident he treated me fairly by explaining that I had to be moved to prove to the other prisoners that you can't talk that way. It was fair 'cause he explained it to me. (Prisoner, Doncaster)

This is not to say that outcomes are irrelevant:

The best I have ever been treated with fairness was the occasion I returned a positive drug test. This was a result of the medication which I have to take and it was revoked after my files were checked. The banter which followed was a massive dose of good humour, which helped me through a stressful time. One officer was a great help to me over this. (Prisoner, Risley)

At work, I was nicked for having something in my box in the workshop under my table that wasn't mine. I was found not guilty on adjudication; that was the right and fair decision; for once the governor believed me. (Prisoner, Wandsworth)

It was not always clear where the line was crossed between fair but unwelcome, and just unfair:

[This prisoner was on the basic regime and had been on it four and a half months] . . . . because I had a bad attitude. It can be for stupid things like passing a smoke. You get one warning before they put you on basic and then if you get three minus's you get seven days added and if you get nicked on basic you have to start on basic from the beginning. It's not necessarily unfair putting you on but it is really hard to get off once you're on. (Prisoner, Holme House)

It was easier to identify unfairness than it was to talk about what fairness was. Unfairness was inconsistency, as well as failure to distinguish among individuals:

Generally we are not treated fairly here because it is so inconsistent, you get different answers from the same officer. (Prisoner, Belmarsh)

It wasn't fair last night. Someone threw an orange juice and everyone got banged up for it—that's not fair. (Prisoner, Doncaster)

Too great a distinction between individuals, and on inappropriate criteria, amounted to discrimination:

Some staff think you're not punished enough; they treat you differently depending on your offence. (Prisoner, Holme House)

Staff do not treat prisoners fairly when distributing privileges. The privileges that are taken all seem to be off certain people only, same when they're given out only to a select few—the staff favourites. (Prisoner, Wandsworth)

I think prisoners on 'own protection' deserve to be treated as normal prisoners because VPs and 'basics' get all the activities and we get nothing and I think it's disgusting. (Prisoner, Holme House)

Failure to stick to one's word was unfair: 'Half of them are fair with you, if you are fair with them. A lot say they'll do something and then never do' (prisoner, Holme House).[15]

Prisoners could distinguish between their perception that the material circumstances of prison life were unfair—due to lack of access to courses or home leave—and their empathy with staff, whom they sometimes saw as the unwilling victims of a 'system' that did not work (see also Sparks *et al.* 1996; Bottoms and Rose 1998):

Some staff try and wind you up on purpose to nick you so I keep myself to myself and only ask if I have to. You get fed up asking for anything. They're fed up too—they're doing cat B duties on a cat C site. We're supposed to have more opportunities to find help here but everything is such a struggle, it puts you off. I do a lot through outside probation now, about home leave and stuff. I asked about it, to my personal officer, and they said 'we don't do home leave in here', he went to the senior officer and they just don't know. But I know some people who get it and they just said something about there being a loophole in the system . . . You think you're getting somewhere and then you get hit with sledgehammers . . . Prison makes you more aggressive, it's helping me become more stoic. (Prisoner, Risley)

Definition of fairness   Free from dishonesty or discrimination. To be treated clearly, consistently, impartially, in conformity with rules or standards, with access to redress, and courteously.

[15] See Raphael (2001, *passim*).

In our survey, the dimension 'fairness' consisted of 15 statements. We wanted to explore this concept in some detail, given the research outlined above, to include regime and staff fairness components, and the notions of clarity and consistency:[16]

Statement 9   Privileges are given and taken fairly in this prison (0.763)

Statement 84   The regime in this prison is fair (0.758)

Statement 7   Staff here treat prisoners fairly when applying the rules (0.733)

Statement 8   Staff here treat prisoners fairly when distributing privileges (0.720)

Statement 20   Overall, I am treated fairly by staff in this prison (0.655)

Statement 24   The rules and regulations in this prison are made clear to me (0.652)

Statement 31   In general, I think that the disciplinary system in here is unfair (0.650)

Statement 38   It is hard for me to obtain information about the prison regime and the rules and regulations in this prison (0.635)

Statement 50   This prison is poor at giving prisoners reasons for decisions (0.623)

Statement 56   I am treated differently by staff on the grounds of my race, offence, or any other characteristic (0.605)

Statement 64   This prison responds slowly to requests and applications (0.601)

Statement 97   This prison is poor at delivering justice and fairness (0.593)

Statement 39   In general, I think most prisoners approve of the way this prison and its regime operate (0.573)

Statement 28   Staff in this prison are not consistent in their interpretation of the rules (0.552)

Statement 74   Staff in this prison are clear in telling you what you can and cannot do (0.522)

---

[16] Had we read the article, 'Do Fair Procedures Matter?', by Paternoster *et al.* we might have included notions of 'competence' (of staff) and 'opportunity to state one's case' as well as more precise tests of 'correctability' and 'ethicality' (by which the authors mean respect and dignity; see further Paternoster *et al.* 1997).

TABLE 6.1. Percentage of prisoners who agree/strongly agree with items relating to fairness

Statement (Fairness)	Belmarsh	Holme House	Risley	Doncaster	Wandsworth
1. Staff here treat prisoners fairly when applying the rules.	47.0	54.2	44.6[b]	66.6[a]	56.6
2. Staff here treat prisoners fairly when distributing privileges.	32.5[b]	45.7	37.7	61.4[a]	40.0
3. Privileges are given and taken fairly in this prison.	26.5[b]	47.9	39.6	57.9[a]	38.4
4. Overall, I am treated fairly by staff in this prison.	67.5	74.5	61.4[b]	81.6[a]	71.6
5. The rules and regulations in this prison are made clear to me.	60.2	78.8	47.5[b]	80.7[a]	68.3
6. Staff in this prison are not consistent in their interpretation of the rules.	59.1[b]	49.0	53.5	33.3[a]	50.0
7. In general, I think the disciplinary system here is unfair.	43.4	52.1[b]	41.6	21.0[a]	38.3
8. In general, it is hard to obtain information about rules and regulations.	44.5[b]	29.8	32.7	11.4[a]	33.4
9. In general, I think most prisoners approve of the way the prison and its regime operate.	12.0[b]	33.0	15.8	59.6[a]	20.0
10. This prison is poor at giving reasons for decisions.	69.8[b]	61.7	57.5	40.3[a]	60.0
11. I am treated differently by staff due to race, offence, or any other characteristic.	30.2[b]	16.0	21.8	7.7[a]	20.0
12. The prison responds slowly to requests and applications.	79.5[b]	49.0[a]	64.4	51.7	71.7
13. Staff in this prison are clear in telling you what you can and can't do.	62.7	81.9[a]	54.4[b]	76.3	68.3
14. The regime in this prison is fair.	33.7	44.7	30.7[b]	75.4[a]	35.0
15. This prison is poor at delivering justice and fairness.	48.2[b]	40.4	33.7	22.8[a]	38.3

Note: Throughout this account, scores accompanied by the letter 'a' indicate the most positive score. Scores accompanied by the letter 'b' indicate the most negative.

TABLE 6.2.   A comparison of prisoner views on fairness: individual item mean scores

Item/statement	Item scores (1–5)					ANOVA (Mean difference)									
	B	HH	R	D	W	B&HH	B&R	B&D	B&W	HH&R	HH&D	HH&W	R&D	R&W	D&W
Staff here treat prisoners fairly when applying the rules.	3.12ᵇ	3.24	3.12ᵇ	3.64ᵃ	3.33	N/s	N/s	0.52*	N/s	N/s	0.40	N/s	0.52*	N/s	N/s
Staff here treat prisoners fairly when distributing privileges.	2.86ᵇ	3.06	2.92	3.51ᵃ	3.02	N/s	N/s	0.65*	N/s	N/s	0.44	N/s	0.59*	N/s	0.49
Privileges are given and taken fairly in this prison.	2.75ᵇ	3.10	2.94	3.46ᵃ	2.88	N/s	N/s	0.71**	N/s	N/s	N/s	N/s	0.52*	N/s	0.57
Overall, I am treated fairly by staff in this prison.	3.64	3.70	3.49ᵇ	3.82ᵃ	3.63	N/s	N/s	N/s	N/s	N/s	N/s	N/s	N/s	N/s	N/s
The rules and regulations in this prison are made clear to me.	3.25	3.70	3.07ᵇ	3.76ᵃ	3.57	N/s	N/s	0.51*	N/s	0.63*	N/s	N/s	0.69**	0.50	N/s
Staff in this prison [are] consistent in their interpretation of the rules.	2.29ᵇ	2.67	2.42	3.02ᵃ	3.57	N/s	N/s	0.73**	N/s	N/s	N/s	N/s	0.60*	N/s	N/s
In general, I think that the disciplinary system in here is [fair].	2.66	2.60ᵇ	2.64	3.22ᵃ	2.82	N/s	N/s	0.56*	N/s	N/s	0.62*	N/s	0.58*	N/s	N/s

In general, it is [not] hard for me to obtain information about rules and regulations in this prison.	2.78^b	3.19	2.93	3.61^a	3.18	N/s	N/s	0.83**	N/s	N/s	0.42	N/s	0.68**	N/s	N/s
In general, I think most prisoners approve of the way this prison and regime operate.	2.19^b	2.74	2.31	3.46^a	2.43	0.55*	N/s	1.27**	N/s	0.44	0.72**	N/s	1.16**	N/s	1.03**
This prison is [good] at giving prisoners reasons for decisions.	2.06^b	2.37	2.32	2.78^a	2.37	N/s	N/s	0.72**	N/s	N/s	0.41	N/s	0.46*	N/s	N/s
I am [not] treated differently by staff on grounds of my race, offence or another characteristic.	3.08^b	3.62	3.33	3.82^a	3.37	0.53*	N/s	0.73**	N/s	N/s	N/s	N/s	0.49*	N/s	N/s
The prison responds [quickly] to requests and applications.	1.93^b	2.62^a	2.22	2.55	1.97	0.69*	N/s	0.62*	N/s	N/s	N/s	0.65*	N/s	N/s	0.59*
Staff in this prison are clear in telling you what you can and can't do.	3.49	3.83^a	3.29^b	3.77	3.70	N/s	N/s	N/s	0.54*	N/s	N/s	N/s	0.48*	N/s	N/s
The regime in this prison is fair.	2.82	3.07	2.78	3.72^a	2.73	N/s	N/s	0.90**	N/s	N/s	0.64**	N/s	0.94**	N/s	0.99**
This prison is [good] at delivering justice and fairness.	2.42^b	2.87	2.84	3.13^a	2.68	0.45*	0.42	0.71*	N/s	N/s	N/s	N/s	N/s	N/s	0.45

Notes: * The mean difference is significant at the p < 0.05 level. ** The mean difference is significant at the p < 0.001 level.

Table 6.1 shows the proportion of prisoners who agreed or strongly agreed with each statement in the 'fairness' dimension.

These results constitute plausible reflections of each prison's 'style', with Belmarsh low on privilege distribution, information, and responses to requests and applications. Holme House was high on clarity and 'responsiveness'. Risley was rated as disorganized and rather unfair. Doncaster was high on most things—although it is not as clear as Holme House on 'staff being clear in telling you what you can and can't do' (statement 13), and not as swift in its responses to requests and applications (statement 12). Wandsworth was rated fairly highly on overall fairness (although still third, of five; statement 4), and not as low as other prisons in most areas, perhaps because of its consistency. There are different types of 'fairness' and 'unfairness' detectable from these figures (see further below). On the two general questions, 'Overall I am treated fairly by staff in this prison' (statement 4), and 'In general I think most prisoners approve of the way this prison and its regime operate' (statement 9), the prisons are ranked on both items by prisoners: Doncaster highest, then Holme House, then Wandsworth, with Belmarsh fourth, then Risley fifth for 'fairness' (statement 4), and Risley fourth, then Belmarsh fifth for 'approval' (statement 9). On this (rough) reckoning, relational aspects of fairness seem rather important. On the other hand, clarity, consistency, and control also contribute significantly to perceptions of fairness, except when a prison is unresponsive, discriminatory, and (therefore) unclear.[17]

Table 6.2 shows the means, and significant differences on individual items. It is important to look at the scores in themselves (i.e. whether they are under or over 3) as well as at the differences between prisons. Some aspects of fairness seem to be easier to achieve than others. No prison is rated at 3 for 'giving reasons for decisions' or 'responding quickly to requests and applications'. Only Doncaster 'scrapes' a 3 on consistency and (slightly more) for

[17] This finding is consistent with the analysis by Bottoms and Rose of Ahmad's data, which showed that perceptions of fairness were higher at the local prison (where a more structured and ordered regime was in place) than at either the category C prison or a dispersal prison. There are several possible explanations for this finding (e.g. dispersal prisoners may be more critical of prison regimes in general), but we can infer support for the notion that order and structure are 'desirable' in prison, on the whole.

its disciplinary procedures. These figures may tell us something important about prisons in general. It seems there is more clarity than consistency in prison. The rules are prominent, even if they are selectively enforced.

TABLE 6.3. Scores on dimension six: fairness

Prison	Reliability	Dimension score
Doncaster	0.8525	3.4175
Holme House	0.8609	3.0929
Wandsworth	0.8776	2.9600
Risley	0.9233	2.8403
Belmarsh	0.8874	2.7566

All of the items, except statement 4, discriminated between the prisons, with most of the differences found between Doncaster and the other establishments (including Holme House), but some interesting differences between, for example, Belmarsh and Holme House, and Holme House and Risley (Table 6.2).

The overall internal reliability of the dimension 'fairness' across all prisons was very high, at 0.90. Two prisons scored 3 or above on fairness. Doncaster was significantly higher on fairness than Holme House. Wandsworth scored just below 3, and Risley and Belmarsh scored slightly, but not significantly, lower.

Fairness was significantly positively correlated with all other dimensions. It was most highly correlated with: humanity (0.774), trust (0.739), relationships and respect (0.730), and order (0.707). As we saw earlier in this chapter, Rawls (and others) have argued that fairness generates trust. There is an empirical relationship between the two dimensions, as well as a strong correlation between fairness, humanity, relationships, and respect. We shall explore these relationships more closely at the end of this chapter. Below, we look within our dimension 'fairness', to see whether distinct factors emerge, and then at what happens when we combine the 'relationships' items discussed in the previous chapter with the 'fairness' dimension.

Three Components of Fairness

We carried out a factor analysis on the 15 items in the original 'fairness' dimension. It was divisible into three key components: a 'staff

fairness' component; a 'clarity' component; and a 'formal procedures' or 'formal justice' component (Table 6.4).

TABLE 6.4.   Three factors arising from the original dimension 'fairness'

Factor One: Staff fairness (five items (0.88)[1])	Factor Two: Clarity (three items (0.71))	Factor Three: Formal justice (five items (0.75))
Privileges are given and taken fairly in this prison (0.845)	The rules and regulations in this prison are made clear to me (0.906)	This prison is poor at giving prisoners reasons for decisions (0.656)
Staff here treat prisoners fairly when distributing privileges (0.814)	It is hard for me to obtain information about the prison regime and the rules and regulations in this prison (0.582)	This prison is poor at delivering justice and fairness (0.646)
Staff here treat prisoners fairly when applying the rules (0.804)	Staff in this prison are clear in telling you what you can and cannot do (5.539)	In general, I think that the disciplinary system in here is unfair (0.611)
The regime in this prison is fair (0.709)		This prison responds slowly to requests and applications (0.604)
Overall, I am treated fairly by staff in this prison (0.676)		I am treated differently by staff on the grounds of my race, offence, or another characteristic (0.538)

Notes: [1] Internal reliability scores for the new dimensions. We have used a cut-off point of 0.500. Items appearing in the factor analysis with lower reliability scores have been excluded from any dimension.

   The mean scores for five prisons on the new dimensions, 'staff
fairness', 'clarity', and 'formal justice' were as shown in Table 6.5.
Doncaster scored highest on 'staff fairness', but all prisons scored
above 3. The lowest scoring prisons on 'staff fairness' were
Belmarsh and Risley. Doncaster scored highest on 'clarity',
although Wandsworth and Holme House also scored well above 3
on 'clarity'. On 'formal justice', Doncaster scored just above 3 and
Holme House was the next highest prison, but below 3, at 2.8.
These variations suggest that it is possible to make meaningful distinctions between these three components of fairness. Prisons score
higher on 'clarity' than on either 'staff fairness' or 'formal justice'.
Taking the analysis of the data on fairness overall, we might
describe the five prisons in our study as 'unresponsive' (Belmarsh),

'controlled/consistent' (Holme House), 'haphazard' (Risley), 'relational' (Doncaster), and 'clear/consistent' (Wandsworth).

TABLE 6.5.   Mean scores on the new dimensions 'staff fairness', 'clarity', and 'formal justice'

Prison	Factor One: Staff fairness	Factor Two: Clarity	Factor Three: Formal justice
Belmarsh	3.0361[b]	3.1767	2.4313[b]
Holme House	3.2362	3.5745	2.8149
Risley	3.0495	3.0957[b]	2.6693
Doncaster	3.6263[a]	3.7164[a]	3.1000[a]
Wandsworth	3.1200	3.4833	2.6400

Notes: Significant differences: staff fairness—D and B ($p < 0.001$), HH ($p < 0.05$), R ($p < 0.001$), W ($p < 0.01$); clarity—D and B ($p < 0.001$), R ($p < 0.001$), B and HH ($p < 0.05$), HH and R ($p < 0.005$). W and R almost reach statistical significance ($p = 0.08$); formal justice—D and B ($p < 0.001$), R ($p < 0.005$), W ($p < 0.005$); D and HH almost ($p < 0.07$). HH and B ($p < 0.05$). The difference between Belmarsh and Risley is almost statistically significant, at $p = 0.09$.

Fairness and Relationships

We combined all items from the 'fairness' and 'relationships' dimensions. Three main factors arose, at least two of which are very similar to those above (suggesting that they are fairly robust). It is interesting to note that an item originally belonging to 'fairness' actually belongs in (correlates highest with) the new 'relations with staff' factor.[18] A new factor, 'distributive fairness', arose, with four items from the original 'fairness' dimension in it, as shown below. Factor 1 ('injustice') is similar to the 'conflict/frustration' factor in Chapter 5, but now has several fairness items in it (Table 6.6).

When the dimension 'relations with staff' has a fairness item within it, Risley's score deteriorates slightly (Table 6.7). Belmarsh scores very poorly on 'injustice' (which is a highly 'relational' factor, as we can see from the items within it) and 'distributive justice'. It is notable that Doncaster scores much lower on 'injustice' (as do the other prisons) than it does on 'relations with staff' and 'distributive justice'. This reinforces our suggestion made earlier that prisoners evaluate (feel more strongly about) negatively worded ('hot') items.

---

[18] The two items most highly correlated with the item 'Overall I am treated fairly by staff in this prison' are 'Relationships between staff and prisoners are good' (0.617) and 'Personally, I get on well with the officers on my wing' (0.629).

TABLE 6.6.   Three factors arising from the original 'fairness' and
'relationships' dimensions

Factor One: Injustice (seven items (0.80))	Factor Two: Relations with staff (13 items (0.94))	Factor Three: Distributive justice (four items (0.87))
I am not being treated as a human being in here (0.776)	Overall, I am treated fairly by staff in this prison (0.791)	Privileges are given and taken fairly in this prison (0.861)
This prison is poor at treating prisoners with respect (0.789)	Staff in this prison show concern and understanding towards me (0.779)	Staff here treat prisoners fairly when distributing privileges (0.854)
Some of the treatment I receive in this prison is degrading (0.648)	I feel that I am treated with respect in this prison (0.775)	Staff here treat prisoners fairly when applying the rules (0.736)
This prison is poor at delivering justice and fairness (0.629)	I receive support from staff in this prison when I need it (0.770)	The regime in this prison is fair (0.666)
I am treated differently by staff on the grounds of my race, offence, or another characteristic (0.613)	Staff here treat me with kindness (0.762)	
Staff in this prison are generally not available to talk to (0.603)	Personally, I get on well with the officers on my wing (0.745)	
There is a strong sense of 'them and us' in this prison (0.660)	Staff address and talk to me in a respectful manner (0.725)	
	Relationships between staff and prisoners in this prison are good (0.711)	
	I am treated as a person of value in this prison (0.696)	
	I trust the officers in this prison (0.661)	
	Staff in this prison often display honesty and integrity (0.626)	
	I feel that I am trusted quite a lot in this prison (0.609)	
	I have been helped significantly by a member of staff in this prison with a particular problem (0.607)	

TABLE 6.7. Mean scores on the revised dimensions, 'injustice', 'relations with staff', and 'distributive justice'

Prison	Factor One: Injustice	Factor Two: Relations with staff	Factor Three: Distributive justice
Belmarsh	2.6609[b]	3.0899[a]	2.8855[b]
Holme House	2.9909	3.1015	3.1197
Risley	2.9547	3.0655[b]	2.9406
Doncaster	3.3684[a]	3.4177	3.5811[a]
Wandsworth	2.8095	3.0731	2.9917

Notes: Significant differences: injustice: D and B (p < 0.001), HH (p < 0.05), R (p < 0.005), W (p < 0.001); HH and B almost (p = 0.06); relations with staff: D and R (p < 0.05); with D and B, HH and W almost (p = 0.06, 0.06 and 0.08 respectively). Distributive justice: D and B (p < 0.001), HH (p < 0.01), R (p < 0.001), W (p < 0.005).

Order

> [T]here must have been a time when there was no government on earth, no political societies; and when all men lived in a state of anarchy, or what Locke called a 'state of nature'. This state of natural anarchy had proved intolerable: for where every man was a law unto himself, life could not be orderly, peaceful and predictable. The weak had no protection against the strong: and the strong themselves were in perpetual fear of their rivals.
>
> (Cranston 1982: 75)

> Order consists of the predictability of human conduct on the basis of common and stable expectations.
>
> (Wrong 1994: 5)

We have seen that fairness in prison is far from straightforward, and that the treatment of prisoners by staff, and the day-to-day decision-making of officers, may influence prisoners' perceptions of fairness to a considerable extent. Bottoms and others have argued that order in prison is strongly related to perceptions of fairness, and to perceptions of *staff* fairness in particular. Why might this be?

Order in society depends on the existence of 'shared meanings' that make possible 'stable, recurrent, and cooperative social interaction' (Wrong 1994: 5). Its essential features are predictability and regularity. It is never perfectly achieved, but persists to different degrees despite unpredictabilities, disruptions, and 'mistaken perceptions' (ibid. 10): 'It coexists with, and influences and is influenced by, individual deviance, group conflict, and cultural innovation' (Wrong 1994: 13).

Lurking behind social order is the threat of violence, civil war, or the collapse of society (ibid.). The problem of order is important precisely because social order is so precarious, and unlikely. It is difficult to account for social cohesion, given the different interests of people, their limited sympathy, and their tendency to compete for scarce resources (Wrong 1994). Order has often been named as the 'fundamental theoretical problem of sociology' (Wrong 1994). Society is: 'nothing but a web of social relations that is constantly being spun, broken, and spun again, invariably (unlike a spider's web) in a slightly different form' (Wrong 1994: 45).

It is spun 'merely' out of 'expectations', and yet 'it binds like chains of steel' (ibid.). These expectations—or 'habit-expectation-norms'—emerge over the course of time.[19] This is the problem standing in need of explanation. Different solutions have been offered by classical political philosophers to this problem: Hobbes' solution was coercive, Locke stressed mutual self-interest, and 'the Rousseau of The Social Contract gave primacy to normative consensus' (Wrong 1994: 9).[20]

Individuals (men, in the classical literature) want and need the esteem, recognition, and approval of their fellows (Wrong 1994: 89).[21] They are dependent economically but also psychologically on others: 'The original resource a human being can offer to another is the capacity to recognise the worth of the other to exist—a resource that cannot be produced if it is not shared' (Wrong 1994: 89, citing Pizzorno).

This need for 'reflected appraisal', or this exchange, may coexist with (and be linked to) more antisocial motivations, such as vanity and rivalry. The 'other is the enemy with whom one is inescapably

---

[19] Wrong uses this analysis to explain why the use of observation and participation in social research is so important (see pp. 46–7).

[20] Rawls and Nozick, more contemporary political philosophers, follow this typical distinction between the normative emphasis (Rawls) and the self-interested (Nozick 1974).

[21] It would be interesting to investigate the extent to which the nature and extent of these needs are mediated by gender.

and compulsively preoccupied' (p. 95). Wrong draws on Schopenhaur's parable of the porcupines: 'in which human society is compared to a colony of porcupines huddling together to keep warm in winter but then pricking one another with their quills and drawing apart repeatedly until they achieve a balance between the need for warmth and a secure distance from pain' (Wrong 1994: 80–1).

Two important ideas stem from Wrong's account. First, the link between psychological needs and the emergence of socially co-operative values. Secondly, the tension individuals may feel between their support for these values and their coexisting egotism, or man's dual nature (see Wrong 1994: 135). As von Hirsch and others have argued, men are not angels, and the 'individual' is in some ways threatened by the 'social' and has 'a powerful share of aggressiveness' (von Hirsch 1993; Freud 1961). We should not assume an 'oversocialized' view of human nature, hence the need for several types of motivation for socially co-operative behaviour. On the other hand, the need for order is powerful:

I have in mind the condition of infantile dependency, the 'premature' thrusting into the world of 'red and wrinkled lumps of flesh' . . . and human survival in that state for a period of several years during which the world and the parents in all their fearsome uncertainty impinge upon the helpless organism, generating a tumultuous emotional life of terror, yearning, and occasional fulfilment. (Wrong 1994: 156)

No wonder, suggests Wrong, that: 'social scientists have been so prone to identify the problem of order with sheer unpredictability rather than with violent conflict' (ibid.).

Others have made the same point (Laing 1965; Giddens 1984 on 'ontological security'; and Liebling 1999 on the painfulness of unpredictability in prison). So we need order, and our perceptions of order and safety may be linked to *predictability* and *trust in the environment*, rather than to actual occurrences of violence (see later).

Bottoms argues, after Wrong, that each of the main classical approaches to order, the normative (i.e. the emergence of shared norms), the coercive, and the instrumental, operate as reasons for social or legal compliance. That order is achieved in any society may require, or depend upon, a different balance between these complementary strategies. So some forms of order are more coerc-ive than others; others are more normative (Bottoms 2002). Some forms of order may mask high levels of conflict, so we need to look beneath the 'facts of predictability', at whether 'the rules' are grounded in shared meanings, before we can be sure that their observance is voluntaristic (Wrong 1994: 38).

It should be clear from this account that order in the prison is constituted by the features and motivations above, with some spe-cial limitations. This case has been made in some detail by Sparks and colleagues: '. . . On a normal day . . . power remains largely "unseen" . . . It is when that flow is interrupted or challenged that the issues of power, and of who holds it, becomes visible' (Sparks *et al.* 1996: 325).

The authors suggest that order is continually worked at through routines, social relations, and some situational 'crime prevention' (opportunity reducing) techniques (Bottoms *et al.* 1991). Different types of order can be achieved, with considerable variation in the deployment of authority, and with different costs and benefits aris-ing from each. They propose that some of these forms of order may be more durable—or legitimate—than others, although they note that more than one version of sustainable order can be found. There is an important (albeit imperfect) relationship between order and fairness.

Prisons are a special case of 'the problem of order', as they gen-erate impulses towards both resistance (prisoners are, after all, held against their will), and towards accommodation and sociability (compliance rarely has to be literally enforced; Sparks *et al.* 1996). Coercive power is held in reserve, and a much reduced form of power 'flows smoothly' between staff and prisoners for much of the time. Order is threatened, interrupted, and repaired constantly, perhaps more visibly than in society at large. There are competi-tions for power, between prisoners and between prisoners and prison staff, but these competitions may be resolved more satisfact-orily in some prisons than in others. This account clearly resonates with Wrong's analysis, where egoism and conflict exist but are con-tinually channelled, averted, or handled. A stark 'control model' of penal order is rarely necessary (although sometimes this model is used; see Kantrowitz 1996; Clare *et al.* 2001; Toch 2002). Order is more than, and should be distinguished from, the absence of con-flict. Conflict is present, but is assimilated in successfully ordered communities (Wrong 1994: 209). So, just as outside, but perhaps more so in the prison, the routinized reproduction of everyday life stands in need of explanation. As Cressey argued:

One of the most amazing things about prisons is that they 'work' at all . . . Any ongoing prison is made up of the co-ordinated actions of hundreds of people, some of whom hate and distrust each other, love each other, fight each other physically and psychologically, think of each other as stupid or mentally disturbed, 'manage' and 'control' each other, and vie with each other for favours, prestige and money. Often the personnel involved . . . are not sure whether they are the managers or the managed. Despite these conditions, however, the social system which is a prison does not degenerate into a chaotic mess of social relations which have no order and make no sense. (Cressey 1961: 2)

The empirical research conducted by Sparks *et al.* was carried out in two establishments with deliberately distinctive identities and histories. Albany had a history of control problems, whereas Long Lartin did not. Albany had a characteristically 'restricted' regime (largely related to its experiences of disorder), whereas Long Lartin was arguably the most 'liberal' regime within the dispersal system (Dunbar 1971). In this sense, the two prisons represented 'polar extremes', each having a distinct 'ethos'. Long Lartin had entered into the dispersal estate with an explicit attention to 'choice, responsibility and self-respect' (Dunbar 1971). Its stable history was attributed to its 'good relationships, good foundations, good training and its innovation', more than a decade later (Jenkins 1987; although see HMCIP 1992a). Staff at the establishment referred to its regime as representing the 'last Radzinowicz prison': a real 'liberal regime within a secure perimeter' (Advisory Council on the Penal System 1968; Liebling 2002). Albany, on the other hand, had a less stable history and emerged, in the late 1980s, with 'control, safety, and supervision' as its key themes. Its distinctive 'restricted regime' was linked to the restoration of staff confidence following a series of major disturbances. This also became an 'ethos' to which staff referred. The culture at Albany was linked to the regime being predictably delivered. Long Lartin had high levels of freedom of movement, and a 'soft-policing' approach to regulation. This depended on a good information flow between staff and prisoners, the avoidance of 'pettiness', and the avoidance of trouble by tact and humour. There was an explicitly 'liberal' perspective on the need for prisoners to retain a certain degree of autonomy and privacy. The authors describe a relatively high level of trust within the prison.

At Albany, a certain level of stringency in rule-enforcement resulted in greater clarity. This was the 'right' kind of regime in which 'right' relationships and practices (rather than 'good relationships'; see Chapter 9) could evolve (except in the vulnerable prisoner unit, where staff deployed their power more heavily; see Sparks *et al.* 1996, chapter 7).[22] Albany tolerated a degree of unpopularity for the sake of higher levels of supervision and opportunity reduction. Importantly, in the light of the above account of fairness, the staff were regarded as relatively fair. Good relationships and 'good service delivery' helped the staff to maintain some degree of legitimate authority. Trust in the regime was generated by specific practices, and the predictability of these, rather than by historical experience or flexible relationships. Whilst these differences were by no means unqualified (some staff felt 'misplaced' in both types of regime), and the actual 'regimes' in place differed somewhat less than staff depiction of them might have indicated, the main difference between the two establishments can be summarized as shown in Figure 6.2.

The 'control model'	The 'negotiation model'
due process	support
efficiency	participation
amenity and service	responsibility and choice
assertive authority	'soft policing' (non-confrontation)
consistency (little discretion)	flexibility (wide use of discretion)
formal (but cordial) relations	close relations
situational control	social control
'control, safety, supervision'	'choice, responsibility, self-respect'

FIGURE 6.2.   Two 'ideal types' of penal order

Sources: This figure has been derived from the descriptions given by Sparks *et al.* of the contrasting regimes at Albany and Long Lartin in Sparks *et al.* (1996: 126–203); and Bottoms *et al.* (1991).

---

[22] As the authors point out, there is an important distinction between 'resignation' and 'assent' (Sparks *et al.* 1996, ch. 6).

There were criticisms of each regime—from inattention to supervision at Long Lartin, to inappropriate conditions for long-term imprisonment at Albany. Albany had some surprising strengths (high levels of perceived staff fairness and considerable predictability) whereas Long Lartin, which on the face of it was the more legitimate prison, had some major lapses of safety and consistency (and was later the site of two of the few murders of prisoners by other prisoners to have occurred in the UK). Interpersonal incidents of violence were far more serious, more likely to take place backstage, and were more deeply 'embedded' at Long Lartin. There can be too little, or too much freedom, participation, and flexibility in the prison.

In addition to their descriptive analysis of these two contrasting forms of order, the authors address the more fundamental question: how was order possible at all, in these places? They draw on Giddens's structuration theory, to illuminate the fact that the structural properties of social institutions are not 'fixed' but are continually reproduced in action by individual agents. This daily 'accomplishment' is achieved almost without thought. This is what Wrong meant by 'habit-expectation-norm' and this routine, reproduced nature of society is given considerable attention by Giddens, and later by Sparks and colleagues. The 'flow' of everyday life depends on knowledgeable human agents operating at a level of 'practical consciousness' which consists of all the things people 'know tacitly about how to "go on" in the contexts of social life without being able to give them direct discursive expression' (see Hay and Sparks 1991; Giddens 1984).[23] The complexity of what prisoners and prison officers do is underpinned by expectations and knowledges which are difficult to articulate because there is little vocabulary for talking about it. The routine in prison is inherently fragile. Yet both staff *and* prisoners are engaged in the reproduction of these structures most of the time (e.g. when prisoners return to their cells at lock-up time), without force. The reproduction of these structures depends on mutual knowledges

---

[23] This is prison officers almost unconsciously drawing on their experience, knowledge, and skills, like good footballers might when they score a goal (see Hay and Sparks 1991). What prison officers describe as 'common sense' or 'jail craft', Giddens and others regard as 'practical consciousness': embedded experience, without which we could not 'go on'. See Sparks *et al.* (1996).

and expectations, and on feeling (i.e. the feeling of willingness). The structures of prison life are made up of formal, but also *informal* rules and resources.

Ensuring reliable reproduction of the regime requires a certain amount of *consent*. This consent depends on perceptions of fairness, or *legitimacy*. As the authors put it: 'Only legitimate social arrangements generate normative commitments towards compliance' (Sparks *et al.* 1996: 87). Legitimacy means, broadly, the fairness of authority. We shall say more about this term in Chapter 10. Here, we simply wish to illustrate the role played in order, by fairness, as indicated above. The legitimate exercise of authority depends on people's experience of the fairness of their treatment, which includes procedures, but also the *manner* of their treatment. Willing compliance (central to 'the problem of order') is achieved via a combination of rational/prudential (instrumental), situational, and normative considerations (Bottoms 1999, 2002). The presence of higher or lower degrees of legitimacy, in *addition* to knowledge of the consequences of disobedience (instrumental motives) and prisoners' awareness of the potential for the use of coercion, together account for the fact that the social order of the prison is 'imposed' and yet is not achieved by complete domination. There may also be elements of socialization (Bottoms 1999, 2002). Fairness or legitimacy plays an important (and varying) role in the accomplishment of order in prison. Different forms of order, drawing upon these various constituent sources of compliance to different degrees, may be perceived as more or less fair.

There are, then, important variations in the ways that order in prison is achieved; and existing prisons may belong in different places along this continuum.[24] This is a largely conceptual scheme, although there was clear empirical evidence to support the case made by Sparks *et al.* for the basic differences between Albany and Long Lartin, and for some of the consequences for order and disorder that flowed from these differences.[25] Critics of the prison have tended to argue that the power prisons use is inherently

[24] Individual establishments may also contain various 'microclimates'—such as the VPU (Vulnerable Prisoner Unit)—which differ again.

[25] Useem and Reisig found that weak management was predictive of disturbances (see Ch. 8 n. 1) but point out that other important factors, such as a 'sense of injustice', have never been operationalized in studies of prison disturbances (Useem and Reisig 1999: 754).

non-legitimate. Sparks *et al.* demonstrate that this assumption is simplistic and that fairness or legitimacy, as well as 'situational' and other 'social' modes of control, are central to the achievement of order. As Wrong argues: 'Fears of disorder and of a totalitarian excess of order are not mere opposites, for the threat or reality of the former is both dreaded in its own right and as lending attraction to the latter as a corrective. They are dialectically related, to employ a once fashionable way of putting it' (Wrong 1994: 241).

As Woolf and others have indicated, there are variable conditions which make it more or less likely that prisoners will accept the authority of their custodians. A reasonable regime and just procedures are two such conditions. There are others:

The institutional climates and local cultures of different prisons result from other, less openly visible sources—the demeanour and routine practices of prison staff, locally held assumptions about the appropriateness of different kinds of relationships, the exercise of discretion—in short precisely those features of daily prison life which the sociology of prisons since Sykes has emphasised (Sparks *et al.* 1996: 306)

Prisons begin with an inherent legitimacy deficit, but some make up this deficit more successfully than others. Few prisons achieve a completely satisfactory resolution of these dilemmas, as we shall see. The work of Sparks *et al.* confirms the case we wish to make: that there is a *moral dimension to penal practice*. A prison should be stable—for unstable prisons are fearful places. But they should be stable for the 'right reasons', just as societies should be (see Rawls 1996: 143). The 'right reasons' may be less visible and less straightforward than we think. These informal dimensions of prison life—which are most likely to escape formal oversight, measurement, and policy intervention—may make the most direct impact on the quality of life in prison.

Our conversations with prisoners reflected the above account. Order could mean predictability and organization: 'The best thing about this prison is that it is good at organising things what they do everyday ... gym and education ... it just seems easily run' (prisoner, Doncaster). Or it could mean 'discipline'. Prisoners often talked about the quiet accomplishment of order:

A lot of things get sorted out verbally here; staff aren't confrontational. The other day there were two prisoners arguing at the servery, like the next thing I expected to hear was the crack of bones. The officers came over and talked them down; they didn't rush in and jump on their back like they would've done in the past but calmly told them verbally and warned them they would go down the block if they carried on. They just parted and walked away and that was that. (Prisoner, Holme House)

It was difficult to separate order from security, as prisoners experienced 'tightening up' in both areas. When we asked about order, prisoners often referred to security and control, seeing them as part of an overall regime 'style'. There could be 'too much' order and security, from a prisoner's point of view:

It's a drugs mad prison. There is security and people, or there's security mad. It is beyond sense. (Prisoner, Belmarsh)

It used to be more laid back, now everything is up-tight. It's a screws' jail, not that everything has to be by the book, but there are pathetic rules ... It's all 'apps', you can't get a haircut without putting in an app, you can't even get another toilet roll without putting in an app. (Prisoner, Holme House)[26]

They are always there; there is too much supervision; we're not going anywhere. (Prisoner, Wandsworth)

Everything has changed due to security; you can't go anywhere without an escort now ... The new system is full of problems; you get a mouthful of abuse when you ask for a November [radio call/request]; getting to the library, education, or going for medical treatment ... things that take five minutes and you can be away for an hour ... You can't go in the different blocks now. To be honest prisoners are pissed off ... (Prisoner, Risley)

The imposition of increasing levels of security and order (a major feature of life at one of our establishments) resulted in a *lack* of organization and predictability:

In——you knew where you stood at least, things change from week to week here at the moment. It wouldn't be too bad if things were brought in gradually but this Governor is trying to change everything at once. We get nothing now, with 'these' [sex offenders]. You didn't used to mind and there were incentives to come here and stay here. We had something to get—parole, home leave, cat D. Someone has told the Governor to do it; it's not just him but I would say he shouldn't take everything at once. Set

---

[26] A formal application or request.

a regime going and stick to it so lads know where they stand. All the changes are very frustrating. (Prisoner, Risley)

So there was a difference between order as *control*, and order as organization or predictability: 'There is some structure to the regime in here, but mostly it is chaotic; one minute you know what is happening, then, with no warning it's all changed' (prisoner, Wandsworth).

Prisoners were aware that order was dependent on their assent:

They [staff] only have control because prisoners here are working towards cat D or parole, otherwise I wouldn't agree that they have a lot of control. (Prisoner, Risley)

This prison is not good at maintaining good order, that's up to us; we could cause chaos if we wanted to, but the thing is, there is no reason to kick off. (Prisoner, Doncaster)

Officers (and sometimes, prisoners) expressed a view that security and order were a first priority. After that, other things could follow: 'You do need security, and clear boundaries. If you can take these for granted, then you can relax about everything else' (officer, Belmarsh).

Definition of order The degree to which the prison environment is structured, stable, predictable, and acceptable.

In our survey, the dimension 'order' consisted of three statements:[27]

Statement 59 This prison is well organized (0.848)
Statement 12 This prison is good at delivering a structured and predictable regime so that you know where you stand (0.804)
Statement 89 This prison is good at maintaining order (0.728)

Belmarsh was a 'carefully watched' prison, with high levels of security and order as a result. There were, however, regular alarms,

---

[27] Our definition reflects the preceding discussion, and the observation that a concentration camp can be structured, stable, and predictable and yet completely inhumane. We attempted to devise a question on compliance or acceptance of the regime but participants found this kind of question difficult to understand. We settled for a suggestion that prisoners would not agree to statements 1 and 3 in particular, if they felt the regime was completely objectionable.

fairly frequent fights, and some acts of organized disobedience or resistance. The prison was more 'secure' and 'controlled' than legitimately 'ordered', according to prisoners. Holme House was rated exceptionally highly on structure and predictability, and good order generally, although Doncaster was seen as 'well organized'. Risley was lowest on structure and predictability, and organization but was higher than Belmarsh on 'maintaining good order' (see Tables 6.8a and 6.9a).

Looking at the item means individually (Table 6.9a), it appears that three of the prisons had different 'strengths' in relation to

TABLE 6.8. Percentage of prisoners who agree/strongly agree with statements about order and safety

Statements	Belmarsh	Holme House	Risley	Doncaster	Wandsworth
(a) Order					
1. This prison is good at delivering a structured and predictable regime so that you know where you stand.	40.9	74.4[a]	36.6[b]	67.6	45.0
2. This prison is well organized.	20.5	42.6	8.9[b]	50.0[a]	23.4
3. This prison is good at maintaining order.	14.4[b]	62.7[a]	37.6	58.8	58.3
(b) Safety					
1. There is hardly any taxing in this prison.	44.5	44.7	38.6	37.7[b]	55.0[a]
2. There is quite a lot of threats/bullying in here.	21.7	33.0	31.6[b]	20.2	16.7[a]
3. I feel safe from being injured, bullied, or threatened by others.	68.7	72.3	52.5[b]	63.2	75.0[a]
4. The level of drug use in this prison is quite high.	39.7	54.2	68.3[b]	38.6	35.0[a]
5. I feel safe from being injured, bullied, or threatened by staff in this prison.	51.8[b]	64.9	58.4	74.5[a]	56.7
6. This prison is good at delivering personal safety.	49.4	47.9	32.7[b]	50.8[a]	45.0
7. Generally I fear for my physical safety.	15.6	5.3[a]	13.9[b]	8.7	13.4

TABLE 6.9. A comparison of prisoner views on order and safety: individual item mean scores

Item/Statement	Item scores (1–5)					ANOVA (Mean difference)									
	B	HH	R	D	W	B&HH	B&R	B&D	B&W	HH&R	HH&D	HH&W	R&D	R&W	D&W
(a) Order															
This prison is good at delivering a structured and predictable regime so that you know where you stand.	2.73^b	3.64^a	2.76	3.62	2.98	0.90**	N/s	0.89**	N/s	0.88**	N/s	0.65*	0.86**	N/s	0.64*
This prison is well organized.	2.45	2.96	2.04^b	3.36^a	2.60	0.51*	N/s	0.91**	N/s	0.92**	N/s	N/s	1.32**	0.56*	0.76*
This prison is good at maintaining order.	3.51	3.54	3.11^b	3.52	3.58^a	N/a	N/a	N/a	N/a	0.43*	N/s	N/s	0.41*	0.47*	N/s
(b) Safety															
There is hardly any taxing in this prison.	3.18	3.02^b	3.05	3.17	3.53^a	N/s	N/s	N/s	N/s	N/s	N/s	0.51	N/s	N/s	N/s
There is [not] a lot of threats/bullying in here.	3.33	3.17	3.05^b	3.25	3.48^a	N/s	N/s	N/s	N/s	N/s	N/s	N/s	N/s	N/s	N/s
I feel safe from being injured, bullied, or threatened by other prisoners in here.	3.73	3.71	3.34^b	3.71	3.80^a	N/s	N/s	N/s	N/s	N/s	N/s	N/s	N/s	0.46	N/s
The level of drug use in this prison is quite [low].	2.88	2.60	2.13^b	2.89^a	2.88	N/s	0.75*	N/s	N/s	0.47	N/s	N/s	0.77**	0.75*	N/s
I feel safe from being injured, bullied, or threatened by staff in this prison.	3.34^b	3.51	3.48	3.82^a	3.47	N/s	N/s	0.49*	N/s	N/s	N/s	N/s	N/s	N/s	N/s
This prison is good at delivering personal safety.	3.30	3.29	3.08^b	3.40^a	3.28	N/s	N/s	N/s	N/s	N/s	N/s	N/s	N/s	N/s	N/s
Generally I [do not] fear for my physical safety.	3.64^b	3.90	3.67	3.94^a	3.70	N/s	N/s	N/s	N/s	N/s	N/s	N/s	N/s	N/s	N/s

order. Holme House was rated as significantly more 'structured and predictable' than most of the other prisons; Doncaster was seen as 'well organized', and Wandsworth was seen as 'good at maintaining order'. Belmarsh and Risley were seen as unpredictable, and disorganized, respectively. It is interesting that Doncaster had a relatively high assault rate (see Chapter 4), and yet it *felt* ordered to most prisoners. This may reflect greater *trust in the environment*, as suggested by Wrong. We shall see below whether this feeling of order extends to feelings of safety.

The overall internal reliability of the dimension 'order' across all prisons was high, at 0.71. The reliability score was lower at Belmarsh, with very few prisoners agreeing that 'This prison is good at maintaining order' (Table 6.10). Three prisons scored 3 or above on order. There were significant differences between Doncaster and Risley and Wandsworth, with Risley attracting significantly lower ratings than Doncaster and Wandsworth. Order was most significantly positively correlated with fairness (0.707).

TABLE 6.10.   Scores on dimension seven: order

Prison	Reliability	Dimension score
Doncaster	0.7148	3.5000
Holme House	0.6117	3.3794
Wandsworth	0.6223	3.0556
Belmarsh	0.5141	2.8956
Risley	0.7152	2.6370

Order and Fairness

We added the three items from the dimension 'order' to the dimension 'fairness', to explore these links further through a factor analysis. Three factors arose. 'Staff fairness' remained the same as in our original 'fairness' factor analysis (see above). The additional items from 'order' separated into two new dimensions, two joining the factor 'formal justice' and one joining the factor 'clarity' (which could be renamed 'clarity and predictability'), as shown in Table 6.11.[28]

---

[28] This resonates with the analysis of order by Elster, who suggests that there are two kinds of disorder in society: lack of *predictability* and lack of *co-operation*. See Elster (1995: 1).

TABLE 6.11. Three factors arising from the original dimensions 'fairness' and 'order'

Factor One: Formal justice (seven items (0.80))	Factor Two: Staff fairness (five items (0.88))	Factor Three: Clarity and predictability (four items (0.76))
This prison is well organized (0.687)	Privileges are given and taken fairly in this prison (0.865)	The rules and regulations in this prison are made clear to me (0.875)
In general, I think that the disciplinary system in here is unfair (0.679)	Staff here treat prisoners fairly when distributing privileges (0.841)	This prison is good at delivering a structured and predictable regime so that you know where you stand (0.660)
This prison is poor at giving prisoners reasons for decisions (0.587)	Staff here treat prisoners fairly when applying the rules (0.805)	It is hard for me to obtain information about the prison regime and the rules and regulations in this prison (0.573)
This prison is poor at delivering justice and fairness (0.577)	The regime in this prison is fair (0.706)	Staff in this prison are clear in telling you what you can and cannot do (0.543)
This prison responds slowly to requests and applications (0.552)	Overall, I am treated fairly in this prison (0.671)	
This prison is good at maintaining order (0.580)		
I am treated differently by staff on the grounds of my race, offence, or another characteristic (0.523)		

This analysis suggests, as expected, that fairness and order are intrinsically related. Order and organization constitute 'formal justice', as well as arising from it.

The mean scores for five prisons on the revised new dimensions, 'formal justice' and 'clarity', are shown in Table 6.12 (we have included the results from 'staff fairness' again). Risley and Wandsworth scored lowest on 'formal justice'. Belmarsh, Risley, and Wandsworth scored lowest on 'staff fairness', but all prisons scored higher on this than on 'formal justice'. Risley and Belmarsh scored lowest on 'clarity and predictability'. It is noticeable that Holme House scored higher on 'clarity' than it did on either 'formal justice' or 'staff fairness'.

TABLE 6.12.   Mean scores on the revised dimensions, 'formal justice', 'staff fairness', and 'clarity and predictability'

Prison	Factor One: Formal justice	Factor Two: Staff fairness	Factor Three: Clarity (and predictability)
Belmarsh	N/a	3.0361[b]	3.0663
Holme House	2.9392	3.2362	3.5904
Risley	2.6421[b]	3.0495	3.0124[b]
Doncaster	3.1967[a]	3.6263[a]	3.6930[a]
Wandsworth	2.7690	3.1200	3.3583

Notes: Significant differences: formal justice: D and HH ($p < 0.05$), R ($p < 0.001$), W ($p < 0.01$); staff fairness: D and B ($p < 0.001$), HH ($p < 0.05$), R ($p < 0.001$), W ($p < 0.01$); clarity: D and B ($p < 0.001$), D and R ($p < 0.001$), B and HH ($p < 0.005$).

Safety

> The person's equilibrium hinges on finding sanctuary from others.
>
> (Toch 1992a: 51)

The feeling of safety in prison, like the feeling of order, may be related to other aspects of prison life (such as trust) other than levels of violence. Stated positively, safety is related to confidence that one can survive the day without fear or loss of property or personal security. A safe environment may be linked to the presence of a relaxed atmosphere, and a stable set of social relations (i.e. to order, as argued above), but there is the added requirement that individuals in that environment can contain their own aggressive impulses. Prisons need effective checks on tension, as safety may be threatened by sudden losses of emotional control in unpredictable others (Toch 1992a: 54). There can be gangs, cliques, and elites in (particularly long-term) prisons (King and McDermott 1995: 133), which make life difficult for many prisoners, or which link safety to the successful handling of predatory relationships with others. Feelings of unsafety led prisoners to carry weapons in self-protection or to exercise constant vigilance for evidence of danger (ibid.: 64). Prisons are 'high risk environments' (Sparks and Hay 1992), in which some locations may be safer (easier to supervise) than others (see King and McDermott 1995: 136–43).

Feelings of safety tend to be linked to security categories, so that prisoners in maximum security prisons feel less safe than prisoners in semi-open prisons, although as Toch points out, some prisoners may have 'higher safety concerns' than others (Toch 1992a). Vulnerable prisoners are called such because they are in need of protection from violence and abuse from other prisoners. There is an apparent 'safety paradox' in prison: that is, studies tend to find both high levels of victimization and relatively low levels of reported fears for safety at a general level (Bottoms 1999: 169; Edgar et al. 2002). This might be due to features of the inmate social world (e.g. the adopting of collective strategies for remaining safe, and norms discouraging disclosure), the predictability of routines, and personal protection strategies (Bottoms 1999: 269–72). Edgar et al. add that familiarity and 'learning that they can survive', if necessary by becoming an aggressor, can increase feelings of safety (Edgar et al. 2002: 84–90). They also suggest that prisoners' experiences of victimization outside, and a lifestyle whereby fighting can sometimes be regarded as entertainment, may mean that, relatively speaking, prison is not generally perceived as an unusually risky environment (Edgar et al. 2002: 89).[29]

There is far more said in the literature about violence in prison and its management (see e.g. Bowker 1980; Bottoms 1999; Edgar et al. 2002) than there is about what safety feels like and under what circumstances it is found. The study by Edgar and colleagues usefully suggests (in line with studies of safety in the community) that feelings of safety in prison may be linked to: 'the experience of crime as a "normal part of everyday life", familiarity with people and places; territory—a sense of belonging, or, more accurately, of ownership of space; a sense of control over one's environment; and networks of support' (Edgar et al. 2002: 89–90).

The KPI which is intended to measure levels of safety in prison is the number of officially recorded assaults. These figures tell us that rates of assault on prisoners are around 30 to 40 per 1,000 prisoners per year. Figures are highest in young offender institutions and remand centres (Bottoms 1999: 215; Edgar et al. 2002). The KPI figures include guilty findings at formal adjudications only. They may therefore be influenced by the visibility of the

---

[29] A recent unpublished study of homicides in prisons in England (there was a total of 15 over 12 years) showed that a disproportionate number took place in high security prisons before 1994 but, since that time, higher proportions have occurred in local prisons (Sattar 2003).

assault, the adjudication process, 'policing behaviour' by prison staff, the nature of the regime (e.g. its 'openness' or the number of hours spent out of cell), the nature of the population (especially age and sentence length), and establishment 'sensitivity' to assault as a category of disciplinary offence (which may be politically related to staffing levels), or the possibility of prisoners being charged with similar but lesser offences so that the prison stays within its KPI requirements. The figures do not reflect variations according to seriousness, victim, perpetrator, or circumstances (Sparks *et al.* 1996).

Other aspects of safety of concern to prisoners, but not reflected by assault rates include: non-adjudicated injuries (e.g. head injuries; see Davies 1982), property theft, verbal threats and intimidation, latent levels of hostility and tension, collective disorder, sexually predatory behaviour, economic and material extortion, staff use of force (such as Control and Restraint), fear (of staff and prisoners, of specific and general kinds), the operation of gangs, drug use, and the presence of mentally unstable prisoners. Staffing levels appear to be related to feelings of safety in a U-curve, so that there can be too few staff (reducing levels of supervision), or there can be too many (resulting in staff 'gangs' or socializing). Some attempts have been made to assess levels of assault, sexual attacks, and threats of violence in prisons in different types of establishments in England using survey data (e.g. King and McDermott 1995; and Bottoms 1999: 218), and to compare results from different studies (Bottoms 1999: 220). The results suggest that between 7 and 30 per cent of male prisoners in closed prisons report having been assaulted; between 3 and 13 per cent report a sexual attack; and between 26 and 49 per cent report threats of violence (ibid.). The higher figures are always from the maximum security estate.[30] A detailed self-report study by Edgar and colleagues in four prisons found that 19 per cent and 26 per cent of adult males had been assaulted and/or threatened with violence in the last month, respectively, and 30 per cent and 44 per cent of young offenders had been assaulted and/or threatened with violence in the last month, respectively (Edgar *et al.* 2002: 29–30). The frequency of cell thefts and verbal abuse was considerably higher (ibid. 30).

---

[30] Contrary to popular assumption, the assault rate in female establishments is very high (115–162 per 1,000 prisoners between 1990 and 1996; Bottoms 1999: 235), although homicide in female prisons is rare.

Our account of order above shows how safety is achieved via daily practices as well as more formal mechanisms, such as disciplinary procedures and the use of control measures such as transfer to special locations (see McDermott and King 1988; King and McDermott 1995: 97–110; Sparks *et al.* 1996, chapter 8).

Logan included safety as one of his measures of the quality of confinement (Logan 1992). The aspects of safety he included were prisoners' perceived likelihood of being assaulted, with or without a weapon; prisoners' estimates of rates of assault and sexual assault in their prison; and the proportion of inmates who said they had been assaulted in a six-month period. His measure included perceived safety of staff, perceived dangerousness of inmates, safety of the environment, and staffing adequacy. Other related safety items were assessed using institutional records (see Logan 1992: 604–5). The results were presented as the total number of favourable 'pairwise' comparisons within each overall dimension. The measure was therefore *relative* and *summary*, and showed that the private prison scored higher than a federal and state prison on safety (as well as order and security; see Logan 1992: 591).[31]

The Federal Bureau of Prisons include a detailed measure of 'personal safety and security' in their Prison Social Climate Survey, which includes questions inviting prisoners to estimate the number, nature, and extent of heated arguments, assaults, fights, sexual assaults, and gang activity over the last six months. The questionnaire also asks for reactions to those incidents (e.g. 'does this bother you so much that you've thought of requesting a transfer to another prison?'). Other questions address actual assaults, the use of physical force by staff, disciplinary incidents, feelings of ease of movement around the establishment, the incidence of searches and shakedowns, and questions about how much influence 'inmates have over what other inmates do here' (Federal Bureau of Prisons 1990). This is the most comprehensive and relevant set of questions about safety that we have found. A survey conducted in 1999 to compare one private with three public prisons showed that staff and prisoner evaluations of safety were positively related and that such measures do differentiate between prisons (Camp *et al.* 2003).

---

[31] Survey data from prisoners were not included in the federal prison (Logan 1992: 581 n). We would argue that it is not satisfactory to conflate prisoner and staff perceptions of safety. See Chapter 2.

The authors report that higher levels of safety from assault were associated with lower reported staffing levels (i.e. where prisoners rated prisons lower on whether there were sufficient staff during different shifts to provide for their safety (ibid.).[32]

Measuring safety in prison is difficult without a clear conceptual and operational definition of the term. There may be important differences between staff perceptions of safety and prisoner perceptions (although see Camp *et al.* 2003), as well as different reasons for these perceptions. Prisoners' feelings of safety seemed to be linked to staff responsiveness, the control of bullying and drug use, and the personal resources of the individual:

I feel safe here; you know staff are aware of everything going on. They might look relaxed but they watch everything. (Prisoner, Belmarsh)

If anything happened, staff are quick to respond; if there is a fight on the yard and an alarm bell, there'll be 15 officers there in 30 seconds. (Prisoner, Belmarsh)

I always feel safe, because I have confidence in myself. I know they wouldn't hurt me, I don't make their job hard, and I know I wouldn't hurt myself. (Prisoner, Belmarsh)

There are drug addicts, there is bullying and assaults, but staff are on top of things here. Prison should be a safe place. TVs make it relaxed; I've not seen a fight in 15 months and that's amazing. (Prisoner, Holme House)

I feel safe . . . because of the way staff make it clear to prisoners . . . bullies will be dealt with severely. (Prisoner, Risley)

Safety was also linked to security:

[INTERVIEWER: What makes you feel safe in this prison?] You get the feeling it is high security and there are cameras. A couple of times I felt intimidation,

---

[32] Camp *et al.* make the important point that the use of surveys to obtain reliable and valid information about operational differences between prisons requires the use of complex statistical techniques including multilevel modelling to demonstrate that responses represent institutional-level performance measures rather than demographic or individual-level differences (see Camp *et al.* 1997, 2002, 2003). We address some of these issues later, including the introduction of individual-level controls. We are concerned here with the prior task of establishing the meaning, and then exploring measurement, of the concepts of interest and of using this exercise to understand more about the nature of prisons and the experience of prison life.

when a new guy came on the wing and was trying to find out the weaker ones. I'm quiet, but I mix well. There is a pecking order, based on crime and your size. (Prisoner, Doncaster)

It was also linked to discipline:

You don't see any taxing or bullying; there is bound to be some but you never see it—you're not out of your cells long enough. Here they are always moving you on and you can't stop at someone's door or anything. (Prisoner, Wandsworth)

I do feel safe. It is a restricted regime, regimented, with good staff response. (Prisoner, Wandsworth)

I feel safe everywhere. What makes me feel safe? Seeing the problems controlled; when you hear the whistle and you see how quick and how many there are to control the problems. (Prisoner, Wandsworth)

The concept of safety had a physical and psychological dimension:

Safety is dependent on who you're locked up with. (Prisoner, Holme House)

I feel safe. Most of the problems here are fighting and bullying but it's just about drugs. If you're just normal, you don't come across problems, it's all the smack heads, but it is a lonely place at night when you're alone. (Prisoner, Risley)

There were safe and unsafe places (like showers and recesses) and times (like evenings), so prisoners did not always feel clearly 'safe' or 'unsafe' in a prison; their perceptions were complex:

I feel safest in my [single] cell, but at the same time vulnerable as people can just come in. I don't feel safe on the yard as there are lots of people I don't know—anything can happen. (Prisoner, Belmarsh)

If you have an argument you would be looking over your back, but basically, yes, I feel safe. Sometimes you think the worst but you get on with it and be strong. (Prisoner, Risley)

The only time you feel safe in here is when you're locked up in your pad. (Prisoner, Risley)

It was difficult to feel completely safe in a prison, as no one could control the environment (however, note the safety paradox, raised earlier, whereby prisoners feel slightly safer overall than might be expected). There was some reassurance in staff presence:

I don't feel unsafe but I feel things could happen anytime, it can turn at any time because we are all mixed and there is a young population who act like 'jack the lad'. A lot of things are covered up here; bullying and drugs are not reported like they are supposed to be. The prison has to make reports on all these things but they don't want to look bad so they are not addressing the problem. Staff are not really there enough. (Prisoner, Risley)

Prisoners talked about efforts they made to get the balance right between 'avoiding trouble' and avoiding intimidation:

You're not safe in any prison anywhere, but I don't annoy anyone or get involved in jail politics. (Prisoner, Risley)

I feel safe. It is easily run . . . on here . . . on the bigger wings it had an element of feeling unsafe and working on the servery you have to assert yourself and say no when prisoners ask for extra portions and so then you have to watch him after. (Prisoner, Risley)

> **Definition of safety**　A feeling of security or protection from harm, threat, or danger, and of physical and psychological trust in the environment.

In our structured survey, the dimension 'safety' consisted of seven statements:

Statement 22　There is quite a lot of threats/bullying in here (0.705)

Statement 11　There is hardly any taxing in this prison (0.642)

Statement 30　I feel safe from being injured, bullied, or threatened by other prisoners in here (0.641)

Statement 68　This prison is good at delivering personal safety (0.631)

Statement 85　Generally, I fear for my physical safety (0.606)

Statement 55　I feel safe from being injured, bullied, or threatened by staff in this prison (0.586)

Statement 48　The level of drug use in this prison is quite high (0.503)

Table 6.9*b* shows single item means and significant differences between the prisons, with all the scores expressed positively.

Looking at the items which make up the dimension 'safety', we can see that at Wandsworth, prisoners feel safe from each other (e.g. compared with Risley), but less safe in relation to staff. At Doncaster, prisoners feel very safe from staff and in general, but there are slightly higher reported levels of taxing and bullying. We have described Holme House, until now, as an apparently controlled prison, but Tables 6.8*b* and 6.9*b* show that it has higher reported levels of taxing than Wandsworth.

Statements 4 and 5 discriminated most between the prisons, with reported drug use significantly higher at Risley than at Belmarsh, Doncaster, or Wandsworth. Prisoners at Doncaster felt significantly safer from being injured, bullied, or threatened by staff than prisoners at Belmarsh. Safety is a complex, multidimensional, and poorly understood concept, especially in the prison. It is interesting that prisoners report quite high levels of perceived safety (compared to levels of trust, for example). Doncaster and Belmarsh had the highest officially recorded levels of assaults (see Chapter 4) but Doncaster was experienced by most prisoners as a relatively safe prison. At Doncaster, 8.7 per cent of prisoners agreed with the statement that 'generally I fear for my physical safety' (see Table 6.8*b*). This figure was lowest at Holme House.

All five prisons scored 3 or above on safety (see Table 6.13). The only significant differences were between Risley and Doncaster, and Risley and Wandsworth, with Risley rated as significantly less safe. Wandsworth and Doncaster competed to be the 'safest' prisons, although the models of safety they accomplished were radically different, as we can see from the responses to individual questions. Wandsworth achieved high levels of safety largely through lack of activity, whereas at Doncaster, conversely, high levels of activity seemed to bring about high levels of perceived safety

TABLE 6.13.   Scores on dimension eight: safety

Prison	Reliability	Score
Doncaster	0.7397	3.4561
Wandsworth	0.6269	3.4500
Belmarsh	0.6881	3.3425
Holme House	0.6896	3.3146
Risley	0.7719	3.1132

(see Table 6.9*b*). The overall internal reliability of the dimension 'safety' across all prisons was high, at 0.73.

Safety was most significantly positively correlated with well-being (0.523) as Johnson and Toch, and Sykes would have predicted (Johnson and Toch 1982; Sykes 1958)[33] and order (0.488). Feelings of unsafety may exacerbate 'major mental health problems such as pervasive fear and chronic anxiety' (Dunn 1982: 10).

Well-being

> My whole heart and soul ache with the pain of being here.
>
> (Boyle 1985: 71)

> Stress can contaminate programmes, undermine adjustment efforts, and leave a residue of bitterness and resentment among inmates. It can make the prison a destructive and debilitating institution.
>
> (Johnson and Toch 1982: 20)

The term 'well-being' arose as a result of discussions about tension. Prisoners (and staff) were trying to express, positively, the absence of the psychological tension often experienced during a period of custody. Because we were attempting to state all of our dimensions positively, we agreed that the term 'well-being' might capture this aspect of the prison experience. This dimension was related to the level of stress, tension, and psychological fear experienced by prisoners. Commentators on the prison often note that they should not inflict 'unnecessary and wanton pain' (e.g. Dunn 1982: 11). We might add to this argument that individual prisons within one system should not be experienced as significantly more 'painful' than others.

It is clear that the experience of imprisonment can be painful for many prisoners (and that it is unbearable for some), despite common public and, occasionally, prison staff perceptions that prison is 'too soft' or that 'it would deter if it were more punishing' (see Liebling 1999; Haney 1997; Johnson and Toch 1982; Toch 1992*b*;

[33] In work arising from this project, we have revised this dimension to incorporate two measures of safety: one relating to bullying and general physical safety, as above; and another related to thoughts of suicide and psychological distress (see Liebling 2002).

Boyle 1985; and Sykes 1958, for accounts of the 'pains of imprisonment').[34] This confounding of the material with the psychological conditions of imprisonment permeates popular commentary on
the prison. The 'effects literature' provides contradictory evidence,
some studies arguing that prison does not damage and may even
repair (see West 1997; Walker 1987). The focus of early sociological studies on 'adaptation' implied that coping with prison was a
relatively straightforward, if differentiated, task. Other studies
have linked the prison experience to suicide (Liebling 1992),
psychological breakdown (Toch 1992b; Cohen and Taylor 1972)
and post-traumatic stress disorder (Karim 2001). Prisoners bring
often limited coping skills to the prison environment (Liebling
1992, 1999). Vulnerabilities are exposed by the social, material,
and psychological conditions of imprisonment, for example, by
prolonged isolation, by fear and tension, or by the pressure to 'save
face' (Liebling 1999; Lindquist 2000). Aspects of prison life which
are found to be particularly painful are entry into custody, solitary
confinement, fear, and having to 'wear a mask' (Adams 1992;
Haney 1997). There is considerable evidence that the early experience of custody is especially traumatic (see Gibbs 1982; Liebling
1992; Harvey forthcoming).

We accept the premise that the deprivation of liberty which
results from a term of imprisonment constitutes the intended punishment, and that any additional suffering is both unintended and
damaging (however, see Johnson and Toch 1982: 18; Carlen 1994;
Garland 2001a; and Gallo and Ruggiero 1991 on the prison as a site
for the expression of rage, and the deliberate infliction of punishment
and pain). A prison should be judged by its consistency with its
declared aim, which is to accommodate prisoners humanely and
without undue suffering. We know that some prison environments
are 'healthier' than others (HMCIP 1999a).[35] Do some prisons
minimize distress? What is it about some penal environments that

[34] Sykes famously argued that five basic deprivations—of liberty, goods and services, heterosexual relationships, autonomy, and personal security—together dealt a
'profound hurt' that went 'to the very foundation of the prisoner's being' (1958: 79;
and see later).

[35] The Inspectorate of Prisons has developed a 'healthy prison' notion that consists of safety, respect, meaningful contact with family, and constructive activities.
See Chapter 2.

preserves or permits well-being? Is a feeling of well-being possible, in a prison? It is important to understand differences between prisons in this respect.

Some prisoners talked about 'feeling OK', or finding the general atmosphere reasonable: 'There is a right relaxed atmosphere, it's not like any prison I've been in before' (prisoner, Doncaster). Others found 'niches' (Toch 1992a) or places where the pressures of imprisonment were less obvious, or one could escape the feeling of being in prison:

Gym is the best thing I do here. It's proper spot on that gym; it's the best one in prison. I got a letter from my mate and he told me to go to the gym . . . I've never been one for going to the gym, I was here six weeks before I went. You have that bit of freedom down there; it's just gym screws, none of this macho-man stuff. It's a proper friendly atmosphere; you almost don't feel like you're in jail and you come straight back and have a shower just like you would if you went to a gym outside; it takes it away. (Prisoner, Holme House)

I've been at war for fourteen years [in prison]; now I'm not on my guard all the time or ready to have a go when my door is opened. I feel relaxed, like a big weight has been lifted. (Prisoner, Doncaster)

Most prisoners described avoidance, escape, or 'special places' when they talked about well-being. Few described feeling 'good' on ordinary prison landings (although some did): 'Life is at its best here when you wake up and the sun is shining. When I'm locked in my cell; then you can take the mask off, switch off and relax in a safe environment. No one bothers you and you can be yourself' (prisoner, Holme House).

The need for escape was sometimes expressed more negatively:

When is life at its best here? When I'm behind my door—it's the only time you have your own privacy and you can do what you want to do, although it is limited, from listening to the radio, to reading, writing, without them watching you, or telling you. It is the only time you can be yourself. You have to put on a front in prison. You can't let your defences drop—it's seen as a weakness. (Prisoner, Risley)

Prisoners described tension in prison, and missing their families as two of the main stresses of imprisonment:

I hate it here, because it is so far away from home and because of the cons. The tension in here is unbelievable . . . I'm always stressed and tense,

because of being away from home. I've never been away from home before
and I've got a wife and three kids . . . With the amount of stress I'm under
I'm surprised I'm not in a psychiatric ward. I cry sometimes, people know
I do, I'll say 'right, I'm off to me pad'. Prison has given me so much time
to think, to worry, and get depressed. (Prisoner, Risley)

I feel tense all the time in here . . . There is a lot of aggression behind everything, even the staff . . . They try and hang on to the old military way. In
other prisons it has gone now, but not here. (Prisoner, Wandsworth)

Part of the distress experienced was, as Gallo and Ruggiero
(1991) have noted, linked to the efforts required to keep distress
under control:

In your cell you become introverted and brood more. You can't discuss
your problems in order to put them into perspective. Both my parents have
died since I have been in here and no one has asked me how I am . . .
I can't grieve in here or I will appear vulnerable to other prisoners.
(Prisoner, Wandsworth)

I get depressed being in my cell alone and watching TV, reminding you of
life outside. (Prisoner, Holme House)

Every now and then things just creep up on you, you feel depressed and
lock yourself away for a couple of days . . . (Prisoner, Doncaster)

Some prisoners talked of 'morale' being low, in a way that was
reminiscent of conversations with staff: 'Morale amongst prisoners? We try but we all have the feeling it's like being on a sinking
ship in this prison' (prisoner, Risley).

There were ways of 'doing prison', which were all about managing emotions, avoiding negative feelings, staying stable when the
atmosphere was tense and volatile:

It's a personal thing; jail is what you make it, if you go in with an attitude
you will get stressed. You can sometimes almost feel the tension in here.
You have to wear your psychological armour. Prison is full of anger, guilt,
and regret. The atmosphere is inconsistent; it will see-saw for all sorts of
reasons. (Prisoner, Doncaster)

Definition of well-being   The condition of being contented, and
psychologically healthy; the provision of an atmosphere or environment in which the welfare and adaptation of prisoners is
achievable.

In our structured survey, the dimension 'well-being' consisted of seven statements:

Statement 70   I feel tense in this prison (0.831)
Statement 77   My experience in this prison is painful (0.818)
Statement 51   My experience of imprisonment in this particular prison has been stressful (0.781)
Statement 86   Generally I fear for my psychological safety (0.717)
Statement 69   I can be myself in this prison (0.655)
Statement 13   The atmosphere in this prison is relaxed and friendly (0.621)
Statement 78   Morale amongst prisoners here is high (0.577)

Table 6.14 shows differences in responses to questions about the atmosphere (note the difference between Belmarsh and Doncaster, for example), which seem very much in line with prisoners' other evaluations of life in each prison. Prisoners described their experience of imprisonment as particularly stressful in Wandsworth and Belmarsh. Prisoners found it easier to be themselves in Doncaster (followed by Holme House), and prisoners felt much more tense in Belmarsh than in the other prisons.[36]

All the items in this dimension discriminated between the prisons (Table 6.15). The results show prisoners at Doncaster, quite closely followed by prisoners at Holme House, reporting higher levels of well-being. That is, they reported a significantly more relaxed atmosphere, less stress, the ability to 'be themselves', less tension, less 'painfulness', higher morale, and less 'fear for my psychological safety'. Belmarsh, at the other end of the scale (and, on some items, Wandsworth), was reported as significantly more painful. Statements 4 and 5 are especially noteworthy, with half of all prisoners at Belmarsh agreeing that they felt tense, and agreeing that 'my experience in this prison is painful'. There were also differences between Holme House and the other three prisons on most of these items. It seems imprisonment feels more painful and punitive at one prison than at another. There are implications arising from this 'differential delivery of punishment'. These findings cast doubt on

---

[36] Overall, fewer than half of all prisoners could 'be themselves' in this prison. Haney argues that 'prisoners who labour both at an emotional and a behavioural level to develop a prison mask that is unrevealing and impenetrable risk alienation, emotional flatness and distance, and withdrawal from social interactions' (Haney 1997: 537).

TABLE 6.14.   Percentage of prisoners who agree/strongly agree with statements about well-being

Statement (Well-being)	Belmarsh	Holme House	Risley	Doncaster	Wandsworth
1. The atmosphere in this prison is relaxed and friendly.	30.1[b]	58.5	44.5	64.0[a]	36.6
2. My experience of imprisonment in this prison has been stressful.	57.8	36.1	48.5	26.3[a]	61.6[b]
3. I can be myself in this prison.	34.9[b]	54.3	39.7	62.3[a]	46.6
4. I feel tense in this prison.	50.6[b]	28.7	39.7	21.1[a]	36.7
5. My experience in this prison is painful.	50.6[b]	25.5	31.7	15.8[a]	35.0
6. Morale amongst prisoners here is high.	24.1	41.5	20.8	48.2[a]	16.7[b]
7. Generally I fear for my psychological safety.	28.9[b]	21.3	24.8	15.8[a]	28.4

a indicates highest score, b indicates lowest.

the fairness of the 'proportionality' thesis, which assumes that length of sentence equals the sum of discomfort or punishment experienced (von Hirsch 1976; see also Walker 1985).

The overall internal reliability of the dimension 'well-being' across all prisons was high, at 0.84. Two prisons scored 3 or above on well-being (Table 6.16). There were significant differences between Doncaster and Holme House, Risley, Wandsworth, and Belmarsh respectively, and between Holme House and Risley and Belmarsh. The difference between Holme House and Wandsworth almost reached a level of statistical significance.

Well-being was significantly positively correlated with all other dimensions. It was most highly correlated with, in descending order: fairness (0.631), humanity (0.603), and power/authority (0.602). This suggests, plausibly, that the experience of unfairness, inhumanity, and coercive power is painful and potentially damaging (see Ahmed et al. 2001; and de Zulueta 1993).

We look next at the concept of 'development', which many suggest is a dimension that seeks to place limits on the painfulness or destructiveness of prison (e.g. Johnson and Toch 1982: 15).

TABLE 6.15. A comparison of prisoner views on well-being: individual item mean scores

Item/statement	Item scores (1–5)					ANOVA (Mean difference)									
	B	HH	R	D	W	B&HH	B&R	B&D	B&W	HH&R	HH&D	HH&W	R&D	R&W	D&W
The atmosphere in this prison is relaxed and friendly.	2.89[b]	3.34	3.08	3.55[a]	2.95	0.45	N/s	0.66*	N/s	N/s	N/s	N/s	0.47*	N/s	0.60*
My experience of imprisonment in this particular prison has [not] been stressful.	2.34[b]	3.06	2.55	3.29[a]	2.42	0.73*	N/s	0.95**	N/s	0.51*	N/s	0.65*	0.74**	N/s	0.87**
I can be myself in this prison.	2.82[b]	3.20	2.94	3.47[a]	3.08	N/s	N/s	0.65*	N/s	N/s	N/s	N/s	0.53*	N/s	N/s
I [do not] feel tense in this prison.	2.54[b]	3.21	2.95	3.46[a]	2.98	0.67*	N/s	0.92**	N/s	N/s	N/s	N/s	0.51*	N/s	N/s
My experience in this prison is [not] painful.	2.63[b]	3.33	3.05	3.66[a]	2.92	0.70*	N/s	1.03**	N/s	N/s	N/s	N/s	0.61*	N/s	0.74*
Morale amongst prisoners here is high.	2.71	3.13	2.76	3.38[a]	2.62[b]	0.42	N/s	0.67**	N/s	N/s	N/s	0.51*	0.61**	N/s	0.76**
Generally I [do not] fear for my psychological safety.	3.14[b]	3.50	3.33	3.68[a]	3.27	N/s	N/s	0.53*	N/s	N/s	N/s	N/s	N/s	N/s	N/s

TABLE 6.16. Scores on dimension
nine: well-being

Prison	Reliability	Score
Doncaster	0.7657	3.9871
Holme House	0.8048	3.2538
Risley	0.8769	2.9519
Wandsworth	0.8221	2.8905
Belmarsh	0.7947	2.7246

Personal Development

What man actually needs is not a tension-less state but rather the
striving and struggling for some goal worthy of him.

(Frankl 1964: 107)

We were encouraged by our discussions with staff, and especially
prisoners, to use the term *development* rather than the more commonly used term 'resettlement' to describe the dimension of prison
life related to activities and work. This reflected two concerns: first,
the varied position of prisoners on remand, those serving very long
sentences, and those who were newly arrived, many of whom were
far from focused on leaving prison. Secondly, a specific meaning
was being expressed. Prisoners found the term 'resettlement' limited. To *re*-settle suggests a prior, settled state. It denotes existing
bonds and a pathway to which the prisoner is reconnected towards
the end of a sentence. Prisoners articulated, instead, a more universal need to learn, grow, and develop, sometimes from a poor
base. Their meaning came closer to Allport's concept of 'becoming'. Allport argued that we are unique and striving beings, whose
central problem of life is to make our lives worth living (Allport
1955). This process is made more difficult for those whose early
affiliative (and educational) needs are unmet: individuals need 'a
basic rapport with the world before proper growth can start'
(Allport 1955: 32). Security and 'affectional relationships' are,
Allport argued, 'the ground of becoming', which depends on the
'possession of long-range goals and an ideal self-image' (Allport
1955: 75). The individual needs to assert herself, but also, ideally,

to reconcile herself with or make sense of the world.[37] In this sense, the individual's need to adjust to and 'master the environment' is innate and continuing, throughout the lifecourse. Psychological health is linked to what Allport calls 'propriate striving', that is, future-oriented development (Allport 1955: 89–91). All opportunities for 'growth' aid in this process of becoming. This analysis makes sense of the link prisoners made between development in prison and humanity. There were also links between this concept of development and the concept of 'meaning', explored in Chapter 7. Becoming or development constitutes, then, a moral value which is strongly linked to humanity. This link has long been recognized:

It is all too easy to construct a regime based on what appear to be the needs (or the deserts) of prisoners. More thought and research is needed to discover what the needs of a human being in prison actually are . . . A prisoner is a human being of individual worth, and the regime should preserve or increase his self-respect. It follows, for example, that he should not have to wear ill-fitting clothes or perform what is obviously useless work . . . He should have the opportunities to engage in activities . . . that may increase his self-respect. (Advisory Council on the Penal System 1968: 28)

In 1993 the Chief Inspector of Prisons published a report, *Doing Time or Using Time*, in which a powerful case was made for a reduction in 'enforced idleness' and the development and delivery of active, relevant activities and programmes for prisoners. The report pointed out that prisoners were experiencing 'a quality of life that varied according to the particular establishment, or the particular part of the system in which they found themselves' (HMCIP 1993a: 10): 'The quality of life for an inmate was often random, haphazard and dependent on accidents of geography and allocation' (ibid. 11).

Many parts of the system (in particular, local prisons) were concerned with little more than 'survival'. Low levels of activity—or 'impoverished regimes'—had been one of the 'common threads running through the [1990s] disturbances'. So, on the grounds of justice and humanity, prisons needed to provide meaningful and constructive activities, within a management framework that

---

[37] This may be why the humanities—philosophical, civic, or political education— are thought by some to aid in the process of reducing recidivism (Gaes *et al.* 1999: 399; Duguid 2000).

supported such activities (HMCIP 1993*a*). An ethic of purposeful activity, sentence planning, and constructive occupation—of using time rather than doing time—was a basic requirement (ibid. 86).

Evaluations of prison life often include some measure of activity or programme delivery, particularly when comparing public and private prisons (see Chapter 2), but for narrower reasons than those outlined above. Thomas, for example, asserted the importance of participation in meaningful work and educational and vocational programmes, on the grounds that 'a busy prison is a safe prison' (Thomas 1997). Logan (1992) included a measure of 'activity' (including work and industry, education and training, recreation, and religious services) in his analysis of the quality of confinement. Moos included a measure of 'involvement and practicality' in his assessment of a prison's social climate. Toch's Prison Preference Index (PPI) included indicators of social stimulation and activity. The Prison Service measures 'hours in purposeful activity' and 'completed accredited offending behaviour programmes' as two of its KPIs. There is considerable emphasis by senior managers (supported by government funding) on increasing the numbers of prisoners attending such structured programmes in the light of some evidence of a reduction in reoffending of 10 to 15 per cent by prisoners who successfully complete such programmes, when compared with matched controls (Hollin 1999, 2003; Friendship *et al.* 2002; McGuire 2002). There is also, however, a stringent critique in the literature of any conflation of the concept of 'personal development' with the neo-liberal, modern, enforced participation in such courses (Hannah-Moffatt 2001; Duguid 2000).[38]

We included several questions for this dimension, some of which were related to previous research on incentives and earned privileges, which explored motivations to engage in activities

---

[38] Newly formed risk categorizations have turned offenders into 'transformative risk subjects' in an exclusionary and non-welfare-like way (Hannah-Moffatt 2004). Within this framework, correctional treatment is narrowly conceived, is a limited resource, and takes a 'responsibilization' approach. What Hannah-Moffatt and others have called 'new rehabilitationism' blends risk and management with control. 'This construction of the offender leaves intact the presumption that crime is the outcome of poor choices or decisions and not the outcome of structural inequalities or pathology . . . new technologies of need management rely on the creation of independent autonomous subjects who have learned how to be a good risk manager responsible for their own self-care and to avoid risky situations' (Hannah-Moffatt 2004). See also Duguid (2000).

(Liebling *et al.* 1997). Others were suggested by prisoners and by staff and were related to participation in courses and attitudes towards time spent in custody.

It was clear that involvement in work or education transformed the prison experience for most prisoners. 'Every day is great here because of my job' (prisoner, Risley). Participation in a regular activity, particularly work and gym, was strongly related to prisoners' perception of their quality of life. Gym was valued as a means to unwind and relieve tension: 'When you go to the gym you can burn off all your energies. There would be less violence if there was more gym. I get achievement from lifting more weights, or doing a faster circuit time; it gives me something to work towards, my own goals' (prisoner, Holme House).

Whilst it was often the case that prisoners did not feel their work was constructive, interesting, or might be useful to them in the future, they still reported that education and work were worthwhile activities: 'I work as a cleaner and on the servery. The job does nothing for rehabilitation but you do get clean clothes, washing, time out of cell and you get to know the officers better . . . and it looks good on your record' (prisoner, Wandsworth).

So activities provided time out of cell, gave prisoners something to do, and helped time pass quickly. Activities gave prisoners greater access to phones and showers and opportunities to interact with other prisoners and staff, as well as providing money:

I've done an industrial cleaning course and now I work in the laundry, which I enjoy. It was all very stressful when I first came in and I was timid, you know? But I've come out of myself since I've been working in the laundry. I enjoy the routine of work, time flies down there, and I get on with the other prisoners. (Prisoner, Holme House)

I was made a cleaner two days ago. It's my first time in prison and I've been here three weeks. I put in for education on my second day here but never heard anything and it's better for me to be a cleaner on the spur anyway as I get access to the phone and get out of my cell more. (Prisoner, Belmarsh)

Some prisoners clearly did feel that the work they were doing would increase their employment prospects on release: '[I do] the painting and decorating and the industrial cleaning course. You get hands on experience and there are job opportunities, definitely.

I was crap at painting and decorating before; it will be really useful when I get out to help me get a job' (prisoner, Holme House).

Most employment was wing-based and of a domestic nature. Prisoners complained often about the lack of constructive activities (including offending behaviour programmes). As prison populations grew, new houseblocks were built but prisons did not provide the extra facilities needed. Waiting lists for courses were long. Prisoners complained of boredom, especially at weekends:

. . . If you're not working you're not allowed to use the association games during the day. It's a working jail but no way is there enough work; you can be unemployed for two to three months. (Prisoner, Risley)

They don't really help you, all they do is hold you here. There are no programmes to go through to rehabilitate you for life. (Prisoner, Wandsworth)

Much of the work off the wing (e.g. in workshops) was described as monotonous and unlikely to provide relevant work experience or training that might be beneficial on release.

Activities were a catalyst for change; they gave prisoners a sense of purpose, built confidence, and developed talent. They often had a therapeutic value, especially in art-related subjects. Much of prisoners' sense of self-development arose from their individual interests, 'cell hobbies', study, reading, and religious activities, and the role of helping others. These activities were not necessarily provided within the prison regime:

The most constructive activity I do is chanting . . . The help and support I get comes from the Buddhist class and Narcotics Anonymous. (Prisoner, Belmarsh)

When I was last here I did an art course in education; that was excellent, but I didn't get to finish it—I did it for twelve months and then got out. I still draw though, in my cell; I do portraits of my family and send them out. (Prisoner, Holme House)

Prisoners wrote letters for one another, learned sign language, started Open University courses, learned how to use computers, devoured books ('I can read about four books a day'; prisoner, Wandsworth) and they taught basic reading skills to other prisoners:

Teaching reading is the best thing I've done, it is rewarding and I've enjoyed that the most; and when I was a Listener. (Prisoner, Wandsworth)

The most constructive thing? . . . The psychology GCSE; I got an A! I want to do an access course now and go to university to do psychology. It has helped me to understand human behaviour and how, in prison, people have to be offensive to be defensive. (Prisoner, Risley)

The provision of accredited offending behaviour programmes (including drug rehabilitation courses) was very limited. Courses attracted long waiting lists but often provided valuable insight and self-knowledge for those who attended:[39]

The most constructive thing I have done here is Enhanced Thinking Skills (ETS). It's made me think better and talk to people better. (Prisoner, Wandsworth)

The Sex Offender Treatment Programme has changed my life. It has opened my eyes to be open and honest—I was on an island before. (Prisoner, Wandsworth)

The Problem Solving Training course; it did a lot for me that course. Before I'd done that I'd be straight in, f'ing and blinding, but the course changed my outlook on things, it made me stop and realize. (Prisoner, Holme House)

The most constructive thing for me has been the ETS course. It gave me more confidence in life; I'm a really shy person. You do role-plays on the course and it helps you look at things in different ways, like if your visit doesn't turn up or your mail goes missing, there may be a good reason. It's about beliefs and not always thinking the worst . . . I'd recommend it to anyone, not just prisoners. (Prisoner, Risley)

---

[39] Many prisoners were crying out for 'rehabilitation' and for 'courses'. Some were very positive about such courses and others were scathing, demanding a more individualized approach to their offending behaviour. Most, however, seemed to want to stop offending, and wanted 'the prison' to help them achieve this. This appeared to us to represent both a genuine wish by many prisoners to change their lives and find new ways of thinking, as well as successful domination by 'responsibilization' and self-governance penal strategies (which include enforced participation in 'tackling offending behaviour' programmes).

Prisoners were comfortable with the term 'rehabilitation' and often expressed a wish for 'more of it':

They are paranoid about security and drug enforcement, but rehabilitation is the other side of the coin. (Prisoner, Belmarsh)

This place is more towards bang 'em away than trying to help people change; they should encourage people to do more activity, but that's not their job. Their prime task is to keep us safe and held away. (Prisoner, Holme House)

Having a job or other activity was positively related to scores on other dimensions: for example, relationships, trust, respect, and fairness. Many prisoners used 'getting a job' as an example of being treated with respect or fairness.

An officer told me he'd got me a job; he stuck his neck out for me really because the others thought I was too boisterous. They had bets that I wouldn't last but this was four months ago. I've proved them wrong so I get on better with them now. (Prisoner, Holme House)

The staff get on with the workers the best—'cause they get to know them. When they finish work they sit around the table together, laughing and joking. Even if prisoners lose their jobs their relationships with staff are still better, 'cause they know them. (Prisoner, Doncaster)

The most constructive thing for me has been being given a trusted job. I'm a drug addict . . . a little goes a long way, builds your confidence; I've not been trusted for years and it feels good—you're spoken to like a human being and it gives you a boost. (Prisoner, Doncaster)

Many of the changes prisoners wanted to see made to prison life were related to activities, development, and the provision of courses:

I'm really scared about when I get out—I need a chat about it, even if someone just sat down and asked me what I wanted to do, but they're not interested. They used to have a pre-release course but they stopped it. I've been in such a long time and I'm used to them doing it all for me, I'm really worried about what will happen when I get out. I don't want to come back. I'm thinking about moving somewhere else so I don't get in with the same crowd and dealing drugs. (Prisoner, Risley)

They should teach you trades . . . they do hairdressing and tiling here but there should be more, like plumbing, bricklaying, painting and decorating, up to City and Guilds so there is more chance of people not reoffending; that would be a big improvement here. (Prisoner, Risley)

You come in a drug addict and get booted out the same as when you come in; there's no help, no courses, no counselling; you go out in the same frame of mind and then come back in two weeks later . . . I want help but just can't get it. (Prisoner, Holme House)

> **Definition of personal development**   The extent to which provision is made for prisoners to spend their time in a purposeful and constructive way, opportunities are available for self-development, and prisoners are enabled to develop their potential, gain a sense of direction, and prepare for release.

In the survey, the dimension 'personal development' consisted of 20 statements:[40]

Statement 33	The work I do in this prison is helping me to develop myself (0.735)
Statement 34	Relationships with staff in this prison are helping me to develop (0.707)
Statement 32	The education I receive in this prison is helping me to develop myself (0.682)
Statement 62	I get a lot out of the activities I take up in here (0.680)
Statement 52	On the whole I am 'doing time' rather than 'using time' (0.679)
Statement 16	I am being helped to lead a law-abiding life whilst in prison (0.675)
Statement 72	I am encouraged to work towards goals/targets in this prison (0.668)
Statement 96	The regime in this prison is constructive (0.665)
Statement 17	I am being helped to lead a law-abiding life on release in the community (0.665)
Statement 36	My participation in courses in here has helped me to develop myself (0.661)
Statement 1	The main activity I do here is interesting (0.658)
Statement 91	My time here seems like a chance to change (0.657)

---

[40] We used 22 items in the last three prisons, but their addition did not increase the reliability of the dimension significantly, so we omitted them for this part of the analysis (we have included responses to the two additional questions in Table 6.17).

Statement 2   The main activity I do here is enjoyable (0.636)

Statement 41   This regime encourages me to think about and plan for my release (0.628)

Statement 25   This prison does well at delivering an interesting and varied regime (0.625)

Statement 3   The main activity I do here is worthwhile to me (0.622)

Statement 61   I feel motivated to get involved in activities in this prison (0.599)

Statement 81   I often feel bored here (0.506)

Statement 35   Relationships with outside organizations are helping me to develop myself (0.506)

Statement 4   I don't put much effort into the main activity I do here (0.341)

Table 6.17 shows that most of the positive responses came from Doncaster and Holme House, but they arose in slightly different ways. For example, a high proportion of prisoners at Holme House felt they were 'being helped to lead a law-abiding life in prison', whereas a higher proportion in Doncaster felt they were 'being helped to lead a law-abiding life on release'. More than half the prisoners at Doncaster felt it delivered 'an interesting and varied regime'—a much higher proportion than at the other prisons. This dimension attracted low scores overall in most areas (Table 6.18). For example, no prison scored 3 on the item, 'I am being helped to lead a law-abiding life on release in the community' or on the item, 'On the whole I am "doing time" rather than "using time". Scores on 'feeling bored' were poor in all prisons. On the other hand, more than half of the items led to significant differences between the prisons, with Doncaster being rated as far more constructive overall. Risley scored very poorly on delivering 'an interesting and varied regime'.

The overall internal reliability of the dimension 'personal development' across all prisons was very high, at 0.92. Only Doncaster scored above 3 on this dimension (Table 6.19). There were significant differences between Belmarsh and Doncaster, Risley and Doncaster, and Wandsworth and Doncaster, with Doncaster scoring significantly higher than these three prisons.

Personal development was most significantly positively correlated with quality of life ('this regime is positive') (0.684), fairness (0.567), and trust (0.560).

TABLE 6.17.   Percentage of prisoners who agree/strongly agree with statements about personal development

Statement (personal development)	Belmarsh	Holme House	Risley	Doncaster	Wandsworth
1. The main activity I do here is interesting.	40.9	42.6	43.6	54.3[a]	36.6[b]
2. The main activity I do here is enjoyable.	42.1	50.0	46.5	61.4[a]	30.0[b]
3. The main activity I do here is worthwhile to me.	45.8[b]	53.2	49.5	67.5[a]	46.7
4. I don't put much effort into the activity I do here.	16.9	11.7[a]	24.7[b]	13.2	13.4
5. I am being helped to lead a law-abiding life whilst in prison.	19.3[b]	44.6[a]	32.7	36.8	28.4
6. I am being helped to lead a law-abiding life on release.	13.2[b]	29.8	29.8	35.1[a]	21.6
7. This prison does well in delivering an interesting and varied regime.	21.7	33.0	16.8[b]	52.6[a]	20.0
8. The education I receive in this prison is helping me to develop myself.	33.7	41.5[a]	32.6	39.5	26.7[b]
9. The work I do in this prison is helping me to develop myself.	22.9	34.1[a]	30.7	31.6	16.7[b]
10. Relationships with staff in this prison are helping me to develop.	15.7[b]	22.3	15.9	38.6[a]	16.6
11. Relationships with outside organizations are helping me to develop.	19.2[b]	27.6[a]	25.8	20.2	26.7
12. My participation in courses here has helped me to develop myself.	28.9[b]	44.7[a]	32.7	32.4	36.6
13. This regime encourages me to think about and plan for my release.	27.7[b]	40.5	31.6	48.3[a]	38.4
14. On the whole, I am 'doing time' rather than 'using time'.	73.5[a]	67.0	66.4	55.2[b]	71.7
15. I feel motivated to get involved in activities in this prison.	28.9[b]	44.7[a]	32.7	32.4	36.6
16. I get a lot out of the activities I take up here.	40.9	51.1	35.7	59.6[a]	35.0[b]
17. I am encouraged to work towards goals/targets in this prison.	18.1[b]	41.5	34.6	43.0[a]	25.0
18. I often feel bored here.	86.8[a]	72.3	69.3[b]	69.3[b]	71.6
19. My time here seems like a chance to change.	40.9	41.5	40.6[b]	57.0[a]	43.3
20. The regime in this prison is constructive.	13.2	26.6	16.8	48.3[a]	11.7[b]
21. I feel I have been encouraged to address my offending behaviour.	—	—	33.6	36.9[a]	30.0[b]
22. I am concerned about what will happen to me when I am released.	—	—	52.5	50.0[a]	56.7[b]

a indicates highest score, b indicates lowest.

TABLE 6.18. A comparison of prisoner views on personal development: individual item mean scores

Item/statement	Item scores (1–5)					ANOVA (Mean difference)									
	B	HH	R	D	W	B&HH	B&R	B&D	B&W	HH&R	HH&D	HH&W	R&D	R&W	D&W
The main activity I do here is interesting.	3.07	3.05	3.08	3.48ᵃ	2.93ᵇ	N/s	N/s	N/s	N/s	N/s	N/s	N/s	N/s	N/s	N/s
The main activity I do here is enjoyable.	3.08	3.20	3.18	3.59ᵃ	2.88ᵇ	N/s	N/s	0.50*	N/s	N/s	N/s	N/s	N/s	N/s	0.70*
The main activity I do here is worthwhile to me.	3.19	3.24	3.11ᵇ	3.74ᵃ	3.12	N/s	N/s	0.54*	N/s	N/s	0.49	N/s	0.63*	N/s	0.62*
I [do] put effort into the main activity I do here.	3.66	3.81	3.44ᵇ	3.85ᵃ	3.80	N/s	N/s	N/s	N/s	N/s	N/s	N/s	0.42	N/s	N/s
I am being helped to lead a law-abiding life whilst in this prison.	2.47ᵇ	2.98	2.77	3.04ᵃ	2.65	0.51	N/s	0.57*	N/s	N/s	N/s	N/s	N/s	N/s	N/s
I am being helped to lead a law-abiding life on release in the community.	2.28ᵇ	2.78	2.71	2.90ᵃ	2.50	0.50	N/s	0.63*	N/s	N/s	N/s	N/s	N/s	N/s	N/s
This prison does well in delivering an interesting and varied regime.	2.47	2.89	2.35ᵇ	3.43ᵃ	2.37	N/s	N/s	0.96**	N/s	0.55*	0.54*	0.53*	1.08**	N/s	1.06**
The education I receive in this prison is helping me to develop myself.	2.89	3.12	2.96	3.14ᵃ	2.70ᵇ	N/s	N/s	N/s	N/s	N/s	N/s	N/s	N/s	N/s	N/s
The work I do in this prison is helping me to develop myself.	2.61	2.97	2.82	3.02ᵃ	2.43ᵇ	N/s	N/s	N/s	N/s	N/s	N/s	0.53	N/s	N/s	N/s
Relationships with staff in this prison are helping me to develop.	2.49	2.68	2.56	3.06ᵃ	2.48ᵇ	N/s	N/s	0.57*	N/s	N/s	N/s	N/s	0.50*	N/s	0.58*
Relationships with outside organizations are helping me to develop.	2.60	2.82ᵃ	2.71	2.80	2.58ᵇ	N/s	N/s	N/s	N/s	N/s	N/s	N/s	N/s	N/s	N/s

TABLE 6.18. (Continued)

Item/statement	Item scores (1–5)					ANOVA (Mean difference)									
	B	HH	R	D	W	B&HH	B&R	B&D	B&W	HH&R	HH&D	HH&W	R&D	R&W	D&W
My participation in courses in here has helped me to develop.	2.87[b]	3.12[a]	2.95	3.09	2.95	N/s	N/s	N/s	N/s	N/s	N/s	N/s	N/s	N/s	N/s
This regime encourages me to think about and plan for my release.	2.66[b]	3.00	2.85	3.15[a]	2.83	N/s	N/s	0.49	N/s	N/s	N/s	N/s	N/s	N/s	N/s
On the whole I am ['using'] time rather than ['doing'] time.	2.18	2.35	2.23	2.55[a]	2.08[b]	N/s	N/s	N/s	N/s	N/s	N/s	N/s	N/s	N/s	N/s
I feel motivated to get involved in activities.	2.98	3.33	2.88[b]	3.47[a]	3.22	N/s	N/s	0.50*	N/s	0.45	N/s	N/s	0.59*	N/s	N/s
I get a lot out of the activities I take up.	3.02[b]	3.38	3.03	3.48[a]	3.03	N/s	N/s	0.46*	N/s	N/s	N/s	N/s	0.45*	N/s	N/s
I am encouraged to work towards goals/targets in this prison.	2.39[b]	3.03	2.92	3.12[a]	2.73	0.65*	0.54*	0.74**	N/s	N/s	N/s	N/s	N/s	N/s	N/s
I [do not] often feel bored here.	1.78[b]	2.17	2.20	2.25[a]	2.13	N/s	N/s	0.47	N/s	N/s	N/s	N/s	N/s	N/s	N/s
My time here seems like a chance to change.	2.95[b]	2.99	2.97	3.38[a]	2.95[b]	N/s	N/s	N/s	N/s	N/s	N/s	N/s	N/s	N/s	N/s
The regime in this prison is constructive.	2.41[b]	2.90	2.54	3.27[a]	2.78	0.49*	N/s	0.86**	N/s	N/s	0.37	0.59*	0.73**	N/s	0.96**
I have been encouraged to address my offending behaviour whilst in this prison.	N/a	N/a	2.93	2.94[a]	2.78[b]	N/a	N/a	N/a	N/a	N/a	N/a	N/a	N/s	N/s	N/s
I am [not] concerned about what will happen to me when I am released.	N/a	N/a	2.67[a]	2.66	2.52[b]	N/a	N/a	N/a	N/a	N/a	N/a	N/a	N/s	N/s	N/s

a indicates highest score, b indicates lowest. * indicates $p < 0.05$; ** indicates $p < 0.001$.

TABLE 6.19. Scores on dimension
ten: personal development

Prison	Reliability	Score
Doncaster	0.9098	3.1598
Holme House	0.9256	2.9912
Risley	0.9181	2.8123
Wandsworth	0.9325	2.7273
Belmarsh	0.8774	2.7011

Four Components of 'Personal Development'

We carried out a factor analysis on the items in 'personal development' to see whether distinguishable sub-dimensions could be identified. Four factors emerged: 'personal development', 'engagement', 'constructive regime', and 'help with offending behaviour' (Table 6.20).

'Personal development' included items relating to constructive activities that foster growth. The factor 'engagement' is similar to the concept used by Bottoms, 'normative involvement in personal projects' (Bottoms 1999: 258). The third factor, 'constructive regime', refers to an active as opposed to inactive regime—and could be said to be similar to the concept of 'positive custody' used by the May Committee (Home Office 1979; but, for its critics, see Bottoms 1990). The fourth factor includes items indicating 'help with offending behaviour', that is, perceptions by prisoners that they are being assisted specifically to 'lead a law-abiding life'.

Looking at these factors separately helps to distinguish between aspects of development being delivered in each prison (see Table 6.21). Belmarsh (closely followed by Wandsworth) scored lowest on 'personal development' (although none of the scores was high). Wandsworth scored lowest on 'engagement' (and Doncaster scored particularly high on this new dimension). Wandsworth scored lowest on 'constructive regime', closely followed by Belmarsh. Belmarsh scored lowest on 'help with offending behaviour'. Again, none of the prisons scored high on this dimension, suggesting that prisons 'do better' at offering an interesting regime (passing the time) than they do at developing prisoners or helping them with their release.

TABLE 6.20. Four factors arising from the original dimension, 'personal development'

Factor One: Personal development (five items (0.84))	Factor Two: Engagement (three items (0.90))	Factor Three: Constructive regime (three items (0.84))	Factor Four: Help with offending behaviour (three items (0.80))
Relationships with staff in this prison are helping me to develop.	The main activity I do here is enjoyable.	Overall, I feel that the regime in this prison is positive.	I am being helped to lead a law-abiding life whilst in prison.
My participation in courses in here has helped me to develop myself.	The main activity I do here is interesting.	The regime in this prison is constructive.	I am being helped to lead a law-abiding life on release in the community.
The work I do in this prison is helping me to develop myself.	The main activity I do here is worthwhile to me.	This prison does well at delivering an interesting and varied regime.	My time here seems like a chance to change.
The education I receive in this prison is helping me to develop myself.			
I am encouraged to work towards goals/targets in this prison.			

TABLE 6.21. Mean scores on the new dimensions, 'personal development', 'engagement', 'constructive regime', and 'help with offending behaviour'

Prison	Factor One: Personal development	Factor Two: Engagement	Factor Three: Constructive regime	Factor Four: Help with offending behaviour
Belmarsh	2.6506[b]	3.1165	2.5020	2.5663[b]
Holme House	2.9830	3.1667	2.9397	2.9149
Risley	2.8436	3.1221	2.4983	2.8185
Doncaster	3.0860[a]	3.6023[a]	3.4123[a]	3.1082[a]
Wandsworth	2.6600	2.9778[b]	2.4611[b]	2.7000

Notes: Significant differences: personal development: D and B ($p < 0.05$), W ($p < 0.05$); engagement: D and B ($p < 0.05$), R ($p < 0.05$), W ($p < 0.01$), HH almost ($p = 0.06$); constructive regime: D and B ($p < 0.001$), HH ($p < 0.005$), R ($p < 0.001$), W ($p < 0.001$); also HH and R ($p < 0.01$), W ($p < 0.05$); help with offending behaviour: D and B ($p < 0.01$).

Family Contact

> Prisoners with strong outside ties have an edge in facing pains of imprisonment, and community ties are essential to humane management of prisons.
>
> (Toch 1982: 35)

There are three reasons for a concern with prisoners' families in the 'moral measurement' of a prison. The first is to pay attention to the unintended consequences of family disruption on family members; the second is the relevance of family contact to the painfulness of the prison experience; and the third is the potential relationship between family ties and recidivism. The literature has more to say about the first and third, clearly important subjects in their own right.[41] We place particular emphasis upon the second in this section.

Maintaining (and developing) relationships with family and friends was clearly an important aspect of prisoners' lives whilst in prison, but primarily (in their view) for reasons relating to the *painfulness of prison*. The provision, or the lack, of opportunities for interaction with families could have an enormous impact on the quality of life they experienced. Prisoners talked a lot about family problems and often expressed a feeling of lack of control over what happened outside, during the interviews. Many prisoners felt that life in prison was at its best when they were in some form of communication with their family, either on a visit, by telephone, or in the sending and receiving of letters (however, see Lindquist 2000).

Life is at its best when I have access to my family . . . but it's hard to get on the phone. Prisoners are anxiously waiting to speak and they don't understand. Once, the day I was sentenced, I was late back and banged up; I asked to talk to my wife and they let me use the phone. I think that was humane. (Prisoner, Belmarsh)

What makes a difference? Visits mainly . . . if you get a visit, when you get mail, if you get a good response on the phone. (Prisoner, Holme House)

Mail does cheer you up. When I get a nice letter from my mum or my girl-friend, it's something to reply to so it makes you feel better. (Prisoner, Doncaster)

---

[41] See e.g. Light (1993); Shaw (1987, 1992); Sampson and Laub (1993); and Farrall (2002: 152–60).

Prisoners said that they were sometimes assisted in maintaining contact with their families, at the discretion of individual officers. Officers let prisoners out of their cell to make a telephone call, or they allowed a (compassionate) private call in an office with a member of staff present. Some prisoners gave examples of being helped to sort out a problem with a visiting order.

[INTERVIEWER: Have you ever been assisted in maintaining contact with your family here?] Yes, they always give extra phone calls, if you can prove you have family problems on the out, or if you can explain why you need to make a call, like if your missus is in hospital and you've run out of phone units they will make a call for you or let you out and give you half an hour on the phone, or the chapel will come over and take you over there to use the phone. They do go out of their way to make sure you know everything is OK; they know that unnecessary worry leads to suicide and violence. (Prisoner, Holme House)

My dad was in and out of hospital and had an operation and they said if I ever needed to call the hospital to speak to the nurses, they would let me use the phone in private, in an office with an officer there but more private than using the phones on the wing. (Prisoner, Risley)

I've not really needed any assistance in maintaining contact; you've got a lot of time to use the phone and you get a lot of association. If you have family problems it is allowed to use a private phone in an office. I did get a phone call when my girlfriend was pregnant with our youngest. (Prisoner, Doncaster)

I've been given a personal phone call in the office by a member of staff, that was very helpful and was risking their job, so I could call my family. They sorted it straight away as I had no phone cards on that day. (Prisoner, Wandsworth)

A couple of weeks ago I sent a VO [Visiting Order] out to my girlfriend but her ex-boyfriend ripped it up. I told an officer on here and he contacted the senior officer in visits who told him to tell me to phone her and tell her to come up anyway and they sorted it out; they reissued a VO at the gate when she got here and I got my visit no problem. (Prisoner, Holme House)

Some prisoners complained about the lack of opportunities for visits, delays in receiving mail, the lack of telephones on the wings, delays in visits starting, the manner in which their visitors were treated (prisoners felt their visitors were criminalized), and the indignity of being subject to searching procedures. This led to some prisoners deciding not to see their friends and family:

The lack of phones is a problem; there are only two for the whole spur of 60. Everyone wants to use them at the same time and the noise is too loud to have a decent conversation because of where they are. (Prisoner, Belmarsh)

It's upsetting the way visitors are treated. My nine-month old daughter was searched for drugs; her nappy was opened and they touched her body and everything. I understand you need to search people for drugs to stop them coming in but the way they search young children is really annoying. (Prisoner, Belmarsh)

My parents had to wait outside for two hours before they could see me and I feel that it's designed to wind me up, which it does. (Prisoner, Risley)

My mum doesn't like coming . . . It takes her days to book a visit and she waits for two hours for to see me. I'd rather not have any visits than put her through that. (Prisoner, Wandsworth)

Distance from home made visits difficult: prisoners blamed the Prison Service for this. If relationships with, and between, family members outside were trouble-free, then life inside was less stressful. This may account for the positive relationship between the dimensions 'family contact' and 'well-being':

Getting a visit cheers me up, but you have mixed feelings really, because you can feel low at the same time, when the visit is over and you have to say goodbye it's painful. (Prisoner, Belmarsh)

I don't receive visits from my family . . . It's depressing when you have a lot of time to think about your family . . . or you've not received mail and everyone else has. It's the same for visits, you feel not wanted . . . I knew about prison visitors so I went to the chapel and asked for one and they picked one out for me. I want contact with someone from outside, to keep me sane, you know? (Prisoner, Holme House)

Definition of family contact The degree to which prisoners are encouraged to maintain links and develop their relationships with their families.

In our structured survey, the dimension 'family contact' consisted of four statements (only one statement was used at Belmarsh):

Statement 87   I am able to receive visits often enough in this prison (0.760)

Statement 88   The length of time for each visit is long enough (0.729)

Statement 100   I am able to maintain meaningful contact with my family whilst I am in this prison (0.672)

Statement 93   My visitors to this prison are treated well (0.569)

Seventy-eight per cent of prisoners received visits (90 per cent at Belmarsh; 79 per cent at Holme House; 77 per cent at Risley; 76 per cent at Doncaster; and 76 per cent at Wandsworth). Those who did not receive visits said that this was because they were too far from home, they had no family to visit them, or they chose not to have visits for 'personal reasons' (e.g. because they did not like their families being subject to searching procedures).

TABLE 6.22.   Percentage of prisoners who agree/strongly agree with statements about family contact and decency

Statements	Belmarsh	Holme House	Risley	Doncaster	Wandsworth
(a) Family contact					
1. I am able to receive visits often enough in this prison.	—	69.1	68.3	74.6[a]	51.7[b]
2. My visitors to this prison are treated well.	—	33.0	36.6	40.4[a]	31.7[b]
3. The length of time for each visit is long enough.	—	50.0	59.4[a]	46.5	33.3[b]
4. I am able to maintain meaningful contact with my family whilst here.	65.1	91.4[a]	75.3	84.2	61.6[b]
(b) Decency					
1. I am given adequate opportunities to keep clean and decent.	—	94.7	95.0[a]	93.0	56.6[b]
2. The quality of my living conditions is poor.	59.0[b]	23.4	22.8	13.2[a]	38.4
3. Prisoners spend too much time locked up in their cells.	89.1[b]	74.5	28.8	22.8[a]	81.7
4. I feel that I have enough privacy here.	—	57.5	55.5	63.2[a]	46.6[b]
5. I am given adequate opportunities to keep my living area clean and decent.	—	83.0	87.1	93.0[a]	53.3[b]

Three of the statements discriminated significantly between the prisons, with Doncaster, Holme House, and Risley rated significantly higher than Wandsworth. The question on how visitors were treated did not discriminate between the prisons, but was raised by prisoners in our discussions as an important matter to them. Question 4 (our original question) discriminated particularly well (Table 6.23a).

The overall internal reliability of the dimension 'family', across all prisons, was acceptable at 0.62. Different aspects of family visits were evaluated rather differently in each prison, so that, for example, the length of visits attracted a relatively low score at Doncaster, despite positive evaluations of the frequency of visits. Three prisons scored 3 or above on 'family contact' (see Table 6.24). There were significant differences between Holme House and Wandsworth, Risley and Wandsworth, and Doncaster and Wandsworth, with Wandsworth scoring significantly lower on this dimension than the other three prisons.

TABLE 6.24.   Scores on dimension 11: family contact

Prison	Reliability	Score
Doncaster	0.5949	3.4759
Holme House	0.5166	3.4229
Risley	0.7017	3.4208
Wandsworth	0.6257	2.9917
Belmarsh	—	—

Family contact was significantly positively correlated with all other dimensions. It was most highly correlated with decency (0.491) and well-being (0.452).

Decency

We introduced a dimension, 'decency', at the first establishment but extended it following further discussions with staff and prisoners. The more detailed discussions about the meaning of this term arose in our workgroup discussions as a result of the 'decency agenda' being launched by the Prison Service (see Chapter 10).

What prisoners meant by the term originally (and so how we have used the term here) was quite 'material':

A prison is decent if it is clean, tidy, and somewhere you can live without picking up diseases. (Prisoner, Holme House)

TABLE 6.23. A comparison of prisoner views on family contact and decency: individual item mean scores

Item/statements	Item scores (1–5)					ANOVA (Mean difference)									
	B	HH	R	D	W	B&HH	B&R	B&D	B&W	HH&R	HH&D	HH&W	R&D	R&W	D&W
(a) Family contact															
I am able to receive visits often enough in this prison.	N/a	3.62	3.57	3.82ᵃ	2.97ᵇ	N/a	N/a	N/a	N/a	N/s	N/s	0.65*	N/s	0.61*	0.86**
My visitors to this prison are treated well.	N/a	2.83ᵇ	3.08	3.13ᵃ	3.00	N/a	N/a	N/a	N/a	N/s	N/s	N/s	N/s	N/s	N/s
The length of time for each visit is long enough.	N/a	3.16	3.40ᵃ	3.03	2.62ᵇ	N/a	N/a	N/a	N/a	N/s	N/s	0.54*	N/s	0.78*	N/s
I am able to maintain meaningful contact with my family whilst I am in this prison.	3.59ᵇ	4.09ᵃ	3.63	3.91	3.38	0.49*	N/s	N/s	N/s	0.45*	N/s	0.70*	N/s	N/s	0.53*
(b) Decency															
I am given adequate opportunities to keep myself clean and decent.	N/a	4.19	4.23	4.26ᵃ	3.25ᵇ	N/a	N/a	N/a	N/a	N/s	N/s	0.94**	N/s	0.98**	1.01**
The quality of my living conditions is [good].	2.43ᵇ	3.39	3.31	3.57ᵃ	2.83	0.96**	0.87**	1.14**	0.40*	N/s	N/s	0.56*	N/s	N/s	0.74*
Prisoners [do not] spend too long locked up in their cells.	1.59ᵇ	2.02	3.16	3.39ᵃ	1.67	N/s	1.57**	1.80**	N/s	1.14**	1.37**	N/s	N/s	1.49**	1.73**
I feel that I have enough privacy here.	N/a	3.16	3.31	3.41ᵃ	2.93ᵇ	N/a	N/a	N/a	N/a	N/s	N/s	N/s	N/s	N/s	0.48
I am given adequate opportunities to keep my living area clean and decent.	N/a	3.97	3.96	4.16ᵃ	3.18ᵇ	N/a	N/a	N/a	N/a	N/s	N/s	0.78**	N/s	0.78**	0.97**

Decent? Clean, drug free, and safe from physical harm. (Prisoner, Holme House)

This is a decent prison. You get association three times a day, you get gym every day, outside exercise seven days a week, you get a TV in your pad, quilts, it's clean, and you get your food. (Prisoner, Doncaster)

Our later discussions included staff attitudes, access to privacy, and the atmosphere: 'This is a decent prison . . . this is as good as any prison could be run; you have choices. Staff make it decent; the regime, the way it is run' (prisoner, Doncaster).

Prisoners knew what was 'indecent':

The physical environment makes people depressed. (Prisoner, Wandsworth)

The simple things here they think is a privilege, like phone calls and showers, but they are the basics. You can't keep yourself clean . . . (Prisoner, Wandsworth)

You never can make prisons decent places because no one wants to be here so they don't care and will still throw tea-bags on the wall and stuff. Like, there are metal toilets in your cell and they always stink, you can't get rid of the smell and we have to eat in the same room as we go to the toilet. (Prisoner, Risley)

You can't make prison decent; it is meant to be there for punishment; jail is still jail. Ninety-nine per cent of the time you'll get the same sort of people even if it's clean, tidy, and you have TVs—they don't make any difference—screws are still screws and cons are still cons. (Prisoner, Risley)

Definition of decency The extent to which prisoners can keep themselves and their living area clean, spend time out of their cells, and have access to privacy.

In our structured survey, the dimension 'decency' consisted of five statements (at Belmarsh only two questions—2 and 3—were asked):

Statement 99 I am given adequate opportunities to keep my living area clean and decent (0.742)

Statement 53 The quality of my living conditions is poor (0.726)

Statement 27 I am given adequate opportunities to keep myself clean and decent (0.710)

Statement 60 Prisoners spend too long locked up in their cells in this prison (0.672)

Statement 98 I feel that I have enough privacy here (0.646)

TABLE 6.25.   Scores on dimension 12: decency

Prison	Reliability	Score
Doncaster	0.6510	3.7632
Risley	0.6604	3.5921
Holme House	0.6879	3.3468
Wandsworth	0.7707	2.7733
Belmarsh	—	—

Table 6.22*b* shows differences in the proportion of prisoners agreeing that they had 'adequate opportunities to keep themselves clean and decent', and so on, with Holme House, Risley, and Doncaster significantly better than Wandsworth (see Table 6.23*b*). Prisoners at Belmarsh and Wandsworth complained most about the amount of time they spent locked in their cells.

The overall internal reliability of the dimension 'decency' across all prisons was high, at 0.74. Three of four prisons scored 3 or above on decency (Table 6.25). Most of the significant differences were between all prisons and Wandsworth, with Wandsworth significantly lower. Belmarsh was lowest on the two questions we asked there. Decency was significantly positively correlated with humanity (0.620).[42]

We reflected as we analysed the data that the term 'decency' could either be regarded quite narrowly (as above) or it could involve broader dimensions of prison life and treatment. We shall consider this broader use of the term in Chapter 10.

Conclusions and Further Analysis

We pause here to consider some of the relationships between the dimensions explored so far. We summarize and reflect on our argument, before taking our analysis in a slightly different direction.

Previous research has highlighted the significance of the concepts of fairness, order, and relationships in prison (Sparks *et al.* 1996; Ahmad 1996; Liebling and Price 2001). Bottoms and Rose (using

---

[42] This confirms the possibility discussed in Chapter 5 that 'humanity' has a material and a relational component. For example, the correlation between the items 'I am being looked after with humanity' (H—humanity) and 'The quality of my living conditions is poor' (Dec—decency) was significant, at 0.437.

Ahmad's data) argued that prisoners' views about 'staff fairness' were central to judgements they made about 'regime fairness' and that staff fairness outweighed formal and material aspects of a prison regime in making these judgements (Bottoms and Rose 1998). We would suggest, further, that even to make a distinction between 'staff fairness' and 'regime fairness' is only sustainable where material regime provision is concerned (e.g. the amount of access to the gym, the number of visits permitted, and so on), in the light of our understanding of staff practices and their inextricable links with 'the regime' as experienced by prisoners. Staff practices are so fundamental to the prison regime that, arguably, 'the regime' and 'the staff' are inseparable. Even 'number of hours unlocked'— a formal measure on paper—varies in practice, according to staff behaviour on the day. There were clearly close links between concepts of fairness, order, and relationships in our study. These links were potentially analytically significant, and so our empirical data allow a closer exploration of the relationship between these key qualities of prison life.

Our factor analysis explored the concepts of fairness, relationships, and order together. Five distinct factors arose: 'relations with staff', 'clarity and predictability', 'conflict/frustration', 'rewards and punishments', and 'order'. Consistent with the analyses above, the item 'Overall, I am treated fairly by staff in this prison' fitted best in the 'relations with staff' factor. Another item, originally in 'fairness', 'Staff here treat prisoners fairly when applying the rules', also fitted well in the revised 'relations with staff' dimension.

Our emerging 'conflict/frustration' factor grew larger, and a new dimension, 'rewards and punishments', arose. Two items from the original dimension 'order' reappeared in this analysis, representing a dimension we could call 'order and organization'. The third item from the original dimension 'order' appeared in (correlated more highly with) 'clarity and predictability'.

Doncaster emerged with the highest score on all dimensions, but Belmarsh was lowest on 'relations with staff', 'conflict/frustration', and 'punishments and rewards', and Risley was lowest on 'clarity' and 'order and organization' (see Table 6.27). Holme House was considerably lower on 'relations with staff' and 'frustration/alienation' than it was on 'clarity'. Given what we know of subsequent events in Holme House and Belmarsh (each had a serious disturbance in 2002), one could hypothesize, drawing on these figures,

TABLE 6.26. Five factors arising from the original dimensions, fairness, relationships, and order

Factor One: Relations with staff (16 items (0.94))	Factor Two: Clarity and predictability (five items (0.77))	Factor Three: Frustration/alienation (11 items (0.88))	Factor Four: Punishments and rewards (four items (0.83))	Factor Five: Order and organization (two items (0.64))
Staff in this prison show concern and understanding towards me (0.799)	The rules and regulations in this prison are made clear to me (0.802)	This prison is poor at treating prisoners with respect (0.744)	Staff here treat prisoners fairly when distributing privileges (0.851)	This prison is good at maintaining order (0.751)
Overall, I am treated fairly by staff in this prison (0.785)	This prison is good at delivering a structured and predictable regime so that you know where you stand (0.655)	I am not being treated as a human being in here (0.743)	Privileges are given and taken fairly in this prison (0.850)	This prison is well organized (0.675)
I feel that I am treated with respect by staff in this prison (0.784)	It is hard for me to obtain information about the prison regime and the rules and regulations in this prison (0.623)	There is a strong sense of 'them and us' in this prison (0.647)	The regime in this prison is fair (0.691)	
I receive support from staff in this prison when I need it (0.771)	Staff in this prison are clear in telling you what you can and cannot do (0.541)	Staff in this prison are generally not available to talk to (0.623)	In general, I think that the disciplinary system in here is unfair (0.489)	
Staff here treat me with kindness (0.767)	Staff in this prison are not consistent in their interpretation of the rules (0.480)	Some of the treatment I receive in this prison is degrading (0.615)		
Personally, I get on well with the officers on my wing (0.747)		I am treated differently by staff on grounds of my race, offence or another characteristic (0.594)		

Staff address and talk to me in a respectful manner (0.728)

I am treated as a person of value in this prison (0.726)

Relationships between staff and prisoners in this prison are good (0.720)

I trust the officers in this prison (0.666)

I feel that I am trusted quite a lot in this prison (0.655)

Staff in this prison often display honesty and integrity (0.649)

Staff here treat prisoners fairly when applying the rules (0.642)

I have been helped significantly by a member of staff in this prison with a particular problem (0.627)

I am being looked after with humanity in here (0.595)

This prison is good at placing trust in prisoners (0.520)

This prison is poor at delivering justice and fairness (0.590)

The level of staff interaction with prisoners here is low (0.577)

This prison is poor at giving prisoners reasons for decisions (0.484)

Staff are confrontational towards prisoners in this prison (0.475)

This prison responds slowly to requests and applications (0.467) that lack of clarity and organization is less frustrating to prisoners than are poor relationships and over-control.

This empirical analysis confirms theoretical links that have been drawn between concepts of fairness, relationships, and order in prison. We might argue, based on these figures, that relationships make a *disproportionate* contribution to the quality of prison life, and also that 'fairness' and 'relationships' are very closely intertwined. Good relationships contribute to the quality of life, and conflict with staff or frustration detracts significantly from the quality of life. On the other hand, staff at Doncaster arguably neglected some of their security tasks in the interests of good relationships (Doncaster suffered two escapes in 2000; see further, Chapter 9). That all too easy mistake had been made before. Getting the balance right between 'relationships', 'security', 'justice', and 'order' in prison is difficult (see Chapter 1). When we came to reflect on the data as a whole (including our more qualitative descriptions of each prison in Chapter 4), and on subsequent events, we could see that none of the prisons in our study had got this balance right. We shall consider this claim, and its implications, in Chapter 9.

TABLE 6.27.   Mean scores on the revised new dimensions 'formal justice', 'relations with staff', 'clarity', 'conflict/frustration', 'punishments and rewards', and 'order and organization'

Prison	Factor One: Relations with staff	Factor Two: Clarity	Factor Three: Frustration/ alienation	Factor Four: Punishments and rewards	Factor Five: Order and organization
Belmarsh	3.0399[b]	2.9108	2.5312[b]	2.7714[b]	N/a
Holme House	3.0924	3.4064	2.8704	2.9574	3.2500
Risley	3.0594	2.8931[b]	2.8020	2.8218	2.5743[b]
Doncaster	3.4260[a]	3.5579[a]	3.2073[a]	3.4759[a]	3.4386[a]
Wandsworth	3.0646	3.2300	2.6500	2.8625	3.0917

Looking at the means for the new dimensions confirms the distinctions we have drawn between the prisons in our study, and adds further subtlety to the characterizations of each. To conclude our analysis of the relationships between the dimensions, and to develop a model of prison quality, we conduct a regression analysis in Chapter 10, casting order, well-being, and fairness as dependent variables in turn.

Reflections on the Argument so far:
Moral Measures and the Purpose of Prison

In his account of 'Moral Measures', Tiles discovers that in an important Buddhist text, there are 16 'qualities' that are to be used as 'measures of the self against the self' or as a means of self-scrutiny (Tiles 2000: 294).[43] We have explored 12 dimensions of prison life in some detail so far, and whilst we do not claim to have exhausted analysis of these important and complex concepts, we are proposing that they constitute a set of qualities against which the moral performance of a prison can be evaluated. We pause here to consider how and why we come to make this case. We argue that it is the dimensions considered up to this point that constitute a prison's 'moral performance'.

Any moral measures or standards by which we approve and disapprove of conduct, or patterns of conduct, require a source. That source can be the law (although the law does not always have high standards), concepts of pleasure and pain (utility), tradition, or some concept of 'right' or 'the good', achieved by discursive thought.[44] Certain exemplary individuals—those we admire and try to emulate—possess these qualities or virtues (Tiles 2000, chapter 10). Measures of the good require an account of *purpose* (for example, what, as a whole, are we seeking to do with our lives, or, returning to our central argument, what is the purpose of imprisonment?). Thus we judge 'how well a pattern of conduct contributes to or interferes with that objective' (Tiles 2000: 302). Whatever general principles can be established, life is sufficiently complex that there will always be considerable scope for deliberation in their application. Despite our hunger for explicit guidance, such guidance cannot 'sustain an individual life nor a culture':

The capacity to represent laws and to conform to them may be the basis of our freedom, but the truly excellent person needs an ability to recognise

---

[43] 'The *bhikku* must examine himself for evil desires, a tendency to exalt himself and disparage others, a tendency to anger (and as a consequence disparage the reprover, answer back, sulk and decline to explain his actions), to become harsh and spiteful, envious and grudging, treacherous and deceitful, stubborn and proud, and finally to seize, grasp tightly and not easily let go of temporal things' (Tiles 2000: 294).

[44] Measures of right are commonly expressed as general imperatives or universal laws, such as Kant's maxim that persons should be treated as ends and not as means (Tiles 2000).

where laws and rules do not apply, the ability that Kant called 'judgment' and which he insisted cannot be reduced to rules . . . The measure of virtue . . . turns crucially on the distinction between judging and judging well. (Tiles 2000: 303)

We have argued in previous work that deliberation in company ('taking counsel') on the daily practices of the prison is an important source of guidance for prison officers faced with complex and competing priorities (see earlier in this chapter).

In order to deliberate well, a clear vision of 'the end' is required, so that we know when we are contributing to this end and when we are 'injudiciously' harming it. This human capacity to 'represent the future to ourselves' (and to adjust our behaviour or control our passions in accordance) is what makes us distinct from animals without such linguistic and reflective capacities (Tiles 2000: 305–6).[45] Sometimes judgement is required about the co-ordination of, or balance between, apparently conflicting means. A consideration of ends helps to settle these questions. Belmarsh was a good example of 'too much' of one duty (security), and the neglect of another (activities and relationships) as a result:

How does one judge 'too little' or 'too much'? One way is by a 'feel for the outcome' . . . [alternatively] . . . This requires an explicitly articulated account of what we should be aiming to do . . . and an accurate assessment of what contribution will be made to this end by a habit of responding in some characteristic fashion. (Tiles 2000: 215)[46]

Goals and their consequences should be evaluated in a deliberative manner, so that for example: 'If to run our business in what we think of as a profitable or efficient manner, we find that we have to lay off half our workforce or pollute the environment, we may reconsider what profitability or efficiency involves or what it is we are in business to achieve' (Tiles 2000: 217). We shall see in the concluding chapter how a 'standpoint of universal concern' (Tiles 2000: 314) or 'respect for others' may provide a moral framework

---

[45] It is this linguistic capacity that determines that humans 'cannot make effective use of their characteristically human capacities without interacting with other human beings' (Tiles 2000: 307; see also Taylor 1985, 1992).

[46] See Tiles (2000: 214–15), for a discussion of the problems of 'yes/no' approaches to values and duties.

for life in the community.[47] A moral framework for the prison requires some further reflection on the notion of purpose.

Prisons have several, often conflicting, purposes and these purposes shift in their importance over time (Bottoms 1990 and Chapter 1). These purposes are custodial, coercive, punitive, corrective (Morgan 1997), and expressive (Garland 1990). The former are largely instrumental aims, and they are much discussed (e.g. Garland 1985). The latter expressive aim is, conversely, often neglected in formal discussions about the role of the prison. Prisons have most difficulty achieving their instrumental aims, and, as Garland suggests, there are other institutions that are better placed to achieve the prison's corrective aspirations. The prison is more effective in its expressive (as well as punitive) role.

Whether we take our cue from Garland's analysis or from the less elaborate claims made in official discourse, there is a convincing case that the role of the prison is a moral and symbolic one. Garland argues that there is no single purpose or aim of institutions of punishment, and that contradictions and tensions are part of the lived reality of penality (Garland 1990). He argues that penality is a deeply social issue and that, as such, a social approach must be taken to any consideration of imprisonment's aims. It was the technical working ideology of the 1960s and 1970s that led to the 'penal pessimism' associated with the loss of a moral framework for the prison (Bottoms 1990). This conclusion, Garland suggests, misses the point. Instead, institutions of punishment serve the sentiments of the dominant moral order, order-maintenance, and class interests. Prisons operate in a broad social and cultural setting, communicating meaning not just about crime and punishment but also about power, authority, morality, personhood, social relations, and a host of other matters (Garland 1990: 252; and Chapter 1). Penal practices 'embody theories of behaviour' (Haney 1997: 519). Garland doubts whether a single 'purpose' can be identified or whether prisons can be criticized for failing to achieve a single utilitarian task.

Garland's analysis relates mainly to the external moral dimensions of imprisonment. If prisons have such an external moral purpose, we should also be interested in evaluation of their internal achievement of these goals, and the relationship between the two. What do they achieve, in practice, in relation to notions of personhood (respect),

[47] Bauman suggests that immorality is 'behaviour which forsakes and abdicates responsibility for others' (Bauman 1989: 183). See pp. 490–1.

legitimacy, relationships, and authority? What is their internal moral configuration? This is what we mean by their moral performance (see further Chapter 10). How does prisoners' understanding of fairness and respect relate to shifting social definitions of these terms? The agenda set by Garland is far broader than the one we have pursued and its fulfilment would require considerably more attention to exterior matters than we have aimed for in this book, but we have, at least, made a start.

Tiles exhorts that 'craftsmen do not get by with a single measuring tool' (Tiles 2000: 303):

It would be folly to dispense with the try square and calipers because one has a satisfactory straight-edge on hand. Intelligent craft requires assessing problems and progress in many qualitative dimensions. It should not be assumed that we can assess the quality of conduct and ignore the contribution of character and goals, or assess people and pay no attention to what they aim at. (Tiles 2000: 98)

We agree with this argument. In Chapters 5 and 6 we have attempted to construct a measuring approach that evaluates 'that something missing' from existing tools. Our account has given some form to the intuitive sentiment that, in the prison and in modern managerialist approaches to evaluation, an inferior role has been 'assigned to our natural tendency to value most highly what we as individual agents can achieve by interacting with persons' (Tiles 2000: 315).

The close relationship between the dimensions in these two chapters, the manner in which they were identified, and their reflection of, or role in, the moral purpose of imprisonment, constitute our case for the terminology we have used. There is perhaps one dimension missing from this framework so far, and having reflected on our results and on subsequent events, we are not surprised that it did not arise in our discussions. We shall return to this 'missing dimension' when we consider the importance of value balance at the end of the book.

In Chapter 7 we take a diversion, with some rather different dimensions that we decided, on reflection, to exclude from our 'moral performance framework'. We consider them briefly, before moving on in our argument, in order to make the distinction between dimensions we have included, and those we have found illuminating in understanding prison life, but less useful within our scheme. They may in fact be *outcomes* arising from the moral measures explored so far. We shall consider this possibility at the end of the next chapter.

7
Social Structure and Meaning

In this chapter we consider two structural dimensions of prison quality: the distribution of power, and the organization of prisoner social life, or relationships among prisoners. These dimensions clearly matter in prison. They are distinct from all of the preceding dimensions in the sense that higher scores do not necessarily indicate higher quality of life. We explore these dimensions for what they tell us in general about the prison and its quality. We discuss later whether or not they can be included in our measure of moral performance.

In addition, we explore a few individual items which we introduced as a result of our discussions in workgroups and which do not belong in any of the dimensions already discussed. The first is the meaning of the prison experience, and the second and third are two general questions on overall prison quality.

Power/Authority

> Power is the capacity of some persons to produce intended and foreseen effects on others.
>
> (Wrong 1997: 2)

> Not necessity, not desire—no, the love of power is the demon of men. Let them have everything—health, food, a place to live, entertainment—they are and remain unhappy and low spirited: for the demon waits and waits and will be satisfied.
>
> (Nietzsche 1881: 262)

The term 'power' has overtones of coercion—it typically means the capacity of one person or group to realize their own will in a social action. But coercion is only one form of power. It is not 'the essence of the phenomenon itself' (Wrong 1997: 261 n.). Wrong argues that a distinction should be drawn between 'power to' (a distributive notion based on the capacity to summon available resources and satisfy wants) and 'power over' (a relational notion, and a special case of 'power to'). He says:

> Power is both a generalised capacity to attain ends that is unequally distributed among the members of a society as a result of the structure of its major institutions, on the one hand, and an asymmetrical social relation among persons manifested directly in social interaction or indirectly through anticipated reactions, on the other. (Wrong 1997, p. xxii)

We were interested in power and the use of authority because of its obvious centrality to prison life. Coercive power is used in prison, but this form of power constitutes only one dimension of the flow of power. Its *threat* may be more significant than its actual use in daily social practices. Assuming that only the threat of coercion underlies prison life may blind us to the significance of other forms of power: such as persuasion, authority, and manipulation (Wrong 1997). It may blind us also to other means of compliance, such as legitimacy, which is based on assent (Bottoms 2002; and Chapter 6). Wrong argues that we are part of 'an age that has condemned coercive power relations and rejected traditional legitimations of authority grounding it in divine commandment, moral absolutes or natural law' (Wrong 1997, pp. xxiv–xxv). This is not quite true in the prison world, for reasons outlined in Chapter 1. Perhaps it is more accurate to suggest that for instrumental and cultural reasons, the use of coercive power stands in greater need of legitimation than formerly.[1] Force is resorted to, in general, when other more effective forms of power cease to work.

What are these more effective forms of power? Control and security flow from 'getting relationships right', as the Control Review Committee and others have famously stated. Scott argues that 'social power has its effects *through social relations*' (Scott 2001: 1; emphasis added). This fact is a key explanation for the centrality of staff–prisoner relationships to prison life (see Chapter 5). The dynamic nature of the prison is due to the essentially *relational* exercise of power in its everyday life. Officers sometimes describe staff–prisoner relationships as a form of 'quiet power' (Liebling and Price 2001: 92). We have demonstrated, in previous work,

---

[1] And, we shall suggest below, that other potentially more effective strategies of power have been devised.

the important link between the relationships officers develop with prisoners and their rule-enforcement decisions (ibid. 93–4). Officers may elect to under-enforce the rules, selectively, based on judgements they make about the demeanour and worthiness of individual prisoners, and the likely effectiveness of their actions in any particular case (see Piliavin and Briar 1964; Banton 1964; and Bittner 1967; Black 1970; on this aspect of policing).

Power, then, is everywhere in the prison, but its use is not obvious, and it is this normally 'invisible' feature of prison life that gives it its distinctive tone. It may flow intentionally and unintentionally, and in many, sometimes counter-intuitive directions. Power is not simply applied,[2] but is resisted, appropriated, redistributed, and subverted (see Lukes 1974; McEvoy 2001; Sparks *et al.* 1996). As Sykes argued, behind the illusion of 'almost infinite' power held by prison officers lies a 'cracked monolith', because prisoners feel no moral obligation to obey. They outnumber prison officers, and prison officers may find it difficult to impose their authority for many reasons, including the possibility that they like their charges and have things in common with them (Sykes 1958; see also Ben-David 1992; and McEvoy 2001, for the distinct Northern Ireland example). There is some reciprocity of influence. There are constraints upon prisoners, which limit their scope, or the options available to them to resist. Prisoners may *anticipate* the use of power, which makes its exercise unnecessary. Reputations, for example, amongst segregation unit staff (or for prison staff and other prisoners, the reputations of particular prisoners), may make these anticipations highly socially significant. What others *believe* about us makes us more or less powerful in practice (Wrong 1997). As Scott argues, 'it is important to distinguish between *exercising* power and *holding* power' (Scott 2001: 4). For prison officers, different power bases can be drawn upon: reward, coercive, expert, referent, and legitimate (Hepburn 1985; Liebling 2000). These different power bases have become the subject of considerable

---

[2] Force, or the use of coercive power, *is* applied (although not simply), for example, in the use of control and restraint, the removal of privileges, or the use of transfers to 'special' locations. 'Raw violence' (Scott 2001: 14) is occasionally used by staff against prisoners, and if exposed, results in criminal sanctions and removal from post. As Scott argues, the use of force tends to be experienced as alienating 'and is especially likely to arouse feelings of hostility and acts of resistance' (Scott 2001: 14).

senior management attention since the mid-1990s. Throughout this period, shifting (mainly increasingly coercive) power bases formed the subject of considerable critical commentary from prisoners. Some of these attempts to increase (regain, or reformulate the basis of) power failed, although in general they were highly effective (see Liebling 2002; and Chapter 1). At the same time, many prisoners become nervous when staff retreat, and leave the maintenance of order and control in the hands of other prisoners.

There are strong grounds for believing that the distribution and use of power varies between prisons, as well as over time (Liebling 2000; and below). The central questions for prison sociology, then, are: (i) what is the balance of power in any particular prison? (ii) what forms of power are used? and (iii) what are the implications of these empirical facts?

We concentrate, in this section, on the use of power by staff upon prisoners, and how this was perceived. In the prison, paradoxically, relatively low levels of formal power are deployed (compared to what is available), but correspondingly high levels of informal power are used. Prisons as organizations can use high levels of Lukes's third facet of power: the prison can shape or distort the 'real interests' of prisoners, so that they believe their interest lies in doing something that might be contrary to their deeper interests (Lukes 1974; Scott 2001).[3] Prisoners may, through self-discipline and 'censoriousness', become instruments of their own domination (Foucault 1977; Burchell 1996; Garland 1997; Mathiesen 1965; and see later).[4]

Not enough happens to bullies; they just get 28 days on basic and when they come out the one who told will be in trouble. There should be a lot

---

[3] Lukes argues that power can be observable and direct (who prevails in decision-making?), less direct (e.g. influencing outcomes by not making a decision) and indirect (e.g. by shaping beliefs and preferences; Lukes 1974).

[4] 'Domination exists where power is structured into the stable and enduring social relations that make up large-scale social structures. [It works] through institutions to produce regular and persistent patterns of action' (Scott 2001: 16). A good example of such domination can be seen in one of the Prison Service's new Dangerous and Severe Personality Disorder (DSPD) units, where long-term prisoners express anxiety about whether or not they will 'pass' the assessment phase and thereby be diagnosed as dangerously personality disordered. Only then will they receive yet to be conceived and delivered treatment, which they imagine might be a reliable route towards their parole.

more punishment for bullies and attackers. There is a lot of that. It's a power thing. (Prisoner, Holme House)

I was threatened by an officer when I was in another [wing], in odd circumstances. I had met the officer on the out. I didn't know he was an officer and I called him a prat. When I came [here] this officer came in my cell and asked me if I remembered him, and threatened to come down on me like a ton of bricks if I put a foot wrong. He said, 'you're in my domain now'. I knew there were two officers waiting outside the door to jump in if I rose to the occasion, but I knew the score and didn't do what they wanted. The potential is always there. (Prisoner, Holme House)

Prisoners saw staff as having significant distributive power. Staff could deliberately influence the 'incentive structure' of costs and benefits faced by prisoners (see Scott 2001: 7):

The landing staff run the prison, not management or headquarters. Officers would never have to be bullies because they have all the power. (Prisoner, Belmarsh)

The regime is fair but they hold it against you with the threat of basic or taking your TV off you . . . they have all the power; to move you off the wing, to move you down the block, to put you on basic. (Prisoner, Doncaster)

You can have some fun, but if you mess about they'll do things like make you move cells, or put you in with a horrible guy. It's silly to play games . . . they hold all the cards. (Prisoner, Wandsworth)

In the eyes of prisoners, the over-use of power could be the application of a rule that is normally overlooked: 'Staff will wander about and then they will suddenly go for the rules' (prisoner, Belmarsh).

Staff had the power not to listen, not to respond, not to carry through action: 'It all boils down to the power of the officers; here they tend to be hardcore, they fob you off and you never hear again' (prisoner, Wandsworth).

Certain areas of the prison, or certain subgroups of prisoners, experienced a different use of power:

If you're in for drugs you're victimised . . . Most of them get a buzz from the power; they like to get a grip on people. They intimidate you and use physical violence on the weaker prisoners and people in for drugs . . . (Prisoner, Holme House)

Houseblock One is more strict than the others. You have less freedom and responsibility. The officers are always around and in your face; on the other wings they leave the cons to themselves. (Prisoner, Holme House)

The way power was used by staff was crucial in prisoner evaluations of the quality of the prison. Power could be used inconsistently, fairly, or it could be over-used.[5] The use of power and authority was linked to respect, so that legitimate power was authority deployed respectfully:

A lot of officers, I think, are on a power trip and talk to you like you are lower than them; if you ask them for something they don't answer and some just ignore you and walk away. They should treat us a bit better, with more respect. Some are all right; it depends on the individual and how you are with them. (Prisoner, Holme House)

The worst thing is the screws, there is no relationship and they try and get one over on you. They do little things that gnaw at you and it drives me mad. They are always trying to be in control and they tell us 'we're in charge'. They only interact with you when they have to, when they have to do paperwork. (Prisoner, Risley)

The fact that staff had considerable, uneven power had implications. Prisoners felt that staff had a moral obligation to 'start' relationships off:

A good officer would understand your plight and your problems and talk in a friendly tone; it makes all the difference. Some even let you use their first names, that creates a sense of, I don't know . . . a nice sense . . . a sense of security. It starts with the staff because they rule, they have the power, they have to break down the barriers, you can't, you're a prisoner so you can't. (Prisoner, Holme House)

Some staff recognized this and were sensitive to the degree of power they held: 'You have to be mature enough to handle the

[5] There is some literature on the abuse of power by prison staff (e.g. Liebling and Price 2001; Scraton 1987; Scraton et al. 1991; Thomas and Pooley 1980; Jameson and Allison 1995) but little empirical analysis of the causes or the extent of this abuse of power. Nietzsche argued that the will to power is man's basic instinct: 'What is happiness?—The feeling that power increases—that a resistance is overcome' (Nietzsche 1881). Others argue that the prison attracts authoritarian personalities and/or provides the relevant structural conditions (Milgram 1974; Haney et al. 1973). These arguments overdetermine what seems to be a more diverse picture.

power that you've got' (senior officer, Belmarsh). Prisoners recognized that staff needed some power, and that the prison would be dangerous if prisoners had too much of it themselves:[6] 'When it first opened we ran it, not the officers. They were not HMP officers and didn't have a clue. It's tighter now, it's got a bit stricter and it's better in a way but they think they've got power, when they give you a direct order. If you need support and help they do give it, I'll give them that' (prisoner, Doncaster).

Prisoners (and more vociferously, senior managers) agreed that there were 'upper limits' on the amount of power prisoners *should* have in a prison, so that, unusually in our conceptual scheme, there was a point beyond which a high score on power would reduce rather than enhance the quality of life.

Definition of power   The actual or perceived use of control, influence, or authority by prison staff; the degree to which prisoners have the capacity to exercise control over their own time, treatment, and lives.

In the structured questionnaire, the dimension 'power' consisted of six statements:

Statement 14   There are quite a lot of opportunities for me to use my own initiative in this prison (0.712)

Statement 66   Prisoners are encouraged to make their own decisions and become involved in/have a say in what goes on in here (0.683)

Statement 92   Prisoners in here have some power (0.662)

Statement 46   I am rarely given opportunities and encouragement to manage my own time and to be independent in this prison (0.591)

Statement 57   My time here seems very much like a punishment (0.572)

Statement 40   Staff in this prison have a lot of power and control over prisoners (0.554)

---

[6] In an earlier study, we found that 'role model' prison officers identified by prisoners as particularly good at the job were in the middle of a continuum on willingness to use coercive power. That is, they were neither *reluctant* to use it, nor *over-eager*. If prisoners knew officers were *prepared* to use coercive power, they rarely had to (see Liebling and Price 2001; Gilbert 1997). As Nietzsche said, 'To exercise power costs effort and demands courage' (Nietzsche 1881).

TABLE 7.1.   Percentage of prisoners who agree/strongly agree with statements about power

Statement (power)	Belmarsh	Holme House	Risley	Doncaster	Wandsworth
1. There are a lot of opportunities for me to use my own initiative here.	21.7[b]	39.4	26.8	53.5[a]	33.4
2. Staff in this prison have a lot of power and control over prisoners.	90.3	89.3	66.4	61.4[a]	91.7[b]
3. I am rarely given opportunities and encouragement to manage my own time and be independent in this prison.	68.7[b]	47.8	31.7[a]	32.5	53.4
4. My time here seems very much like a punishment.	83.1[b]	46.8[a]	53.4	49.1	61.7
5. Prisoners are encouraged to make their own decisions and have a say in what goes on here.	13.2	12.7[b]	12.9	37.7[a]	13.4
6. Prisoners in here have some power.	10.8[b]	25.5	13.9	42.1[a]	16.7

Note: Throughout this account, scores accompanied by the letter 'a' indicate the most positive scores. Scores accompanied by the letter 'b' indicate the most negative.

Table 7.1 shows the proportion of prisoners who agreed or strongly agreed with each statement, whichever way round it was expressed. Table 7.2 shows single-item means, and any significant differences between prisons, with all the scores expressed positively. The five prisons differed significantly in the extent to which prisoners felt they had some power or autonomy, with the highest scores at Doncaster. There were significant differences between Doncaster and all the other establishments, and between Belmarsh and Holme House, and Belmarsh and Risley (Table 7.3).

Most prisoners thought that staff had a lot of power and control over prisoners, but this varied considerably between establishments, with prisoners at Wandsworth and Belmarsh feeling staff had most power (closely followed by Holme House), and prisoners

TABLE 7.2.   A comparison of prisoner views on power/authority in five prisons: individual item mean scores

Item/statement	Item scores (1–5)					ANOVA (Mean difference)									
	B	HH	R	D	W	B&HH	B&R	B&D	B&W	HH&R	HH&D	HH&W	R&D	R&W	D&W
There are quite a lot of opportunities for me to use my own initiative in this prison.	2.36^b	2.85	2.67	3.27^a	2.57	0.49	N/s	0.91**	N/s	N/s	N/s	N/s	0.60*	N/s	0.71*
Staff in this prison [do not] have a lot of power and control over prisoners.	1.72^b	1.77	2.23	2.43^a	1.72^b	N/s	0.50*	0.71**	N/s	0.46*	0.66**	N/s	N/s	0.51*	0.71**
I am [often] given opportunities and encouragement to manage my own time and be independent in this prison.	2.28^b	2.73	2.94	3.00^a	2.57	0.46	0.66*	0.72**	N/s	N/s	N/s	N/s	N/s	N/s	N/s
My time here [does not seem] very much like punishment.	1.89^b	2.73	2.60	2.75^a	2.28	0.84**	0.71*	0.85**	N/s	N/s	N/s	N/s	N/s	N/s	N/s
Prisoners are encouraged to make their own decisions and have a say in what goes on here.	2.13^b	2.26	2.31	2.99^a	2.25	N/s	N/s	0.86**	N/s	N/s	0.74**	N/s	0.68**	N/s	0.74**
Prisoners in here have some power.	2.10^b	2.48	2.32	3.18^a	2.32	N/s	N/s	1.08**	N/s	N/s	0.70**	N/s	0.86**	N/s	0.86**

Notes: *The mean difference is significant at the p < 0.05 level. **The mean difference is significant at the p < 0.001 level.

at Risley and Doncaster reporting significantly lower levels. Few prisoners thought they had many opportunities to use their own initiative (lowest at Belmarsh and highest at Doncaster). Likewise, few thought they were given opportunities to manage their own time and be independent in the establishments (again fewest at Belmarsh and most at Risley and Doncaster). Only 13 per cent at Belmarsh and Holme House, but 38 per cent at Doncaster thought they were encouraged to make their own decisions and become involved in, or have a say in, what went on in the prison (Table 7.1): 'We have an inmate committee, I used to be on it—you have your say but nothing gets done' (prisoner, Risley). 'On the servery you have power . . . With my job I get a lot more leeway and I know how to use that and abuse that' (prisoner, Wandsworth).

The proportion of prisoners who said their time in the establishment felt very much like a punishment varied significantly, from 46.8 per cent at Holme House to 83.1 per cent at Belmarsh. As the following prisoner put it:

There is a misunderstanding on behalf of the officers—they think everyone is out to subvert the prison . . . I think it is fear that makes prison officers adversarial in their attitudes . . . If the only way to treat us is to humiliate us then they will continue to destroy our self-esteem, we'll see no reason to change, and continue to hide behind a false front. (Prisoner, Wandsworth)

In this dimension, items were scored positively if prisoners said they felt they had some power or autonomy. All of the items discriminated between the prisons, with the highest scores at Doncaster and the lowest scores at Belmarsh. Power was most significantly correlated with fairness (0.646).

TABLE 7.3.   Scores on dimension
13: power/authority

Prison	Reliability	Score
Doncaster	0.4535	2.9357
Risley	0.7169	2.5116
Holme House	0.6173	2.4699
Wandsworth	0.6550	2.2833
Belmarsh	0.7107	2.0803

Partly because we devised our questions deductively from discussions and other explorations with prisoners and staff, we have arguably produced a restricted concept of power based on its more overt and coercive properties. The dimension includes items about opportunities for prisoners to use their initiative and manage their own time (statements 1, 3, and 5),[7] the experience of staff power (statements 2 and 6) and the feeling of being punished in prison (statement 4).[8] These questions relate mainly to the staff–prisoner interface, as we might expect. These aspects of power and its flow tell us much about each prison.

There are other ways of thinking about the flow of power in prison, however, including how governors govern and shape the regime (see Chapter 8), the role of routines (see Sparks *et al.* 1996) and the ways in which prisoners engage with or resist new penal 'technologies of the self' (Garland 1997), both consciously and unconsciously. These modes of governance 'operate lightly and unobtrusively' and seek to 'align the actors' objectives with those of the authorities' (Garland 1997: 187). This makes them less visible, more difficult to articulate, and yet more effective as a means of securing penal order. IEP schemes, offending behaviour programmes, risk assessment procedures and their consequences, sentence planning, and other 'responsibilizing' strategies all form part of the modernizing penal project (see Liebling *et al.* 1997; Hannah-Moffatt 2000; O'Malley 1996; Barry *et al.* 1996). Simon suggested that modern penal governance operates 'around' the social. Garland proposes, on the contrary, that attempts to govern are best achieved by acting through the actors involved (Simon 2000; Garland 1997: 188), although in ways that stand in complete contrast to more 'social' penal regimes of the 1960s and 1970s (Simon 2000; Liebling 2002). These analyses raise some of the most important questions we should be asking about the late modern prison, including the question of just who possesses power in the prison, and how it is transmitted. How is conduct regulated 'within the encounters that make up the everyday experience of individuals?' (Rose 1996: 37). The ways in which prisoners become 'active partners in the business of security and crime control', and the extent to which

[7] These are, as Garland points out, questions about *agency* (which is shaped and constrained) rather than about *freedom* (Garland 1997: 197).

[8] Statement 4 is highly correlated with an item in 'well-being': 'My experience in this prison is painful' (0.435**).

they experience this as one of the new pains of imprisonment, deserves a separate study (see Garland 1997: 207–8). How far are prisoners consumers of opportunities for release (or 'entrepreneurs of [their] own personal development . . . and rehabilitation' (ibid. 191)? How far must they align their behaviour 'with the goals of the prison authorities' (ibid. 192)? What kind of 'self' is being shaped by prison programmes and by the new therapeutic interventions (Duguid 2000)? Modern penal power has a new configuration as well as a 'new set of objectives' (Garland 1997: 188). As Garland suggests, a 'governmentality analytic' might help to open these lines of enquiry for criminologists (Garland 1997: 192).[9] We shall return to this point briefly in Chapter 10.

Despite the above qualifications, the overall internal reliability of the dimension as we devised it, across all prisons, was high at 0.70. It was, however, relatively low at Doncaster. Table 7.2 shows how, even at Doncaster, prisoners felt subject to staff power (discretion) and experienced being in prison as quite punishing. Prisoners at Doncaster were much more likely than prisoners at other establishments to acknowledge that 'prisoners in here have some power'. We shall come to some events in Doncaster that illustrate this starkly in Chapter 9. All of the dimension scores on 'power' are relatively low, as we might expect in a prison. At Belmarsh in particular, but at most of the other prisons too, prisoners felt almost totally powerless (see statement 6 above).

Power/authority was significantly positively associated with all the other dimensions and was most significantly associated with fairness (0.646) and well-being (0.602). It is a complex concept to explore, and although we could see from further analyses that levels of power experienced by prisoners were important in their overall judgements of the quality of life, it was not a simple linear relationship.[10] The distribution of power is clearly important in evaluations of prison quality but it is possible that we can infer

---

[9] Although, as he warns, the rationalities and technologies identified by the governmentality approach are partially achieved, they will be corrupted in practice, and they may produce unforeseen consequences. These are the sociological issues of interest and, as such, the governmentality literature provides a 'basis for empirical analysis, not a substitute for it' (Garland 1997: 199).

[10] Few empirical investigations of 'concrete configurations of power' (Scott 2001: 25) in prison currently exist. We hope to remedy this in future work (Crewe forthcoming).

power configurations from responses to other dimensions already considered, such as 'fairness'. This requires further reflection.

Prisoner Social Life

Prison is a place where people live.

(Clemmer 1940)

The society of prisoners ... is not only physically compressed; it is psychologically compressed as well, since prisoners live in an enforced intimacy where each man's behaviour is subject both to the constant scrutiny of his fellow captives and the surveillance of the custodians. It is not solitude that plagues the prisoner but life *en masse*.

(Sykes 1958: 4)

A series of questions about prisoners' relationships with each other was used to form a dimension 'prisoner social life'. This did not function as our other dimensions did, as higher and lower scores could have very different meanings. We were interested to explore how the dimensions reported earlier (e.g. trust, fairness, and order) were related to the structural properties of prisoners' relations with each other. Sykes suggested that (in a maximum security prison, at least) prisoner social life, with its well-developed code, developed as a response to the pains of imprisonment: 'Subjected to prolonged material deprivation, lacking heterosexual relationships, and rubbed raw by the irritants of life under compression, the inmate population is pushed in the direction of deviation from, rather than adherence to, the legal norms' (Sykes 1958: 22).

The earliest studies of the sociology of the prison applied the ecological insights of the Chicago School of Sociology to the 'prison community'. These studies found inmate leaders, various groupings or social roles played by prisoners, and a 'cool rejection' by prisoners of prison staff (e.g. Clemmer 1940; Sykes 1958; McCorkle and Korn 1954; Grusky 1959; Berk 1966; and Sykes and Messinger 1960). Three key themes to emerge from the early prison sociology literature were: the notion of the prison as a sustained social community, with a flow of power operating through it in complex ways; the division of prisoners into social roles; and the concept of solidarity—or rather the question of whether such solidarity existed and, if so, what function it served.

Sykes argued that, alongside the variation existing between types of establishments for different populations, there were basic similarities. Prisons showed: 'a remarkable tendency to override the variations of time, place, and purpose. Prisons are apt to present a common social structure . . . prisons appear to form a group of social systems differing in detail but alike in their fundamental processes, a genus or family of sociological phenomena' (Sykes 1958, p. xiii).

Sykes overemphasized the similarities between prisons as social organizations at the expense of important differences (e.g. in their cultures and management). However, his analysis of the prison is a valuable one. He showed, by prolonged observation, that the social control exerted by the prison was not predominantly overt but rather, it was covert and invisible. The prison was not just about confinement, but constituted a series of movements between partial releases and reconfinements (unlock, lock up, unlock, lock up). It was this pattern of incomplete 'captivity' which created the society of captives, and the constantly renegotiated relationship between staff and prisoners: 'The prison exists in an uneasy compromise of liberty and restraint' (Sykes 1958: 7).

The prison's multiple functions—containment, reformation, punishment, and self-maintenance—created a community of both conformity and resistance. After five o'clock, when specialist staff left, the wings and corridors of the prison world return to their ordinary state, of action and interaction, of movement and manoeuvre. The hidden world of the prison, known only by staff and prisoners, re-emerged. It was often mundane, drab, or monotonous, but it could also be sporadically infused by intense activity, violence, and pain, and occasionally by shared pleasure and relief, as a situation passed or an emergency was resolved. This social world did not operate apart from the wider community but instead interacted with it—absorbing this political and social context. This can be seen, sometimes vividly, as in the case of a riot, a suicide, or an escape; and sometimes in legal challenges, letters to loved ones, or organized newsletters and campaigns (Jacobs 1977).[11]

[11] A re-reading of Sykes in the light of the Woodcock and Learmont Reports (Home Office 1994 and 1995, respectively) suggests that their insights relating to dynamic security, and the significance of prison staff practices to the internal aspects of security, were already available: 'A ladder constructed of dental floss which can be hidden in the palm of one hand; a fight in another part of the prison to serve as

Sykes argued that prisons essentially create a situation of relative scarcity and deprivation. A code arises from these deprivations (the 'pains') of imprisonment, which accounts for the regular nature of the system of action in prison (see Chapter 6, p. 305). Arising from these, and intended to secure some relief from them, there existed a pattern of relationships, roles, and activities characterized by its own set of values, attitudes, and beliefs (Sykes 1958). A special language existed which reflected the conflicts and tensions inherent in the prison situation: 'It is the language of the dispossessed, tinged with bitterness and marked by a self-lacerating humour' (Sykes 1958: 84).

This code included resistance to staff, and 'solidarity' among prisoners (see below). We saw, in the dimension 'personal development', that prisoners put little effort into the activities or work they undertook. This was despite constant pleas for more of both. Sykes showed how resistance by prisoners to hard work—apathy, minimal effort ('the traditional answers of the slave'), and sabotage—constitutes one of many subtle forms of rebellion 'and [the officer's] limited means of coercion cannot prevent them from occurring' (Sykes 1958: 28–9).

The unskilled and monotonous nature of most of the work available to prisoners, the low level of wages, the lack of promotion, the consequences of too ready compliance, and the lack of other 'distant rewards of the free community' offered little to motivate prisoners.

> The custodians, it is true, can push their prisoners into the semblance of work but beyond this point they move with difficulty. Unlike the masters of a concentration camp, the prison officials are barred from using extreme penalties, such as brute force or starvation, to extract high levels of effort. Unlike the managers of an industrial enterprise in the free community, they are denied the use of the common rewards of work incentives, such as meaningful monetary rewards or symbolic forms of recognition. The result tends to be minimal effort on the part of the prisoner—a form of inefficiency which is economically feasible only because the production of goods and services in the prison is but loosely linked to the discipline of the open market. (Sykes 1958: 30)

> a momentary diversion; the prisoner waiting in the exercise yard for the welcome cover of darkness; a prison uniform stripped of its distinguishing marks to serve as civilian dress—these are the preparations for escape which must be detected long before the final dash for freedom occurs. To the prison officials, then, the guards on the wall form the last line of the institution's defences, not the first, and they fight their battle at the centre of their position rather than at its perimeter' (Sykes 1958: 19).

Sykes saw the organizational task of prison staff as a battle for compliance—for internal order—a 'within-walls' objective far removed from more aspirational goals of rehabilitation. Such compliance was more doubtful than certain, as staff power was, in reality, limited: 'In the prison, power must be based on something other than internalised morality and the custodians find themselves confronting men who must be forced, or cajoled into compliance' (Sykes 1958: 47).

One way in which this could be accomplished was through a system of rewards and punishments. Sykes argued that such rewards and punishments as are available to the authorities were meaningless. The available punishments 'do not represent a profound difference from the prisoner's usual status' (Sykes 1958: 50). This may be less the case in the modern prison, where highly prized goods (such as televisions in cells and own clothes) are available. Perverse incentives, such as prestige, might follow from punishments: 'The control measures of the officials may support disobedience rather than decrease it' (Sykes 1958: 51).

According to Sykes, prisoners are classified, labelled, approved, or disapproved by each other, according to certain key 'axes': their orientation to staff and towards their own imprisonment; and towards the expressed 'moral code'. The 'rat' or 'squealer' is the prisoner who 'betrays his fellows by violating the ban on communication'. This betrayal is a general and severe one, for the 'rat' (in the UK, 'grass') is 'denying the cohesion of prisoners as a dominant value when confronting the world of officialdom' (Sykes 1958: 87). Loyalty to each other is a key dominant value in the prison. There are other ways of betraying this value: by identifying with the values of the staff (the 'centre man'). This more open form of betrayal destroys 'the unity of inmates as they face their rejectors' (Sykes 1958: 90). 'Gorillas' take what they want from others by force; 'merchants' trade; 'fish' are the newly received prisoners; and 'wolves', 'punks', and 'fags' are the aggressive-masculine, passive, and 'feminine' varieties of those engaged in homosexual acts in prison. The 'wolf' retains his masculine dignity by seeking sexual satisfaction only, being 'unmoved by love' or the softer sentiments of the despised feminine prisoner. 'Ball busters' are openly defiant, and uncontrolled. The 'real men' attract greater prestige due to their greater self-containment and 'dignity and composure under stress':

[T]he *real man* regains his autonomy, in a sense, by denying the custodians' power to strip him of his ability to control himself—it is also true that his role is of vital functional significance for the social system of imprisoned criminals. In the emphasis on endurance with dignity, the inmates have robbed the rebel of their support; it is the man who can stop himself striking back at the custodians that wins their admiration and thus their image of the hero functions wittingly or unwittingly to maintain the *status quo*. (Sykes 1958: 102)

'Toughs' and 'hipsters' make the prison environment fearful, as they prey on their own kind: the 'tough' acts out his threats, where the 'hipster' projects a false front. Both provoke violence and may use it 'expressively' rather than 'instrumentally'. These types are, as Sykes argues, 'social roles rather than personality traits' (Sykes 1958: 106). Prisoners adopt them, move into and out of them: 'It is the structure of social relationships formed by imprisoned criminals which concerns us; an inmate may enter these relationships in a variety of capacities for varying periods of time, but it is the structure itself which lays the main claim on our attention' (Sykes 1958: 106).

So inmate cohesion or solidarity is maintained by the 'real man'. His is a cohesive response to imprisonment, which makes life tolerable for the majority:

A cohesive inmate society provides the prisoner with a meaningful social group with which he can identify himself and which will support him in battles against his condemners—and thus the prisoner can at least in part escape the fearful isolation of the convicted offender. Inmate solidarity, in the form of mutual toleration, helps to solve the problems of personal security posed by the involuntary intimacy of men who are noteworthy for their seriously antisocial behaviour in the past. Inmate solidarity, in the form of 'sharing' or a reciprocity of gifts and favours, attacks one of the most potent sources of aggression among prisoners, the drive for material betterment by means of force and fraud . . . scarce goods will at least be distributed more equitably in a social system marked by solidarity and this may be of profound significance in enabling the prisoner to better endure the psychological burden of impoverishment. (Sykes 1958: 107–8)

Solidarity denotes something quite different from 'friendship' but means the propensity of prisoners to act collectively, or to be bonded by common deprivations and a need to resist authority. Cohen and Taylor (amongst others) argued that resistance is important to prisoner psychological survival (Cohen and Taylor 1972). Mathiesen argued, conversely, that prisoners are atomized and relatively weak, and dependent upon staff (Mathiesen 1965). Other sociological studies of prison life have described prisoner culture as utilitarian, oppositional, and exploitative (Grapendaal 1990; Bondeson 1989).

There has been considerable speculation in the prison world about the erosion of 'prisoner solidarity', as prisoners have become more interested in drugs, or in their own material circumstances. The introduction of IEP, and the development of more stringent, risk-laden parole decision-making, have been credited with contributing to this overall decline in collective activity and sentiment amongst prisoners. We have little empirical evidence by which to test these assertions. There have been few major sociological studies of the prison world and its interior social life since the pioneering studies by Clemmer (1940), Sykes (1958), Irwin and Cressey (1962), Jacobs (1974, 1977), and others in the USA, and Mathiesen (1965) in Norway. Sociological studies of prisons in the UK have been carried out by, for example, Morris and Morris (1963), Cohen and Taylor (1972), King and McDermott (1989, 1995), McDermott and King (1988), Sparks *et al.* (1996), and Jewkes (2002). Few of these studies have attempted to characterize the ways in which the prison community has changed since the modernizing penal developments described in Chapter 1.

Our questions were intended to explore, albeit briefly, the nature of relationships between prisoners. Did trust exist? Were friendships formed? Were aspects of the prison's functioning linked to the social system that arose amongst prisoners?

There was evidence of both solidarity and of 'atomism' in all of our prisons, with low levels of trust amongst prisoners but small groups where 'friendships' were developed. Prisoners were reluctant to use the word 'friend' and often qualified what they said about their 'mates' with comments about the transitory and superficial nature of these relationships. Glaser (1964: 111) found that in four of five prisons he studied, most prisoners expressed some ambivalence towards their fellow prisoners and 'wariness' about commitment to friendships with them (see also Sykes 1958: 117–18; Sparks *et al.* 1996: 39). Evidence of a basic set of values and beliefs amongst prisoners was apparent. As one prisoner said:

a sub-culture has to exist, because the rules are too strict. You have to survive. There is a kind of undercurrent of how to survive things. (Prisoner, Belmarsh)

... as far as I'm concerned, inmates have got to stick together, you know, if there's a problem, we keep it to ourselves, we're not supposed to go and tell the officers that someone's smoking, or this and that—that is grassing, as far as we're concerned, which is wrong. (Prisoner, Belmarsh)

There were variations, 'sub-groups', and divisions, however—between young/volatile and 'mature'/old-timer, drug-using and non-(hard)-drug-using prisoners, and between short-term and long-term prisoners. Drug users were in breach of prisoner morality. Prisoner beliefs were (according to our group discussions): don't grass; don't act for yourself alone; don't be *too* friendly with staff; keep your head; don't show weakness; 'be a man' (and sexualize all women); look after your material interests; don't thieve (and certainly don't get caught); keep fit; show autonomy; and don't interfere with others' activities.[12] The young were seen as 'hot-headed', destructive, and unpredictable.

Few prisoners felt safe enough to 'relax'. Fewer than half of the prisoners we interviewed thought they could 'be themselves' in prison. Large proportions thought they 'wore a mask' most of the time. Prisoners described having to behave in new ways to survive prison—some said their behaviour could be 'worse' inside than outside. They had to be smart to avoid conflict. They had to be 'secretive and cunning', to 'watch their backs', and not to react to provocation. 'There are convict morals, one is not to show suffering;

---

[12] Prisoners in a dispersal prison we studied for other reasons were much more overtly organized. They cooked together—the cleaners struggled to keep their 'right' to cook in the afternoons on the wings—a right which they lost towards the end of the project (see Liebling 2002). Long-term prisoners looked after each other's pet birds when they went 'down the seg'. They shared the valuable commodities of newspapers, non-stick pans, sugar, tea, and coffee. But, on most wings, prison life involved violence, intimidation, and the fear of violence, which was unpredictable and serious: 'You usually find the people at the top on the main wings are the bullies, the so-called gangsters who've only got there through violence and through being a bit quicker than the other cons' (prisoner). Prisoners paid each other to burn out a prisoner's cell, or assault someone with unpaid debts. A subculture of heavy drug use impinged on any cohesive spirit on many wings—those who were addicted to heroin, and who acted as desperate individuals, with no sense of any prison code of conduct, were regarded as sick, immoral, volatile, and self-seeking: 'I don't like junkies—it's a terrible weakness; the dealers are not even honest; they dilute it; they can make hundreds a week' (prisoner). There was a much more developed prisoner social world than we found in any of the five prisons in this study (although Doncaster came closest to having the long-term prisoner culture described briefly here).

but there is too much pressure not to express myself' (prisoner, Belmarsh).

Relationships with each other were complex. Prisoners did develop groups, as well as friendships, but these friendships were wary:

I will help others, mostly practical, like ring someone up and mediate or talk to someone if they are depressed. It's better then because you get his trust. You give but you never get it back, you don't pay back kindness, it's all a chess game. (Prisoner, Belmarsh)

I've not had any problems, I look after myself. On here it's dead relaxed, there are different factions of prisoners but they all talk to each other. Prisoners do generally help each other, lending tobacco and things. I trust some of them to keep to their word and for them to pay me back exactly what they borrowed and that they were telling the truth about waiting for some money to come in etc. You can tell when other prisoners feel down; we ask each other if we're OK. Someone might have had a bad visit and other lads will sit with them and have a chat. (Prisoner, Holme House)

I haven't got mates, they're 'prison associates'. You can't express your feelings in here. Only the strong survive. (Prisoner, Holme House)

We all look after each other, but we've all got our own problems. (Prisoner, Doncaster)

Other prisoners from my home town would help me, say if I was getting bullied, as we all stick together. (Prisoner, Doncaster)

Lifers all stick together because you know one day you will meet up again in the system. (Prisoner, Doncaster)

You always get a sense of solidarity, especially amongst the old school prisoners. (Prisoner, Doncaster)

Prisoners give each other support. On the first day I was totally lost and alone and on the yard, but it was only for a day. (Prisoner, Wandsworth)

Definition of prisoner social life   Social relationships among prisoners; the extent of trust, companionship, and solidarity; and the existence of subdivisions.

In our structured survey, the dimension 'prisoner social life' consisted of six statements:

Statement 82   Relationships amongst prisoners in this prison are poor (0.738)
Statement 83   I don't have friends in this prison I can go to for help (0.701)

Statement 54   Prisoners here generally do not help and support each other (0.692)

Statement 73   I feel that I am treated with respect by the other prisoners in here (0.649)

Statement 80   I don't trust other prisoners in here (0.613)

Statement 42   I get on well with the other prisoners in this prison (0.580)

More than three-quarters of the prisoners (85 per cent) said they got on well with other prisoners. This was a relatively superficial measure of the nature of relationships, however, as despite the high numbers saying they 'got on well with the other prisoners in here', fewer than half at all five prisons said they trusted other prisoners. The similarity of the answers in all five establishments offers some support for Sykes's argument that certain features of prison social life are related to (inherent in) the prison as a social institution, regardless of differences in regime, management, and so on. Alternatively, this dimension does not explore deeply enough the dynamics of prisoner social life.

Some interesting differences were found on individual items: so that, for example, over 70 per cent of prisoners at Belmarsh and Holme House felt they were treated with respect by other prisoners, compared to 53 per cent at Risley (a statistically significant difference; see Table 7.4*a* below) and just over 60 per cent at Doncaster and Wandsworth. Prisoners at Wandsworth were least likely to feel they could go to other prisoners for help. Levels of trust were, predictably, quite low. The mean score was highest at Wandsworth and Holme House (possibly an indication of feelings of solidarity). But as Table 7.4*b* shows, the proportions of prisoners who say they 'get on well with other prisoners' or can go to friends for help are much higher than the proportions willing to say they 'trust' other prisoners. This precarious balancing act (friendship that is not friendship, and that is held in check by lack of trust) is one of the complexities or pains of prison life for prisoners generally (as Glaser noted in 1964; see pp. 90–3) and may be related to the 'dual' or 'suspended' identity developed by prisoners to survive in prison (Jewkes 2002: 134). Relationships among prisoners are guarded and low in trust (see Table 7.4*b*). In Belmarsh and Doncaster, prisoners trusted staff far more than they trusted prisoners (see Chapter 5). In the other three prisons, levels of trust of staff and other prisoners were similarly low, at around a quarter each.

TABLE 7.4*a*. Percentage of prisoners who agree/strongly agree with statements about prisoner social life

Statement (Social life)	Belmarsh	Holme House	Risley	Doncaster	Wandsworth
1. I get on well with other prisoners in the prison.	80.8	92.5[a]	80.2	90.4	78.3[b]
2. Prisoners here generally do not help and support each other.	32.5	27.6	26.7	24.5[a]	33.4[b]
3. I feel I am treated with respect by other prisoners here.	72.3	75.5[a]	53.4[b]	64.0	61.6
4. I don't trust the other prisoners here.	48.2[b]	39.4	41.6	42.1	36.6[a]
5. Relationships amongst prisoners in this prison are poor.	18.1	21.3	19.8	12.3[a]	26.7[b]
6. I don't have friends in this prison I can go to for help.	15.6	12.7[a]	14.9	17.5	25.0[b]

TABLE 7.4*b*. Percentage of prisoners who trust other prisoners and have friends they can go to for help

Statement (Social life)	Belmarsh	Holme House	Risley	Doncaster	Wandsworth
1. I trust the other prisoners in here.	15.7[b]	30.8[a]	23.8	21.1	23.4
2. Prisoners in here do help and support each other.	44.5	45.7[a]	38.7	42.1	36.7[b]
3. I have friends in this prison who I can go to for help.	60.3	74.4[a]	65.3	71.9	50.0[b]

The overall internal reliability of the dimension 'prisoner social life', across all prisons, was high at 0.75. There were no significant differences between the prisons, although the score at Wandsworth was lower than the scores for other prisons. On this dimension, whilst all the scores represent positive answers (i.e. whichever way round the question was posed, a positive response attracts a positive score) a higher score may not always reflect the quality of life in the

TABLE 7.5.   A comparison of prisoner views on prisoner social life: individual item mean scores

Item/statement	Item scores (1–5)					ANOVA (Mean difference)									
	B	HH	R	D	W	B&HH	B&R	B&D	B&W	HH&R	HH&D	HH&W	R&D	R&W	D&W
I get on well with the other prisoners in the prison.	3.95	4.17ª	3.93	4.13	3.90ᵇ	N/s	N/s	N/s	N/s	N/s	N/s	N/s	N/s	N/s	N/s
Prisoners here generally [do] help and support each other.	3.11	3.18	3.08	3.22ª	2.98ᵇ	N/s	N/s	N/s	N/s	N/s	N/s	N/s	N/s	N/s	N/s
I feel that I am treated with respect by the other prisoners here.	3.73	3.83ª	3.48ᵇ	3.68	3.67	N/s	N/s	N/s	N/s	0.35*	N/s	N/s	N/s	N/s	N/s
I [do] trust the other prisoners here.	2.59ᵇ	2.84	2.79	2.68	2.85ª	N/s	N/s	N/s	N/s	N/s	N/s	N/s	N/s	N/s	N/s
Relationships amongst prisoners in this prison are [good].	3.27	3.29	3.14	3.40ª	3.12ᵇ	N/s	N/s	N/s	N/s	N/s	N/s	N/s	N/s	N/s	N/s
I [do] have friends in this prison I can go to for help.	3.55	3.67	3.58	3.68ª	3.33ᵇ	N/s	N/s	N/s	N/s	N/s	N/s	N/s	N/s	N/s	N/s

TABLE 7.6.   Scores on dimension 14: prisoner social life

Prison	Reliability	Score
Holme House	0.7632	3.4965
Doncaster	0.7314	3.4649
Belmarsh	0.7021	3.3675
Risley	0.7669	3.3333
Wandsworth	0.7668	3.3083

prison, as some authors have suggested that prisoner 'solidarity' increases with the pains of imprisonment. It seems to be the case that relationships among prisoners are slightly better in the better quality prisons (Holme House and Doncaster), and worse in the prisons where staff and prisoners were more antagonistic (Belmarsh and Wandsworth). Consistent with Sykes's propositions, prisoner social life is an outcome rather than a component of prison quality, but the direction of influence may be complex: trust and friendship seem to be greater where a better quality of life exists. However, solidarity and collective protest (which should be distinguished from friendship and trust) may be more likely where staff–prisoner relationships are more confrontational.

We concluded that this dimension provided useful beginnings, but could not tell us in sufficient depth what the nature of relationships between prisoners was like, nor if it was a clear indicator of the quality of life in an establishment. We therefore excluded it from our prison quality scale.[13]

The Meaning of Imprisonment

Meaning is the extent to which individuals see their life as having some purpose and that life tasks are worthy investments.

(Chamberlain et al. 1992: 302)

Meaninglessness is a condition which the mind finds it hard to tolerate. It leads to boredom, depression, neurosis and even suicide. On the other hand, as [Viktor Frankl] is fond of quoting, 'He who has a why to live can bear with almost any how'.

(Weatherhead 1964, p. vii)[14]

[13] The study referred to in n. 10 aims to remedy this.
[14] The quote is from Nietzsche.

During the workgroup exercises outlined in Chapter 3, and in our individual conversations with prisoners, we were struck by the number of times reference was made to concepts of meaninglessness and alienation (e.g. Galtung described an 'air of irrelevance' in prison, shared by 'few other institutions'; Galtung 1961: 107).[15] We devised an exploratory item: the extent to which prisoners found meaning in their experience of imprisonment (where meaning indicates the positively expressed opposite of the more familiar concept of 'alienation' or 'anomie'; see Clark 1959; Dean 1961; Nettler 1957; Seeman 1959; and Blauner 1964).[16] Lack of meaning is linked to powerlessness: if a person is 'an object controlled and manipulated by other persons or by an impersonal system (such as technology)', then it is difficult to experience meaning (Blauner 1964: 16). The opposite 'non-alienated pole' is freedom and control. Retaining some control (e.g. in the workplace) is 'a kind of affirmation of human dignity' (Blauner 1964: 16 and 21).

Whilst there is some evidence that meaning is a personality construct (Chamberlain *et al.* 1992), there is also evidence that levels of meaning vary according to circumstances. Frankl suggested that finding meaning in difficult circumstances (by which he meant an 'inner hold on their moral and spiritual selves') is a means of survival (Frankl 1964: 69). Others have suggested (e.g. Bettleheim 1943, 1960, 1979) that meaning is important for psychological survival and that the person: 'is capable of enduring incredible burdens and taking cruel punishment when he has self-esteem, hope, purpose, and belief in his fellows' (Wolff 1957: 45, in Dean 1961: 755).

Clearly, the prison is not as extreme as the concentration camp experiences that led to these insights, but prisoners and critics have argued that it demands this kind of meaning-making (Cohen and

---

[15] Galtung suggests that one of the reasons prison is 'irrelevant' is because it does not *restore* anything (Galtung 1961: 109).

[16] Alienation is described as a psychological state reflecting a form of estrangement from one's self (i.e. one's rightful role), or a 'feeling of the lack of means (power) to eliminate the discrepancy between his definition of the role he is playing and the one he feels he should be playing in a situation' (Clark 1959: 849). The term is often used in relation to working conditions (to describe the 'worker's "separation" from effective control over his economic destiny'; Dean 1961: 754) and other conditions of unequal power relations. It has also been used to denote 'normlessness' or a lack of values that might give purpose or direction to life (Dean 1961).

Taylor 1972). Feelings of alienation and meaninglessness are associated with mental and emotional disorder, and suicide (Nettler 1957). Central to Frankl's sense of meaning is 'a future' and 'a goal' (Frankl 1964: 71), which may differ for individuals.[17] This brings it close to Allport's notion of 'becoming', discussed in Chapter 6. Antonovsky proposed a broader but related term, 'sense of coherence', to denote three dimensions associated with positive coping: meaning, manageability, and comprehensibility (Antonovsky 1983). It has been demonstrated that individuals with higher scores on a 29-item sense of coherence scale recover better from illness, cope better with life, and adjust positively to stressful circumstances. Low scores are associated with higher degrees of suicide risk (Petrie and Brook 1992). In a study of 150 suicide attempters in New Zealand, the subscale 'meaning' was most highly related to suicidal thoughts at follow-up (Petrie and Brook 1992). We were interested in whether prisoners experienced different levels of meaning in different establishments.

This item provided us with some interesting results, but it did not discriminate significantly between establishments. Thirty-eight per cent of prisoners thought their experience of imprisonment was meaningless. Finding meaning in the prison experience was linked to the feeling of 'being listened to' and to activities:

On the best days I feel as if there is meaning in being here, especially when someone eventually listens to what I have to say. I feel that there is a light at the end of a long tunnel and that I am not just locked up and forgotten about. I can also feel that at times I am a person and I do matter. (Prisoner, Risley)

I've got full-time Physical Education coming up; I'm doing an NVQ in Sports and Recreation. It's a twelve week course and at the end I'll have

---

[17] Frankl's perspective of life's meaning, deeply influenced by the loss of most of his family and his own long-term experience in concentration camps, has to do with 'responsibleness' and self-transcendence, through which self-actualization is possible. Life is given meaning through activity ('by doing a deed'); by 'experiencing a value'; by suffering; and by love. 'Everything can be taken from a man but one thing: the last of the human freedoms—to choose one's attitude in any given set of circumstances, to choose one's way' (Frankl 1964: 65). 'So live as if you were living already for the second time and as if you had acted the first time as wrongly as you are about to act now! . . . This maxim . . . invites him to imagine that the past may yet be changed and amended. Such a precept confronts him with life's *finiteness*' (Frankl 1964: 111–13).

something to show for my nine months behind bars so it won't have been a waste of time. (Prisoner, Belmarsh)

The most constructive activities I've done here are education and courses. They gave me both a sense of purpose and achievement. (Prisoner, Doncaster)

There were other ways in which the prison experience could be meaningful for prisoners, including staying off drugs, or staying alive:

The most constructive thing I've done is I've stayed off drugs; but that's just me. I had a bad first week but now I've never felt better in years. This is the break I needed; the way I was going outside I would be dead by now . . . I just look at my ID card from when I first came in, I looked awful, so that helps to remind me . . . (Prisoner, Holme House)

In a way prison has saved my life; I'd be dead by now on the out, the amount I drank. (Prisoner, Holme House)

Is it meaningful? Well, before I came in I would have either killed myself or someone else. (Prisoner, Risley)

I've found myself since I've been in this prison; I'd lost my sense of reality. (Prisoner, Doncaster)

To prove I've changed [gives me a sense of purpose], that I beat the system and bettered myself. Prison has given me insight into who I am. (Prisoner, Belmarsh)

Forty-one per cent of prisoners at Belmarsh, 42.6 per cent at Holme House, 38.6 per cent at Risley, 36.9 per cent at Doncaster and 30.0 per cent at Wandsworth agreed or strongly agreed that 'my experience of prison is meaningless'. Most prisoners neither agreed nor disagreed, or disagreed with this statement (suggesting that they found it difficult to respond to in this structured way). The single-item means did not discriminate between establishments (see Table 7.7) and we found it difficult to account for the slightly higher score in Wandsworth than in the other prisons. Although these results are of interest, and the concept is important, we excluded it from our revised prison quality scale as it did not form part of a dimension, it did not discriminate significantly between establishments, and we felt that this was not the most valuable way to set about exploring the meaningfulness of the prison experience (see Buffry et al. 1992 for an interesting early attempt). It was most highly correlated with the dimension 'personal development' (0.391).

Quality of Life

Finally, we devised two overall quality of life scores. One asked prisoners to score the prison out of ten; the other asked to what extent prisoners found that 'overall, the regime in this prison is positive'. We invited them to talk about this overall evaluation, and to identify one or two areas of prison life they thought were good:

> For a lock-up jail it's as good as you're going to get in a prison. It is a model prison. (Prisoner, Holme House)

> I quite like it here; it's better than——, it's cleaner, there is less bullying, and prisoners aren't all mixed together; the VPs [Vulnerable Prisoners] are segregated here. There are smaller wings and staff try to help you. There is quite a bit to do here; there are a lot of courses you can take, some trade qualifications, and work. (Prisoner, Holme House)

> It is a good size, you have a single cell, it is clean, furniture is in good repair—it would be a cracking jail if the attitude of staff changed. (Prisoner, Risley)

> It is like being in a civilized world instead of a crocodile pit. (Prisoner, Doncaster)

Individuals rated each prison differently, according to their circumstances, but the overall pattern was confirmed: Doncaster was regarded as 'positive' by most prisoners, with Holme House regarded as 'positive' by 40 per cent. A quarter regarded the regime as positive in Belmarsh and Wandsworth, respectively, and Risley's regime was very poorly regarded by most prisoners (even though its relationships were seen as 'not that bad'; Table 7.7(b).

The results discriminated between prisons, with Doncaster rated significantly higher than all the other prisons, and the difference between Holme House and Risley almost reaching a level of statistical significance on the second item. The responses to the two 'quality of life' questions matched the composite scores for the other dimensions. It is clear that prisoners are drawing on their views about the regime, relationships, and facilities, as well as comparisons with other prisons, when they make this overall assessment. We concluded that it was valuable to retain an overall quality of life question in the questionnaire, as a useful general assessment (although only one question was needed).

TABLE 7.7. A comparison of prisoner views on meaning and quality of life: individual item mean scores

Item/statement	Item scores (1–5)					ANOVA (Mean difference)									
	B	HH	R	D	W	B&HH	B&R	B&D	B&W	HH&R	HH&D	HH&W	R&D	R&W	D&W
(a) Meaning															
My experience of prison is [not] meaningless.	2.82[b]	2.83	2.88	2.97	3.18[a]	N/s	N/s	N/s	N/s	N/s	N/s	N/s	N/s	N/s	N/s
(b) Quality of life															
Overall, on a scale of 1–10, how would you describe the quality of life in this prison?[1]	2.45	2.83	2.52	3.37[a]	2.39[b]	N/s	N/s	1.84**	N/s	N/s	1.08*	N/s	1.70**	N/s	1.96**
Overall, I feel that the regime in this prison is positive.	2.63	3.02	2.60[b]	3.54[a]	2.71	N/s	N/s	0.91**	N/s	0.42	0.51*	N/s	0.93**	N/s	0.84**

[1] The responses are expressed as mean scores on a 1–5 scale.

TABLE 7.8.   Percentage of prisoners who agree/strongly agree with
statements about quality of life

Statement (Social life)	Belmarsh	Holme House	Risley	Doncaster	Wandsworth
1. I feel the regime in this prison is positive.	25.3	40.5	19.8[b]	60.5[a]	36.1

Conclusions

In this chapter we have reported on some dimensions and individual items that we wished to pursue, following our discussion
with staff and prisoners about 'what matters' in prison. Although
these dimensions of prison life are important and sociologically
interesting, we excluded them from our prison quality scale. The
dimension 'power' was difficult to use in the context of our overall
scheme, as there was no clear way of knowing, from the research
as we conducted it, the point at which prisoners had too much control and autonomy (for the safety of other prisoners, for example).
Several prisoners expressed surprise that they seemed to have as
much autonomy and freedom at Doncaster, and a few commented
that staff infrequently searched their cells. We shall return to this
point in Chapter 9. Power did play a role in perceptions of fairness
and relationships in particular, however. It was also related to
perceptions of trust, development, well-being, and order. In better
prisons, there will be a reasonable balance of power. More thought
needs to be given as to what this 'balance' might look like.

The 'prisoner social life' dimension was also less useful in measuring prison quality. Certain aspects of relationships amongst prisoners may be a result of other features of prison quality. But this is
far from straightforward. It seems that *trust* and *companionableness*
increase with better staff–prisoner relationships, but that *solidarity*
and *preparedness to take collective action* increase in response to
staff antagonism, and other deprivations of imprisonment, as Sykes
argued. There is scope for considerably more work, of a more ethnographic nature, in this area of prison life.

Both dimensions are analytically interesting and tell us important
things about the structure of prison life. They are complex sociological phenomena, which are less amenable to evaluation in this

quantitative way. They are not captured adequately by our prison quality measure. Likewise, evaluating the 'meaning' of the prison experience is difficult, and is better addressed by the questions we have asked in the dimension 'personal development'. It is helpful to have a single 'quality of life' item in the questionnaire, and responses on this item closely matched the overall scores.

Before drawing our analyses together, we turn in the next chapter to the world above prisoners. What does the late modern, managerialist world look like for those trying to run and manage prisons? How do prison staff perceive those above them? What are relationships like between staff and managers? What is the role of trust in this part of prison life? We consider how prisons have *emotional* as well as *moral* climates, and we suggest that emotions have a moral importance that is often overlooked.

PART III

Penal Values and Prison Management

8

Managing Late Modern Prisons and their Performance

People feel the lack of sustained human relations and durable purposes.

(Sennett 1998: 98)

One does not have to be a moral philosopher to subscribe to the notion that the best correctional institution is to be found in a society that does not have correctional institutions. In the real world, however, these institutions exist, and they vary in their goals and norms. The variations in outlook of their administrators and the resulting attitudes of the inmates are profound.

(Janowicz 1966, p. vi)

I believe firmly that it is a key task of leaders to articulate clearly the values of the organisation.

(Pilling 1992: 8)

Introduction

In Part II of this book we looked almost exclusively at the prison world as perceived by prisoners, and at the role of key value dimensions as we and prisoners made sense of them. This part of the book returns to some contextual issues raised in Chapters 1 and 2 and to some of the questions of power and governmentality, explored briefly in Chapter 7. Who possesses power above prisoners, and how is power deployed, in the late modern prison? How do prison staff perceive their working environment, and their treatment by those above them? How do the conditions of late modernity impact on the world of the prison? What is shaping prison life, and therefore the experience of imprisonment for prisoners? Who determines the 'values of the organisation' and how are these values secured in practice?

This chapter explores the links between a prison's quality of life or moral performance and its management. What does 'sharper performance management' (Home Office 1999a: 6) mean in practice?[1] We shall return, in this account, to some of the historical developments introduced in Chapter 1. These developments have produced an important dialogue about values in prison. The central question is whether modern managerialist approaches to prisons, or to any traditionally public sector organization, improve that organization's quality, or whether there are risks to certain values in these approaches. We argued in Chapter 2 that the concept of quality tends to be rather impoverished in managerialist assessments of performance. Part II of our book tried to replace, or at least supplement, existing approaches to the measurement of prison quality with a set of dimensions we suggest reflects a prison's 'moral performance'. We return in this chapter to the modernization of prison management during the 1990s, current senior management organization, and then to our five prisons, to look at five governors, and at how the prison staff in our study saw the world above them. We ask, are there limits to the need for efficiency, or to the level of control that should be exerted over the workforce? How far does trust extend in the late modern prison, and how relevant are levels of trust to prison quality?

The role of governors in shaping the quality of life in prison is crucial. This is despite a widespread belief that governors are increasingly constrained by senior management control and direction, and by a powerful managerialist hold on their actions and priorities.

---

[1] Studies of prison management are few and far between. Some useful historical material can be found in, for example, Barak-Glantz (1981); Jacobs (1977, ch. 4); and DiIulio (1987). More contemporary reflections are included in Adler and Longhurst (1994); Vagg (1994); Bryans and Wilson (2000); and McEvoy (2001). Useem and Reisig argue in their US study of protests, disturbances, and riots in prison that 'weak, divided or unstable management' is a key variable (Useem and Reisig 1999). Rifts between management and officers, low morale amongst officers, perceived incompetence amongst officers, and 'agitation between officers and inmates' are associated with inmate collective action (Useem and Reisig 1999). 'Strong, coherent administration is the crucial ingredient in avoiding disturbances' (Useem and Kimball 1989: 227). The authors add that this is difficult to accomplish as 'prisons are impinged upon by the political upheavals of the outside world' (p. 227). Empirical research on management outside penology suggests, for example, that high self-efficacy, or high confidence, is independently related to successful outcomes on official measures of performance (J. Braithwaite 1998: 346; also G. Morgan 1997). The themes we touch on here are in need of much further empirical study.

How do they see this framework? Does it help them to achieve better quality prisons? How much influence does 'managerial action' have on a complex organization such as a prison (see Smith and Goddard 2002)? Governors are managers and 'leaders' of the prison. Their abilities, interpretations of their role, and the values they bring to it influence life in an establishment to a very significant extent.

The account to follow provides a descriptive and 'appreciative' account of the world-view of staff and senior managers and places that world-view into context. We did not formally interview the governors of our five prisons in this study, nor have we asked them to complete management-style questionnaires, tempting though that idea became as we analysed our results. Our account draws on the many informal conversations we had with the governors and other senior managers in each prison, on our own observations and notes, and on what staff said. We have sought, in the interests of anonymity, to provide general observations, rather than to provide a full account of each prison, in order. A few parts of our story could identify individuals, and we have asked each governor (four of whom have now been promoted to more senior positions) to read and comment on our account.

Managing and Being Managed in the Late Modern Context

As we saw in Chapters 1 and 2, managerialism is a term used to describe radical changes in the style of prison management from the 1980s onwards (McEvoy 2001: 254–8). It is a 'distinct set of ideologies and practices' (McEvoy 2001: 254), representing a pragmatic, future-oriented, technologically supported approach to the management of organizations which emphasizes strategic planning, 'service delivery', efficiency, and value for money. It is 'neither apolitical nor ideology free' (McEvoy 2001: 252) and has an in-built tendency towards instrumentalism and quantification (e.g. so that what can be measured becomes important, rather than vice versa). It is characterized by strong central direction, but also by devolution-within-parameters to local managers. This form of 'government-at-a-distance' by the centre is made possible by newly powerful mechanisms of accountability, such as performance targets, described in Chapter 2. Managerialism is one of several characteristics of late modernity which alter the sources of trust for those who work in organizations, from concrete individuals with known track records, to abstract future-oriented systems generated by unknown and remote 'others' (Giddens 1990; Bottoms 1995; and Chapter 1).

We suggested in Chapters 1 and 2 that managerialism has exerted a considerable influence on prison life since the mid-1980s. Much has been written about managerialism in criminal justice generally and its impact on those caught up in criminal justice processes. Feeley and Simon, amongst others, have argued persuasively that managerialist or actuarial practices fail to take seriously the moral agency of individuals, often treating them as units to be classified and managed rather than individuals with futures (Feeley and Simon 1992, 1994; Bottoms 1995). Fewer commentators have addressed the impact of managerialism on the deliverers of criminal justice: those who work in the new performance culture, and those who manage it.[2] Some social theorists have analysed the impact of the new economy on the organization of the public sector (e.g. Pollitt and Bouckaert 2000) and on the workplace in general. Sennett, for example, argues that the human consequences of the 'new flexibility' are profound. Our new high-risk, low-loyalty, lean workplaces corrode our moral identity, as we are forced to abandon habits of dependability, service, and routine and the concept of 'the career', and must embrace a modern work identity consisting of short-term, short-notice, outcomes-driven 'projects' (Sennett 1998; see also Pollitt and Bouckaert 2000: 162–3).[3] Such an environment, Sennett argues, breeds anxiety and brings in its wake new controls

---

[2] There is a distinction to be drawn between managerialism as a social development, and the characterization of individuals in strategic managerial positions as essentially managerialist in nature. As one interviewee observed, 'I have difficulty in seeing myself as a new managerialist . . . What I say and think about imprisonment and governing has remained remarkably consistent over twenty and more years. It is not, in fact, very new' (pers. comm.). This seems a fair remark to make, and illustrates the complex interplay between the individual protagonists of this chapter, how they see themselves, and the broader social developments in which they play a part.

[3] Pollitt and Bouckaert argue that, at the highest levels, there is a contradiction between a strategy of downsizing alongside a simultaneous strategy of 'unleashing the creative talents' of the workforce. They suggest that it is possible to envision a 'smaller, less bureaucratic, more highly skilled, and perhaps even better remunerated public service within which morale could be restored and a new performance-oriented culture solidly entrenched', but that this vision depends on a perception that 'a new phase of relative stability has been attained' (Pollitt and Bouckaert 2000: 163).

which are hard to understand. Character, a term linking personality to civic or public ties, is lost in this new short-term, non-linear environment.[4] Loyalties and commitments cannot be fostered. The iron cage of bureaucracy with its reward of upward social mobility for the diligent time-serving worker has given way to a less predictable and individualized form of work, where 'the qualities of good work are not the qualities of good character' (Sennett 1998: 21). The market is impatient, and rapid institutional change is part of this dynamic, redefinable, flexible, and flatter world of work. This environment is not conducive to trust, loyalty, and commitment—and may be dysfunctional for the individual (and for the organization):

Take the matter of commitment and loyalty. 'No long term' is a principle which corrodes trust, loyalty, and mutual commitment. Trust can, of course, be a purely formal matter, as when people agree to a business deal or rely on another to observe the rules in a game. But usually deeper experiences of trust are more informal, as when people learn on whom they can rely when given a difficult or impossible task. Such social bonds take time to develop, slowly rooting into the cracks and crevices of institutions . . . The short time frame of modern institutions limits the ripening of informal trust. (Sennett 1998: 24)

In this world, power can easily be wielded over the necessarily co-operative (because expendable) workforce, whose own needs and desires (e.g. for a reasonable home life and for security of work) can be denied legitimacy (Charlesworth 2000).[5] So the practice of management becomes an 'exercise of domination' (Sennett 1998: 115).

Sennett's analysis is applicable to the late modern prison,[6] and this framework may account for the general sensitivity of staff to

---

[4] By non-linear, Sennett refers to the changing directions that late modern organizational life can take. In the prison, contracts with one company can be ended and a new company might be invited to take over; the public sector can 'win back' contracts to run certain prisons; prisons change their function in order to adapt to rapidly changing compositions in the prison population; the policy climate in which prisons operate can take a completely new direction, and so on.

[5] Charlesworth argues that these 'elementary solidarities' are basic requirements of human decency (Charlesworth 2000: 5).

[6] Where, to return to Rutherford's credos (see Ch. 1), at the level of senior management emphasis, the 'humanity' credo was largely challenged and replaced by the 'efficiency' credo during the 1980s and 1990s.

issues of trust, commitment, and loyalty and, in part, for the generally low scores on these dimensions that were found in our study.[7] The dynamics he describes can be found in both private and public sector prisons, for example, as senior management teams move increasingly quickly through establishments, and where individuals (including governors) risk removal if their performance is poor.[8]

There may be other explanations, however, for problems of trust between staff and managers in prison. Most organizations contain some conflict and division between staff and managers, or between the 'ownership class' and 'workers'. But this fairly common feature of the workplace may be exaggerated in the prison, for particular reasons. We have written elsewhere about the importance for prison staff of in-group loyalty and trust, their conservative and pragmatic 'habits of thought', and their quite understandable resistance to change (Liebling and Price 2001: 145–72). Prison officers, rather like the police, work in a high-risk, tradition-oriented, place-based world, where the consequences of a wrong decision can be dire. They are regularly required to 'face situations where the risk lies in the unpredictable outcome of encounters with other people' (Reiner 1992: 110; Chan 1996). So, 'if it ticks, why change it?' (Liebling and Price 2001: 145). The key facts shaping the prison officer working personality are authority and danger (Liebling and Price 2001: 149, drawing on Skolnick 1966). Prison officers possess authority and must enforce it, much of the time. Doing so can be dangerous. But resolving dangerous situations is accomplished by using various forms of authority—an intrinsically dangerous act, particularly where officers are vastly outnumbered by prisoners. Cohesiveness or camaraderie among officers in this situation is

---

[7] For example, most of the governors had been in post at each of our establishments for relatively short periods of time: from a matter of months to an average of less than two years.

[8] Twenty-four governors left their posts following early and medical retirements during Martin Narey's reign (Roddan, pers. comm.). One of the commentators on an early draft of this chapter suggested that a study might be warranted on the reasons for removing governors. 'As well as the obvious one of kick-starting improvement (like the sacking and replacing of a football club manager), there may be the perfectly honourable one of moving a burnt-out executive for his or her own sake as much as that of the prison' (pers. comm.).

essential to survival. No officer wants to feel they are alone: 'Defining the prison as a conflict situation leads to a demand for unequivocal commitment and loyalty to the officer group' (Colvin 1977: 128).

Officers are judged amongst themselves by their willingness to uphold this norm (Kauffman 1988; Liebling and Price 2001: 153–7). A ready response to an alarm bell is a test of this tight camaraderie (Colvin 1977: 127). Officers frequently mention this highly prized 'ability to work together' as one of the key satisfactions of the job (Liebling and Price 2001: 158). Meanwhile (and increasingly, as the complexity of the job requires many senior managers to be office-bound), they somewhat cynically watch distant governors and other senior managers come and go.

There may be other reasons for the highly cynical 'meta-narrative'[9] detectable in the Prison Service as an organization. Elliott has suggested that two possible explanations for a negative bias in prison staff constructions of prison management are the organization's hierarchical structure; and the high levels of dependency of individuals on those above them (Elliott 2002). These negative constructions (which may be profoundly out of touch with reality as they exclude experiences which are positive) tend to flow consistently upwards, from prisoners to staff, staff to managers, managers to headquarters, and headquarters to ministers. The role of the governor, for example, has grown in size and complexity, partly because 'the days when governors just ran prisons that stayed the same, have gone' (Wheatley 2001: 2). The role is now about implementing continuous change and improvement. This frustrates prison staff for reasons we shall discuss further below, but governors also clearly experience frustrations in their relationships with Prison Service Headquarters as a result. As Carlen found in her study of this relationship in the women's estate:

Despite innovations within the Prison Service in recent years, there is still a general frustration on the part of many governors about the ways in which they themselves are governed by a PSHQ which often seems more meticulous about the ordering of policies on paper than about the implementation of policies in prisons. (Carlen 2002a: 28)

---

[9] An overarching storyline or narrative structure, which defines the properties of other organizational storylines on the basis of the information contained in it.

The Prison Service is seen by those working within it as a *low trust* organization. This is partly due to the special nature of prisons, and partly (we suggest) because of the particular impact that many modern managerialist techniques (including frenetic policy activity and the capacity to demand compliance with it) have upon those who work in a prison environment. There is also a tendency within managerialism towards 'componentiality', where the overall picture may contain contradictions and tensions, as described in Chapters 1 and 2.

Managerialism and late modernity together arguably make it harder for managers to generate trust in prison. The risk-laden environment in which prison staff work means they have short and tradition-oriented time-horizons. Getting to the end of the day peacefully (like they did yesterday) is their primary interest (Liebling 1999). Their confidence in accomplishing this is grounded in experience (Liebling and Price 2001: 173; Liebling 1999). Senior managers, on the other hand, inhabit and create a world of future-oriented plans and aspirational targets. They seek to innovate and to change, with a fast-developing model of 'improvement' (parts of which are sometimes imported from jurisdictions elsewhere) that is difficult for staff to trust. The day-to-day role of the prison officer may not have changed dramatically since the prison first emerged in its modern form, but the 'organisation of their role and work' certainly has (Liebling and Price 2001: 183). Change is necessary, and now inevitable, but whereas senior managers largely understand and have access to the bigger picture, prison staff often do not. They fill in the gaps with guesswork, anxiety, and cynicism (G. Morgan 1997, chapter 7).

Variation *between* establishments within an overall framework of low levels of trust between staff and senior management has a separate explanation, which we shall explore below. Before we embark on this part of our account, we set out the current senior management structure of the Prison Service, a structure which changed dramatically just as we were completing the book. We consider the role of area managers: key players on the performance stage and yet, paradoxically, barely visible to prison staff or to the public. We shall then return to our findings from the five prisons, as well as considering extensive supplementary interviews carried out with governors from additional prisons and others for the purpose of this chapter.

The Senior Management of the Prison Service: Efficiency, Decency, and Delivery

> The culture of the Service is gradually changing with a much stronger focus on setting and delivering agreed objectives.
>
> (Prison Service 1994*a*)

> A strong message received while taking evidence was that there has been an improvement in leadership over the last eighteen months. Progress was attributed to the leadership of the Director General and the work of the Deputy Director General.
>
> (Home Office 2000: 26)

What kind of organization is the Prison Service? What kind of leadership does it have, and how does this influence life in establishments? There are two answers to this question, and we shall attempt to address both. We shall outline the formal organizational structure of the Prison Service, before discussing what we have learned about how the senior leadership of the Prison Service is seen by those working in it. We outlined the important move to agency status, and the modernizing framework within which this development took place, in Chapter 1. The account below provides a more detailed description of the senior management of the Prison Service. The remainder of the chapter focuses on our five establishments: in particular, on the key figure in individual establishments—the governor—and on the complex art of governing.

We described some contradictory impulses in relation to the management of the Prison Service in Chapters 1 and 2. On the one hand, for political reasons, it is important to keep the Prison Service 'in the Whitehall family' (pers. comm.). On the other hand, for reasons of sound modern managerial practice, the Prison Service has formally retained its agency status. This is despite considerable unease about 'what goes on' in prison, amongst ministers and senior civil servants.[10] The Home Secretary symbolically took back the answering of Parliamentary Questions following the Quinquennial Review of Agency Status in 1999, in order to express

---

[10] In 2004, the Carter Review of Correctional Services established a new framework for the Prison Service which ended its Agency Status and returned its senior management to the Home Office (see Home Office 2004). A new National Offender Management Service was established, with Martin Narey as its Chief Executive.

or reassert ministerial accountability (Prison Service 1997).[11] The relationship between the Prison Service, the wider Home Office, and ministers is extraordinarily complex (see Prison Service Review 1997; Home Office 1999*b*, section 5: 'Serving Ministers'; and Home Office 2000), and is continually under review. Ministers need to be involved 'in the strategic development of the Service and in some lower level decisions' (Home Office 2000: 7). Decisions at an individual case level (e.g. whether to allocate certain high profile or notorious prisoners to open conditions) can attract considerable public and parliamentary interest (Home Office 1999*b*: 27). As the Quinquennial Review stated:

The organisational status of the Prison Service needs to be consistent with the political and wider policy context already determined by Ministers; the effective delivery of services; the effective formulation of policy; cost-effectiveness; and good relationships with other criminal justice (and specifically correctional) agencies. (Home Office 1999*a*: 2)

The Quinquennial Review concluded that agency status 'has brought clear advantages, in particular a more business-like focus on management and service delivery' (Home Office 1999*a*: 6). A related review of performance concluded that there had been 'tremendous improvement' between 1992–3 and 1997–8, particularly in security, the introduction of programmes, and staff training. It attributed these changes to the greater flexibility and freedom delegated to the Director General, the clearer focus on outputs and targets, and clearer leadership (Home Office 1999*b*: 2–3).

An additional limitation on agency status in practice is the fact that the Prison Service is part of an increasingly 'joined up' criminal justice system, whose overarching objectives have been set by the Home Secretary (see below). The Quinquennial Review predicted that 'the future organisational arrangements made for the Prison Service will need to be consistent with continuing close working relationships between it and the wider Home Office and the criminal justice machinery' (Home Office 1999*a*: 7). Reintegration back into the Home Office for the Prison Service 'could stifle innovation and have a deleterious effect on morale and future performance' (Home Office 1999*a*: 7). It would be seen as a 'rebuke'. The Prison

---

[11] This means, in practice, that Parliamentary Questions about the Prison Service are answered by a Home Office minister. From the adoption of Agency Status, in 1993, until 1997, Questions were answered by the Chief Executive.

Service therefore operated until 2003 as an agency with unusually strong oversight, and with renewed but modernized public sector leadership.

Merger with the Probation Service was considered during 1999–2000, but regarded at the time as a 'bridge too far'. A national Probation Service was established instead as a 'first stage' in this restructuring programme. In 2003, the Prison and Probation Services were brought together under a single Commissioner for Correctional Services. It is significant that Martin Narey, the Director General of the Prison Service from 1999 to 2003, was selected for this role, largely in recognition of the success of his leadership in the modernizing of the Prison Service. He had presided over a period during which prisons became no longer 'the overwhelming anxiety for a Home Secretary or Prisons Minister' (Narey 2003: 2). His deputy, Phil Wheatley, took up the slightly revised and more explicitly operational role as Director General in his place. This is likely to strengthen Narey's leadership role and confirm the management direction described in this chapter. Narey and Wheatley made it clear at the Prison Service Conference 2003 that their joint agenda, of continuous improvement and the pursuit of decency, would continue (Wheatley 2003).

The Formal Organizational Structure of the Prison Service

The Home Secretary is accountable to Parliament for the Prison Service (now the Correctional Services, including private sector prisons) in England and Wales. The Home Secretary 'sets the strategic direction of the Prison Service, specifies the outputs and targets which it is required to achieve and allocates resources to it accordingly' (Home Office 2000: 7). A newly joined up criminal justice strategy states that the overarching purpose of criminal justice is public protection and the reduction of crime (Home Office 2001c). The Prison Service is expected to work within this framework.

The Prison Service, the National Probation Service, and the Youth Justice Board now come under the direction of the Commissioner for Correctional Services (see Fig. 8.1).[12] There is a

---

[12] It is interesting to note that the Commissioner for Correctional Services retains responsibility for the management of private sector prisons (this establishes a distinction between the 'purchaser' of services and the 'provider', albeit with a continuing line management role in respect of the leads of the Prison Service and National Probation Service).

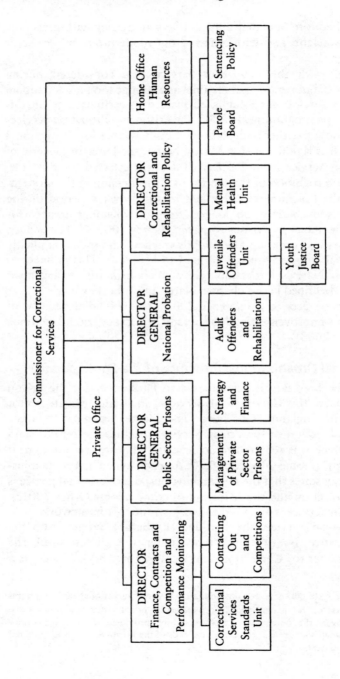

FIGURE 8.1.   Correctional Services, 2003.[1]

[1] From 1 June 2004, the Commissioner for Correctional Services becomes the Chief Executive of the National Offender Management Service. See Home Office 2004.

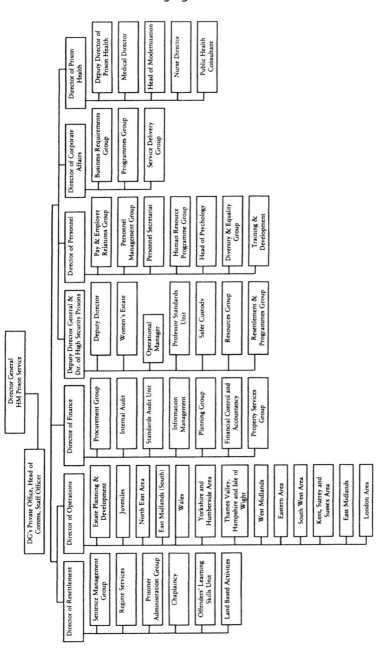

FIGURE 8.2.   HM Prison Service, 2003.

Correctional Services Strategy Board (chaired by the designated minister and also consisting of the Commissioner for Correctional Services, the Prison Service Director General, Director of the National Probation Service, and the Director General, Criminal Justice Group). This is underpinned by the Correctional Services Management Board, consisting of the Commissioner, the two Director Generals, the Directors of Finance Correctional Policy, and a legal adviser. There is also a Prison Service Management Board (PSMB), consisting of the Director General, the Directors of Resettlement, Operations, Finance and Procurement, Personnel, Health, Corporate Affairs, and the Deputy Director (who is also the Director of High Security Prisons; see Fig. 8.2). About half of these people are career civil servants, who (in the eyes of operational people, but not themselves) tend to see their primary role as serving ministers. The Board also has four non-executive members.[13] The PSMB is a forum for discussing the strategic direction of the Services, and performance. The Director General of the Prison Service is responsible for the delivery of those aspects of policy that relate to the Prison Service. Day-to-day operational leadership lies with him. The Director General is appointed by the Home Secretary, with the approval of the Prime Minister (Home Office 2000: 8). The policy leadership of the Prison Service rests with the Commissioner of Correctional Services (soon to become Chief Executive of a new single organization; see Home Office 2004).

Below the PSMB the Operational Policy Group, which consists of senior operational and policy managers (Area Managers and Heads of Group), meets monthly to comment on draft policy or operational proposals.[14] If there are major issues to consider, Area Managers might take them to their own governors for further discussion, through Area Meetings. Area Managers (see further below) all report to the Operational Director.

---

[13] They currently comprise a Legal Adviser from the Home Office, a Media Relations Officer, the Board Secretary, and a Race Equality Adviser. They are not non-executives in the normal sense of that description: persons from a different area of activity and employment. There are 'real non-executives' on the Correctional Services Strategy Board (pers. comm. 2003).

[14] Governors see it as an important but unfulfilled function of this forum to 'filter out unworkable policy' (in Dickinson 2002: 71).

The two key figures throughout the period 1999–2003, Martin Narey and Phil Wheatley, exerted an immensely powerful influence on the tone and the direction of the Prison Service and arguably shaped it in quite an unprecedented way. Narey's leadership was described by journalist David Rose as 'messianic' (Rose 2002). He was a very visible, relatively young, and emotionally engaged Director General,[15] who clearly had the confidence of his Board and of ministers. An ex-National Health Service manager, assistant prison governor (although never a *governing* governor), private secretary to Earl Ferrers (then Minister of State), and Director of Security and then Regimes, he secured substantial additional funding from the Treasury for educational and cognitive-behavioural programmes, 'with the assistance of a skilled financial manager' and other contributions from the Prisons Board. He made the decency agenda his key legacy.

The management task for a Director General requires upwards as well as downwards leadership. Narey described his role as follows:

Increasingly I think my job falls into two parts: to give the philosophical or moral direction for the Service; and secondly to defend its interests with Whitehall and the press and the public. I spend a lot of my time dealing with the Home Office and with Ministers, and I try very hard to protect Phil and the rest of the Service from a great deal of that . . . 'managing the environment'. To allow them to concentrate on managing the Service. (Narey, pers. comm. 2002)

This has changed under the new leadership arrangements, with Narey continuing to manage the relationship with Whitehall and ministers, and the Director General spending more time leading the Service. The relationship between the Prison Service and ministers depends, to some extent, on the personalities of and interaction between the key players: the Commissioner for Correctional Services, the Home Secretary, the Prisons Minister and the Director

---

[15] 'Something early on made me realise you have to do this job with a bit of passion . . . If you want an organisation to change, if the staff don't think that you care about it, then you're lost' (Narey, pers. comm.). As one commentator observed: 'Martin's enthusiasm was easily transmitted down the line too. As a working class lad who supports Middlesbrough F.C., he had an appeal to staff. I guess uniquely, for someone in Martin's position, his higher education was at a polytechnic which also marked him out from the more conventional mandarin mould.'

General. One of the difficulties is a constant change of ministerial office. Narey described a constant effort to develop working relationships and build up confidence with the five prisons ministers he encountered since taking up his post. With each of them there was a significant 'effort in trying to start again'. They 'don't necessarily pick up the baton from where the other one left off'. And you don't start with 'credit in the bank' from previous ministers:

I think there's some nervousness about the role of Director General on the part of ministers, which contributes to it being a difficult role. It's probably significant that the day I got this job Joe Pilling phoned me and reminded me that no Director General has left happily since the mid-70s . . . One of the things which makes the job difficult certainly in recent years, is trying to get the balance right between leadership of the Service, which has got to be done very visibly, and working to ministers. (Narey, pers. comm. 2002)

What would he change about the way business gets done?

I wish there was a clearer distinction about what was for me and what was for ministers, if you like, between policy and operations, but I have concluded that there simply can't be such a distinction. I think Jack Straw got the balance between what was for ministers and what was for me dead right. He said I should make sure he knew anything he had to know and not bother him with anything he didn't have to know. (Narey, pers. comm. 2002)

Narey describes a distinction in practice, then, between 'what ministers need to know' and 'what they should not be troubled with'.[16] This complex distinction (and the ability to make it) is a key thread running through all management roles, from the Director General to area managers, governors, and staff.

The aspiration to find a clearer distinction between policy and operations, widely discussed at the time of Derek Lewis's dismissal (see Chapter 1), has arguably been addressed under the new organizational arrangements, despite Narey's feeling, expressed whilst he was Director General, that it simply can't be made. The

---

[16] Clear judgement is also needed about what is acceptable and what is not acceptable. Both of these abilities require moral as well as strategic judgement, and involve the skill of *discernment*. See Chapter 6.

Commissioner of Correctional Services clearly leads on the implementation of 'policy' and the Director General now leads on 'operations'. To be at all workable, there is of course a need for policy (perhaps especially policy instructions) to be directly informed by operational need and experience.

The leadership of the Prison Service has been seen by most of those working in it over recent years as powerful (i.e. strong). Two aspects of this 'strength' are first, the clarity of the messages to the field about what is wanted (good performance); and secondly, the proactive approach taken towards the appointment and removal of governors: 'I am interested in good prisons before public prisons. I am convinced that we are getting better at getting the right governors in the right places. Area managers have an unprecedented grip on establishments' (Narey, speech to Prison Service Conference 2002).

Terms like 'robust' and 'firm' are often used by those working in senior positions about the current leadership of the Prison Service. Some governors and staff feel the modern performance framework has led to impatience and criticism, and to constant challenge. A controversial 'decency' video inviting prison staff who did not like the message to resign, several removals of governors and other staff who underperform, and a hard line taken on failing prisons (i.e. performance testing; see Chapter 2) have together resulted in a slightly nervous organization. Other European prison services (e.g. in Belgium and Denmark) seem to have a less 'disciplined' senior management atmosphere.[17] The unprecedented grip on establishments described above operates through area managers, but was actually held convincingly by Narey and his former Deputy Director of the Service,

[17] Drawing on language used by Adler and Longhurst in their study of the reorganization of the management of the Scottish Prison Service up to the early 1990s, it seems that a more or less single discourse can be identified among governors in England and Wales, which has been shaped by senior Prison Service managers. That is, there is a single relatively coherent set of ideas about both means and ends in prison management. This involves the wholesale adoption of managerialist means to achieve the ends of control and 'neo-rehabilitation' (the challenging of offending behaviour via basic skills and accredited programmes). It is less clear whether the decency agenda is part of this instrumentalist framework, or whether it represents a genuinely deontological project at an organizational and institutional level (see Ch. 10). Some critics (and practitioners) see it as part of what Bottoms calls 'control-oriented criminology' (Bottoms 2002: 44; Carlen 2002a). Others (including Bottoms) suggest that it represents a departure from both control-oriented criminology (Bottoms 2002: 44) and from instrumentalism (Bottoms, pers. comm.).

and is likely to continue with the same individuals in enhanced roles in the future. This is modern managerialism in practice. The newly appointed Director General, assisted by technology, a Deputy, and his area managers, has an extraordinary level of knowledge about the culture and performance of individual establishments. Paradoxically, this firm approach to the scrutiny of and demand for performance from the top has brought with it a renewed but related emphasis on moral practices within establishments. The version of managerialism adopted by the Prison Service since 1999 is arguably a version of 'managerialism-plus', whereby deontological values are loudly declared, rather than simply replaced by narrowly conceived performance indicators. 'Performance' on decency, respect, and relationships is (partly as a result of our own work, set out in this book) currently being measured, albeit in an inevitably mechanistic way. To what extent this 'third way' (a less utilitarian version of managerialism, with a declared value base) can possibly reconcile the tensions, difficulties, and moral problems of the prison is a question to which we shall return in Chapter 10.

The Role of the Area Manager: Accountants or Moral Watchdogs?

> I'm very clear what my responsibility is; I am accountable for what is delivered in each of the establishments for which I am responsible. Others are directly accountable to me for managing those establishments and therefore the critical thing . . . is to ensure that each establishment is delivering what it is supposed to deliver and [is] developing and improving to meet our overall aims and objectives. That is the primary role for me.
>
> (Area manager, interviewed in Dickinson 2002: 57)

There are 14 area managers of whom 11 have responsibility for a number of prisons in their geographical area, and whose role is to oversee those establishments. They have responsibility for between four (in Wales) and 13 establishments (in the south-west); an average of nine establishments each. The geographical areas are coterminous with the nine government regions. Some area managers of smaller areas carry responsibilities for additional functions, such as oversight of policy development for local prisons. The remaining three area managers have responsibility for the high security estate, juveniles, and women, on a functional, as opposed to geographical, basis.[18]

Area managers provide 'the link between Headquarters and the "field" and between policy and operations' (Home Office 2000: 28). They are all (since 1996) senior civil servants, and are usually ex-governors, with considerable operational experience. The role has been described as 'rather invisible' (compared to the high profile role of the governor), but it has representation, liaison, co-ordination, and pan-area decision-making elements (Home Office Notice, in Dickinson 2002). The role includes 'setting performance targets, managing the area's resources and ensuring that area governors and senior managers work effectively together' (HM Prison Service HON 45/2001). They manage governors 'to ensure that the Prison Service's strategy, contained in its Corporate and Business Plans, is delivered in each establishment' (ibid.). Two of the current total of 14 area managers are women.

Area managers visit the establishments in their area about every six weeks (they have a target of eight visits a year). During each visit, the area managers discuss performance-related issues with the governor. Area managers will arrive equipped: that is, knowing how the establishment is 'doing on the performance scale'. They will have detailed data on KPIs, KPTs, finance, and personnel through the available management information systems (PUMIS—Prisons Unified Management Information System). They will satisfy themselves about progress being made towards audit standards compliance. They normally walk around the prison, sometimes with the governor, and sometimes quite deliberately without, to test out the 'health of the prison', to check the governor's account, pick up concerns from staff and prisoners, and to soak up the atmosphere: are there high levels of discontent, is it busy, and so on? Each visit results in a written report with action points. Area managers arguably focus on the 'measurables'; there will be limits on the extent to which they can know what is going on in their establishments

---

[18] The first functional area manager role was created in 1995 in order to improve accountability in the maximum security estate via a newly established High Security Directorate, following the escapes from Whitemoor and Parkhurst (Home Office 1994, 1995). The area managers for juveniles and women's establishments were created in response to a recognition of their different needs, brought to the Prison Service's attention by (amongst other things) two HMCIP thematic reviews. See HMCIP (1997c, 1997d).

outside of this framework. They hold governors accountable, providing support and encouragement where appropriate, but making it clear that targets have to be met.

They also meet in Prison Service Headquarters in London twice a week to discuss policy, meet with the Deputy Director General in regular bilaterals, and hold themed reviews on policy-related subjects of interest and concern.

Laming argued in 2000 that the role of the area manager was crucial, but ineffective (Home Office 2000). His critique, and the determination of senior management to establish 'a firm grip', has led to considerable attention being focused on their role. Discussion and review of this has continued since its inception in 1990, when they replaced their predecessors, regional directors. The regional management structure had been developed originally because governors were thought to be too isolated from Headquarters (Dickinson 2002; see also Home Office 1979; Prison Service 1997). The problem with the first regional structure, under which four regional directors were based in their areas, was that as natural operational players, most 'went native' and were therefore also regarded as remote from Headquarters. Their successors (three operational directors) were located in London, together with the first generation of area managers. Area managers were relocated to their geographical areas during the last reorganization in 2001. These moves represent an attempt to achieve the right balance between operational oversight and policy responsibility. The key issue at this level of management has always been how to ensure both operational effectiveness (i.e. making sure that governors are operating effectively) and relevant policy input (which requires that area managers spend sufficient time at Headquarters to be part of the policy shaping process). There are complex questions about the delineation between policy and operations, as illustrated in Chapter 1. For example, once a policy instruction is 'released into the field', where does responsibility lie for ensuring that it is effected? When disasters have occurred within establishments (i.e. the high profile escapes of 1994–5, or major disturbances), the question of the nature and extent of the personal accountability of area managers has arisen (see Home Office 1994, 1995, 2000; also Prison Service 1997). Can an area manager be held accountable for shortcomings in establishments? If so, then what does this say of the role of the governor?

This process of building operational knowledge more systematically into the policy-making process, whilst allowing area managers to provide effective oversight of performance in individual prisons, was under way at the time of writing. Laming argued that:

The managerial responsibilities of the Area Managers should be clearly defined and they should be held personally accountable for the performance of each prison in their areas. Specialist staff should be relocated from Headquarters to their areas to enable the Area Managers to fulfil their new and demanding duties. (Home Office 2000: 29)

Dickinson pointed out, in her interview-based study of the role of area managers, that unlike chief constables, with whom they might naturally be compared, area managers have a relatively low public profile (Dickinson 2002; also Reiner 1992). As far as prison staff are concerned, the individual who 'matters most' is their governor. Prison officers are often rather vague about who their area manager is, although some clearly acquire reputations ('Oh, you mean Mr Calculator?').[19] Some area managers see their role as mainly advisory, others assume considerable authority. Derek Lewis argued, following his frustrating experience as Director General, that: 'Some Governors claimed that the 1952 Prison Act gave them freedom of action and immunity from instruction from their bosses, and some Area Managers behaved as though they believed that to be the case' (Lewis 1997: 78).

Since Derek Lewis was removed from his post in 1995, and the Deputy Director General has taken on stringent line-management responsibility for area managers, governors are described, sometimes cynically by prison staff, as 'looking upwards'. However, this change of style is regarded by many as both a constraint and an improvement. In Dickinson's study, many governors reported that they found strong line management by their area managers supportive; and that, conversely, a 'hands-off' style could be regarded as a lack of interest (Dickinson 2002). Others complained that area managers acted as 'super-governors', were too controlling, and that the performance culture raised anxiety and implied blame (ibid. 62). Governors differ, then, in their relationships with, and attitudes

---

[19] Many prison officers may also be vague about who the Director General is. Their main concern is with *their* prison.

towards, their area manager. Area managers manage the performance of the governors (or rather, the performance of the prisons in
which these governors work) much more closely than they used
to.[20] Let us look next at this key role within each of the five establishments in our study.

The Role of the Governor and the Nature of Governing

> No organisation is perfect, omnicompetent, in control of its envi-
> ronment. But few deserve more scrutiny and more commitment
> to be as meaningful to the society it serves than the organisation
> which takes liberty away from its citizens ... Instead of having
> yet another external change agent drive internal reform, let's
> drive internally toward an outward-looking, connecting Service.
>
> (Rimmer [Prison Governor] 2000: 27)

> The brutality which is sometimes shown to the prisoner by the
> warder is often only a reproduction of the brutality which the gov-
> ernor exhibits to the warder; and the brutality of the governor is
> often the result of the brutality of the Commissioners to him.
>
> (Morrison, cited in McConville 1998: 712)

Prison governors undoubtedly perform the key leadership role in a
prison. They are one of the prison's three statutory post-holders
(Prisons Act 1957(1)), the others being the chaplain and the medical officer. They are the visible, accountable 'keepers of the prison',
and as far as prison staff are concerned, they matter more than anyone else. The 'number one' is the one who counts: the figurehead,
for whom everything should be 'right'. The role of the governor has
changed with the onset of managerialism, financial accounting, and
perhaps especially performance measurement, since the days of
charismatic 'mavericks' and individual 'fiefdoms' described by
Jacobs during the 1950s and by Adler and Longhurst and others
during the late 1980s (Jacobs 1977; Adler and Longhurst 1994;

[20] The Prison Service has been asking itself, for example, partly as a result of
repeated Inspectorate criticism, how specific instances of staff brutality at several
local and young offender establishments during 1998–2001 went apparently unno-
ticed by area managers. One reason might be that staff attitudes and brutality are
not in any way indicated by poor performance on any existing targets (HMCIP
2001*d*; see also Ch. 2).

Scottish Prison Service 1990; Barak-Glantz 1981: 47). Governors have to be financially aware, and prepared to work to agreed targets, many of which are set nationally and the remainder of which may be negotiated with area managers. The nature of governing has become more 'business-like' and more focused on targets and outcomes. Professional accountants now play a major role in senior management teams (see Barak-Glantz 1981: 45–7). Some governors have described the modern role as rather like the role of a 'chief executive', combining management with leadership (McDonnell 2000). In private prisons the leadership role is given the title 'Director' (and is, in practice, usually filled by ex-Prison Service governors).

Governors are accountable for what happens in their establishments. They have to devise and develop strategy, manage systems, and control a tightly constrained budget, a shift in focus which has resulted in: 'A reduction in the direct management of prisoners by governors. Governors have been forced to limit the amount of time they spend conducting adjudications, hearing applications and touring the prison. The days of the "hands on" governor who knew the names of all their prisoners and staff are long gone' (Bryans 2000: 7).

This sentiment has some basis in reality, but, put as above, may constitute a romantic view of how the majority of governors behaved in the past, as well as a naïve view of how increasingly large and complex prisons can be managed. It also omits any account of the dismal history of prison quality and management throughout most of the twentieth century, and the weak accountability that modern managerialist approaches seek to address. There are problems with performance management, as argued in Chapter 2, particularly when 'the tenor is one of smooth management rather than moral mission' (Rutherford 1993: 13). One of its unintended side-effects is to increase levels of competitiveness between governors and to reduce co-operation between establishments seeking to preserve their own performance targets. We agree with Bryans's case that 'humanitarian managerialism' (i.e. management 'in the service of human rights or other liberal and humanitarian goals') is to be preferred to managerialism as an end in itself (Bryans 2000; see also Cavadino *et al.* 1999; Raine and Willson 1995). Governors and staff want to be part of a 'genuinely *values-driven organisation*' (Rimmer 2000: 26; emphasis in original). Wilson has argued that an important but less clearly articulated part of the role of the governor is to 'fashion and reshape an essentially punitive structure into one that [is] positive and optimistic' (Wilson 2000: 12). There is increasing talk of the need for governors to be 'morally resilient', to constitute the 'secular conscience of the establishment', to set the moral tone and shape the organizational culture of the establishment (Wilson 2000):

We need pretty sophisticated managers. We are very short of cash, so governors have to be very good in terms of managerial skills, at being financial, human resource managers. They need to be very good at planning, but on top of those things, which you might replicate in a hospital, every governor has a job of moral leadership, setting the tone in saying what will and will not be acceptable. And sometimes doing that when overcrowding is increasing, when money is very short, when it almost looks as if you're about to be overwhelmed ... that's when you need moral resilience ... (Narey 2002)[21]

This aspiration was often impossible to deliver in practice, in a climate of increasing population growth, staffing shortages, cell sharing, transfers to obscure locations, and a lack of facilities for suicidal prisoners:

Two of my governors have written to me recently, saying, 'You've talked an awful lot about morality since you've been the DG, and now you're making me do things of which I am ashamed ...' My response to them has been, that's why morality is even more important. It would be so easy under those circumstances [e.g. overcrowding] to let it go and I think that's what makes the job different. (Narey 2002)[22]

It has been argued, in the past, that the Prison Service has been short of outstanding governors, by which critics mean governors with well-developed business and 'person management' skills. Rutherford's 'Credo Three' practitioners are sometimes seen as in conflict with 'Credo Two' practitioners (Wilson 2000; Rutherford

---

[21] However, too much emphasis on 'setting the tone' without attention to strategy can be disastrous. See Jacobs (1977: 89).

[22] One of the governors asked to read a draft of this chapter commented that the importance of resources should not be underestimated: 'Governors are not magicians and if they don't have the buildings, facilities or (crucially) the people, then moral performance will be affected ... what you can achieve is unquestionably reduced' (pers. comm.).

1993). One way of addressing this shortage of talent in management skills has been to operate an accelerated promotion scheme for graduate entrants and talented staff. Over half of the graduates of this scheme in recent years have been women.

It is possible to detect a distinction between older and younger generations of governors, with governors recruited and trained 'in the old days' (i.e. those who attended the pre-managerialist version of the assistant governors' course) more likely to express idealistic aspirations and slightly more liberal perspectives, and younger (new generation) governors more likely to speak the language of performance.[23] Using Adler and Longhurst's characterization, more prison governors of older generations might have belonged in the 'professionalism–rehabilitation' cell of their means–ends discourse matrix, and more younger prison governors could be characterized as belonging in the 'bureaucracy–control' cell of this matrix today (see Adler and Longhurst 1994: 44–7).[24]

Older generation governors seem more likely to concern themselves with (or speak the language of) changing individuals, than with 'improving systems'. Governors sometimes describe themselves as 'not systems people' to emphasize their interest in the lives and futures of individual prisoners (and see Jacobs 1977: 89).[25]

At the Prison Service Conference 2000, Phil Wheatley, then Deputy Director General, described the role of the governor as 'the key senior manager'. He argued that the role could be divided into

[23] Although in practice 'the new breed may actually be more likely to change people . . . as a result of their more effective management' (pers. comm.). See similar characterizations from a different era throughout Stateville (e.g. Jacobs 1977: 89). Jacobs's 'new administrators' are our 'old school' variety.

[24] A survey carried out by the Prison Governors' Association of its then 1,080 members (90% of eligible governor grades) achieved a (low) response rate of 25%. Of those who responded, 30% had degrees; 40% had worked through the ranks; and the remainder (19%) were from the APS scheme, and 18% from one of the old AG Training schemes. Nine per cent were direct entrants or had transferred from other positions and organisations (PGA 2002). The Prison Governors' Association was established in 1988, to represent the interests of prison governors. It publishes a magazine (*The Key*) and has a manifesto calling for constructive regimes, an end to prison privatization, and a reduced prison population. See www.prisongovernors.org.uk.

[25] The role of the deputy governor is important, too, and in some cases 'the dep' may have (or develop) strengths the governor lacks. This role may be especially important in large prisons (such as Belmarsh, Wandsworth, and Doncaster). For significant periods (leave, official duties elsewhere, sickness) the dep *is* the governor.

three main components: first, 'organising the internal environment'. This included ensuring discipline, control, and security; staff recruitment, leadership, and motivation; communication and industrial relations; and the maintenance and development of the prison and its regime. Secondly, the role involved 'managing processes and outputs'. This involved setting and achieving targets; decision-making; budget management; using management information effectively; and driving and controlling change. Governors' effectiveness would be measured by how successfully they could organize their establishment's human and other resources to achieve these targets. The third component of the role was 'managing the external environment'. This included representing the prison to the wider public; forming working relationships with other agencies; and keeping alert to changes in the wider political, social, and economic environment (the local economy is influential in staff recruitment and retention, for example). This outward-looking part of the role had grown, and required sensitivity to the political climate as well as an awareness of the power and role of the media. These tasks were all accomplished with the aid of the rest of the senior management team, but again, despite the fact that incoming governors usually inherited a team not of their choosing, the governor's competence tended to be judged by how effectively the whole team operated.[26]

To achieve all of the above well required 'clarity about the prison's direction', an effective mode of communication with staff, a 'firm and decisive' style, a sharp eye for resources, and important personal qualities, such as resilience, persistence, and 'integrity' (Wheatley 2000, *passim*). Governors needed to be visible, consistent, and knowledgeable, and they needed to be respected (and regarded as competent) rather than 'likeable' (see Tyler and Blader 2000). Being likeable was an added bonus, if all the other requirements were met, but, on its own, could be a positive hazard. One senior manager summed up the role as follows: 'It's not mechanistic. What a governor's got to do is find all the energy and get it all pointing in the right direction' (senior manager, pers. comm.).

By 2001 the message had become firmer. Governors had to exert their legitimate authority. Tackling poor performing prisons was

---

[26] This required developing a team, and sometimes bringing people in, with complementary skills, placing individuals in appropriate roles, making sure each individual was clear about their role, and so on. The ability to create and motivate an effective senior management team was an important skill.

'operationally . . . very hard work' (Narey 2001: 4). As Narey said in his challenging speech to the Prison Service Conference:

> Overwhelmingly your response to the demands has been magnificent. You have delivered more for less at prison after prison. But I acknowledge that at some places the challenge facing individual governors appeared . . . to be too much and we have moved governors on . . . I know that I am asking a lot. I know the job used to be easier. I know the job used to be more fun. But I also know that we used to tolerate inhumanity. (Narey 2001: 5–7)

The demands have been extraordinary. Partly as a result of the rapid changes in ideology outlined in the introductory chapter, but partly also as a result of the highly visible and politically sensitive nature of penal policy, far too much policy activity (i.e. change and development) goes on at Headquarters. As Carlen found in her study of governors' views about life above them, and as the Learmont Report pointed out bluntly (Home Office 1995: 103), establishments end up with:

> An overload of managerialist baggage from different eras, with a proliferation of objectives and tasks going way beyond the functional and financial capacity of prisons, and with accretions of paperwork . . . that made several respondents pessimistic about the Service's capacity for coherent and consistent policy implementation—as opposed to piecemeal responses to political whim. (Carlen 2002a: 35)

Certainly the feeling in contemporary prisons is of 'constant change and managerialist overload', and of fragmentation of policy initiative (Carlen 2002a: 35; Bottoms 1995). There is considerable cynicism about 'Headquarters' and a cultural divide between 'operational' and 'policy' people, despite some movement across this gulf (see Pollitt and Bouckaert 2000).[27] An ongoing review (*Reinventing the Centre*) seeks to streamline, strengthen, and improve the role of Headquarters (Prison Service 2002c). This review aims to bring about a 'slimmer', more effective and 'responsive' structure, with clear central direction,

---

[27] In Pollitt and Bouckaert's international comparative study of attempts by governments to change the culture of their civil services in the interests of modern managerialism, the UK is characterized as a self-styled 'world leader' in reform, that has made modest progress (Pollitt and Bouckaert 2000, esp. chs. 4 and 5). Ferlie *et al.* suggest that the UK change process may have been 'top down' and 'power led' (Ferlie *et al.* 1996: 22).

but with the intention of reducing the amount of detailed prescription from the centre (Prison Service 2002c).[28]

The governor in late modernity is situated uncomfortably between the pressure for change 'downwards' and the complex social organization into which he or she walks. Governors have only a limited range of disciplinary and motivational tools available to them, and an equally limited range of situational measures (e.g. the redeployment elsewhere in the prison of unsuitable staff) at their disposal. It is no wonder that other sources of compliance (or motivation), for example their moral and leadership approach, take on such significance in this complex social world, as we shall see (and further, Bottoms 2002: 29–38).[29]

The Prison Officers' Association

> Managing a complex Industrial Relations climate requires as much ability and strength of character as managing difficult prisoners.
>
> (Bryans and Wilson 2000: 88)

This study has not looked in any detail at the role of the Prison Officers' Association (for a brief history, see Liebling and Price 2001: 161–70).[30] It is fair to say that the role of the POA historically has been very important in placing constraints on modernization (see e.g. Home Office 1979; Rock 1996: 267–73, 320–43; Lewis 1997; Home Office 1991a, para. 13.230). The POA has traditionally been a powerful trade union which has taken industrial action on a number of occasions, usually with damaging effects (King and McDermott 1995: 36–7; Home Office 1987). Their motto is 'unity in strength' (see website, below). There are frequent disputes between the POA and managers over staffing levels, pay rises, and the use of privatization and performance testing, but it is

---

[28] This review was announced in response to resource constraints, and criticisms from the field that too many initiatives, some of which conflicted with each other, were emanating from a remote headquarters (see Carlen 2002a; also Prison Service 1997).

[29] Bottoms argues that these mechanisms *interact* and that 'among the principal mechanisms underpinning . . . compliance [of which legitimacy is a subtype] normative compliance can be said to occupy a pivotal position' (Bottoms 2002: 33). He also suggests, however, that 'the normative dimension is also the one that is least obviously deliverable by technical and managerialist approaches' (Bottoms 2002: 45). See p. 491.

[30] For an account of their role and membership, see www.poauk.org.uk.

also clearly the case that, compared to the 1970s and 1980s, prisons operate in a considerably changed industrial relations climate.

The vast majority of prison staff are members of the POA (although in some establishments there may be alternative organizations, such as the Prison Service Union, on offer). Staff say they join unions mainly for legal protection, but the more active members and officials clearly see their role as protecting the working conditions of prison officers against infringement by managers. It is well established that the Conservative government of 1979–97 had, as part of its aim, the reduction of trade union power through increased private sector involvement in industry.

The culture or climate of a prison is influenced to a significant extent by the activities and perspectives of local POA branches, as well as by aspects of the working environment described earlier. The local industrial relations climate can vary considerably, from the co-operative to the intransigent (Tallentire 2002). The 'collective working personality' of staff in individual prisons may be shaped by national and local POA attitudes. There are 'subcultures' (e.g. on different wings or among specialist groups), but there is also an identifiable 'way we do things around here' in most prisons (Bryans and Wilson 2000: 76). It is possible that there exists a roughly proportionate relationship between the extent of POA resistance to change and the degree of negative attitudes held towards managers, and sometimes prisoners.[31] A certain amount of 'cultural indoctrination' takes place on residential training courses (Bryans and Wilson 2000: 76; and Arnold forthcoming) and then newly trained officers are more or less assimilated into the culture of the first establishment in which they work. There are many other reasons for prison officer resistance to change besides unionization, which include a tradition-oriented investment in 'what worked yesterday', as argued above. In a volatile prison environment, staff are naturally reluctant to trust in abstract, future-oriented strategies which bear little resemblance to their own concerns to make it peacefully through the day (see Liebling and Price 2001: 173, and chapter 7; Jacobs and Crotty 1978; Bottoms 1995).

---

[31] Duffee suggests that the officer subculture is antagonistic to the policy and values of senior management, but that the nature of this subculture is directly related to the way in which officers perceive themselves to be managed (Duffee 1974). A subculture, he argues, arises as a 'group response to commonly felt conflict' (Duffee 1974: 156).

Governors' handling of POA matters is clearly relevant to their success. Several initiatives have 'tamed' the traditionally resistant POA and increased managerial power (e.g. the removal of the right to strike, then its reinstatement, but alongside increased use of the Advisory, Conciliation, and Arbitration Service (ACAS) in partnership agreements, and private sector competition). This apparent 'breaking of the spell' (Bryans and Wilson 2000: 85) depends to some extent on who the elected officials are at any one time. The current position is, some would say, 'progressive' (pers. comm.). Official statements (e.g. recent Corporate Plans) declare a commitment to building trust, increasing consultation, and resolving disputes at local level. We shall see briefly below how this formal position works in practice.

Staff–Governor Relationships in Five Prisons

It seems to be the case that establishments require different governing styles at different stages, depending on the specific management priorities of the time (e.g. a 'failing prison' may need a much tougher approach than a well-performing prison). Some prisons are more difficult to manage than others. The language of 'difficult prisons' and 'failing prisons' acknowledges this, and may explain why several of the prisons in our sample had the particular governors they had: three prisons had relatively newly arrived governors, each of whom had been carefully picked for the post. It was interesting to learn, in discussions with senior managers about the prisons in our study: 'You may have a good spread of prisons, you have got a good range of performance there. But in [three of the prisons in our study], you have probably got three of the best young governors in the Service' (pers. comm.).

The governors of the five prisons (and the relationships they had with their staff) were all quite different. Belmarsh was governed by a young female, who had come to Belmarsh from a maximum security prison in the north-east of England on promotion. She was the first female governor of a high security prison—a fact that some of her staff held against her. Holme House was governed by an older, male governor, who showed no sign of moving on, and who expressed a quiet pride in his establishment and his staff. Risley was governed by a young, 'high flier' governor who was known to be tough, and whose brief when he arrived was to 'turn this failing prison around'. Doncaster (a private prison) had, unusually, been managed by the same male director for eight years, since it had opened in 1994. This symbol of loyalty was appreciated by staff, who shared the 'family-oriented approach' their director favoured.[32] Wandsworth was governed by a newly arrived, young, male, very well-regarded governor, who was to achieve promotion, and therefore a transfer, towards the end of our study. He stayed for just two years.[33]

All of these office-holders had significant strengths. Three were regarded as especially bright; and as young, capable, energetic people with successful careers ahead of them. Two were regarded as 'solid performers', who were very loyal to their establishments. Some of the concerns expressed by staff about 'their governors' were linked to 'governors in general', but their comments were also linked to aspects of their governors' personal style. So, for example, one governor was seen as 'too remote, emotionally', and another was seen as 'too prisoner-oriented'. One establishment seemed to be yearning for 'stronger, tougher leadership', where another was yearning for 'a gentler touch'. There was a complexity to the 'establishment-leadership fit', then, whereby different governing styles might suit different types of establishment at different stages in their evolution. How staff and prisoners regarded governors depended a great deal on where the establishment was in its development, who had held the post before, how long they were likely to stay, and what their reputations were like.

Staff declared, on the one hand, that 'governors come and go', and that they brought their 'pet issue' with them, for a while—as if they were only peripherally relevant to the establishment's continuing life. On the other hand, governors did matter. There was something of a parental yearning in staff, to the extent that one prisoner described staff as 'orphans, looking for a father figure'. Staff wanted a governor to provide leadership, direction, security, and a sense of worth. They had a symbolic importance, which outstripped

[32] The longer duration of this director's leadership was not an inherent characteristic of privately managed prisons, although we are aware of other cases where directors have stayed for fairly long periods (more than four years). This may be due to the length of time taken for new contracts to be won.

[33] The three 'high flier' governors had moved on (all on promotion) by the time we had completed our research. Another governor was moved 'sideways' to sort out problems in another establishment. The governor of the fifth establishment in our study was also moved to a new position at the time of writing.

any individual judgement officers may have made about their competence in the varied roles they were expected to play. Governors embodied authority, and had to be seen to be prepared to use it (e.g. at adjudications). Trust in governors was shaped in part, just as it was by prisoners in staff, by judgements made about competence, fairness, ethicality, and opportunities to be heard (see Chapter 6). These judgements were, in turn, influenced by what kinds of power governors used, and the ways in which they used such power (see Chapter 7; and Gilbert 1997). Coercive power was often used in relation to procedures that were auditable, and was more likely to be used by governors of struggling establishments. Expert power was increasingly used, as governors became the experts in vision, direction, and strategy, and staff were partly discouraged from trusting in their own old ways. Reward power was rarely used, as governors had limited rewards available to them. The management tone was set at an organizational level by the language of 'tackling failing prisons' and 'robust leadership' (see Chapter 1). Rather like the policy on IEP for prisoners, it was somehow easier and more urgent for the 'stick' part of policy to be implemented than the 'carrot' part (Liebling *et al.* 1997; Bottoms 2003*b*).

We found the three governors in the more difficult prisons in our study struggling to various degrees with their senior management teams, trying to ease out 'unhealthy influences' and bring in, or empower, those with the most energy, ability, and credibility. Each of these teams reported conflict ('power struggles') within the senior management team at the time we arrived, for example, between 'the old guard' and the 'new revolutionaries'. The slightest sign of such divisions gave staff the ability to resist or undermine change, by playing to or seeking the support of different senior management audiences. Coherence (at least 'in public') was crucial. Staff generally understood and were knowledgeable about what was going on at senior management level. They registered every tension, and detected every weak link (rather as prisoners did, with staff). Confidence, then, was also crucial.

Governors struggled to tackle 'lazy and incompetent staff', to use disciplinary procedures against them, or to 'tackle poor performance', and often their judgement in particular cases was challenged by staff. Officers were collectively sensitive about such practices, despite often saying to us (e.g. in our workgroup exercises) that there was nothing they wanted more than to 'ease out the poor performers', and to be surrounded by reliable colleagues.[34] This might be one example where staff held a genuinely conflicted position (see G. Morgan 1997, chapter 7). Staff wanted, almost above all else, to *matter* to governors, and this was judged on both individual and collective levels. The robust treatment of their colleagues (even if they were performing poorly) was experienced by staff as a rebuff. Staff were collectively particularly sensitive to any sign or statement that indicated that 'prisoners matter more than we do'. They were sensitive, in other words, to whether or not they felt treated with respect. But this was extraordinarily difficult to achieve for individual governors in an environment where they might have over 500 staff and in a climate where individual (or departmental) poor performance was being challenged.

Governors needed to establish and retain legitimacy in the eyes of staff, in a complex environment with serious external constraints and demands, and this was difficult. They also had to exert a considerable level of managerial control and direction, particularly where the prison was not performing well, and this often meant moving staff 'in the right direction', away from practices they wanted to defend. Belmarsh was an interesting example of this, where staff were 'over-achieving on security' and wanted to be 'better than the security manual'. Other aspects of prison life (the 'prisoner management bits') were subordinated to this goal. Staff were untrusting of senior management (and, in two of our prisons, said they trusted prisoners more than senior managers—a response they noticed with alarm as they completed our questionnaires). Considerable cultural 'suspicion of senior management', in the two large London prisons in particular, made it especially difficult for governors to 'win staff over'. The governor of Wandsworth clearly made some headway, with his very visible, inclusive style. For example, he persuaded 16 staff, including a key member of the POA, to become involved with us in an AI or 'best practice development process' (see Liebling *et al.* 2001; Rimmer 2002). Staff changed their shifts, cancelled their leave, and showed 'an amazing level of responsiveness', because they wanted to see, and be part of,

---

[34] Staff in one establishment expressed awareness that they 'colluded' with lack of respect towards prisoners, and with poor performance, and said that the culture made it very difficult to challenge other staff. Similar points were made in two of the other prisons.

the prison's improvement.[35] Comparisons we were able to make with an earlier survey showed that some progress was clearly made over the 18 months of his reign (Liebling and Arnold 2002). The governor was quite quickly promoted in 2001, leaving staff confirmed in their rather cynical original position: 'We are just a stepping stone', and 'managers take the credit for good officer work. That's how it works in industry'. This echoed feelings expressed in other prisons: 'This prison is *used*, as a means to an end. The governors have no long-term commitment to the place. There's no loyalty between staff and prisoners. No trust' (officer). 'There's a very big divide between uniform and suits here' (officer).

We see here an unintended consequence of the kinds of tensions between modernization and the *moral identity of the person* that we began with in this chapter, and which has emerged as a theme throughout the book. The human consequences of the new workplace include a feeling expressed by many working people that highly prized values of trust, respect, commitment, loyalty, and security, which are inherently in short supply in the prison, are seriously under threat. As we have argued throughout, these values have an instrumental value (without legitimacy, workers will not work) but also a deontological value. They need inserting into the apparently actuarial language of prison and other organizational management in the sense intended here (i.e. in relation to the treatment of workers by managers) as well as in the sense intended by recent analyses of 'public service' (i.e. in relation to the provision of efficient and effective services to clients).

Perhaps for some of the reasons outlined above, it was easier for senior managers to give in to staff than to manage them firmly. Managers who used staff appraisal ratings carefully (i.e. avoiding over-use of the category 'exceeded') were regarded as bullies. The transition from a 'lazy management culture' to a demanding and robust one caused considerable organizational anxiety. Staff felt—sometimes with reason (it was not always clear how policies worked in practice) and sometimes for other reasons—that 'governors don't know what they are doing'. Staffing shortages, and accumulated 'time owed', added to this feeling that unreasonable

---

[35] On the other hand, a second POA member declined the invitation, with thanks, because (as he explained to us) he was 'afraid of being sucked in to the governor's agenda'.

demands were being made, that staff continually made 'impossible requests work', and that only problem staff came to senior management's attention. Staff disliked not feeling trusted by senior management, particularly when they saw themselves as 'decent, hard-working honest people', doing the job for security and a wage. They particularly resented the feeling that senior managers 'only came on to the wing to pick holes in us'. Their wish was for senior managers to 'train us and trust us', and 'give people more to aim for'. Very occasionally, staff saw that 'governors are under pressure too and they need results' (principal officer). A specific recruitment and retention problem was being faced by London prisons at the time of our research. Staff felt attention was focused on 'the deficits', and they did not always understand why a change of direction was needed: 'We are the second-best London prison after Pentonville. The way we care for people needs tweaking, not an overhaul' (officer).

The sheer size of prisons like Wandsworth and Belmarsh made it very difficult for governors to communicate effectively to staff. Where governors did try to communicate to staff collectively, for example at full staff meetings, there were inevitably rows of uniformed officers who 'stood at the back' looking cynical. Staff had a 'collective position' on senior managers, and understood each other more readily than they understood their somewhat distant governors. The strong bonds between staff were, as we suggested above, partly related to the nature of the job, and concerns for safety: 'I will put my life in danger for my mates, but not for the governor' (officer). This kind of solidarity or mutual loyalty is a crucial part of what it means to be a prison officer, and whilst it has advantages and a functional utility, it means that the risks for governors of 'governing-at-a-distance' are considerable.

Staff were (quite deliberately) 'not easily impressed' by anyone not wearing a uniform (this included researchers like us). They thought governors understood very little about 'how things work on the wing', and there were particularly strong views about young, 'non-operational' governors, with 'hardly any time in': 'They should have two types of governors. Your APS people,[36] who can do finances and budgets; and your residential people, who should come up through the ranks, who've got "jailcraft"' (senior officer).

[36] Accelerated Promotion Scheme.

These feelings were understandable in the light of the importance of experience, and 'practical consciousness' in the work of prison officers (see Chapter 6). In practice, governors were often unfairly stereotyped, and were sometimes fatally judged by early 'mistakes'. One serious blunder (usually signifying a lack of regard for staff) could lead to a significant legitimacy deficit that was difficult to make up (see Bottoms 2002: 39). Officers had very little under-standing of the constraints under which governors operated. There was, as we have noted before, a particular tension between the sight and time horizons of staff (the wing, and the end of this shift, respectively) and those of senior managers (the establishment, the area, and the end of the financial year—or the next inspection or audit). Officers and managers also had different goals, staff priori-tizing today's peace, and governors prioritizing this year's targets. This placed an in-built tension into relationships between staff and senior managers, and may have explained why each group felt as though they were failing to communicate effectively to the other.

Table 8.1 shows that staff relationships with each other were positively related to their relationships with senior managers on the whole. It shows that relations among staff are manifestly cohesive (as Duffee suggested; Duffee 1974).[37] If we rank each prison on its relationships among staff, and staff relationships with senior man-agers (using positive responses), we see that Doncaster had good relationships among senior managers and with director grades. Holme House had slightly lower levels of officers saying they had a good relationship with their officer colleagues, but higher levels saying they had quite good relationships with senior managers. Belmarsh staff reported very good relationships with each other but less favourable relationships with senior managers. Risley staff reported the least 'good' relationships with staff (although still very high, at 59.2 per cent, responding 'very good'), but relatively poor relationships with senior managers.

---

[37] As we stated in Chapter 3, our interviews with staff were less structured. Although we did use a structured questionnaire, we did so tentatively as the project was primarily intended to develop a prisoner survey. The questionnaire was not standardized and the numbers of staff included were relatively small. We therefore draw on these results selectively and do not attempt to pursue any complex analy-ses. We have done so in work arising from this study and will report on this in future publications.

TABLE 8.1. Staff relationships with colleagues, line managers, and senior managers

Question (relationships)	Belmarsh	Holme House	Risley	Doncaster	Wandsworth
1. Do you feel you have a good relationship with officer colleagues?	(3)	(4)	(5)	(1)	(2)
Very good	73.7	66.7	59.2	84.8	82.4
Quite good	26.3	25.0	28.6	12.1	17.6
OK	0	8.3	4.1	3.0	0
Quite poor	0	0	6.1	0	0
Very poor	0	0	0	0	0
2. Do you feel you have a good relationship with management?	(2)	(3)	(5)	(4)	(1)
Very good	42.1	45.8	30.6	33.3	35.3
Quite good	42.1	37.5	36.7	39.4	52.9
OK	15.8	12.5	20.4	21.2	11.8
Quite poor	0	0	10.2	3.0	0
Very poor	0	4.2	2.0	3.0	0
3. Do you feel you have a good relationship with governor grades?	(5)	(2)	(4)	(1)	(3)
Very good	0	20.8	12.2	24.2	17.6
Quite good	21.1	33.3	24.5	33.3	23.5
OK	26.3	37.5	38.8	18.2	35.3
Quite poor	26.3	8.3	14.3	12.1	17.6
Very poor	26.3	0	8.2	12.1	5.9

Note: Ranking in parentheses.

Tables 8.1 and 8.2 show that staff at Doncaster, closely followed by staff at Holme House, had fairly positive feelings about their treatment by senior managers. Staff at Belmarsh were particularly negative at the time of our research, although rather like prisoners at Holme House, they were prepared to say they were treated reasonably fairly, despite low levels of perceived respect, value, and trust (Table 8.2). Even at Doncaster, trusting senior managers was uncommon. Staff at Wandsworth and Risley gave rather mixed replies. They were not completely alienated, but they were not comfortable either.[38]

TABLE 8.2.   Staff perceptions of treatment by senior managers (those agreeing 'very much' and 'quite a lot')

Statement (Relations with senior managers)	Belmarsh	Holme House	Risley	Doncaster	Wandsworth
1. Do you feel you are respected by senior managers?	0[b]	29.1	36.8	57.6[a]	41.2
2. Do you feel supported in your work by senior managers?	0[b]	29.2	30.6	42.4[a]	23.5
3. Overall, do you feel you are fairly treated by senior managers?	47.4	75.0[a]	61.1	60.6	41.1[b]
4. Do you feel you are valued as a member of staff by senior managers?	5.3[b]	33.3	36.8	51.5[a]	35.3
5. How much do you trust senior managers?	15.8[b]	41.7[a]	30.6	33.4	35.3

Note: Scores accompanied by the letter 'a' indicate the most positive score. Scores accompanied by the letter 'b' indicate the most negative.

The majority of staff said their primary loyalty was 'to their colleagues' (see Table 8.3). Duffee suggested that one of the 'favourite pastimes' of correctional officers was 'identifying dishonesty and hypocrisy in those above him' (sic), just as prisoners did (Duffee 1974: 155). Loyalties varied slightly at each establishment, so that staff at Doncaster and Risley were most committed to 'the prison';

---

[38] It is interesting to note that in Herzberg et al.'s studies of worker morale and motivation, feelings of unfairness appeared frequently in the 'low morale' stories: 'The individual became unhappy on the job because he perceived what had happened as an indication of a *lack of concern* that his superiors or the company in general had *for him as an individual*. Often this was a feeling that the company *lacked integrity*' (Herzberg et al. 2002: 76; emphasis added). This early work foreshadows the links between fairness, respect, and trust that emerged in our study, and illustrates the importance of these values to staff as well as to prisoners. As they conclude, 'the basic need of the worker is to be treated with dignity' (ibid. 108). The authors also show that examples of unfairness are easier to give than examples of fairness. Their analysis suggests that workers experience fairness as (or via) respect (ibid. 76–9).

and staff at Doncaster were noticeably more committed to 'the company' than prison staff at other prisons said they were to the Prison Service. Very few staff at any establishment were prepared to say their primary loyalty was 'to the governor', despite high levels of commitment to 'the prison' (see Table 8.3).

TABLE 8.3.   Staff commitment and loyalty

Question (Loyalty)	Belmarsh	Holme House	Risley	Doncaster	Wandsworth
1. To whom is your primary loyalty?					
The prison	10.5	16.7	18.4	21.2	17.6
The governor/the director	0	4.2	4.1	9.1	0
Officer colleagues	84.2	58.3	34.7	69.7	76.5
The Prison Service/ company	0	20.8	40.8	0	5.9
2. How committed are you to this prison?					
Very committed	52.6	66.7	55.1	72.7	64.7
Quite committed	36.8	25.0	38.8	21.2	29.4
Not very committed	5.3	8.3	4.1	6.1	5.9
Not committed at all	5.3	0	0	0	0
3. How committed are you to the Prison Service/Premier Prison Services?					
Very committed	36.8	41.7	55.1	21.2	17.6
Quite committed	36.8	45.8	38.8	33.3	58.8
Not very committed	10.5	12.5	4.1	30.3	23.5
Not committed at all	10.5	0	0	12.1	0

The Nature and Significance of Staff–Governor Relationships

Staff often behaved as though they were exclusively interested in material rewards, but, during our interviews, one of the striking themes was the very personal nature of their relationships with governors. If they were individually recognized, invited to do something, or involved in something that brought them into contact with governors, staff appreciated this, and one or two explained that they had been transformed by the experience:

I would have been a dinosaur—I was heading that way, the momentum was, if you like, to be a dinosaur. It is difficult to stand against this momentum without confidence, individuality, or time out. Then a senior manager just noticed that I had an interest. I was asked to take on suicide prevention. I suppose it was a bit of an honour . . . I found where my forte lies, and through supporting, recognizing, encouraging . . . That conversation changed the course of my career. (Principal officer)

Visibility was valued because staff felt recognized and appreciated if they were 'known' and relationships developed:

PRINCIPAL OFFICER. Visible management. Yes. I'm a firm believer in it. I can't quite say why, I just know it's important. If a wing is short, I'll do the job myself. It's really important to show that you're prepared to do any job you'd ask anyone else to do.

INTERVIEWER. Are you saying that this shows that your role is valuable, valued?

PRINCIPAL OFFICER. Yes. This is not a very visible management prison. We had an incident the other day, and it took a long time to find someone in charge. The senior managers don't seem to get out and about enough. When I go round, people ask if there's something wrong. That shouldn't happen. They think visibility is a bad sign.

INTERVIEWER. So it's a certain sort of visibility you are looking for?

PRINCIPAL OFFICER. Non-threatening.

Staff liked interest, of a generally supportive kind, albeit with high expectations (just as governors expressed quite favourable views about this kind of area manager). This is close to the meanings of 'trust' and 'respect' outlined in Chapter 5. They wanted to be provided with a clear agenda, and to *feel* that they were expected and encouraged to live up to high standards, but then they wanted to be 'trusted to deliver'; to be stretched, but only just. Lack of trust, in either direction, was destructive: 'Officers are distrusting of inmates, but managers are much more untrusting of staff' (officer).

Staff judged governors by their personal style, physical presence, level of visibility, orientation towards staff and prisoners, 'whether or not they know who you are', the key messages they communicate, and their apparent bargaining power with those above them. Reputations also shaped staff perceptions of incoming governors. They did notice whether or not their own establishment was doing well or badly in the performance league, and liked to feel they had a governor who was 'taking them forward'. Prison officers' greatest 'wish' was for: 'A clear, stable, strong senior management structure, with clear lines of accountability, and a visible management style' (officer, Wandsworth).

Officers used terms like 'determined leadership' and 'commitment' to express how they saw senior managers at their best. The values prized by 'the managed', in senior management, were: fairness, truthfulness, consistency, experience, communication, approachability, hard work, visibility, focus, supportive leadership, and decisiveness. Staff were demotivated by bullying, signs of any lack of truthfulness, and any indication that they did not matter as individuals. Apparently 'liberal preference' for prisoners was not prized. Those governors who solicited the support of their staff made it clear that staff were valued *and* that they were expected to provide a good service to prisoners.

Governors had to work out the sensitivities of their staff, and form a clear idea about how to tackle aspects of staff behaviour they wanted to change (see Sparks *et al.* 1996: 136). This was dangerous territory:

There's a willingness to do well here, everywhere. I'd say that's the majority. They are almost over-eager. But the picture is getting less rosy, the longer I am here. That's partly the nature of the job. What comes to your attention is what's not going well. I hear the worst of staff. I am becoming aware of a culture of the treatment of prisoners. It's a darker thread. It's a culture [this prison] created . . . it's like a mantra: 'my job is so difficult and dangerous I can't tell you my name'. They have created it. The use of C and R is very high. They almost push prisoners so they can C and R them. Things get 'paid back', at IEP reviews.[39] It is security with knobs on. But then the staff are a bit bitter. There is a lot of organizational anxiety. They are expressing a feeling of not being valued. Jobs in security are highly valued. It is a very difficult one to unpick. They are feeling challenged, bullied. The way they challenge management's power is to go sick. (Governor)[40]

Changing a recalcitrant prison meant challenging the staff over 'who's got the legitimate agenda' and, inevitably, in a stringent financial climate, asking staff to work in a new way, including more evenings and weekends: '[This] will impact on their quality of life.

---

[39] This meant that staff sometimes used a quasi-formal power to reduce a prisoner's privilege level for the wrong reasons, or in discriminatory ways.

[40] High levels of sick leave cause major difficulties for senior managers and for performance targets, but also for colleagues. 'Managing sick' is one example of a complex task involving individual judgement but inviting the application of an aggregate strategy. Sickness levels for each establishment, often taken to be an indication of the health of staff–management relationships, are included in Chapter 4. Private companies are not required to divulge this information.

There are fewer perks, they will be held accountable, they will be managed more rigorously. They know it's got to go this way ... ' (governor).

This meant that staff did have to understand the national agenda, and to accept the diagnosis when they were told: 'This prison has performed badly for most of its life. It has a well-known history of being POA-driven, so I have inherited an ambivalent, controversial approach to management. Most management initiatives have been seen off, or just not implemented' (governor).

However, unlike the two London locals, where both staff–management and staff–prisoner relations were mixed, at Risley: 'They have comfortable relationships between staff and prisoners. There is little challenging of offending behaviour, but there's a *laissez-faire* approach. There's nothing coherent' (governor).

Staff and prisoners were united in what looked to the governor like apathy. He had been charged by his seniors with challenging this. Relations with the governor at Risley, then, were tense, and, for the first time, there had been an 'imposed solution to a failure to agree' issued by the POA. The governor had the full and active support of his area manager and the Deputy Director General, but his was a lonely and demanding task. Staff told us individually that 'his vision for the future gives staff hope'. But collectively, they were more sceptical, and they noted every confrontation. Effective communication was very difficult:

I have tried appealing to reason, and to hearts and minds. I have used emotional language. I have asked them to look behind the suit, at me the man, trying to do a job. Even some of the management team are locked into how Risley is. It's like they are in an alliance to maintain the status quo. There's a question about whether Risley will survive in the public sector. It is one of the worst performing cat C's around. So it's in the firing line. Threat has been the only effective tool. (Governor)

But threats were experienced as coercive and alienating. Staff were deeply anxious about the changes being made, and were divided amongst themselves. 'Rumour control' played a powerful role in the prison. Those who were willing were sensitive to being stereotyped as 'the resistant enemy' by management. Officers described being 'chastised by colleagues' for 'liking prisoners', and being 'punished and ridiculed' for finding drugs. Many staff saw the governor as 'a bit confrontational', although 'his plans for the prison are good' and 'things are no longer swept under the carpet'. Staff respected him, liked the fact that he was 'tackling sick and corruption'. They understood that he was under pressure from those above him. He was 'the prison's saviour, cutting edge . . . but he's the devil incarnate': 'We need a sea change for survival. We've got to make it work. Staff want to make the changes but not have the evening duties. There is no time for luxury and there's no alternative' (governor).

Many of the staff felt 'it's only a matter of time before we are privatized'. They said, 'we are not a service anymore, we're a business'. They expressed feeling undervalued, and they referred with some regrets to 'the dinosaur era', when 'we did long working hours but there was good teamwork'. The governor was working to 'a clear brief, with little time to deliver', and he expressed finding his role necessary but uncomfortable and difficult. He acknowledged that his task was: 'to go through the angst . . . Someone else will come here after me and do the healing. I have to accept that some demonizing has to take place' (governor).

In the two 'higher performance' prisons, which were both in the north of England, staff were more well disposed towards their governors, and towards senior managers in general. This was slightly undermined at Doncaster by the atmosphere referred to in Chapter 4, of impending cuts (this may explain the lower findings on 'trust'). The director was under considerable pressure to reduce costs, and staff inevitably reacted to this with disillusion. They began to say that 'management just aren't listening any more', partly because they had some fears about their own safety, and about the pressure they felt under to 'cut corners'. The governor and the director at both of these prisons expressed pride in their staff, and seemed well informed about areas of the prison that were operating well. Without the cultural difficulties (of resistance and continuing industrial relations matters), they were more able to focus on programmes, the fine-tuning of the regime, drug treatment communities, and other constructive activities. It was not always clear how this freedom from resistance had come about: 'I am not sure how we've done it. The atmosphere is important. It's a mixture of procedures and atmosphere. There is a dissatisfaction amongst staff that we can't do more. The re-profiling will address this' (governor).

Both prisons had experienced difficulties in their early years, as new prisons often did, with new staff, routines not yet established, and prisoners constantly challenging boundaries. Both prisons had staff who felt generally supported by senior management: 'I feel very loyal to staff. They have given us such a lot. I have been here when it was hard. I slept here for 24 nights in the early days. We've got mutual support here. I try not to be tied down by paperwork. I have got a secretary and a PA. That means I can be visible' (director).

It was noticeable at Doncaster that, despite the quite specific complaints above, staff said similar things about management: 'This is a very comfortable place to work. I've got the best boss I've ever had. Nothing's too much trouble. He tries to make you feel human' (officer).

This was also reflected in what prisoners said: 'This is the best prison I've ever been in. It is very civil, polite. They treat me like a human, and I reciprocate. I never give them any grief. If you've got something to give, they'll let you develop it. It's a good place to leave from. You flourish. It frightens you at first' (prisoner).

There was much similarity in how prisoners, staff, and managers described the positive ethos of the prison. For example: 'The policy is that you are here *as*, not *for* punishment' (prisoner). 'The way the organization relates to you affects the way you relate to each other, which affects the way you relate to your job' (officer).

There were some difficulties, for example, some concerns about under-policing, experienced staff being moved out to open a new prison, some impending reductions in already low staffing levels, and staff working out that they would be 'better off' if they were taken over by the public sector, where pay and conditions were better. We shall return to these difficulties in Chapter 9. The context of continuing financial cuts had implications for staff views of senior management. As we have argued in Chapter 5, trust is easier to lose than to win. Staff talked of getting more 'appreciation and recognition from prisoners' than from management, despite the very high levels of job satisfaction generally. The director was constrained by 'the company', and by the 'penalty points' system, so that 'profit overrides people'. Some staff were beginning to express some negative attitudes towards prisoners at meetings, but others persisted: 'We are feeling a bit hard done by, but we know we have good interpersonal relationships. So we don't take it on to the wing. We'd be back to fighting them every day' (officer).

As staff became closer to prisoners, so senior managers could be perceived as 'the common enemy'.

We have seen in this chapter so far how complex the social organization of the prison above staff–prisoner relationships can be, and how relevant notions of trust, fairness, respect, and loyalty are to the management of the prison environment. Late modern managerialist techniques pose some risks to the establishment of trust between officers and senior managers, in an already low trust environment. Whilst trust on its own is not necessarily the key to prison quality, the legitimacy of senior managers in the eyes of prison staff, in which trust plays a part, forms a key part in the motivation and willing assent of prison officers in their work (see Bottoms 2002). Many commentators have suggested that the way staff treat prisoners (or nurses treat patients, and so on) is related to the way they feel treated themselves (Liebling *et al.* 1997; Coyle 2002). If the newly appointed Director General is right in his assertion that 'Relationships [between staff and prisoners] are central to developing our work . . . [they] require active management . . . ' (Wheatley 2003: 5–6), then how governors model the treatment of staff may be one way in which they can influence the staff–prisoner interface. Governors' legitimacy in the eyes of staff (and therefore their orientation to their work, and to prisoners) is likely to be related to their levels of attachment, involvement, and commitment, and to their beliefs about 'governors in general' and about 'this governor in particular' (Bottoms 2002: 38–9).

Prisons, their Cultures, and their Emotional Climates

> To understand people and cultures, whether ourselves and ours or others . . . we need to know their values.
>
> (Stocker 1996: 83)

A theme has appeared in our account so far, which should be made more explicit. From the Commissioner of Correctional Services, to the Director General of the Prison Service, to the staff, to prisoners, we hear that the emotional tone of prison life is raw, real, and distinctive. There *is* an emotional tone, different in every prison.[41] This is partly shaped by the position adopted by the POA in each prison, but it is also shaped by staff culture more broadly, the governor's personal style, the mood of prisoners, and the collective memory of the institution. We attempt below to describe this aspect of the five prisons in our study and to reflect on what this means.

A Note on Penal Cultures

[C]ulture refers to all those conceptions and values, categories and distinctions, frameworks of ideas and systems of belief which human beings use to construe their world and render it orderly and meaningful.

(Garland 1990: 194)

Culture is a 'learned product of group experience' (Schein 1985: 57) or a 'collective construction of social reality' (Sackmann 1991: 21). The existence of a culture suggests that members share ideas, theories, or 'habits of thought' about their world, and about what should and should not be done in it (Chan 1997: 68). Cultures bind people together, encouraging stereotyping, bonding, and solidarity among groups. They provide core beliefs, or the 'codes and frames that people use in building and articulating their own world views, their attitude to life and social status' (Alasuutari 1995: 26; Willis 1977).[42] The language used, and the patterns of interactions among individuals, provide clues as to the culture of a group or organization (G. Morgan 1997: 130) and often serve as a key mode of its transmission. Individual actors participate in the production and reproduction of culture, via storytelling, relationships, codification, and 'common-sense' rules (Chan 1997: 65–80). Language occupies a central position in culture. Karstedt argues that the term culture

---

[41] Crawley has conducted some interesting work on the emotional labour required by prison officers to perform their work, demonstrating that prisons are 'emotional arenas' in which emotion-work is done, according to certain 'feeling rules' (Crawley forthcoming and 2000). She suggests: 'The new recruit to the Prison Service must also learn the organisation's "emotional map"' (Crawley in press). Our argument relates mainly to *establishments* (and to differences between them).

[42] When we say that researchers have 'gone native', we mean that they have taken on this world-view, and can no longer critically reflect on it, or even recognize it (see Liebling 1999). The social norms have been fully absorbed.

implies external difference and internal homogeneity (Karstedt 2001), although organizations can have multiple cultures (Schein 1985), for example, with managers having one set of assumptions and workers having a different set of assumptions about 'the way things are done around here' (Chan 1997: 69). Cultures arise partly as a means for making sense of and addressing 'certain structural strains, contradictions and anomalies of their prescribed role and task' (Manning and Van Maanen 1978: 116; Chan 1997).

Morgan argues that '[Culture] must be understood as an active, living phenomenon through which people jointly create and recreate the worlds in which they live' (G. Morgan 1997: 141). *Values* form an important part of culture and may be an outward manifestation of it (Mullins 1999: 803). Identifying and describing cultures is methodologically and epistemologically difficult (Clifford and Marcus 1986). Depictions, particularly in unfamiliar territory, are 'inherently partial' and incomplete (Clifford 1986: 7).

Penal cultures consist of 'conceptions, values, categories, distinctions, frameworks of ideas and systems of belief' (Zedner 2002: 359). They also consist of *emotions* (or 'sensibilities', as Garland put it; Garland 1990). The social practices of the prison are deeply shaped by such 'cultural forms' (Garland 1990: 199). 'Dominant cultures' (structural forms and senior management practices) matter as well as 'subcultures' (the 'working rules' of officers and the codes of prisoners) in the climate of the prison (Downes and Rock 1986: 180).

The five prisons in our study can be said to have a distinctive culture (as we began to demonstrate earlier). It might be useful to characterize this culture as representing an emotional as well as a 'moral' climate, of which governors formed a part, and which they had to navigate (see also Scheff and Retzinger 2001: 23).[43] Barbalet argues that emotional climates (e.g. fears 'experienced and shared by members of a social collectivity') are both 'social influences on individual behaviour' and 'a source of collective action' (Barbalet 1998: 158-9): 'Emotional climates are sets of emotions or feelings which are not only shared by groups of individuals implicated in common social structures and processes, but which

---

[43] A few early explorations of emotional reactions of staff to difficult prisoner-clients can be found, such as Weber's 'Emotional and Defensive Reactions to Cottage Parents', published in 1961.

are also significant in the formation and maintenance of political and social identities and collective behaviour' (ibid. 159).

Emotional climates are sociologically constructed, and they are embedded in organizations. Although climates are shared, 'individual participation in them will be patterned and therefore unequal' (ibid.): 'An emotional climate is not a blanket which equally covers each member of the group associated with it. Each group member will contribute differently to the formation of the climate and will experience it in terms of their particular place in the group' (ibid. 160).

If we try to identify the emotional climate in each establishment, we might tentatively offer the following (see Table 8.4).[44] We have also reflected on the model developed by Sparks *et al.* 1996 (p. 328), to include a column in this table indicating how prisoners were regarded, that is, on what basis social order was founded in each prison. It is interesting to note that staff and prisoners shared a similar (negative) emotional climate at Belmarsh and Wandsworth, and also at Risley. Belmarsh allowed the least respect to prisoners, seeing them as subjects rather than as agents who might be self-determining (see further Sparks *et al.* 1996: 327–9). At Doncaster, staff and prisoners shared a more positive emotional climate, but prisoners were arguably under-policed (Table 8.4; also Chapter 9). At Holme House in particular, staff and prisoners inhabited quite different emotional worlds (they were poorly *attuned*, in the language of Scheff and Retzinger 2001: 38).

TABLE 8.4.   Five prisons and their emotional climates

Prison	Staff	Prisoners	Basis of social order
Belmarsh	Nervous, under siege, powerless	Angry, powerless	Dangerous subject
Holme House	Content, confident	Controlled, disrespected	Malleable agent
Risley	Anxious, pessimistic	Uncertain, frustrated	Docile agent
Doncaster	Valuable, committed	Self-actualizing, confident	Thinking, feeling agent
Wandsworth	Demoralized, weary	Resigned, powerless	Dangerous agent

Stocker (1996) argues that emotions and values are deeply intertwined; that emotions (such as anger or joy) *reveal* values. Emotions

[44] We recognize that prison will have 'emotional zones', that is 'places or settings which become understood in terms of different emotions' (Crawley 2000: 53; and 146–70).

also *contain* values—that is, they tell us something about a person and their character. Emotions help us to *discover* our values, for example: 'I found out how much I valued you, my nationality or my religion by seeing how angry undeserved slights made me' (Stocker 1996: 73).

What makes us angry is related to what we think is unjust, which helps us to identify what we think justice is (a little like the 'reframing' exercise described in Chapter 3). Certain acts may cause offence by indicating lack of respect. This can happen for different reasons (e.g. malice or undue inattention), but our reaction is a source of knowledge and understanding. Stocker argues that emotions are 'evaluatively informative'; that is, important 'as a means of revealing value' (Stocker 1996: 83).[45] Emotions of certain kinds can cloud our judgement, but *not* having certain emotions (such as interest or involvement) can reduce the quality of our judgement. Emotions underlie and guide moral conduct (Evans 2001: 64). Wisdom is more than 'cleverness' and includes 'reality testing' with some contribution made by affect (feeling)—something like the term 'emotional intelligence' made popular by Goleman and others (Goleman 1996; but see the much deeper analysis by Stocker 1996: *passim* and 121). Emotions may be particularly important where conflicting goals exist (Evans 2001: 161). Not being able to take account of relevant feelings (denying or avoiding them) can amount to a disorder:

A person without emotions, or without a large enough range of adequate emotions, will be unable to make and act on evaluation. Emotions [are] directly essential for evaluations . . . People who have correct emotions, because they are such people, are typically well placed to make correct evaluations, and people who have incorrect emotions are, because they are such people, typically poorly placed to make correct evaluations. (Stocker 1996: 135–6)

Not *all* emotions are important for *all* values or for *all* evaluations (ibid. 140). Whether or not a prisoner trusts a member of staff, for example, will determine the extent to which his or her oversight makes the prisoner angry. Whether or not one has fellow-feeling amongst colleagues will determine the extent to which poor

[45] Garland makes the interesting observation that collective emotions and value-driven frameworks of action often drive penal policy, but in ways that are difficult to observe and analyse (Garland 1997: 202–3).

treatment of a colleague makes us angry. As Stocker puts it, 'different emotional configurations can lead to different judgments' (Stocker 1996: 144). The emotional climate within an organization (or within a family) will impact on perceptions of one's treatment. It is, if you like, part of the moral climate.[46] Emotional configurations shape attitudes, and attitudes influence and therefore constitute part of treatment. When we react to a benefit or injury, we react mainly to the 'manifestation of attitude' that the behaviour suggests. What we call kindness is often a kind attitude rather than (just) a specific act (Stocker 1996: 158, citing Strawson 1962). Respect 'involves one's *manner*, which goes beyond speech' (Scheff and Retzinger 2001: 65).

Stocker argues that emotions have a *moral importance* that is often overlooked. They are 'constitutively relevant for act evaluations' (Stocker 1996: 160). Our working as well as our personal lives are made up of emotional structures that 'help determine whether our life is going well' (ibid. 165). Emotions *give rise to* values (Stocker 1996: 179); some criminologists have argued that there are 'moral emotions' (Katz 1988). Good institutions, then, require correct emotional climates.[47]

Stocker's work takes us a step further in understanding how and why the manner of one's treatment, for example, is so important in evaluations of fairness, and why disregard for one's person leads to negative 'affect' or feelings. He uses the example of cancer patients responding to medical treatment:

Patients with cancer might judge a surgeon in just the ways they would judge a drug or a computer-driven, automated laser . . . simply in terms of costs and benefits, as determined by survival rates, gains or loss of functions, pain . . . Many complain that their surgeons are too technocratic, too concerned with mere effectiveness and survival rates. These patients, thus, do not view their surgeons as mere means, mere mechanisms for ridding them of cancer. This is correlative of how they want their surgeons to view them. They want their surgeons to be concerned and involved with

[46] There are highly individualized 'ways of seeing' which are also important, and which shape perceptions of treatment, but we suggest that emotional configurations also exist at the organizational level (see Stocker 1996: 167).

[47] Several studies on the relevance of 'emotional intelligence' to prison life are under way, including one on managers (Cross 2003) and another on prison staff (Arnold forthcoming). This relationship between values and emotional climates clearly has relevance to other organizations and social institutions.

them as people, not just as sites for operations. And they want this, not because, or just because, they think that doctors give better care to those they care about personally . . . They also see their doctors' acts as human acts, with emphasis on both 'human' and 'acts' . . . For the acts, themselves, not just their outcomes, are valued. (Stocker 1996: 139)

We are social beings, in need of validation and recognition by others. Emotions 'make acts and relations good' (or bad) and they are 'continually at work in good decisions' (Stocker 1996: 177 and 191). They are necessary for evaluative knowledge (see Liebling 1999). Staff may be right when they say, 'you had to be there' to understand what happened (see Stocker 1996: 192–3). Barbalet's sociological analysis suggests that emotional climates and categories are related to social-structural issues and that the study of emotions can 'offer an understanding of the linkage between the micro and the macro domains' (Barbalet 1998: 4). Emotions have 'a social nature' (ibid. 8) and 'patterns of emotional experience are different in different societies' (ibid. 9) and institutions. They may be an 'outcome or effect of social processes' (ibid. 9) as well as a cause of social behaviour. The late modern penal-organizational climate may, for example, emphasize systems, aggregates, and sanctions over individual moral agents and rewards, with unintended consequences for the emotional climates of individual establishments. Our account constitutes a beginning, and not a complete portrayal, of these dynamics.

Our account above throws additional light on the truism that 'prisons are all about relationships'. How staff, prisoners, and managers *think* and *feel* about each other seems powerfully related to the quality of life experienced by prisoners (and staff), with positive emotions generally linked to 'high performance' and negative emotions generally linked to 'poor performance' (albeit with some important qualifications; see later). These emotional climates have implications for the vision of the prisoner to which staff are inclined to work.

Our findings, and our reflections on them, suggest that the way staff and prisoners perceive their treatment has both an emotional component and emotional *effects*. The account of prison life we have developed may illuminate what is meant by the 'feeling' of a prison: this 'feeling' is the prison's moral and emotional climate. This is, we propose, 'what matters' (aided by staff and prisoners, and now senior managers). The scheme above, albeit tentative and schematic, develops our understanding of what matters in prison a step further, and it illuminates one aspect of 'governing' (managing an emotional climate) often left undeveloped. This proposition is complex, however, and there are some important caveats to our analysis so far. We shall return to the five establishments and some catastrophic events in the next chapter.

Conclusion: The 'Performance Culture' and Values

To be effective, governors need a 'task' or systems and structures orientation and a 'relationship' orientation (White 1995). They also need an effective and complementary senior management team, and an astute sense of history and mood. The nature and extent of their contribution to the quality of life in a prison (the effectiveness of their power and authority) may depend on the match between their style and the prison's current state, as well as on their own personal and professional qualities. Some prisons will be much more difficult to lead than others. Many governors enter their careers with a 'strong' sense of 'moral purpose' (Carlen 2002a: 45), and many retain this sense, despite setbacks and frustrations in their work. Some governors complain that the 'current requirements of the Service' (ibid. 46) make it impossible to fulfil, or remain true to, this sense of purpose. In any prison, governing is a 'high involvement' exercise.

The term 'performance' in the modern managerial context means the accomplishment of specified goals, normally set by those at the top of the organization and elsewhere (White 1995). It is interesting to note that the term 'performance' has a quite different meaning outside of that framework (e.g. Goffman 1990) but is often regarded as an accurate description of the emphasis on 'impression management' characteristic of modern management styles (and approaches to measurement; see Chapter 2). Managing a prison in the modern performance framework means effectively controlling and directing both the processes aimed at achieving these goals, and the individuals who make up the organization, who in turn carry out these processes. In management language, the paradigm associated with these developments is 'command and control' rather than 'trust and empowerment' (Pollitt 1995). This paradigm has been associated with calls for increased levels of accountability for public spending, and a drive for continuous improvement in public services. Many critics have noted that this development has threatened some of the values they feel matter in organizational life.

The Relationship between Prison Governing and Values

What values actually underpin this performance management framework? It is clear that one key value is the efficient use of public money. The modern managerialist approach has been characterized as a cultural revolution (Carter *et al.* 1995) which has transformed the behaviour of organizations and individuals. It has also been, in some ways, a moral revolution. It has challenged traditional Civil Service values, and replaced *theta-type* values (such as fairness and due process) by *sigma-type* values (such as efficiency; see Hood 1991). The management problem was that theta-type values were not actually 'delivered' in inefficiently managed establishments, which often had well-meaning governors, but no structures or systems to support the delivery of a specified regime.[48] In practice, these desirable values, on their own, became associated with tardiness, delay, carelessness, weak financial accountability, and complacency (Raine and Willson 1997). There are many examples of 'liberal well-meaning regimes' which went wrong (Home Office 1995; Liebling 2002; Home Affairs Select Committee 2001). On the other hand, critics accuse the performance management framework of encouraging a preoccupation with window-dressing or impression management, and the production of 'feel good documents'. Attention is detracted from important but less quantifiable aspects of performance, such as 'trust', 'fairness', and 'respect'. Another criticism of the concept of 'performance' is that it is a *relative* concept—that is, organizations are compared with each other in league tables, or with themselves over time, rather than against any reasoned or 'objective' standard.

We agree that effective management requires the clarification of key objectives and the use of measures to evaluate progress towards their achievement (see Pollitt and Bouckaert 2000). But there is also a feeling that something important has been lost (see Raine and Willson 1997). Our account so far suggests that trust may be undermined by many of these modern management strategies and

[48] As one governor said, there is a considerable difference at governor level between 'caring for prisoners', and '*delivering* care to prisoners'.

that, counter-intuitively given modern outlooks, trust may be an important component (alongside principles and structures) of what makes an organization work. Braithwaite and colleagues have demonstrated, for example, that stigmatizing forms of regulation increase non-compliance and non-engagement, whereas recognizing and sanctioning non-compliance within a 'reintegrative' and supportive framework ('responsive regulation') improves compliance (Braithwaite and Braithwaite 2001; also Braithwaite 2002). Nurses who participated in the generation of their own outcome standards were more likely to implement those standards (Braithwaite 2002). Self-efficacy, praise, and interest were important to sustaining continuous improvement. Conversely, deviance or non-compliance is high in low trust organizations (ibid.), and may be motivated by feelings of injustice. We have shown in previous chapters how this might be the case.

The performance management agenda in criminal justice (and elsewhere) has been 'privileged' (Humphrey *et al.* 1993), in the sense that its impact on the effectiveness of organizations is assumed to be positive. Some critics argue that this is more a question of faith than evidence (Pollitt 1995). Evidence of improvement is, overall, favourable but patchy (Jenner 2001; Sinclair 2002; Home Affairs Committee 1997). The measurement tools are far from infallible. There is a powerful feeling, expressed by practitioners, critics, and often managers themselves, that 'something is missing' from this framework. This 'something missing' has, we have found, something to do with values, perhaps especially the values of trust and respect. These features of the prison's working environment may in turn be (counter-intuitively, in an age of robust management) linked to staff motivation and compliance with the increasing demands made upon them (Bottoms 2002; Braithwaite 2002).

What seems evident from our account and from the empirical data we have explored in this chapter is that 'prison quality' is linked to 'fairness' or 'legitimacy' in relation to staff as well as prisoners. One of the reasons given by civil servants asked why they worked in the public sector was that they liked the way they were treated (Wilson, pers. comm.). Legitimacy for prison staff includes high expectations, clear structures and systems, reliable procedures, and decent interpersonal treatment. This balance is particularly difficult to achieve in 'poor performing prisons', where a climate of distrust, anxieties about employment, and nervousness about change are inevitable, and the scale of change is enormous. There are tensions between the will to empower staff and the need for increased accountability. There are decreasing promotion opportunities as management structures flatten. There are tensions between some of the targets (e.g. between the need for tight security and preparation for release). There are external influences on prison life (such as increases in the size of the prison population) which sometimes make the concept of performance management and 'effectiveness' seem rather remote. There is also a tendency for 'maverick managerialism' (Carlen 2002a: rapid, unprioritized, and sometimes conflicting policy directives which are difficult to implement) to undermine the apparent rationalism of modern management (see also Pollitt and Bouckaert 2000: 163).[49] This is a particular problem for a public sector organization that is continually in the public eye, is of major concern to ministers, and that serves multiple symbolic, expressive, and political functions (Garland 1990, 2001a). How these tensions are approached, resolved, or avoided has a considerable impact on levels of trust between staff and senior management, and between governors and Prison Service Headquarters. As Carlen argues, prisons constitute 'rather peculiar microcosms' of the 'disciplinary, risk and audit society' (Carlen 2002a: 30). She argues that: 'managerialism's main effect was to erode the traditional ethics and discretion of professionalism; and . . . impede the development of the more sophisticated definitions and assessments of performance required when the manufacture of justice (or health or education) is at stake, rather than the manufacture of cars (or frozen peas)' (Carlen 2002a: 34).

We suggest that the 'traditional ethics and discretion of professionalism' had its weaknesses in practice, and we have argued in this chapter that managerialism has a role to play in modern, accountable organizations, and in making certain values real. We also suggest that used as a *means* (where the end or purpose is clearly specified) rather than as an end in itself, managerialism can,

---

[49] Particularly as each new policy arrives with new measures to check its implementation. President Clinton introduced a Paperwork Reduction Act in 1995 in the USA. All prison governors decry the proliferation of paperwork. 'The trade is between, on the one hand, simple, light monitoring controls which permit subtleties and complexities and "gaming" to squeeze round or through them, and, on the other, detailed, heavy systems which capture more of the complexities and ploys, but which are burdensome and expensive to operate' (Pollitt and Bouckaert 2000: 165).

if properly limited, assist in the 'delivery' of less damaging penal regimes. If prisons are to modernize, it is the behaviour of prison officers—those who influence the quality of life experienced by prisoners the most—that needs to change. The private sector has found some techniques for achieving this (at least in some establishments) but we wonder if they are the right techniques. There are some remaining values and tensions to consider.

We have been considering moral values and the question of 'what matters' in the prison throughout this book. Our main message in this chapter is that as human values, they are as relevant to staff (and governors)—to the workforce—as they are to prisoners. However, this straightforward statement skates over what is in practice a far more complex state of affairs. As Pollitt and Bouckaert argue in their analysis of civil service public sector reform: 'Administrative "principles" often come in matching pairs, with advantages and disadvantages trading off as one moves from one polar principle to its opposite' (Pollitt and Bouckaert 2000: 151).

Information technology, management systems and the substitution of the magical word 'management' for the unfashionable 'administration' do not resolve the dilemmas of competing priorities in contemporary organizational management (Pollitt and Bouckaert 2000: 149–51; and 154–71). The shortening of institutional memories brought about by future-oriented 'can-do' management is one of many trade-offs settled in one direction, without sufficient regard for what is lost.[50] The corporate memory, held by long-standing advisers and a source of wise advice to whatever government is in power on the day, has all but crumbled in the forward-looking, future-oriented late modern Prison Service.

This account is by no means intended to sound nostalgic. In our attempt to describe, and express the feelings of, those staff and governors we watched and conversed with in the workplace, we simply support their need for both high standards and an emotionally intelligent organization. The workforce require the same balance between 'discipline', 'reward', 'development', and 'human agency' as anyone else. We show in the concluding chapters how *value balance* is a critical concept in this framework.

[50] Over the course of many years, we have seen a policy of incentives and earned privileges appear, run into difficulties, improve, and then reappear, with much of the corporate memory of those early difficulties lost. In several other areas of practice, oscillations (e.g. between security and 'regimes', between flexibility and control, and so on) seem to characterize penal policy and practice.

9

Security, Harmony, and 'What Matters' in Prison Life

> Virtue is a mean state between two vices, one of excess and one of deficit.
>
> (Aristotle, *Ethics*, II. vi. 15)

Introduction

So far we have reported our results rather evenly and, perhaps, uncritically. There are important questions still to be addressed, one of which we shall consider in this chapter. This question relates to a distinction we have drawn in previous work, and which emerged towards the end of our research, between 'good' and 'right' relationships (Liebling and Price 2001: 75–84), or between a theory of the moral and a theory of 'being nice' (McEvoy 2003). 'Good' relationships can be flexible, tolerant, harmonious, and respectful. They can also be overly lenient, sometimes resulting in inconsistency, perceptions of unfairness, and a lack of safety, order, and security in prison, as we suggested in Chapter 1. Staff can get too close to prisoners, identifying with their needs and concerns to the exclusion of other considerations. Or they can be distant, with staff withdrawing from informal, negotiated forms of order. As one prisoner said in an earlier study on the nature of staff–prisoner relationships: 'Relationships are good. Staff are alright. You never see them on the wing!' Here 'good' means 'unobtrusive'. We have argued that respect, trust, humanity, and relationships are crucial in evaluations of fairness. Interpersonal treatment of prisoners by staff forms a major part of their overall judgement about their treatment in prison. This is all undoubtedly true. But where are the limits?

'Right' relationships are a route through which the prison is accomplished (and yet remains a prison), and the individual prisoner retains a sense of moral agency (and yet remains imprisoned). Right relationships are respectful, yet they incorporate a 'quiet flow of power' (Liebling and Price 2001: 92). They have boundaries and principles so that departures from the rules can be justified and, where appropriate, repeated in similar circumstances (Liebling and Price 2001: 104–8, 140–3; Bottoms 1998) and conflict can be addressed rather than avoided (McEvoy 2003). As we argued in Chapter 5, respect may include certain kinds of challenges to the behaviour of others, and a holding to account for one's actions. The 'firm, confident and humane approach' described by the Control Review Committee in the mid-1980s, and favoured by many prisoners in practice, is a very difficult approach to get right. What, then, is a reasonable rationale for 'right' rather than 'good' relationships and what limits might this place on 'pleasing the prisoners'? We shall return to the analysis in Chapter 1 of the distinction between laxity and justice, and to some subsequent events, in order to explore this distinction and its implications for our moral performance framework.

What Matters in Prison

First, we shall return to the question of what matters in prison. Table 9.1 shows what prisoners felt most strongly about. Most of the items appearing in the column 'strongest negative evaluations' belong to the dimensions 'personal development', 'power and authority', and 'fairness'. One item each from 'decency', 'order', and 'safety' arose. Aspects of prison life that concerned prisoners most were: boredom, being locked up, staff having a lot of power and control over them, slow responses to requests and applications, the feeling of 'doing rather than using' time, staff never apologizing to prisoners when they got things wrong, not being given reasons for decisions, prison feeling like punishment, not being involved in decisions, a lack of order and organization, and the presence of drugs. The material conditions of imprisonment seem less pressing: a quarter strongly agreed that they were given adequate opportunities to keep themselves clean and decent.

Prisoners' strongest positive evaluations were related to how they approached activities. Many strongly disagreed with the suggestion that they put little effort into the main activity they did. They were also fairly positive about cleanliness, how they got on

Strongest Negative Emotions

Rank	Question No.	%	Item	Dimension
1	81	32.5 SA	I often feel bored in this prison	Personal development
2	60	30.5 SA	Prisoners spend too long locked up in their cells in this prison	Decency
3	40	29.4 SA	Staff in this prison have a lot of power and control over prisoners	Power & Authority
4	64	26.8 SA	This prison responds slowly to requests and applications	Fairness
5	52	26.1 SA	On the whole I am 'doing time' rather than 'using time'	Personal development
6	42	22.3 SA	In general, staff here do not apologize to prisoners	N/A
7	50	20.1 SA	This prison is poor at giving prisoners reasons for decisions	Fairness
8	57	19.5 SA	My time here seems very much like a punishment	Power & Authority
9	66	18.8 SD	Prisoners are encouraged to make their own decisions and have a say in what goes on here	Power & Authority
10=	59	18.4 SD	This prison is well organized	Order
10=	48	18.4 SA	The level of drug use in this prison is quite high	Safety

Strongest Positive Evaluations

Rank	Question No.	%	Item	Dimension
1	4	25 SD	I don't put much effort into the main activity I do here	Personal development
2	27	24.8 SA	I am given adequate opportunities to keep myself clean and decent	Decency
3	43	20.8 SA	I get on well with the other prisoners in this prison	N/A
4	99	17.9 SA	I am given adequate opportunities to keep my living area clean and decent	Decency
5	85	17.9 SD	Generally, I fear for my physical safety	Safety
6	30	16.8 SA	I feel safe from being injured, bullied, or threatened by other prisoners in here	Safety
7	100	16.4 SA	I am able to maintain meaningful contact with my family whilst I am in this prison	Family contact
8	18	15.9 SA	Personally, I get on well with the officers on my wing	Relationships
9	3	15.5 SA	The main activity I do here is worthwhile to me	Personal development
10	74	15.3 SA	Staff in this prison are clear in telling you what you can/cannot do	Fairness
11	19	14.6 SA	I have been helped significantly by a member of staff in this prison with a particular problem	Support

with other prisoners, feeling safe (although remember the 'safety paradox'; p. 297), maintaining contact with families, how they got on with officers on their wing, how worthwhile their main activity was, clarity, and being helped significantly by a member of staff with a particular problem. Positive evaluations were found in the 'safety', 'decency', and 'personal development' dimensions (their *responsiveness* to what was provided rather than to *what* was provided), in the 'family contact' dimension, and one each in 'relationships', 'fairness' (the clarity component), and 'support'. The strongest negative evaluations were weighted more heavily than the strongest positive evaluations (i.e. the percentage of prisoners who strongly agreed or strongly disagreed with statements in a negative direction was higher than the percentage who strongly supported positive evaluations).

We did not ask prisoners to rank the dimensions in importance, but we can infer from the above analysis that clarity, safety, and organization are important in prison as well as respectful interpersonal treatment. Prisoners valued predictability, a drug-free environment, regular access to services, and a feeling of order as well as freedom from arbitrary power and control. They did not appreciate chaos, any more than staff did. This balancing act (between 'excess' and 'deficit') was tricky.

In the year following our data collection exercises, the two apparently 'high performing' prisons in our study suffered from, in one case, a major disturbance on two wings and four suicides (Holme House) and, in another, two escapes (Doncaster). A third prison suffered from a major disturbance on one wing (Belmarsh). It was a period of dramatic population increase, with the additional pressures such growth brings. But we felt that these serious events were in some ways consistent with our understanding of each prison. We had noted that Holme House had, like some other prisons, performed well on its official targets but did less well on many of our relational measures (such as 'respect' and 'humanity'; see Fig. 4.1). We had to reflect seriously on our account so far of 'good moral performance' in order to make sense of these events.

We already knew, from the analysis of prisoners' comments and the literature reviewed in Chapters 5 to 7, that concepts like respect and fairness, properly understood, brought limits with them on what staff and prisoners could do. Our account in Chapter 1 sought to make a clearer distinction than often is the case in practice between liberal or 'lax' regimes and 'just regimes', as envisaged by Woolf. Were there also limits to trust between staff and prisoners, in a moral prison? There were, but the question of where this limit should be (and the narrowness of the distance between 'too much' and 'too little') was vexed.

Security, Harmony, and Moral Performance

In our discussions, we wondered whether we had underestimated the importance of security values (i.e. values relating to order, authority, control, and security) in our 'moral performance' framework. Inevitably in the prison, where behaviour is closely regulated and individuals feel constrained, and as a result of our methodology, we were unlikely to generate much attention to security during our workgroup exercises with prisoners in particular (although clearly order, which we did measure selectively, was a 'good'). We did generate measures of order, safety, and power, but arguably there was a built-in assumption (shared at the time by ourselves and prisoners) that too much security was 'a bad thing'. Security issues (such as regular searching) are often regarded as major irritants of prison life. It is difficult to construct survey questions that produce positive scores for tight attention to security matters in prison. We can see, however (and prisoners said, in group discussions), that security *values* are important in assessments of prison quality, up to a point, if the relevant processes are carefully conducted. Security became such an irritant, and such a dominant value in prisons post-1995, that it is difficult to find prisoners who have a good word to say about security procedures. It tends to be seen, and arguably during 1994–7 became, inherently in opposition to other important values. How do we disentangle this 'problem of security'? Have we under-represented some important aspects of prison quality in our overall scheme?

Security values seemed important for different reasons: in the case of Doncaster, because there was too little attention paid to them, and in the case of Holme House and Belmarsh, because there was too much.[1] As the then Deputy Director of the Prison Service

---

[1] Recall our descriptions of each prison in Chapter 4, as well as the results presented in Chapters 5 to 7. Camp and Gaes suggested that staff in private prisons have a particular difficulty with security procedures (Camp and Gaes 2001). Their account (of lack of experience and high turnover) has relevance to life as we found it at Doncaster during the time of our fieldwork. It is also significant that at

argued, in his public account of our findings and subsequent events:

The research assessment of Doncaster indicates that it is a prison where staff have very close relationships with prisoners. Doncaster staff are genuinely liked by prisoners who regard them as good and caring. The closeness of the relationship and the extent of the joint identification of staff and prisoners is surprising. This gives Doncaster some major advantages. The downside is that sometimes staff over identify with prisoners and become their supporters and protectors. Staff may not always maintain a sufficient degree of scepticism and detachment. There are risks to security in this. It is probably not unconnected that [shortly after Doncaster was assessed] . . . there were two escapes. One escape was from escort. The other using impersonation from reception. In both cases, the escapes involved 'conning' staff who were successfully 'conned'. The obvious task for Doncaster was to build on the really good relationships but to inject slightly greater detachment and scepticism into them. (Wheatley 2003: 5)

As soon as words like 'scepticism' and 'detachment' are used, the opposite problems arise.[2] They infer lack of attention to individual need; at worst, a lack of respect. At Holme House, where relationships were less close:

The results . . . show a staff who were seen as fair by prisoners but not liked and also that staff at Holme House made use of their formal position and power more than other staff at other prisons.[3] Holme House staff were not seen as treating prisoners with respect. This year Holme House ran into difficulties . . . which coincided with increased population pressures. The net effect . . . was to cause the Governor to restrict the regime so that the delivery of the regime for prisoners ceased to be predictable. It was at this point that Holme House experienced control problems with two very major incidents within a number of months. . . . With the benefit of hindsight, it is likely that relationships that staff and prisoners had operated well when the prison was delivering a better than average regime but staff/prisoner relationships lacked the closeness and strength to withstand the

Holme House, material life for prisoners deteriorated as the prison population rose, and a wing that was unoccupied at the time of our research became full. Dissatisfaction with staff attitudes may have increased (and staff attitudes towards prisoners may have declined in practice) as a result of this change.

[2] Other commentators have suggested that 'the more fundamental challenge is for public sector prisons to develop greater respect for prisoners' (pers. comm. 2003).

[3] See Chapter 4, pp. 181–2; HMCIP 2002c; and Table 7.2, item 2.

regime reduction. At least some prisoners found it easy to blame the staff for the problems they were facing and to take it out on staff. The relatively austere and formal relationships probably made that easier. (Wheatley 2003: 4–5)

The incident at Belmarsh had a similar explanation. Poor relationships, and an overall lack of respect, resulted in a hostile reaction from prisoners when they were fed up with increasingly restricted access to association. We know from other research that staff can 'sell' a restricted regime to prisoners (up to a point), if they treat prisoners fairly and respectfully (Sparks *et al.* 1996). On the other hand, a regime that is too relaxed can mask violence between prisoners, and inattention from staff.

Here we have an illustration of the difference between legitimacy and something approaching 'appeasement' at Doncaster (Sparks *et al.* 1996: 329–36), and the difference between control verging on coercion and 'willing assent' at Holme House. Prisoners complied with a materially fair regime, until population pressures limited their access to activities. Their consent to the regime was largely instrumental (rather than normative) and did not survive the transition to more limited provision. Legitimacy is neither about 'pleasing the prisoners' when they make far-fetched demands, nor is it about the imposition of order without paying attention to their moral agency, and their heartfelt critiques (Sparks *et al.* 1996: 330). This balancing act—between security and harmony values (and practices), as we shall call them below—is extremely difficult. The gap between too much and too little power, trust, or safety in prison may be narrow. The 'mean between excess and deficit' is elusive.

The possibility that there was too much emphasis on one set of values at the expense of another, apparently competing, set of values in each of the above prisons made sense when we read the work of Braithwaite and colleagues on value balance. Successful 'moral performance' included respectful interpersonal treatment, but it also included placing certain constraints on prisoner (and staff) behaviour.[4]

Braithwaite argues, in her studies of political values in the general population, that two relatively independent value

---

[4] Levi shows, for example, that 'citizens are more likely to trust a government that ensures that others do their part' (Levi 1998: 90).

orientations—security and harmony—tend to be prioritized by different individuals (with security favoured by conservatives and harmony favoured by liberals). These value orientations bring together personal and social goals and modes of conduct (Braithwaite 1998*b*) and can be characterized as follows:

Security values	Harmony values
Self-protection	Peaceful coexistence
Rule of law	Mutual respect, human dignity
Authority	Sharing of resources
Competitiveness	The development of individual potential
Tough law enforcement	Wealth redistribution

The term 'security values' includes security practices in a prison, but might also incorporate rule enforcement, the use of authority, risk management, control practices, privilege removal, and routine. Harmony values, applied to the prison, might include respect, humanity, trust, support, relationships, activities or personal development, and contact with family.[5]

Most people favour security values, or harmony values, and these preferences are linked to voting behaviour. According to Braithwaite, each value orientation implies a conception of the 'other' (e.g. as a competitor or as an equal, worthy of respect). In general, and at a personal rather than organizational level, harmony values are 'other oriented' and security values are 'self-protective' (Braithwaite 1994).[6] Braithwaite also found that two additional

---

[5] Braithwaite found that harmony values (which were related to personal values such as being tolerant, considerate, understanding, helpful, forgiving, and generous) were highly correlated with each other. Security values (which were related to personal values such as propriety in dress and manners, being polite, clean, prompt, neat, refined, and reliable) were less highly correlated with each other. She suggests that security values are more strategic, and may be valued because they are believed necessary to achieve more basic values (e.g. 'peace through strength'; Braithwaite 1994).

[6] 'Materialist values are the concern of those who have experienced economic or physical insecurity: They give priority to order and stability, and to economic and military strength. In contrast post-materialists [who in this part of Braithwaite's analysis represent those with higher harmony values] have been exposed to greater security and are likely to place a higher value on ideas, brotherhood, greater citizen involvement in decision-making at government and community levels, and environmental protection' (Braithwaite 1994: 84, referring to work by Inglehart 1971). This account suggests that security values must be satisfied before harmony values will be prioritized.

'types' of people—dualists and moral relativists—favoured *both* as ideals or goals, in the case of dualists, or had a weaker commitment to either, in the case of moral relativists (Braithwaite 1998*a*, 1994). Dualists have high commitment and balanced values, and must engage in the more complex moral reasoning in order to 'solve the value balance dilemma' (Braithwaite 1998*a*: 227; see also Abbey 2000: 130).[7] Sometimes choices must be made which are in conflict with an individual's values, because of the constraints of (in the case of Braithwaite's work) political institutions (Braithwaite 1998*a*).

Let us reflect on how this discerning proposition about value orientations might apply to the prisons in our study. Table 9.2 is schematic and draws on our empirical results, and on other information we have gleaned about each prison. In this case, 'security values' might include order, stability (including resistance to change), security, and the rule of 'rules'. 'Harmony values' include attention to human dignity, respect, relationships, co-operation, democracy (or 'rule by the people'), equality, opportunity, and progress. This conceptual distinction between value orientations usefully reflects the oscillating organizational priorities outlined in Chapter 1 (the liberal penal project versus security and control), as well as the institutional-level differences in 'ethos' or orientation found in individual establishments. Most establishments tend to emphasize one more than the other.

TABLE 9.2. Five prisons and their value orientations

Prison	Security values	Harmony values	Basis of social order
Belmarsh	+ + +	−	Dangerous subject
Holme House	+ +	−	Malleable agent
Risley	−	+	Docile agent
Doncaster	− ?	+ +	Thinking, feeling agent
Wandsworth	+ + +	−	Dangerous agent

We have included each prison's 'conception of the prisoner' (or the basis of social order), as indicated in Chapter 8 earlier (developed

---

[7] Jacobs points out that, historically, when traditional authoritarian prison regimes were 'liberalized', the 'harmony' or rehabilitation role was given to civilian staff such as counsellors (and psychologists; see also Thomas 1972). This resulted in a new moral division of labour. Previously, there had been some 'moral balance' to the prison officer's role (Jacobs 1977: 96–7).

from Sparks *et al.* 1996) in order to draw out the implications for prisoners of each position in this spectrum.

Duffee suggests that the prison officer 'value complex' involves a 'flight from ambiguity' (Duffee 1974: 157). Prisons tend (not just as a result of officer behaviour) to lean in one direction or the other, towards 'security' or 'harmony' priorities, just as people do. The most complex position of all is the dualist position, where strong adherence to apparently conflicting values often results in an ongoing value balance dilemma. The complexity of holding this position is borne out by Table 9.2, where we have been unable to characterize any prison as evenly balanced.

These characterizations bear some resemblance to the 'Albany/Long Lartin', 'situational/social control' distinctions identified by Sparks *et al.* in their study of different forms of order. The authors concluded that an 'excess of caution' in situational control measures might be counter-productive (Sparks *et al.* 1996: 319). They also suggested that getting the balance right between situational and social modes of order was a 'wonderful trick' (ibid. 319).

The Doncaster model is closest to the 'negotiation model' described by Sparks and colleagues at Long Lartin, and Belmarsh is closest to the imposed or 'situational' form of order characteristic of Albany and some other, particularly high security and local prisons. The escapes from Doncaster were consistent with an overly negotiated form of order, in which highly desirable harmony values were in place without certain desirable security values. More formal forms of order secure important freedoms (from risks from other prisoners, for example). In Holme House, a firm approach to security and order seemed to exclude some important harmony values, despite a materially reasonable regime. As we described in Chapter 4, some prisoners at Holme House complained about staff attitudes and the threatening language used by some officers. There was some discrepancy between staff and prisoner perceptions and feelings, as we suggested in Chapter 8 (Table 8.4). Staff considered relationships with prisoners to be good, but prisoners had mixed feelings, and some felt treated disrespectfully. In Belmarsh and Wandsworth, a lack of freedom of movement (very high levels of situational control) plus some identification between staff and prisoners (both groups felt powerless) ruled out major protest or resistance (there was some, at Belmarsh), despite low levels of harmony values. At Risley, prisoners did not feel strongly that they were over-controlled. There was a lack of predictability, but not a lack of co-operation (see Elster 1995; and Chapter 6).

Value balancing is crucial to prison life. We have arguably measured more 'harmony' than 'security' values, although we did include a measure of order, in our survey. There must be a distinction between positive prisoner evaluations *despite* staff doing 'the difficult bits' (maintaining security and order), and positive prisoner evaluations because staff have *given up* doing 'the difficult bits' (conditioning or appeasement, in the ill-fated Woodcock and Learmont terminology; see Chapter 1; and Liebling 2002). It seems that morality is about more than 'face-to-face personal relations' (Emmett, cited in Part 1) and that there is a moral argument for using power carefully. Prison officers have to be in the 'right place' on several dimensions, including the use of formal and informal power, the use of discretion, confidence, optimism-realism, and involvement (Liebling and Price 2001: 132, 47; Gilbert 1997). Officers with a 'professional orientation' are open and non-defensive, make exceptions when warranted, prefer to gain co-operation through communication, but are willing to use coercive power or force as a last resort (Gilbert 1997: 50). They balance empathy, dignity, due process, security, and control. None of the prisons in our sample had the 'right' value balance.

Two kinds of value balance mistakes are easily made in prison. First, there can be too much emphasis on 'security values', at the expense of other values. This orientation includes security procedures but also includes a position taken towards prisoners, that casts them as not to be trusted, as threatening and deserving of punishment. Braithwaite and colleagues show how punitive and stigmatizing (disrespectful, degrading, or outcasting) punishments, arising from a security orientation, threaten the individual and may lead to destructive forms of shame, and rage (Ahmed *et al.* 2001): 'The identity degradation of stigmatisation destroys healthy identities' (Braithwaite and Braithwaite 2001: 16).

Defensive strategies follow, which deflect 'blame' on to others. Disrespect begets disrespect (Chapter 5, and Zehr 1991*a*). Too great a preoccupation with security reduces legitimacy and perceptions of fairness.

On the other hand, tolerance on its own, and beyond a certain limit, leads to unregulated conduct. Wachtel and McCold show how permissiveness (excessive leniency) or low social control can represent neglect and a lack of necessary support (Wachtel and McCold 2001). Effective social discipline requires 'supportive limit setting'. Both order without freedom (tyranny) and freedom without order (anarchy) result in unfavourable outcomes (ibid.). Too much trust has many dangers, perhaps especially in a prison (see e.g. Rutherford 2000; Home Affairs Select Committee 2001; also Home Office 1994, 1995). Acts may need to be sanctioned, and limits found, but in ways that develop healthy identities (Wachtel and McCold 2001; see also Maruna 2001). Order and security have a place in prison life: 'Moral balance requires both processes' (Braithwaite and Braithwaite 2001: 16).

Braithwaite and colleagues argue that: 'We need institutions of justice that allow respectful moral reasoning in which the defendant is not dominated, and can think aloud with those who can help her to think' (ibid. 17).

Whilst this morally balanced approach to law-breaking behaviour in general is inherently limited in the prison (for the prison constitutes a place of domination), this analysis, and the understanding of the effects of degradation it allows, supports our case that the prison is a morally dangerous environment. It is dangerous precisely because of the need for power to be used and security to be accomplished. Security values are, however, relevant to prison quality. There is a moral case for not taking the easy way out 'for a quiet life'. Because power is corruptible, and security values inherently involve scepticism and detachment, it is extraordinarily difficult to pursue respect and security values simultaneously. It is this kind of precarious value balance that underpins good moral performance.

Towards a Model of Moral Performance

With all of the above in mind, and some questions as yet unresolved, what have we learned about prison quality or moral performance so far? How were the dimensions ranked overall? How much trust, safety, order, or respect did we find, and did some have 'upper limits'? How were the dimensions related to each other, and did some seem causally related to others? Let us return to the data and to some additional analyses, in order to draw together some of the themes we have developed.

The dimensions were ranked, overall, as follows:

1. Decency (3.4482)
2. Family contact (3.3679)
3. Safety (3.3284)
4. Support (3.1875)
5. Order (3.1608)
6. Well-being (3.1027)
7. Respect (3.0715)
8. Relationships (3.0624)
9. Humanity (3.0571)
10. Fairness (3.0389)
11. Personal development (2.9360)
12. Trust (2.8258)
13. Power (2.5004)

It is interesting to note the decline from 'decency', 'family contact', and 'safety', to 'support' and 'order', and to the next two dimensions ('well-being' and 'respect'). The four key 'relationships' dimensions are only just above the 'neutral' score of 3. 'Fairness' is particularly close to 3—suggesting that these prisons overall 'only just' accomplish a positive evaluation from prisoners. Of the three dimensions below 3, 'personal development', 'trust', and 'power', perhaps the low scores on the latter two are least surprising. But the former dimension, 'personal development', would need to be well above 3 if current claims being made about the prison were being achieved. Prisoners could not, on the whole, evaluate their prison experience as constructive, or as helping them to develop. There may be limits to 'trust' and 'power', but where these limits are may depend on the function, architecture, ideology, and goals of the establishments concerned. These limits may have been reached at Doncaster, but we are aware of other prisons where levels have been higher (e.g. Boyle 1977; Genders and Player 1995; HMCIP 1993c). Drawing on the conversations reported throughout Chapters 5 to 7, we would want to reiterate the positive effects that trust and autonomy have on well-being and personal development, and the dangers of their absence.

We conclude, then, that, even in the better prisons, 'moral performance', as we have measured it so far, was limited. We have left unanswered the complex questions of what scores might be 'good enough' (there will always be a 'legitimacy deficit', or a shortfall in moral performance), or whether some dimensions should carry greater weight than others. We propose that there can hardly be too much 'decency', 'family contact', 'safety', 'support', 'order', 'well-being', 'respect', 'relationships', 'humanity', 'fairness', or 'personal development' in prison (others might disagree; but see the account by Sparks of the now disbanded Barlinnie Special Unit; Sparks 2003). There is room for further reflection on the measurement of 'right relationships' and on the evaluation of security aspects of prison regimes. The latter might be one dimension of prison life where audit procedures constitute a more suitable approach to evaluation.

The dimensions were closely related to each other, as we have shown throughout. We argue that the dimensions are conceptually separate (as individual establishments can achieve a reasonable score on 'fairness' but a lower score on 'respect'), but that they reflect or constitute facets of a broader underlying dimension, which we have called 'moral performance'. The dimensions, 'humanity', 'respect', 'staff–prisoner relationships', and 'fairness' were particularly closely related and form a core component in our 'moral performance' framework. We might suggest (based on the work of Sparks *et al.* 1996; and Bottoms 1999) that the key prison quality or 'moral performance *outcomes*' are 'order' and 'well-being'. We turn now to the question of whether our model has a causal shape, or predictive value.

We conducted a multiple linear regression analysis (using enter and forward methods), designating 'order' and 'well-being' as the dependent variables, in turn. When 'order' was designated as the dependent variable, the strongest predictors were 'fairness' ($p < 0.001$) and 'safety' ($p < 0.001$) followed by 'support' ($p < 0.05$) and 'personal development'($p < 0.05$). Prisons with lower scores on 'fairness', 'safety', 'support', and 'personal development' would, according to this model, be more likely to suffer from disorder, or be considered disorderly by prisoners.

When 'well-being' was designated as the dependent variable, the strongest predictors were 'fairness' ($p < 0.001$), 'safety' ($p < 0.001$), 'support' ($p < 0.05$), 'family contact' ($p < 0.05$), and 'decency' ($p < 0.05$). According to this model, prisons with lower levels of 'fairness' and 'safety', 'support' and meaningful 'family contact' would be more likely to suffer from elevated levels of prisoner distress, and from suicides.

'Fairness' and 'safety' are clearly key dimensions, on which 'order' and 'well-being' depend. We are taking a considerable leap here in assuming a direct relationship between 'well-being' (i.e. where low well-being is 'distress') and suicide risk.[8] But let us pursue this mode of analysis further.

'Fairness' could itself be both a cause of and a result of other dimensions (such as 'relationships'). We therefore designated 'fairness' as the dependent variable. In this analysis, 'fairness' was predicted most strongly by 'order' ($p < 0.001$), 'relationships' ($p < 0.005$), and 'humanity' ($p < 0.05$), followed by 'support' ($p < 0.05$), and 'trust' ($p < 0.05$). This suggests that 'fairness' and 'order' are mutually dependent, or reciprocal, and that 'relationships' (and the other relational dimensions) are crucial in the accomplishment of 'order', 'fairness', and 'well-being'.

We have brought together these relationships between the dimensions in our study in an interactive model (drawing on our multiple linear regression, above) in Figure 9.1.

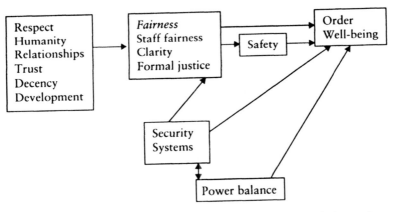

FIGURE 9.1. Prison quality and penal outcomes: a speculative and interactive model

---

[8] Moral philosophers have long known that moral values are related to human well-being (see Hollis 1998: 6; Berlin 1969: 157). We are exploring these links more systematically in ongoing work.

The model draws together what we can say with some confidence, in the form of a hypothetical model, based on our empirical results and the literature reviewed so far. The concept of 'power balance' requires further elaboration, to establish whether there is in fact a preferable distribution of power among prison staff, prisoners, and senior managers in a prison.[9] It would be interesting to test this model for different prisons, perhaps using outcomes (such as suicides or incidents of disorder) as dependent variables in the model. We have not developed staff dimensions in this model, or attempted this kind of further analysis, but we hope to do so in the future. It should be borne in mind that we are exploring cross-sectional data in this study, and this places limits on what we can say about causality.

We have established, conceptually and with empirical support, that if the prison is to do less harm, it must take the ethical identity of its inhabitants, including its staff, seriously, as well as 'keep them safe' (Logan 1992). Several commentators on our work have hypothesized that prisoners released from prisons with higher mean scores on these measures may 'do better' on release than prisoners released from prisons with lower scores. Prisoners who feel treated fairly and respectfully may leave prison with healthier identities than those who feel abused. This would be a valuable hypothesis to test in further developments of our work.[10]

A Model of Prison Quality and Moral Performance

It has a lot to do with staff attitudes. What you want are staff who will deliver the regime . . . They look at who's on today and they know what they're going to get.

(Senior officer)

---

[9] Tittle and others describe efforts made by offenders to escape control exercised by others or by circumstances, suggesting that 'a fundamental meaning of crime for the criminal is to escape the control of others' (Vold et al. 2002: 219; Tittle 1995; see also Liebling 1999; and Gallo and Ruggiero 1991). People who are controlled by others tend to engage in deviance to escape that control' (Vold et al. 2002: 308). Tittle refers to this as a 'control-balance' theory. Too much, and too little, can be damaging. We would expect this theory to have some relevance to prison staff and to prisoners, along the lines suggested by Cohen and Taylor (1972), other 'resistance' theorists, and throughout this chapter.

[10] We referred in Chapter 2 to a study by Lanza-Kaduce et al. (1999) which suggested that better organizational cultures seemed to be associated with slightly better prospects for released prisoners. More careful evaluations of this nature are needed.

There must be consistent delivery and there isn't. . . . There is an element of 'care' in 'delivery'.

(Officer)

Staff generally deliver a regime properly—for example, unlocking prisoners on time—when they have some respect and concern for prisoners. At two of our lower scoring prisons, staff acted out their generally indifferent attitude towards prisoners by finding reasons to delay unlock, lock up early, or cancel association and exercise. We have established elsewhere that prison officers have, like the police, high levels of low visibility discretion (Liebling 2000). What shapes the use of this discretion is, amongst other things, their relationships with prisoners, their vision of the prisoner, the moral messages they understand from their managers, their colleagues, and broader social trends. The apparent distinction between service delivery and professional values is much less clear-cut than critics have assumed.

The concept of regime delivery is morally relevant, if we consider the experience of imprisonment from the prisoner's point of view. Woolf was right about the lack of justice felt by prisoners about certain key aspects of their treatment, including the attitude of many staff. It can be argued that the 'service delivery' concept forces establishments to manage better quality regimes more effectively.[11] We have demonstrated that regime delivery depends on relational aspects of prison life. 'Quality' as we define it (as moral performance) cannot be *reduced* to the concept of service delivery, but there is an important relationship between the two. We demonstrated the complexity of the relationship between staff–prisoner relationships and regimes in Chapters 5 and 6.

The reality of prison life is anything but morally neutral (Sparks 1994; Carlen 2001). We need to return to the dialogue entered into in Chapter 8 (pp. 420–6) about what a moral prison might be. What are the limits to what might be justifiable under a declared moral agenda? The service delivery model, as typically conceived, avoids addressing the moral dangers of imprisonment and the moral realities of regime delivery, and seeks to construct the notion of 'performance' around hours out of cell (see Chapter 2). Meanwhile, professional

---

[11] This does not mean that the concept does not have other moral dangers (see Sparks 1994 and Liebling submitted).

practitioners suffer moral dilemmas as their own performance becomes tied to targets rather than to ideals. As one governor recently said, 'if they asked us to run Dachau, we'd probably do it'.[12] Critics have pointed out that penological debate has drifted away from these important questions of morality, in the name of performance. Our study brings together these apparently separate spheres: 'morality' and 'performance', and shows how they are related.

None of the prisons in this study was without flaws. Those two which we (and prisoners) regarded as better than others carried significant risks. There are tensions between some of the desirable qualities required of prison staff: respectful attitudes may be in tension with rigid adherence to important security procedures. A good prison achieves high scores on both relational ('harmony') *and* procedural ('safety/security') aspects of prison life. Good management techniques and a sound value base are important in the delivery of a decent prison. As the officers argued above, 'the regime' delivered in practice does depend to some extent on whether staff want to deliver it, and what they think it is *for*. Taking the five prisons in our study together (and leaving aside for now the problem of over-population), we develop below a composite picture of 'what a reasonable prison might be' (Table 9.3). We suggest in this model that 'relationships' and 'fairness' dimensions, together with security and management procedures, constitute acceptable moral performance, with safety, order, and well-being representing *outcomes* of better quality prisons.[13] Moral performance includes security-related issues *and* fairness and relationships, and good moral performance leads, in general, to safety, order, and well-being as outcomes. We are back in the realm of the sociology of order, and of political theory.

The concept of power balance includes the balance within the organization (among senior managers, between senior managers and staff, among staff, and between staff and prisoners, as well as among prisoners); and externally (between ministers, managers, and the public; see Pollitt and Bouckaert 2000: 155). As Pollitt and Bouckaert argue, power is not a zero-sum. Each constituent can

---

[12] The governor concerned subsequently left the Prison Service.

[13] This model by no means supplies a comprehensive theory of prison performance, but might constitute one of the 'incremental steps' towards the development of such a theory. Camp and Gaes argue that 'a comprehensive theory of prison performance . . . may take some time to develop', but must be attempted if comparative analyses of prison quality are to make sense (Camp and Gaes 2001: 297).

have greater control, in their different corners, but this is a 'fairly demanding' condition (Pollitt and Bouckaert 2000: 156).

TABLE 9.3.   Towards a model of prison quality and 'moral performance'

	Poor performance	Good performance

Qualities	Lack of respect
	Inhumanity
	Poor relationships
	
	Lack of fairness
	  (formal justice, staff
	  fairness and clarity)
	Laxity and disorganization
	Weak management
		Respect
		Humanity
		Good/right staff–prisoner
		  relationships
		Fairness (formal justice,
		  staff fairness and clarity)
		
		Security and management systems
		Strong leadership

Symptoms	Poor industrial relations Demoralized staff Uncertain identity No 'care' in delivery Threats to safety Disorder Distress	Meets performance targets High morale and job satisfaction Clear identity Professional standards of delivery Safety Order Well-being

Underlying
causes
	Changes of management
	Confusion of function
	Lack of trust in management
	Absent or imbalanced values
	Power imbalance
	Dilapidated or unsuitable
	  physical conditions
		Stability of competent management
		Clarity of function and direction
		Trust in line and senior management
		Value balance
		Power balance
		Reasonable physical/
		  architectural conditions

The concept of value balance—a complex 'ideal'—refers to the dual adherence to security and harmony values identified earlier. It is interesting to note that adherence to values in tension is common in political life, and that preferences for one (security) rather than another (harmony) are related to political and economic conditions:

Thus, in times of high unemployment and economic recession, people may become more conservative because they are sensitive to arguments about the need to 'tighten the belt', to control crime, to cling to tradition, and to strengthen the nation. They have received the message that the nation is in trouble and that values relating to self-protection, that is national strength and order, must be given priority. This is not to say, however, that the community values harmony and cooperation any less. (Braithwaite 1994: 86)

The current public mood—and political reaction to and manipulation of it—may be the single most destructive influence on the size, scale, and moral reality of the late modern prison (see Caplow and Simon 1999; Garland 2001a; and Chapter 1). Too much use of the prison—and too high a priority being given to security values— makes the 'moral performance of the prison', always a morally dangerous place, significantly more difficult to deliver.[14]

Returning to our discussion of 'what matters', we might argue that social capital (including trust, hope, norms, and civil relations) is possible in the prison as well as in the community, within limits (see Strang and Braithwaite 2001: 5–7). Using the kind of analysis reported in this book, we can arrive at a richer vision of what legitimate penal practices might be, and where they are lacking. It may be possible, using techniques like AI, and the 'undominated storytelling' also characteristic of restorative justice (Strang and Braithwaite 2001), to transform penal practices so that less harm is done (Liebling *et al.* 2001; see also McEvoy 2003 for an example of such a transformation in the Northern Ireland community). There is support for the existence of a shared moral community, even in the prison, in which stability and respect for individuals are key values. As Pepinski argued: 'The principles that create or destroy peace are the same from the Smith family kitchen to the Pentagon and the prison' (Pepinski 1991: 305).

There are difficulties with the idea of a shared conception of the good in the penal context, but if we use the language of civil society (or 'public good'; see Loader and Walker 2001; or legitimacy; see Chapter 10), we have a greater purchase on what it is that makes one prison better or worse than another. We use the term here, in its original sense, to mean the internal organization of a society. It means 'to be ordered or well governed' (*New Shorter Oxford English Dictionary* 1993); to have a 'secure, reliable, predictable legal order' (Kaviraj and Khilnani 2001: 2).[15] At its strongest, it denotes 'a community, a collection of human beings

---

[14] Garland argues, for example, that the emergent neo-conservative 'criminology of the other' (which is, in Braithwaite's language, security- rather than harmony-oriented) transforms the values on which penal modernism was built. It prioritizes order and authority, social defence, punishment and retribution, and exclusion. These values replace the values of inclusion, social reform, and a welfarist form of criminal justice (Garland 2001a: 184–7; and *passim*).

[15] Contemporary uses of the term tend to mean the activities taking place in the space between the state and the individual: uncoerced community life and values, or the opposite of atomized individualism (see Deakin 2001: 4 and *passim*).

united within a legitimate political order' (Khilnani 2001: 17); or
'the *just society*' (Deakin 2001, p. xiv). It is the opposite of the
'state of nature' (ibid. 19), bringing with it personal security and
'freedom from unlawful violence' (Black 2001: 33). There cannot
be 'unity' in prison, but there seems to exist something like a common set of goals and purposes, at least in relation to how a prison
should be socially organized. 'Order', civil society, or legitimacy is
never perfectly achieved in the free community: 'civil society is not
a determinate end-state, nor can it ever be a secure acquisition for
any group of human beings' (Khilnani 2001: 25).

It is this imperfect or aspirational quality of the term that makes
it a useful evaluative notion to apply to prison life. Unlike vague
and one-sided terms like 'good relationships', thinking about legitimacy and civil society usefully reconciles the tension between security and harmony values outlined earlier, or between 'tyranny and
anarchy' (Sacks 1997: 30). It helps us to sever the apparent link
between morality and *leniency* that the Prison Service has struggled
with in the past. There is a moral case for security and safety as
well as for respect in civil society (McEvoy 2003; and see Abbey 2000:
103–49).[16] As others have said before, we should disaggregate humanitarianism from sentimentalism (Home Office 1966; Liebling 2002;
Frank 1986).[17] There are many moral hazards in naïve optimism,
but it is possible to apply social-humanitarian principles to prison
life without falling prey to 'romanticism'. Such principles need to
be clearly articulated in order to avoid the moral confusions
described in the first chapter of this book.

We should consider the possibility that, in our exercises, prisoners (and staff) identified values that would generate maximum
benefits *for them*, if followed by others. We did not reflect, with

[16] McEvoy suggests that peacemaking criminologists, for example, propose compassion and empathy as a route to a better society, but this proposition has limited
application in situations where conflicts exist. He proposes a 'new' peacemaking
criminology in which humanizing interventions in conflict are possible (using
restorative justice principles). McEvoy 2003: 334–6.

[17] 'One must love the people, but not with a sentimental love acquired in the
study' (Dostoevsky, in an article cited by Frank 1986: 199) nor with the 'patroniz-
ing and self-serving' assumption that 'I can do what I like with him . . . for I know
what is for his own good' (ibid. 200). 'Starting from unlimited freedom, I arrive at
unlimited despotism' (Frank 1995: 449). Dostoevsky served as 'the voice of the
national conscience' at a time when the great public issues were freedom (modernism, atheism, and nihilism) and tyranny (see Frank 1995).

prisoners or with staff, on the *implications* of these values for their own practice, either as individuals or collectively. In so far as values provide 'cues for behaviour' (Deakin 2001: 73), or 'guides to conduct' (Frank 1995: 341), this research exercise, and the results flowing from it, might provide a platform on which to take forward such a 'civic' development programme. Such a programme might make more explicit the implications of 'what I value' for 'my own behaviour'.[18] We agree with O'Neill's argument that duties and obligations as well as rights should inform our political thinking (O'Neill 2002: 31). This is to raise again the distinction drawn by Sparks *et al.* between 'legitimacy' and 'appeasement' (Sparks *et al.* 1996: 329–36). Privileges and freedoms require a defensible moral basis, and there are limits to the demands that can reasonably be made in prison. The analysis of our interview data in Chapters 5 to 7, as well as our review of the literature, makes instrumentalism an unlikely explanation for the values chosen. Our dialogue did not, after all, take us beyond 'standards that can be defended externally in moral and political argument' (ibid. 330).

This brings us, finally in this chapter, and briefly, to the problem of rights. The question of the impact of human rights discourses and practices and their contribution to the moral functioning of a prison *system* deserves fuller reflection than we can offer here (see McEvoy 2001: 152; Cavadino and Dignan 2002: 55–8, 344–5; Creighton and King 2000; Livingstone *et al.* 2003: 543–66; and Haney 1997: 552–86). The terms 'respect', 'dignity', and 'humanity' are common to international instruments (such as the United Nations Standard Minimum Rules for the Treatment of Prisoners; see further Coyle 2002: 31–48). Such instruments provide an important baseline, or common and impartial framework, against which specific practices can be evaluated in individual prisons (see, generally, Coyle 2002; McEvoy 2003). Taylor argues that the 'language of rights provides a shorthand for the sorts of moral discriminations a culture makes . . . it is a shorthand for "strong evaluation"' (in Abbey 2000: 129; and see later). It is important to note that most of the values identified by staff and prisoners in our 'appreciative inquiry' exercise find some expression in human rights principles. The interpretation of these terms in practice, however, for example

---

[18] Some offending behaviour courses touch on related themes, in a less political-theoretical way.

by the European Court of Human Rights, tends to be conservative (see Creighton and King 2000: 290, on the use of segregation). Most prisoners would not contemplate resorting to the courts except in extreme cases and when serving long sentences. The existence of statutory instruments clearly exerts some pressure on policy-makers to take account of their requirements (but see Dixon 1997 on the role of the law, in practice, in policing). Creighton and King suggest that even this kind of impact is limited. We might also bear in mind O'Neill's warning (referred to above, and discussed more fully in Chapters 2 and 5) that rights discourses may need supplementing with a discourse of responsibilities (and see Taylor, in Abbey 2000: 127–33, on some other problems of rights discourse).

Livingstone *et al.* suggest that experience from other jurisdictions (e.g. Canada) suggests that the courts take 'a few years' to begin to use new rights in new ways (Livingstone *et al.* 2003: 563). They propose that overcrowding and its consequences (lack of opportunities, increasing threats to prisoner safety, and so on) may offer scope to challenge 'what happens in prison', particularly in relation to Article 3 of the Human Rights Act (the obligation to prevent torture, inhuman or degrading treatment or punishment; ibid. 562–4). We hope that the kind of analysis we have developed here offers an additional way of deliberating on what the terms 'inhuman' or 'degrading' might mean. We hope it may also contribute to a clearer understanding of what a 'lawful and non-violent' penal system might look like (see McEvoy 2003: 327) and what limits might be set, under the pursuit of order and security. Prison work is particularly socially significant, as complex considerations of fairness, security, and safety are intrinsic to it (see Loader and Walker 2001, on the police). We hope we have, by now at least, reframed the concept of prison evaluation from the narrow and technical account we started with in Chapter 2, towards a more moral and political, and meaningful, exercise (see McEvoy 2003: 335; and the next chapter).

10

Legitimacy, Decency, and the Moral Performance of Prisons

The deepest roots of discontent with the political leadership do not grow out of perceptions of their incapacity to manage affairs but rather from their (perceived) untrustworthiness or low moral standards.

(Pollitt and Bouckaert 2000: 145)

On a practical level, it warrants recognition that the specific practices of any prison system stem from penal ideology, and for as long as the underlying assumptions and supporting ideology of the penal system remain unexamined and unchallenged, then that system will successfully resist all but the most superficial of changes.

(McHugh 1978: 3)

Slaves are, so to speak, socially dead: they are not recognised as persons at all.

(Rawls 1996: 33)

We began, in this book, by setting out the important role played by ideas about prisons in prison life. We have demonstrated in subsequent chapters that prisons have moral and emotional climates, and that these climates are shaped by values, ideas, and relationships. What matters in prison, according to the analysis presented so far, is a set of values which are essentially *interpersonal* (see Stocker 1996: 166) and *civic*. These values matter internally in the sense that prison life is experienced and prison quality understood, by those who live and work there, in terms of 'performance' in these areas. We have sought to substitute narrow concepts of measurement and performance with a more satisfactory and analytically helpful concept of 'moral performance'. This concept fully incorporates, we suggest, these important but complex relational aspects of the prison, in a way that might apply to any organization. They are related to (and may reveal) exterior changes in the structure, culture, and values of the larger society (Jacobs 1983: 12).

Where does this account, and the findings we have presented here, take us? We have two main questions to answer, before we reflect more fully on the extent to which our analysis resonates with broader criminological developments. The first question is broad and sociological: having looked for differences between prisons, what 'essential similarities' have we found? What has this exercise told us about the prison? The second question is conceptual. In our exploration of 'what matters', how and why have we alighted on the term 'moral performance'? What is included in this term; how does it relate to the concept of legitimacy, and the Prison Service's own 'decency' agenda? What do *we* mean by 'quality' and can there be a 'moral prison'? If there is a moral agenda being pursued at senior levels in the Correctional Services and above, what limits does it set? Are the moral questions about the prison restricted to process issues, or are there specific outcomes that raise moral problems for the prison too? We reflect on some of these questions, in the light of our own research, below. First, let us summarize our work so far.

Summary of the Book

We argue that some important transformations have taken place in penal practices, values, and sensibilities over the period 1990–2003. Part of this transformation included a serious flirtation with a liberal penal project that went wrong. A significant factor in this unfortunate turn of events was a lack of clarity, on the part of those working in and managing prisons, about important terms like 'justice', 'liberal', and 'care', and how they might apply in daily penal practice. The escapes from two maximum security prisons in the mid-1990s, and the exposure of inappropriately regulated privileges in the high security estate, coincided with a dramatic 'punitive turn', to produce one of the most turbulent periods of penal policy in recent history. The period since 1995 has brought about first, a reconfiguration in the power base of prison life, with power shifting upwards, and secondly, a concerted managerial effort to improve the performance of, and to modernize and regulate, the prison. These shifts have taken place within a context of increasing public punitiveness, the re-responsibilization of the offender, and increasingly individualized explanations for crime (see Wiener 1994). The tensions and oscillations between bureaucratic-managerial, punitive, and humanitarian values throughout this period have been striking.

By 2003 some seemingly insoluble problems, including 'painfully slow progress' in modernization and reform, have apparently been solved. Meanwhile new problems face the late modern prison, including its apparent attractiveness to an increasingly punitive populist audience, and some concerns about the meaning and effects of performance measurement.

The prison of the 1980s was characterized by insanitary, inactive, and inhumane conditions, and the level of management knowledge about the nature and extent of the problem, as well as its likely causes, was poor.

In contrast, the reinvented, late modern prison of 2003–4 is a more sanitary and apparently purposive place, and its performance is much more carefully scrutinized and managed. This is despite an unprecedented period of population growth (which some critics suggest might be causally linked to these modernizing, relegitimation efforts). The modernization project, in which privatization plays a significant role, is part of a search for rapid organizational progress, in which better, firmer management aims to secure better, more efficient, and more effective public services. This new reform ethic brought with it the new, but flawed, craft of performance monitoring and measurement. We explore the arrival and the impact of the concept of performance throughout our early chapters, critically, but, we hope, with more balance than we have found amongst either its critics or supporters to date.

We consider the links apparently forged between managerialism and moral values, in relation to both the use of privatization to deliver better quality regimes, and the development of the Prison Service's decency agenda. These relationships are complex, as managerialism has an inherent tendency towards instrumentalism, and privatization comes with some significant moral risks. As Harding (2001) suggests, we may be led towards different conclusions depending on the strength and effectiveness of the accountability mechanisms in place, and the quality of provision in the public sector, including the treatment of prisoners and staff. There are some dangers when deontological values become linked to instrumentalist goals, as they did (we suggest) in the era following the Woolf Report. The oscillations between justice and humanity on the one hand, and security and austerity on the other, were made all the more likely because there was no clear moral base to the managerialist agenda of the early 1990s. Some things may be right because they are right and not just because they may 'work', despite the conditions of late modernity.

In Chapter 2 we argued that the information revolution has generated unprecedented knowledge about individual prisons, as well as providing a management reach into establishments from a distance, and a capacity for 'chronic revision' (Giddens 1991: 20), that was unimaginable fifty years ago. Compared to the emotive language of some studies or inquiries, and of critical Chief Inspectors' Reports, official measures of the prison seem to lack relevance, both to many who live and work in prison and to its critics. Whilst key performance measures have their strategic uses (including strengthening accountability), and they are certainly not irrelevant to prison quality, they also have limitations, and some dangers. They may measure 'progress through the jungle', but contrary to the declared ethos of managerialism, they do not necessarily indicate whether this is 'taking [us] further into or out of the jungle' (Sinclair 2002: 11). The art of performance measurement has been developed much faster than performance management. Standards auditing, a means of checking whether specified procedures are followed, has been heralded both as an effective means of investigating and improving practice, and by critics as a 'ritual of verification' which has reached pathological levels in many organizations (Power 2001, p. xvi). Such sociologically significant practices may have unintended consequences, including a reaction of distrust in employees, evasive behaviour, and cynicism towards managers. There is, however, evidence to suggest that establishments that are good at meeting official targets are generally good at other things too, with some significant exceptions. Inspectorate Reports often provide a more qualitative (and morally relevant) source of information about individual prisons, but some such reports, especially where critical, have been regarded as methodologically flawed. This, we suggest, is a pity, as they often contribute significantly to the flow of information about prison life and quality and they retain the sense of observed practices that other official measures seem to have lost.

Academic studies of prison quality have tended to be linked to an outdated model of treatment and other questions of effects, to a limited version of 'performance', as above, or to be constructed around management concerns. Conceptually and methodologically, there is a case for stronger integration between diverse evaluation efforts, together with more innovative, unconstrained comparative explorations of the practices, values, management activities, and influence of the private sector.

The true test of the meaning and usefulness of performance measurement, we propose, is in a careful analysis of what staff and prisoners have to say about their contemporary experience of prison life, and the question of quality, in a range of carefully chosen establishments. We found that what matters to those who live and work 'where the action is' in prison is a set of concepts that are all about relationships, fairness, and order, and the quality of their respective treatment by those above them. We devised and measured 14 of these kinds of dimensions in five prisons, using an 'appreciative' interview protocol and survey tool for prisoners, derived (and in some cases, administered) with considerable assistance from staff and prisoners. We found significant differences between establishments in these important areas of prison life (as well as some significant similarities), and we found some departures from the official vision of the prison supported by the performance framework. We devote considerable time in the second part of the book to exploring the meaning of these concepts in the penal setting, drawing on an extensive review of the literature and on what staff and prisoners had to say. We try to arrive at a satisfactory definition, via our exploratory account, of such terms as 'respect', 'humanity', 'fairness', 'order', 'personal development', and 'well-being' in prison. We call this framework the 'moral performance' or 'moral climate' of a prison. We shall reflect at greater length about this choice of terminology below.

Our analysis, in Chapters 5 to 7, shows the value of engaging in conversations about, and attempting to quantify, these important aspects of prison life. We might argue that our methodology constitutes a form of 'strong evaluation', moving beyond utilitarian calculations, supported as it is by shared values and views about what is 'right' (Seligman 1997: 68; Taylor 1985,

1992).[1] Our attempt to capture the meaning in practice of these important terms represents a beginning in a process we hope might continue. We can learn a great deal about prisons and how they work (and go wrong) as well as about how people co-operate socially from being clearer about what respect, trust, and fairness are and what they are not, where prisons fall short, and how they differ. It is, surely, more responsible and valid to show that, despite a generally poor quality of life at any one prison, some examples of fair interactions can be found. Staff, and others, are more responsive to this kind of analysis than to a general statement that there is a 'culture of brutality' or 'culture of institutionalized racism' in their prison. If we are to be honest about the kinds of places that prisons are, we need to be honest about the just transactions that take place in them, as well as frank and critical about abuses of power, and expressions of indifference.

Whilst the dimensions were highly inter-correlated overall, individual prisons could have quite different profiles, for example scoring well on 'fairness' but badly on 'respect', or delivering a distinct type of 'safety'. These differences seemed to be plausibly related to 'outcomes'. Prisoners in establishments scoring lowest on moral performance experienced punishment as more painful than did prisoners in better prisons, contravening any claim that there is 'uniformity of punishment' (Wiener 1994: 308; Haney 1997: 581). Prisons differ, in complex ways, and these differences in the delivery of punishment (and services) are deeply relevant to the prison experience. We saw in the data an empirical illustration of the possibility mooted in the literature that fairness generates trust, that respect and relationships are intrinsic to fairness, and that fairness and safety may be causally related to well-being. This part of our analysis provides a framework for work that will continue, and that others might develop. There is already an extensive literature on the ways in which fairness is inextricably bound up with the quality of the behaviour of individuals, especially of people in

---

[1] This is the idea that we can evaluate our evaluations and make qualitative distinctions between them. We are aware, as human beings, that some of our desires, goals, or aspirations are superior to, or more worthy than, others (Taylor 1985, 1992). Some have a 'stronger pull' (Abbey 2000: 23) and attract attitudes of admiration rather than contempt. Reflection, articulation, and strong evaluation (bringing highly valued goods from tacit to foreground understanding) are reflexively linked (as in AI).

power. The dimension 'fairness' 'strained to be in' our relationships category. It was correlated most highly with humanity, trust, relationships, respect, and order. Fairness is about both rules and rights, and relationships, and this finding is less gendered in the prison than some contemporary justice theorists suggest. We have emerged from this research with a much greater understanding of the maxim that 'staff–prisoner relationships matter'.

We found that even in apparently high-performing prisons, levels of perceived fairness, respect, humanity, and safety were low. None of the prisons reached the 'passmark' on personal development. Regime delivery was closely related to the nature and quality of relationships in prison. There were some similarities between prisons of different natures, so that trust was always low, and prisoners saw staff as having 'all the power'. Trust plays an important and underestimated role in prison life, at several levels, as well as constituting one of the central problems of contemporary social and political thought (Seligman 1997). On the other hand, the gap between too little and too much of dimensions like trust was narrow. The balancing act between 'security values' and 'harmony values' should not be regarded as a zero-sum business: what Doncaster prison needed was more vigilance, not less respect. This is an extraordinarily difficult balancing act to get right, in prison.

In Chapter 8 we explored the consequences of the new performance framework (and its new moral overtones) for those managing and being managed in the late modern context. The radical changes that have taken place in prison management since the 1980s have resulted in some significant reshapings of the power base in prison. A form of 'government-at-a-distance', involving strong central direction, and future-oriented improvement, is experienced by the workforce (as in many other organizations) as somewhat alienating. The constantly redefinable world of work is not conducive to trust. Given that this is already a fragile commodity in the prison, modern managerialist techniques may pose additional problems for governors and staff. There may, however, exist an over-romanticized vision of what prisons and prison management were like before this revolution. Asking prison staff to deliver 'respect' and 'fairness' (and then ensuring that they do so) is not as straightforward as it sounds.

We proposed in Chapters 8 and 9 that, for prison staff, clearly understanding such open-textured but important terms as justice, respect, humanity, care, order, security, and safety, and then balancing some of these 'principles in tension' is difficult. Prison staff have some moral needs and claims of their own, which are often overlooked in an era of 'turbo-charged capitalism' and 'sharper performance management'. The pragmatic, future-oriented approach to organizations taken by modernizing managers is experienced uncomfortably by tradition-oriented officers, whose time-horizons are inevitably shorter and whose priorities are quite different. For senior managers, navigating and shaping the moral and, we suggest, emotional climate of individual prisons is a thorny task. It is made all the more difficult as governors enter (and often quickly leave) an already existing social world, with its own collective memories and ethos, and sometimes somewhat cynical position on senior managers. Prisons are special moral environments in which *how people feel treated* (i.e. how prisoners *and staff* feel treated) has serious consequences, first, for what happens in them, and secondly, for the claims that can be made about them.

We suggest that although the prison has some special characteristics, which we shall summarize below, our analysis reaches well beyond the prison, to other organizations and social institutions, including government. The public's relationship to government is affected more by emotional investments and degrees of trust than by their ability to measure its performance (Braithwaite and Levi 1998; Tyler 1998). The roles of trust and of moral values in economics, organizations, and social and political life have become major topics of inquiry (van Deth and Scarbrough 1998; O'Neill 2002; Kramer and Tyler 1996; Braithwaite and Levi 1998; Halpern 2001; Karstedt 2001; Levi and Pithouse forthcoming). This emergent view of the social institution as a place where fragile but largely collective values can be nurtured or threatened (Levi 1998) has a particular relevance to the prison: an inherently low trust organization. Too little interpersonal trust within an institution leads to pathology (Levi 1998) and self-interested actions and values (Halpern 2001). This is quite a separate matter from institutionalizing the kind of formal distrust recommended by Braithwaite in his studies of the regulation industry (e.g. J. Braithwaite 1998) or encouraging the 'responsible disengagement' from violence described by McEvoy in the Northern Ireland context (McEvoy 2003: 332–3).

We shall return below to the two outstanding questions we promised to address in the remainder of this chapter. We looked mainly in our study for differences between prisons, but have we found any 'essential similarities' and what do these resemblances tell us about the prison? Why have we chosen the term 'moral performance', and how does this term relate to concepts of legitimacy, and 'decency'?

Prisons and their 'Essential Similarities'

Prisons are, primarily, places of punishment. They are (unusually, in the late modern context) place-based communities, where one party closely observes another. Prisons are special communities (but communities nevertheless), which exist at once outside and inside the social community. Their form is shaped by social and political ideas held about crime, punishment, social order, and human nature. Many of the practices within them are also shaped by these ideas. Prisoners are generally held against their will. In this sense, but also in others, prisons suffer from an 'inherent legitimacy deficit'. They are not consensual communities; and, as such, they are susceptible to abuses of power and to breakdowns in order. They are hierarchical, and normally a single individual is in charge. Compliance (of staff as well as prisoners) needs to be worked at. There are many constraints on freedom; for example, there are routines, which are made up of the daily practices of individuals. Power flows in prison, sometimes in subtle ways and sometimes in unexpected directions. By entering prison, prisoners lose much of their subject-agent status, and become depersonalized. Prisons are sensitive, sometimes 'raw', and potentially volatile places, where values are in tension. They contain, and produce, pain. Prisons are moral and emotional communities in which (except in a very few cases, such as some segregation units in some super-maximum prisons (see King 1999) or close supervision centres) relationships exist. Prisons have many moral dangers: they are dominating institutions in which respect is continually under threat.

We have elaborated in this book on the underdeveloped maxim that 'staff–prisoner relationships' are at the heart of prison life. These relationships are, we have shown, central to the prison's nature, functioning, and quality of life. What goes on in prison is shaped by structures, systems, ideas (held by those outside and those with influence inside), and physical layout. Prisons are also, and crucially, shaped by relationships. These relationships are formed over time, by values, practices, memories, and feelings, and by the way these interact.

On all of these basic characteristics, however, prisons differ by degree. The nature and quality of each prison's daily existence is detectable by those who know prisons. There is often a remarkable (if barely articulate) consensus amongst staff, prisoners, senior managers, and relevant external bodies about what a prison is like. This sense of the character of each prison is not reflected in KPIs or KPTs, as we hear continually. This character, ethos, or culture is difficult to conceptualize as well as difficult to measure.

Figure 4.1. (in Chapter 4) shows that the range of scores is widest for 'decency', 'power', and 'order', and narrowest (particularly among the four public sector prisons) for 'respect', 'support', 'trust', 'safety', 'prisoner social life', and 'meaning'. The narrow range of scores in these areas among the four public sector prisons in this study, despite some important differences, is interesting in itself. It suggests the presence of an overarching public sector culture that is distinctive (and relatively low on 'respect' and 'relationships'), perhaps especially in four prisons of a similar type. (Risley had been a local prison and had not made the transition, culturally, to a category C.) The persistence of an unwilling, and in places, hostile, public sector culture despite plainly declared values at senior levels in the civil service raises managerial and moral questions, which do not have straightforward answers. We have found greater variation (and some outperforming of private sector prisons) in ongoing work. Some aspects of prison life and quality clearly vary more than others. We are only one step along the way towards an explanation of these differences, and similarities. Low levels of respect (and so on) have consequences, including damaging effects on individual well-being.

Within an overall framework of increasing modernization and control, prisons with similar roles differ in identifiable ways (albeit within a relatively narrow range). They pursue distinct organizational goals which are linked to history and (to some extent) management.[2] We suggested in Chapter 1 that ideas and beliefs shape practice, that is, they shape the deep structures of penological action. These differences can be broad and historically contingent

---

[2] 'Formal leaders do not have any monopoly on the ability to create shared meanings' (G. Morgan 1997: 137).

(as Garland's work illustrates), and they may also exist at an intra-institutional level. We may characterize these intra-institutional differences as, in part, differences in ethos or culture.

We suggested tentatively in Chapter 4 that individual prisons have 'value cultures'. Prisons have some essential features, but they also differ by degree in their treatment of and orientation towards prisoners (and staff). Each prison is, in this sense, unique. Our account of five prisons supports the assertion that cultures and values are inextricably linked, and that they together constitute a major component of the quality of prison life. We have also shown that relational aspects of treatment in prison are deeply influenced by, as well as constitutive of, value cultures. We have tried, in this book, to put some shape on this 'essence of the prison', precisely because this invisible but essential aspect of prison life matters. We had to work from staff and prisoners upwards, to achieve this.

The Empirical Findings and their Significance

We should reiterate our basic belief that this 'prison quality' survey has value only because we engaged in a detailed attempt to involve staff and prisoners in the generation of the framework (i.e. the dimensions) and in the identification and wording of many of the items in the questionnaire. Staff and prisoners are undoubtedly experts on the prison. We could argue that they are better informed about the prison than 'the public' is about issues addressed in most public opinion surveys. The use of highly correlated dimensions (multi-item scales) is more satisfactory for this purpose than the reliance on single-item measures of complex concepts (Braithwaite 1994). Single-item measures can exacerbate the problems of multiple or ambiguous interpretations.[3] Prisoners often asked questions, for example, about whether they should complete the questionnaire as they saw prison life for those around them (particularly if they knew other prisoners were 'having a harder time') or for themselves. They understood, once we explained, that they should complete it from their own experience—but that we would 'capture'

---

[3] We would have certain minimum methodological requirements for an exercise like this: the questionnaire should be administered to a random sample of at least 100 prisoners in each prison; there should be opportunities for elaboration and discussion, and support for those who ask for clarification of questions, or who have difficulty reading (e.g. in English).

a representative experience of this prison overall from continuing the survey process with others, throughout the establishment. They were satisfied with this answer. We were informed often that the results had high face validity (they 'rang true'), they reflected subtle detail ('colour rather than monochrome'), and that the process as well as the results were 'more constructive' than other measurement attempts. Better use could be made of the data at an explanatory level if such surveys included an equivalent set of data from staff of all grades and types. We only made a start on this part of our work in this study.

We can use the data generated from these surveys in five ways:

1. To provide a detailed evaluation of life in an individual prison; in our proposed language, to assess the moral performance of a prison.
2. To explore the effectiveness of specific policies and procedures (for example, the impact of an anti-bullying policy on feelings of safety).
3. To identify, with some precision, differences between prisons.
4. To measure differences longitudinally in particular establishments.
5. To understand the nature and dynamics of prison life and the prison experience.

We have concentrated on the first and third of these, and we hope that this book makes a significant contribution to the last, throughout. We have addressed the second and fourth in other publications (Liebling *et al.* 2001; Liebling and Durie forthcoming). The research identifies different compositions (for example, of safety) as well as differences in 'scores'. We suggest, in addition, that this kind of research allows exploration of the relationships between important concepts so that we see, for example, that trust is linked to predictability, that fairness is related to relationships, and that personal development in prison constitutes part of what it means to treat prisoners humanely.

The Limitations of the Survey and this Analysis

There are several limitations to our analysis, which we need to make clear and which require us to continue to develop our work. First, the survey tool as we have developed it here is by no means the 'end of the story'. We can improve on several of the dimensions. We can add other conceptually important dimensions (we have done both in work currently in progress). Some important and difficult to operationalize dimensions are missing, such as security procedures, and aspects of the psychological experience of custody. We have arguably addressed more of the 'harmony'-type values than 'security'-type values described by Braithwaite (Braithwaite 1994). The differences we found between the four public sector prisons in this study were statistically relatively small. Using the survey in additional prisons has demonstrated that greater variation exists when more prisons are studied in this way. To 'make sense' of prison quality, as evaluated by prisoners, at an explanatory level, we need equally rigorous data from staff[4] as well as KPI and KPT data.

We have only included one private prison so far, so we cannot draw conclusions about the merits of privatization *per se*, nor attribute the results to distinctive or unique features of private sector management, but again we hope to pursue this question further. We have not attempted to take into account material differences (such as age and design) between the prisons in our study. Future research should develop from our attempt to identify what matters, towards *accounting* for the differences found in a less speculative and more theoretically informed way. Ideally, this kind of data would form the basis of a longitudinal study, and would be supplemented by detailed ethnographic work. This would allow us to develop more satisfactory explanations for differences in prison quality between prisons, and within prisons over time.

The account we have developed provides a methodological and conceptual foundation, upon which we and others may continue to work. We have concentrated on getting the identification of 'what matters' right. Methodologically, there are inevitably some limitations, once we move from our 'grounded theory' of what matters in prison, to quantitative analysis of survey data. We are using individual-level data to tell us about life in organizations (see Camp

---

[4] Duffee demonstrated that staff perceptions of the style of management, such as openness versus autocracy, were related to prisoner evaluations of the social climate in prisons (Duffee 1974). Healthy social climates were significantly associated with 'more democratic organisational profile scores' (Duffee 1974: 167–8). More autocratic styles were associated with more negative evaluations. On the other hand, 'officers feel very uncomfortable if they . . . are asked to behave in a democratic manner with their own subordinates, the inmates' (Duffee 1974: 166). These relationships would be interesting to explore in the current managerial climate.

1999; Camp *et al.* 1999; and see Horney *et al.* 1995 on the use of multi-level analysis).[5] We are comparing prisons, when we have argued convincingly that prisons may all have such distinct functions and characteristics that any attempt to compare them is flawed. However, we were ourselves surprised by the relevance of the survey to prisoners at Risley (a training prison) when we had originally developed it in a local prison. We have used the survey in female establishments and in young offenders establishments, and we have been assured that the questions, and dimensions, are relevant. This suggests that we have identified areas of prison life that matter, regardless of the prison's function. This is an important step. The *interpretation* of the scores from different types of establishments with different types of populations may, however, require caution.[6] There is evidence to suggest that women and young prisoners may be less critical about some aspects of prison life, for example, than prisoners in the high security estate (Liebling *et al.* 1997). We know that prisons fluctuate, and that within-prison differences can be found, for example, between wings.[7] There are always risks that, with breadth, we lose depth. We have not explored whether our dimensions are ordered hierarchically (see

[5] Mayton *et al.* argue that 'values have another uncommon characteristic in that they are relevant at both the micro or individual levels, and at the macro or societal and institutional levels' (Mayton *et al.* 1994: 1). We are aware of a vibrant tradition in the study of values (e.g. Rokeach 1973; van Deth and Scarbrough 1998), as well as a sophisticated literature on the use of individual-level data to make inferences about organizations. In this sense, our work constitutes a beginning, or a first empirical contribution from penology, to a broader theoretical project.

[6] For example, when we compared the responses of the White British participants in our sample (80.7%) with the Non-White/Non-British participants (19.3%), the Non-White/Non-British group scored significantly lower on perceptions of fairness ($p < 0.05$), relationships ($p < 0.05$), power ($p < 0.01$), decency ($p < 0.05$), and one of the family contact items ($p < 0.05$). This was 'I am able to maintain meaningful contact with my family whilst I am in this prison'. Other differences within the sample overall (unlikely to be accounted for by prison differences) included IEP status and having a job (prisoners on enhanced status and those with employment scored most things better). These group differences in perceptions of prison quality require further exploration, in studies with larger and more varied samples.

[7] There is a problem inherent in the use of scales in this context. The mean score omits variation between individuals (and groups) within each prison. We have found, for example, that mean scores often do vary by wing, and that these differences are plausible and informative. The data are amenable to analysis in this more detailed way, but we have not included those analyses here. This problem is true of all attempts to evaluate prison quality. See e.g. Liebling (2000).

Mayton *et al.* 1994), nor have we embarked on the tantalizing project of exploring the extent to which values are, in practice, linked to attitudes and behaviour in the prison.[8] We wonder whether working with prisoners (and with staff) on the implications of their value-orientations ('People can . . . change their behaviour to conform to their values'; ibid. 6) might be a promising way of developing what we have found.[9] The results from these surveys can be used at an organizational level to guide the strategic planning process (see Wozniac *et al.* 1998: 27). The hostility created among the regulated towards regulators using sanctions and deficit approaches, which generates resistance and leads to a decline in organizational performance (Braithwaite and Makkai 1994; Braithwaite 1998), may be avoided using this kind of approach. Even at Belmarsh, generally a poorly rated prison in our survey, we were able to represent empirically the existence of some trust, some respect, some humanity, and a considerable degree of support. There is considerable evidence that this represents a more strategic approach to the measurement of organizations than the deficit approach.

We started out in this book with a detailed account of the changes to have taken place in prisons over the period 1990–2003, with an argument that was primarily focused on the exploration of longitudinal changes in prisons and their relationship with changes in the external environment. The study we have reported on since then establishes relevant baselines, but we have not so far carried out (with one minor exception) any longitudinal studies using this framework. This kind of work is where our research has naturally led us. We hope to report on some longitudinal studies in future publications. What we hope we have achieved in this book is a framework, an analysis, and a methodology through which studies of this kind might be encouraged.

Penological debate needs to take into account the nature of the prison experience, and the extent to which values are practised, as

---

[8] A study by Camp found that using inmate surveys did provide reliable indicators of prison quality and conditions. He found that relevant differences between prisons persisted, for example, after controlling for different prisoner characteristics (Camp 1999).

[9] The AI technique, used fully, is intended to bring about organizational transformation (see Elliott 1999; Liebling *et al.* 2001). Consistent with AI's theory of change, Kluckhorn suggests that encouraging individuals to talk about their values can change their behaviour in the direction of those values (Kluckhorn 1951).

well as the prison's formal legal structure. There may be some idealization of the 'professional ethics' which managerialism has apparently eroded, as well as some lack of clarity about whether the liberal-welfare model of prison life ever delivered justice or humanity (see Liebling 2002; also Bottoms 1998; von Hirsch 1986), at least in the English context (see Downes 1988). Without management systems and abilities, and some appreciation of the importance of value balance, such aspirations lack foundation.

Prisons and their Moral Performance

Let us reconsider why we embarked on this work and how it led us where it did. The research had its origins in several pieces of previous research, which together suggested that the *relational* aspects of a prison's life, and its *ethos*, were crucial to the prison experience. These aspects of prison life are recognized by all who live and work in the prison, but they did not seem to be adequately reflected in official approaches to measurement or 'performance'. The prisoner who was 'not entitled to a pillow' (cited in Chapter 3) argued that indifferent treatment 'can turn you into a different person'.[10] Prisons differed, beyond their formal and material properties, in the extent to which they treated individuals harshly, or with respect. Our primary interest was in capturing accurately, using imaginative methods where we could, this aspect of the prison experience: that is, how it is *lived* and understood. The research, as we continue to develop it, is beginning to show that there is a significant empirical link between aspects of a prison's moral performance and (*a*) levels of psychological distress, anxiety, and depression found amongst prisoners; and (*b*) its suicide rate (Liebling *et al.* submitted).[11] Poor treatment leads to negative emotions. It is distressing and

---

[10] Conversely, difficult prisoners in small units saw 'being treated fairly', and as a 'human being' as the most significant factor in their progress—a number mentioned specifically that 'they came to see staff in a completely different light as a consequence of their time in the [Barlinnie Special] unit' (Scottish Prison Service 2002: 4). See also Bottomley *et al.* (1994).

[11] This early exploration, which we shall pursue in more detail, raises important questions about which (especially negative) emotions are generated by what aspects of one's treatment in prison. Feelings of confidence, and its lack, safety, and its lack, anxiety, and resentment are crucial components of the prison experience (see Barbalet 1998; Scheff and Retzinger 2001).

damaging for individuals (see e.g. Harris 2001: 84–6; de Zulueta 1993; Scheff and Retzinger 2001).

Why were these dimensions originally identified in our conversations? We have described *how* they arose in Chapter 3. The dimensions identified *matter* for four main reasons. First, they are seriously under threat in the prison. The 'essential similarities' described above make it highly likely that these issues will arise. They have practical consequences: 'a good day is a day when you get everything you're entitled to' (prisoner). Whether or not this happens is closely related to attitudes of staff. As one senior officer put it, 'there is an element of care in delivery'. When staff respect prisoners, they unlock them on time, they respond to calls for assistance, and they try to solve problems.[12] Staff are more likely to take this approach when they feel treated with respect themselves. Secondly, the absence of respect and fairness (and so on) is psychologically painful, as other prison studies have shown. Being treated disrespectfully or without dignity generates negative emotions (anger, tension, indignation, depression, and rage). Thirdly, and related to the arguments of Sparks *et al.* (1996), these dimensions constitute a set of principles to which we aspire in law and in contemporary moral and political philosophy. They are 'first virtues', the foundation of our social life. Fourthly, they are also, MacIntyre has argued, virtues that human beings need (MacIntyre 1999).

We began with the first two of these issues, and they have led us to the third and fourth: 'The officer on that houseblock didn't believe me. That's where there is a lack of respect. You are automatically assumed to be a liar. Prisoners cannot be thought to tell the truth and that hurts. I pleaded guilty to murder, why should I lie about other things?' (prisoner, Belmarsh).

The framework offered in this book represents a conceptual scheme, which attracts considerable *consensus* among staff and prisoners, against which a prison can be empirically examined. The survey we have devised expresses a shared understanding of 'what matters'. We were informed, but not constrained, by the empirical and theoretical literature. We may argue in retrospect that many of the dimensions we have included together constitute something of

[12] Sparks *et al.* make a similar point: 'it would be difficult, perhaps false, to disentangle the order of priority between a certain level of material provision and the particular posture or set of values held by staff in the day-to-day running of the prison' (Sparks *et al.* 1996: 171).

an approximation to, or operationalization of, the concept of 'legitimacy' used by Sparks *et al.* (1996) and others in their analysis of the prison. This point, and our use of the term 'moral performance' instead, calls for further elaboration.

Prisons and Legitimacy

We have seen that the term 'legitimacy' has been applied to prison life, and particularly in relation to the concepts of fairness and order, in a way that has illuminated how things 'go on' in the prison (Sparks 1994; Sparks *et al.* 1996). Legitimacy is a concept concerned mainly with authority and power relations. Bottoms and colleagues argue that 'legitimacy is a characteristic that may or may not attach to those in positions of power' (Bottoms 2002: 36). Formal structures, moral justifications (in terms of the beliefs of the population in question), and expressed support are all necessary constituents of the fairness of any authority (Beetham 1991). Legitimacy requires that authority is legally valid, that officials act fairly, and that they justify what they do to those affected by their decisions (see Bottoms 1999: 255; also Tyler 1990; Paternoster *et al.* 1997). Legitimacy includes the nature and status of the formal rules, the existence of shared beliefs which support these rules, and the *manner* of one's treatment (see Sparks and Bottoms 1995; Bottoms 2002: 36–8). Other terms might include moral credibility (Sparks 1994: 17), penal probity (Carlen 2001), or, simply, justified authority (Beetham 1991; Sparks *et al.* 1996). The concept of legitimacy has been linked theoretically, and at an exploratory empirical level, with levels of order and disorder in the prison (see Chapter 6; Sparks *et al.* 1996; Bottoms 1999). It is essentially a political-theoretical term: 'The problem of legitimacy is an abiding concern of political theory' (Sparks 1994: 14).

Its extensive use in the penal context originated with Woolf, who did not use the term himself, but who laid out the argument, taken up by others. Following the disturbances at Manchester Strangeways and other prisons in England and Wales during 1990, Lord Justice Woolf took the view in his report that prisoners experienced a general *sense of injustice* about aspects of their treatment. This, he argued, had contributed in a major way to their willingness to become involved in the disturbances on such a massive scale. This sense of injustice had several sources, and included material conditions, the manner of prisoners' informal treatment by staff, and their views on formal procedures, including grievance and disciplinary procedures. Woolf argued that order would be more sustainable in prison if prisoners could be persuaded that these aspects of their treatment were reasonable and fair, that is, that people in general are more likely to comply with authority if they believe that authority is legitimate (Home Office 1991a; Bottoms 1999; see also Cavadino and Dignan 2002). Sparks argues similarly that systems of social power generate moral requisites: 'To the extent that people confer consent they do so for a complex of moral as well as self-interested reasons, and rarely through coercion alone' (Sparks 1994: 15).

The absence of legitimacy 'carries large consequences for all parties in a system of power relations' (ibid. 15). The prison faces special legitimation problems, as it operates as an 'autocracy within a democratic polity' (Sparks 1994: 15). Sparks points out that it is important to consider both the interior life of the prison and its related 'exterior' settings. As he argued, especially in relation to their interior workings, some prisons are more legitimate than others. That is, there are 'differences in the power balances between the governed and the governing' (Garland 1992: 411); there are different material conditions; radically different informal practices; different cultures or 'working ways'; and sometimes subtly different attempts being made at legitimation.

Sparks *et al.* elaborated in some detail on the legitimacy of the *interior* life of prisons in their book, *Prisons and the Problem of Order* (Sparks *et al.* 1996). They demonstrated that different forms of order could be identified in long-term prisons, and that some forms of order were more sustainable and legitimate than others. The core issue is whether: '[P]risoners come to see the behaviour of their custodians as being justifiable, comprehensible, consistent and hence, fair—or, alternatively, unwarranted, arbitrary, capricious, and overweening' (Bottoms and Sparks 1997: 22).

Legitimacy should be clearly distinguished from 'appeasement' or 'pleasing the prisoners'. Sparks *et al.* point out that prisoners (often) know the difference between reasonable expectations (that a visit will be preserved) and unreasonable or 'unjustifiable' requests ('don't patrol our exercise yard'). These are expectations which can be justified in relation to a wider set of largely shared beliefs about what is reasonable. Legitimacy requires reference to standards that can be defended externally in moral and political argument. There are constraints on what can be done inside prison (in the name of interior legitimacy) by considerations of exterior legitimacy, for example public opinion, which can be hostile both to apparently highly punitive measures and to what might be seen as overly lenient measures (see Bottoms 2003b). Legitimacy in prison therefore includes the perceived fairness of staff, the perceived fairness of the regime, and procedural justice. We have seen in Chapters 5 to 9 that the dimension 'relationships' was very highly correlated with the dimension 'fairness' and that fairness is in itself a complex concept with many distinguishable components.

So can we distinguish the term 'legitimacy' from our use of the term 'moral performance'? What do *we* mean by the term 'moral performance'? Some aspects of moral performance overlap with the concerns of legitimacy; but there are also some distinctions.

Defining Moral Performance

By moral performance we mean those aspects of a prisoner's mainly *interpersonal* and material treatment that render a term of imprisonment more or less dehumanizing and/or painful. Prisons should perform well because it is important to treat human beings well. We took seriously the case that the concept of *quality* had not been satisfactorily defined in previous or current official measures of the prison. The concept of moral performance is an important aspect of quality, in the sense communicated to us by those with whom we worked at the earliest stages of our research. As one prisoner said: 'Respect, right? It's something about what I was saying with that cup of tea. An officer got me a cup of water at lock up so I could make myself one. Someone wanted to recognize that I'm a person. Do you know what I mean?' (prisoner, Belmarsh).

We alighted on the term 'moral performance' towards the end of our research: this terminology appealed because it 'rang true'. It indicates that we are interested in how prisoners (and staff) *feel* they are morally treated in and by the prison.[13] We believe that the term 'moral performance' takes us beyond legitimacy (in itself a complex concept), in a way that indicates that prisons are about

---

[13] The *emotional* tone of many of our workgroup exercises, as well as our interviews, was high. This supports our argument made earlier that prisons have emotional as well as moral climates.

474 Penal Values and Prison Management

more than power relations. They are, or can be, despite the stark imbalance of power, almost civic communities. Prisons can be moral communities and can be experienced as such, under certain conditions.

We used a combination of deductive and inductive reasoning (i.e. the literature and our structured and unstructured conversations with staff and prisoners) to develop our conceptual scheme. Some of the dimensions we explored may have a causal relationship with others (e.g. respect and relationships may lead to increased order and well-being), but we have only explored these possible causal relationships tentatively in this research. The scheme bears some resemblance, but is not identical, to a political theory of prison life. Janowicz argued that, in some correctional institutions, the language of the political scientist can be used to describe leadership, power balance, coalition formation, and communication patterns (Janowicz 1966, p. 7). As this language suggests, and as we have seen briefly in Chapters 2 and 7, much of the attention of early prison sociology focused on describing relationships *between prisoners*, with only selected attention paid to relations between prisoners and staff. We wanted to include broader issues of practice and value, including the moral status ascribed to the individual within the institution. We were more interested in the way prisoners saw staff, and in how they felt treated, than in their relations with each other. This was a result of their clear identification of what matters and of what should be evaluated when thinking about prison quality.

We have been primarily concerned with what prisoners *said* (largely inductive reasoning) rather than with what legitimacy theorists, or early prison sociologists, claim. We seem to have identified a slightly more complex and explicitly relational model of what matters in the prison, which avoids, for the time being, some of the *exterior* matters raised by Sparks (Sparks 1994; but see further below) and some of the *inner* 'social life' matters raised in more ethnographic studies. This scheme should be distinguished from Sparks's version of 'weak' legitimacy, however, whereby the most 'visible features of the problem' can simply be 'fended away' for the time being (Sparks 1994: 19) and where the key issues are presented in purely consequentialist terms (ibid. 22). It is also more than a variation on the 'Portia'/'Persephone' debate, whereby interpersonal matters contribute more than we typically assume towards perceptions of justice (see Heidensohn 1986; Gilligan 1982; Pilling 1992). Our scheme places the treatment of the individual, in ways that really matter, at the heart, rather than the periphery, of evaluative knowledge. This is arguably because, in part, it operationalizes the key concept of legitimacy. But it also incorporates broader questions of personal development, psychological well-being, the delivery of pain, interpersonal treatment outside the flow of power, and meaning, not all of which are explained by or fully conditional upon power relations. We are arguing that prisons are a special case of other civic and moral communities, in which the risks of abuses of power are high, but the 'smooth flow of power' is not all that goes on in them. They always fall short, for this is their nature, but we should concern ourselves with the nature, extent of, and explanations for these various shortfalls.

This framework, with its many dimensions, and its positive and critical components,[14] requires us to reflect in more detail about the implications of prisoner (and staff) evaluations of their treatment. The term 'performance' attracted us because the exercise had an evaluative aim, but (we hope) this aim explicitly incorporates a more meaningful and conceptually informed set of dimensions than standard performance attempts. The data generated in this way provide us with a clear and important set of issues to think about. We would argue that the term constitutes the beginning of an empirical 'grounded theory' of the prison experience, whereby official measurement or evaluation approaches can be challenged and an empirical-moral framework can be generated. This arises precisely because the moral constitutes such a significant part of 'what goes on' in prison life. The scheme inevitably has normative implications. Our data and this framework has a descriptive and explanatory role, and may also be used as an empirical test, or mode of exploration, of the role of legitimacy (and its constituent parts) in the prison experience. But it also aims to achieve more than this. We have shown that even (perhaps especially) in the prison, the values of civil society matter. Our vision of the 'civic',

[14] Bottoms distinguishes between positive morality (what 'is') and critical morality ('what should be, against this standard'). Our account, and the 'moral performance' survey we have devised, can be regarded as addressing 'what should be' at the design stage, and 'what is, against a standard', at the survey stage (see further p. 489; and Bottoms 2002: 23–4).

devised from our detailed empirical work, has slightly less emphasis on 'safety and order' (especially as seen from above) than the models developed by Logan, DiIulio, and others (US Department of Justice 1993), with their more managerialist framework. This was an important departure from prior studies. We recognize in the light of our discussion in Chapter 9, however, that there is still considerable thinking to be done about just how to include safety and security dimensions in this kind of research, in ways that grow out of, and remain true to, the prisoner experience.

So how does our conceptual scheme relate to the 'decency agenda'? The three terms (legitimacy, moral performance, and decency) have often been used interchangeably by those with whom we have discussed our work. We need to develop some further clarification of our term 'moral performance' by distinguishing it from the term 'decency' as used in recent Prison Service discourse. There are, of course, also some important areas of overlap.

Prisons and Decency

The term 'decency' first appeared in official Prison Service language in the 1991 White Paper (1991b: 59),[15] but was adopted in a rather different spirit by Michael Howard, as part of his claim that prisons should be 'decent but austere'. The term was used in Martin Narey's first speech to the Prison Service Conference as the incoming Director General, in 1999, to mean 'fair and humane' (Narey 1999). The decency agenda received a more formal launch following the exposure of abuse by prison officers in several local and young offender establishments during 2000 and 2001 (HMCIP 2001d). Attention was targeted at 'failing prisons', by which senior managers meant prisons with impoverished regimes, poor industrial relations, and poor treatment of prisoners (Home Office 2000 and Chapter 1). Narey declared, in 2001, that he wanted to make prisons 'decent and reformative places'. His speech to the Prison Service Conference in 2001 was both controversial and ground-breaking. He described it as 'the most important I have made'. He challenged governors not to accept that intolerable prisons were places that could not be changed: 'Year after year, governor after governor, inspection after inspection, prisons like these have been exposed. Year after year the exposure has led to a flurry of hand-wringing,

---

[15] Where it was said that conditions should be 'decent **but** not lavish'.

sometimes a change of governor, a dash of capital investment, but no real or sustained improvement' (Narey 2001: 1).

Staff became resigned in such prisons, and couldn't 'be bothered' to fill education or workplaces. They lied about whether rooms had been cleaned, and they 'sorted out prisoners' in completely unacceptable ways. This had to change. These establishments were morally outrageous. He said:

The point I'm trying to make is that we have to decide, as a Service, whether this litany of failure and moral neglect continues indefinitely or whether we are going to reform places, whatever the difficulties, whatever the burden of overcrowding, whatever the resource constraints, whatever the middle management inadequacies, whatever the POA opposition. I want to tell you frankly that I have no wish to be a Director General of a Service which is going to duck these issues . . . I tell you now: unless, in addition to the unequivocal support of Ministers and the backing of an outstanding, committed and cohesive Board, I believe I have the support, encouragement and determination of all of you in this audience, I'll find an easier way to earn a living . . . The only reason, the only justification for my doing this job, the only thing that can make it remotely worthwhile, is a passionate belief that the apologies and the abject explanation will no longer be necessary. (Narey 2001: 3)

The speech was represented in the press as 'DG threatens resignation'. One or two governors left the conference hall, upset by the naming of their establishments or exhausted by the challenge that it was all 'a matter of determination':

The choice is straight forward. We take on the challenge. We make a reality of the rhetoric of decency and dignity. Or we accept the unacceptable. We tolerate filth, appalling healthcare, treating prisoners as a sub-species, doing virtually nothing to prepare them for release. We tolerate these things because they are too difficult to change. (Narey 2001: 3)

Most governors welcomed the decency agenda, however, and described it as 'what we should have been doing all along'. The challenging speech came alongside the introduction of performance testing for bottom of the league establishments, as described in earlier chapters.

The term 'decency' is being used variously, and sometimes broadly, in a sense that might incorporate concepts of fairness and minimum standards, but that tries also to incorporate security, order, the challenging of offending behaviour, and a reduction in the availability and use of drugs (Wheatley 2001). Some might ask how a word like decency can mean all these things. The word means, literally, 'not indecent', or 'fit and appropriate'. In the prison context it can mean as little as 'reasonable basic conditions' (see Chapter 6) or a more aspirational concern with respect and hope. Some argue that its advantage over other terminology is this very flexibility, and the acceptability of most of its possible definitions to prison staff. Others see this vagueness as its main flaw. The word 'decency' is arguably acceptable to most prison staff (although they tend to agree to its material implications more readily than to its 'human rights' and 'relationships' implications; Mulholland 2002), who are more comfortable with this word than with related terms like 'justice', 'humanity', and perhaps especially, the term 'liberal' (Liebling 2002).[16] Use of the term is, amongst other things, an attempt by the Prison Service to add, to the narrowly conceived performance agenda described earlier, a concern with respect for prisoners and the culture of a prison. Narey (and his successor, Wheatley) is publicly insisting on a 'firm, fair, courteous and competent' approach, especially in those prisons that have had a reputation for many decades of staff over-control and under-management. This 'change of tone' is part of an internal drive for a 'different sort of Service . . . in which no establishment is seriously failing with the basics—where a safe and decent environment is given for all in our care' (Narey 2002: 8).

This is the stated objective. Some senior managers, and many academic commentators, are deeply sceptical and see it as 'old wine in new bottles' or as a strategic attempt to justify increasing use of the prison (see e.g. Carlen 2002a). Simon and Feeley warn (drawing on Edelman 1977) that 'words can succeed even though policies fail . . . Images generated by public policies can create a sense of confidence that problems are being attended to even when little or no concrete progress is being made' (Simon and Feeley 1995: 151).

There are, between the lines, much less benevolent messages to governors and area managers about keeping a 'tight managerial

[16] Not necessarily because there is anything intrinsically wrong with the words, but because they are infuriatingly difficult to be clear about and they are more difficult still to translate into practice in the complex environment of the prison.

grip', which some feel might be long overdue, and which is consistent with the public sector efficiency drive and performance agenda more broadly, as suggested in Chapter 8. Some governors experience this as a brutal form of leadership. Others argue that strong leadership of this kind is the only way to deliver significant moral improvement. It is significant that, at the level of rhetoric at least, civic and pro-social values are newly appearing (or newly *reappearing*) in Prison Service vocabulary (and in other criminal justice agencies; see Macpherson 1999; HMCIC 1999).[17] Managerialism has been claimed as the route by which this moral agenda can be most effectively pursued.

The question of empirical practice is of course to be distinguished from the rhetoric, and we have explored this empirical question throughout. We prefer the term 'moral performance' for our empirical exercise, because it makes explicit the broader values we heard reflected in our discussions. It is more precise, more amenable to operationalization, and it gives priority to those relational aspects of prison life about which people had the most to say. It cannot easily be used to mean material provision alone, in the way that the term 'decency' can. We consider below what conclusions can be drawn from our work.

Values, Performance, and Prison Privatization

We have not formally studied the structural or exterior conditions of imprisonment, but we suggest there are in our account some implications for the public–private sector debate, as well as for the increasing use of imprisonment, to which privatization is often thought to be logically connected. Our analysis of competing values in Chapter 9 applies to the debate about privatization, introduced in Chapter 2. It is over-simplistic to suggest that the public sector has the monopoly on 'public sector values' or, conversely, that only the private sector has the management expertise to make values real in practice. It is naïve to imagine that for-profit enterprise will

---

[17] Some individual prison establishments have publicly expressed a commitment to taking this agenda forward: '[Our new] curriculum ['The Civic Prison'] will enable prisoners to develop the capacity to behave in accordance with civic rules and to learn, through personal experience, their role as a citizen within an environment in which personal growth is encouraged and valued' (HMP Risley, n.d.). See also US Department of Justice (1993) on the measurement of 'civic ideals' in criminal justice.

regulate itself morally, but this is not to suggest that many individuals working in private companies do not operate with a fairly fully developed moral framework in mind. In the end some careful consideration of what services are required (outside any narrow performance framework), and for what purposes, in order to resemble a just institution, must take place. We need then to reflect on the question of what mechanisms might best secure these 'just institutions', with what attendant risks of different approaches to the task. This questioning should include the issue of prison population size, and should be informed by serious empirical study of the role and impact of private sector activities and values on population growth, its possible reversal, and on public attitudes towards the prison. This is much more than a question of management.

We are persuaded by Pollitt and Bouckaert, and by our own observations, that the public sector reform agenda has been necessary but harsh (especially in the UK). Whilst 'sluggish, centralised bureaucracies, their preoccupation with rules and regulations, and their hierarchical chain of command, no longer work very well' (Osborne and Gaebler 1992: 11), there is no 'global recipe which will reliably deliver "reinvented" governments' (Pollitt and Bouckaert 2000: 60). There are some positive characteristics of the public sector ('continuity, honesty and a high commitment to equity'; ibid.)—the theta-type core values—which matter. These values are broader, more carefully balanced, and they exist at a higher level, than those values we found being practised at Doncaster, despite this establishment's undeniably impressive achievements. The private sector, and the new image public sector, have produced a new discourse of reform, and a feeling of culture change, but detailed empirical studies of 'micro-improvement' or of management action in the private sector are rare (Pollitt and Bouckaert 2000: 191). There are no studies that we know of that test the impact of newly opening prisons (private or otherwise) on sentencing practice. Again, the concept of value balance might be important here. We reject the ideological claim that 'private is better', whilst hoping that the public sector might learn from both its successful and its disastrous experiments with privatization. We should never forget the dangers of public sector bureaucracies (Bauman 1989), and in this sense we welcome the attention to comparison and quality that public–private sector competition has brought with it. We have become persuaded, however, that the empirical studies of individual prison regimes favoured by Harding and others do not address the most important distinction between public and private sector prisons: the nature, quality, and stability of the value base on which prison quality is built.

In Chapter 2, in the light of our discussion of existing evaluations of prison quality, we raised the question of what a just institution might be. We have seen, particularly in Chapters 5 and 6, that relational matters are extremely important in people's evaluations of justice. We find considerable support for our findings in the analysis by Tyler and Blader, who suggest that: 'Interpersonal treatment is important because it communicates a message to the person about their status in relation to the group' (Tyler and Blader 2000: 90).[18]

A just institution has trustworthy motives, fair procedures, neutral decision-making, and it treats individuals with dignity (Tyler and Blader 2000: 89–90). In it, people receive 'status recognition' or 'treatment that is consistent with ethical standards' (ibid. 90). The quality of decision-making and the quality of treatment make crucial and distinct contributions to evaluations of fairness. Relational treatment serves as 'information that speaks to a person's value as an individual' (ibid. 90). Tyler and Blader propose that 'people use their interactions with the group to assess their social status' (ibid.). This means that people are concerned to a significant extent (primarily, according to Tyler and Blader) with relational aspects of procedures in their assessments of fairness (ibid. 92). Participation in decision-making is also important. As we saw in Chapter 6, neutrality may not be quite the right word in the prison, where individual rights and dignities are under threat. What prisoners want is to be treated without discrimination, but as favourably as possible in the circumstances (a version of Harrison's term, mercy). We established in Chapter 8 that just institutions also extend these principles to staff. Due consideration should of course be given to outcomes as well as processes, in any moral scheme. This is where, amongst other things, prison population size, post-release survival, and the collateral consequences for communities, staff, and prisoner well-being, and public trust in government, all need to be taken into account in our moral reckoning with the prison.

[18] See also Scheff and Retzinger (2001: 65).

Towards a Comparative Moral Evaluation of Prisons

Many criminologists characterize the prison as a place of punishment, exclusion, and authoritarian power. In 1983, David Garland and Peter Young lamented the incoherent and unstable state of knowledge in the field of penality: the diversity of types of analysis and of approaches to 'the power to punish' made 'research and the production of useful knowledge uneven and fragmented' (Garland and Young 1983, p. ix). They identified a need to shift from a predominantly technical or administrative penology towards a more fully social analysis of punishment. Garland's subsequent work has gone a long way towards achieving this, especially at the broad theoretical and historical level (Garland 1985, 1990, 1997, 2001*a*). Our understanding of the functions and nature of the penal system has been transformed by his project and the work of others. But what of those concrete, historically specific investigations into particular penal practices, which, Garland continues to argue, ground or help us to explore the broad sociological concepts of interest: power, discipline, and punishment? Is there, in the study of punishment, an intellectually vibrant dialogue between empirical studies of specific sanctions and practices and broader sociological analyses within criminology and beyond? There are few. Part of the explanation for this is the way the prison is often misrepresented in much criminology as *simply* a place of illegitimacy, exclusion, and administrative practice. We need, as Garland has suggested, to integrate fully close empirical scrutiny of the new powers and technologies of penal practices with critical and sociological models of explanation. We should fuse careful accounts of what *is*, with normative evaluations of what *should be*.

We have long had a concern that the significance of the prison (for example, in criminological analysis) is too easily reduced to power and to size. Of course the question of what drives prison populations and how we account for (and reverse) the unprecedented increases in the size of the prison population matters (see Blumstein and Beck 1999; Caplow and Simon 1999; Garland 2001*b*). However, a preoccupation with, for example, the number of prisoners housed in supermax facilities (King 1999) is a disturbing diversion from the equally important qualitative question of what supermaximum custody. *signifies*, and how it operates. Just how illegitimate is it—and if moral values survive in these places, how is this so? Why is it our chosen route—and what price is being paid for its apparent benefits (Clare *et al.* 2001)? Who are 'the new prisoners' (Ruggiero 1999)? Are they, as Simon speculates, a less literate generation than before (Simon 2000)? Are they, as a recent ONS (Office of National Statistics) survey suggests, a drug-dependent and disordered population, a quarter of whom have attempted suicide in their lifetime, and half of whom have thought about it (Singleton *et al.* 1997)?[19] The growing and cumulative vulnerability of the prison population may be as significant as the population's increasing size. Once in prison, they become 'those we are afraid of' (Riveland 2000: 193)—and then many of them live up to it (see Clare *et al.* 2001).

In addition to the quantitative increase, then, there have been important qualitative changes in the nature of the prison population. There have also been major qualitative changes in the way punishment is *administered* in prisons in England and Wales. We may be beyond austerity, but fiscal as well as moral considerations are leading towards a 'no frills' and hyperdisciplinary trend in imprisonment (McDonald 1999; also Bottoms 1983). What are the consequences of this transition—for prisoners, staff, and those who advocate a different model? There are new modes of exercising power in prison—do we know enough about what they are, how they are practised, what their consequences might be? These developments are linked in complex ways to the broader social practices of an increasingly exclusionary, authoritarian, and punitive kind identified by many criminologists, but analysis tends to stop at the prison gate. In prison, as well as outside, there are new categories: 'roughest', 'rough', and 'respectable' or 'deserving' and 'undeserving'; 'basic', 'standard', and 'enhanced', as earned privileges schemes proliferate (Liebling *et al.* 1997). Just how are prisoners divided into the 'deserving' and the 'undeserving'?

When comparing the prison research of the 1970s and early 1980s with most subsequent work, we cannot fail to note the relative silence of the radical paradigm in the late modern era (see for a review van Swaaningen 1997; also Sim 1990). There has been an almost complete depoliticization of explanations for crime and of the position of prisoners. Contrast today's language of performance with

[19] Between 5–8% male prisoners and 4–10% female prisoners had 'no evidence of any disorder' (Singleton *et al.* 1997).

the struggles and protests of the 1970s, the contested discourse on prisons and the challenges to secrecy mounted by Cohen and Taylor (1972), Fitzgerald and Sim (1982), campaigning organizations, and the prisoners' rights movement. Jacobs argues that the prisoners' rights movement of the 1960s and 1970s in the USA has to be understood in the context of a 'fundamental democratization'; as part of a 'broadscale effort to redefine the moral, political, economic as well as legal status of prisoners in a democratic society' (Jacobs 1980: 431–2; also Jacobs 1977). Alongside this transformation in citizenship, there was the movement's other project: a sustained exposure of the myth of benevolent rehabilitation, of unaccountable and arbitrary power; and a desire to make visible the excluding and disciplinary function of the prison. Order in prison was fragile, the system was in crisis, prisons and many sources of penal powers—medical, psychiatric, disciplinary, symbolic, and ideological—were challenged by prisoners with voices and by other critics. There was clearly resistance. Jacobs argued, in 1980, that the increasing role of the courts in challenging prison practices 'spelled the end of the authoritarian regime in American penology' (Jacobs 1980: 434).

Certainly there has been a transformation in the basic living conditions that prisoners endure. Some more recent academic commentators argue that 'the prison offers a potentially humane and legal way to address violent offenders that society must be protected from', that it remains 'a potential locus of accountability and rights' (Caplow and Simon 1999: 111). There is greater access to families, goods and services, and redress. There is good reason to believe that the case for prisoner protest is less urgent, for the majority. But there is a peculiar tension between these improvements in basic conditions and the corresponding increase in what Garland has called the 'expressive' function of prison—as a site of public revenge. The empirical trends described in Chapter 1 make precisely this point.

Where does this leave prisoners? Do they meekly assent to the modern penal scheme? What of resistance today? This has been the largely undocumented penal project of the last decade or so: to eliminate residual resistance and secure a new mode of compliance. Our detailed account in this book began in the early 1990s, but arguably the 'new compliance' mission began with prison staff in the late 1980s and then continued into the early 1990s, with Fresh

Start and then privatization and market-testing. Officers in many establishments were resistant to the liberalization of regimes brought about by an increasing concern with civil rights, and by the shift in penological thinking from rehabilitation to normalization and 'humane containment' (Bottoms 1990). But, as we suggested in Chapter 1, what might be characterized as 'the great compliance project' extended to prisoners once they failed to appreciate the more liberal regimes conceived in one way by Woolf and others, but delivered in quite another by prison staff. Far from improving order, as promised, the liberal interpretation of the justice model seemed to bring new problems of high assault rates, increased drug use, and idleness (HMCIP 1993a; Prison Service 1994a). Perhaps prisoners' expectations rose uncontrollably (see Jacobs 1980: 460).[20] Staff underenforcement of the rules in the interests of good relationships with demanding, well-organized, powerful prisoner groups culminated in the escapes from Whitemoor and Parkhurst. How did all this take place? What were the consequences?

We do not know, but in a 'reassertion of penal authority' (Simon 2000), the apparently post-social prison emerges, where no accommodation of prisoner hierarchies can be sanctioned, the formal takes precedence over the informal, and we witness a return to the rules (ibid.). Even prison governors were subject to a strict regime from the mid-1990s. The new robust management approach has resulted in the departure of several governors and area managers. Punitive discipline is now applied to the suppliers of punishment as well as its objects. What does this mean? Order, of a quite specific kind, has been largely achieved—so that prisons are, in the words of one prisoner, 'safer, in a tense sort of way' (in Liebling and Price 1999).[21] What accounts do we have of this will-to-order? How has the relative quietness or submissiveness of prisoners been achieved (if, indeed, it has)? What part has been played by public sentiments

[20] Jacobs argues that prisoners' rights movements may intensify grievances as rising expectations outpace reform, and may demoralize and embitter prison staff. He detects links between these possibilities and the need for 'less punitive' but 'more intrusive' modes of control; and increasing bureaucratization (Jacobs 1980: 460–3). He also points out, however, that the prisoners' rights movement 'has contributed greatly to the reduction of brutality and degradation, the enhancement of decency and dignity, and the promotion of rational governance' (ibid. 466).

[21] We quite recently witnessed one category C prison, for example, proudly declaring that the last guitar had finally been removed—a symbolic act of victory over the permissive era of 1992–5.

and political opportunism in the 20-year shift from questions about whether prisons are humane enough, to the question, are they punitive enough (see Haney 1997)? How have prisoners become fully engaged in the management of their own incarceration (Garland 1997)? Has the authoritarian regime described by Jacobs re-emerged, in a different guise? Is it sustainable? Is the apparently compliant behaviour achieved masking resentful hostility amongst prisoners who argue that: 'They've killed it. Gone overboard. All that trust is gone . . . They're not gaining, but losing what they had. Sad, isn't it?' (prisoner, cited in Liebling 2002).[22]

The anger and resentment previously expressed periodically through organized channels and by large groups of prisoners became transferred to a small group of the super-resistant: those who challenged their placement and treatment in the UK's answer to supermax, in Woodhill Prison's Close Supervision Centre.[23] Sherman's 'defiance theory of criminal sanctions' might be usefully applied to this group (Hagan and Dinovitzer 1999: 127; Sherman 1993)—a proud and angry emotion driving retaliation for the rejection and stigmatization entailed. Have they now succumbed? Or has the prison reasserted its legitimacy in this symbolically crucial place too?

The disciplinary web is not fragile, as characterized by critics in the 1970s (see Sim 1990). It is composed of multiple new knowledges and techniques: incentives and earned privileges, discretionary release and curtailed home leave, enhanced internal and perimeter security, CCTV, mandatory drugs testing, the volumetric control of personal possessions, computerized security information, and so on (Liebling 2000). Prisoners are, in ways Mathiesen could not have envisaged, 'atomized and depressed', divided and self-regarding (see Mathiesen 1965). There can be little solidarity with so much power to punish available. Is it not significant that we seem to have stopped hearing the word 'crisis' in relation to

---

[22] A study of the introduction of a policy of incentives and earned privileges found that prisoners in a tightly controlled young offender institution, operating with high levels of discretion, secured superficial compliance from disempowered prisoners. Their attitudes towards the staff and the regime of the prison were, however, negative (see Liebling et al. 1997; also Bottoms 2003b; and Table 1.3).

[23] Considerable changes have taken place in the operation of Close Supervision Centres, now in 'Phase Three' of their lifetime. D Wing—the ill-fated segregation unit within the CSC system—was emptied and disbanded in 2002.

prisons, despite unprecedented population growth, and some disturbing new practices? Where does power lie now? Prison officers have more power of a certain discretionary kind, but perceive themselves as powerless in other regards, and as expendable. Prisoners have more rights, but arguably less power. Their status has been transformed. It is almost no longer possible to think of a prisoner as a victim, certainly not as a hero or revolutionary (Jacobs 1980: 439; and Garland 2001a, on the shifting moral status of the offender). Prisoners are 'unreliable partners for prison management' (Simon 2000: 297). As Simon argues, any mild bias in their favour has been replaced by 'an inverse bias associated with the victims' rights movement that has successfully marked interest in inmate expression as morally perverse' (Simon 2000: 290).[24] The entitlement of prisoners to moral agency and status is an earned privilege.

There have been some other significant shifts, which are worthy of analysis: for example, the seeming decline in (or control of) medical power in prisons, alongside the corresponding increase in managerial power. What kind of power is this, and how does it operate? Is it, unlike medicine, a power without an ideology, without an obvious professional group? How does it feel to work in a prison where a line manager receives a sick warning notice for one of his staff, an officer who had died the week before? As van Swaaningen argues in his appeal for a modern critical criminology, something disturbing is happening to civilization (1997: 233). We are failing to consider the actions of the powerful, both for and against civilization, as Jefferson and Grimshaw advocated in relation to the police (see Jefferson and Grimshaw 1984). There is surely a case for studying these questions in relation to the prison.

There is little analysis of the rise in knowledge and power of the prison psychologist—a dramatic rise which is disproportionately true of those psychologists who work in prison.[25] This development,

[24] It is interesting that the first National Prison Survey in 1990 sought prisoners' views on all aspects of prison regimes. This study has not been repeated in England and Wales, although it was extensively adopted in Scotland. A national prisoner survey carried out more recently focused exclusively on criminality. Standards Audit Unit, an internal Prison Service Unit, has recently adopted a modified version of the prisoner questionnaire developed in our research, as part of their audit procedure.

[25] Although paradoxically, in relation to medical officers, prison psychologists have very little power—much less than their National Health Service colleagues, for example, in relation to access to medical files (personal communication). See Haney (1997) on a call for this kind of analysis of the role of psychology in prison.

although stark, remains under-theorized, at the micro and macro level, or as they interweave (Layder 1994). The 'exercise of penitentiary practice' (Foucault 1977; Sim 1990) is heavily regulated by a new professional group whose knowledge is narrow and yet whose power is now almost unchecked. Diagnoses of risk—the new God (see Hannah-Moffatt 2004)—have prominence over judgements about desert, fairness, or (especially) mercy. Such normative language seems to have no place in late modern penology, despite the efforts of Narey and his followers. It is not normality and abnormality, but dangerousness and undangerousness, which have entered the new discourse of punishment. This discourse has been readily adopted by prisoners, eager to secure their own release and all too aware of the constraints ahead of them: 'I know I sometimes dress in women's clothes', said the elderly prisoner, shyly and seriously at his Discretionary Lifer Panel in front of the Parole Board, . . . but it's not criminogenic!' (see Padfield and Liebling 2000).

To return to our main argument, whilst radical and realist criminology seems to have neglected the prison, for it is distasteful and obvious, the prison has grown, deepened, and been reshaped. Once the point had been established that the prison had an excluding and disciplinary function, it seemed that there were new practices of interest and little incentive to reform the prison through critique. But we would argue that the changing shape of this particular power to punish, contain, change, and coerce must surely form a major component of contemporary criminology. This is an empirical and theoretical project—part of the construction of a rounded sociological account of penality launched by David Garland and in need of integration with other lines of inquiry. We should not overlook the importance of everyday practices (as argued by Sparks *et al.* 1996, after Giddens 1984), nor fail to connect our analyses with the past. Perhaps, as Garland argues (Garland, pers. comm.) empirical scholars in particular need to pay more attention to the key concepts of power and discipline: what are their effects, their sources, their shape, and their rationale? It should be possible to make these broad themes a self-conscious part of our inquiries, present at the outset, rather than reflected on, if at all, at the end, so that there is an accumulation of evidence and argument at this level (ibid.; see also King and Wincup 2000; and Bottoms 2000).

So how is power deployed, resisted, understood, in the very different, and yet structurally related penal environments of the world? What is the nature of the prison experience? How painful

is the prison? Can prisons be moral places? These are the new—
and old—questions we should be asking about the prison. This
book offers a modest start on some of these complex and important themes.[26]

Morality, Public and Penal Policy

We want finally to return to the title of this book and to its central
argument. We have used the term 'moral performance' in order to
make our case that the prison is a moral place, and that prisons
differ in their moral practices. To say that an authority or an institution lacks legitimacy is to subject it to moral criticism. Bottoms
has argued that 'the normative or moral dimension (in both its positive and its critical sense)[27] is of central importance to criminology'
(Bottoms 2002: 1; also McEvoy 2003). The 'implicit derogation of
moral discourse' by criminological positivists has had 'adverse
consequences for criminology as a discipline' (ibid. 3). All communities have rules which arise in order for some form of order and
living together, or 'normal social relations', to be sustainable. These
rules may shift over time and communities and individuals will
both experience and express different levels of assent to these rules.
Normative understandings change, but clearly exist.[28] Institutions
differ in precisely this way. Rutter and colleagues have suggested,
for example, that schools with better behaved children tend to have
a distinct 'ethos' or climate, which makes an independent contribution to order in the school.[29] This ethos consists of:

Good models of teacher behaviour (with respect to time keeping, personal
interactions, and responsivity to pupil needs); appropriately high expectations

---

[26] Several individuals have suggested that this type of work should be conducted
on an international comparative basis, in order to explore baselines further and place
each system in perspective.

[27] Positive morality is the identification and articulation of existing moral positions
('what *is*'); critical morality refers to the general moral principles by which actual
social practices or institutions might be judged (what '*ought* to be') (see further p. 475;
Bottoms 2002: 23–4; and Hart 1963).

[28] As Bottoms argues, attempts may be made to revive normative compliance by
Victorian moral preaching or an 'authority model' of social morality, but this model
is 'structurally obsolete'. This does not mean that the normative is irrelevant to
contemporary criminal policy (Bottoms 2002: 42).

[29] The term 'ethos' comes from the same linguistic root as 'ethics' (Bottoms
2002: 36).

of pupils with helpful feedback; interesting, well-organised teaching; good use of homework and monitoring of progress; good opportunities for pupils to take responsibility and show autonomy, with a wide range of opportunities for all to experience success; an orderly atmosphere with skilled, noncoercive classroom management; and a style of leadership that provides direction but is responsive to the ideas of others and fosters high morale in staff and pupils. (Rutter *et al.* 1998: 223)

These factors seem to produce a sense of belonging, engagement, or meaning in their pupils.

We can use the analysis offered by Bottoms to see that the critical morality of the 1960s and 1970s was 'very negative about many aspects of the "authority model" of social morality in which its advocates had been reared' (p. 23). In other words, the liberal model (touched on in Chapter 1) was a result of a much-needed critical morality of its time. Applied to the prison, it had unintended and unexpected effects. Some of these unintended effects were, we have argued, related to a poorly worked-out conception of important concepts like justice and humanity. The reaction to this crisis of the liberal humanitarian model was to abandon it. As Sparks has argued, this tendency to repudiate the past at critical moments (the 'rhetoric of reaction'; Sparks 2001: 167) tends to have other disastrous consequences. Recurrent dilemmas arise, apparently in cycles. A careful accumulation of knowledge and experience is needed in order to move beyond the kinds of oscillations for which prison systems are famous.

Bottoms suggests that a new positive morality can be built instead (and can be detected in formulation) upon 'the moral meaning of respect for others' (Boutellier 2000; Bottoms 2002: 24). Thus, Bottoms argues, the Macpherson Report[30] on the police and the prisons decency agenda (the argument, for example, that 'failing prisons' are due to 'moral neglect') can be seen as examples of a re-emergence of the moral in the social and the criminal justice spheres. They constitute critical morality, and they depart from what Bottoms describes as 'control oriented criminology' precisely because of their use of explicitly moral language. We do not need to abandon liberalism, but we should consider a 'third way', or

[30] The Macpherson Report examined the circumstances surrounding the racially motivated murder of black teenager Stephen Lawrence and its handling by the Metropolitan Police.

normative liberalism, which includes notions of respect for the other, equality, individual dignity, and tolerance (Boutellier 2000: 150) and which pays attention to what these words mean. The normative late or post-modern state achieves or supports morality to the extent that it connects just practices to the competitive market, whilst paying attention to the sympathetic individual (ibid. 153). The new morality requires a sensitivity towards and respect for others. This places limits on our freedom, and yet might also secure it. The notion of value balance is critical to this future.

Public policy (especially but not exclusively on crime or prisons) 'needs to take seriously all four potential main mechanisms of legal compliance, and the ways that they interact with each other'.[31] The normative dimension, Bottoms argues, is 'pivotal . . . since it is the dimension which interacts most frequently and with the greatest practical effect with the other mechanisms' (Bottoms 2002: 25). Criminal justice policy in the UK and elsewhere has been increasingly attracted 'by technical and managerialist approaches to tackling crime' (Bottoms 2002: 25).[32]

Returning to the prison, there are other reasons for the relevance of this analysis to the penal setting. The question remains, is it possible to construct a form of imprisonment whose basic structure and daily practices are more or less acceptable to those who endure it, despite their domination and commonly low social position? Are prisoners slaves or citizens? If they retain their citizenship, then certain things follow. If it were possible to construct a form of imprisonment whose basic structure and daily practices are more or less acceptable to those who endure it, then the effects of this form of imprisonment might be less damaging and more socially constructive. Whilst the imprisoned cannot easily perceive themselves as citizens because of the conditions of their confinement, it is surely important to preserve (or try to generate) a notion of citizenship even within the prison. Generating commitment to civic virtues must be a better strategy, even in the prison, than 'crowding them out' (Tyler 1998: 290).

---

[31] i.e. instrumental reasoning, constraint-based compliance, normative compliance and habit or routine (see Bottoms 2002).

[32] These include situational crime prevention, CCTV, electronic tagging, risk assessment, and so on (Bottoms 2002). These strategies 'make good sense' but omit other morally relevant strategies that build upon attachments, commitment, and involvement in social communities (see further Bottoms 2002; Boutellier 2000).

There are critics who would chastise us for our exploration of values in the prison. Gallo and Ruggiero argue that: 'Perhaps because prisons are so hated that one fears to make them even better: it would be monstrous if one tried to render them more humane' (Gallo and Ruggiero 1991: 287).

Seeking improvements to the prison is like putting 'pink curtains on the bars'. They argue that 'even the most reformed and "humane" ones, produce psycho-physical handicaps' (ibid.). We have some sympathy with this position. Our book is not an argument for prison, but as realists, and as human beings, we are in contact with those who survive and endure the prison experience, and those who deliver it. We hope our investigation helps to shape much less prison, of a more palatable kind.

We have not, meanwhile, resolved the moral problems of imprisonment, but we have shed some light on the prison's nature, its dangers, and its moral and emotional properties. Perhaps we should return to the governors who were ashamed of what they were doing. It was, as we described in Chapter 1, such a feeling in 1995–6 that led to the moral reflexivity those working in the Service now practise, and to the abandonment of some immoral practices. Those who live and work in prisons know better than anyone else that the rate of imprisonment in England and Wales has reached immoral and dangerous proportions. These feelings are, as we have shown, an important guide to action. Our last words we have borrowed from another:

We seldom reflect high values in action, and because of their unreal elevation and their internal inconsistencies our best values cannot be adequately reflected in action. The maintenance of high values involves sin, i.e. a discrepancy between values and actions. And if norms which are not or cannot be adapted to action are to be advocated, some hypocrisy is called for. Sin and hypocrisy are necessary to the creation and preservation of high morals. Those without sin or hypocrisy are those who pursue or advocate realizable goals, trading in their morality in exchange. (Brunsson 1989: 233–4)

Appendix: A Comparison of Prisoner Views on the Quality of Life in Five Prisons: Dimension Scores and Significant Differences

Dimension	Dimension scores (1–5)					ANOVA (Mean difference)									
	B	HH	R	D	W	B&HH	B&R	B&D	B&W	HH&R	HH&D	HH&W	R&D	R&W	D&W
Respect (3)	2.8956[b]	2.9397	3.0594	3.4094[a]	2.9000	N/s	N/s	0.5138*	N/s	N/s	0.4696*	N/s	0.3500*	N/s	0.5094*
Humanity (5)	2.7398[b]	3.0383	3.0396	3.3842[a]	2.9333	N/s	N/s	0.6445**	N/s	N/s	0.3459*	N/s	0.3446*	N/s	0.4509*
Relationships (5)	2.9133	3.0149	2.9743	3.4000[b]	2.8500[b]	N/s	N/s	0.4867**	N/s	N/s	0.3851*	N/s	0.4257**	N/s	0.5500**
Trust (4)	2.6386[b]	2.7181	2.7153	3.1557	2.8125	N/s	N/s	0.5171*	N/s	N/s	0.4376*	N/s	0.4404*	N/s	N/s
Support (4)	3.1807	3.1676	3.0891	3.3991[a]	2.9917[b]	N/s	N/s	N/s	N/s	N/s	N/s	N/s	0.3100*	N/s	0.4075*
Fairness (15)	2.7566[b]	3.0929	2.8403	3.4175[a]	2.9600	0.3363*	N/s	0.6609**	N/s	N/s	0.3246*	N/s	0.5773**	N/s	0.4575*
Order (3)	2.8956	3.3794	2.6370[b]	3.5000[a]	3.0556	N/s	N/s	N/a	N/s	0.7425**	N/s	0.3239	0.8630**	0.4816*	0.4444*
Safety (7)	3.3425	3.3146	3.1132[a]	3.4561[a]	3.4500	N/s	N/s	N/s	N/s	N/s	N/s	N/s	0.3430*	0.3368*	N/s
Well-being (7)	2.7246[b]	3.2538	2.9519	3.4987[a]	2.8905	0.5292**	N/s	0.7741**	N/s	N/s	0.3633	N/s	0.5468**	N/s	0.6083**
Personal development (20)	2.7011[b]	2.9912	2.8134	3.1956[a]	2.7350	0.2901	N/s	0.4945**	N/s	N/s	0.3822*	N/s	0.3822*	N/s	0.4606**
Personal development (22)	N/a	N/a	2.8123	3.1598[a]	2.7273[b]	N/a	N/a	N/a	N/a	N/a	N/a	N/a	0.3432*	N/s	0.4282**
Family contact (1)	3.5904	4.0851[a]	3.6337	3.9123	3.3833[b]	0.4947*	N/s	N/s	N/s	0.4514*	N/s	0.7018*	N/s	N/s	0.5289*
Family contact (4)	N/a	3.4229	3.4208	3.4759	2.9917[b]	N/a	N/a	N/a	N/a	N/s	N/s	.4312*	N/s	0.4291*	0.4820*
Decency (2)	2.0120[b]	2.7074	3.2327	3.4825[a]	2.2500	0.6954**	1.2206**	1.4704**	N/s	0.5252*	0.7750**	0.4574*	N/s	0.9827*	1.2325*
Decency (5)	N/a	3.3468	3.5921	3.7632[b]	2.7733[b]	N/a	N/a	N/a	N/a	0.2453	0.4128*	0.5735*	N/s	0.8187*	0.9863*
Power/ authority (6)	2.0803[b]	2.4699	2.5116	2.9357[a]	2.2833	N/s	0.4312*	0.8554**	N/s	N/s	0.4658**	N/s	0.4241**	N/s	0.6523*
Prisoner social life (6)	3.3675	3.4965[a]	3.3333[b]	3.4649	3.3083	N/s	N/s	N/s	N/s	N/s	N/s	N/s	N/s	N/s	N/s
Meaning (1)	2.8193[b]	2.8298	2.8812	2.9737	3.1833[a]	N/s	N/s	N/s	N/s	N/s	N/s	N/s	N/s	N/s	N/s
QOL 1 (1)	2.6265	3.0213	2.6040[b]	3.5351[a]	2.7000	N/s	N/s	0.9086**	N/s	0.4173	0.5138*	N/s	0.9311**	N/s	0.8351**
QOL 2 (1)	2.4465	2.826	2.515	3.368[a]	2.388[b]	N/s	N/s	1.843**	N/s	N/s	1.084*	N/s	1.706**	N/s	1.961**

Notes: B: Belmarsh; HH: Holme House; R: Risley; D: Doncaster; W: Wandsworth. Scores accompanied by the letter 'a' indicate the most positive score. Scores accompanied by the letter 'b' indicate the most negative. N/s: not significant. N/a: not applicable. *The mean difference is significant at the p < 0.05 level. **The mean difference is significant at the p < 0.001 level. Statistically significant differences are presented in bold.

References

Abbey, R. (2000) *Charles Taylor*, Teddington: Acumen.

Adams, K. (1992) 'Adjusting to Prison Life', in M. Tonry and J. Petersilia (eds.), *Crime and Justice: A Review of Research*, xvi, Chicago: University of Chicago Press, 275–361.

Adler, M., and Longhurst, B. (1994) *Discourse, Power and Justice: Towards a New Sociology of Imprisonment*, London and New York: Routledge.

Advisory Council on the Penal System (1968) *The Regime for Long-Term Prisoners in Conditions of Maximum Security*, London: HMSO.

Ahmad, S. (1996) 'Fairness in Prisons', Ph.D. thesis, University of Cambridge.

Ahmed, E., Harris, N., Braithwaite, J., and Braithwaite, V. (2001) *Shame Management through Reintegration*, Cambridge: Cambridge University Press.

Alasuutari, P. (1995) *Researching Culture: Qualitative Method and Cultural Studies*, London: Sage.

Albrecht, T. L., and Adelman, M. B. (1987) 'Communicating Social Support: A Theoretical Perspective', in T. L. Albrecht and M. B. Adelman (eds.), *Communicating Social Support*, London: Sage.

Allard, P. (1991) 'Respect in the Community', in *Respect in Prison: The Transcript of a Conference held 11–14 July at Bishop Grossteste College, Lincoln*, Lincoln: The Bishop's House, 14–26.

Allport, G. W. (1955) *Becoming: Basic Considerations for a Psychology of Personality*, New Haven: Yale University Press.

Antonovsky, A. (1983) 'The Sense of Coherence: Development of Research Instrument', S. Schwartz Research Center of Behavioral Medicine, Tel Aviv Newsletter and Research Reports, No. 1: 1–11.

Argyle, M. (1987) *The Psychology of Happiness*, London and New York: Routledge.

Aristotle (1976) *The Nicomachean Ethics*, trans. J. A. K. Thompson; notes by H. Tredennick, introd. by J. Barnes, London: Penguin.

Arnold, H. (forthcoming) 'Identifying the High Performing Prison Officer', Ph.D. thesis, University of Cambridge.

Bagnall, N. (2000) 'Words: Appreciate', *Independent on Sunday*, 9 July, p. 12.

Banister, P., Heskin, K. J., Bolton, N., and Smith, F. V. (1973) 'Psychological Correlates of Long-Term Imprisonment. I. Cognitive Variables', *British Journal of Criminology*, 13/4: 312–23.

Banton, M. (1964) *The Policeman in the Community*, London: Tavistock.

Barak-Glantz, I. L. (1981) 'Towards a Conceptual Schema of Prison Management Styles', *Prison Journal*, 61/2: 42–60.

Barbalet, J. M. (1998) *Emotion, Social Theory and Social Structure: A Macrosociological Approach*, Cambridge: Cambridge University Press.

Barry, A., Osborne, T., and Rose, N. (eds.) (1996) *Foucault and Political Reason*, London: University College Press.

Barry, B. (1989) *Theories of Justice*, London: Harvester Wheatsheaf.

Bauman, Z. (1989) *Modernity and the Holocaust*, Cambridge: Polity Press.

Beck, A. T., Weisman, A. W., Lester, D., and Trexler, L. (1974) 'The Assessment of Pessimism: The Hopelessness Scale', *Journal of Consulting and Clinical Psychology*, 42: 861–5.

Becker, H. (1970) *Sociological Work: Method and Substance*, New Brunswick: Transaction Books.

Beetham, D. (1991) *The Legitimation of Power*, Basingstoke: Macmillan.

Ben-David, S. (1992) 'Staff-to-Inmate Relations in a Total Institution: A Model of Five Modes of Association', *International Journal of Offender Therapy and Comparative Criminology*, 36/3: 209–21.

—— and Silfen, P. (1994) 'In Quest of a Lost Father? Inmates' Preferences to Staff Relation in a Psychiatric Prison Ward', *International Journal of Offender Therapy and Comparative Criminology*, 38/2: 131–9.

—— —— and Cohen, D. (1996) 'Fearful Custodial or Fearless Personal Relations: Prison Guards' Fear as a Factor Shaping Staff-Inmate Relation Prototype', *International Journal of Offender Therapy and Comparative Criminology*, 40/2: 94–104.

Berger, P. L., Berger, B., and Kellner, H. (1977) *The Homeless Mind: Modernisation and Consciousness*, Harmondsworth: Penguin.

Berk, B. (1966) 'Organizational Goals and Inmate Organization', *American Journal of Sociology*, 71: 522–34.

Berlin, I. (1969) *Four Essays on Liberty*, London: Oxford University Press.

Bettelheim, B. (1943) 'Individual and Mass Behavior in Extreme Situations', *Journal of Abnormal and Social Psychology*, 38: 417–52.

—— (1960) *The Informed Heart: A Study of the Psychological Consequences of Living under Extreme Fear and Terror*, New York: The Free Press.

—— (1979) *Surviving and Other Essays*, London: Thames and Hudson.

Biggam, F. H., and Power, K. G. (1997) 'Social Support and Psychological Distress in a Group of Incarcerated Young Offenders', *International Journal of Offender Therapy and Comparative Criminology*, 41/3: 213–30.

—— —— (2002) 'A Controlled, Problem-Solving, Group-Based Intervention with Vulnerable Incarcerated Young Offenders', *International Journal of Offender Therapy and Comparative Criminology*, 46/6: 678–98.

Bittner, E. (1967) 'The Police on Skid Row: A Study of Peace Keeping', *American Sociological Review*, 32/5: 699–715.

Black, A. (2001) 'Concepts of Civil Society in Pre-Modern Europe', in S. Kaviraj and S. Khilnani (eds.), *Civil Society: History and Possibilities*, Cambridge: Cambridge University Press, 33–9.

Black, D. (1970) 'Production of Crime Rates', *American Sociological Review*, 35: 733–48.

Blauner, R. (1964) *Alienation and Freedom: The Factory Worker and his Industry*, Chicago: Chicago University Press.

Blumstein, A., and Beck, A. (1999) 'Population Growth in U.S. Prisons, 1980–1996', in M. Tonry and J. Petersilia (eds.), *'Prisons', Crime and Justice: A Review of Research*, xxvi, Chicago: University of Chicago Press, 121–62.

Bolton, N., Smith, F. V., Heskin, K. J., and Banister, P. A. (1976) 'Psychological Correlates of Long-Term Imprisonment: A Longitudinal Study', *British Journal of Criminology*, 16/1: 38–47.

Bondeson, U. V. (1989) *Prisoners in Prison Societies*, New Brunswick, NJ: Transaction.

Bottomley, A. K., James, A., Clare, E., and Liebling, A. (1997) *Monitoring and Evaluation of Wolds Remand Prison*, Home Office Report, London: Home Office.

—— Liebling, A., and Sparks, R. (1994) *Barlinnie Special Unit and Shotts Unit: An Assessment*, Scottish Prison Service Occasional Paper No. 7/1994, Edinburgh: Scottish Prison Service.

Bottoms, A. E. (1983) 'Some Neglected Features of Contemporary Penal Systems', in D. Garland and P. Young (eds.), *The Power to Punish*, London: Heinemann.

—— (1990) 'The Aims of Imprisonment', in D. Garland (ed.), *Justice, Guilt and Forgiveness in the Penal System*, University of Edinburgh, Centre for Theology and Public Issues, Occasional Paper No. 18.

—— (1995) 'The Philosophy and Politics of Punishment and Sentencing', in C. Clarkson and R. Morgan (eds.), *The Politics of Sentencing Reform*, Oxford: Clarendon Press, 17–49.

—— (1998) 'Five Puzzles in von Hirsch's Theory', in A. Ashworth and M. Wasik (eds.), *Fundamentals of Sentencing Theory: Essays in Honour of Andrew von Hirsch*, Oxford: Oxford University Press, 53–100.

—— (1999) 'Interpersonal Violence and Social Order in Prisons', in M. Tonry and J. Petersilia (eds.), *'Prisons', Crime and Justice: A Review of Research*, xxvi, Chicago: University of Chicago Press, 205–82.

—— (2000) 'The Relationship between Theory and Research in Criminology', in R. King and E. Wincup (eds.), *Doing Research on Crime and Justice*, Oxford: Oxford University Press, 15–60.

—— (2002) 'Morality, Crime, Compliance and Public Policy', in A. E. Bottoms and M. Tonry (eds.), *Ideology, Crime and Criminal*

Justice: A Symposium in Honour of Sir Leon Radzinowicz, Cullompton: Willan Publishing, 20–51.

—— (2003*a*) 'Some Sociological Reflections on Restorative Justice', in A. von Hirsch, J. Roberts, A. E. Bottoms, K. Roach, and M. Schiff (eds.), *Restorative Justice and Criminal Justice: Competing or Reconcilable Paradigms?* Oxford: Hart Publishing, 79–114.

—— (2003*b*) 'Theoretical Reflections on the Evaluations of a Penal Policy Initiative', in L. Zedner and A. Ashworth (eds.), *The Criminological Foundations of Penal Policy: Essays in Honour of Roger Hood*, Oxford: Oxford University Press, 107–98.

—— Gelsthorpe, L., and Rex, S. (eds.) (2001) *Community Penalties: Change and Challenges*, Cullompton: Willan Publishing.

—— Hay, W., and Sparks, R. (1990) 'Control Problems and the Long-Term Prisoner', unpublished report submitted to the Home Office.

—— —— —— (1991) 'Situational and Social Approaches to the Prevention of Disorder in Long-Term Prisons', *The Prison Journal*, 70: 83–95.

—— and McClintock, F. H. (1973) *Criminals Coming of Age: A Study of Institutional Adaptation in the Treatment of Adolescent Offenders*, London: Heinemann Educational.

—— and Rose, G. (1998) 'The Importance of Staff-Prisoner Relationships: Results from a Study in Three Male Prisons', in D. Price and A. Liebling, 'Staff Prisoner Relationships: A Review of the Literature', unpublished report submitted to the Prison Service.

—— and Sparks, R. (1997) 'How is Order in Prison Maintained?' in A. Liebling (ed.), *Security, Justice and Order: Developing Perspectives*, Cambridge: Institute of Criminology, 14–31.

—— and Stelman, A. (1988) *Social Inquiry Reports: A Framework for Practice Development*, Aldershot: Wildwood House.

—— and Wiles, P. (1996) 'Crime and Insecurity in the City', in C. Fijnaut, J. Goethals, T. Peters, and L. Walgrave (eds.), *Changes in Society, Crime and Criminal Justice in Europe: A Challenge for Criminological Education and Research*, Dordrecht: Kluwer Law, 1.1–1.38.

Bourgois, P. (1995) *In Search of Respect: Selling Crack in El Barrio*, Cambridge: Cambridge University Press.

Boutellier, H. (2000) *Crime and Morality: The Significance of Criminal Justice in Post-Modern Culture*, Dordrecht, Boston, and London: Kluwer Academic.

Bowery, M. (1994) *Junee: One Year Out: A Study Undertaken for the NSW Department of Corrective Services*, Sydney: NSW Department of Corrective Services.

—— (1996) *Private Prisons in NSW: Junee—Year Two: A Study Undertaken for the NSW Department of Corrective Services*, Sydney: NSW Department of Corrective Services.

—— (1997) *Private Prisons in NSW: Junee—Year Three: A Study Undertaken for the NSW Department of Corrective Services*, Sydney: NSW Department of Corrective Services.

—— (1999) *Private Prisons in NSW: Junee—A Four-Year Review*, Sydney: NSW Department of Corrective Services.

Bowker, L. H. (1980) *Prison Victimisation*, New York: Elsevier.

Bowlby, J. (1969) *Attachment and Loss*, London: Hogarth Press.

—— (1979) *The Making and Breaking of Affectional Bonds*, London: Tavistock Publications.

Boyle, J. (1977) *A Sense of Freedom*, London: Penguin.

—— (1985) *The Pain of Confinement: Prison Diaries*, London: Pan, 1985; 1st pub. 1984.

Braithwaite, J. (1998) 'Institutionalising Distrust, Enculturating Trust', in V. Braithwaite and M. Levi (eds.), *Trust and Governance*, New York: Russell Sage Foundation, 343–75.

—— (2002) *Restorative Justice and Responsive Regulation*, New York: Oxford University Press.

—— and Braithwaite, V. (2001) 'Shame, Shame Management and Regulation', in E. Ahmed, N. Harris, J. Braithwaite, and V. Braithwaite (eds.), *Shame Management through Reintegration*, Cambridge: Cambridge University Press, 3–72.

—— and Makkai, T. (1994) 'Trust and Compliance', *Policing and Society*, 4: 1–12.

—— and Strang, H. (2001) 'Introduction: Restorative Justice and Civil Society', in H. Strang and J. Braithwaite, *Restorative Justice and Civil Society*, Cambridge: Cambridge University Press, 1–13.

Braithwaite, V. (1994) 'Beyond Rokeach's Equality-Freedom Model: Two-Dimensional Values in a One-Dimensional World', *Journal of Social Issues*, 50/4: 67–94.

—— (1998a) 'The Value Balance of Political Evaluations', *British Journal of Psychology*, 89: 223–47.

—— (1998b) 'Communal and Exchange Trust Norms: Their Value Base and Relevance to Institutional Trust', in V. Braithwaite and M. Levi (eds.), *Trust and Governance*, New York: Russell Sage Foundation, 46–74.

—— and Levi, M. (eds.) (1998) *Trust and Governance*, New York: Russell Sage Foundation.

Brown, G., and Harris, T. (1978) *Social Origins of Depression: A Study of Psychiatric Disorder in Women*, London: Tavistock.

Brunsson, N. (1989) *The Organisation of Hypocrisy: Talk, Decisions and Actions in Organisations*, Chichester: Wiley.

Bryans, S. (2000) 'The Managerialisation of Prisons—Efficiency without a Purpose?' *Criminal Justice Matters*, 40: 7–8.

—— and Wilson, D. (2000) *The Prison Governor: Theory and Practice*, Leyhill: Prison Service Journal.

Bryman, A., and Cramer, D. (1999) *Quantitative Data Analysis with SPSS Release 8: A Guide for Social Scientists*, London: Routledge.

Buffry, A., Hutchinson, W., and Semple, J. (1992) 'The Meaning of the Prison Experience: An Analysis of the Prison Experience in HMP Blantyre House and Other Secure British Prisons: Based on a Questionnaire of Inmates', unpublished script.

Burchell, G. (1996) 'Liberal Government and Techniques of the Self', in A. Barry, T. Osborne, and N. Rose (eds.), *Foucault and Political Reason*, London: University College Press, 19–36.

Burnside, J., and Baker, N. (1994) *Relational Justice: Repairing the Breach*, Winchester: Waterside Press.

Caird, R. (1974) *Good and Useful Life: Imprisonment in Britain Today*, London: Hart-Davis.

Camp, S. D. (1994) 'Assessing the Effects of Organizational Commitment and Job Satisfaction on Turnover: An Event History Approach', *The Prison Journal*, 74/3: 279–305.

—— (1999) 'Do Inmate Survey Data Reflect Prison Conditions? Using Surveys to Assess Prison Conditions of Confinement', *The Prison Journal*, 79/2: 250–68.

—— and Gaes, G. G. (2001) 'Private Adult Prisons: What Do We Really Know and Why Don't We Know More?' in D. Shichor and M. J. Gilbert (eds.), *Privatisation in Criminal Justice: Past, Present and Future*, Ohio: Anderson Publishing, 283–98.

—— —— (2002) 'Growth and Quality of U.S. Private Prisons: Evidence from a National Survey', *Criminology and Public Policy*, 1/3: 427–50 (http://www.bop.gov/orepg/oreprres_note.pdf).

—— —— Klein-Saffran, J., Daggett, D. M., and Saylor, W. (2003) 'Using Inmate Survey Data in Assessing Prison Performance: A Case Study Comparing Private and Public Prisons', *Criminal Justice Review*, 27/1: 26–51.

—— —— and Saylor, W. (2002) 'Quality of Prison Operations in the Federal Sector: A Comparison with a Private Prison', *Punishment and Society*, 4/1: 27–53.

—— Saylor, W. G., and Harer, M. (1997) 'Aggregating Individual-Level Evaluations of the Organizational Social Climate: A Multilevel Investigation of the Work Environment at the Federal Bureau of Prisons', *Justice Quarterly*, 14/4: 739–61.

—— —— and Wright, K. N. (1999) 'Creating Performance Measures from Survey Data: A Practical Discussion', *Corrections Management Quarterly*, 3/1: 71–80.

Caplow, T., and Simon, J. (1999) 'Understanding Prison Policy and Population Trends', in M. Tonry and J. Petersilia (eds.), *'Prisons', Crime and Justice: A Review of Research*, xxvi, Chicago: University of Chicago Press, 63–120.

Carlen, P. (1983) *Women's Imprisonment: A Study in Social Control*, London: Routledge and Kegan Paul.

—— (1994) 'Why Study Women's Imprisonment? Or Anyone Else's?—An Indefinite Article', in R. D. King and M. Maguire (eds.), *Prisons in Context*, Oxford: Oxford University Press, 131–40.

—— (2001) 'Death and the Triumph of Governance? Lessons from the Scottish Women's Prison', *Punishment and Society*, 3/4: 459–72.

—— (2002*a*) 'Governing the Governors: Telling Tales of Managers, Mandarins and Mavericks', *Criminal Justice*, 2/1: 27–49.

—— (2002*b*) 'Carceral Clawback: The Case of Women's Imprisonment in Canada', *Punishment and Society: The International Journal of Penology*, 4/1: 115–22.

Carter, N., Klein, R., and Day, P. (1995) *How Organisations Measure Success*, London: Routledge.

Cavadino, M., Crow, I., and Dignan, J. (1999) *Criminal Justice 2000: Strategies for a New Century*, Winchester: Waterside Press.

—— and Dignan, J. (1997) *The Penal System: An Introduction*, 2nd edn., London: Sage.

—— —— (2002) *The Penal System: An Introduction*, 3rd edn., London: Sage.

Cawley, C. (2000) 'A Crisis of Identity? Role Conflict and Managerial Style amongst Female Prison Governors: A Qualitative Study', M.St. thesis, Institute of Criminology, University of Cambridge.

Chamberlain, K., Petrie, K., and Asariah, R. (1992) 'The Role of Optimism and Sense of Coherence in Predicting Recovery Following Surgery', *Psychology and Health*, 7: 301–10.

Chan, J. (1992) 'The Privatisation of Punishment: A Review of the Key Issues', *Australian Journal of Social Issues*, 27/4: 223–47.

—— (1996) 'Changing Police Culture', *British Journal of Criminology*, 36: 109–34.

—— (1997) *Changing Police Culture: Policing in a Multicultural Society*, Cambridge: Cambridge University Press.

Charlesworth, S. J. (2000) *A Phenomenology of Working Class Experience*, Cambridge: Cambridge University Press.

Christie, N. (1981) *Limits to Pain*, Oxford: Martin Robertson.

—— (1993) *Crime Control as Industry: Towards Gulags, Western Style?* London: Routledge.

Clare, E., Bottomley, A. K., Grounds, A., Hammond, C. J., Liebling, A., and Taylor, C. (2001) *Evaluation of Close Supervision Centres*, London: Home Office.

Clark, J. P. (1959) 'Measuring Alienation within a Social System', *American Sociological Review*, 24: 849–52.

Clarke, J., and Newman, J. (1997) *The Managerial State: Power, Politics and Ideology in the Remaking of Social Welfare*, London: Sage.

Clarke, R. V., and Martin, D. N. (1971) *Absconding from Approved Schools*, Home Office Research Studies, London: HMSO.

Clemmer, D. (1940) *The Prison Community*, New York: Holt, Reinhart and Winston, 1958; 1st pub. 1940.

Clifford, J. (1986) 'Partial Truths', in J. Clifford and G. E. Marcus (eds.), *Writing Culture: The Poetic and Politics of Ethnography*, Berkeley: University of California Press, 1–26.

—— and Marcus, G. E. (1986) *Writing Culture: The Poetic and Politics of Ethnography*, Berkeley: University of California Press.

Cohen, L., and Holliday, M. (1982) *Statistics for Social Scientists*, London: Harper and Row.

Cohen, S., and Taylor, L. (1972) *Psychological Survival: The Experience of Long-Term Imprisonment*, Harmondsworth: Penguin.

Collins Dictionary of the English Language (1979) ed. P. Hanks, London: Collins.

Colvin, E. (1977) 'Prison Officers: A Sociological Portrait of the Uniformed Staff at an English Prison', Ph.D. thesis, University of Cambridge.

Colvin, M. (1982) 'The 1980 New Mexico Prison Riot', *Social Problems*, 29/5: 449–63.

Coyle, A. (2002) *A Human Rights Approach to Prison Management: Handbook for Prison Staff*, London: International Centre for Prison Studies.

—— (2003) *Treating Prisoners with Humanity: Some Questions of Definition and Audit*, London: International Centre for Prison Studies.

Cranston, M. (1982) 'John Locke and Government by Consent', in D. Thompson (ed.), *Political Ideas*, Harmondsworth: Penguin, 67–80.

Crawley, E. (2001) 'The Social World of the English Prison Officer: A Study in Occupational Culture', Ph.D. thesis submitted to Keele University.

—— (in press) 'Emotion and Performance: Prison Officers and the Presentation of Self in Prisons', *Punishment and Society*.

Creighton, S., and King, V. (2000) 'Human Rights Act 1998 and the European Commission on Human Rights', in S. Creighton and V. King, *Prisoners and the Law*, 2nd edn., London, Dublin, and Edinburgh: Butterworths.

Cressey, D. R. (1958) 'Foreword', in D. Clemmer, *The Prison Community*, New York: Holt, Reinhart and Winston, pp. vii–xi.

—— (1961) (ed.) *The Prison: Studies in Institution Organization and Change*, New York: Holt, Rinehart and Winston.

Crewe, B. (forthcoming) *A New Society of Captives*.

Cross, R. (1971) *Punishment, Prison and the Public: An Assessment of Penal Reform in Twentieth Century England by an Armchair Penologist*, London: Stevens.

Cross, S. (2003) 'Do the Leadership Qualities of Prison Governors Influence Performance?' unpublished Masters thesis submitted to Oxford Brookes University.

Cunningham, K. (1996) 'Justice in Prison', M.Phil. thesis, Institute of Criminology, University of Cambridge.

Daniels, N. (ed.) (1975) *Reading Rawls: Critical Studies on Rawls' A Theory of Justice*, Oxford: Basil Blackwell.

Dasgupta, P. (1988) 'Trust as a Commodity', in D. Gambetta (ed.), *Trust: Making and Breaking Cooperative Relations*, Oxford: Basil Blackwell, 49–72.

Davies, H., Nutley, S., and Smith, P. (eds.) (2000) *What Works? Evidence-based Policy and Practice in Public Services*, Bristol: Policy Press.

Davies, W. (1982) 'Violence in Prison', in M. P. Feldman (ed.), *Developments in the Study of Criminal Behaviour*, ii, New York: John Wiley, 131–63.

De Vaus, D. A. (1999) *Surveys in Social Research*, 4th edn., London: University College Press; 1st pub. 1985.

de Zulueta, F. (1993) *From Pain to Violence: The Traumatic Roots of Destructiveness*, London: Whurr.

Deakin, N. (2001) *In Search of Civil Society*, Basingstoke: Palgrave.

Dean, D. (1961) 'Alienation: Its Meaning and Measurement', *American Sociological Review*, 26: 753–8.

Dickinson, C. (2002) 'The Role of the Area Manager', unpublished M.St. thesis submitted to the University of Cambridge.

DiIulio, J. (1987) *Governing Prisons: A Comparative Study of Correctional Management*, New York: The Free Press.

Dinitz, S. (1981) 'Are Safe and Humane Prisons Possible?' *Australian and New Zealand Journal of Criminology*, 14: 3–19.

Ditchfield, J. (1990) *Control in Prisons: A Review of the Literature*, London: HMSO.

—— and Duncan, D. (1987) 'The Prison Disciplinary System: Perceptions of Fairness and Adequacy by Inmates, Staff and Members of Boards of Visitors', *Howard Journal of Criminal Justice*, 26/2: 122–38.

Ditton, J., Bannister, J., Gilchrist, E., and Farrall, S. (1999) 'Afraid or Angry? Recalibrating the "Fear" of Crime', *International Review of Victimology*, 6: 83–99.

Dixon, D. (1997) *Law in Policing: Legal Regulations and Policing Practices*, Oxford: Clarendon Press.

Dobash, R. P., Dobash, R. E., and Gutteridge, S. (1986) *The Imprisonment of Women*, Oxford: Basil Blackwell.

Downes, D. (1988) *Contrasts in Tolerance: Post-War Penal Policy in the Netherlands and England and Wales*, Oxford: Oxford University Press.

—— and Morgan, R. (2002) 'The Skeletons in the Cupboard: The Politics of Law and Order at the Turn of the Millennium', in M. Maguire,

R. Morgan, and R. Reiner (eds.), *The Oxford Handbook of Criminology*, 3rd edn., Oxford: Oxford University Press, 286–322.

—— and Rock, P. (1986) *Understanding Deviance: A Guide to the Sociology of Crime and Rule Breaking*, Oxford: Oxford University Press, 1986; 1st pub. 1982.

Duffee, D. (1974) 'The Correction Officer Subculture and Organizational Change', *Journal of Research in Crime and Delinquency*, 11: 155–71.

—— (1975) *Correctional Policy and Prison Organisation*, Beverley Hills, Calif.: Sage.

Duguid, S. R. (2000) *Can Prisons Work? The Prisoner as Object and Subject in Modern Corrections*, Toronto: University of Toronto Press.

Dunbar, I. (1971) 'Long Lartin: the Development of a Concept', *Prison Service Journal*, 3: 6–8.

—— (1985) *A Sense of Direction*, London: Home Office.

—— (1992) Letter to Prison Service Establishments accompanying copies of Pilling's 1992 lecture.

—— (2002) Personal communication.

—— and Langdon, A. (1998) *Tough Justice: Sentencing and Penal Policies in the 1990s*, London: Blackstone.

Dunn, C. (1982) 'Foreword', in R. Johnson and H. Toch (eds.), *The Pains of Imprisonment*, London and Beverley Hills, Calif.: Sage.

Dworkin, R. (1975) 'The Original Position', in N. Daniels (ed.), *Reading Rawls: Critical Studies on Rawls' A Theory of Justice*, Oxford: Basil Blackwell, 16–52.

—— (1977) *Taking Rights Seriously*, London: Duckworth.

Edelman, M. (1977) *Words that Succeed and Policies that Fail*, New York: Academic Press.

Edgar, K., O'Donnell, I., and Martin, C. (2002) *Prison Violence: The Dynamics of Conflict, Fear and Power*, Cullompton: Willan Publishing.

Elias, N. (1996) *The Civilizing Process*, Oxford: Blackwell; 1st pub. 1939.

Elliott, C. (1999) *Locating the Energy for Change: An Introduction to Appreciative Inquiry*, Winnipeg: International Institute for Sustainable Development.

—— (2001) Personal communication.

—— (2002) Seminar to M.St. students, University of Cambridge.

Elster, J. (1995) *The Cement of Society: A Study of Social Order*, Cambridge: Cambridge University Press; 1st pub. 1989.

Emery, F. E. (1970) *Freedom and Justice within Walls: The Bristol Prison Experiment*, London and New York: Tavistock Publications.

Emmett, D. (1966) *Rules, Roles and Relations*, London: Macmillan.

Ericson, R., and Haggerty, K. (1997) *Policing the Risk Society*, Oxford: Clarendon Press.

Erikson, E. H. (1995) *Childhood and Society*, London: Vintage; 1st pub. 1950.

Evans, D. (2001) *Emotion: The Science of Sentiment*, Oxford: Oxford University Press.

Evans, M. D., and Morgan, R. (1998) *Preventing Torture: A Study of the European Convention for the Prevention of Torture and Inhuman or Degrading Treatment or Punishment*, Oxford: Clarendon Press.

Fairweather, L., and McConville, S. (2000) *Prison Architecture*, Oxford: Butterworth-Heinemann.

Falconer (2003) Lord Falconer, Secretary of State for Constitutional Affairs and Lord Chancellor, Speech to the Prison Service Conference, February 2003.

Farrall, S. (2002) *Rethinking What Works with Offenders: Probation, Social Context and Desistence from Crime*, Cullompton: Willan Publishing.

Farrington, D., Ditchfield, J., and Howard, P. (2002) *Two Intensive Regimes for Young Offenders: A Follow-Up Evaluation*, London: Home Office Research, Development and Statistics Directorate.

Faulkner, D. (2001) *Crime, State and Citizen: A Field Full of Folk*, Winchester: Waterside Press.

Federal Bureau of Prisons (1990) *The Prison Social Climate Survey: Inmate and Staff Versions*, Washington: US Department of Justice.

Feeley, M. (2002) 'Entrepreneurs of Punishment: The Legacy of Privatisation', *Punishment and Society*, 4/3: 321–44.

—— and Simon, J. (1992) 'The New Penology: Notes on the Emerging Strategy of Corrections and its Implications', *Criminology*, 30: 449–74.

—— —— (1994) 'Actuarial Justice: The Emerging New Criminal Law', in D. Nelken (ed.), *The Futures of Criminology*, London: Sage, 173–201.

Ferlie, E., Ashburner, L., Fitzgerald, L., and Pettigrew, A. (1996) *The New Public Management in Action*, Oxford: Oxford University Press.

Ferrell, J., and Hamm, M. S. (1998) *Ethnography at the Edge: Crime, Deviance, and Field Research*, Boston: Northeastern University Press.

Fisher, G., Semko, E. M., and Wade, F. J. (1995) 'Defining and Measuring Hostile Environments: Development of the Hostile Environment Inventory', in S. Sauter and L. Murphy (eds.), *Organizational Risk Factors for Job Stress*, Washington: American Psychological Association.

Fitzgerald, M., and Sim, J. (1979) *British Prisons*, Oxford: Blackwell.

Flanagan, J. (1954) 'The Critical Incident Technique', *Psychological Bulletin*, 51: 327–58.

Fogel, D. (1975) *We are the Living Proof: The Justice Model for Corrections*, Cincinnati: W. H. Anderson.

Ford, N. (1999) 'Foreword', in C. Elliott, *Locating the Energy for Change: A Practitioner's Guide to Appreciative Inquiry*, Winnipeg: IISD.

Foucault, M. (1977) *Discipline and Punish: The Birth of the Prison*, New York: Vintage.

Frank, J. (1986) *Dostoevsky: The Stir of Liberation 1860–1865*, London: Robson.

—— (1995) *Dostoevsky: The Miraculous Years, 1865–1871*, Princeton: Princeton University Press.

Frankl, V. E. (ed.) (1964) *Man's Search for Meaning: An Introduction to Logotherapy*, trans. by Ilse Lasch, London: Hodder and Stoughton; 1st pub. 1959.

Friendship, C., Blud, L., Erikson, M., and Travers, R. (2002) *An Evaluation of Cognitive Behavioural Treatment for Prisoners*, London: Home Office.

Freud, S. (1961) *Civilization and its Discontents*, trans. and ed. by J. Strachey, New York: W. W. Norton.

Friedman, L. J. (1999) *Identity's Architect: A Biography of Erik Ericson*, London: Free Association Books.

Gaes, G. G., Flanagan, T. J., Motiuk, L. L., and Stewart, L. (1999) 'Adult Correctional Treatment', in M. Tonry and J. Petersilia (eds.), *'Prisons', Crime and Justice: A Review of Research*, xxvi, Chicago: University of Chicago Press, 361–427.

Gaita, R. (1998) *A Common Humanity: Thinking about Love and Truth and Justice*, London: Routledge.

Gallo, E., and Ruggiero, V. (1991) 'The "Immaterial" Prison: Custody as a Factory for the Manufacture of Handicaps', *International Journal of the Sociology of Law*, 19/3: 273–91.

Galtung, J. (1961) 'Prison: The Organisation of Dilemma', in D. Cressey (ed.), *The Prison: Studies in Institutional Organisation and Change*, New York: Holt, Rinehart and Winston, 107–45.

Gambetta, D. (ed.) (1988) *Trust: Making and Breaking of Cooperative Relations*, Oxford: Basil Blackwell.

Garland, D. (1985) *Punishment and Welfare: A History of Penal Strategies*, Aldershot: Gower.

—— (1990) *Punishment and Modern Society*, Oxford: Clarendon Press.

—— (1992) 'Criminological Knowledge and its Relation to Power: Foucault's Genealogy and Criminology Today', *British Journal of Criminology*, 32/4: 403–22.

—— (1996) 'The Limits of the Sovereign State: Strategies of Crime Control in Contemporary Society', *British Journal of Criminology*, 36/4: 445–71.

—— (1997) ' "Governmentality" and the Problem of Crime: Foucault, Criminology, Sociology', *Theoretical Criminology*, 1: 173–214.

—— (2000) Personal communication.

—— (2001a) *Culture of Control: Crime and Social Order in Contemporary Society*, Oxford: Clarendon Press.

—— (ed.) (2001*b*) 'Special Issue on Mass Imprisonment in the USA', *Punishment and Society*, 3/1: 5–199.

—— and Sparks, R. (eds.) (2000) *Criminology and Social Theory*, Oxford: Clarendon Press.

—— and Young, P. (1983) *The Power to Punish: Contemporary Penalty and Social Analysis*, Aldershot: Gower.

Gatrell, V. A. C. (1994) The *Hanging Tree: Execution and the English People 1770–1868*, Oxford and New York: Oxford University Press.

Geis, G., Mobley, A., and Shichor, D. (1999) 'Private Prisons, Criminological Research, and Conflict of Interest: A Case Study', *Crime and Delinquency*, 45/3: 372–88.

Gelsthorpe, L., and Padfield, N. (eds.) (2002) *Exercising Discretion: Decision Making in the Criminal Justice System and Beyond*, Cullompton: Willan Publishing.

Genders, E. (2002) 'Legitimacy, Accountability and Private Prisons', *Punishment and Society*, 4/3: 285–303.

—— and Player, E. (1989) *Race Relations in Prisons*, Oxford: Oxford University Press.

—— —— (1995) *Grendon: A Study of a Therapeutic Prison*, Oxford: Clarendon Press.

Giallombardo, R. (1966) *Society of Women: A Study of A Women's Prison*, New York: John Wiley.

Gibbs, J. J. (1982) 'The First Cut is the Deepest: Psychological Breakdown and Survival in the Detention Setting', in R. Johnson and H. Toch, *The Pains of Imprisonment*, London and Beverley Hills, Calif.: Sage.

Giddens, A. (1984) *The Constitution of Society*, Cambridge: Polity Press.

—— (1990) *The Consequences of Modernity*, Stanford, Calif.: Stanford University Press.

—— (1991) *Modernity and Self-Identity: Self and Society in the Late Modern Age*, Stanford, Calif.: Stanford University Press.

—— (ed.) (2001) *The Global Third Way Debate*, Cambridge: Polity Press.

Gilbert, M. J. (1997) 'The Illusion of Structure: A Critique of the Classical Model of Organisation and the Discretionary Power of Correctional Officers', *Criminal Justice Review*, 22/1: 49–64.

Gillespie, S. (2002) Personal communication.

Gilligan, C. (1982) *In a Different Voice: Psychological Theory and Women's Development*, Cambridge, Mass.: Harvard University Press.

Glaser, D. (1964) *The Effectiveness of a Prison and Parole System*, Indianapolis: Bobb-Merill.

—— and Strauss, A. L. (1967) *The Discovery for Grounded Theory: Strategies for Qualitative Research*, New York: Aldine de Gruyter.

Glover, J. (1999) *Humanity: A Moral History of the Twentieth Century*, London: Jonathan Cape.

Goffman, E. (1961) 'On the Characteristics of Total Institutions', in D. R. Cressey (ed.), *The Prison: Studies in Institutional Organisation and Change*, New York: Holt, Rinehart and Winston.

—— (1962) *Asylums: Essays on the Social Situation of Mental Patients and Other Inmates*, Chicago: Aldine Publishing.

—— (1967) 'Where the Action is', in E. Goffman, *Interaction Ritual: Essays on Face-to-Face Behaviour*, New York: Doubleday Anchor, 149–270.

—— (1987) *Asylums: Essays on the Social Situation of Mental Patients and Inmates*, London: Peregrine; 1st pub. 1961.

—— (1990) *The Presentation of Self in Everyday Life*, Harmondsworth: Penguin Books; 1st pub. 1959.

Goleman, D. (1996) *Emotional Intelligence*, London: Bloomsbury.

Grapendaal, M. (1990) 'Inmate Subculture in Dutch Prisons', *British Journal of Criminology*, 30: 141–57.

Grimshaw, R., and Jefferson, T. (1987) *Interpreting Policework*, London: Unwin.

Grosser, G. H. (1960) 'Introduction', in R. Cloward, D. R. Cressey, R. McCleery, L. E. Onlin, G. Sylees, and S. L. Messinger, *Theoretical Studies in the Social Organization of the Prison*, New York: Social Science Research Council, 1–5.

Grusky, O. (1959) 'Some Factors promoting Co-operative Behavior among Inmate Leaders', *American Journal of Corrections*, 21/2: 8–21.

Gunn, J., Robertson, G., Dell, S., and Way, C. (1978) *Psychiatric Aspects of Imprisonment*, London: Academic Press.

Hagan, J., and Dinovitzer, R. (1999) 'Collateral Consequences of Imprisonment for Children, Communities and Prisoners', in M. Tonry and J. Petersilia (eds.), *'Prisons', Crime and Justice: A Review of Research*, xxvi, Chicago: University of Chicago Press, 121–62.

Halpern, D. (2001) 'Moral Values, Social Trust and Inequality: Can Values Explain Crime?' *British Journal of Criminology*, 41: 236–51.

Haney, C. (1997) 'Psychology and the Limits to Prison Pain: Confronting the Coming Crisis in the Eighth Amendment Law', *Psychology, Public Policy and Law*, 3/4: 499–588.

—— Banks, C., and Zimbardo, P. (1973) 'Interpersonal Dynamics in a Simulated Prison', *International Journal of Criminology and Penology* 1: 69–97.

Hannah-Moffatt, K. (2000) 'Prisons that Empower: Neo-Liberal Governance in Canadian Women's Prisons', *British Journal of Criminology*, 40/3: 510–31.

—— (2001) *Punishment in Disguise: Penal Governance and Federal Imprisonment of Women in Canada*, Toronto: University of Toronto Press.

—— (2004) 'Criminogenic Need and the Transformative Risk Subject', *Punishment and Society*, 7/1.

Hansard (1999) House of Lords, 22 Mar., col. WA 131.

Hansen, C. (2000) 'Classical Chinese Ethics', in P. Singer (ed.), *A Companion to Ethics*, Oxford: Blackwell, 69–81.

Harding, R. (1997) *Private Prisons and Public Accountability*, New Brunswick, NJ: Transaction Publishers.

—— (2001) 'Private Prisons', in M. Tonry and J. Petersilia (eds.), *Crime and Justice: A Review of Research*, xxviii, Chicago: University of Chicago Press, 265–346.

Harris, N. (2001) 'Three Conceptual Approaches to the Emotions of Shame', in E. Ahmed, N. Harris, J. Braithwaite, and V. Braithwaite, *Shame Management through Reintegration*, Cambridge: Cambridge University Press, 78–93.

Harrison, R. (1992) 'The Equality of Mercy', in H. Goss and R. Harrison (eds.), *Jurisprudence: Cambridge Studies*, Oxford: Oxford University Press.

Hart, H. L. A. (1961) *The Concept of Law*, Oxford: Oxford University Press.

—— (1963) *Law, Liberty and Morality*, Oxford: Oxford University Press.

Harvey, J. (2002) *The Psychological Experience of the First Month in Prison*, paper presented at the Prison Research Centre Steering Group Meeting, 11 Dec. 2002, Cambridge.

—— (forthcoming) 'Social Support, Psychological Distress, and Self-Harm among Young Offenders in Prison', Ph.D. thesis, University of Cambridge.

Hawkins, G. (1976) *The Prison: Policy and Practice*, Chicago and London: University of Chicago Press.

Hawkins, K. (1992) *The Uses of Discretion*, Oxford: Clarendon Press.

Hay, W., and Sparks, R. (1991) 'What is a Prison Officer?' *Prison Service Journal*, 83: 2–7.

—— —— (1992) 'Vulnerable Prisoners: Risk in Long-Term Prisons', in K. Bottomley, T. Fowles, and R. Reiner (eds.), *Criminal Justice: Theory and Practice*, British Criminology Conference 1991, selected papers vol. ii. London: British Society of Criminology.

Heal, K., Sinclair, I., and Troop, J. (1973) 'Development of a Social Climate Questionnaire for use on Approved Schools and Community Homes', *British Journal of Sociology*, 24/2: 222–35.

Hecht, T. (1998) *At Home in the Street: Street Children of Northeast Brazil*, Cambridge: Cambridge University Press.

Heffernan, E. (1972) *Making it in Prison: The Square, The Cool and The Life*, New York: Wiley-Interscience.

Heidensohn, F. (1986) 'Models of Justice: Portia or Persephone? Some Thoughts on Equality, Fairness and Gender in the Field of Criminal Justice', *International Journal of the Sociology of Law*, 14/3–4: 287–98.

Hennessy, P. (2001) *Whitehall*, London: Pimlico; 1st pub. 1989.

Hepburn, J. R. (1985) 'The Exercise of Power in Coercive Organisations: A Study of Prison Guards', *Criminology*, 23/1: 145–64.

Herzberg, F., Mausner, B., and Snyderman, B. B. (ed.) (2002) *The Motivation to Work*, New Brunswick, NJ: Transaction Publishers; 1st pub. 1959.

Hillyard, P., Sim, J., Tombs, S., and Whyte, D. (2004) 'Leaving a "Stain Upon the Silence": Critical Criminology and the Politics of Dissent', *British Journal of Criminology* 44: 1–22.

HMCIC (1999) *Police Integrity: Securing and Maintaining Public Confidence*, London: Home Office.

HMCIP (1987) *Report of an Inquiry by Her Majesty's Chief Inspector of Prisons for England and Wales into the Disturbances in Prison Service Establishments in England between 29 April–2 May 1986*, London: HMSO.

—— (1990a) *Report of a Review by HM Chief Inspector of Prisons for England and Wales of Suicide and Self-Harm in Prison Service Establishments in England and Wales*, London: Home Office.

—— (1990b) *Annual Report of HM Chief Inspector of Prisons for England and Wales 1989–1990*, London: Home Office.

—— (1992a) *HM Prison Long Lartin: Report by HM Chief Inspector of Prisons*, London: HMSO.

—— (1992b) *HM Prison Wolds: Report of an Inspection by HM Inspectorate of Prisons*, London: Home Office.

—— (1993a) *Doing Time or Using Time: Report of a Review by Her Majesty's Chief Inspector of Prisons for England and Wales of Regimes in Prison Service Establishments in England and Wales*, Presented to Parliament by the Secretary of State for the Home Department by Command of Her Majesty, January 1993, London: Home Office.

—— (1993b) *Report of an Unannounced Short Inspection: HM Prison Wormwood Scrubs*, London: Home Office.

—— (1993c) *HM Prison Blantyre House: Report of an Inspection by HM Inspectorate of Prisons*, London: HMSO.

—— (1995) *HM Prison Holme House: Report*, London: Home Office.

—— (1996) *Report of HM Chief Inspector of Prisons: HM Prison and Young Offender Institution Doncaster*, London: Home Office.

—— (1997a) *HM Prison Blantyre House: Report of an Unannounced Short Inspection: 3–4 March 1997*, London: Home Office.

—— (1997b) *HM Prison Wormwood Scrubs: Report of a Full Inspection*, London: Home Office.

—— (1997c) *Women in Prison: A Thematic Review*, London: Home Office.

—— (1997d) *Young Offenders: A Thematic Review*, London: Home Office.

—— (1998) *HM Prison Belmarsh: Report of a Full Inspection 11–20 May 1998*, London: Home Office.

—— (1999*a*) *Suicide is Everyone's Concern: Report of a Thematic Inspection on Suicides in Prison*, London: HMSO.

—— (1999*b*) *HM Prison Blakenhurst: Report of a Short Unannounced Inspection 5–7 October 1998*, London: Home Office.

—— (1999*c*) *HM Prison Wandsworth: Report on a Short Unannounced Inspection of HM Prison Wandsworth 13th–16th July 1999*, London: Home Office.

—— (1999*d*) *Report of an Unannounced Inspection of HM Prison Wormwood Scrubs 8–12 March 1999*, London: Home Office.

—— (1999*e*) *Report on a Short Unannounced Inspection of HM Prison and YOI Doncaster 3–5 November 1998*, London: Home Office.

—— (1999*f*) *Annual Report of HM Chief Inspector of Prisons for England and Wales 1997–1999*, London: Home Office.

—— (2000*a*) *Feltham: Report on a Short Unannounced Inspection of HM Young Offender Institution and Remand Centre Feltham 28–30 September 1999*, London: Home Office.

—— (2000*b*) *HM Prison Wandsworth: Report of an Unannounced Inspection of HM Prison Wandsworth 20–23 November 2000*, London: Home Office.

—— (2000*c*) *HMP Wormwood Scrubs: Report of a Full Unannounced Inspection 7–17 February 2000*, London: Home Office.

—— (2000*d*) *Report of an Unannounced Short Inspection of HM Prison Wandsworth 13–19 July 1999*, London: Home Office.

—— (2000*e*) *Inspection of Close Supervision Centres: A Thematic Inspection, August–September 1999*, London: Home Office.

—— (2001*a*) *Her Majesty's Young Offender Institution and Remand Centre Feltham: An Unannounced Inspection 23–26 October 2000*, London: Home Office.

—— (2001*b*) *Report on a Full Announced Inspection of HM Prison Risley 4–8 December 2000*, London: Home Office.

—— (2001*c*) *Report of an Unannounced Follow-Up Inspection of HM Young Offender Institution Portland 5–8 December 2000*, London: Home Office.

—— (2001*d*) *Annual Report of HM Chief Inspector of Prisons for England and Wales 1999–2000*, London: Home Office.

—— (2002*a*) *HM Prison Wormwood Scrubs: Report of an Unannounced Inspection of HM Prison Wormwood Scrubs 10–19 December 2001*, London: Home Office.

—— (2002*b*) *HMP and YOI Ashfield: Report on a Full Announced Inspection of HMP and YOI Ashfield 1–5 July 2002*, London: Home Office.

—— (2002*c*) *Report of a Full Announced Inspection of HM Prison Holme House 26 February–3 March 2001*, London: Home Office.

512   References

HMCIP (2002d) *Report on an Unannounced Follow-Up Inspection of HM Prison Dartmoor 17–21 September 2001*, London: Home Office.
—— (2003) *HM Prison Wandsworth: Report of an Unannounced Inspection of HM Prison Wandsworth 20–24 January 2003*, London: Home Office.
HMI Press Service (2002) 'Chief Inspector Condemns Dartmoor's "Outdated Culture of Disrespect and Over-Control" ', www.homeoffice.gov.uk/hmiprison.htm.
HM Government (1982) *Efficiency and Effectiveness in the Civil Service*, Cm. 8616, London: HMSO.
HMP Risley (n.d.) *The Ascent of Decency*, Warrington: HMP Risley.
HM Treasury (2001) *Choosing the Right Fabric: A Framework for Performance Information*, www.hm-treasury.gov.uk/media//BB5BC/229.pdf.
Hobbs, G. S., and Dear, G. E. (2000) 'Prisoners' Perception of Prison Officers as Sources of Support', *Journal of Offender Rehabilitation*, 31/1–2: 127–42.
Hofstede, G., and Bond, M. H. (1984) 'Hofstede's Cultural Dimensions: An Independent Validation using Rokeach's Value Survey', *International Journal of Cross-Cultural Psychology*, 15: 417–33.
Hollin, C. (1999) 'Treatment Programs for Offenders: Meta-Analysis, "What Works and Beyond" ', *International Journal of Law and Psychiatry*, 22/3–4: 361–72.
—— (2003) 'An Overview of Offender Rehabilitation: Something Old, Something Borrowed, Something New', *Australian Psychologist Special Issue: The Rehabilitation of Offenders: Issues and Models*.
Hollingdale, R. J. (1998) *A Nietzsche Reader: Selected and Translated with an Introduction by R. J. Hollingdale*, Harmondsworth: Penguin, 1998; 1st pub. 1977.
Hollis, M. (1998) *Trust within Reason*, Cambridge: Cambridge University Press.
Holmes, J. (1993) *John Bowlby and Attachment Theory*, London: Routledge.
Home Affairs Committee (1987) *Contract Provision of Prisons, Fourth Report from the Home Affairs Committee, Session 1986–87*, London: HMSO.
—— (1997) *Second Report: The Management of the Prison Service (Public and Private): Volume I Report together with the Proceedings of the Committee*, London: Stationery Office.
Home Affairs Select Committee (2001) *First Special Report—Blantyre House Prison: Government Reply to the Fourth Report from the Home Affairs Select Committee Session 1999–2000, House of Commons*, London: Stationery Office.
Home Office (1959) *Penal Practice in a Changing Society*, Cmnd. 645, London: HMSO.

—— (1966) *Committee of Enquiry into Prison Escapes and Security* (Mountbatten Report), London: HMSO.

—— (1977) *Prisons and The Prisoner: The Work of the Prison Service in England and Wales*, London: HMSO.

—— (1979) *Committee of Inquiry into the United Kingdom Prison Service—The May Inquiry*, Cmnd. 7673, London: HMSO.

—— (1982) *Home Office Statement on the Background, Circumstances and Action subsequently taken relative to the Disturbance in 'D' Wing at HM Prison Wormwood Scrubs on 31 August 1979; together with the Report of an Inquiry by the Regional Director of the South East Region of the Prison Department*, London: HMSO.

—— (1984) *Managing the Long-Term Prison System* (The Report of the Control Review Committee), Cmd. 3175, London: HMSO.

—— (1985) *Report of the Committee on the Prison Disciplinary System (Prison Committee)*, London: HMSO.

—— (1987) *Report of an Inquiry by HM Chief Inspector of Prisons for England and Wales into the Disturbances in Prison Service Establishments in England between 29 April–2 May 1986*, London: HMSO.

—— (1988) *Categorisation and Allocation of Adult Male Prisoners in Categories B, C and D* (Circular Instruction 7/1988), London: Home Office Prison Department.

—— (1991a) *Prison Disturbances April 1990: Report of an Inquiry by the Rt. Hon. Lord Justice Woolf (Parts I and II) and his Honour Judge Stephen Tumim (Part II)*, London: HMSO.

—— (1991b) *Custody, Care and Justice: The Way Ahead for the Prison Service in England and Wales*, London: HMSO.

—— (1994) *Report of an Enquiry into the Escape of Six Prisoners from the Special Security Unit at Whitemoor Prison, Cambridgeshire on Friday 9th September 1994 by Sir John Woodcock*, London: HMSO.

—— (1995) *Review of Prison Service Security in England and Wales and the Escape from Parkhurst Prison on Tuesday 3rd January 1995—The Learmont Report*, London: HMSO.

—— (1999a) *Quinquennial Review of Prison Service: Prior Options Report*, London: Home Office.

—— (1999b) *Quinquennial Review of Prison Service: Evaluation of Performance 1992–3 to 1997–8*, London: Home Office.

—— (2000) *Modernising the Management of the Prison Service: An Independent Report by the Targeted Performance Initiative Working Group—The Laming Report*, London: Home Office.

—— (2001a) *Review of the Boards of Visitors: A Report of the Working Group Chaired by Rt Hon Sir Peter Lloyd MP*, London: Home Office.

—— (2001b) Strategic Plan.

Home Office (2004) *Reducing Crime—Changing Lives: The Government's Plans for Transforming the Management of Offenders*, London: Home Office.

Hood, C. (1991) 'A Public Management for All Seasons?' *Public Administration*, 69/1: 3–19.

Horney, J. D., Osgood, W., and Marshall, I. H. (1995) 'Criminal Careers in the Short-Term: Intra-Individual Variability in Crime and its Relation to Local Life Circumstances', *American Sociological Review*, 60: 655–73.

House of Commons (2002) Home Affairs Public Administration Select Committee, *The Public Service Ethos*, Seventh Report of Session 2001–2 263-II, London: Stationery Office.

Howard, J. (1929) *The State of the Prisons*, abridged edn., London: J. M. Dent.

Howe, A. (1994) *Punish and Critique: Towards a Feminist Analysis of Penality*, London: Routledge.

Ignatieff, M. (1978) *A Just Measure of Pain: The Penitentiary in the Industrial Revolution 1750–1850*, London: Macmillan.

Inglehart, R. (1971) 'The Silent Revolution in Europe: Intergenerational Change in Post-Industrial Societies', *The American Political Science Review*, 65: 991–1017.

Irwin, J. (1980) *Prisons in Turmoil*, Boston: Little Brown.

—— and Cressey, D. R. (1962) *Thieves, Convicts and the Inmate Culture*, New York: McGraw-Hill.

Jacobs, J. (1974) 'Street Gangs behind Bars', *Social Problems*, 21/3: 395–409.

—— (1977) *Stateville: The Penitentiary in Mass Society*, Chicago: University of Chicago Press.

—— (1980) 'The Prisoner Rights Movement and its Impacts', in N. Morris and M. Tonry (eds.), *Crime and Justice: A Review of Research*, ii, Chicago: University of Chicago Press, 429–70.

—— (1983) *New Perspectives on Prisons and Imprisonment*, Ithaca, NY: Cornell University Press.

—— and Crotty, N. (1978) *Guard Unions and the Future of the Prisons*, Ithaca, NY: Institute of Public Employment, New York State School of Industrial and Labor Relations.

James, A. K., Bottomley, A. K., Liebling, A., and Clare, E. (1997) *Privatizing Prisons: Rhetoric and Reality*, London: Sage.

Jameson, N., and Allison, E. (1995) *Strangeways 1990: A Serious Disturbance*, London: Larkin.

Janowicz, M. (1966) 'Foreword', in D. Street, R. D. Vinter, and C. Perrow, *Organisation for Treatment: A Comparative Study of Institutions for Delinquents*, New York: Free Press, pp. v–xiv.

Jefferson, T., and Grimshaw, R. (1984) *Controlling the Constable: Police Accountability in England and Wales*, London: Frederick Muller Ltd.

Jenkins, M. (1987) 'Control Problems in Dispersals', in A. E. Bottoms and R. Light (eds.), *Problems of Long-Term Imprisonment*, Aldershot: Gower.

Jenkins, S. (1995) 'Another Fine Mess of Porridge', *The Times*, 18 Oct.

Jenner, S. (2001) 'Perspectives on the Impact of Performance Management within the Prison Service since Agency Status: Progress—Real or Illusory?' M.St. thesis, University of Cambridge.

Jewkes, Y. (2002) *Captive Audience: Media, Masculinity and Power in Prisons*, Cullompton: Willan Publishing.

Johnson, R. (1996) *Hard Time: Understanding and Reforming the Prison*, 2nd edn., Belmont, Calif.: Wadsworth.

—— and Price, S. (1981) 'The Complete Correctional Officer: Human Service and the Human Environment of the Prison', *Criminal Justice and Behaviour*, 8/3: 343–73.

—— and Toch, H. (1982) *The Pains of Imprisonment*, London and Beverley Hills, Calif.: Sage.

Jones, H., and Cornes, P. (assisted by Stockford, R.) (1977) *Open Prisons*, London: Routledge and Kegan Paul.

Jones, T., and Newburn, T. (forthcoming) 'Comparative Criminal Justice Policy-Making in the US and the UK: The Case of Private Prisons', *British Journal of Criminology*.

Kantrowitz, N. (1996) *Close Control: Managing A Maximum Security Prison: The Story of Ragen's Stateville Penitentiary*, Guilderland, NY: Harrow and Heston.

Karim, N. (2001) 'Post-Traumatic Stress Disorder and the Psychological Effects of Long-Term Imprisonment: A Cross-Sectional Sample of Long-Term Offenders in the Pacific Region of Canada', Ph.D. thesis, University of Cambridge.

Karstedt, S. (2001) 'Die moralische Stärke schwacher Bindungen: Individualismus und Gewalt im Kulturvergleich' (The Moral Strength of Weak Ties: A Cross-Cultural Comparison of Individualism and Violence), *Monatsschrift für Kriminologie und Strafrechtsreform*, 84: 226–43.

Katz, J. (1988) *Seductions of Crime: Moral and Sensual Attractions in Doing Evil*, New York: Basic Books.

Kauffman, K. (1988) *Prison Officers and their World*, Cambridge, Mass. and London: Harvard University Press.

Kaviraj, S., and Khilnani, S. (eds.) (2001) *Civil Society: History and Possibilities*, Cambridge: Cambridge University Press.

Khilnani, S. (2001) 'The Development of Civil Society', in S. Kaviraj and S. Khilnani (eds.), *Civil Society: History and Possibilities*, Cambridge: Cambridge University Press, 11–33.

King, D. (1999) *In the Name of Liberalism: Illiberal Social Policy in the United States and Britain*, Oxford: Oxford University Press.

King, R. D. (1991) 'Maximum Security Custody in Britain and the USA: A Study of Gartree and Oak Park Heights', *British Journal of Criminology*, 31/2: 126–52.

King, R. D. (1994*a*) 'Order, Disorder and Regimes in the Prison Services of Scotland, England and Wales', in E. Player and M. Jenkins (eds.), *Prisons after Woolf: Reform through Riot*, London and New York: Routledge.

—— (1994*b*) 'Russian Prisons after Perestroika', in R. D. King and M. Maguire (eds.), *Prisons in Context*, Oxford: Oxford University Press, 1–13.

—— (1997) 'Can Supermax help solve Security and Control Problems?' in A. Liebling (ed.), *Security, Justice and Order in Prison: Developing Perspectives*, Cambridge: Institute of Criminology.

—— (1999) 'The Rise and Rise of Supermax: An American Solution in Search of a Problem?' *Punishment and Society: The International Journal of Penology*, 1/2: 163–86.

—— (2000) 'Doing Research in Prisons', in R. D. King and E. Wincup (eds.), *Doing Research on Crime and Justice*, Oxford: Oxford University Press, 285–310.

—— and Elliott, K. W. (1977) *Albany: Birth of a Prison—End of an Era?* London: Routledge and Kegan Paul.

—— and McDermott, K. (1989) 'British Prisons 1970–1987: The Ever-Deepening Crisis', *British Journal of Criminology*, 29: 107–28.

—— —— (1995) *The State of Our Prisons*, Oxford: Oxford University Press.

—— and Morgan, R. (1980) *The Future of the Prison System*, Farnborough: Gower.

—— and Wincup, E. (eds.) (2000) *Doing Research on Crime and Justice*, Oxford: Oxford University Press.

Kirby, P. (2000) *Report of the Independent Investigation into the Management and Operation of Victoria's Private Prisons*, Melbourne: Minister for Corrections.

Kluckhorn, C. (1951) 'Values and Value Orientations in the Theory of Action: An Exploration in Definition and Classification', in T. Parsons and E. A. Shils (eds.), *Toward a General Theory of Action*, Cambridge, Mass.: Harvard University Press, 388–433.

Kramer, R. M., and Tyler, T. R. (1996) *Trust in Organizations: Frontiers of Theory and Research*, Thousand Oaks, Calif.: Sage, 196–215.

Kruttschnitt, C., Gartner, R., and Miller, A. (2000) 'Doing Her Own Time? Women's Responses to Prison in the Context of the Old and New Penology', *Criminology*, 38/3: 301–37.

Kumar, K. (1981) *Prophecy and Progress: The Sociology of Industrial and Post-Industrial Society*, 2nd edn., Harmondsworth: Penguin.

Lacey, N. (1994) 'Government as Manager, Citizen as Consumer: The Case of the Criminal Justice Act 1991', *Modern Law Review*, 57: 534–54.

Laing, R. D. (1965) *The Divided Self: An Existential Study in Sanity and Madness*, Harmondsworth: Penguin.

Lanza-Kaduce, L., Parker, K., and Thomas, C. (1999) 'A Comparative Recidivism Analysis of Releases from Private and Public Prisons', *Crime and Delinquency*, 45: 28–47.

Lawson, N., and Sherlock, N. (2001) *The Progressive Century: The Future of the Centre-Left in Britain*, Basingstoke: Palgrave.

Layder, D. (1994) *Understanding Social Theory*, London: Sage.

—— (1998) *Sociological Practice: Linking Theory and Social Research*, London: Sage.

Lesley Brown, W. (1993) *The New Shorter Oxford English Dictionary*, Oxford: Oxford University Press.

Levi, M. (1998) 'A State of Trust', in V. Braithwaite and M. Levi (eds.), *Trust and Governance*, New York: Russell Sage Foundation, 77–101.

Levi, M. and Pithouse, A. (forthcoming) *White Collar Crime and its Victims*, Oxford: Clarendon Press.

Lewin, K. (1997) *Field Theory in Social Science*, London: Harper and Row; 1st pub. 1951.

Lewis, D. (1997) *Hidden Agendas: Politics, Law and Disorder*, London and New York: Hamish Hamilton, Penguin Books.

Liebling, A. (1992) *Suicides in Prison*, London: Routledge.

—— (1999) 'Doing Research in Prison: Breaking the Silence', *Theoretical Criminology*, 3/2: 147–73.

—— (2000) 'Prison Officers, Policing and the Use of Discretion', *Theoretical Criminology*, 4/3: 333–57.

—— (2001) 'Whose Side are We On? Theory, Practice and Allegiances in Prisons Research', in E. Stanko and A. Liebling (eds.), 'Researching Violence: Methodological and Ethical Issues', *British Journal of Criminology Special Issue*, 472–82.

—— (2002) 'A "Liberal Regime within a Secure Perimeter"?: Dispersal Prisons and Penal Practice in the Late 20th Century', in A. E. Bottoms and M. Tonry (eds.), *Ideology, Crime and Criminal Justice: A Symposium in Honour of Sir Leon Radzinowicz*, Cullompton: Willan Publishing, 97–153.

—— (submitted) 'Prisons, Privatisation and the Problem of Moral Values', paper under review.

—— and Arnold, H. (2000) 'Measuring the Quality of Prison Life', report submitted to the Home Office (2 vols.).

—— —— (2002) *Measuring the Quality of Prison Life: Research Findings 174*, London: Home Office.

—— and Durie, L. (in progress) *Do Processes Secure Outcomes? Audit and the Quality of Prison Life*.

—— Harvey, J., and Durie, L. (forthcoming) *An Evaluation of a Safer Prisons Initiative*.

—— Elliott, C., and Arnold, H. (2001) 'Transforming the Prison: Romantic Optimism or Appreciative Realism?', *Criminal Justice*, 1/1: 161–80.

Liebling, A., Elliott, C., and Price, D. (1999*a*) 'Appreciative Inquiry and Relationships in Prison', *Punishment and Society: The International Journal of Penology*, 1/1: 71–98.

—— Elliott, C., Arnold, H., Moore, C., and Grossman, R. (1999) 'Measuring the Quality of Prison Life: A Brief Study of HMP Wandsworth', unpublished study submitted to Prison Service.

—— and Krarup, H. (1993) *Suicide Attempts and Self-Injury in Male Prisons: A Report Commissioned by the Home Office Research and Planning Unit for the Prison Service*, London: Home Office.

—— Muir, G., Rose, G., and Bottoms, A. E. (1997) 'An Evaluation of Incentives and Earned Privileges: Final Report to the Prison Service', unpublished report to Home Office, London.

—— and Price, D. (1999) *An Exploration of Staff-Prisoner Relationships at HMP Whitemoor*, Prison Service Research Report No. 6.

—— —— (2001) *The Prison Officer*, Leyhill: Prison Service and Waterside Press.

—— and Sparks, R. (eds.) (2002) 'Editor's Preface', *Punishment and Society*, 4/3: 283–4.

Light, R. (1993) 'Why Support Prisoners' Family-Tie Groups', *Howard Journal of Criminal Justice*, 32/4: 322–30.

Lilly, J. R., and Knepper, P. (1993) 'The Corrections-Commercial Complex', *Crime and Delinquency*, 39/2: 150–66.

Lindquist, C. H. (2000) 'Social Integration and Mental Well-Being among Jail Inmates', *Sociological Forum*, 15/3: 431–55.

Livingstone, S., Owen, T., and Macdonald, A. (2003) *Prison Law*, 3rd edn., Oxford: Oxford University Press.

Lloyd, M. (2002) Personal communication.

Loader, I., and Walker, N. (2001) 'Policing as a Public Good: Reconstituting the Connections between Policing and the State', *Theoretical Criminology*, 5/1: 9–35.

Logan, C. H. (1990) *Private Prisons: Cons and Pros?* Oxford and New York: Oxford University Press.

—— (1992) 'Well-Kept: Comparing Quality of Confinement in Private and Public Prisons', *Journal of Criminal Law and Criminology*, 83/3: 577–613.

—— (1993) 'Criminal Justice Performance Measures for Prisons', in J. DiIulio, J. Q. Wilson, C. H. Logan, G. F. Cole, M. H. Moore, G. P. Alpert, and J. Petersilia, *Performance Measures for the Criminal Justice System: Discussion Papers from the BJS-Princeton Project*, Princeton: Diane Publishing.

Lomas, M. (2001) 'Market Testing as Management: A Case Study of the Market Test Process and its Impact on the Public Sector', M.St. thesis, University of Cambridge.

Loucks, N. (1994) 'Methods of Dealing with Perceived Misbehaviour in Prison: A Comparative Study of Sweden, France and England', Ph.D. thesis, University of Cambridge.

—— (1995) 'Anything Goes . . .': The Use of the 'Catch-All' Disciplinary Rule in Prison Service Establishments, A Report for the Prison Reform Trust, London: Prison Reform Trust.

Lucas, J. R. (1980) On Justice, Oxford: Clarendon Press.

Ludema, J., Cooperrider, D., and Barrett, F. (2001) 'Appreciative Inquiry: The Power of the Unconditional Positive Question', in P. Reason and H. Bradbury (eds.), Handbook of Action Research, London: Sage, 189–99.

Lukes, S. (1974) Power: A Radical View, London: Macmillan.

Lygo, Admiral Sir R. (1991) Management of the Prison Service, London: Home Office.

McCleery, R. H. (1960) 'Communication Patterns as a Basis for a System of Authority', in R. Cloward, D. R. Cressey, R. McCleery, L. E. Ohlin, G. Sykes, and S. L. Messinger, Theoretical Studies in the Social Organization of the Prison, Social Science Research Council, New York.

—— (1961) 'The Governmental Process and Informal Social Control', in D. R. Cressey (ed.), The Prison: Studies in Institution Organization and Change, New York: Holt, Rinehart and Winston.

McConville, S. (1998) English Local Prisons 1860–1900: Next Only to Death, London: Routledge.

McCorkle, L., and Korn, R. (1954) 'Resocialization within Walls', The Annals of the American Academy of Political and Social Sciences, 293: 88–98.

McDermott, K., and King, R. (1988) 'Mind Games: Where the Action is in Prisons', British Journal of Criminology, 28/3: 357–77.

—— —— (1989) 'A Fresh Start: The Enhancement of Prison Regimes', The Howard Journal, 28/3: 161–76.

McDonald, D. (1999) 'Medical Care in Prisons', in M. Tonry and J. Petersilia (eds.), 'Prisons', Crime and Justice: A Review of Research, xxvi, Chicago: University of Chicago Press, 427–78.

McDonnell, D. (2000) 'Managerialism, Privatisation and the Prison Scene', Criminal Justice Matters, 40: 13–14.

McEvoy, K. (2001) Paramilitary Imprisonment in Northern Ireland: Resistance, Management and Release, Oxford: Oxford University Press.

—— (2003) 'Beyond the Metaphor: Political Violence, Human Rights and "New" Peacemaking Criminology', Theoretical Criminology, 7/3: 319–46.

McGuire, J. (2002) Offender Rehabilitation and Treatment: Effective Programmes and Policies to Reduce Re-offending, Chichester: John Wiley.

McHugh, G. A. (1978) Christian Faith and Criminal Justice: Towards a Christian Response to Crime and Punishment, New York: Paulist Press.

MacIntyre, A. (2000) *After Virtue: A Study in Moral Theory*, 10th edn., London: Duckworth; 1st pub. 1981.

—— (1999) *Dependent Rational Animals: Why Human Beings Need the Virtues*, London: Duckworth.

Macpherson, W. (1999) *The Stephen Lawrence Inquiry: Report of an Inquiry by Sir William Macpherson of Cluny advised by Tom Cook, The Right Reverend Dr John Sentamu, Dr Richard Stone*, London: The Stationery Office.

Maher, L. (1996) *Sexed Work: Gender, Race and Resistance in a Brooklyn Drug Market*, Oxford: Oxford University Press.

Mandaraka-Sheppherd, A. (1986) *The Dynamics of Aggression in Women's Prisons in England*, Aldershot: Gower Publishing.

Manning, P. K., and Van Maanen, J. (eds.) (1978) *Policing: A View from the Street*, Santa Monica, Calif.: Goodyear Publishing Company.

Maruna, S. (2001) *Making Good: How Ex-Convicts Reform and Rebuild Their Lives*, Washington: American Psychological Association.

Mathiason, N. (2001) 'Crime Pays Handsomely for Britain's Private Jails', *Observer*, 11 Mar.

Mathiesen, T. (1965) *The Defences of the Weak*, London: Tavistock.

—— (1974) *The Politics of Abolition*, Oslo: Scandinavian University Books.

Matza, D. (1969) *Becoming Deviant*, Englewood Cliffs, NJ: Prentice-Hall.

Mayton, D. M., Ball-Rokeach, S. J., and Loges, W. E. (1994) 'Human Values and Social Issues: An Introduction', *Journal of Social Issues*, 50/4: 1–8.

Midgley, M. (2000) 'The Origin of Ethics', in P. Singer (ed.), *A Companion to Ethics*, 1st edn., Oxford: Blackwell, 3–13.

Milgram, S. (1974) *Obedience to Authority: An Experimental View*, London and New York: Harper and Row.

Misztal, B. (1996) *Trust in Modern Societies: The Search for the Bases of Social Order*, Cambridge: Polity Press.

Mobley, A., and Geis, G. (2001) 'The Corrections Corporation of America aka The Prison Reality Trust, Inc', in D. Shichor and M. J. Gilbert (eds.), *Privatisation in Criminal Justice: Past, Present and Future*, Ohio: Anderson Publishing, 207–26.

Moos, R. H. (1968) 'Assessment of the Social Climates of Correctional Institutions', *Journal of Research in Crime and Delinquency*, 5: 174–88.

—— (1974) *Evaluating Treatment Environments: The Quality of Psychiatric and Substance Abuse Programmes*, 1997 edn., New Brunswick, NJ: Transaction Publishers.

—— (1975) *Evaluating Correctional and Community Settings*, New York: Wiley.

Morgan, G. (1997) *Images of Organizations*, London: Sage; 1st edn. 1996.

Morgan, R. (1985) 'Her Majesty's Inspectorate of Prisons', in M. Maguire and R. Morgan (eds.), *Accountability and Prisons: Opening up a Closed World*, London: Tavistock, 106–23.

—— (1991) 'Review of David Garland's Punishment and Modern Society', *British Journal of Criminology*, 31/4: 431–3.

—— (1992) 'Following Woolf: The Prospects for Prisons Policy', *Journal of Law and Society*, 19/2: 231–50.

—— (1997) 'Imprisonment: A Brief History, The Contemporary Scene, and Likely Prospects', in M. Maguire, R. Morgan, and R. Reiner (eds.), *The Oxford Handbook of Criminology*, 2nd edn., Oxford: Oxford University Press.

—— (2000) 'The Politics of Criminological Research', in R. D. King and E. Wincup (eds.), *Doing Research on Crime and Justice*, Oxford: Oxford University Press, 61–85.

Morris, T., and Morris, P. (1963) *Pentonville: A Sociological Study of an English Prison*, London: Routledge and Kegan Paul.

Mott, J. (1985) *Adult Prisons and Prisoners in England and Wales 1970–1982*, HORS No. 84, London: HMSO.

Moyle, P. (1993) 'Privatization of Prisons in New South Wales and Queensland: A Review of Some Key Developments in Australia', *The Howard Journal*, 32/2: 231–50.

—— (1995) 'Private Prison Research in Queensland, Australia: A Case Study of Borallon Correctional Centre 1991', *British Journal of Criminology*, 35/1: 34–62.

—— (2000) *Profiting from Punishment: Private Prisons in Australia: Reform or Regression?* Annandale, New South Wales: Pluto Press.

—— (2001) 'Separating the Allocation of Punishment from its Administration: Theoretical and Empirical Observations', *British Journal of Criminology*, 4/1: 77–100.

Muir, G., and Liebling, A. (1995) 'A Staff Survey at HMP Belmarsh', unpublished study.

Muir, W. K. (1977) *Police: Streetcorner Politicians*, Chicago: University of Chicago Press.

Mulholland, I. (2002) Personal communication.

Mullins, L. J. (1999) *Management and Organisational Behaviour*, 5th edn., Harlow: Prentice Hall.

Murray, H. A. (1938) *Explorations in Personality*, New York: Oxford University Press.

Narey, M. (1999) Speech to the Prison Service Conference 1999, Harrogate, Feb. 1999.

—— (2001) Speech to the Prison Service Conference 2001, Nottingham, Feb. 2001.

—— (2002) Interview conducted in Cambridge, 11 May 2002.

—— (2003) Speech to the Prison Service Conference, Harrogate, Feb. 2003.

National Advisory Council (2003) *Advice to Independent Monitoring Boards*, Guidance Paper No. 2, London: Home Office.

National Audit Office (2003) *The Operational Performance of PFI Prisons Report by the Comptroller and Auditor General, HC Session 2002–3: 18 June 2003*, London: The Stationery Office.

Neal, P. (1997) *Liberalism and its Discontents*, Basingstoke: Macmillan.

Neier, A. (1998) *War Crimes: Brutality, Genocide, Terror and the Struggle for Justice*, New York: Times Books.

Nellis, M. (1999) 'Towards the Field of Corrections: Modernising the Probation Service in the 1990s', *Social Policy and Administration*, 33/3: 302–23.

—— (2000) 'Renaming Probation', *Probation Journal*, 47/1: 39–44.

—— (2001) 'Community Penalties in Historical Perspective', in A. E. Bottoms, L. Gelsthorpe, and S. Rex (eds.), *Community Penalties: Change and Challenges*, Devon: Willan Publishing.

Nettler, G. (1957) 'A Measure of Alienation', *American Sociological Review*, 22: 670–7.

New Shorter Oxford English Dictionary (1993) ed. L. Brown, Oxford: Clarendon Press.

New Statesman (2001) 'Nick Cohen follows Tony Blair to Prison and finds him determined to be the First Prime Minister to go into an Election promising more Convicts', *New Statesman*, 114/646: 11–13.

—— (2002a) 'The Chief Inspector of Prisons fears that Squalid Conditions and Overcrowding breach the Human Rights of Some Inmates', *New Statesman*, 15/718: 783–91.

—— (2002b) 'The Head of Prisons admits that Suicide Rates are "Hideous" and Overpopulation Rife, yet he wants more Children Locked Up', *New Statesman*, 15/718: 30–1.

Nietzsche, F. (1881) *Daybreak*, cited in R. J. Hollingdale (1998), *A Nietzsche Reader*, Harmondsworth: Penguin.

Nozick, R. (1974) *Anarchy, State and Utopia*, New York: Basic Books.

Nussbaum, M. (1997) *Cultivating Humanity: A Classical Defence of Reform in Liberal Education*, Cambridge, Mass.: Harvard University Press.

Office of the Inspector of Custodial Services (2001) *2000–2001 Annual Report*, Perth: OICS.

O'Grady, S. (2002) 'Out of the Shadows: Profile of Michael Howard', *The Independent*, 13 Apr.: 5.

Ohlin, L. E. (1956) *Sociology and the Field of Corrections*, New York: Russell Sage Foundation.

O'Malley, P. (1996) 'Risk and Responsibility', in A. Barry, T. Osborne, and N. Rose (eds.), *Foucault and Political Reason*, London: University College Press, 189–208.

—— (1999) 'Volatile and Contradictory Punishment', *Theoretical Criminology*, 3: 175–96.

O'Neill, O. (2000) *Bounds of Justice*, Cambridge: Cambridge University Press.

—— (2002) *A Question of Trust*, The BBC Reith Lecture Series, Cambridge: Cambridge University Press.

OPCS (1992) *The National Prison Survey 1991* by P. Dodd and P. Hunter, London: Office of Population Censuses and Surveys.

Osborne, D., and Gaebler, T. (1992) *Reinventing Government: How the Entrepreneurial Spirit is Transforming the Public Sector*, Reading, Mass.: Addison-Wesley Publishing.

Padfield, N., and Gelsthorpe, L. (2003) *Exercising Discretion: Decision-Making in the Criminal Justice System and Beyond*, Cullompton: Willan Publishing.

—— and Liebling, A., with Arnold, H. (2000) *An Exploration of Decision-Making at Discretionary Lifer Panels*, Home Office Research Study 213, London: Home Office.

Park, I. (2000) *Review of Comparative Costs and Performance of Privately and Publicly Operated Prisons 1998–1999*, Home Office Statistical Bulletin 6/00, London: Home Office.

Paternoster, R., Brame, R., Bachman, R., and Sherman, L. W. (1997) 'Do Fair Procedures Matter? The Effects of Procedural Justice on Spouse Assault', *Law and Society Review*, 31/1: 163–204.

Pepinski, H. (1991) 'Peacemaking in Criminology and Criminal Justice', in H. Pepinski and R. Quinney (eds.), *Criminology as Peacemaking*, Bloomington, Ind.: Indiana University Press.

—— and Quinney, R. (eds.) (1991) *Criminology as Peacemaking*, Bloomington, Ind.: Indiana University Press.

Perrow, C. (1967) 'A Framework for the Comparative Analysis of Organizations', *American Sociological Review*, 32: 194–208.

Petersilia, J. (2000) 'Parole and Prisoner Re-entry in the United States', in M. Tonry and J. Petersilia (eds.), *'Prisons', Crime and Justice: A Review of Research*, xxvi, Chicago: University of Chicago Press, 479–531.

Petrie, K., and Brook, R. (1992) 'Sense of Coherence, Self-Esteem, Depression and Homelessness as Correlates of Reattempting Suicide', *British Journal of Clinical Psychology*, 31: 293–300.

Pettit, P. (1993) 'Analytical Philosophy', in R. E. Goodin and P. Pettit (eds.), *A Companion to Contemporary Political Philosophy*, 1995 edn., Oxford: Blackwell.

PGA (2002) *Prison Governors Association Manifesto*, London: Horseferry House.

Piliavin, I., and Briar, S. (1964) 'Police Encounters with Juveniles', *American Journal of Sociology*, 70: 206–14.

Pilling, J. (1992) 'Back to Basics: Relationships in the Prison Service', Eve Saville Memorial Lecture to the Institute for the Study and Treatment of Delinquency, reprinted in *Perspectives on Prison: A Collection of Views on Prison Life*, supplement to Annual Report of the Prison Service for 1991–2, London: HMSO.

Player, E., and Jenkins, M. (eds.) (1994) *Prisons after Woolf: Reform through Riot*, London and New York: Routledge.

Pollitt, C. (1991) 'A Public Management for All Seasons?' *Public Administration*, 69/1: 3–19.

—— (1995) *Managerialism and the Public Services: Cuts or Cultural Change in the 1990s?* Oxford: Blackwell; 1st pub. 1993.

—— and Bouckaert, G. (2000) *Public Management Reform: A Comparative Analysis*, Oxford: Oxford University Press.

—— Sirre, X., Lonsdale, J., Mul, R., and Summa, H. (2002) *Performance or Compliance? Performance Audit and Public Management in Five Countries*, Oxford: Oxford University Press, 2003; 1st pub. 1999.

Pollock, J. M. (1998) *Ethics in Crime and Justice: Dilemmas and Decisions*, 3rd edn., Belmont, Calif.: Wadsworth.

Polsky, H. W. (1962) *Cottage Six: The Social System of Delinquent Boys in Residential Treatment*, New York: Russell Sage Foundation.

Poole, E. P., and Regoli, R. M. (1980) 'Role Stress, Custody Orientation, and Disciplinary Actions: A Study of Prison Guards', *Criminology*, 18/2: 215–26.

Power, M. (2001) *The Audit Society: Rituals of Verification*, Oxford: Clarendon Press.

Pratt, J. (1998) 'Towards the "Decivilizing" of Punishment', *Social and Legal Studies*, 7/4: 487–515.

—— (2000) 'Emotive and Ostentatious Punishment: Its Decline and Resurgence in Modern Society', *Punishment and Society*, 2/4: 417–39.

—— (2002) *Punishment and Civilization: Penal Tolerance and Intolerance in Modern Society*, London: Sage.

Pratt, T. C., and Maahs, J. (1999) 'Are Private Prisons More Cost Effective than Public Prisons? A Meta-Analysis of Evaluation Research Studies', *Crime and Delinquency*, 45/3: 358–71.

Preston, R. (2000) 'Christian Ethics', in P. Singer (ed.), *A Companion to Ethics*, Oxford: Blackwell, 91–105.

Price, D. (1999) 'Categorisation and Allocation', unpublished Ph.D. thesis, Institute of Criminology, University of Cambridge.

—— and Liebling, A. (1998) 'Staff-Prisoner Relationships: A Review of the Literature', unpublished report to the Prison Service.

Prison Privatisation Report International (various) www.psiru.org.justice.

Prison Service (1993) *Framework Document*, London: Prison Service.

—— (1994a) *Corporate Plan 1994–97*, London: Prison Service.

—— (1994b) *Caring for the Suicidal*, London: Prison Service.

—— (1995) *Instruction to Governors 74/95: Incentives and Earned Privileges*, London: Prison Service.

—— (1997) *Prison Service Review*, London: Prison Service.

—— (2000a) *Prison Service Annual Report 1999–2000*, London: Prison Service.

—— (2000*b*) *Prison Service Business Plan 2000–2001*, London: Prison Service.

—— (2001) *Prison Service Annual Report 2000–2001*, London: Prison Service.

—— (2002*a*) *Prison Service Annual Report 2001–2002*, London: Prison Service.

—— (2002*b*) *Corporate Plan 2002–3 to 2004–5: Business Plan 2002–3*, London: HM Prison Service.

—— (2002*c*) *Reinventing the Centre—Major Directorate Change*, London: Prison Service.

—— (2002*d*) *Prison Service Performance Standards Manual*, 3rd edn. PSO 0200, London: Home Office.

—— (2003) www.hmprisonservice.gov.uk.

Quinn, P. (1993) 'Adjudications in Prison: Custody, Care and a Little Less Justice, Disciplinary Procedures', *Howard Journal of Criminal Justice*, 32/3: 191–202.

Quinton, A. (1991) 'A Philosophical Basis for Respect', in *Respect in Prison: The Transcript of a Conference held 11–14 July at Bishop Grosseteste College, Lincoln*, The Bishop's House, Lincoln, 37–48.

Raine, J. W., and Willson, M. J. (1995) 'New Public Management and Criminal Justice', *Public Money and Management*, 15/1: 35–40.

—— —— (1997) 'Beyond Managerialism in Criminal Justice', *The Howard Journal*, 36/1: 80–95.

Raphael, D. (2001) *Concepts of Justice*, Oxford: Clarendon Press.

Rawls, J. (1980) *A Theory of Justice*, Oxford: Oxford University Press; 1st pub. 1971.

—— (1996) *Political Liberalism*, New York and Chichester: Columbia University Press.

Reiner, R. (1992) 'Police Research in the United Kingdom', in N. Morris and M. Tonry (eds.), *Modern Policing*, Chicago: University of Chicago Press.

—— (1997) 'Policing and the Police', in M. Maguire, R. Morgan, and R. Reiner (eds.), *The Oxford Handbook of Criminology*, 2nd edn., Oxford: Clarendon Press, 997–1034.

—— (2000) 'Police Research', in R. King and E. Wincup (eds.), *Doing Research on Crime and Justice*, Oxford: Oxford University Press, 205–27.

Rex, S. A., Lieb, R., Bottoms, A. E., and Wilson, L. (2003) *Accrediting Offender Programmes: A Process-Based Evaluation of the Joint Prison/Probation Services Accreditation Panel*, Home Office Research Study 273, London: Home Office.

Richards, D., and Smith, M. (2002) *Governance and Public Policy in the United Kingdom*, Oxford: Oxford University Press.

Richardson, G. (1993) 'From Rights to Expectations', in E. Player and M. Jenkins (eds.), *Prisons after Woolf: Reform through Riot*, London and New York: Routledge.

Rimmer, S. (2000) 'The Prison Service and Culture Change', *Prison Service Journal*, 128: 25–7.

—— (2002) 'Leading the Development of Wandsworth Prison: Some Personal Reflections', *Probation Journal*, 49/2: 151–4.

Riveland, C. (2000) 'Prison Management Trends, 1975–2025', in M. Tonry and J. Petersilia (eds.), *'Prisons', Crime and Justice: A Review of Research*, xxvi, Chicago: University of Chicago Press, 163–204.

Rock, P. (1979) *The Making of Symbolic Interactionism*, London: Macmillan.

—— (1996) *Reconstructing a Women's Prison: The Holloway Redevelopment Project, 1968–88*, New York: Clarendon Press.

Roddan, D. (2002) Personal communication.

Rokeach, M. (1973) *The Nature of Human Values*, New York: Free Press.

Rose, D. (2002) 'It's Official—Prison does Work after all', The Observer, 5 May: 20–1.

Rose, N. (1996) 'Governing in "Advanced" Liberal Democracies', in A. Barry, T. Osborne, and N. Rose (eds.), *Foucault and Political Reason: Liberalism, Neoliberalism and Rationalities of Government*, London: University College Press, 37–64.

Ruggiero, V. (1999) Personal communication.

Rutherford, A. (1993) *Criminal Justice and the Pursuit of Decency*, Winchester: Waterside Press.

—— (1996) *Transforming Criminal Policy: Spheres of Influence in the United States, the Netherlands and England and Wales during the 1980s*, Winchester: Waterside Press.

—— (2000) 'A Self-Inflicted Injury by the Prison Service', *New Law Journal*, 150 (1 Dec.): 1796.

Rutter, M. (1982) *Maternal Deprivation Reassessed*, Harmondsworth: Penguin.

—— Giller, H., and Hagell, A. (1998) *Anti-Social Behaviour by Young People*, Cambridge: Cambridge University Press.

Ryan, A. (ed.) (2001) *Justice*, Oxford: Oxford University Press; 1st pub. 1993.

Ryan, M. (1992) 'The Woolf Report: On the Treadmill of Penal Reform?' *Political Quarterly*, 63/1: 50–6.

—— and Ward, T. (1989) *Privatization and the Penal System: The American Experience and the Debate in Britain*, Milton Keynes: Open University Press.

Rynne, J. (2004) 'The regime impacts of the private sector on custodial services in Queensland', Ph.D. under preparation for submission to Griffith University.

Sackmann, S. (1991) *Cultural Knowledge in Organizations: Exploring the Collective Mind*, Newbury Park, Calif.: Sage.

Sacks, J. (1997) *The Politics of Hope*, London: Jonathan Cape.

Sampson, R. J., and Laub, J. H. (1993) *Crime in the Making: Pathways and Turning Points through Life*, London and Cambridge, Mass.: Harvard University Press.

Sandel, M. J. (1982) *Liberalism and the Limits of Justice*, Cambridge: Cambridge University Press.

Sattar, G. (2001) *Rates and Causes of Death among Prisoners and Offenders under Community Supervision*, Home Office Research Study 231, Home Office Research, London: Development and Statistics Directorate.

—— (2003) Personal communication.

Saylor, W. G. (1984) *Surveying Prison Environments*, Washington: Federal Bureau of Prisons.

—— (2002) Personal communication.

—— and Wright, K. N. (1992) 'Status, Longevity, and Perceptions of the Work Environment among Federal Prison Employees', *Journal of Offender Rehabilitation*, 17/3–4: 133–60.

Scheff, T., and Retzinger, S. (2001) *Emotions and Violence: Shame and Rage in Destructive Conflicts*, Lexington, Mass.: Lexington Books; 1st pub. 1991.

Schein, E. H. (1985) *Organizational Culture and Leadership*, San Francisco: Jossey-Bass Publishers.

Scott, J. (2001) *Power*, Cambridge: Polity Press.

Scottish Prison Service (1990) *Opportunity and Responsibility: Developing New Approaches to the Management of the Long Term Prison System in Scotland*, Edinburgh: Scottish Office.

—— (2002) *Small Units in the Scottish Prison Service*, Research Bulletin Issue 7, Edinburgh: Scottish Prison Service.

Scraton, P. (ed.) (1987) *Law, Order and the Authoritarian State*, Milton Keynes: Open University Press.

—— Sim, J., and Skidmore, P. (1991) *Prisons under Protest*, Crime, Justice and Social Policy Series, Milton Keynes: Open University Press.

Scrivens, E. (1994) *Accreditation: Protecting the Professional or the Consumer?* Buckingham: Open University Press.

Seeman, M. (1959) 'On the Meaning of Alienation', *American Sociological Review*, 24: 783–91.

Seligman, A. B. (1997) *The Problem of Trust*, Princeton: Princeton University Press.

Sennett, R. (1998) *The Corrosion of Character: The Personal Consequences of Work in the New Capitalism*, New York: W. W. Norton.

—— (2003) *Respect: The Formation of Character in an Age of Inequality*, London: Allen Lane.

Shapira, R., and Navon, D. (1985) 'Staff-Inmate Co-operation in Israeli Prisons: Towards a Non-functionalist Theory of Total Institutions',

International Review of Modern Sociology, 15 (spring–autumn): 131–46.

Shaw, R. (1987) *Children of Imprisoned Fathers*, London: Hodder and Stoughton.

—— (1992) *Prisoners' Children: What are the Issues?* London: Routledge.

Sherman, L. (1993) 'Defiance, Deterrence, and Irrelevance: A Theory of the Criminal Sanction', *Journal of Research in Crime and Delinquency*, 30: 445–73.

Shichor, D. (1993) 'The Corporate Context of Private Prisons', *Crime, Law and Social Change*, 20: 113–38.

—— (1999) 'Privatizing Correctional Institutions: An Organizational Perspective', *Prison Journal*, 79/2: 226–49.

—— and Sechrest, D. K. (2002) 'Privatization and Flexibility: Legal and Practical Aspects of Interjurisdictional Transfer of Prisoners', *Prison Journal*, 82/3: 386–407.

Siegal, M. (1982) *Fairness in Children: A Social-Cognitive Approach to the Study of Moral Development*, London: Academic Press.

Sim, J. (1990) *Medical Power in Prisons: The Prison Medical Service in England and Wales 1774–1989*, Buckingham: Open University Press.

—— (1994) 'The Abolitionist Approach: A British Perspective', in A. Duff, S. Marshall, R. E. Dobash, and R. P. Dobash (eds.), *Penal Theory and Practice: Tradition and Innovation in Criminal Justice*, Manchester: Manchester University Press, 263–84.

Simon, J. (2000) 'The Society of Captives in the Era of Hyper Incarceration', *Theoretical Criminology*, 4/3: 285–308.

—— and Feeley, M. (1995) 'True Crime: The New Penology and Public Discourse on Crime', in T. Blomberg and S. Cohen (eds.), *Punishment and Social Control*, New York: Aldine de Gruyter, 147–80.

Sinclair, A. (2002) 'A Study of How and the Extent to Which, KPIs Drive Performance in the Prison Service', unpublished M.St. thesis, Institute of Criminology, University of Cambridge.

Sinclair, I. (1971) *Hostels for Probationers*, Home Office Research Studies, London: HMSO.

Singleton, N., Meltzer, H., and Garward, R. with Coid, J., and Deasy, D. (1997) *Psychiatric Morbidity among Prisoners: A Survey carried out by the Social Survey Division of ONS on behalf of the Department of Health*, London: Office for National Statistics.

Sitkin, S. B., and Stickel, D. (1996) 'The Road to Hell: The Dynamics of Distrust in an Era of Quality', in R. M. Kramer and T. R. Tyler (eds.), *Trust in Organizations: Frontiers of Theory and Research*, Thousand Oaks, Calif.: Sage, 196–215.

Sixsmith, M. (2002) *Control Freaks*, Channel Four Documentary, 29 Sept.

Skolnick, J. (1966) *Justice without Trial: Law Enforcement in Democratic Society*, London and New York: Wiley.

Smith, C. (1996) 'The Imprisoned Body: Women, Health and Imprisonment', Ph.D. thesis, University of Wales, Bangor.

—— and Wincup, E. (2000) 'Breaking In: Researching Criminal Justice Institutions for Women', in R. D. King and E. Wincup (eds.), *Doing Research on Crime and Justice*, Oxford: Oxford University Press, 331–50.

Smith, P. C., and Goddard, M. (2002) 'Performance Management and Operational Research: A Marriage made in Heaven?', *Journal of the Operational Research Society*, 53/3: 247–56.

Solicitor General Canada (1999) *The Effects of Prison Sentences on Recidivism*, Canada: Government Services.

Sparks, R. (1971) *Local Prisons: The Crisis in the English Penal System*, London: Heinemann.

Sparks, R. (1994) 'Can Prisons be Legitimate?' in R. King and M. McGuire (eds.), *Prisons in Context*, Oxford: Clarendon Press.

—— (1996) ' "Penal Austerity": The Doctrine of Less Eligibility Reborn?' in R. Matthews and P. Francis (eds.), *Prisons 2000*, London: Macmillan.

—— (1997) 'Recent Social Theory and the Study of Crime and Punishment', in M. Maguire, R. Morgan, and R. Reiner (eds.), *The Oxford Handbook of Criminology*, 2nd edn., Oxford: Clarendon Press.

—— (2001) 'Degrees of Estrangement: The Cultural Theory of Risk and Comparative Penology', *Theoretical Criminology*, 5(2): 159–76.

—— (2003) 'Out of the Digger: The Warrior's Honour and the Guilty Observer', *Ethnography—Special Issue: 'In and Out of the Belly of the Beast: Dissecting the Prison'*, 3/4: 556–82.

—— (in progress) *The Meaning of Humanity in the Penal Context*.

—— and Bottoms, A. E. (1995) 'Legitimacy and Order in Prisons', *British Journal of Sociology*, 46/1: 45–62.

—— —— and Hay, W. (1996) *Prisons and the Problem of Order*, Oxford: Clarendon Press.

Steinberg, J. (1991) *All or Nothing: The Axis and the Holocaust 1941–1943*, London and New York: Routledge.

Stenson, K. (2001) 'The New Politics of Crime Control', in K. Stenson and R. Sullivan (eds.), *Crime, Risk and Justice: The Politics of Crime Control in Liberal Democracies*, Cullompton: Willan Publishing, 15–28.

Stenson, K., and Sullivan, R. (eds.) (2001) *Crime, Risk and Justice: The Politics of Crime Control in Liberal Democracies*, Cullompton: Willan Publishing.

Stern, V. (1993) *Bricks of Shame: Britain's Prisons*, 2nd edn., London: Penguin Books, 1993; 1st pub. 1989.

Stocker, M. with Hegeman, E. (1996) *Valuing Emotions*, Cambridge Studies in Philosophy, Cambridge: Cambridge University Press.

Stohr, M. K., Hemmens, C., Marsh, R. L., Barrier, G., and Palhegyi, D. (2000) 'Can't Scale This? The Ethical Parameters of Correctional Work', *The Prison Journal*, 80/1: 56–79.

Strang, H., and Braithwaite, J. (2001) *Restorative Justice and Civil Society*, Cambridge: Cambridge University Press.

Strawson, P. (1962) 'Freedom and Resentment', *Proceedings of the British Academy*, 48: 187–211; repr. in G. Watson (ed.), *Free Will*, Oxford: Oxford University Press.

Street, D., Vinter, R. D., and Perrow, C. (1966) *Organisation for Treatment: A Comparative Study of Institutions for Delinquents*, New York: Free Press.

Sykes, G. (1958) *The Society of Captives*, Princeton: Princeton University Press.

—— and Messinger, S. (1960) *The Inmate Social System: Theoretical Studies in the Organization of the Prison*, Social Science Research Council Pamphlet No. 15, New York.

Sztompka, P. (1999) *Trust: A Sociological Theory*, Cambridge: Cambridge University Press.

Tallentire, A. (2002) 'Getting the Measure of Industrial Relations', M.St. thesis, University of Cambridge.

Tavuchis, N. (1991) *Mea Culpa: A Sociology of Apology and Reconciliation*, Cambridge: Cambridge University Press.

Taylor, C. (1985) 'What is Human Agency?' in *Human Agency and Language: Philosophical Papers I*, Cambridge: Cambridge University Press, 15–44.

—— (1992) *Sources of the Self: The Making of the Modern Identity*, Cambridge: Cambridge University Press.

Taylor, I. (1999) *Crime in Context: A Critical Criminology of Market Societies*, Oxford: Polity Press.

Taylor, M. (2001) Contribution to 'A Roundtable Discussion on the Prospects for a Progressive Century', in N. Lawson and N. Sherlock, *The Progressive Century: The Future of the Centre-Left in Britain*, Basingstoke: Palgrave.

Thomas, C. W. (1997) 'Comparing the Cost and Performance of Public and Private Prisons in Arizona', Report for the Arizona Department of Corrections.

—— and Petersen, D. M. (1977) *Prison Organisation and Inmate Subcultures*, Indiana: Bobbs-Merrill.

Thomas, J. E. (1972) *The English Prison Officer since 1850: A Study in Conflict*, London and Boston: Routledge and Kegan Paul.

—— and Pooley, R. (1980) *The Exploding Prison: Prison Riots and the Case of Hull*, London: Junction Books.

Thomson, J. A. K., and Barnes, J. (1976) *The Ethics of Aristotle: The Nicomachean Ethics*, trans. [from the Greek] by J. A. K. Thomson; introductions and bibliography by Jonathan Barnes, Harmondsworth: Penguin.

Thornton, D. (1987) 'Assessing Custodial Adjustment', in B. J. McGirk, D. M. Thornton, and M. Williams (eds.), *Applying Psychology to Imprisonment*, London: HMSO, 445–62.

Tiles, J. E. (2000) *Moral Measures: An Introduction to Ethics West and East*, London: Routledge.

Tittle, C. R. (1995) *Control Balance: Toward a General Theory of Deviance*, Boulder, Colo.: Westview Press.

Toch, H. (1982) 'Studying and Reducing Stress', in R. Johnson and H. Toch (eds.), *The Pains of Imprisonment*, London and Beverley Hills, Calif.: Sage, 25–44.

—— (1992a) *Living in Prison: The Ecology of Survival*, New York: The Free Press; 1st pub. 1977.

—— (1992b) *Mosaic of Despair: Human Breakdown in Prison*, rev. edn., Washington: American Psychological Association. 1st pub. as *Men in Crisis*, 1975.

—— (1997) *Corrections: A Humanistic Approach*, New York: Harrow and Heston.

—— (2002) 'Ameliorating Purgatory', seminar given to M.St. students at the Institute of Criminology, University of Cambridge.

—— and Adams, K. with Grant, J. D. (1989) *Coping: Maladaptation in Prison*, New Brunswick, NJ: Transaction Publishers.

Tonry, M., and Petersilia, J. (eds.) (2000) 'American Prisons at the Beginning of the Twenty-First Century', in M. Tonry and J. Petersilia (eds.), *'Prisons', Crime and Justice: A Review of Research*, xxvi, Chicago: University of Chicago Press, 1–16.

Train, C. (1985) 'Management Accountability in the Prison Service', in M. Maguire, J. Vagg, and R. Morgan (eds.), *Accountability and Prisons: Opening Up a Closed World*, London and New York: Tavistock Publications, 177–87.

Twining, W., and Miers, D. (1982) *How to do Things with Rules: A Primer of Interpretation*, London: Wiedenfeld and Nicolson.

Tyler, T. (1990) *Why People Obey the Law*, New Haven: Yale University Press.

—— (1998) 'Trust and Democratic Governance', in V. Braithwaite and M. Levi (eds.), *Trust and Governance*, New York: Russell Sage Foundation, 269–94.

—— and Blader, S. L. (2000) *Cooperation in Groups: Procedural Justice, Social Identity, and Behavioural Engagement*, Philadelphia: Taylor and Francis.

US Department of Justice (1993) *Performance Measures for the Criminal Justice System: Discussion Papers from the BJS-Princeton Project*, Bureau of Justice Statistics, Washington: US Department of Justice.

Useem, B., and Kimball, P. (1989) *States of Siege: U.S. Prison Riots 1971–1986*, Oxford: Oxford University Press.

Useem, B., and Reisig, M. D. (1999) 'Collective Action in Prisons: Protests, Disturbances and Riots', *Criminology*, 37/4: 735–59.

Uslaner, E. M. (2002) *The Moral Foundations of Trust*, Cambridge: Cambridge University Press.

Vagg, J. (1985) 'Independent Inspections: The Role of the Boards of Visitors', in M. Maguire, J. Vagg, and R. Morgan, *Accountability and Prisons: Opening Up a Closed World?* London: Tavistock.

—— (1994) *Prison Systems: A Comparative Study of Accountability in England, France, Germany and the Netherlands*, Oxford: Clarendon Press.

Van Deth, J., and Scarbrough, J. (eds.) (1998) *The Impact of Values*, Oxford: Oxford University Press.

van Swaaningen, R. (1997) *Critical Criminology: Visions from Europe*, London: Sage.

Van Zyl Smit, D. (2002) *Taking Life Imprisonment Seriously in National and International Law*, The Hague and New York: Kluwer Law International.

Vold, G. B., Bernard, T. J., and Snipes, J. B. (2002) *Theoretical Criminology*, 5th edn., Oxford and New York: Oxford University Press.

von Hirsch, A. (1976) *Doing Justice: The Choice of Punishments: Report of the Committee for the Study of Incarceration*, New York: Hill and Wang.

—— (1986) *Past or Future Crimes: Deservedness and Dangerousness in the Sentencing of Criminals*, Manchester: Manchester University Press.

—— (1993) *Censure and Sanctions*, Oxford: Clarendon Press.

Walker, N. (1985) *Sentencing: Theory, Law and Practice*, London: Butterworth.

—— (1987) 'The Unwanted Effects of Long-Term Imprisonment', in A. E. Bottoms and R. Light (eds.), *Problems of Long-Term Imprisonment*, Aldershot: Gower.

Wachtel, T., and McCold, P. (2001) 'Restorative Justice in Everyday Life', in H. Strang and J. Braithwaite (eds.), *Restorative Justice and Civil Society*, Cambridge: Cambridge University Press, 114–29.

Weatherhead, L. D. (1964) 'Introduction', in V. E. Frankl, *Man's Search for Meaning: An Introduction to Logotherapy*, trans. Isle Lasch, London: Hodder and Stoughton.

Weber, G. H. (1961) 'Emotional and Defensive Reactions to Cottage Parents', in D. Cressey (ed.), *The Prison: Studies in Institutional Organisation and Change*, New York: Holt, Rinehart and Winston, 189–228.

Wenk, E. A., and Moos, R. H. (1972) 'Social Climates in Prison: An Attempt to Conceptualize and Measure Environmental Factors in Total Institutions', *Journal of Research in Crime and Delinquency*, 9: 134–48.

West, T. (1997) *Prisons of Promise*, Winchester: Waterside Press.

Wheatley, P. (2001) Speech to the Prison Service Conference, Nottingham, Feb.

—— (2002) Speech to the Prison Service Conference, Nottingham, Feb.

—— (2003) Speech to the Prison Service Conference, Harrogate, Feb.

White, A. (1995) *Managing for Performance: How to Get the Best out of Yourself and Your Team*, London: BCA.

White, S., Howard, L., and Walmsley, R. (1991) *The National Prison Survey 1991: Main Findings*, London: HMSO.

Wiener, M. J. (1994) *Reconstructing the Criminal: Culture, Law and Politics in England, 1830–1914*, Cambridge: Cambridge University Press.

Willis, P. (1977) *Learning to Labor: How Working Class Kids get Working Class Jobs*, New York: Columbia University Press.

Wilson, D. (2000) 'Whatever Happened to "The Governor" ', *Criminal Justice Matters*, 40: 11–12.

Wilson, E., and Doig, A. (1996) 'The Shape of Ideology: Structure, Culture and Policy Delivery in the New Public Sector', *Public Money and Management*, 16/2: 53–61.

Windlesham, D. (1993) *Responses to Crime Volume 2: Penal Policy in the Making*, Oxford: Clarendon Press.

Wolff, H. G. (1957) 'What Hope Does for Man', *Saturday Review*, 40 (5 Jan.): 45.

Wood, B. S., Wilson, G. G., Jessor, R., and Bogan, J. B. (1966) 'Troublemaking Behavior in a Correctional Institution: Relationship's Definition of their Situation', *American Journal of Orthopsychiatry*, 36: 795–802.

Woodbridge, J. (1999) *A Comparison of the Costs of Public and Privately Managed Prisons*, London: HMSO.

Woodman, J., and Dale, S. (2002) *National Staff Survey 2001*, London: Prison Service.

Wozniac, E., Dyson, G., and Carnie, J. (1998) *The Third Prison Survey*, SPS Occasional Paper No. 3, Edinburgh: Scottish Prison Service.

—— Gemmell, M., and Machin, D. (1994) *The Second Prison Survey*, SPS Occasional Paper No. 10, Edinburgh: Scottish Prison Service.

—— and McAllister, D. (1992) *The Prison Survey*, SPS Occasional Paper No. 1, Edinburgh: Scottish Prison Service.

Wright, K. N. (1979) 'The Conceptualization and Measurement of the Social Climate of Correctional Organizations', *Journal of Offender Counselling Services and Rehabilitation New York*, 4/2: 137–52.

—— (1985) 'Developing the Prison Environment Inventory', *Journal of Research in Crime and Delinquency*, 22/3: 257–77.

—— (1993) 'Prison Environment and Behavioural Outcomes', *Journal of Offender Rehabilitation*, 20/1–2: 93–113.

—— and Boudouris, J. (1982) 'An Assessment of the Moos Correctional Institutions Environment Scale', *Journal of Research in Crime and Delinquency*, 19/2: 255–76.

Wright, K. N., and Goodstein, L. (1989) 'Correctional Environments', in L. Goodstein and D. L. MacKenzie (eds.), *The American Prison: Issues in Research and Policy*, iv, London and New York: Plenum Press, 253–66.

—— and Saylor, W. G. (1991) 'Male and Female Employees' Perceptions of Prison Work: Is There a Difference?', *Justice Quarterly*, 14/3: 525–46.

—— —— Gilman, E., and Camp, S. (1997) 'Job Control and Occupational Outcomes among Prison Workers', *Justice Quarterly*, 14/3: 525–46.

Wright Mills, C. (1970) *The Sociological Imagination*, Harmondsworth: Penguin Books.

Wrong, D. H. (1994) *The Problem of Order: What Divides and Unites Society*, New York: The Free Press.

—— (1997) *Power: Its Forms, Bases and Uses*, Somerset, NJ: Transaction Publishers.

Young, P. (1987) *The Prison Cell: The Start of a Better Approach to Prison Management*, London: Adam Smith Institute.

Zamble, E., and Porporino, F. J. (1988) *Coping, Behavior and Adaptation in Prison Inmates*, New York: Springer Verlag.

Zedner, L. (2000) 'The Pursuit of Security', in T. Hope and R. Sparks (eds.), *Risk and Insecurity*, London: Routledge, 200–14.

—— (2002) 'Dangers of Dystopia in Penal Theory', *Oxford Journal of Legal Studies*, 22/2: 341–66.

—— (2003) 'The Concept of Security: An Agenda for Comparative Analysis', *Legal Studies*, 23/1: 153–76.

Zeeman, E. C., Hall, C. S., Harrison, P. J., Marriage, G. H., and Shapland, D. H. (1977) 'A Model for Prison Disturbances', *British Journal of Criminology*, 17/3: 251–63.

Zehr, H. (1991a) *Changing Lenses: A New Focus for Criminal Justice*, Scottsdale, Calif.: Herald Press.

—— (1991b) 'Respect in the Home', in *Respect in Prison: The Transcript of a Conference held 11–14 July at Bishop Grossteste College, Lincoln*, Lincoln: The Bishop's House, 1–13.

Index

Lightning Source UK Ltd.
Milton Keynes UK
17 July 2010

157160UK00004B/6/P